Home, School

NINTH EDITION

& Community Relations

CAROL GESTWICKI

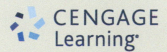

CENGAGE
Learning®

Australia • Brazil • Mexico • Singapore • United Kingdom • United States

Home, School & Community Relations, Ninth Edition
Carol Gestwicki

Product Director: Marta E. Lee-Perriard

Product Manager: Mark Kerr

Content Developer: Kate Scheinman

Product Assistant: Julia Catalano

Marketing Manager: Jennifer Levanduski

Content Project Manager: Tanya Nigh

Art Directors: Jennifer Wahi, Marissa Falco

Manufacturing Planner: Doug Bertke

Compositor and Production Service: Integra

IP Analyst: Jennifer Nonenmacher

IP Project Manager: Brittani Morgan

Photo and Text Researchers: Lumina Datamatics

Cover and Text Designer: Jeff Bane, CMB Design Partners

Cover Image: Illustrated by Jeff Bane, CMB Design Partners

For product information and technology assistance, contact us at
Cengage Learning Customer & Sales Support, 1-800-354-9706.

For permission to use material from this text or product,
submit all requests online at **www.cengage.com/permissions.**
Further permissions questions can be e-mailed to
permissionrequest@cengage.com.

Library of Congress Control Number: 2014948593

Student Edition:
ISBN: 978-1-305-08901-3

Loose-leaf Edition:
ISBN: 978-1-305-49687-3

Cengage Learning
20 Channel Center Street
Boston, MA 02210
USA

Cengage Learning is a leading provider of customized learning solutions with office locations around the globe, including Singapore, the United Kingdom, Australia, Mexico, Brazil, and Japan. Locate your local office at **www.cengage.com/global.**

Cengage Learning products are represented in Canada by Nelson Education, Ltd.

To learn more about Cengage Learning Solutions, visit **www.cengage.com.**

Purchase any of our products at your local college store or at our preferred online store **www.cengagebrain.com.**

Printed at CLDPC, USA, 02-20

Brief Contents

Contents

SECTION II Teacher-Family Partnerships in Early Education

SECTION III Methods for Developing Partnerships

SECTION IV Making a Partnership Work

Preface

The Goal of This Book

It is not unusual in classes for teachers and students preparing to become teachers to hear the statement "I do just fine with the children; it's the parents who …

- make me crazy."

- I can't stand."

- I could do without."

- make me think about quitting."

As more families and teachers share the care of young children, it becomes obvious that disruptive tensions are more common than rare. Learning the skills of communicating effectively with families about matters both routine and emotionally charged has become an important part of a teacher's preparation. In fact, the standards set by the National Association for the Education of Young Children (NAEYC) for college programs that prepare early childhood teachers require that teachers become skillful in building family and community relationships. Likewise, the NAEYC Early Childhood Program Standards for accreditation of good schools for young children specifically mandate that "program staff establish intentional practices designed to foster strong reciprocal relationships with families" (NAEYC, 2007, p. 56).

In addition, in today's society, attention is increasingly focused on the stress experienced by the contemporary family. Television specials and politicians have found it appropriate to speak out about the dilemmas of working parents—caught between choices of unaffordable or inadequate child care and stretched between home and work responsibilities. Schools feel inadequate to the task of filling in the gaps in children's lives created by families under stress. Efforts are being made in public and private sectors to offer some external support to alleviate family stresses, as the understanding dawns that family breakdown is responsible for many of the ills plaguing the community at large. Conversely, it may also be stated that the breakdown of the community, with escalating incidences of drug use, violence, unemployment, and economic hardships for families, may contribute to many of the ills that plague families. As part of the community, teachers are active participants in the initiatives of family support that are becoming more numerous.

As families with two working parents become the norm and single-parent families are ever more numerous, teachers are challenged to find ways to support and cooperate with families who depend on them to help educate and care for their children. Various mandates also demand that teachers in public schools and teachers working with particular funding sources develop family involvement plans. This is a large issue and perhaps more philosophical in its nature than merely practical: Once teachers are convinced about the necessity and benefits of working with families, they will find their own ways to do so—ways appropriate for their own situations.

This is not merely a pleasant possibility for those teachers who choose to work with families. Rather, the reality is teachers find that their own practice and work with children is much enhanced by working effectively with their families. The standards of early childhood professional organizations indicate the recognition that working with families is in fact an essential role for the early educator—difficult though this frequently is, given the changing nature of families today.

The purpose of this ninth edition of *Home, School, and Community Relations* is to continue to raise some of these larger issues—to sensitize teachers and prospective teachers to the complex nature of parenting in today's world—so teachers' basic stance will not become "us against them" but instead "we're all in this together." Therefore, your retention of particular small facts is less important than understanding larger concepts, incorporating into your personal teaching philosophies the idea that supporting families to do an optimum job with their own children is a worthy and essential goal. In this way, you will begin to perceive your role in communication with individual families so as to help parents become stronger in their parenting skills and to make appropriate decisions for their children's care and education. This is not the old view of the teacher as an all-knowing professional who will tell parents what they should be doing—a somewhat daunting figure who could usually not be said to be in any sort of relationship with families. Rather, this new view recognizes that early childhood teachers, schools, and programs are part of the community systems to support the development of healthy families and enhance development and education of their children by creating working partnerships and engagement with families.

Themes of the Text

Readers will encounter several specific themes running through the text.

Emphasis on Diversity

Emphasis in the text is placed on developing the ability to empathize with parents and developing the communication skills and techniques that will support real partnerships. In the ninth edition of this book, particular emphasis has been placed on encouraging teachers to understand the diversity of experience, values, and functioning to be found in today's families. The idea that teachers must prepare themselves to work with families whose culture, language, and beliefs about raising children may be very different from their own is an important awareness for new and experienced teachers. Throughout the text, you will find icons to indicate attention to the topic of diversity.

Legislation Recognizing Families as Partners

Attention is also given to the aspect of working along with parents as advocates for children and families. Considerable discussion is included about some of the stresses and circumstances that affect today's families. There is recognition of current moves within the business and legislative communities to support families. There is also discussion of the most recent education legislation—No Child Left Behind and Race for the Top—that mandates family involvement and choices as part of the educational reforms. The far-reaching implications of this legislation mean that teachers at all levels will be working closely with families.

Full Family Engagement

The dual nature of teachers' roles in working with parents and children is emphasized, with the inclusion of books and resources to use with children who have diverse family backgrounds and needs. The many practical problems that must be addressed in working with families are considered. But perhaps the most important overriding theme is the idea of the necessity for working partnerships and full family engagement, and the need for persistence in the face of often difficult circumstances and responses. Hopefully, you will complete your coursework and text reading with the conviction that this is a necessary teacher role. Coming to such an understanding is a process that occurs over time.

This ninth edition of the text continues to stress the specific attitudes, philosophies, and practical techniques that teachers in any setting can find useful in building relationships with families. The underlying philosophy of the book is that those relationships are crucial in providing appropriate educational experiences and success for children. The text also recognizes that some family situations today create real challenges for teachers trying to create partnerships with families, and that such efforts are often frustrating and seem almost hopeless. Rather than giving up, which means failure to support children with the connections among home, school, and community, teachers are encouraged to develop a strong belief in the importance of partnership and family involvement and to keep returning to this philosophy to find new strength and inspiration in the face of bleak situations.

Continuing Strengths of the Text

Also included in this ninth edition is a strong focus on local and national community efforts and organizations to remind teachers that they have responsibilities to work with and support families beyond the walls of the schools or centers in which they work with children. The federal No Child Left Behind legislation has implications for families and for teachers, as well as larger implications for schools and communities. This legislation and its significance to teacher–family concerns are addressed in Chapters 4 and 12. There is an expanded discussion of the many components that constitute family engagement, as well as a look at the history of parent involvement in this country.

Also presented are specific techniques teachers can use to be sure of conveying an attitude of welcoming acceptance to every family. Discussions of dealing with common problems that arise between teachers and parents, including the current issues of testing young children for "readiness" and changes in parenting concerns, have been expanded. Additional aspects of various models of parent education are included. Updated references and suggestions for further reading will be helpful to students who wish to go beyond the text.

Working with families will always be one of the more challenging tasks for educators. Students are encouraged to realize that this is not a separate role but one that is integrated into the concept of working with the whole child—and one for which they need to prepare fully.

The Intended Audience

This book is intended for you—as a student, a new or experienced teacher, or any professional working with families of children in public and private schools and kindergartens, elementary schools, early childhood programs, family child care homes, afterschool care programs, and other settings. The principles of partnership and communication with families remain constant—whether you are a teacher who is concerned about relationships with families of kindergarten students, fourth-grade students, or toddlers in a child care setting. If you read an example in this book that seems relevant to younger (or older) children, ask yourself how the ideas would apply in your particular situation. Good professional communication practices are the same, even though the content may differ.

The philosophy and practical techniques discussed in this textbook are appropriate for use no matter where you work with children and their families. Examples of elementary and pre-K teachers help make this clear, as well as information about the No Child Left Behind legislation and requirements that affect public schools and all families with children. Indeed, this important piece of legislation has far-reaching effects on every community and citizen.

Organization and Content

Section I, "Introduction to Families," is designed to introduce readers to the experience of parenting. Chapter 1 introduces the subject by taking a close look at what life is like for two families, reminding students of the need to prepare to work respectfully with families of diverse backgrounds and experiences and with unique needs. Chapter 2 considers families in our modern world and the factors that shape their lives. Chapter 3 describes the various roles of parents in bringing up children and creating families.

Section II, "Teacher–Family Partnerships in Early Education," explores the subject of teacher–parent partnerships in early education. Chapter 4 examines the various models and motivations for family involvement. Chapter 5 identifies benefits for children, parents, and teachers when parents and teachers work in partnership, as well as potential barriers to teacher–parent relationships. Chapter 6 describes the attitudes and conditions that create the foundations for successful partnerships and offers examples of schools that are trying to implement partnership philosophy in their practice.

Section III, "Methods for Developing Partnerships," moves the student into a discussion of the various techniques that teachers can use to involve families in the educational process. Chapter 7 describes the orientation process for children and parents to begin the process of exchanging information and supporting one another during the separation experience. Chapter 8 introduces a number of informal communication methods, including newsletters, bulletin boards, electronic communication, and other personal methods. Chapter 9 outlines how to plan and conduct effective parent–teacher conferences. Chapter 10 focuses on involving families in their children's classrooms in a variety of ways. Chapter 11 considers parent education. Chapter 12 describes ways that parents and teachers can collaborate to affect community policy and action on family and children's issues as we recognize the need to support families' efforts. It also discusses current legislation and community movements that affect families and schools, and it describes the use of community resources.

Section IV, "Making a Partnership Work," moves to a discussion of working with families with specific needs and issues. Chapter 13 examines ways to welcome and include all families—no matter how richly diverse their language, culture, race, religion, or family structure. Chapter 14 considers working with families in particular circumstances: Families experiencing separation and divorce, families with infants, families with children who have special needs, families who have experienced abuse and neglect, and adoptive families are discussed in particular. Chapter 15 identifies strategies for teachers who face particularly challenging attitudes and situations.

Each chapter begins with clearly defined learning objectives, linked with the specific criteria from the NAEYC program standard for accreditation of programs for young children and from the NAEYC Licensure standards. These standards are printed on the front and back inside covers of this book for handy reference. Specific examples and dialogues from teachers and parents, who may be quite like those encountered by students, make ideas and suggestions real, as in the previous editions. The exercises for students listed at each chapter's end and in the Instructor's Guide are designed to help students grapple actively with the concepts. Bibliographies of suggested readings can help students examine the issues further; in this edition, they are found on the website.

Teaching and Learning Tools

- **Use of color throughout the text.** The ninth edition uses full-color photographs, illustrations, tables, and graphs, and to draw attention to examples and other important features. We are excited to offer you this attractive new format.

- **Stronger emphasis on NAEYC standards.** As mentioned earlier, the standards for NAEYC program accreditation for early childhood programs and for professional preparation programs inform the objectives and content of each chapter. You will find the standards themselves printed on the inside covers of this book for easy reference, and you can find them linked after each objective. Throughout the text, you will find icons to denote NAEYC standards and statements.

- **Learning Objectives.** The learning objectives correlated to the main sections in each chapter show students what they need to know to process and understand the information in the chapter. After completing the chapter, students should be able to demonstrate how they can use and apply their new knowledge and skills.

- **Digital Downloads.** Downloadable and often customizable, these practical and professional resources allow students to immediately implement and apply this textbook's content in the field. The student downloads these tools and keeps them forever, enabling preservice teachers to build their library of practical, professional resources. Look for the TeachSource Digital Downloads label that identifies these items.

- **TeachSource videos** feature footage from the classroom to help students relate key chapter content to real-life scenarios. Critical-thinking questions provide opportunities for in-class or online discussion and reflection.

- **Strengthened coverage of working with families from diverse backgrounds.** Throughout this book, readers will encounter an extended understanding of the importance of working respectfully with families of very diverse backgrounds and beliefs. A feature to further highlight this emphasis is the specific points of "Cultural Considerations" to be found in each chapter. Each feature concludes with a personal reflective question to stimulate thought on the topic and to evaluate one's own beliefs/thinking. Watch for these specially marked boxes.

- **MindTap for Education** is a first-of-its kind digital solution that prepares teachers by providing them with the knowledge, skills, and competencies they must demonstrate to earn an education degree and state licensure, and to begin a successful career. Through activities based on real-life teaching situations, MindTap elevates students' thinking by giving them experiences in applying concepts, practicing skills, and evaluating decisions, guiding them to become reflective educators.

- **What Does Brain Research Tell Us feature boxes.** Where relevant, discussions of brain research have been added to broaden reader understanding of the practical implications of research on brain development for working with children and families. Watch for these specially marked features.

- **Opportunities for Self-Reflection** are intended to encourage you to consider your personal attitudes and experiences related to the concepts discussed in each chapter. Thought-provoking questions are included to promote your individual reflection and class discussion.

- **Ideas for Teachers** boxes contain practical considerations, highlighted at appropriate points.

- **Cultural Considerations** sections are found in each chapter to further highlight the text's emphasis on diversity and are accompanied by personal reflective questions to help students evaluate their own beliefs regarding the topic.

- **List of books for both children and adults.** Books that are appropriate for important issues, such as family diversity, divorce and stepparenting, living with children with special needs, child abuse, and adoption, are noted.

- **Key Terms** are printed in **bold type** where they first appear in the chapter and are defined in the margins and again in the glossary at the back of the book. Reinforcement and cross-referencing enhance comprehension.

- A bulleted **Summary** concludes each chapter.

- **Student Activities for Further Study** may be used for in-class or out-of-class assignments.

- An exercise titled **Apply the Concepts: Case in Point** encourages the application of particular concepts to classroom practice and teacher experience. Questions may be used for individual thought and group discussion. In addition, most chapters include realistic scenarios of interaction and attitudes of teachers and parents.

- **Review Questions** check students' mastery of the chapter content.

- **Helpful websites** are offered to recognize the important role that technology plays in today's world in expanding resources for learning. Due to the fluid nature of the Internet, we are not providing web addresses, but instead we describe the relevant agencies and organizations. Students may then use their search engine to locate websites.

- **References**, containing a vast amount of new and updated research, are now found at the end of the textbook.

- **Appendix on Home Visits with Parents and Children** is a newly expanded appendix, which offers information about the topic of home visits, recognizing that some programs and schools may consider using this strategy for family involvement. (This was included as a chapter in earlier editions.)

- A comprehensive **Glossary** and **Index** conclude the text with reader-friendly cross-references.

Chapter-by-Chapter Coverage and Updates

- Chapter 1 is an introduction to the dominant theme of the text—the need to work respectfully with very diverse families, and the need to understand the unique needs of every family. The chapter has been expanded to help students more easily identify the learning objectives in the chapter. Other new additions include updated information on diversity in America and a new TeachSource video activity.

- Chapter 2 is an in-depth study of modern families and the factors that shape their lives. All statistics and figures in this chapter have been updated. With the numbers of families living in poverty increasing, two new additions to this chapter include a summary of the effects of poverty on brain development and a TeachSource video activity related to homeless families.

- Chapter 3 focuses on the various roles of parents in creating families and bringing up children in order to heighten teacher awareness of the challenges facing parents.

A new section on parenting and brain development has been added. All statistics and references have been updated.

- Chapter 4 offers a discussion of the various models and motivations to include families in the education of their children. A new TeachSource video activity explores the effects of one of the intervention programs that involved parents. One new addition to this chapter is a summary of the benefits of family engagement in their children's education, as identified by the National PTA, as well as an expansion of Hart and Risley's study on the effects of supporting parents to adopt new behaviors with their children. The recommendations of NAEYC are discussed.

- Chapter 5 identifies benefits for children, parents, and teachers when parents and teachers work in partnership, as well as potential barriers to teacher–parent relationships. This chapter has been streamlined to present cogent arguments for working with families, as well as promoting teacher awareness of attitudes and behaviors that prevent real partnership.

- Chapter 6 describes the attitudes and conditions that create the foundations for successful partnerships and offers examples of schools that are trying to implement partnership philosophy in their practice. Realistic examples are offered throughout the chapter.

- Chapter 7 describes the orientation process for children and parents to begin the process of exchanging information and supporting one another during the separation experience. Helpful questionnaires, suggestions for teachers, and handouts are offered for digital download in addition to being embedded in the text.

- Chapter 8 introduces a number of informal communication methods, including newsletters, bulletin boards, electronic communication, and other personal methods. Again, very practical examples are given, as well as a number of video activities to increase understanding and digital downloads for future classroom use.

- Chapter 9 offers a comprehensive look at parent–teacher conferences, with many practical tips for effective communication. The chapter includes a video activity for application.

- Chapter 10 explores the various methods for involving families in the classroom and recognizes other ways that families can support the teacher's efforts outside the classroom.

- Chapter 11 discusses the various facets of parent education and offers many practical suggestions for teachers planning such efforts. A new video case allows students to apply the concepts from the chapter.

- Chapter 12 considers how home and schools work with and within communities. The role of advocate is discussed, and a discussion of service learning for children within the community also is included.

- Chapter 13 focuses entirely on the issue of working with diverse families, including both linguistic and cultural diversity. Some of the issues that often arise are explored, and a detailed example of working with diverse families in a particular program is given, along with another that is available on the website.

- Chapter 14 helps students understand ways of working with families in unique circumstances, such as divorce and remarriage, parenting children with special needs or in adoption, families with infants, and families where abuse and neglect have occurred. Specific examples help clarify the teacher role. New additions to this chapter include information on how brain development is impacted.

- Chapter 15 deals with the recognition that teachers have to work with all parents, including those who are difficult to work with or reach. Helpful strategies are offered, along with tools for considering things from the parent's viewpoint.

Accompanying Teaching and Learning Resources

The ninth edition of *Home, School, & Community Relations* is accompanied by an extensive package of instructor and student resources.

MindTap™: The Personal Learning Experience

MindTap for Gestwicki *Home, School, & Community Relations* 9e represents a new approach to teaching and learning. A highly personalized, fully customizable learning platform, MindTap helps students to elevate thinking by guiding them to do the following:

- Know, remember, and understand concepts critical to becoming a great teacher.

- Apply concepts, create tools, and demonstrate performance and competency in key areas in the course.

- Prepare artifacts for the portfolio and eventual state licensure, to launch a successful teaching career.

- Develop the habits to become a reflective practitioner.

As students move through each chapter's Learning Path, they engage in a scaffolded learning experience, designed to move them up Bloom's Revised Taxonomy, from lower- to higher-order thinking skills. The Learning Path enables preservice students to develop these skills and gain confidence by:

- Engaging them with chapter topics and activating their prior knowledge by watching and answering questions about TeachSource videos of teachers teaching and children learning in real classrooms

- Checking their comprehension and understanding through *Did You Get It?* assessments, with varied question types that are autograded for instant feedback

- Applying concepts through mini-case scenarios—students analyze typical teaching and learning situations and create a reasoned response to the issue(s) presented in the scenario

- Reflecting about and justifying the choices they made within the teaching scenario problem

MindTap helps instructors facilitate better outcomes by evaluating how future teachers plan and teach lessons in ways that make content clear and help diverse students learn, assessing the effectiveness of their teaching practice, and adjusting teaching as needed. The Student Progress App makes grades visible in real time so students and instructors always have access to current standings in the class.

MindTap for Gestwicki *Home, School, & Community Relations* 9e helps instructors

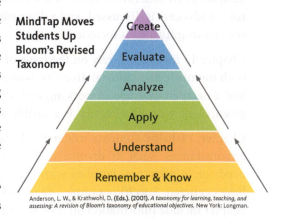

MindTap Moves Students Up Bloom's Revised Taxonomy

Create
Evaluate
Analyze
Apply
Understand
Remember & Know

Anderson, L. W., & Krathwohl, D. (Eds.). (2001). *A taxonomy for learning, teaching, and assessing: A revision of Bloom's taxonomy of educational objectives.* New York: Longman.

easily set their course since it integrates into the existing Learning Management System and saves instructors time by allowing them to fully customize any aspect of the learning path. Instructors can change the order of the student learning activities, hide activities they don't want for the course, and—most important—add any content they do want (e.g., YouTube videos, Google docs, links to state education standards). Learn more at www.cengage.com/mindtap.

PowerPoint® Lecture Slides

These vibrant Microsoft® PowerPoint lecture slides for each chapter assist you with your lecture by providing concept coverage using images, figures, and tables directly from the textbook.

Online Instructor's Manual with Test Bank

An online Instructor's Manual accompanies this book. It contains information to assist the instructor in designing the course, including sample syllabi, discussion questions, teaching and learning activities, field experiences, learning objectives, and additional online resources. For assessment support, the updated test bank includes true/false, multiple-choice, matching, short-answer, and essay questions for each chapter.

Cognero

Cengage Learning Testing Powered by Cognero is a flexible online system that allows you to author, edit, and manage Test Bank content from multiple Cengage Learning solutions; create multiple test versions in an instant; and deliver tests from your LMS, your classroom, or wherever you want.

About the Author

Carol Gestwicki was an instructor in the early childhood education program at Central Piedmont Community College in Charlotte, North Carolina, for over 30 years. Her teaching responsibilities included supervising students in classroom situations as they worked with families. Earlier in her career, she worked with children and families in a variety of community agencies and schools in Toronto, New York, New Jersey, and Namibia (Southwest Africa).

She received her MA from Drew University. She has been an active member of the NAEYC for many years, including making numerous presentations at state and national conferences. She has been a Fellow in the Early Childhood Leadership Development Project at the University of North Carolina at Chapel Hill, and she has been associated with the T.E.A.C.H. Model/Mentor program.

Her other publications include more than two dozen articles about child development and family issues and scripts and design for 14 audiovisual instructional programs. She has three other books on topics in early education published by Delmar Learning: *Developmentally Appropriate Practice: Curriculum and Development in Early Education*, Fifth Edition (2013); *Essentials of Early Education* (1997); and *Authentic Childhood: Exploring Reggio Emilia in the Classroom* (2002). Currently, she writes a regular column titled "Grandma Says" for *Growing Child*.

Acknowledgments

Students and colleagues in Charlotte and throughout North Carolina have been enormously helpful in the continuing discussion of working to support children and their families. I have been fortunate to have an ongoing relationship with the children, families, and staff at the Children's Educational Center of the Islands in Sanibel, Florida. I would also like to acknowledge longtime friends and colleagues at Central Piedmont Community College in Charlotte. Thank you also goes to the reviewers of the text for their helpful comments. They include:

Jennifer Briffa, Merritt College

Cheryl Bulat, Morton College

Joannie Busillo-Aguayo, California State University–Northridge

Jennifer Carsten, University of the Incarnate Word

Marilyn Cavazos, Laredo Community College

Mary Jo Cherry, Ursuline College

Amy Davis, Nashville State Community College

Evia Davis, Langston University

Katharine Delavan, Lake Erie College

Janet Fisher, Western Piedmont Community College

Peggy Gallagher, Georgia State University

Shanna Graves, University of Houston–Clear Lake

Ginger Harris-Mcginty, Central Carolina Community College

Kathy Head, Lorain County Community College

Jeanne Helm, Richland Community College

Annemarie Hindman, Temple University

Patricia Hutton, Judson University

Mary Larue, J. Sargeant Reynolds Community College

Laurie McAdams, Tarrant County College South

Michelle Moen, El Camino College

Mary Ruth Moore, The University of the Incarnate Word

Sandra Owen, Cincinnati State Technical and Community College

Laine Rieger, Minnesota West Community and Technical College

Heather Seagle, Jeff Davis Community College

Lois Silvernail, Spring Hill College

Kerri Tobin, Marywood University

Marye Vance, Durham Technical Community College

Reece Wilson, University of Pittsburgh–Bradford

Loraine Woods, Mississippi Valley State University

Robin Zinsmeister, College of the Albemarle

And as always, I appreciate the support and love from my own family, who taught me everything I know about the complexity and importance of family.

CHAPTER 1

A Day with Two Families: Diversity of Experience

Digital Vision/Photodisc/Getty Images

Learning Objectives

After reading this chapter, you should be able to:

1-1   Identify circumstances in families' lives that influence parents and children.

1-2   List several external factors causing stress in the families portrayed.

1-3   List several emotional responses evidenced in the parents portrayed.

1-4   Describe why teachers have an obligation to understand family life and how family life impacts teaching.

1-5   Identify types of diversity that may be found in typical communities.

naeyc

Related NAEYC Standards

Accreditation Standards (see inside text back cover for full listing of the Accreditation Standards for exemplary early childhood programs)

1.A.01, 1.A.02, 1.A.03, 1.A.04; 2.A.08; 7.A.01, 7.A.02, 7.A.04

Licensure Standards (see inside text front cover for full listing of the Licensure Standards for this chapter)

2a, 2b, 2c

Building partnerships with families is a complex process. The most important way for teachers to begin learning how to work effectively with families is to become sensitive to the needs and pressures of every family. This requires an authentic appreciation of the strengths and challenges inherent in each situation. Families that teachers encounter may be difficult to understand in their diversity. The ideas, emotions, and cultural experiences of unique individuals are what create families. Their living places, their family traditions, and their styles of communicating and living together are familiar and comfortable to those within the family and to no one else. Even families who share the same cultural, linguistic, or religious traditions will not be alike because of the unique inner and outer views of the individuals involved. And in contemporary society, with the myriad cultures, family structures, and lifestyles that exist side by side, interacting within the same schools, workplaces, and communities, it is vital that this assumption and celebration of uniqueness be made explicit and accepted by all teachers.

The differences in families create divisions with teachers only when those differences are seen as frightening, threatening, and mysterious. When they are seen as interesting and enriching to society in general and to the lives they touch in particular, differences are to be valued. When individuals come together to form relationships and communicate in the spirit of openness that is vital for effective family–teacher partnerships, a first step is to attempt to understand the other and to convey an attitude of respect and acceptance. Understanding and acceptance are products of knowledge and an attitude of openness. In this chapter, an examination of the hypothetical lives of two of the case study families we will meet throughout the book may help to heighten awareness of the demands and stresses in the lives of families and of the individual circumstances of each family's life. The more sensitivity that teachers can develop to the complex lives of different families, the more likely they can approach those families with true empathy.

As a teacher working with children, it is important to be mindful of the absolute significance of the families from which they come. Family is the preeminent force in developing us as people. Families are unique in their circumstances, but they are related by the common roles and experiences of parenthood. No one who is just an onlooker to the living drama of any family can come close to appreciating the thousands of details, interactions, and emotional nuances that comprise a family's experience. Researchers (or teachers) frequently do not have the opportunity to record the actions of family members as they live their daily lives, but it is probably only through such methods that the individual threads of the family fabric can be perceived and appreciated. Children and their families may face enormous individual and social pressures, which may not be perceived or understood by teachers. This is why teachers must become as familiar as possible with the story of each family.

Such familiarity has nothing to do with being intrusive; rather, it helps a teacher become as professionally helpful as possible. Appreciating the contribution of each family is a good starting place to consider how to build effective partnerships with them. Throughout the book, you will find references to the diverse fictional families that will be introduced in detail in Chapter 2. They represent the many family structures, cultural backgrounds, and particular circumstances that you may find among families in your own classrooms. Here is a closer look at two of our case study families as they move through a day. Consider their challenges and their needs as you reflect on the stories. (If you want details on each family, read the section in Chapter 2 beginning on page 23 now.)

1-1   Case Study: Meet Two Families

1-1a   The Lawrence Family

When the alarm went off at 6 a.m., no one moved. Fannie stayed quite still, hoping Otis would remember it was his morning to get the children up and start the dressing and breakfast process. She felt so tired that she could not get up yet anyway, stifling the guilty reminder that it was 11 the night before when Otis got home from his class, and he must be pretty tired, too. But the past month, she seemed to be completely exhausted at the start of each day. She wondered how she would get through the next three months. She again considered whether it might be a mistake to work right up until the birth, but that was the only way she could take three months off after the baby was born. In her head, she reviewed the decision, but there appeared to be no other options. Their income looked fine on paper, but when you subtracted the child support that Otis sent for the boys—and it would soon increase because Danny had to get braces—there just was no extra money for her to take additional unpaid leave.

She groaned, but Otis still did not move. In a burst of exasperation, she maneuvered out of bed and banged the bathroom door louder than was necessary. Otis stretched and turned over, feeling guilty about Fannie but also telling himself he needed the extra rest after the late night at class and the late night he would have tonight at work. He would get up in a few minutes and help Fannie get the kids ready.

Fannie laid out breakfast things and went to wake the children. Four-year-old Pete was tired and hard to get moving, so she practically had to dress him, and eight-year-old Kim was impatient to get her hair done. By the time they were eating breakfast, Fannie looked at the clock and realized she would have to skip hers and dress quickly or she would be late again. In the still-dark bedroom, she fumbled for clothes and shoes and then went into the bathroom to shower quickly and dress.

She returned to the kitchen to find the table a mess of cereal and milk and heard the TV blaring in the living room. "Kim, when I leave you in charge, I don't expect you to let Pete watch TV. Just look at this mess. Turn that off and at least put the milk in the fridge and get your teeth brushed, and Petey, see if you can't tie your shoes to help Mama out today."

Kim said, "Mama, I want a lunch packed. It's that awful fried chicken for lunch at school today, and I hate it."

"Kim! I told you before, I have to fix lunches at night. I don't have the time. We've got to leave right now, so don't start that." Kim's lip trembled, and Fannie turned away abruptly. She did not have time for one of Kim's scenes; besides, she was getting pretty sick of them because Kim was doing this more and more often. Last night, she spent an hour whining that she did not have any friends in her class and she hated Miss Yates. This was not like Kim, Fannie thought distractedly. She had always been a happy child.

Otis appeared in the kitchen just in time to see Kim burst into tears. "Hey, what's the matter here?" he asked cheerily. Fannie glared at him as Kim sobbed that Mama would not make her a lunch and that she could not eat the lunch at school. "Oh, won't she—" Otis began teasingly, but Fannie snapped, "Just be quiet, Otis. I haven't had one second this morning. I haven't even had time for breakfast, so if she wants a lunch, you'd have to make it, but we have to leave right now!"

Otis handed some change to Kim and said, "Well, at least you can eat some ice cream, OK? Now leave your mama alone." He patted Fannie's shoulder apologetically. "Slow down, babe. You'll make it. You shouldn't be skipping breakfast. Come on, Petey, hurry up. Your mom's in a hurry. Don't forget I work late tonight, Fannie. See you by 10. Try to be awake," he joked, patting her again.

"Fat chance," muttered Fannie and she hustled the children to the car, with Kim still sniffling loudly. As she drove along, Fannie again wondered why they had even gotten married. With work and his college classes, Otis was never home in the evenings. Instantly, she stifled the thought and wished she had at least given him a hug. He did work hard. She knew this was a good marriage—better than the too-young one with Kim and Pete's father that had left her a single mother for two years before she met Otis, who was also recently divorced.

She dropped Kim off at her school with a determined smile. Kim walked off sullenly, and Fannie tried not to mind. She noticed that no one else was entering the door with Kim. It was early, she knew, but she had to drop Kim off, then Pete, and still arrive at her own school by 7:45 a.m. She would not have felt right leaving Kim to wait for the bus, but this was another one of Kim's complaints—all the other kids got to ride the bus. She made a mental note to try to see Kim's teacher soon and ask her whether Kim was justified in saying she had no friends. Perhaps she could arrange for a girl to come with Kim after school—on a day when her own schedule allowed Kim to skip going to afterschool child care. Anyway, she would have to ask Miss Johnston if Kim being dropped off early created a problem; she was a little afraid to do that because the teacher was young and single and probably would not understand hectic morning schedules. Heaven knows it would be worse next year because Pete's school did not offer infant care; that would mean three stops before 7:45 a.m. She had been tempted to move Pete to another school but decided that he already had to adjust to a lot of changes in his young life—and the baby would be yet another one. She sighed and then realized they were at Pete's school. Thank goodness he had been quiet—unusual for him.

"Oh, no," she whispered as they passed the classroom bulletin board with its reminder that they needed toothpaste. "I forgot again." Fannie helped Pete take off his jacket and smiled toward a teacher who approached her.

"Oh, Mrs. Lawrence, I see Pete's got one of his cars again. We really can't let the children bring their own toys; it creates such problems. Please take it with you."

Confused, Fannie looked down and realized Pete was clutching a tiny car in his hand. She started to explain that she did not realize he had brought it, but then she fell silent as she realized that made her sound like a pretty careless mother. Pete put his hand behind his back, and Fannie looked for help from the teacher, who moved down the hall. Fannie realized she had to take the car away. She had a nasty thought about the teacher while she pried the car out of Pete's fingers. Pete burst into tears, and Fannie's stomach tightened. She gave him a quick hug and muttered a few words in his ear, looked appealingly at the teacher—who now looked even more annoyed—and quickly dashed down the hall. She felt like crying herself as she listened to Pete's wails and thought about what a horrible morning it had been for all of them. She was so preoccupied with thinking about the kids' reactions and making resolutions for a tranquil evening that she walked right past another parent, who called hello after her. Sheepishly, she waved and then hurried on, her face hot with embarrassment.

Stoplights and blocked lanes punctuated the trip to her own school, and she found herself almost running from her parked car, aware that several busloads of children had already arrived.

The day went fairly smoothly for Fannie, although with 28 third-graders to look after—plus her turn at playground duty—she was worn out when the final bell rang.

A parent who came to pick up her child wanted to talk about the new reading program, but Fannie had to cut her off to get to the weekly faculty meeting on time. As she hurried down the hall, she reminded herself to make an appointment with Kim's teacher so she would not start off by annoying the teacher showing up unannounced. The faculty meeting dragged on, and Fannie found herself glancing repeatedly at her watch, estimating how long it would take to pick up Kim and get her to her dancing class.

The meeting finally ended and she rushed to her car, noticing with longing the group of young women who stayed back, chatting and planning to go out for a drink.

Her heart lifted when she saw Kim playing happily with another girl at the afterschool child care where the bus dropped her each afternoon. The college student in charge of the group apologized for not remembering that it was Kim's dancing class day and having her already changed. Fannie swallowed her irritation, but it became more difficult to control because rather than change into her dancing clothes, Kim dawdled with her friend until Fannie had to brusquely order her to leave and hurry up and change. Kim began to whine, but she stopped when she saw the look on her mother's face.

Fannie tried to relax and make pleasant conversation about Kim's day as they drove to the dancing class. Kim chattered happily about her new friend at child care and asked if she could come to their house to play one afternoon. Fannie promised, thinking uneasily of the logistics problems of rides and permission that might entail. She dropped Kim at the door, promising to try to be back in time to watch the last few minutes of the class. Checking her watch, she tried to organize her errands to fit them into the hour time slot—drop off the dry cleaning, cash a check at the bank, pick up a few groceries, and get to the post office for stamps. That would cut it pretty close for picking up Pete. She hated his day to be so long, but she knew from experience that it was worse to drag a tired child with her. Trying to ignore her own fatigue, she hurried on.

Pete looked up hopefully as she walked into his room at the child care center, and she realized with a pang that he had probably been doing that as each parent entered the room for the previous half hour. His teacher said that he had had a good day after the upsetting beginning. Fannie was annoyed that she brought that up again. She wished this young woman could understand that it was bad enough having to rush Pete in the morning, let alone strip him of all his favorite things for the day.

An accident held up traffic on the way to the dancing studio, and by the time they arrived, Kim was waiting in the parking lot with the dancing teacher, who looked in a hurry to leave. Kim's face was stormy as she accused Fannie with "You promised." Fannie tried to explain but felt helpless and angry at the eight-year-old's indignation. Impulsively, changing the mood and giving in to her own fatigue, she suggested supper at McDonald's.

Amid the kids' squeals of glee, she thought glumly about the nutritional consequences and decided she would not ask them what they had eaten for lunch. Some mother, she thought, conjuring up an image of her own mother's plentiful dinner table. And there would be nothing to keep warm for Otis. Well, maybe she would fix him a nice omelet if he was not too late.

The kids were cheerful and chatty over hamburgers, so Fannie relaxed and enjoyed their stories. "We're doing OK," she told herself. "They're really fine."

It was after 8 p.m. when they got home. Fannie put Pete in the bathtub and started Kim on her reading homework in the bathroom to watch him so Fannie could unpack the groceries and start a load of laundry. At least Otis had cleaned up the breakfast mess; that was more than she could have stood 12 hours later!

She read Pete a bedtime story and then tucked him in. He was tired and settled down easily. Fannie looked at him tenderly. He was growing so quickly; pretty soon, he would no longer be the baby. For the thousandth time, she wondered how he would feel when the new baby arrived.

Kim wanted to watch some television, but Fannie reminded her to first find her clothes for the morning and decide if she wanted a lunch, which she did. Making the sandwiches, Fannie thought, "Maybe tomorrow will be a better day." At bedtime, Kim asked her to be sure to give Daddy a kiss for her. Fannie wished again that Otis could be home more at night so they could feel like a real family. She knew what Otis would say if she brought it up again. "The classes are important if I'm ever going to be able to stop selling cars at night. It's only a couple more years. And in the meantime, selling cars is giving us a good living." He was right, of course, but the kids practically never saw him. For that matter, it was tough on all of them.

Fannie folded the laundry, washed her hair, spread out her clothes for the morning, and lay down on the bed to read the morning paper. Within 10 minutes, she had fallen asleep. When Otis came in at 10 p.m., she was still sleeping. He sighed, turned out the light, and went to see if there were any leftovers in the kitchen.

1-1b The Ashley Family

Sylvia Ashley, mother of six-year-old Terrence and four-year-old Ricky, got up quickly when the alarm went off at 6 a.m. She had washed out Terrence's shirt the previous night and wanted to iron it before it was time for him to get up. Anyway, she liked having time in the early morning when the building was still quiet. The rest of the day, there was hardly a moment when someone was not yelling or throwing something. She turned on the kitchen light cautiously, knowing the roaches would scurry away from the sink.

She ironed carefully. She felt bad that Terrence had to wear the same clothes over and over, but at least he was always clean and tidy. She hoped the teacher would notice that and not treat him badly. He had recently made some comments about boys bullying him on the playground, and she hoped it was not because of his clothes. She hated the way some people treated people without money. She also did not want her kids to grow up thinking they were not as good as everyone else just because they lived in subsidized housing and were in a single-parent family.

She sighed, remembering she had to return to the social services office today to talk to the social worker. She dreaded it, but their check had been reduced two months earlier and she simply could not make it on the lower amount. Last week, she had to borrow $5 from her neighbor across the hall to get some macaroni and milk for the kids' supper. She knew she could not do that again—the woman barely spoke to her anyway. Because she was entering that job-training program, she also knew she had to get a new pair of shoes. Ricky's sneakers had a hole right through the toe, too.

She unplugged the iron and glanced at the clock. Time to get the boys up. They were cheerful and chattered away, and Terrence helped Ricky get dressed. Ricky ate a bowl of cereal; Terrence drank a glass of milk to have something in his stomach until he got to school. He preferred to have breakfast at home, and she had always let him until things got so tight. Because he was eligible for the free breakfast at school, she took advantage of that small opportunity to save money.

She dressed quickly and cleaned up the kitchen. Terrence was ready at the door, hair neatly combed, when she got there. He grumbled a bit every day about his mother and little brother having to go with him to school, but she was afraid to let him walk alone six blocks through this neighborhood where shots frequently rang out.

Ricky struggled to keep up. They waved to Terrence from the street as he climbed the school stairs by himself. Sylvia worried about him; he never mentioned a friend, and after school, she and Ricky walked him home and then he played with Ricky. She knew he needed friends his own age, but she kept him in the apartment unless she could go to the playground with them. She had seen and heard plenty of fights and wildness from some of the kids in their building, and she knew some of them were already in serious trouble with the police. She was going to keep her boys free from that. Terrence was a good student—a smart boy; he would grow up differently from those other kids.

She and Ricky waited at the corner for the bus that would take them downtown to the square, where they could transfer to the one that would take them out to the social services building. She barely heard Ricky chattering and pointing out cars and asking questions as they rode along because she was busy rehearsing what she had to say.

The waiting room was full; she found one chair and held Ricky on her lap for a while until he got wiggly. Then, she let him sit on the floor beside her. She kept listening for the woman to call her name, knowing that Ricky was getting restless. He asked her for something to eat as he watched a man eat crackers he had bought from the vending machine. Sylvia did not want to waste 85 cents and wished she had remembered to bring something for him. Fortunately, they called her name just then, and moving into the small office distracted Ricky.

At least this social worker was kinder than the last one, who had positively glared every time Ricky moved. Sylvia had been furious underneath; the woman had to have known there was no money for babysitters and that nobody could help them out, but it would not have done to let that anger show.

By the end of the discussion, Sylvia felt very depressed. She hated the questions about whether she had heard from either of the boys' fathers; she always wanted to say she was thankful she had not and would not take a penny from either of them anyway. Now that she was starting the job-training program, Ricky's child care would be paid for until after she was working full time.

Sylvia worried about whether her wages would be enough to support all of them when she was no longer receiving assistance and whether the children's medical expenses would be covered, but she was hopeful about what her work could mean for her small family. Maybe she would make enough to get them into a little apartment somewhere nicer, and she would have some friends from work, and Terrence could have friends to play with, and things would be better. She had to do it. Her kids deserved more.

Ricky was tired and cranky as they waited for the bus home. He started to cry, and she shook him a little—not very hard, but she just could not stand to listen to it or have the bus driver stare at her when she got on with a crying child.

He fell asleep on the bus, and she pulled him against her shoulder, knowing he would wake up when they had to transfer. It had been a long morning for him. Neither of them said much as they rode the last bus and walked home for lunch. Ricky finished his soup, and she put him in bed for a nap. She sat and thought about Ricky going to child care and about herself starting the training program. She hoped she could do it. It had been a long time since she had been in school—and she did not have kids and everything else to worry about. She worried about how it would be for Ricky; he had never been away from her at all. The social worker told her that the preschool was a good one, but that did not reassure her that Ricky would not get upset.

She glanced at the clock; in a few more minutes, she would have to wake up Ricky to go get Terrence. He was so worn out that she wanted to let him sleep, but there was nobody to ask to stay with him. She worried briefly about Terrence, who would have to undergo yet another change when she started her job-training program. He would have to come home to an empty apartment and stay by himself for a couple of hours until she finished her class, picked up Ricky, and arrived home. She had already lost sleep worrying about that, but there was nothing else to be done. She would warn him about not answering the door, staying away from the windows, not using the stove, and everything else she could think of and then just hope he would stay in the apartment, safely, by himself.

Terrence was quiet on the way home. In the apartment, he unfolded a note and handed it to her. It was a reminder that parents needed to send $5 the next day to pay for a ticket to a play at the children's theater next week. Sylvia avoided Terrence's eyes as she said that she could not send the money, so he could stay home from school the day of the play. Terrence said nothing.

She gathered the laundry, her wallet, and keys and then took the boys with her to the basement laundry room. The children sat and argued. When another woman came in, Sylvia snapped at the kids to be quiet, and they sat glumly until she asked Terrence to help her match the socks. Back upstairs, the boys watched cartoons while she made hamburgers for supper. After supper, Terrence did his homework at the kitchen table, and Ricky sat beside him and colored in a coloring book. She put them in the bath together while she tidied the kitchen. After the children watched some more TV, she put them in bed and sat by herself in the living room, on the couch where she would sleep. There was nothing she wanted to see on TV, but she left it on to keep her company. After an hour or so, she turned out the light and went to sleep.

Stop now and consider the various external sources of stress in the lives of these two families, as well as some of the typical emotional responses of the parents.

1-2 External Factors That Cause Stress

Socioeconomic status is an evident factor. In the case of the Lawrence family, two fully employed adults are needed to maintain their middle-class lifestyle, especially with the demands of child support after divorce. Work hours and a two-parent working family conflict with family life, and parents usually feel stretched and tense. In the case of the Ashley family, there is the constant struggle of poverty, involving concerns about adequate housing and food, and pressures on the parent to try to improve her socioeconomic status. The demands and functions of other institutions, such as the social welfare system and the school and child care systems, impact families. The complexity of modern life, with time spent commuting and driving children, as well as the errands necessary to maintain a household, is another stressor. Community factors, such as unsafe or violent neighborhoods, add stress, as does the isolation of families, caused by all these factors. The dynamic of marital and family relationships may add additional stress, to say nothing of the minutiae of daily life. No family is immune from these stressors.

1-3 Emotional Responses

As you considered the emotional responses of the parents portrayed, surely love and concern for the well-being of their children were most evident. Each of these parents genuinely cared about doing the best possible for their individual children. Even when parents were stressed, their children brought them joy. Guilt was another emotion portrayed in several instances—a feeling that they were not able to do the best for the children that they wanted to do. All were proud of their children and recognized that they deserved good things. Exasperation and frustration were present as well, with the daily annoyances. The feeling of loneliness also was evident.

- Irritability/Anger
- Restlessness
- Sadness
- Moodiness
- Grief / Depression
- Fear
- Overwhelmed

CULTURAL CONSIDERATIONS

Gender roles

One thing that culture defines is the gender roles played by male and female family members. Create a list for family responsibilities that you expect both males and females to carry out. Then, compare and discuss your assumptions with a fellow classmate. Consider the source of your understandings. Also consider the assumptions about gender roles of each adult family member in these two stories. A teacher's awareness of the diversity of cultural assumptions should be constant.

1-4 Implications for Teachers

It is a good idea to try to comprehend the lives of the families with whom you will work. Perhaps this has been a useful exercise to help you be aware of the circumstances of individual families that may affect so many of their interactions with teachers and schools. It is often too easy for teachers to be critical of parents who pick up their children late, forget the rules about bringing toys from home or signing reading records, or seem unwilling to cooperate with field trip plans. Seeing only one's own perspective is a common problem that disrupts relationships and communication.

When viewed more closely, both families have unique living circumstances and experiences, but both also have a common thread of stress with the various roles and responsibilities of parenthood, the isolation that comes from concentrating on children's care, and the deeply felt concerns for the children's lives. The families are alike in that, as with every other family you will encounter, they have both strengths and challenges.

You, the teacher, may or may not be a parent. If you are, then you have had daily experiences from a parent's perspective and do not need further convincing of the astonishing task of blending and fulfilling these various roles. But add to that understanding the awareness that variety in family structure, socioeconomic circumstances, individual abilities, and needs affect all families. Separately and on the printed page, parenting roles appear demanding; when experienced together in the particular context of daily life, they can be staggering. Even so, it is not unusual for teachers to use their own experiences as a standard against which to measure all other families: "If I could do it as a single parent, why can't she do a better job?" This is dangerous because each individual situation is unique.

For those of you who are not parents, recollections of your parents' lives during your childhood may be faint and will not reflect the enormity of life's demands. Even acquaintance with the parents of children in your classroom probably does not fully expose you to the extent of the demands on them. An active imagination will help you best here. On a sheet of paper, jot down any facts you know about several families' lives: the family members' ages, jobs or schools, hobbies and interests, and special family circumstances.

Now mentally take yourself through a sample of their days—and nights. (Parenting does not have a neatly prescribed limit on working hours!) Remember to include the details of daily life, such as doctors' visits, haircuts, and trips to the library and bank, as well as the unforeseen emergencies that pop up—the car breaking down, the babysitter getting sick, and the additional assignment at work.

Choose a cross section of families to contemplate; remember that the socioeconomic circumstances of any family may add additional strains—whether they are the daily struggles of a poverty-level family or the demands on an upwardly mobile professional family. If you are doing this right, you will likely soon be shaking your head and growing tired in your imagination.

This might be a useful exercise to repeat whenever you find yourself making judgments or complaining about families. It is virtually impossible for a teacher to work effectively with classroom families until he or she is able to empathize with them. Remember, this is only an attempt to mentally understand possible situations; no outsider can fully appreciate what really goes on in any one family. Every family truly stands alone in its uniqueness.

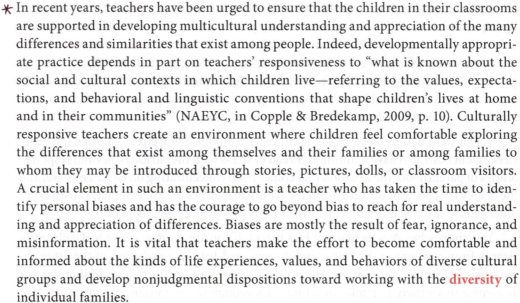

1-5 The Importance of Understanding Diversity in Classrooms

In recent years, teachers have been urged to ensure that the children in their classrooms are supported in developing multicultural understanding and appreciation of the many differences and similarities that exist among people. Indeed, developmentally appropriate practice depends in part on teachers' responsiveness to "what is known about the social and cultural contexts in which children live—referring to the values, expectations, and behavioral and linguistic conventions that shape children's lives at home and in their communities" (NAEYC, in Copple & Bredekamp, 2009, p. 10). Culturally responsive teachers create an environment where children feel comfortable exploring the differences that exist among themselves and their families or among families to whom they may be introduced through stories, pictures, dolls, or classroom visitors. A crucial element in such an environment is a teacher who has taken the time to identify personal biases and has the courage to go beyond bias to reach for real understanding and appreciation of differences. Biases are mostly the result of fear, ignorance, and misinformation. It is vital that teachers make the effort to become comfortable and informed about the kinds of life experiences, values, and behaviors of diverse cultural groups and develop nonjudgmental dispositions toward working with the **diversity** of individual families.

Culture is a comprehensive term that includes the various understandings, traditions, and guidance of the groups to which we all belong. "In essence, it is a lens through which each of us views and interprets the world" (Espinosa, 2010). This includes the cultures of family; ethnic, linguistic, and racial groups; religious groups; gender and sex role identifications; and geographical and community orientations.

In Chapter 13, we will explore in more detail ways that teachers can incorporate classroom practices that indicate the welcoming of each unique family and the valuing of the contributions their culture can make for rich classroom experiences and positive dialogue. Welcoming each family lays the groundwork for the development of positive identity formation and self-esteem for children and for respectful communication with their parents. In the context of this chapter's appreciation of unique family orientations, it is vital that teachers see the importance of taking the initiative in attempting to understand the backgrounds and circumstances of the families with whom they work (see Figure 1-1). The information to do this may come from published accounts written by members of particular cultural backgrounds.

diversity
State of being varied, as by family structure, race, religion, socioeconomic class, primary language, ethnic background, and so on.

culture
The various understandings, traditions, and guidance of the groups to which we all belong; the ways of living developed by a social group and transmitted to succeeding generations; the social backgrounds that imbue children with particular forms of knowledge, values, and expectations for behavior.

Published accounts, as in the case of imaginary accounts of the daily lives of families found in this chapter, may be less than perfect sources of understanding. They can, however, certainly heighten teacher awareness of cultural patterns of behavior and communication styles that might otherwise be misinterpreted or even offensive.

Teachers preparing to work with the diverse cultures represented in America or Canada today should become familiar with literature about working with at least the following cultural groups: African American, Native American or indigenous people, various Latino cultures, various Asian cultures, new immigrant families (whether legal or not), interracial and biracial families, gay, lesbian, and transgender families, and inner-city, homeless, single-parent, teenaged, and migrant families (see Figure 1-2). In addition, the populations of particular schools may reflect unique characteristics related to their geography, parents' occupations, or class composition. Such understanding will at least begin to open the doors of knowledge that will increase within relationships with members of the particular cultures; each family will still have its own specific interpretation of its particular culture. Teachers are also cautioned that learning about other cultures is not for the purpose of further separating groups into subjects to be studied but rather to bring people closer together through increased understanding and respect. As Janet Gonzalez-Mena warns in *Diversity in Early Care and Education Programs: Honoring Differences* (2008), "cultural labels are necessarily generalizations." Teachers must always remember that the best source of information about any individual family comes from the relationship with the family itself. And only as families perceive a genuine spirit of welcome and acceptance conveyed by a teacher will they become willing to share information about themselves.

It is important for a teacher to consider ideas about families actively. Recording thoughts about families in a notebook is a good starting place. Throughout this textbook, you will find suggestions titled "Opportunity for Self-Reflection."

FIGURE 1-1
Teachers must go beyond their own cultural experiences to understand the circumstances of all families with whom they work.

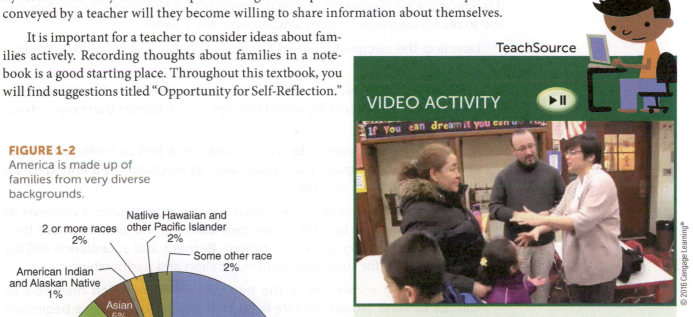

TeachSource

VIDEO ACTIVITY ▶❚❚

After viewing the video *Teachers Share their Experiences of Building Understanding of Families*, consider these questions:

1. How do the personal experiences of these teachers influence their understanding of diversity?

2. How do you see that these teachers' awareness would enhance their relationships with diverse families?

3. What strategies are presented to help teachers when encountering cultural diversity?

FIGURE 1-2
America is made up of families from very diverse backgrounds.

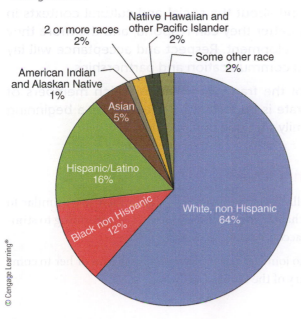

2 or more races
2%

Natiive Hawaiian and other Pacific Islander
2%

Some other race
2%

American Indian and Alaskan Native
1%

Asian
5%

Hispanic/Latino
16%

Black non Hispanic
12%

White, non Hispanic
64%

© Cengage Learning®

Thinking in a journal offers teachers opportunities to reflect actively on the attitudes and experiences that will shape practice and to ask questions that will help them decide on future actions. Here is the first "Opportunity for Self-Reflection." Watch for more in later chapters. Your instructor may assign these to you.

OPPORTUNITY FOR SELF-REFLECTION

How would you rate your experiences of the diversity that exists in America? So far in your life, have you been fairly removed from individuals who reflect America's diversity or have you had some encounters?

If you have been removed, reflect on the circumstances that have created this absence. If you have encountered diverse lifestyles and values, what was your response? What does this imply about areas on which you will have to concentrate or enhance in your professional development?

SUMMARY

It is important for teachers to realize the stresses that come with daily family life, and to recognize the unique circumstances of every family.

- Learning the circumstances of family lives helps teacher understanding and effectiveness.

- Time, socioeconomic stresses, and family structure, as well as the specific interpersonal relationships within families, are all factors that create stress within families.

- Most parents are devoted to their children and feel overwhelming love, along with pride, guilt, frustration, and exasperation. Parenting is an intensely emotional experience.

- The more teachers understand about the social and cultural contexts in which their families live, the better they can respond, and the more they can support learning and development. Respect and acceptance will lay the foundation for successful communication and partnerships.

- Understanding something of the framework within which members of various cultural groups operate is important for teachers as a beginning place to appreciating the family's unique perspective.

Student Activities for Further Studies

1. Consider a family you know well. Create an imaginary day in their life—similar to the stories you read early in the chapter. Work with a partner, brainstorming to stimulate your thinking. Share your account with the class.

2. Invite a parent of a young child to join your class discussion. Ask him or her to come prepared to present a sample diary of the family's daily life.

3. Read an account of a family or cultural group that might increase your understanding of various cultures or segments of society. For ideas, refer to the "Suggestions for Further Reading" box. Then, small groups of students could create a day in the life of a particular family, such as a newly immigrated Asian family, a Latino family, a family with two mothers, and so forth.

SUGGESTIONS FOR FURTHER READING

Birckmayer, J., Cohen, J., Jensen, I., & Variano, D. (2005). Kyle lives with his granny—Where are his mommy and daddy? Supporting grandparents who raise grandchildren. *Young Children, 60*(3), 100–104.

Bloom, L. (2001). I'm poor, I'm single, I'm a mom and deserve respect: Advocating in schools as/with mothers in poverty. *Educational Studies,* (32), 30–36.

Burt, T., Gelnaw, A., & Lesser, L. (2010). Do no harm: Creating welcoming and inclusive environments for lesbian, gay, bisexual, and transgender (LGBT) families in early childhood settings. *Young Children, 65*(1), 97–102.

Clay, J. (2007). Creating safe, just places to learn for children of lesbian and gay parents. *Spotlight on Young Children and Families.* Washington, DC: NAEYC.

Copple, C. (Ed.) (2003). *A world of difference: Readings on teaching young children in a diverse society.* Washington, DC: NAEYC.

DeJong, L. (2003). Using Erikson to work more effectively with teenage parents. *Young Children, 58*(2), 87–95.

Deparle, J. (2004). *American dream: Three women, ten kids, and a nation's drive to end welfare.* New York: Viking Books.

Duarte, G., & Rafanello, D. (2001). The migrant child: A special place in the field. *Young Children, 56*(2), 26–34.

Eggers-Pierola, C. (2006). *Connections and commitments: Reflecting Latino values in early childhood programs.* Portsmouth, NH: Heinemann.

Ehrenreich, B. (2002). *Nickled and dimed: On (not) getting by in America.* New York: Owl Books.

Elliott, K., & Fujiwara, S. (2005). Working with homeless young children and families. *Exchange,* (166), 45–48.

Hale-Benson, J. (1986). *Black children: Their roots, culture and learning styles* (rev. ed.). Baltimore: Johns Hopkins University Press. (2001). *Learning while black: Creating educational excellence for African-American children.* Baltimore: Johns Hopkins University Press.

Hildebrand, V., Phenice, L., Gray, M., & Hines, R. (2007). *Knowing and serving diverse families* (3rd ed. [most cultural groups]). Englewood Cliffs, NJ: Prentice Hall.

Howard, G. (2006). *We can't teach what we don't know: White teachers, multiracial schools* (2nd ed.). New York: Teachers College Press.

Huntsinger, C., et al. (2000). Understanding cultural contexts fosters sensitive caregiving of Chinese American children. *Young Children, 55*(6), 7–15.

Joshi, A. (2005). Understanding Asian Indian families: Facilitating meaningful home–school relations. *Young Children, 60*(3), 75–79.

Lamme, L., & Lamme, L. L. (2002). Welcoming children from gay families into our schools. *Educational Leadership, 59*(4), 6–11.

Lipper, J. (2004). *Growing up fast* [teenaged mothers]. New York: Picador.

Louie, V. (2004). *Compelled to Excel: Immigration, education and opportunity among Chinese Americans.* Palo Alto, CA: Stanford University Press.

Lundgren, D., & Morrison, J. (2003). Involving Spanish-speaking families in early education programs. *Young Children, 58*(3), 88–95.

Lynch, E., & Hanson, M. (2004). *Developing cross-cultural competence: A guide for working with young children and their families* (3rd ed.). Baltimore: Paul H. Brooks.

Rosier, K. (2000). *Mothering inner-city children: The early school years.* Piscataway, NJ: Rutgers University Press.

Shipler, D. (2004). *The working poor: Invisible in America.* New York: Knopf.

Swick, K., & Bailey, L. (2004). Communicating effectively with parents and families who are homeless. *Early Childhood Education Journal, 32*(3), 211–215.

Thompson, G. (2004). *Through ebony eyes: What teachers should know but are afraid to ask about African American students.* San Francisco: Jossey-Bass.

Walker-Dalhouse, D., & Dalhouse, A. D. (2001). Parent–school relations: Communicating more effectively with African American parents. *Young Children, 56*(4), 75–80.

Wardle, F. (2001). Supporting multiracial and multiethnic children and their families. *Young Children, 56*(6), 38–39.

Washington, V., & Andrews, J. D. (Eds.). (2010). *Children of 2020.* Washington, DC: NAEYC & Council for Professional Recognition.

4. Read the children's book *On the Day I Was Born* by Debbi Chocolate (Scholastic Press, 1995). Discuss with your classmates the specific ways your family celebrates the birth of a new baby. How do the celebrations you hear about differ from the customs in the book? How are the family's emotional responses like the emotional responses you hear described by your classmates? Write a brief summary of the differences and similarities among various family experiences.

5. With your classmates, generate a list of questions that would help you conduct a respectful interview with a person from another cultural or religious background. For example, you might want to formulate some questions that ask about family customs and holidays, religious observances, the roles played by family members, how discipline is approached within the family, and so on. Conduct the interview and then share some of your learning with your classmates. You may find the person to interview among your classmates, among the faculty at your college, in your neighborhood, or in one of your community institutions.

Apply the Chapter Concepts: Case in Point

This chapter is about the case studies of two families. Now that you have finished reading the case studies, consider these questions to further your understanding:

1. Identify the distinct emotions felt by Fannie Lawrence. What situations caused these emotions?

2. Identify the distinct emotions felt by Sylvia Ashley. What situations caused these emotions?

3. Identify some sources of stress for the children in the Lawrence family. Identify some sources of stress for the children in the Ashley family. What effect did the children's stress have on the parents?

4. In addition to the stress felt by the children, what are some other causes of stress for each mother?

Review Questions

1. List several external factors causing stress in the families portrayed.

2. List several emotional responses evidenced in the parents portrayed.

3. Describe why it is important for teachers to understand family life.

4. Identify the various kinds of diversity teachers may encounter.

Helpful Websites

- The National Association for the Education of Young Children. This website contains the NAEYC position statement "Responding to linguistic and cultural diversity, recommendations for effective early childhood education."

- National Black Child Development Institute. NBCDI initiates positive change for the health, welfare, and educational needs of all African American children. Visit this website to find helpful resources.

- Culturally & Linguistically Appropriate Services. The CLAS Institute identifies, evaluates, and promotes effective and appropriate early intervention practices and preschool practices that are sensitive and respectful to children and families from culturally and linguistically diverse backgrounds. The site has information for consumers (e.g., practitioners, families, and researchers) about materials and practices that are available and the contexts in which they might select a given material or practice.

Families Today

Learning Objectives

After reading this chapter, you should be able to:

2-1 Define family and consider several characteristics of families.

2-2 Describe seven characteristics of contemporary life that influence the nature of modern families.

2-3 Describe the importance of teacher understanding of contemporary trends that affect families.

naeyc

Related NAEYC Standards

Accreditation Standards (see inside text back cover for full listing of the Accreditation Standards for exemplary early childhood programs)

7.A.01

Licensure Standards (see inside text front cover for full listing of the Licensure Standards for this chapter)

2a

For a teacher, one very important role is collaborating with families. Although many teachers might prefer to concentrate only on the children who enter the classroom each day, children live in the context of their families—and their families are the most important and lifelong influence on their development. Teachers must understand those family contexts and respect the uniqueness of each family while bringing them into the child's educational world as full partners.

The families with whom a teacher works may not resemble the teacher's own and may be quite unlike each other in their structure, family lifestyles and values, cultural influences, and relationships. As America grows increasingly diverse, teachers need to prepare themselves to recognize, appreciate, and work with such diversity.

In this chapter, we begin to consider some of the reasons for the diversity and changes in family structure and appearance that are apparent in most American classrooms.

2-1   What Defines a Family?

The family is the most adaptable of human institutions and is able to modify its characteristics to meet those of the society in which it lives. Certainly, the family has adapted to much in recent decades: urbanization, a consumer-oriented economy, economic uncertainty, wars and terrorist attacks, changes in traditional religious and moral codes, increasing cultural diversity, and changes in all relationships basic to family life—including but not limited to those between male and female and young and old. Such changes have been occurring in every corner of the world, although our primary concern here is the American family.

Consider the families you might meet within any classroom or community: single-father families and single-mother families, with parents who may be widowed, divorced, or have never married; blended families from second marriages that bring together children from unrelated backgrounds; unmarried couples with children; gay and lesbian parents; adoptive families; grandparents functioning as parents in the absence of the intermediate generation; foster families; and families of mixed racial heritage—either biological or adoptive.

Such a wide range of families and relationships may make us feel uncomfortable in the distance from our values or ideals or comforted by the realization that our families are not the only ones that do not fit the perfect image of 1970s families in *The Cosby Show* seen on late-night cable reruns.

The word *family* has always meant many things to many people. What comes to mind when you think of the traditional family? Social historian Stephanie Coontz reminds us that this answer has changed depending on the era and its particular myths (2000). Despite the obvious fact that the phrase *the American family* does not describe one reality, it is used sweepingly. Many creators of television commercials seem to think it usually means a white, middle-class, monogamous father and mother at work, children busy with school and enrichment activities family—one that lives in a suburban one-family house, nicely filled with an array of appliances, a minivan or SUV in the driveway, and probably a dog in the yard. Such a description excludes the vast majority of American families, according to the last census (which does not enumerate dogs or minivans but found less than 7 percent of households conforming to the classic family headed by a working husband with a wife and two children at home). A recently made comment was that whereas most families used to have 2.6 children, many children now have 2.6 parents.

The entire Western world has experienced similar changes in family life during the past several decades.

Rather than suggest that the family is under siege, it is more accurate to suggest that our image of family may need to be broadened to accept diversity. It may be more important to concentrate on what families do rather than what they look like. Family may be more about content than about form (see Figure 2-1).

FIGURE 2-1
Families come in all shapes and sizes.

(a)

(b)

(c)

(d)

(e)

(f)

(g)

(h)

(i)

(j)

2-1a "Ideal" Family Images

What image comes to mind when you see the word *family*? People's mental images vary greatly, based in large part on their individual life experiences.

Try an experiment while you think about family. On a piece of paper, draw stick figures to represent the members of the family you first knew as a young child. Who represented family to you? Then, do the same to represent your family when you were a teenager. Had your family changed? Was anyone added or removed? What were the reasons for any changes?

Now draw the family in which you presently live. Who are your family members? What does this say about any changes in your life? If, as an adult, you have lived in numerous family structures, represent them, too.

Now, for one last picture. Imagine that you could design the ideal family for yourself. Draw what it would look like.

Sorting through your pictures may generate some thinking about family. One prediction is that most of the ideal pictures include a father, mother, and two children (probably a boy first and then a girl). If you are like most students who have done this, the ideal family usually includes these members—regardless of the actual composition of the families in which individuals have participated or presently live. Real experiences are often passed over in favor of the ideal two-parent, two-child home.

For many, the image of an ideal family is influenced less by real experiences than by subtle cultural messages that have bombarded us since childhood. The Vanier Institute reports that 86 percent of high school students surveyed, including 78 percent of the teens whose own parents had not stayed together, expect a lifelong marriage. From magazine advertisements to children's books—and, even more pervasively, from television shows— the attractive vision of husband, wife, and children beams at us. These inescapable messages influence our thinking about desirable family characteristics, and may produce guilt and negative feelings when the reality does not match the ideal.

Interestingly, students surveyed are aware that their ideal image is just that and are also aware of the societal influences that helped produce it.

FAMILY IMAGES

1. Draw the family you lived in as a child.
2. Draw the family you lived in as a teenager.
3. Draw the family in which you presently live.
4. Draw the ideal family you would design for yourself.
5. Share your pictures with two classmates.
6. Considering all the pictures, what statements can you make about family and the influences that have created your sense of an ideal family?

But they may be less aware of how insidiously this subliminal image can influence their encounters with real families. If an ideal lurking unknowingly in a teacher's value system is considered "right," then a negative evaluation can be made of any family that does not measure up to this standard. The problem with assessing this one **nuclear family** model as "good" is that it may prevent us from considering alternative family structures as equally valid.

nuclear family
A social unit composed of parents and children.

It is too easy for a teacher to feel more affinity and comfort with a family that approaches his or her ideal than with one that is clearly outside the teacher's individual frame of reference.

2-1b Samples of Diverse Family Structures

If personal images of family cannot convey a complex enough picture, perhaps brief descriptions of families you might meet and work with will help. In Chapter 1, you followed two fictitious families through a day. Here, we will meet them and others—as a sample of families any teacher may encounter—to consider the diversity in structure that corresponds to the differing values, customs, cultural influences, and lifestyles that appear in our world. Watch for these same families later in this book when we consider different relationships and techniques in teacher-parent communication.

A. From Chapter 1, you will recall meeting Sylvia Ashley, 29, who lives alone with her sons Terrence (nine) and Ricky (three). Her marriage to Ricky's father ended in divorce before Ricky's birth; she did not marry Terrence's father, who was in one of her classes in college before she dropped out during the first semester. She has had no contact with her parents since before Terrence's birth. Although she lives in a subsidized housing apartment, she rarely has contact with her neighbors; hers is the only white family living in the area. Before Ricky was born, she worked in a department store. Since then, her income has come from **TANF** (Temporary Aid to Needy Families) funds and food stamp payments as well as the subsidized housing. She is now beginning a job-training program, hoping to follow through with her plan to become a nurse's assistant. Ricky has been home with Sylvia, but he will enter a child care program when his mother begins the job-training program.

B. You have also met Otis and Fannie Lawrence, each married before. Otis has two sons from his first marriage—14 and 10—who visit one weekend each month and for about six weeks each summer. Fannie's seven-year-old daughter Kim and four-year-old son Pete see their father, who has moved out of state, only once or twice a year and have called Otis "Daddy" since their mother married him three years ago. Fannie is six months pregnant, and they have recently moved into an attractive new four-bedroom house, knowing even that will be too small when the boys visit. Fannie teaches third grade and will take a three-month maternity leave after the baby is born; she is on the waiting list at four centers for infant care. Otis sells new cars and is finishing up a business degree at night. Kim goes to an afterschool child care program that costs $115 a week. Pete is in a private child care center, operated by a national chain, that costs $175 a week. The Lawrence family income is $98,000 annually. The Lawrence family is African American.

C. Bob and Jane Weaver have been married five years. They married the day after Jane graduated from high school. Sandra, blonde and blue-eyed just like her parents, was born before their first anniversary. Bob and Jane live in an apartment down the street from Jane's parents and around the block from her married sister. Jane has not worked outside the home much during their marriage. They are hoping to have another child next year. A second pregnancy ended in stillbirth last year. Bob earns $49,750 on the production line at a furniture factory. Jane started working part-time this year to help save for a down payment for a first home purchase. Her mother cares for Sandra while Jane works. Her income of $950 a month after taxes would not go far if she had to pay for child care. They are concerned that Bob's hours could be decreased in the economic downturn.

D. Salvatore and Teresa Rodriguez have lived in this country for six years. Occasionally, one of their relatives comes to stay with them, but the rest of the family has stayed in

TANF
Temporary Aid to Needy Families—the welfare reform legislation passed in 1996.

Mexico. Right now, Sal's 20-year-old brother Joseph is here taking an auto mechanics course; he plans to be married later this year and will probably stay in the same town. Teresa misses her mother, who has not seen their two children since they were babies. Sylvia is seven and has cerebral palsy; she attends a developmental kindergarten that has an excellent staff for the physiotherapy and speech therapy that she needs. Tony is four. Teresa works part-time in a bakery. Her husband works the second shift on the maintenance crew at the bus depot so he can be home with the children while she is at work. This is necessary because Sylvia needs so much extra care. They rent a six-room house, which they chose for the safe neighborhood and large garden.

E. Mary Howard is 16 and has always lived with her parents in a predominantly middle-class neighborhood of African American families. Her grandmother had a stroke and now lives with them, too. When Mary's daughter, Cynthia, was born last year, her mother cared for the baby so Mary could finish the tenth grade. Cynthia is now in a church-operated child care center because Mary's mother needed to return to work to cover increased family expenses. Mary still hopes she might someday marry Cynthia's father, who is starting college this year. He comes to see her and the baby every week or so. Mary also wonders if she will go on to train in computer programming after she finishes high school, as she had planned, or if she should just get a job so she can help her mother more with Cynthia and with their expenses.

F. Susan Henderson celebrated her thirty-ninth birthday in the hospital the day after giving birth to Lucy. Her husband Ed is 40. After 13 years of marriage, they have found adding a child joyful and shocking. Lucy was very much a planned child. Susan felt established enough in her career as an architect to be able to work from her home for a year or so. Ed's career as an investment counselor has also demanded a lot of his attention. Some of their friends are still wavering over the decision to begin a family. Ed and Susan are quite definite that this one child will be all they will have time for. Money is not the issue in their decision; their combined income last year was well over $350,000. Susan's major complaint since being at home with the baby is that the condominium where they live has few families with children, and none of them are preschoolers. She has signed up for a Mother's Morning Out program for infants one day a week and has a nanny who comes to their home each day so she can work.

G. Sam (age two) and Lisa (age four) Butler see their parents a lot—they just never see them together. Bill and Joan separated almost two years ago, and their divorce is about to become final. One of the provisions calls for joint physical custody of their two preschoolers. What this means right now is spending three nights one week with one parent and four with the other. The schedule gets complicated sometimes because Bill travels on business, but so far, the adults have been able to work it out. The children seem to enjoy going from Dad's apartment to Mom and the house in which they have always lived, but on the days they carry their suitcases to the child care center for the midweek switchover, they need lots of reassurance about who is picking them up. Joan worries about how this arrangement will work as the children get older. Sam and Lisa attend a child development center run by the local community college. Joan is already concerned about finding good afterschool care for Lisa when she starts school in the fall, and she knows that it will further complicate her schedule when she has to make two pickup stops after work. She works as a secretary for the phone company and needs to take some computer courses this fall, but she does not know how she can fit them in and the kids, too—let alone find time to date a new man she has met.

H. James Parker and Sam Leeper adopted a one-year-old Korean boy, Stephen, four years ago. They have been together in a committed relationship for 10 years, although they do not live in a state that recognizes gay marriage or legal civil unions. They live a fairly quiet life and visit with Sam's family, who lives in the same town, as well as a few friends, including another family they met at an adoptive parents' support group. Many of their gay friends have also expressed the desire to adopt but are concerned about the prejudices sometimes directed toward gay fathers. Stephen attends prekindergarten in an early childhood program at a church in their neighborhood. Sam is an emergency room doctor at the local hospital. James sells insurance with a national company. When asked if they are worried about their son growing up without a relationship with a mother figure, James responds that Stephen has a grandmother and aunt with whom he is close and that they are more concerned about helping him come to know something of his native culture, as well as for him to be free of some of society's myths regarding sexuality.

I. Justin Martin (age five) lives with his grandparents. His grandfather retired this year after working for the city as a horticulturalist for 30 years. His grandmother has never worked outside the home, having raised five children of her own. Justin is the child of their youngest daughter. She left high school after his birth and has drifted from one minimum wage job to another. On several occasions, she left Justin alone rather than find a child care arrangement for him, and she was reported for neglect by neighbors in her apartment building. Justin's grandparents felt they could provide a better home environment for him, so they petitioned the court for his custody. Neither Justin nor his grandparents have much contact with his mother—she did not come to the house for his last birthday, and she sent some money for Christmas. Justin is in a public school kindergarten. His grandfather takes him to school. His grandmother is quite homebound with arthritis and often finds a lively five-year-old exhausting as well as financially draining on their retirement income.

J. Nguyen Van Son has worked very hard since he came to this country with his uncle 12 years ago. After graduating from high school near the top of his class, he completed a mechanical drafting course at a technical college. He has a good job working for a manufacturing company. His wife Dang Van Binh, a longtime family friend, came from Vietnam only six years ago, and they were married soon after. Her English is still not good, so she takes evening classes. Their three-year-old son Nguyen Thi Hoang goes to a half-day preschool program because his father is eager for him to become comfortable speaking English with other children. Their baby daughter Le Thi Tuyet is at home with her mother. On weekends, the family spends time with other Vietnamese families, eager for companionship and preserving their memories of Vietnam. None of their neighbors talk much with this family, assuming they cannot speak English.

K. Richard Stein and Roberta Howell have lived together for 18 months. Richard's six-year-old son Joshua lives with them. Roberta has decided she wants no children; she and Richard have no plans for marriage at this time. Roberta works long hours as a department store buyer. Richard writes for the local newspaper. On the one or two evenings a week that neither of them can get away from work, Joshua is picked up from a neighborhood family child care home by a college student Richard met at the paper. Several times, this arrangement has fallen through and Joshua has had to stay late with his caregiver, who does not like this because she cares for Joshua and five other preschoolers from 7 a.m. until 6 p.m. each day.

L. Ted Sawyer winces when a member of his Thursday night basketball team calls him "Mr. Mom." He does not like the name, but he admits it is often difficult for others to understand why he is the primary caregiver in his family while his wife Jana works for a large corporation. She also travels with her job—and often is gone for most of the workweek. Ted cares for their first-grader Jacob and their toddler daughter Emma. Between getting Jacob to school and watching out for his active daughter, Ted rarely has time for part-time plumbing jobs—the work he did before the children were born. He has already decided that he will likely not return to full-time employment until both children are in high school because he and his wife believe that one parent should be available as much as possible during children's early years. He sometimes wonders if some of the digs he receives are because his wife, who is the main family breadwinner, is white and he is black, or whether it is just because others do not seem to understand the reasoning they used to make their choices about roles inside and outside the home. Jana is happy and very successful in her work, providing for a comfortable lifestyle, although she misses being home with the family. When out of town, she tries to talk with the children on Skype every night.

In this sample, as in any other you might draw from a cross section in any school, the family some might call "traditional"—with a father who works to earn the living and a mother whose work is mostly rearing the children and caring for the home—is a distinct minority in the variety of structures; in fact, well over 60 percent of American children under age eighteen live in what used to be considered as unconventional families (Downer & Myers, 2010).

The last census indicated the diversity and continuing change in patterns of living situations. The proportion of children living with two married parents continues to steadily decrease, falling from 77 percent in 1980 to less than 25 percent in 2011 (Coontz, 2011). Among children younger than age 18 today, about one-quarter live only with their mothers, 5 percent live only with their fathers, and another 4 percent live with neither parent—often in the care of grandparents, other relatives, or foster care (Coontz, 2011).

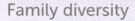

CULTURAL CONSIDERATIONS

Family diversity

As you read the descriptions of the various families, you may be focusing only on the most obvious cultural differences, as in families who have come from other countries or speak different languages. But when we define culture broadly to include the values, beliefs, and usual behaviors passed on to individuals by the segment of society around them, we realize that each of these families will have its unique culture, related to the specific environment that surrounds each one. Cultural beliefs are influenced by educational and socioeconomic experiences, ethnic and racial backgrounds, and individual community and family interpretations of societal norms.

To reflect on the reality of this awareness, think about answers to the following three questions and then discuss your answers with two classmates to discover how your unique family culture influences your own thinking:

1. What one food would you be astonished *not* to see on the table during a family celebration?
2. What is one thing you would expect only a mother to do? Only a father?
3. What is the correct way to fold a bath towel?

Each of us comes from a unique cultural background, no matter what our ethnic or language background.

The Vanier Institute defines family as any combination of two or more persons who are bound together over time by ties of mutual consent, birth, and/or adoption of placement and who, together, assume responsibilities for variant combinations of some of the following:

- Physical maintenance and care of group members
- Addition of new members through procreation or adoption
- Socialization of children
- Social control of members
- Production, consumption, and distribution of goods and services
- Affective nurturance—love

How do we define *family?* The Census Bureau definition of "two or more people related through blood, marriage, or adoption who share a common residence" seems too narrow to include all the dynamics of these sample families. *Webster's Eleventh New Collegiate Dictionary* suggests a broader interpretation and no fewer than 22 definitions that seem more applicable when considering these sample families: "a group of people united by certain convictions or common characteristics" or "a group of individuals living under one roof and usually under one head." Perhaps the most inclusive definition of a family is "a small group of intimate, transacting, and interdependent persons who share values, goals, resources, and other responsibilities for decisions; have a commitment to one another over time; and accept the responsibility of bringing up children." Or simply, from the definition in a survey by the Massachusetts Mutual Life Insurance Company, "a group of people who love and care for each other." The organization Family Support America says that "family is a group of people who take responsibility for each other's well-being, and defining the family is up to the family itself." What about the idea that *family* is "not only persons related by blood, marriage, or adoption, but also sets of interdependent but independent persons who share some common goals, resources, and a commitment to each other over time" (Hildebrand et al., 2007)? Mary Pipher (1996) adds these thoughts:

Family is a collection of people who pool resources and help each other over the long haul. Families love one another even when that requires sacrifice. Family means that if you disagree, you still stay together.... All members can belong regardless of merit. Everyone is included regardless of health, likability, or prestige.... Families come through when they must.... From my point of view, the issue isn't biology. Rather the issues are commitment and inclusiveness.

CONSIDER THE TRUTH OF THIS STATEMENT

A family is like no other family, like some other families, and like all other families.

No matter how we define it, family is important to us (see Figure 2-2). Families may include more than just parents and children. Mary Howard's family includes her parents, grandmother, and child, and the Rodriguezes have Uncle Joseph. The development of the nuclear family is more for affection and support than for the self-sufficient economic unit that the traditional extended family created. Families may include people not related by blood and hereditary bonds. The Parker-Leeper and Stein-Howell households include parents and children and others whose relationship is based on choice, not law.

FIGURE 2-2
Family defined as caring.

We may be related by birth or adoption or invitation.

We may belong to the same race or we may be of different races.

We may look like each other or different from each other.

The important thing is, we belong to each other.

We care for each other.

We agree, disagree, love, fight, work together.

We belong to each other.

© Cengage Learning®

WHAT DOES BRAIN RESEARCH TELL US ABOUT POVERTY AND BRAIN DEVELOPMENT IN EARLY CHILDHOOD?

With millions of American children spending their first years living in families with incomes below the poverty line, the concern arises for their greater risk of impaired brain development. This is due to the number of risk factors associated with poverty that can influence the brain through multiple pathways. During the sensitive early years, children's brains are most vulnerable to deficits and negatives in their environments. These include the following: inadequate nutrition, both prenatally and in the early years; effects of nicotine, alcohol, and drugs; exposure to environmental toxins; trauma and abuse; maternal depression; and the quality of daily care. Any or all of these risk factors may have a direct impact on the neurological development within the brain, becoming evident later in delayed motor skills and in much lower test scores related to vocabulary, reading comprehension, math, and general knowledge. America's poor children are disproportionately exposed to these risk factors.

1. Consider how quality child-care experiences for America's poor children can help mitigate some of these specific risk factors.
2. What is being done in your community to alleviate the effects of poverty on children's development?
3. Learn more about the work of the Children's Defense Fund by visiting their website.

OPPORTUNITY FOR SELF-REFLECTION

Think about our case study families just described. Are there any families with whom you would be uncomfortable? What is causing this discomfort? How would you work with this family, given the discomfort? Which families seem closest to you in values? How do you define *family*?

GOOD BOOKS TO READ WITH CHILDREN TO CELEBRATE FAMILY DIVERSITY

Ackerman, K. *By the Dawn's Early Light.* (Mom works the night shift)

Adoff, A. *Black Is Brown Is Tan.* (interracial family)

Aldrich, A. *How My Family Came to Be—Daddy, Papa and Me.* (adoption, biracial family, two dads)

Aylette, J. *Families: A Celebration of Diversity, Commitment, and Love.* (photos and descriptions of all kinds of families)

Bauer, C. *My Mom Travels a Lot.* [self-explanatory]

Baum, L. *One More Time.* (child going between Mom's house and Dad's house)

Blain, M. *The Terrible Thing That Happened at Our House.* (Mom takes a job)

Blomquist, G., & Blomquist, F. *Zachary's New Home: A Story for Foster and Adopted Children.* [self-explanatory]

Bosch, S. *Jenny Lives with Eric and Martin.* (two fathers)

Boyd, L. *Sam Is My Half-Brother.* [self-explanatory]

Brisson, P. *Mama Loves Me From Away.* (mother in prison)

Brownstone, C. *All Kinds of Mothers.* (mothers who work in and out of the home)

Bunting, E. *Can You Do This, Old Badger?* (living with grandparent)

Bunting, E. *Fly Away Home.* (homeless child and father)

Cowen-Fletcher, J. *Mama Zooms.* (mother in a wheelchair)

Crews, D. *Bigmama's.* (extended family)

Davol, M. *Black, White, Just Right.* (biracial family)

Downey, R. *Love Is a Family.* [self-explanatory]

Drescher, J. *Your Family, My Family.* (different shapes and sizes)

Eichler, M. *Martin's Father.* (nurturing single father)

Eisenberg, P. *You're My Nikki.* (new working mother)

Falwell, C. *Feast for 10.* (large family)

Galloway, P. *Good Times, Bad Times—Mummy and Me.* (working single mother)

Galloway, P. *Jennifer Has Two Daddies.* (child alternates weeks with her mom and stepdad and her father)

Garden, N. *Molly's Family.* (two moms)

Gonzalez, R. *Antonio's Card/La Tarjeta de Antonio.* (two moms; bilingual book)

Hayes, M., & Witherell, J. *My Daddy Is in Prison.* [self-explanatory]

Hickman, M. *Robert Lives with His Grandparents.* [self-explanatory]

Hines, A. *Daddy Makes the Best Spaghetti.* (father cooking)

Jenness, A. *Families.* (family diversity)

Juster, N. *The Hello, Goodbye Window.* (grandparents)

Kroll, V. *Wood-Hoopoe Willie.* (African American family)

Kuklin, S. *How My Family Lives in America.* (real stories of different ethnic backgrounds)

Lasker, J. *Mothers Can Do Anything.* (many jobs mothers do)

Loewen, I. *My Mom Is So Unusual.* (contemporary American Indian)

Maslac, H. *Finding a Job for Daddy.* (unemployed father)

McPhail, D. *The Teddy Bear.* (homelessness)

Merriam, E. *Mommies at Work.* (mothers who work in and out of the home)

Moore, E. *Grandma's House.* (spending the summer with an active, nontraditional grandmother)

Newman, L. *Gloria Goes to Gay Pride.* (child in gay family)

Parr, T. *The Family Book.* (different types of families, including two moms and two dads)

Pelligrini, N. *Families Are Different.* (family diversity)

Quinlan, P. *My Dad Takes Care of Me.* (unemployed father at home)

Richardson, J., & Parnell, P. *And Tango Makes Three.* (two dads)

Rotner, S., & Kelly, S. *Lots of Moms.* (the many appearances of American mothers, and what they do)

Schlein, M. *The Way Mothers Are.* (unconditional love)

Schwartz, A. *Oma and Bobo.* (mother, grandmother, and child)

Simon, N. *All Families Are Special.* (different types of families)

Simon, N. *All Kinds of Families.* (diverse family structures)

Skutch, R. *Who's in a Family?* (multicultural contemporary families)

Soto, G. *Too Many Tamales.* (Mexican American family)

Spelman, C. *After Charlotte's Mom Died.* (single father)

Stinson, K. *Mom and Dad Don't Live Together Any More.* (divorce)

Tax, M. *Families.* (variety of families)

Valentine, J. *One Dad, Two Dads, Brown Dad, Blue Dads.* (all kinds of dads)

Vigna, J. *My Two Uncles.* (child with uncle and his partner)

Wickens, E. *Anna Day and the O-Ring.* (two mothers)

Wild, M. *Space Travelers.* (homeless)

Willhoite, M. *Daddy's Roommate.* (divorced parent, gay father)

Williams, V. *A Chair for My Mother.* (families; generations of urban working-class family)

Woodson, J. *Visiting Day.* (father in prison)

New relatives, like those acquired in a stepfamily, such as the Lawrences, may be added. Families may omit a generation, such as Justin Martin and his grandparents. In Justin's case, as with increasing numbers of children—now about 4 percent (Childstats, 2013), he is being raised by grandparents in the absence of his own parents. Aunts, grandparents, and other family members as well as thousands of foster parents who are not related to children by blood are some of the adults who head modern families.

Families may consist of more people than those present in a household at any one time. The Butler joint custody arrangements and the "blended" Lawrence family are examples of separated family structures.

Families change. Their composition is dynamic, not static. It is assumed that Uncle Joseph will form his own household when he and his fiancée marry; Mary Howard hopes to marry and establish her own household. The Butler family may have additions when the parents remarry, as both say they would like to. The Weavers hope to have another baby. Change occurs as family members grow and develop. Family members are continually adjusting to shifts within the family dynamics that challenge earlier positions. It is important that teachers and classrooms always convey an understanding that each family is unique. For ideas, refer to the "Good Books to Read with Children to Celebrate Family Diversity" box. Families are complex systems, and such outside systems as schools, businesses and employers, neighborhoods, communities, religious organizations, subcultures, and society all influence the functioning of families. In recent years, all these systems have been undergoing turbulence and change. It is time to look at some of those changes (see Figure 2-3).

FIGURE 2-3
Modern families are often complex.

"It's a note from my parents, my former parents, my step-grandmother, and my dad's live-in."

2-2 Demographics of Modern Families

Is it harder or easier to be a parent today than it was a generation or two ago? There is no question that today's families are functioning under conditions different from those of their grandparents or even parents. Changes in family forms and functions are not necessarily bad or worrisome—unless one insists on clinging to the past, maintaining the exclusive rightness of bygone ways. Almost all the changes discussed in this chapter have had both positive and negative impacts on today's families.

Some recent trends in contemporary life influencing the nature of families include the following:

- Marital instability and rising numbers of single parents
- Changes in gender role behavior
- Mobility, urbanization, and economic conditions
- Decreasing family size
- Increased rate of social change
- Development of a child-centered society
- Stress in modern living

Each of these will be discussed in this chapter.

2-2a Marital Instability and Single Parents

Statistics tell us part of the story. The proportion of children living with two married parents fell from 77 percent in 1980 to 64 percent in 2012, the last year for which we have government statistics (Childstats, 2013). Currently, it is estimated that nearly 50 percent of marriages begun today will end in divorce. Between 60 and 70 percent of second marriages will collapse. According to Census Bureau predictions, it is likely that at least half of all children born in this decade will spend a significant part of their childhood in single-parent homes. In the Western world, fewer than two-thirds of parents who are legally married when their first child is born are still together when their youngest child graduates from high school.

TOP 10 TRENDS IN MODERN FAMILIES

The Vanier Institute reports these trends:

1. Fewer couples are getting legally married.
2. More couples are breaking up.
3. Families are getting smaller.
4. Children experience more transitions as parents change their marital status.
5. Adults are generally satisfied with life.
6. Family violence is underreported.
7. Multiple-earner families are now the norm.
8. Women still do most of the juggling involved in balancing work and home.
9. Inequality is worsening.
10. The future will have more aging families (Sauve, 2004).

FIGURE 2-4
The majority of single women who become mothers today are older—some in their late 30s or early 40s.

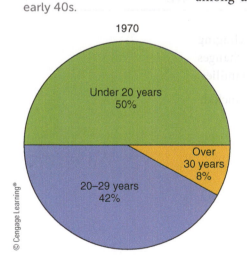

1970

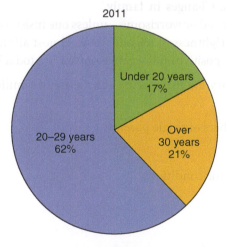

2011

© Cengage Learning®

Between 1970 and 2012, the proportion of children growing up in single-parent families more than doubled to about 35 percent. The majority of these single-parent families are created by divorce. But divorced parents—70 to 80 percent—often remarry. One child in five lives in a stepfamily or blended family. In many areas, children living with two biological parents are a distinct minority.

In addition, some of the single-parent families are the result of a rising birthrate among unmarried women (see Figure 2-4). Births to unmarried women continue to increase—now over 40 percent of all births each year (NCHS, 2013) compared with just over 3 percent of births in 1940. What is interesting is that the birthrate to teenaged mothers continues to drop, with the majority of unmarried mothers being in their 20s. Even so, in some hospitals in poor urban areas, well over half of the women giving birth are single teenagers (see Figure 2-5).

Although there is no question that many single parents do a remarkable job of parenting, a single-parent family can face additional difficulties. A growing body of social and scientific data indicates that children in families disrupted by divorce and birth outside marriage often do worse than children in intact families in several respects. They are two to three times as likely as children in two-parent families to have emotional and behavioral problems and more likely to drop out of high school, get pregnant as teenagers, abuse drugs, and get in trouble with the law. They are also at much higher risk for physical or sexual abuse. But single-parent families are as diverse as any other. When all things are equal—when a single mother has a job that pays a decent wage, is basically contented with her life, and is not overly stressed—there are no major behavioral differences between children raised by single parents and those raised by two. But for purposes of considering **demographics** and families, here we note that family structure may be linked to children's well-being. In the absence of one parent, families often have less social and human capital to draw upon.

demographics
The statistical data of a human population.

Poverty

The term *single parent* does not fully convey the reality that mothers head most of these families. About one-quarter of all American children (50 percent of all black children) live only with their mothers; about 5 percent of all children live with their fathers alone, although this figure is an increase of 25 percent over the previous census—perhaps indicating changes in how custody is granted to parents and more social acceptance of single fathering (Childstats, 2013).

Poverty affects more than 22 percent of all children (Addy, et al., 2013) and makes the United States a shocking leader in the percentage of poor children in the world. In addition, poverty disproportionately affects children who live in mother-headed households.

Children younger than six who are living with single mothers are five times more likely to be poor than children who live in two-parent households. Children living with single fathers are two and a half times more likely to live below the poverty line. Of children being raised by grandparents, the Children's Defense Fund reports that from 10 to 30 percent are living in poverty. Figure 2-6 indicates how poverty among children is divided by specific factors. Research indicates that three factors indicate particular risk for poverty:

1. Single parenthood
2. Low educational attainment
3. Part-time or no employment

In the current economic climate, these factors may intertwine and make it very difficult for single-parent families to escape poverty. Surprisingly, nearly 70 percent of poor young children live in families in which a parent is employed.

Single-parent families created by divorce may precipitously plunge children into poverty. In the years following divorce, living standards for ex-wives and their children

FIGURE 2-5
The birthrate among adolescent girls is declining.

© Aaron Belford/Shutterstock.com

FIGURE 2-6
America's poor children are everywhere.

Who Are America's Poor Children?	
Poor children are	Over 20% of total of children
Of all poor children:	
Living in single mother families	56.1%
Living in single father families	8.6%
Living in married couple families	35.3%
White poor children	12.3 %
Black poor children	37.9%
Hispanic poor children	33.8%
Asian poor children	13.8%
American Indian	29%
Living with grandparents	27%
Living with neither parent	32%

© Cengage Learning®

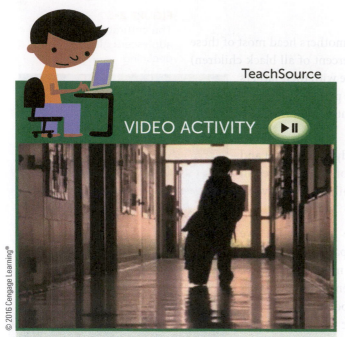

TeachSource

VIDEO ACTIVITY ⏯

After viewing the video clip *Hard Time Generation*, reflect on these questions:

1. What are some of the challenges faced by homeless children and their families?

2. What are some of the challenges faced by the schools serving homeless children and families?

3. How does this information influence what you will do in your classroom?

drop by an average of 30 percent, whereas those for the men involved rise 8 percent. Only half of all families with an absent parent have child support orders; of these families, only half receive the full amount ordered. About a quarter receive partial payment, and a quarter receive nothing. Despite successful efforts in some states to enforce such legal obligations, a majority of fathers' scheduled payments are still in arrears.

Child support accounts for only 15 percent of the total income of single-parent families. Financial stress is a major complaint of divorced women. Many single-parent families are not able to provide adequate support services they need, such as child care while a mother works, as well as recreation or other social relief for a parent.

Poverty in the United States is increasingly linked to family structure. This is the first decade in the nation's history in which a majority of all poor families are headed by women—in what has been called the *feminization of poverty*. In female-headed families, the poverty rate is over 40 percent; in families headed by a parent younger than age 30, this rate is even higher. African American and Latino families are disproportionately represented among poor and single mother–headed households. Currently, one child in 50 is homeless, forced by economic disaster into sleeping with their families in shelters, motels, campgrounds, or cars. Children and families are the fastest-growing group among the homeless population—now representing about 40 percent of all homeless (Hubert, 2009).

Cuts in social spending have included drastic reductions in the food stamp program. Increasingly, government safety nets for poor families have been torn away. Families that are particularly affected by this are single-parent families, especially those headed by young parents.

Stress

A family that began with two parents and shifts to single-parent status will undoubtedly experience increased stress for some time—if not permanently.

Adjustments must be made by all family members when any of the following changed living patterns occur:

- The loss of a relationship, regardless of how negative

- A move and new job or school arrangements

- Other changes necessitated by the constraints of a more limited budget

- Less contact with one parent

- Changed behaviors in both parents

We will talk more about this stress in Chapter 14. Although custody arrangements now often include joint physical custody for both parents and more divorcing fathers are granted custody than previously, the majority of single-parent families created by divorce are headed by women. A mother in a single-parent family is under the additional strain of adding the father role to her parental responsibilities. Not only do many divorcing fathers abandon their children financially, but they also do so emotionally; half of all divorced fathers do not see their children. The mother may easily overload herself while trying to compensate for her concern induced by social attitudes that a single-parent family is a pathological family. The mixed data in this area are scarcely reassuring, and real or feared changes in children's behavior can add appreciably to a parent's burden at this time. Social attitudes toward divorce may have undergone a shift toward acceptance, but attitudes toward what some have unfortunately called a "broken family" still leave many single parents with an additional burden of guilt.

If a single-parent family is merged to create a new blended family, additional stress may be created. A new family may begin with financial problems created when the income must support more than one family and with emotional burdens created by the multiplicity of possible new relationships as well as the striving to create an "instant" family, warm and close, to make up for the earlier pain and banish the "ugly stepparent" fears. Unfortunately, these burdens may be too heavy: Up to 60 percent of blended family marriages end in divorce within four years. This means that many children may experience divorce, remarriage, and all the attendant stresses two or three times before they become adults.

Never-wed single-parent families may also face stress in the form of a possible lack of cultural, social, or economic support for the family, but teachers do well to remember that every situation is unique.

2-2b Changes in Role Behavior

In the reruns of television series from the 1960s, Beaver Cleaver's mom was home baking cookies, and Aunt Bea raised Opie while Andy worked to support the family. Today, however, most moms—in both television sitcoms and real life—are working outside their homes (see Figure 2-7).

Current census figures indicate that the majority of women in the workforce are mothers of children living at home. To put this in perspective, in 1900 only one wife in 20 was in the labor force, by 1950, the ratio was one out of five, and now it is more than three out of five, with more than 40 percent of women being the main or sole breadwinner in the family. But labor statistics show that more mothers are now staying home when they have a choice. According to the last census, the number of working mothers has declined for the first time since 1976, declining 4 percent for mothers of preschool children and 6 percent for mothers of infants, including mothers at all education levels. Demographers note that many mothers who are members of so-called Generation X—now in their 20s and 30s—are looking for a sense of realistic balance, wanting to be good workers and good mothers (Howe, Strauss, & Matson, 2000). Howe sees these mothers at the cutting edge of a generation that is "very protective of family life." On the other hand, the Center for WorkLife Law at the University of California Hastings College of Law pointed out that "workplace inflexibility, the lack of family supports and workplace bias" may be forcing American mothers out of the workforce—whether they can really afford to "opt out" or not (Warner, 2006). And with the most recent economic downturn, many mothers and fathers have lost work—without any choice at all.

Women's Roles

Statistics alone cannot describe all that has occurred since the 1960s with the redefinition of women's roles. Since the publication of *The Feminine Mystique* (Friedan, 1963), women the world over have urged each other to find equality in their relationships with

FIGURE 2-7
Over half of all infants and preschoolers have mothers working outside the home.

men and in their places in the community and at work. This has not been an easy change for anyone involved. For women, it has meant adding new roles while often retaining much of the responsibility for household maintenance and child rearing. If a woman tries to combine all the roles she saw her mother play at home with her new work roles, she is in danger of falling into the "Superwoman" syndrome, with exhaustion and stress spilling over into all aspects of her life. Four out of every 10 women "often" or "very often" report feeling "used up" at the end of the workday. Working mothers are more likely to get sick than their husbands. Although women have cut back their household work from about 30 hours a week two decades ago to 18 hours a week today, their working husbands have not made up the difference, increasing their household work only from 5 hours to 10 hours, according to a recent report on American time use (BLS, 2013).

Today, women work so they can contribute to the necessities for their families, as well as the items considered important for a rising family living standard. Recent statistics have found that an increasing number of married women are now the primary breadwinners in the family (Rampell, 2013). But it is more than a dollars-and-cents issue. Many women would not give up the satisfaction of work even if money were not an issue. Mothers working outside the home are likely here to stay. But this creates complexity in blending real and mythical issues about social roles.

Work is not the only aspect of women's lives to be reconsidered. The language of the women's movement in the 1960s and 1970s spoke of women as one of society's minorities, without equality at home or outside the home. Issues of sexuality and reproduction and of sex role stereotypes and limitations were discussed nationwide. Some real changes were effected, and awareness was raised. The increase in marital instability may be partly attributable to this questioning of traditional relationships, and the women's movement may have been a major and permanent influence on the nature of families and society. Whether or not women and men agree with the push toward equality, it is virtually impossible for anyone in the country to remain untouched by the debate and its repercussions on lifestyles. But change comes through turmoil, and this environment of changing relationships and role behaviors has pushed women and men in the family into less comfortable territory.

FIGURE 2-8

Many fathers now participate with mothers in their infants' births.

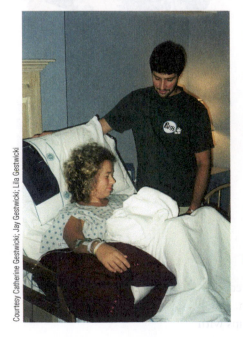

Courtesy Catherine Gestwicki; Jay Gestwicki; Lila Gestwicki

Men's Roles

Men's family roles are on similarly challenging new ground. Not only are they asked to share positions and power in the workplace with women, but also at home, more is expected of them than was expected of their fathers. They may still not be carrying their equal share of household chores, but the days of hiding guilt-free behind the newspaper until dinner is on the table are gone. Gone also are the models of paternal behavior they knew as children. But after all, this is what happened to their fathers before them. As fathers received more leisure time due to changing work patterns and as the expert advice to parents continued to change from stern rigidity to concern with children feeling loved and happy, fathers became people with whom their children could have fun.

Today's father plays with his child, but he also takes his turn sitting in the pediatrician's office, cooking dinner, supervising homework, and carpooling. Frequently, he is involved before his child's birth—attending childbirth classes with his wife to learn how to coach her through prepared childbirth (see Figure 2-8). But is this involvement as pervasive as some articles in women's magazines portray?

The answer appears to be increasingly *yes* in families where mothers are "work committed"—that is, who work full time and share financial decisions.

In these families, men are beginning to shrink the labor gap in the household and are becoming more involved with their children. One report says that men are now the primary caregivers in one out of every five dual-earner households with preschool children (Halle, 2002). This suggests that many more men have significant child care responsibilities than is usually thought.

Certainly, the pressure for men to become more involved with household and child care responsibilities has come from women, especially those with growing economic power. But fathers themselves are frequently looking for a new lifestyle—one that allows them to be more involved with their families. Trying to find a balance between job and family responsibilities creates new stress for some fathers today.

Although increased participation is occurring in many households, the primary responsibility for house and child care remains the mother's—perhaps due to the constraints of role behavior norms for men and women and the signals sent by society that moms are the parents who really count, while dads are in minor roles. One writer (Helms, 2000) offers the example of a school secretary trying to get in touch with the mother of a sick child. When asked by a coworker whether she had already called the father, she said she did not like to interrupt him. The implication is that Mom's work is more easily interruptible and anyway it is really her job to care for a sick child (an additional source of stress for working mothers) but also that Dad is either less caring or less capable of handling the emergency rather than equally competent and caring as Mom. Such implicit messages weaken men's attempts to be fully involved parents.

Certainly, there are not a lot of models of highly participant fathers, and the few fathers who do participate equally as parents receive little recognition and support—at least in their perceptions. Many men who try to take time off to attend a teacher conference or school play get the impression that the boss and coworkers see them as slackers and expect the mothers—working or not—to handle such matters.

Some research projects also show that men who attempt to take on more family responsibilities get increased negative feedback from grandparents and even from wives. The legacy of the model of male as breadwinner and female as caregiver may create stress for men trying to find new roles. But it is probably fair to say that today's father is often called on to share with his wife all aspects of the children's care and to display many of the nurturing behaviors previously associated only with mothers (see Figure 2-9).

Indeed, one phenomenon that occurs in many communities is fathers becoming stay-at-home parents while their wives work outside the home. These fathers assume the full responsibility for the household and care of children that was previously thought to be the woman's role. To define what it means to be a man, major shifts in thinking are required. However men feel about it—and most fathers are pleased with their new roles—the change in women's roles in contemporary society has changed their own. Chapter 3 will look more at recent research on the absolute importance of fathers' involvement with their children's lives.

It should also be noted that agreement about the desirability of this sharing of father and mother roles is not universal. A strong conservative orientation is currently advocating a return to "paternalism"—fathers being the strong voice in running the family and women returning to the home for primary responsibility in child rearing. It will be interesting to see whether this becomes a trend in our culture.

FIGURE 2-9
Many fathers are more involved in all aspects of parenting today.

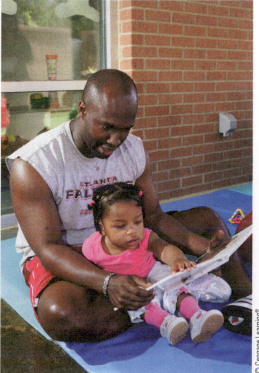

© Cengage Learning®

Slowly, society has been pushed to alter its expectations regarding the roles of family members, and individuals are caught between trying to balance the external realities and demands and the internal psychological conflict caused by attempting a new social pattern. The jury is still out on what impact the different patterns of family roles and parenting have on family members. Certainly, there are more opportunities for personal growth, with alternatives from which to choose freely. Children have a more inclusive family model as an increasing number of fathers take on the loving and nurturing aspects of parenthood and an increasing number of mothers take on leadership roles outside as well as inside the home. Changes in roles have opened doors for everyone—men and women alike.

2-2c Mobility, Urbanization, and Economic Conditions

With changing economic and employment patterns, many workers and their families move frequently in the search for new and better jobs. The average American moves more than 11 times in a lifetime, according to Census Bureau estimates. And in contemporary America, far more families live in urban than rural settings.

What does this mean to present-day families? When earlier families worked together on economic production in the home and on the family farm, parents were much more available to their children. The shift to urban occupations enabled many families to improve their economic status. Recent changes in the structuring of business and industry have made family job security more fragile, and families have had to move where jobs dictate. This increased geographical mobility has brought less sense of community and more isolation. It probably means that the nuclear family—the parents and their children—are far removed from the physical presence of others who may have acted as sources of support in earlier times. With the increasing number of immigrants—legal and illegal—even more numbers of families are living far from family supports.

A mother coming home from the hospital with her new baby may know little about how to care physically for the infant, let alone how to deal with the anxiety that arises about 3 a.m. Her only support is her husband, who may be as ignorant and anxious as she is. In a bygone day, her mother, mother-in-law, aunts, cousins, sisters, and neighbors who had known her since she was a baby may have surrounded her.

As time goes by, the young couple needs babysitters to be able to shop in peace or have some recreation time away from the child, someone to care for the sick child when the parents have to work, and someone to delight along with them in the child's success at school or commiserate and calm them when the child begins to throw temper tantrums or have learning problems. Increasingly, parents have to turn to others to fill functions that could have been performed by the extended family were they not so far away. For example, they might hire the neighbor's teenaged daughter to look after the baby so they can have an evening out, or they might decide they cannot afford the expense or the anxiety and just stay home instead.

FIGURE 2-10

Many nuclear families are so far from grandparents and other family that children have to show on the map where they occasionally visit.

© Cengage Learning®

The isolation caused by moving far from traditional sources of support causes stress for today's parents. Parents are totally responsible for everything, creating an ambivalent situation in their home and family. In one sense, the nuclear family so created has a special sense of solidarity that separates this unit from the surrounding community; its members feel more in common with one another than with anyone outside the family. Although this may produce some warm feelings of closeness, cold feelings of isolation and anxiety may also be present (see Figure 2-10).

Part of this isolation is self-induced. Taught to value independence, American families feel that seeking help beyond the family circle is an admission of failure. Today, without the traditional backup system, this lingering myth further isolates families. This isolation may be exacerbated by linguistic differences in immigrant families or fear of discovery by authorities when the family's status is illegal. Families struggle to learn how to adapt to a new culture while preserving their own traditions and ideas.

Rearing children in an urban setting offers its own problems for parents in addition to isolation. Although the diversity of cultural, religious, and racial backgrounds offers richness and variety in today's world, it can also be a potential source of conflict as children are exposed to such a pluralistic society. And cities continue to offer the main environment for child rearing. Cities grew nearly twice as fast as other communities in the past decade, with that growth bringing problems of pollution, crime, and stress for families. Lest this be misinterpreted as a condemnation of cities, it should be recalled that our cities have become the major repositories for current culture and knowledge.

The current economic climate has brought enormous stress to contemporary families. Unemployment and underemployment have become common problems in families from all social and economic classes. The resultant financial and emotional problems have increased stress for parents and children and often created other reasons for mobility and isolation.

WHAT DO STRONG FAMILIES HAVE IN COMMON?

Characteristics of strong families:

- Caring and appreciation
- Time together
- Encouragement
- Commitment
- Communication
- Ability to cope with change
- Spirituality
- Community and family ties
- Clear roles

From Jamieson and Wallace, 2010.

2-2d Family Size Decreasing

According to the Census Bureau, a family household is two or more persons related by blood, marriage, or adoption. Current statistics indicate the average family has shrunk over the years, from 4.76 people in 1900 to just 2.58 currently—in both Canada and the United States—with black, Hispanic, and Asian family sizes being about 3.5. (Figures are from the U.S. Census Bureau's current population reports and the Vanier Institute.) This decrease is due to fewer children younger than age 18 in each household—from about 2 in 1970 to a current average of about 1.5. There are numerous reasons for this.

A major reason is delayed marriage and childbearing, with increased standards of education and career expectations. As recently as 1975, 63 percent of women between the ages of 20 and 24 were married; by the 2010 census, this figure had shrunk dramatically to about a quarter. Currently, the median age for American men marrying is 28.7 years, and for women, it is 26.5 (Cohn et al., 2011).

Besides the need for prolonged education and career expectations, reasons for decreasing family size include the following:

- The economic burden of raising children in times of inflation with no corresponding asset of children's economic contribution to the family unit
- Changing attitudes about women's roles in the home and workplace
- Increased expectations for the family living standards and material wants
- Changing views about marriage and cohabitation
- The move from rural to urban environments
- Current views about parent–child relationships

FIGURE 2-11

Many families now have only one child.

There are also more single-child families (see Figure 2-11). In practical terms, this means that it is possible to become a parent without ever having touched a small baby or having had any share of responsibility for caring for younger brothers and sisters, leaving today's parents anxious and confused in their new roles. The earlier form of a larger family offered its members more experience as they grew up with other children.

Another factor contributing to the decrease in family size is the increasing absence of adults other than parents living in the home. In the 1920s, more than 50 percent of American households had at least one other adult living in the home—grandparents, aunts, or uncles. It was common for young families to begin married life living with their own parents. Before the most recent economic downturn, only about 3 to 4 percent of homes had multigenerations or extended family; this figure has increased recently as foreclosures and other economic hardship have forced changes in living arrangements. If families include grandparents today, they are likely to be single-parent families that have moved into the grandparents' home for economic and social support—clearly a role reversal of the old pattern of living with extended family, when younger families were helping maintain the older generation. More than half of young men between ages 18 and 25 were living in their parents' homes in the last census. This may well reflect the delaying of marriage and tight economic times.

Or grandparents may have included their grandchildren in their families but the children's parents are not present, as is the case for more than 6 percent of American children.

The Census Bureau notes the phenomenon of a marked increase in the number of people living alone—people older than 55 and people in their 20s. In the past, these people would have been members of an extended family household. This implies that the smaller nuclear family is without the additional supportive resources of time, money, and companionship that other adults in the household could offer.

It is somewhat difficult to get an accurate reading on family composition today. When reading the results of the latest census, we can see that families and their composition are far too complex for simple classification or counting. For example, families that are counted as being headed by a single father often include a female adult who is likely functioning in many ways as the other parent. And of those classified as unmarried cohabiting partners, two-fifths are also likely to include children.

Again, the most important aspect of considering demographics is to realize how much change families are undergoing, and often without additional supports for stressed parents.

2-2e Increased Rate of Social Change

Parents in a relatively static society encounter less difficulty than those in a society where social change occurs rapidly and drastically, as in our country for the past four decades and more. A generation gap develops when adults play increasingly complex roles in a world for which their own parents could not prepare them, and when parents try to help their own children face a world they cannot yet imagine. It is not a comfortable world where parents can simply produce children like themselves but a new world where parents are unsure about their best actions and decisions—a world of challenge and potential, but also of stress, for today's fathers and mothers.

They themselves grew up in the world of yesterday—a world that is now largely dead—and they internalized that world; they rear their children in the world of today—a world they only partially understand and only partly accept—but they are trying to prepare their children for the world of tomorrow—a world that nobody yet understands.

The rate of change is dizzying as upheaval occurs in every major institution in society. Major discontinuities in relationships among people develop as changing values, laws, and norms of behavior result in a different way of life.

Beginning with the civil rights movement, the women's movement, and the Vietnam War (and the turmoil from groups opposing and supporting it), society has continued to be beleaguered by anxieties:

- Disillusionment with government leaders with questionable practices or moral beliefs
- Worry about the educational system
- Turmoil in the world overseas and at home
- Fears of terrorist attacks at home as well as abroad
- Worry about keeping children safe at school and in the community
- Concerns about environmental deterioration
- Fears about drugs invading our lives
- Concerns about diseases without cures becoming epidemic
- Worry about what inflation, debt, and pollution mean to the future

An endless succession of new ideas and images has bombarded us during recent decades. Closer to home, the structure and appearance of the family, the roles family members play, attitudes toward sexual activity, contraception, abortion—all are different now. There are new life span events, created by the need to respond to increased longevity and the psychosocial identity adjustments within ever more complex family arrangements. Just imagine the mental adjustments that have to be made by a grandparent raising his or her own grandchild in the absence of parents (see Figure 2-12).

Playing the dual roles of parent and grandparent is something for which there is no model; perhaps this promotes role conflict and additional family stress.

All this change makes parents unsure of themselves, and they worry about almost everything that touches their lives and their children's. They worry about whether they are too permissive or expecting too much in a changing world; they worry about the influence of television, video games, and violence and the quality of education; most of all, they worry because they are making decisions alone—they are reluctant to seek advice from others.

FIGURE 2-12
Many grandparents are now raising their grandchildren.

© Cengage Learning®

Parents are not the only ones unsure in a world that has changed so quickly. The society that surrounds them is equally confused. In a recent Gallup poll, Americans supported seemingly contradictory family values. Eighty-seven percent reported they held "old-fashioned values about family and marriage," and 68 percent believed that "too many children are being raised in child care centers today." At the same time, 66 percent rejected the idea that "women should return to their traditional roles in society," and 64 percent also rejected the idea that "it's more important for a wife to help her husband's career than to have one herself." Clearly, change has happened too quickly for some of our values and beliefs to catch up. Families are caught in the dilemma of rapid change in very real ways. Most jobs are still designed as if there were a homemaker to provide support for a working husband, and many institutional practices assume that all children live with two biological parents. Social structure has changed rapidly; changes in social and personal values and feelings lag behind.

2-2f Child-Centered Society

More than one expert has pointed out how the child's role in the family and in society has evolved over the centuries, particularly in current times in the Western world. In earlier times, a child was measured harshly by the yardstick of the adult world and restricted to fit into it.

FIGURE 2-13

Increasingly, we are a child-centered society, with children the darlings of their worlds.

But in modern America, a child is the darling of his or her world (see Figure 2-13). Whole industries have sprung up to cater to children's wishes—toys, children's television, designer clothing, and breakfast cereals. The efforts of psychologists and other researchers are directed more toward telling parents what they should and should not be doing to nurture their children. A large part of current research and thinking concerning child development is now available in forms popular and technical. Bookstores have many shelves of books of advice to parents—often suggesting conflicting views of a variety of experts (Hull, 2003). Parenting magazines, blogs, and websites abound.

Parent education classes are available in almost every community. Anyone who has taught a parent education class has heard two frequent reactions from the parents involved. One is to marvel that parents in earlier times did an acceptable job of parenting without possessing this knowledge: "My mother raised five kids, and we all turned out pretty well, and she never even heard of Erikson or Piaget!" The other reaction is from the parent who concentrates, with guilt, on what he or she has already done or missed the chance to do. "If only I'd known this five years ago." Whether parents decide on their own that they could have done a better job or whether the society around them does, the result is that parents come out as the "bad guys" in a culture that centers on the child.

Many educators have noted the increasing tendency of parents today to center their attention solely on their children, doing everything in their power to protect and control their children's lives toward guaranteed success. So-called "helicopter parents" may have taken the child-centered society to an extreme that may not be healthy for optimum child development.

It should also be noted, ironically, that alarming figures suggest our rhetoric may be more child centered than our practices. Children's Defense Fund (2012) notes that the United States—first among industrialized countries in gross domestic product, the number of millionaires and billionaires, health and military technology, and military exports and defense spending—is twenty-second in rates of low birth weight, twenty-ninth in infant mortality, and last in the relative number of children in poverty and in protecting our children against gun violence. These facts make us question the genuineness of our so-called child-centered society.

2-2g Stress in Modern Living

A generation ago, it seemed that shorter workweeks due to modern technology would make life easier for many families. Unfortunately, that dream was never realized. Today, adults are working harder than ever. According to a recent study, the average workweek jumped from under 41 hours in 1973 to nearly 47 hours today, with many professional and higher-level jobs demanding 50 or more hours each week. A *Wall Street Journal* study found that almost all top executives were working 10 or more hours a day and that nearly one in five was working 12 or more hours. As parents feel overloaded at work, their emotional well-being suffers (Galinsky et al., 2001; Brownfield, 2001). It is no wonder that there seems to be so much stress on the family and individuals when the adults are spending so much time competing to keep their jobs in a time of employment insecurity. Much of this stress is related to economic changes: declines in real wages, demands for a more highly skilled and educated workforce, increasing technology creating competition for jobs, and an increased cost of raising children. Parents may not have real choices about the time spent in work and apart from family.

Obviously, the fallout affects adults and children under such conditions. It creates a parental time deficit when parents spend more time earning a living, and the resulting overload and exhaustion mean they do not do not have time to parent their children (see Figure 2-14).

The UCLA Center on Everyday Lives of Families has spent the past four years observing families to examine the intersection between family life and work. Finding that parents and children live apart at least five days a week—reuniting only for a few hours at night—the researchers suggest that the nonstop pace seems to erode families from within, resulting in playtime, conversation, and intimacy falling by the wayside. Most families have no unstructured time (*News-Press*, 2005). In her study of how children perceive their parents' negotiation of work and family life, Galinsky (1999) found that the quantity of time mothers and fathers have with children matters a great deal. When children spend more time with their parents on workdays and nonworkdays, they see their parents as putting their family first. Nevertheless, many children mention that the time they spend with their parents feels rushed and hectic, and they comment on the lack of focus from many parents, indicating that families today need to find ways of getting out from under the stress to make changes that will benefit all.

FIGURE 2-14
With so many responsibilities and so much stress, it is not surprising that parents may get a little confused.

"Mom!"

© Cengage Learning®

In fact, in recent years, modern parents are not only increasing their time at the workplace but also have greater demands on their nonworking time. There is increased pressure from society for individuals to fulfill self-centered goals. Finding and fulfilling oneself are acceptable and necessary activities that demand time. The highly organized community offers more choices and demands more participation from adults and children. Someone recently commented that most modern children are being brought up by appliances and in moving vehicles; this does seem an apt image for the on-the-go style of modern families. Those who point out the extremely busy life of the suburban child, moving from swimming lessons to Boy Scouts to doctors' appointments to playdates organized with friends, fail to also mention that behind this busy child are parents who make all the arrangements and drive the child around! A parent who works full time at a job has only begun to fill the expected responsibilities at the end of the working day.

For many families in lower socioeconomic circumstances, stress may be caused not by fulfilling responsibilities to children's social lives but by carrying a heavy workload to provide necessities of daily life for their children. Often, parents are working more than one job, working odd shifts, and keeping appointments with community agencies for needed support, so they have little time for either their children or themselves. Such a schedule brings burdens to all.

Chapter 3 looks more carefully at the various roles a parent plays; at this point, it is important to realize that a contemporary parent's day is filled with more demands and expectations than there are hours. Societal attitudes and lack of support may add stress to some family structures.

The real stress in all this is that parenting, when done properly, takes much more time and energy than almost anything else. "Children can't thrive if their families are stressed and, at every point on the socioeconomic spectrum now, it seems that American families are cracking at the seams" (Warner, 2006). As long as modern parents are pulled in so many directions, stress will accompany the family.

2-3   Why Study Sociological Trends?

Beginning teachers may wonder why the conditions in society that currently affect families are a topic that deserves their attention. In fact, it is vital to effective relationships with families to understand the conditions and circumstances in which they live. It is too easy for teachers to set up a kind of oppositional stance—an "us against them" mentality—to judge parents as somehow not measuring up to some sort of ideal standard of what parents are "supposed to do." But when the larger picture of changes in our entire society is considered, it becomes clear that all of us are caught up in and affected by the trends that change the face and functioning of families. Rather than judging families against some artificial standard or perhaps the way we never were, it is vital that teachers be able to recognize the forces that influence the thinking of us all. Empathy and the compassion needed to work with people very different from ourselves are the result of seeing contemporary families against the backdrop of the real world in which we now live.

Two student teachers were once heard describing their common experience in "both coming from **dysfunctional** families." When pressed for elaboration, they clarified that they had both been raised by single parents—one as a result of divorce; the other as a result of a parent's death. So influenced were they by the dominant social images of typical families that they confused form with function; because their families did not resemble the usual image, they labeled them "dysfunctional." In fact, both of their families had functioned well to raise the children with caring, protection, and helpful communication.

dysfunctional
Impaired in function.

Studying sociological trends may keep other teachers from making the error of confusing the form of a family with its ability to carry out its functions. It is important for teachers to focus not on family composition but rather on family disposition, such as beliefs, values, and behaviors.

A family functions successfully when it supports and nurtures its members so everyone's needs are met. Members of a successful family feel emotional and social attachment to one another. They understand the importance of independence and interdependence. They know how to communicate effectively, to resolve conflicts, and to cope with problems that cannot be solved. They know how to provide a secure and protective environment in the home. They provide a safe base for family members to grow and develop, expecting the best from each other (Gonzalez-Mena, 2008).

On the other hand, dysfunctional families are those where something has gone wrong; thus, all family members' needs are not met. Combinations of personal, psychological, and environmental factors may produce homes that do not support healthy growth and relationships.

OPPORTUNITY FOR SELF-REFLECTION

What do you think is the most important function of family? What do you think families need most to be able to fulfill this function? How can communities best support families? How can an individual teacher support families to fulfill their functions?

METAPHORS FOR FAMILY

If the family were a container, it would be a nest—an enduring nest, loosely woven, expansive, and open.

If the family were a fruit, it would be an orange—a circle of sections held together but separable, with each segment distinct.

If the family were a boat, it would be a canoe that makes no progress unless everybody paddles.

If the family were a sport, it would be baseball—a long, slow, nonviolent game that is never over until the last out.

If the family were a building, it would be an old but solid structure that contains human history and appeals to those who see the carved moldings under all the plaster, the wide plank floors under the linoleum, the possibilities.

From L. C. Pogebrin in Schlesinger, 1998

Modern families are beset by difficulties related to new social patterns that have evolved from without and by the psychological pressures from within that arise when individuals' life experiences differ from the models they have learned or the ideals for which they strive.

Parenting is already a complex task, and within the context of modern American culture, the challenge of parenting is heightened. Teachers who will work effectively with families will be sensitive to this understanding.

SUMMARY

The new demographics mean that the American family and the growing-up experiences of many of our nation's children and their families have been drastically altered.

- Definitions of family have been broadened to include many family structures and ways of functioning
- Factors that influence family life include:
  - Marital instability and rising numbers of single parents
  - Changes in role behavior
  - Mobility, economic conditions, and immigration
  - Decreasing family size
  - Increased rate of social change
  - Development of a child-centered society
  - Stress in modern living

Student Activities for Further Study

1. Do your own ministudies to consider the nature of social influences on contemporary families.

   a. Involve a group of parents of your acquaintance in an informal discussion. What are the differences between their and their parents' experiences as parents? Which cultural conditions discussed in this text do you find in their comments?

   b. With parents who are willing to discuss their lifestyles, try to learn family patterns of sex role participation. Who shops, cleans, cooks, cares for children, and takes them to the doctor, to the library, or for haircuts?

   c. Ask several parents of your acquaintance where they were born and raised and where their extended families now live. How do your findings agree or disagree with the text discussion of mobility?

   d. Note the family structure of children in any classroom. Figure out the percentage of traditional two-parent families, families with two working parents, single parents, stepparents, or other arrangements. What about family size? Are there additional family members in the household? How do your findings compare with the text discussions of marital instability, changing roles of women, and family size?

2. Interview three generations of a family: your grandparents, your parents, and yourself or your spouse or others who would be of those generations. Ask questions that will give you insights regarding their views and concerns about family structure and changes, the number of times they have moved, issues of balancing work and family time, who was in charge of what aspects of home life, and the joys and challenges of family life at each stage. Share some of these insights with your classmates.

3. In class discussion, consider some of the causes of divorce and other changes in family patterns.

4. In small groups, discuss the following questions:

   a. Would you rather be a parent today than in 1960? Why or why not?

   b. Would you plan to stay at home with children, work, or do both if you were a parent? If you already are a parent, what would be the ideal living situation for you?

   c. What do you consider some of the biggest challenges families face today?

Apply the Chapter Concepts: Case In Point

Reread the stories of the 12 fictional families described in this chapter. Concentrate on two families in particular as you answer these questions:

1. How do these families illustrate the concept that contemporary families are under stress? Identify the sources of stress in each family.

2. How do these families illustrate the concept that family structure takes many forms? Identify the types of families on which you are concentrating.

3. How do these families illustrate concepts about changing male and female roles?

4. How do these families illustrate concepts about the influence of culture on families?

5. Name any other social changes discussed in this chapter that are illustrated by the two families you chose.

Review Questions

1. Define family and then describe several characteristics of a family.

2. List and discuss several trends in contemporary life that influence the nature of modern families.

3. Discuss why teachers should be aware of contemporary trends affecting families.

Helpful Websites

- Council on Contemporary Families (CCF) is a nonprofit organization dedicated to enhancing the national conversation about what contemporary families need and how these needs can best be met.

- The mission of the Children's Defense Fund is to Leave No Child Behind and to ensure every child a healthy start, a head start, a fair start, a safe start, and a moral start in life and successful passage to adulthood with the help of caring families and communities.

- The primary purpose of the Future of Children is to promote effective policies and programs for children by providing policymakers, service providers, and the media with timely, objective information based on the best available research.

- The website of the Vanier Institute of the Family in Canada provides information on important issues and trends critical to the well-being and healthy functioning of Canadian families.

- Check out the website for Generations United, the national center on grandparents and other relatives raising children.

- The website for the Grandparent Information Center at AARP offers information for grandparents raising grandchildren, including a guide to public benefits for grandparent caregivers and other resources.

Learning Objectives

After reading this chapter, you should be able to:

3-1 Discuss seven roles that parents play and the implications for teachers.

3-2 Describe seven emotional responses of parents and the implications for teachers.

Related NAEYC Standards

Accreditation Standards (see inside text back cover for full listing of the Accreditation Standards for exemplary early childhood programs)

7.A.01

Licensure Standards (see inside text front cover for full listing of the Licensure Standards for this chapter)

2a

In Chapter 2, we considered the sociocultural context of modern parenting in this country. Parenting has never been a simple task, no matter what the societal conditions. Taking on the responsibilities of parenting involves adjusting to numerous roles and profound emotional responses that are quite often surprising. No one is ever quite prepared for parenthood and the resultant adjustments in relationships, lifestyle, and responsibilities that require major reorientations and adaptations. Unfortunately, our society does little to assist parents through current and future changes as they continue to fill complex roles with their developing children. As teachers working with parents who are in the midst of these major adjustments, it is important to understand and recognize the nature of parenting responsibilities in order to support parents optimally. It is also crucial to recognize the deep emotional responses to parenthood that necessarily impact relationships with others. In this chapter, we consider roles and emotional responses of parents.

Teachers working with families may become frustrated by the parents' apparent inability to focus their attention fully on matters regarding the children. It is sometimes difficult for teachers to remember that parenting involves many complex behaviors and roles and that parents may be preoccupied with matters beyond one particular child in a particular classroom situation. It is important that teachers continually try to remain aware of the complexity of parents' lives to avoid making assumptions that parents are not truly interested in their children's welfare.

Consider the following situation. Does the teacher sound at all familiar?

Jane Briscoe is becoming impatient. As she describes it to her director, "These parents, I don't get it. I'm trying to take time to talk with them, and that's tough, believe me, with everything else I've got to do. But some of them just don't seem interested. The other day, Mrs. Lawrence kept looking at the clock when I was talking. And Mary Howard this morning—she looked as if she wasn't even listening to me. I've tried, but if they don't care about their own kids, what am I supposed to do?" The director, Mrs. Forbes, is sympathetic. She knows Jane's frustration arises partly from her concern for the children as well as from the human reaction of wanting response when initiating communication. But she also realizes that Jane is seeing only one perspective and needs to remind herself of how life may seem from the parents' viewpoint to increase her compassion and effectiveness. A teacher who assumes parents are not interested decreases her effort; a teacher who recognizes the multiple pulls on the time and attention of a parent keeps trying.

"I know that's frustrating for you, Jane, when you're trying hard. There's no one easy answer, I'm sure. Sometimes, I try to imagine what life must be like for some of our parents—all the things that could be on their minds when they walk in here. There's your Mrs. Lawrence—she has all the concerns of her work with 28 third-graders on her mind this Monday morning as well as her own two. And I happen to know her two stepsons visited this past weekend, and that always makes it difficult—crowded and hectic. And she's been looking tired now that her pregnancy's further along. Must be a lot to think about, trying to get both her children and his children used to the idea of a new baby.

Her husband works long hours, too—must be hard to find time to relax together, let alone finish up all the chores in that new house."

Jane looked thoughtful. "You're right, you know. And I guess if I think about it, I can figure out some things that might keep Mary Howard's attention from being completely on me. It's exam time at the high school, and I know she's trying to do well in case she decides to go on to college. And she is still a high school kid—mother or not. I sure remember the million-and-one problems my friends and I had—from figuring out how to get enough money to buy the latest fashions to how to get along with our parents. It must really be hard for her to be living with her parents—still an adolescent as well as a young mother who needs our help in looking after her own child. There just wouldn't be room for rebellion, would there? I wonder if she gets excluded at school because of her baby. Keeping the baby must have been a big decision for her to make, and she's still so unsure of what's ahead for her." Jane broke off and smiled ruefully. "I guess I've been spending too much time being annoyed with the parents and too little trying to get inside their skin to see life from their perspective. Thanks, Mrs. Forbes."

Mrs. Forbes smiled as Jane went out, thinking that the young teacher would be all right; she had made the first big step in working effectively with parents. She had begun to try to understand the experience of parenting, including the many roles a parent plays and the emotional responses of parenting.

3-1   Roles Parents Play

Although the teacher was thinking about two mothers, it should be noted that changes in social attitudes have encouraged people to think of **androgynous** adult roles—those that are shared by men and women and have similar functions. While recognizing that fathers and mothers likely relate and interact differently with their children because of the differences in their biology and past experiences, many parents no longer separate aspects of parenting and family living into male and female tasks. Following that model, this text will examine these roles and briefly consider the implications for teachers. There are seven of these roles, and although they can be discussed as separate entities, each of the roles overlaps and influences the others.

3-1a   The Parent as Nurturer

The **nurturing** role encompasses all the affectionate care, attention, and protection that young children need to grow and thrive. This implies caring for the physical needs of children before and after birth, but perhaps the greatest needs for healthy development are emotional support and caring. Being a nurturer is the parent's primary role in providing a psychological environment of warm, emotional interaction in which the child can thrive (see Figure 3-1). Nurturing involves most of the family's developmental tasks, as listed in Figure 3-2. Researchers have found important correlations between warm and responsive parenting in infancy, including close physical contact between parent and baby and attention to needs, and the development of **attachment**, which is defined as the strong, affectional, mutual tie formed in the two years following birth and enduring over time

androgynous
Having the characteristics of both sexes.

nurturing
Encouraging, supporting, caring, nourishing.

attachment
The strong, affectionate, mutual tie formed in the first two years following birth and enduring over time.

FIGURE 3-1
An important parental role is to provide warm, emotional nurturing.

FIGURE 3-2
Nurturing involves most of the family's developmental tasks.

Family Developmental Tasks

- Physical maintenance—shelter, food, clothing, health care, safety

- Allocation of resources—meeting family needs, authority, affection

- Division of labor—earning income, managing household, caring for family members

- Socialization of family members—learning acceptable behavior and standards for moral behavior

- Maintaining order within family system—communication and interaction

- Reproduction, rearing, and release of family members

- Inclusion of family members in larger society—community activities

- Maintaining motivation and morale—satisfying individual needs for acceptance and sense of family loyalty

From Duvall & Hill, 1948

FIGURE 3-3
Warm, responsive parenting in infancy leads to secure attachments.

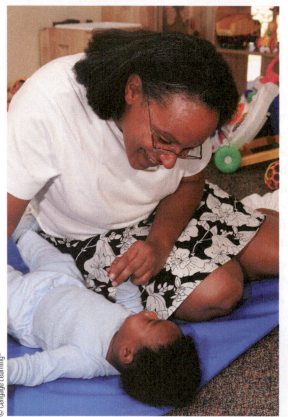

© Cengage Learning®

Touchpoints model
Model developed by T. Berry Brazelton to support families at key points of disruption during their children's development.

(see Figure 3-3). Attachment is felt to be critical to optimum development in every other aspect of development. The basis for differences in behavior and development related to attachment may be that a positive attachment relationship offers the child a secure base from which to venture forth to explore the world and learn how to interact. Older, school-aged children with whom teachers work are still the product of the quality of that earlier attachment.

Ainsworth, one of the leading attachment theorists, reports that by toddlerhood, children's responses in observed "strange situations" indicate that attachment is already formed (Mooney, 2009). Indeed, variations in parents' nurturing behaviors determine the kind of attachment the child will have with the parent. Variations in attachment include secure attachment, anxious-avoidant, or anxious-ambivalent attachments. See Figure 3-4 for related parent responses and behaviors in children.

Two of the most recognized names among Americans working with young children and their families are Dr. T. Berry Brazelton and Dr. Stanley Greenspan. In a joint work—*The Irreducible Needs of Children: What Every Child Must Have to Grow, Learn, and Flourish* (2001)—the two underline the vital importance of consistent, caring relationships in the early years to foster the emotional interaction that is the most critical primary foundation for social and intellectual growth. Brazelton points out that emotional learning comes first through warm interaction, and cognitive learning follows (Brazelton & Greenspan, 2001). The ongoing nurturing work of parents continues throughout the child's years of development, leading to growth in all areas. Brazelton's work in developing the **Touchpoints model**—a model developed to support families at key points of disruption during their children's development—helps teachers, caregivers, and other professionals learn how to support families in developing their nurturing roles.

Recent research on brain development corroborates the connection between emotional nurturing and the actual physical development of the brain in the earliest months

FIGURE 3.4
Variations in Attachment

Type of Attachment	Indicators	Parental Behaviors
Secure attachment	■ Easy separation from mother ■ Friendly behavior to stranger ■ Crying when mother leaves and then friendly to stranger ■ Warm greeting when mother returns	■ Responsive feedback, with correct interpretation of baby's signals ■ Sensitivity to baby's activity, without interfering
Anxious-ambivalent attachment	■ Shows resistance to mother and clinginess ■ Wary of new people and situations ■ Very upset when parent leaves and will not be comforted ■ Seems angry when mother returns	■ Respond inappropriately to baby's cues ■ Little emotional warmth ■ No consistent pattern of responsiveness
Anxious-avoidant attachment	■ Doesn't care whether mother or stranger is present, leaves both easily ■ No distress when mother leaves ■ Avoids reunion contact with mother	■ Ignore baby's cues ■ Little physical contact ■ No consistent pattern of responsiveness

© Cengage Learning®

and years. It has been noted that the parts of the brain that process emotions grow and mature relatively early in a child and are very sensitive to parental feedback and handling. There is a growing body of research confirming that parents' attitudes and actions are central to children's emotional adjustment to learning at home and at school.

THE SEVEN IRREDUCIBLE NEEDS OF CHILDREN

1. The need for ongoing nurturing relationships
2. The need for physical protection, safety, and regulation
3. The need for experiences tailored to individual differences
4. The need for developmentally appropriate experiences
5. The need for limit setting, structure, and expectations
6. The need for stable, supportive communities and cultural continuity
7. Protecting the future: commitment of rich, developed nations to children in less developed parts of the world

From Brazelton & Greenspan, 2001

In recent years, there have been concerns about whether full-time child care placements in the infant's first year will disturb the attachment relationship between parent and child. Studies since the mid-1980s (Belsky, 1986; Clarke-Stewart, 1989; NIHCD Early Child Care Research Network, 1997; Caldwell, 2001; Belsky et al., 2007) have suggested possible negative results of mothers working and leaving their young children in child care—mainly related to cognitive achievement and behavior seen later in school. But the most recent report (Lucas-Thompson et al., 2010), an analysis of 69 studies conducted

FIGURE 3-5
The jury is still out on the long-term effects of full-time child care for the very young.

over a 50-year period, found that children of working mothers have outcomes not dissimilar from stay-at-home mothers—related to academic achievement and behavior issues. The exception to this was some negative findings related to very early full-time child care (see Figure 3-5).

Faced with such good news/bad news, it is important for all adults who care for young children to realize the importance of early emotional nurturing and to support parents in whatever life circumstances they do their parenting. As caregivers understand the critical importance of parents and children forming attachment bonds, they will recognize that one of their own roles is to support the development of attachment.

Teachers should be aware that children can develop different kinds of attachment to key adults in their lives. For example, two-year-old Enrico might have developed an anxious attachment with his mother—perhaps due in part to his mother's two lengthy hospitalizations and ill health during much of his infancy. However, when Enrico is observed with his grandmother—a warm woman sensitive and responsive to his needs and personality—Enrico appears securely attached.

OPPORTUNITY FOR SELF-REFLECTION

One of the things teachers have to recognize is that they likely have some images and feelings related to the nurturing role that could get in the way of full acceptance of parents. Consider how you feel about men as nurturers: Are you as comfortable seeing fathers in the same nurturing role as mothers? Consider how you feel about mothers who leave their small children in the care of others. Do you worry about their children's attachment? Attitudes are neither right nor wrong; they just are. When teachers are aware of attitudes, they are less disruptive to forming relationships.

FIGURE 3-6
Fathers may be as nurturing as mothers toward children.

For years, such nurturance has been equated with "mothering." Little research was done on fathering until the 1980s. Recent research indicates that fathers are important in children's development.

The consensus of research findings is that fathers do not differ significantly from mothers in being interested in infants and children; they become involved with their offspring if encouraged to do so; they are as nurturing as mothers toward children (see Figure 3-6); and they may engage less frequently in active caregiving but are competent in carrying out the activities they perform (Bigner, 2009).

Fathers are not only competent but also absolutely crucial, according to other findings. Research is showing that the involvement of fathers with their children has important influences at every stage of child development (Brotherson & White, 2006). At six months of age, babies with actively involved fathers score higher on the Bailey test of mental and motor development; in the preschool years, children with involved fathers show greater ability to take initiative and direct themselves and a sense of competence; father involvement in children's school life increases the chances that a child will excel by as much as 42 percent; father involvement in adolescence reduces risks of juvenile delinquency, teen pregnancy, and drug use while increasing the amount of education completed.

Studies find that the more time fathers spend with their children and the more supportive their relationship is, the fewer childhood behavior problems there are. (This is also true of stepfathers and divorced fathers without custody.) A U.S. Department of Education study reconfirms the important role fathers play in the school achievement of their children. The research focused on the involvement of fathers in school programs of children in grades 6 through 12.

The study found that children from two-parent homes whose fathers participated in school activities were more likely to receive As on assignments, participate in extracurricular activities, enjoy school, and be less likely to repeat a grade (National Center for Education Statistics, 2001). Although the report recognized the importance of mothers to the social and emotional adjustment of the child, father involvement may be more important for academic achievement.

Some of the more recent involvement of fathers is certainly due to societal shifts over recent decades, not least of which are the number of women working outside the home and changes in the definitions of social roles.

This may be best exemplified by changes beginning in the early 1970s in practices related to pregnancy and childbirth that permitted and encouraged fathers to become more involved from the beginning. This contributed significantly to changing fathers' perceptions of their own role in the family. Several studies conclude that the father's participation at birth helps the mother assume her role; the birth itself may be a strong stimulus for nurturing behaviors from fathers and mothers as well as a time for attitude formation (Bigner, 2009). When fathers assist in the delivery room, they go on to change diapers, be involved with toilet learning, drive carpools, and supervise homework. Children may be strongly attached to both fathers and mothers.

FIGURE 3-7
Parents with several children may have differing demands at the same time.

Most findings concur that the parenting role most crucial for a child's optimum development is the nurturing role. It is within the context of family that children learn about intimate and personal relationships. This is probably one of the most demanding roles a parent plays; it includes myriad prompt responses to an infant's needs at any hour of the day or night during the long period of infant helplessness, and the frequent setting aside of adult needs in favor of growing children's requirements and demands.

The need for nurturing in its various forms does not diminish as young children become older; parents are still the people children look to for comfort, security, and approval. Parents with several children may have differing demands placed on them at the same time—the infant crying to be picked up, the preschooler fearful of being left, the school-aged child needing comfort after an encounter with peers (see Figure 3-7). It is no wonder that many parents feel "burned out" from time to time—so depleted by filling the nurturing needs of their children that they have little time or energy to meet some of their own needs.

Implications for the Teacher

- Teachers can help by understanding the importance of the parents' nurturing role and the many demands this places on mothers and fathers. Emotional support from sources outside the family allows parents to devote more energy to nurturing.

- Teachers can supplement the nurturing role without violating the parent–child bond.

- Teachers who are familiar with behaviors in children associated with secure and insecure attachments can be alert to situations that indicate trouble and can help parents learn about the specific nurturing responses that are related to developing secure attachments.

- Caregivers of infants can promote particular classroom practices to enhance attachment (see Chapter 14).

- Teachers of children of all ages can encourage involvement and nurturing activities that include fathers and mothers as well as any other key adults in children's lives.

- Teachers can also be sensitive to broadening activities to be sure they include stepparents, grandparents, and all other nurturing people in the family, excluding no family structure of any child.

3-1b The Parent in Adult Relationships

Parents are people first, and there is evidence that those who are fulfilled and contented as individuals are better able to function effectively as parents than those who are disappointed in their personal lives. It is evident that the support one parent gives to the other facilitates the development of the parenting role as well as optimizing conditions for nurturing the child. Forty-eight percent of mothers report that their spouse or partner is the primary source for emotional support for parenting. Although the primary adult relationship may be with a marriage partner or cohabiting adult, the adult's life may be crisscrossed with a network of adult relationships—parents, friends, and former spouses. In fact, many parents also help arrange for their own parents' health or living conditions and must make complicated arrangements with former spouses to share custody and negotiate financial matters. The relationship with one's child is an extremely important relationship, but it begins in the context of relationships with other adults.

Before an individual becomes a parent, there is first a relationship with another adult. One of the demands on a parent is to foster the continuance of that relationship or of another that may have replaced the original relationship.

One of the long-standing myths surrounding parenthood is that children give meaning to a marriage, improve the relationship between a couple, help a troubled relationship, and actually prevent divorce. In fact, the addition of parenthood roles to a marriage introduces a time of abrupt transition. Many researchers report this as a time of some degree of crisis. The severity of the crisis may depend on the degree of a couple's preparation for parenthood and marriage, the degree of commitment to the parenthood role, and patterns of communication. Whether or not the transition is a time of severe crisis, a couple is unquestionably going to have to reorganize their relationship and interactions; changes will occur in a marriage with an altered lifestyle and the addition of new role images and behaviors associated with parenthood (see Figure 3-8). Nora Ephron wrote: "When you have a baby, you set off an explosion in your marriage, and when the dust settles, your marriage is different from what it was. Not better, necessarily; not worse, necessarily; but different" (Ephron, 2013).

These changes are linked to a decrease in marital satisfaction. Studies report a U-shaped pattern in the degree of satisfaction, declining from after the birth of a child and as children grow older and then gradually increasing as children are raised and begin to lead independent lives. One reason offered for this decline in satisfaction is role strain. This appears when the following occurs:

- There are incompatible expectations for a person holding several roles at the same time—recall the earlier discussion of the Superwoman syndrome.

- The demands of one social role are in conflict simultaneously with those of another social role—imagine a candlelit dinner disrupted by the baby's cries.

- Strong demands for performance are placed on all social roles— that Superwoman image again!

It is difficult for spouses to pay close attention to the needs of their adult relationship while caring for the needs of their developing children.

FIGURE 3-8
The demands of children may interfere with adults being able to pay close attention to adult relationships.

© Mjth/Shutterstock.com

All these studies support the idea that using children as a means to improve a marriage is a mistake. The parent as a nurturer of children may discover that the parent as an adult in a relationship may neglect and be neglected. Although the divorce rate has gone down, the percentage of couples saying they are in less-than-happy marriages has gone up (Warner, 2005).

Actually, the probability of divorce is doubled when couples have children during their first year of marriage; evidently, many couples are too unsettled to face parenthood before they can work out some of the marital behaviors. However, if children do not improve a marriage, their presence may serve to cement it together a little longer. The median duration of marriages among childless couples before divorce is about four years; couples with several children stay together about 14 years (Bigner, 2009).

Although there is statistical evidence that children stabilize marriages for at least a while, this is not the same as improving them. Some married couples have their worst disagreements over their actions as parents!

Implications for the Teacher

- Teachers learn to relate to parents as interesting adults in their own right, not just in the role of parent. For example, knowing that a father is training for an upcoming marathon, a teacher might give him an article she read about diet to improve muscle. Aware that a grandfather who raises his grandson alone has an extensive collection of baseball cards, another teacher can invite him to participate in the neighborhood hobby show.

- When opportunities arise in conversation, teachers can convey acceptance, approval, and encouragement of parents' efforts to enhance their marriages, to engage in hobbies, and to pursue personal and social enrichment.

■ It is easy for teachers to be critical when parents do not seem to be devoting all their time and attention to their children, but it is important to remember that a significant gift that parents can give their children is a stable home and the model of caring relationships.

3-1c The Parent as an Individual

Americans have come to value the development of the individual person. We are now aware that this personal development is a lifelong process. Parents concerned with nurturing their children's development are also encountering growth in their own lives.

It is relevant for teachers to consider how Erikson's theory examines the psychosocial tasks of adulthood that must be resolved. Many young parents are preoccupied with issues of identity. Erikson speaks of this as the fifth stage, beginning in adolescence. With the prolonging of education and financial dependence on parents and with the confusing multiplicity of roles, careers, and lifestyles from which to select, many identity issues are still being actively worked on in young adulthood. One measure of this may be the postponing of marriage—perhaps seen as an entry step into the adult world and a sign that a young person has settled some issues and is ready to embark on adult life. The events of marriage and parenthood cause many young people to reexamine identity issues as they take on two roles symbolic of adult life. It is not just real-life events that have to be assimilated into an individual's self-concept but also expectations and attitudes from within the individual and from society that set the standards used to measure the new view of self. There are several problems here. One is that most of today's parents grew up with daily facts of life and social role expectations that are radically different from those of the present.

Many mothers find their self-esteem being attacked—whether they have chosen to fill the traditional role of homemaker or have joined the majority of mothers working outside the home. "In the national conversation we have been having in this country about work and family life, having a working mother alternates between being seen as being either good *or* bad for the children" (Galinsky, 2000).

FIGURE 3-9
Many mothers are challenged by combining the roles of mother and career.

In what Galinsky refers to as the "mommy wars," at-home mothers feel they are being dismissed and devalued, and they resent having to "pick up the slack" as classroom volunteers or emergency child care for mothers who have chosen to work. At all income levels, stay-at-home mothers report more sadness, anger, and episodes of diagnosed depression than their employed counterparts (Coontz, 2013). Working mothers feel the stress of having to succeed on two fronts. The media continue to subtly indict working mothers for increasing family stress and sacrificing their children for materialism and success now that they have added to their traditional roles. Working mothers are themselves caught in conflict and ambivalence. A majority of working mothers and fathers feel that it is bad for the family for mothers to be at work. When mothers return to work, they do so in a climate of subtle societal disapproval. And some of the criticism is directed back and forth between working mothers and stay-at-home mothers, each resenting the others' choice and judging their performance and contribution (Hattery, 2000) (see Figure 3-9).

Actually, a major finding of Galinsky's study on work and family life (1999) is that there is no difference in the assessments of children with employed mothers and those of children with mothers at home. What matters most is how children are being parented rather than whether their parents are working outside the home. A current phenomenon is that women's and mothers' groups are finding common ground on issues that span women's concerns as parents and family breadwinners (Shellenbarger, 2005).

FIGURE 3-10
Contemporary fathers have new roles to fit into their identity.

© 2016 Cengage Learning®

In the Ask the Children study, Galinsky found that certain job factors created better mental attitudes in parents and gave them more energy for their interactions with their children:

- Having reasonably demanding jobs
- Having jobs that permit parents to focus on their work
- Having meaningful, challenging jobs that provided opportunities for learning and job autonomy
- Having workplace environments with good interpersonal and supportive relationships, where parents do not feel they have to choose between job and parenting

A father's task of assimilating his new role into his identity is no easier (see Figure 3-10). Although more recently he is gaining attention as part of the family, for many years he has been considered nonessential to the functioning of the family.

After identity, Erikson's next task of adulthood coincides with the stage of establishing family life until early middle age. The previous attainment of a sense of personal identity and engagement in productive work leads to a new interpersonal dimension of intimacy at one extreme and isolation at the other. By this, Erikson means the ability to share with and care about another person without fear of losing oneself in the process. Family relationships are based on this kind of interdependency. Parents are called on to share their world freely with their children and each other in caring relationships. It seems obvious from our earlier discussions about identity and nurturing that these tasks actually occur simultaneously.

Older parents may have added the dimension of Erikson's seventh stage in middle age, when the task may be to work from a sense of what Erikson calls "generativity" rather than negative self-absorption and stagnation. **Generativity** involves the adult's concern

generativity
A concern for establishing and guiding the next generation.

WHAT MAKES A GOOD PARENT?

In Galinsky's survey, eight critical parenting skills emerged:

- Making the child feel important and loved
- Responding to the child's cues and clues
- Accepting the child for who he or she is but expecting success
- Promoting strong values
- Using constructive discipline
- Providing routines and rituals to make life predictable and creating positive neural patterns in developing brains
- Being involved in the child's education
- Being there for the child

From Galinsky, 1999

© Rena Schild/Shutterstock.com

FIGURE 3-11
Many adults are concerned with issues beyond the immediate family.

with others moving beyond the immediate family to active striving to make the world a better place for future generations (see Figure 3-11). Parents with this perspective may become involved beyond the narrower focus on their own children and jobs, working for issues that may improve prospects for other families, schools, and communities.

Issues of identity are never closed. As life circumstances change, a reexamination of roles and relationships and the resulting implications for an individual is necessary. A person's identity as a parent is not fixed either. As children move through successive stages of development, parents are presented with new challenges. For example, skills and behaviors that served well with an infant must be abandoned in favor of new strategies to live compatibly with a toddler or a school-aged child and then an adolescent. Parents' feelings of competence may fluctuate as their ability to adapt to the changing child fluctuates.

Traditional theories used in recent decades describe family life in stages usually marked by children's ages. The best known of these was the eight-stage model outlined by Duvall and Hill (1948):

- Married couples (no children)

- Childbearing families (oldest child aged birth to 30 months)

- Families with preschool children (oldest child aged 21.2 months to six years)

- Families with school-aged children (oldest child aged six to 13 years)

- Families with teenagers (oldest child aged 13 to 20 years)

- Families launching young adults (this stage begins when the oldest child leaves home and ends when the youngest child leaves home)

- Middle-aged parents (this stage begins with an "empty nest" and ends at the start of retirement)

- Aging family members (this stage begins with spouses' retirement and ends at their deaths)

There are some obvious problems when using this common and traditional stage theory. One is that this theory best fits the traditional family, with assumptions about what constituted the tasks of the family at a particular stage. Considering the diverse family forms in contemporary society, it is difficult to apply the stage theory, especially if families are going through stages out of order or repeating stages due to remarriage. Nevertheless, stage theory allows us to quickly convey the particular concerns of the people living within a particular family. For example, when mentioning "the family with infants and toddlers," it is safe to assume we all understand at least some of the issues of that family.

Galinsky's more recent theory looks at family life from the parent's perspective, outlining a six-stage model to describe parent development (Galinsky, 1987):

- The image-making stage of the prenatal period

- The nurturing stage for the first two years—a period of attachment and questioning

- The authority stage when the child is between two and four to five years and the parents decide what kind of authority to be

- The interpretive stage from the child's preschool years to the approach of adolescence, where parents are interpreting the world to their children

- The interdependent stage during the teen years, where parents form new relationships with almost-adult children

- The departure stage when children leave home and parents evaluate the whole of their parenting experience

Implications for the Teacher

- Parents need additional support from teachers as they develop parenting skills to match the changing needs of their developing children.

- Parents develop a positive sense of themselves as parents when their skills are recognized and they receive positive feedback.

- Teachers can form relationships that allow them to learn from parents and not have to rely on theories of parenthood.

- Teachers will be challenged to work with parents at many different ages and stages of adult development.

- Parents of all ages are struggling with issues of parental identity. Very young parents may be struggling with issues of personal identity; others are focused on forging relationships of intimacy; still others can look beyond their own families with concern for society at large. Teachers need to learn as much as they can about adult development to understand and accept individual responses.

3-1d The Parent as Worker

The stage in the life cycle when parenting usually occurs is a time of concern with being productive. Most adults find their means to this goal in one or both of the two channels of parenting and work. However, the two are often in competition with each other, as parents try to navigate work and family life and try to do both well.

About two-thirds of mothers with children younger than age six are currently employed outside the home; nearly 80 percent of mothers of school-aged children are working—41 percent of them full time. This is an increase of more than 10 percent over the previous decade, with the sharpest increase being for married women in two-parent families with children younger than age six. There are several reasons for this increase in the number of working mothers:

- Increased costs in rearing children and living expenses

- An expanded economy with the creation of new job opportunities

- Earlier completion of families, so women are younger when their children start school

- Reduced amount of time needed for housework

- Better education of women

- Expectations of a better lifestyle

- Changes in basic attitudes toward roles, with new social perspectives

CULTURAL CONSIDERATIONS

Parenting roles in diverse cultures

As you read about the various parenting roles, be aware that these are derived from the current thinking and practices in our society and generalized to portray current conditions in the dominant culture. Also be aware that individuals from specific cultures may define these roles very differently or not accept all these roles as being part of their definition of parenthood. For example, some cultural definitions would not see parenting roles as being androgynous but instead have specific separations for mothers and fathers. Other cultural views might not see the parent's individual identity or adult relationships as relevant to the parenting role. Still others might not find the mother as worker role relevant.

This is yet another reminder that teachers must be aware of individual families' cultural definitions of parenting roles and then respond accordingly.

Take a minute to reflect how your own cultural background has affected your understanding of parenting roles. If possible, compare your viewpoints with another student to confirm yet again the importance of sensitivity to cultural diversity.

Economic reasons are dominant for most women: The number of families below the poverty line would increase by 35 percent if both parents did not work. One study reported that mothers want to be employed but in positions that demand less of their time; only 16 percent of mothers would prefer full-time work if they could have their ideal.

Despite the fact that a majority of mothers work outside the home along with fathers, much in our society indicates we are still operating on two related assumptions: that it is the natural role of men to work as providers and that it is equally natural for women to take care of children. One measure of this is that no national statistics are kept on the number of working fathers, although careful note is made of the number of working mothers. With similar bias, studies are done on how mothers' working affects children; no such research is done when fathers work. Although such attitudes may annoy many women in the workplace, their effect is more than mere bother; the attitudes frequently translate into equally outmoded working hours and conditions that are neither helpful nor supportive to a parent working and carrying out home responsibilities.

The majority of these parents have an inflexible working schedule of around 40 hours per week. About a quarter of all employees have flextime schedules, according to Department of Labor statistics, despite the fact that when working mothers are polled, flexible work schedules are the benefit they most desire (Boushey, 2011). The U.S. government as an employer does set an example here; over 40 percent of government agencies allow their employees to flexibly schedule their hours.

The option of job sharing—eminently suited to many parents who would like to decrease the demands of their working life—is still available to only a handful. About 15 to 20 percent of adults are able to work from their homes at least part of the time. This number is growing regularly now that technology allows some work to be done from home—mainly by those in management, professional, and related positions. But many parents are in jobs that require travel away from home. Worse yet, many American workers are asked to change their jobs and move often, disrupting family arrangements. In times of recession, unemployment may add additional stress to the family.

Perhaps the place where we see most clearly how the roles of parent and worker may come into conflict is when the parents are involved in the birth or adoption of a new child into the family. At a time when the family unit is most under the stress of change and new roles, many parents find their employers are not able to give them the time to adapt and adjust.

Contrast the difference in the policies regarding maternity and paternity leave in the United States and other countries. At this most crucial and stressful period of a young family's life, structures are rarely in place in the United States to support the parents leaving the workplace temporarily to have time with their new child. Out of 178 nations, the United States is one of only three that does not offer paid maternity leave benefits, to say nothing of paid leave for fathers, which is offered by more than 50 of these countries. Canada and Norway offer generous benefits of close to a year that can be shared between the father and the mother. See Figure 3-12 for the amounts and length of time currently available in selected countries. It was reported in 2011 that only 11 percent of private sector workers and 17 percent of public workers reported they had access to paid maternity leave through their employer (Beadle, 2012).

The Family and Medical Leave Act offers the only possibility for leave—unpaid though it is—for many American parents. Since the passage of the Family and Medical Leave Act in 1993, parents working for businesses with at least 50 employees are eligible to take an unpaid protected leave of up to 12 weeks for circumstances in the family that

FIGURE 3-12
Government-funded
maternity leave in selected
countries.

require their attention, such as the birth or adoption of a baby or illness of a child or parent. About 40 percent of workers are not eligible even for this because they work for employers with fewer than 50 employees, or they may not have worked for the company the required minimum of a year. Unfortunately, economic realities also prohibit many families from being able to take unpaid leave. A recent study reported that the act has not increased leave-taking by new fathers at all, and it has increased new mothers' leaves only slightly. It seems likely that parents are unable to take substantially more unpaid leave when a new child is born, even when they are given the right to do so (Han & Waldfogel, 2003). In the United States, California and New Jersey are the only states to have enacted a paid-leave insurance law for maternity or paternity leaves, for which only certain workers are eligible. Only 20 states and the District of Columbia have laws that give some female employees the right to job-protected maternity leaves.

What do these employment facts mean to parents? In practical terms, parents as workers spend the majority of their waking hours going to or from work, working, or being tired from working. Their young children, who are likely to be awake during these same hours, are of necessity cared for by someone else during the parents' workday. Their older school-aged children are probably in school during many of the same hours, but before and after school, the long vacations, and other days off all necessitate making arrangements for child care or leaving the children unsupervised. Numerous special events will be hard for parents to either fit in or miss: the kindergarten field trip, the fifth-grade band concert, the mothers' breakfast at the preschool. Employers know that they can expect an increased absentee rate for mothers of preschoolers during the winter months, when colds and other infections run rampant. Parents who feel they cannot spare another day off are faced with the dilemma of leaving a sick child at school (pretending the child is not sick because most schools will not accept sick children) or facing the employer's wrath. Pulled between the displeasure of the employer and the caregiver and the needs and schedule of the child, parents may feel resentful, exhausted, guilty, and inadequate to all the tasks. And this stress does not go unnoticed by children. In Galinsky's study, she found that about two-thirds of children worry about their parents. They worry because they feel their parents are tired and stressed.

No matter what changes have occurred in the relationship of men and women and in their child-rearing participation, it is still true that in most families, the "psychological" parent—the one who takes primary responsibility for the children's well-being—is the mother. This means that most women never leave for work with a clear sense of division between home and office; the concerns of home and family remain with them through the working day, and when working mothers return home, they have less free time than their husbands (Hochschild & Machung, 2003).

No wonder it is more common to speak of stress in working mothers than in working fathers, although many women keep their stress a private matter rather than let anyone think they are not equal to these new tasks.

Considering work–family conflict as only a women's issue ignores the pressures on today's fathers. Recently, there has been a move for some fathers to file charges with their employers on the basis of workplace gender discrimination (Bernard, 2013). When they step outside traditional gender roles, fathers may be penalized by a whole range of negative repercussions, some experts have found (Bernard, 2013).

The conflict between work and family responsibilities is an issue that goes beyond gender (Rapoport, Bailyn, Fletcher, & Pruitt, 2001). Employers who see the worker as more than one-dimensional and provide for family needs in some measure are often rewarded by increased productivity and loyalty from workers relieved of some of their dilemma. Companies that provide on-site child care (unfortunately, under 20 percent of large companies) have found there is less absenteeism, and employees stay longer in their jobs (Connelly, DeGraff, & Willis, 2004). Generally, even as conditions improve (Galinsky, 2002), American parents find that work frequently conflicts with parenting demands, and they must deal with the life shaped by their work schedules.

Rather than see such data as completely negative regarding working mothers, we should note that a recent study found that employed mothers are generally more satisfied with their family lives than mothers who do not work outside the home, who report more sadness, anger, and episodes of diagnosed depression than their employed counterparts (Cherlin & Krishnamurthy, 2004; Coontz, 2013). As seen in Figure 3-13, working mothers get less sleep, watch less TV, spend less time with their children, and generally have less free time than at-home mothers. But they clearly protect their family time; employed mothers spend only five hours fewer a week with their children. But the percentage saying they got a "great deal" or "a very great deal" of satisfaction from their family lives is somewhat higher for mothers who work than for those who do not. Perhaps a busy life that combines employment and child rearing is also a fulfilling one.

Implications for the Teacher

- Teachers can support community and business attempts to alleviate stress for working parents by providing care for sick children or personnel policies that support families' attempts to care responsibly for their children.

- Teachers can try to schedule events for parents at times that may best fit into their working schedules—conferences during after-work hours, programs during lunch hour, and so on.

- Teachers and schools can have open visitation policies so parents feel able to come for lunch, story time, or any other times they are free to volunteer.

- Teachers can encourage parents to learn techniques for managing stress and share ideas for homecoming rituals to allow them to smooth the transition from home to work.

3-1e The Parent as Consumer

With inflation rates that increase every year, the real buying power of modern families continues to decline. Economic survival with the multiple material demands and expectations of our time has been a major factor in establishing the two-working-parent family structure.

FIGURE 3-13
How mothers spend their time (hours per week).

	Employed	Nonemployed
How mothers spend their time		
Total free time	28	41
With children	27	32
Sleeping	53	58
Watching TV	10	16
Housework	16	24
How mothers feel about family life (percent)		
Always feel rushed	51	26
Get a great deal of satisfaction	85	77

A good deal of the family income is devoted to rearing children. Children at one time were considered to be an economic asset—more available workers in a rural, self-sufficient family—but must now be considered economic liabilities. Recent statistics show it costs well over $250,000—depending on the family's income—to raise a child, with a whopping $32,000 spent in just the first two years (Lino, 2013). That figure is just for basic household expenses from birth through age 17. This is an increase of more than 20 percent since 1960. (The estimates include providing for basics of food, shelter, clothing, transportation, and medical care plus an annual inflation rate.) College demands many more thousands of dollars for tuition and expenses, with annual increases far outstripping the inflation rate. Note that these estimates cover only the basics—no piano lessons or summer camp.

When both parents work outside the home, a large proportion of income pays for child care. Child care is one of the most significant expenses in many working families' budgets, particularly for low-income families, often exceeding costs for food and even housing. Although there are variations by region or city or type of care, the annual cost of care for one child ranges between $4,100 and $10,920, with the average being over $6,423 per preschooler; costs for infant care are much higher, with a 2013 report indicating that the cost for full-time infant care in a child care center was greater than a year's tuition and fees at a four-year public university in the same state (Wood & Kendall, 2013). The U.S. Department of Health and Human Services considers 10 percent of a family's income to be a benchmark for affordable care, yet most families pay a far greater percentage (see Figure 3-14 and Figure 3-15). In some cases, mothers find that nearly all their additional family income is spent on child care, plus the purchases necessitated by employment—additional clothing, transportation, and food while away from home. In this case, continuing employment is probably either for maintaining career continuity or for personal fulfillment.

Costs of child care in many European countries are paid for by government support, with families sometimes making a small contribution. In Sweden and Denmark, nearly half of all children under age three are in full-day, publicly supported child care; about 85 percent of three- to five-year-olds are in full-time, publicly supported child care. In France and Belgium, nearly 100 percent of preschool children are in high-quality *ecoles maternelles*, mostly paid for by public funds. Italy has similar public expenditure for high-quality preschool child care. The U.S. government supplements costs of child care only for poor parents; the number of children getting government help is only about two million. The U.S. Department of Defense subsidizes child care for military dependents. Middle-class families receive a maximum tax credit for child care of $1,000 annually.

Without government support, families have to shoulder the full cost of child care and are often forced to choose lower-quality, more affordable alternatives. Some have suggested that the federal government should institute a system of copayments for child care (that parents choose) to expand coverage to 17 million more children, helping the United States catch up with policies in European countries. But in times of strained federal budgets and economic downturn, this may be merely a dream.

FIGURE 3-14
Center-based care is often the greatest family expense.

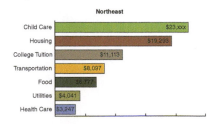

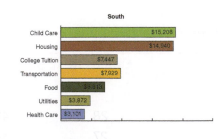

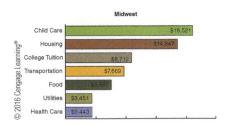

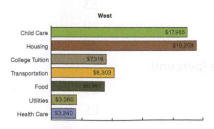

© 2016 Cengage Learning®

FIGURE 3-15
Representative average annual child care fees at programs in selected states.

State	Infant (12-month-old)	Preschooler (four-year-old)	School Age (five–eight-year-olds)
Massachusetts	16,430	12,176	4, 378
Minnesota	13,876	10,664	NA
Washington	12,108	9,240	5,412
Texas	8,495	6,547	3,119
NorthCarolina	8,868	7,501	4,298
Colorado	12,736	9,619	5,177
Arizona	8,671	7,398	6,198
Michigan	10,114	7,930	4,576
Illinois	12,697	9,261	5,877
Florida	8,299	6,571	3,822

Find your state and other information from Parents and the High Cost of Child Care: 2013 Report *Downloaded from www.usa.childcareaware.org*

Parents are caught in a child care **trilemma**. Even when their children enter the school system, it is usually necessary to pay for some kind of afterschool care until parents return home from work. In too many communities, parents on tight budgets are allowing dangerous **latchkey child care** arrangements for their school-aged children. It is not a question of whether parents should work; they are working, and the income figures quoted illustrate why they need to work. Nor is it an issue of whether child care is good or bad for children; many studies support the idea that good care is good and bad care is bad for them. The real trilemma for society is how to balance quality care for children, decent and fair living wages for child care staff, and affordability for parents. Child care professionals are still providing an unseen consumer subsidy by earning low salaries and few benefits. The result of this involuntary financial assistance to working parents is that child care workers have high rates of job turnover—around one-quarter every year—thereby lowering quality (Cost, Quality, and Outcomes Study, 1995, 1999, 2000; Wood & Kendall, 2013).

All sides of the consumer trilemma need urgent attention. It has become obvious that the solution to the problem will have to come from sources beyond the triangle. Although a few employers are beginning to see the need to supplement employee payments for quality child care and the government still considers various tax assistance plans, parents are caught paying too much while child care workers are earning far too little (see Figure 3-16).

It is no wonder that many parents feel they are on a financial treadmill. A major concern stated by most parents is money; a leader in the causes of marital friction is arguing about money. The parent in the role of consumer is stretched thin; when the economic health of the nation is shaky—whereupon many parents lose jobs temporarily or permanently—the family may be thrown into crisis.

trilemma
A dilemma that affects three parties, as in the parent, the child, and the school.

latchkey child care
Children caring for themselves at home after school.

Implications for the Teacher

- Because child care is an expensive item in the average family budget, parents often feel pressed to be sure they are receiving their money's worth. This may help the teacher understand the demands they make for nutritious foods and clean diapers and the annoyance they express for missing mittens or damaged clothing. Teachers need to be sympathetic to the financial pressures on parents.

■ It is in the best interests of parents, teachers, and children for parents and teachers to support each others' efforts to gain financial relief through support of community or government plans to subsidize the cost of quality child care.

3-1f   The Parent as Community Member

With the increasing complexity of modern life, a growing number of family functions have been taken over by community institutions and organizations: education by the school system and recreation and entertainment by the Y and other clubs as well as the church, which has often expanded its purely religious function. There are as many organizations as there are interests in any given community. The community itself has become more highly structured as groups of people coming together have dictated more rules, legislation, and decision making—public and private. But institutions and organizations do not run themselves; community members have many demands placed on them for their time as volunteers and for their money and other supportive efforts. Parents are asked to support the organizations that benefit their children as well as themselves.

It would not be unusual to find a week where families are asked to bake cupcakes for the PTA carnival, spend an hour staffing a booth at the carnival, driving children to and from the church junior choir practice, assisting children in magazine sales to aid the Y in getting new uniforms for the basketball team, coaching the team, making telephone calls to remind others about a local environmental group meeting, and soliciting funds door to door on behalf of a local branch of a national charity—as well as turning down several requests to participate in similar ways for other organizations (see Figure 3-17). For some parents who must work several jobs to make ends meet, there is enormous pressure to still find time to involve themselves and their children in the community or else be seen as not participating fully within the community. The wider the age range of the children, the broader and more fragmenting are the demands on parents. Most parents today face constant tension between outside demands on time and energy and the amount available for personal and family needs.

As community members, parents may not only give but also receive help from the social network of community organizations. If families do not isolate themselves from the larger community, they receive assistance and provide models for children of interacting within a broad base of support. Learning about and utilizing community resources is an important role for parents.

FIGURE 3-16
The child care trilemma.

Parents want quality child care.

Trained child care workers support families.

Quality child care needs trained workers.

Parents can't afford cost of quality care.

Low wages provide hidden subsidy for parents.

Quality child care suffers from turnover due to inadequate wages.

© Cengage Learning®

It is also important for parents to realize that their actions within the community can help shape opinion and policies on issues of importance to teachers and families. Parents need communities that care for children and families and that make children a high priority. As advocates in their own communities, families speak out on behalf of their children and themselves as well as on behalf of all children and families. No one has as much interest in their children as do parents; therefore, they have a right and obligation to stand up for their children. Parents who advocate within their communities for children's and families' rights stay informed about children's issues and involved in their educational institutions, talk to legislators and vote, speak out in the workplace for family benefits and supports, and support improved working conditions for those who care for their children. Through such active advocacy, they can have a powerful influence in the community. An expanded discussion of parents' roles in the community is found in Chapter 12.

FIGURE 3-17
Parents may have community responsibilities.

© Tammykayphoto/Shutterstock.com

Implications for the Teacher

- Any requests for parent participation add another thing to make time for. Teachers must realize this and be sure the idea is worth what it will cost the parent in time and pressure.

- Schedule activities with consideration of other regularly scheduled community events that involve parents or siblings.

- Teachers must guard against assuming that parents are too busy to become involved and thus never make the effort or invitation. Parents have the right to make the decisions about how they spend their time and not to have such decisions made for them arbitrarily.

- It is vital for teachers and parents to build alliances for mutual education on common issues and for support in trying to reach common goals within the community.

3-1g The Parent as Educator

Perhaps the role for which parents feel most unprepared is the role of educator, used here to mean guiding and stimulating the child's development and teaching the skills and knowledge that children need to eventually become effective adults in society. Nevertheless, families teach their children from the time they are babies and continue to teach them what they consider important throughout their life in the home.

They first teach responses, personal hygiene habits, safety rules, and how to be friendly and polite. And schools expect parents to teach certain skills to children before they enter school and then offer support, encouragement, and opportunities to practice as children continue their education. As other institutions take over many of the family's educative functions, the primary tasks of parents are the socialization of their children to the values held by the family as well as assisting and monitoring children's development as learners and providing preparation for schooling.

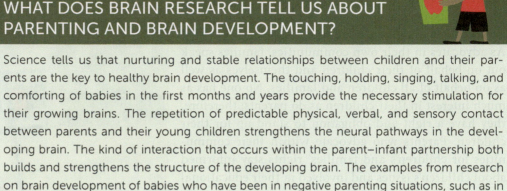

WHAT DOES BRAIN RESEARCH TELL US ABOUT PARENTING AND BRAIN DEVELOPMENT?

Science tells us that nurturing and stable relationships between children and their parents are the key to healthy brain development. The touching, holding, singing, talking, and comforting of babies in the first months and years provide the necessary stimulation for their growing brains. The repetition of predictable physical, verbal, and sensory contact between parents and their young children strengthens the neural pathways in the developing brain. The kind of interaction that occurs within the parent–infant partnership both builds and strengthens the structure of the developing brain. The examples from research on brain development of babies who have been in negative parenting situations, such as in the Communist-era Romanian orphanages or in abusive environments, illustrate the results of the lack of such positive parenting interactions, demonstrable by MRI as underdeveloped areas of the brain.

The idea that the early years are crucial for brain development has, unfortunately, led some parents to misinterpret this to mean that they should be actively teaching their young children—often by very inappropriate methods—lest the opportunity to give their children a superior brain be lost. Whole industries have been started to develop and sell DVDs, educational toys, and books to capitalize on this urge of parents to push. What this approach fails to take into consideration is that it is not direct instruction that builds the neural pathways essential for later learning. Rather, it is the sensory stimulation and active exploration that forges the links between synapses, all done through dynamic interaction with the child's environment, not delivered by instruction. We have always had pushy parents, but a misunderstanding of the science of early brain development may have exacerbated the problem.

1. Consider how you might help parents understand appropriate use of brain development information.
2. Develop a list of appropriate materials and interactions to support brain development of a one-year-old child.
3. Find more information online about the effects on the brain of harshly negative parenting.

Socialization of Children

Education toward socialization is such a difficult task for parents for two main reasons. The first was alluded to in Chapter 2. In today's rapidly changing world, it is difficult for a parent to be sure what life will be like even in the near future. Childhood experiences of today's parents were quite different from what they see their children experiencing; their memories of what their own parents did will probably not serve them well in their present situations. Values and cultural mores have changed, and parents are sometimes unsure how to help their children fit into this new world.

The second reason parents often find the role of educating their own children overwhelming is that the only on- or off-the-job training most receive is through having been parented themselves. Children learn through living with parents most of the basic information they will ever get for their future role as parents. Adults tend to parent as they were parented, and this pattern may be inadequate in the changing world (see Figure 3-18). Studies indicate that the characteristics, values, beliefs, and, most important, the practices of our own parents have the greatest influence on our child rearing.

It seems ironic that our society has become skillful at imparting technical knowledge and education to prepare workers for a career but has made little headway in similarly devising methods to prepare young people for the tasks of parenthood. Most parenting skills are learned by trial and error on the job, giving rise to the not-so-funny old joke about parents wanting to trade in their firstborn because that was the one they learned on! No wonder many parents are overwhelmed by the enormous task of parenthood with so little preparation.

It is important that teachers become aware of positive parenting models and practices to be able to assist parents in their growth as effective parents. The discussion of parent education in Chapter 11 includes a list of books about parenting issues and effective parenting skills. Although these skills cannot necessarily be acquired by reading a book, this can nevertheless be an important starting place. The models of parenting that many parents and teachers have experienced may often be the only sources for learning, unless adults deliberately seek additional information. Although there are as many styles of parenting as there are humans, many psychologists refer to two extremes and a middle ground; most parents likely fall somewhere along a continuum between the descriptions. Teachers should realize that parenting style has significance for healthy or unhealthy development of children.

One style that has been defined is the **authoritarian** parent. This parent requires complete obedience to authority and seems to feel that it is essential to hold very tight reins to control children. Such a parent retains all the power in the parent–child relationship, maintaining rigid rules and punishing when the rules are broken. Children are not given information or choices that would help them learn how to manage their own behavior. Anger and harshness may color the communication between parent and child. Unfortunately, the results of this extreme in parenting style are often fear of the parent, little development of the child's ability to control his or her own behavior, and diminished self-esteem. This style of parenting has been used all over the world for generations and may be effective in societies that experience little change and where there is one way to do things. However, it may be a mismatch for a rapidly changing society that values change and innovation.

At the other extreme is the parent who is overly **permissive** with the child, failing to provide clear and firm guidance about appropriate behavior. Whether because of lack of experience and understanding about children's needs, little self-confidence, or attention directed elsewhere in their lives, these parents simply allow their children inappropriate amounts of power to regulate their own lives long before the children are capable of doing so. Many teachers today express concerns that modern parents err in being too permissive, with the result that their children are unfamiliar with limits and discipline. This creates unhappy situations for children, who give evidence of craving some limits. They are unable to develop self-control when they have no boundaries, and they suffer diminished self-esteem because no one seems to care enough about them to provide necessary parenting. Children raised with permissive parenting may have trouble fitting in with the expectations of others in school, the community, or the workforce. Some have referred to the uninvolved parent. In today's world, there may exist a fine line between permissive

FIGURE 3-18
Children learn to parent by watching their own parents.

© 2016 Cengage Learning®

authoritarian
Requiring complete obedience to authority.

permissive
Having a low level of demands or expectations for children's behavior; tolerating behavior outside of bounds; a hands-off style of interaction.

TeachSource

VIDEO ACTIVITY ▶❚❚

© 2016 Cengage Learning®

Watch *Parenting Style: the Views of Three Mothers.*

After viewing the clip, reflect on these questions:

1. How would the various values of the parents in the video affect parenting styles and decisions?

2. What similarities do you see between the values and goals of the mothers? What differences?

3. How would understanding parental values and goals for their children help a teacher in working with a family?

and neglectful parenting, where parents are so immersed in their own interests that they are rather uninvolved and do not provide the kinds of attention and guidance that children need.

Happier situations for children result when parents exercise **authoritative**—sometimes also called **assertive/ democratic**—and warm relationships, recognizing children's needs for guidance and direction while understanding and accepting the slow process of children's learning about the world. These parents are more likely to explain reasons for behavior and teach more appropriate behaviors than to punish for the inevitable mistakes growing children make. These children get lots of practice with decision making and are guided to see the consequences of their choices. These parents help children slowly assume more and more control over their lives as they become able, supporting the children with firm but loving evidence that parents are in control but available to help children learn. There is pleasure in such parent–child relationships for everyone because parents perceive their children's gradual growth and children see their own expanding abilities. Warm, assertive, and authoritative parents are usually somewhat knowledgeable about children's development as well as secure enough in their adult lives to be able to share power as children need their worlds to expand. This style of parenting seems appropriate in a society where change is constant and choices must be made, with no one right way to do things (for further discussion of parenting styles, see Brooks, 2009). For a comparison of parenting styles, see Figure 3-19.

OPPORTUNITY FOR SELF-REFLECTION

Reflect on the parenting style your parents used. What is the parenting style you use or would like to use with your own children? Why is this your choice? Discuss your thinking with another student.

authoritative or assertive/democratic
Showing confident power and the right to command. See also *assertive/democratic.*

Preparation for Schooling

The issue of assisting children's development as learners and providing preparation for schooling has as many facets as there are opinions about appropriate early childhood education. Basically, there are two broad viewpoints.

One represents the idea that early childhood is a time for allowing children to learn and develop through play, exploration, and child-initiated discovery. These proponents advocate home and school environments that provide varieties of open-ended materials with opportunities to manipulate, create, and learn with the whole self—body and mind—in direct encounters with materials, activities, and people. The idea is that through play, a child learns best to understand the world, others, and his or her own capacities; this preparation lays the foundation for the more formal academic learning of later childhood.

Many teachers and parents strongly believe that young children should be allowed their childhoods and that anything else is "miseducation" (Elkind, 1987). (See Figure 3-20.)

Guidelines for developmentally appropriate curricula for children from birth through age eight as defined by the National Association for the Education of Young Children (NAEYC) (Copple & Bredekamp, 2009) support this viewpoint.

The major alternative viewpoint is that the sooner adults begin to "teach" young children the skills, concepts, and tasks necessary for academic success, the greater the likelihood of achieving that success. Concerned by reports of declining reading and SAT scores and just about everything else that has been tested in recent years, some parents and teachers believe that school skills should be taught earlier and more intensely. Information from brain research is often misinterpreted and used to justify early instruction. The emphasis on accountability and end-of-grade tests legislated by the No Child Left Behind

FIGURE 3-19
Continuum of parenting styles.

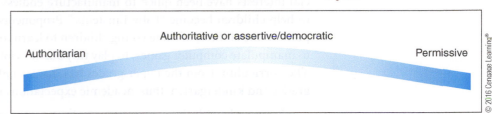

FIGURE 3-20
Children need time to learn about friends (a), time to become lovers of books (b), time to explore their own ideas through the use of materials (c), and time for vigorous play (d).

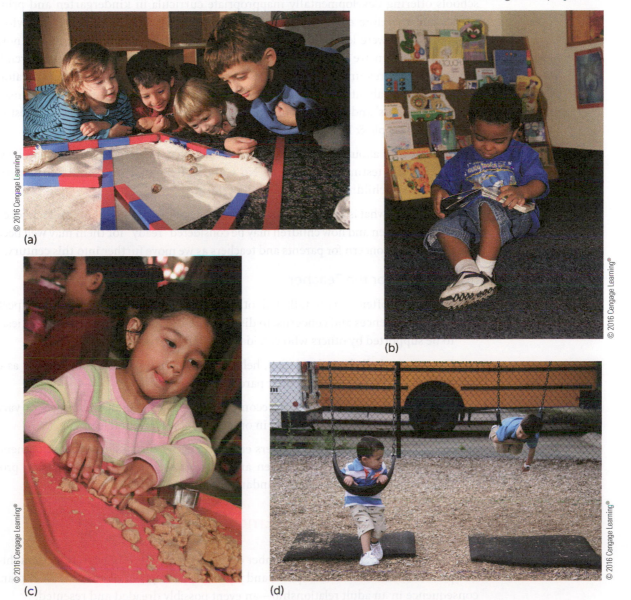

(a)

(b)

(c)

(d)

Act only exacerbates adult concern to start academic learning as soon as possible. Eager to capitalize on parents' desire to give their children an early start in learning, commercial interests have been quick to manufacture endless numbers of products guaranteed to help children become "baby Einsteins." Proponents of teaching at younger ages also point to the abilities of some young children to learn to read at unprecedented early ages, to manipulate computer games, to play tiny Suzuki violins, or to speak foreign languages. The curriculum from the upper grades has increasingly been pushed down to the lower grades and kindergarten; thus, academic expectations have risen.

But people with the opposite viewpoint are concerned about the effects on children and families when developmentally inappropriate demands are made on young children. A major danger is that with the increase in teaching young children, there is a need for testing and extremes, such as flunking kindergarten.

The entire assessment process has serious implications for children, parents, and early childhood education professionals. Born from the prevailing trend to evaluate children's progress as a measure of school accountability, standardized tests are now frequently used to test children's readiness to move on from or even enter a particular program. Actually, the increased reliance on test scores for school placement points to the bigger problem of schools offering developmentally inappropriate curricula in kindergarten and primary grades and therefore expecting young children to enter kindergarten "ready" with the skills that once were learned there. Parents become caught in the dilemma of knowing that their children are chronologically eligible for school but being told the children have not passed the "readiness test." NAEYC urges parents, teachers, and administrators to make decisions about children's readiness based on multiple sources of information, including parents' and teachers' observations, and never on the basis of a single test score (NAEYC in Copple & Bredekamp, 2009).

The concern about advancing children's learning pervades the schools as well as the preschools. The testing mandated by No Child Left Behind makes all adults nervous about how their children and schools will perform.

The issue of what is developmentally appropriate practice in preschool and school experiences for children and how children may be considered "ready" for them may well become a major issue of concern for parents and teachers as we move further into this century.

Implications for the Teacher

- Parents are often eager to talk with other parents as well as with education experts to share experiences and concerns, to discover they are not alone in their anxieties, and to be supported by others who can identify with their positions.

- Parents need all the information, help, and emotional support they can get as they work toward competence in their parental roles.

- It is important for teachers to become knowledgeable about the effects of various parenting styles and interactions in order to support parental learning.

- It is vital that parents and teachers engage in active discussions of developmentally appropriate curricula for children and support each other in attempts to protect children from anxieties about standardized tests.

3-2 Parenthood as an Emotional Experience

People arrive at parenthood via a number of routes. For some, it is a carefully thought-out and planned venture—an anticipated and joyful happening. For others, it is an unplanned consequence in an adult relationship—an event possibly dreaded and resented.

Having children means very different things to different people. There may be one or more possible motivations at work when people decide to become parents or adjust to the concept after the fact. These motivations include the following:

- Validation of adult status and social identity

- Expansion of self—a continuance of the family

- Achievement of moral value—contributing something or sacrificing in parenthood

- Increasing sources of affection and loving ties

- Stimulation, novelty, fun

- Achievement, competence, creativity

- Power and influence over another

- Social comparison and competition

- Economic utility

Raising children is not always fun, nor are all children cute or necessarily appreciative and loving toward their parents much of the time. Not all married couples should necessarily have children nor are all childless married couples unhappy. Despite the fact that many adults today consider having children to be an option—which increasing numbers are choosing not to exercise—there is still considerable pressure on women particularly to consider parenthood an essential experience of adult life. The increasing number of women who give birth to their first child when approaching 40 is testimony to the inner pressure of what has been called the "biological clock" as well as cultural attitudes.

Some of the assumptions people make when deciding to become parents are removed from the reality they will discover. No matter what their motivation was to have children, there are common realities and emotional responses for all parents.

3-2a Irrevocability

There is no turning back. From the time of birth on, parents discover that the responsibility for the care and support of this human being will be entirely theirs for a period of approximately 20 years or longer. Even when other institutions are available to share the task, as in education, the ultimate responsibility rests with the parents. This responsibility may be willingly and joyfully undertaken, but it is always there—24 hours a day, 7 days a week—constantly to be reckoned with. This is a staggering thought for a parent who, when faced with the reality of the developing child's needs, may feel unequal to the task. However, it is too late—the child is here and the parenting must go on. But the feeling of total responsibility often causes parents to worry considerably about matters large and small. Anxiety seems to be an inevitable part of being a parent—anxiety about the child's welfare and the adequacy of the parents' efforts. The increasing complexity of the modern world has given parents new causes for concern and even fear as they think about protecting their children. Paradoxically, whatever mistakes parents make and however burdened they feel, most find it difficult to hand the job over to anyone else.

Implications for the Teacher

- Teachers can indicate understanding and empathy for the parents' position. Many parents feel greatly burdened by the demands and responsibilities of parenthood and alone in their concerns. They will respond positively to someone who cares about their position—someone with whom they can talk freely.

- Teachers can help by indicating willingness to support them and their children in ways parents decide are helpful for their families.

- Teachers can help parents be realistic about dangers requiring protection and the current tendency to overprotect or smother children.

3-2b Restriction, Isolation, and Fatigue

One of the more dramatic changes in becoming a parent is the near total restriction on activity that comes with caring for a totally dependent being. Instead of acting spontaneously, a parent must make elaborate plans to leave the child even briefly. (There are periods in a child's early development when it is difficult to go into the bathroom alone.) And when the child is accompanying the parent, myriad preparations must be made and paraphernalia dragged along. It is no wonder that many parents restrict their activity, preferring not to bother with it all.

Along with this restriction in activity comes the isolation in which many parents live. Separated from extended family and by the physical housing of the modern city, hampered by the difficulty of finding free time for social arrangements, further restricted by the expenses of the child, and psychologically isolated in coming to grips with situations and emotions, many parents feel alone. Preoccupied with the care of a small child and the experience of parenthood, many parents even become isolated from each other, suffering a loss of the intimacy they knew when they were just a couple. Many parents are reluctant to admit they need help because becoming a parent is supposed to be a measure of adult status.

Most parents, especially mothers, complain of fatigue. From early morning until late at night, they are responding to the needs of others—children, spouse, employer, and as many more as can be squeezed into the schedule. When mothers are asked what they want most, the common response is "time by myself." For most, this is an impossible dream.

Implications for the Teacher

- Teachers should take care not to make it seem as if they are adding still heavier demands on the parent; parents will protect themselves and avoid such teachers.

- Teachers can realize that parents do not have excess time to waste. Activities in which they are involved need to be meaningful and streamlined.

- Teachers can provide opportunities for parents to meet other parents for mutual support and socialization to help them feel less isolated as they discover common experiences (see Figure 3-21).

3-2c Conflicts with Parenting Myths and Images

Despite the fantasies promoted by magazine advertisements and movies, many parents do not always feel love for their children. Humans operate beyond the level of instinct, and much parenting behavior and response, including love, comes after time, experience, repeated contact, and learning. Many parents feel ambivalent about their children some of the time, with feelings ranging from exasperation to resentment, with anger occasionally overshadowing feelings of love.

Because parents labor to some extent under the delusions of the "perfect parent," many do not consciously admit these less-than-positive feelings about their children to themselves or anyone else. They are left concerned about their "unnaturalness" and perhaps feel a little guilty.

FIGURE 3-21
Parents are often eager to talk with other parents.

(a)

(b)

Implications for the Teacher

- Teachers can subtly educate parents to try to remove some of the myths and images under which many parents labor.

- Teachers can comment on the real and positive things they see parents doing with their children.

- Teachers can empathize, displaying understanding that children can be exasperating and frustrating, even for the most caring adult.

3-2d Guilt

It is astonishing how frequently today's parents refer to guilt. Many factors precipitate this feeling, including the following:

- The ideal parent imaged in the various media

- The changes in lifestyles and role behaviors, which mean that many parents live quite differently than their parents did

- The prevalent feeling that parents should produce children who will do better than they have done

- The social attitude that "there are no bad children—only bad parents"

FIGURE 3-22
Parents sometimes feel guilt for leaving a crying child.

The parent most susceptible to guilt is the mother, probably because she realizes society views her as the most powerful parent. It does not matter whether she has chosen to work outside the home; employed and stay-at-home mothers are equally susceptible. The working mother may feel guilt because she is breaking a known pattern and is aware of the mixed reviews coming in from researchers and society. Probably a good portion of the Supermom phenomenon is fed by this guilt, pushing her to make sure her child misses no right or privilege. Much of today's materialism and marketing frenzies feed off this emotion of guilt. If the child has been deprived of time and interaction, at least he or she can have the latest item advertised (see Figure 3-22).

Implications for the Teacher

- Teachers would do well to remember that guilt may lie below the surface in many conversations and encounters with parents. Such awareness helps the teacher consciously weigh actions and words, ensuring that nothing on the teacher's part increases any sense of inadequacy that parents may feel.

- Teachers show support when they affirm the child and parent with small appreciative comments as often as possible, especially because teachers may sometimes have to increase the guilt load by sharing something worrisome about the child.

THE GUILT TRAP

Working mothers feel guilt when

- Leaving a crying child with a substitute caregiver
- Being apart from child for long hours
- Being short-tempered at the end of a tiring day
- Feeling inadequate at mothering
- Failing to receive supportive attitudes from others
- Struggling with the decision of whether to work

At-home mothers feel guilt when

- Worrying that children may become too dependent
- Considering the extras that additional income could provide
- Feeling that society expects more than "just a housewife"
- Feeling tired of being restricted to home and children
- Knowing that their spouses bear the financial burdens
- Realizing that their children are not perfect despite full-time mothering

3-2e Satisfaction

Despite the obvious negative aspects of total responsibility and restriction, most parents find many reasons to rejoice. There is great satisfaction in watching children grow and develop, especially when one has played a large part in nurturing that growth. For many parents, the achievements and characteristics of their children give feedback to be incorporated into the parents' own self-esteem; to some extent, the degree to which the child does well (or badly) reflects how well the parents feel they are doing. Most parents feel no one else can know their children as well as they do and care for them quite as well.

Another source of parental satisfaction is the affectionate mutual attachment that forms between adult and child. It is a very positive feeling to know you are the most important person in the world to another. Because it is so important, many parents fear any event or person that could be conceived of as disruptive to that relationship. Many parents experience jealousy or resentment when others become important in the loved child's life, although frequently, these emotions are disguised or not even recognized by the parent.

Implications for the Teacher

- Teachers need to respect the closeness of the parent–child bond. Ensure that classroom attitudes and practices nurture and preserve attachment and do not create excessive emotional dependence in children.

- Teachers can be aware that jealousy may lie behind some of their encounters with parents and avoid any actions on their part that might increase feelings of competition. Think about this in the next journal entry.

- Teachers can learn to present comments in ways that avoid personal evaluation and reaction. Parents frequently react defensively if they feel their children (and therefore their parenting skills) are criticized.

- Teachers can offer tangible and reassuring evidence that the child is cared for adequately by the supplemental caregiver—and, at the same time, offer reassurance that the parent is number one in their child's life.

3-2f Uncertainty

Each child has a unique response to the world; no matter how knowledgeable a parent is about child development and parenting skills, it is often a different matter putting principles into practice in specific situations with a specific child! As children change, parents must also change, and parenting techniques that worked well at one point must be discarded and new ones learned. Often, what worked with one child's personality has no effect on a sibling. Usually, parents do not feel totally confident that they are performing their tasks correctly. With the changes within the family and the surrounding culture (discussed earlier in Chapter 2), today's parents are doing the job without role models, clear directions, or firm approval from society. No wonder most parents often feel unsure of the situation. Societal values imply that responsible adults know what they are doing. Parents feel they should not be uncertain.

Because every parent feels deep inside that child rearing is not quite so simple, real feelings of uncertainty trigger an unproductive cycle of feeling unsuccessful against this false societal standard.

Implications for the Teacher

- Parents need someone who understands the uncertainties involved in the situation. They do not need people who believe there is only one right answer in child rearing or who convey the impression that they are totally certain of their own actions at all times.

- Teachers are helpful when they convey the impression of looking for answers together.

- Teachers are supportive when they do not immediately assign blame for children's difficulties to parenting.

3-2g Real Concern and Caring for Children

However it may appear to an outsider, most parents love and care for their children. In fact, most parents care passionately. Parenting is about these strong connections with children—a continuity over time. Parents want the best for their children, whether this means physical care, education, or future plans. Parents act to the best of their ability on behalf of their children—nevertheless acting within the context of their culture, beliefs, and current situation. However it may seem to others, they do care, and they care deeply. Teachers must believe in and value that parental caring, using this passion to bring parents into partnership.

Implications for the Teacher

- It helps when teachers understand that parents genuinely care and are concerned for their children. Even when parental behavior strikes them as indifferent or uncaring, they must believe that caring exists. Many factors may cause behaviors that convey negative impressions. (Some of these will be discussed in Chapters 5 and 15.)

SUMMARY

An awareness of the possible roles and emotional responses that accompany parenthood will help teachers work with parents.

- Several distinct roles make up a parent's life:
  - Nurturer
  - Part of adult relationships
  - Individual
  - Worker
  - Consumer
  - Community member
  - Educator

- Several common emotional responses have implications for the teacher working with parents. Most parents experience the following:
  - Irrevocability of parenthood, accompanied by anxiety
  - Restrictions, isolation, fatigue
  - Dealing with parenting myths and images
  - Guilt
  - Satisfaction related to self-esteem
  - Uncertainty
  - Real concern for their child

Student Activities for Further Study

1. Read a personal account written by a parent and then write a journal entry with your reflections. Here are some suggestions:

   - Almond, B. (2010). *The Monster Within: The Hidden Side of Motherhood.*
   - Ashworth, T., & Nobile, A. (2007). *I Was a Really Good Mom Before I Had Kids.*
   - Black, K. (2005). *Mothering Without a Map: The Search for the Good Mother Within.*
   - Cooper, E. (2006). *A Father's First Year.*
   - Crittenden, A. (2010). *The Price Of Motherhood: Why the Most Important Job in the World Is Still the Least Valued.*
   - Doocy, S. (2009). *Tales From the Dad Side: Misadventures in Fatherhood.*
   - Enright, A. (2004). *Making babies: Stumbling into motherhood.* New York: W. W. Norton.
   - Eschlima, A., & Oshirak, L. (2010). *Balance Is a Crock, Sleep Is for the Weak: An Indispensable Guide to Surviving Working Motherhood.*
   - Jacobsen, D. (2007). *Rookie Dad: Thoughts on First-Time Fatherhood.*
   - Leibovich, L. (2007). *Maybe Baby: 28 Writers Tell the Truth about Skepticism, Infertility, Baby Lust, Childlessness, Ambivalence, and How They Made the Biggest Decision of Their Lives.*

- Lewis, M. (2010). *Home Game: An Accidental Guide to Fatherhood.*
- Mead-Ferro, M. (2004). *Confessions of a Slacker Mom.*
- Peri, C., et al. (Eds.). (2000). *Mothers Who Think: Tales of Real-Life Parenthood.*
- Schwarzer, E. (2006). *Motherhood Is Not for Wimps: No Answers, Just Stories.*
- Senior, J. (2013) *All Joy and No Fun.*
- Stern, T. (2007). *CEO Dad: How to Avoid Getting Fired by Your Family.*
- Warner, J. (2005). *Perfect Madness: Motherhood in the Age of Anxiety.*

2. Talk with several parents. If possible, choose parents whose children include infants, toddlers, preschoolers, and school-aged children. Talk with at least one father. Discuss their reactions to parenthood: adjustments, negative aspects, positive aspects, and changes in adult relationships and lifestyle. Share your findings with your classmates. Try to identify which of Galinsky's stages of parenthood these parents are in.

3. Talk with a professional in an agency that works to support and educate parents. What are some major concerns, difficulties, and needs of parents that he or she reports?

4. In small groups, brainstorm additional practical ways for classroom teachers to support parents in the seven different roles of parents as defined in this chapter.

5. Interview your own parents if possible. Ask them to describe their satisfactions from parenting and what they were most proud of in being your parents.

Apply the Chapter Concepts: Case in Point

Andrea Sutton is a single mother of a four-year-old and an 18-month-old. She works as a secretary at the local electric company. She is also active in her church, working with the youth choir and teaching Sunday school. Her children attend a child care center run by the church. When her children visit her ex-husband every other weekend, Andrea goes to visit her parents, who are elderly and increasingly frail. Recently, she has begun to date a man whom she met at work, who also has two young children. She hopes to begin taking classes next year at the local community college so she can work toward her lifelong dream of becoming a nurse.

1. What roles do you see or can you guess that Andrea plays as a parent?

2. Knowing what you know about Andrea's life, what emotional responses might you imagine?

3. Knowing what you know about Andrea's responsibilities, what challenges can you identify to bringing Andrea into partnership with her child care teachers?

4. In what ways is Andrea's life the same as every parent's? Different from some other parents?

Review Questions

1. List seven roles that parents play and then discuss the implications of these roles for a teacher working with parents.

2. List seven emotional responses of parents and then discuss the implications of these emotional responses for teachers.

Helpful Websites

- The Families and Work Institute is a nonprofit center for research, providing data to inform decision making on changing the workplace, changing families, and changing communities.

- The National Parent Information Network, sponsored by ERIC, offers access to research and information about the process of parenting and family involvement in education.

- This website for the National Parenting Center provides information for parents from renowned child-rearing authorities.

CHAPTER 4

What Is Family Involvement?

Learning Objectives

After reading this chapter, you should be able to:

4-1 Describe what is meant by family involvement.

4-2 Outline a history of family involvement in education.

4-3 List three motivations and models for family involvement.

4-4 Discuss how research on child development and academic achievement influences inclusion of families in their children's education.

4-5 Describe mandated parent involvement.

4-6 Discuss how community concern for family support motivates family involvement in education.

naeyc

Related NAEYC Standards

Accreditation Standards (see inside text back cover for full listing of the Accreditation Standards for exemplary early childhood programs)

7.A.01

Licensure Standards (see inside text front cover for full listing of the Licensure Standards for this chapter)

2c

When the term *parent* or *family involvement* is used, different individuals may think of very different activities and characteristics that define the involvement of families in schools. There is no standard requirement or philosophy that can be applied to working with families; indeed, many schools seem to feel this is the least important aspect of their function, paying only perfunctory attention to parents, whereas others work hard to include families in as many aspects of their programs as they can. In this chapter, we will explore the various motivations that impel schools to bring families into the educational process for their children, as well as the models of programs that you might find defined as family involvement.

4-1   Perspectives on Family Involvement

Jane Briscoe again. "You know, I'm really confused. At a meeting I attended recently, the subject of parent involvement came up. After several people discussed what they thought about parent involvement, I realized I have been using that term differently from most of them. One of them implied that parent involvement was parents meeting together and making the decisions in a program. Another spoke as if parent involvement meant parents volunteering as assistants in the classroom. Somebody else mentioned the early intervention programs in which parents are being taught more about their children so they can expand the ways they help their own children develop. I've been thinking parent involvement is when I try to let parents know as much as I can about what's going on in their children's classroom lives. And now my director is using the term family engagement *instead of parent involvement. As I said, I'm confused."*

FIGURE 4-1
Parents may assist teachers by participating in the life of the classroom.

Small wonder that Jane is confused. In program descriptions, research, and conversational usage among teachers, the term *parent involvement* is used to describe all these patterns of family participation in early childhood education. *Parent involvement* is an all-purpose term used to describe all manner of family–school interaction: policy making, parent education, fund-raising, volunteering time, and even the simple exchange of information of various sorts with staff.

As the preceding description implies, there is no single model of family involvement. Schools have chosen to address the issue of engaging families in a variety of ways, ranging from a low level to a high level of involvement.

Schools with a low level of family engagement allow parents to take part in activities that do not challenge the expertise of a teacher or the decision-making power of the school. Such activities as newsletters, parent meetings, or individual parent conferences tend to keep families at a distance, learning secondhand about their children's life at school. Schools with a high level of family involvement provide opportunities for families to make their presence known, particularly in the educational setting, by parent visits, observations, or parent volunteer assistance of many kinds; here, parents are perceived as a source of help (see Figure 4-1). The highest levels of family involvement occur in

© Cengage Learning®

schools that believe teachers and parents have expertise, and that families and the school both have decision-making rights. Communicating via many channels, parents have the power to make decisions concerning the education of their children.

Joyce Epstein, a leader in school–family–community research, discusses the overlapping spheres of influence of home and school, with both centered on the child. She suggests that the ideal is more family-like schools and more school-like families, and therefore identifies six types of family involvement, with successful programs incorporating all six. Many schools are now following this model. Here are the six types of involvement:

- **Parenting:** Here, schools help families with parenting and child-rearing skills, child development knowledge, and creating home conditions that support children at each grade level. Reciprocally, schools have to learn to understand families.

- **Communicating:** The school involves parents by communicating about school programs and student progress through effective two-way channels that may include memos, notices, conferences, newsletters, phone calls, and electronic messages.

- **Volunteering:** Schools work to improve recruiting, training, and schedules to involve families and community members as volunteers and as audiences to support students and school programs.

- **Learning at home:** Schools involve families with their children in learning activities at home and in the community, including homework and other curriculum-related activities.

- **Decision making:** Schools include families as participants in school decisions and governance through the PTA, advisory councils, committees, and other leadership opportunities.

- **Collaborating with the community:** Schools coordinate services and resources for families and the school with businesses, agencies, and other groups. Schools also provide services to the community (Epstein, 2011; Epstein et al., 2009).

In Chapter 6, you will read more about how one early education program uses the Epstein model to frame family involvement activities.

TeachSource

VIDEO ACTIVITY

© 2016 Cengage Learning®

Watch *Family Involvement: One School's Perspective.*
After viewing the film, reflect on these questions:

1. Consider how this school is implementing Epstein's ideas in their family involvement plan.

2. How do these components meet needs for families and for teachers?

3. How do these strategies support children's development and education?

4-2 A Brief History of Family Involvement

An interest in the involvement of parents in early childhood education is not new. Parents were involved in some of the first preschool education movements in America in the earliest decades of the twentieth century. For middle-class parents, parent cooperative nursery schools blossomed throughout the 1920s, 1930s, and 1940s, reached a peak around 1960, and continue today to a lesser degree. Often appearing in such middle-class enclaves as university or suburban towns, these schools welcome parents, primarily traditional stay-at-home mothers, who often undergo some training. The parents frequently take the position of paraprofessional in the preschool classroom, assisting a professional teacher. Such close involvement in their children's classroom lives offers opportunities for parents to enrich the lives of their children and themselves (see Figure 4-2).

FIGURE 4-2
Working together.

Unity

I dreamt I stood in a studio and I watched two sculptors there.

The clay they used was a young child's mind

And they fashioned it with care.

One was a teacher—the tools he used

Were books, music, and art.

The other, a parent, worked with a guiding hand

And a gentle, loving heart.

Day after day, the teacher toiled with touch

That was deft and sure,

While the parent labored by his side and when at last, their task was done,

They were proud of what they had wrought,

For the things they had molded into a child

Could neither be sold nor bought.

And each agreed they would have failed

If each had worked alone,

For behind the teacher stood the school,

And behind the parent, the home.

—*Anonymous*

Parent cooperatives usually provide opportunities to participate in the life of the school—from defining the philosophy and practices to contributing to the care and maintenance of the facility. The belief is that parents know what they want for themselves and their children and therefore should be involved in the school. (The parent cooperative model has been used more recently even in child care facilities for parents employed full time. The contributions of parents decrease budget costs for such items as cleaning, accounting, purchasing, and laundry, as well as strengthen the ties between parent and school.) Many of today's charter schools work from the parent cooperative model, with parents involved in the initial philosophy and design of the school and in its organization and management.

Parents from lower socioeconomic backgrounds were involved in the nursery schools and child care centers set up by the government to supply children's nutritional and health care needs in families disrupted by the Great Depression (Works Progress Administration, or WPA, centers). Later, during World War II, the Lanham Act child care centers funded by the government as well as private employer-sponsored centers—notably the Kaiser Shipbuilding Company in Oregon (MacKenzie, 2011)—offered child care for parents working in the war effort. More than just child care, these centers offered on-site infirmaries with registered nurses, care for school-aged children on weekends and during school holidays, and the service of prepared food that workers could buy for take-home family meals. Even with the demands of those stressful times and coming from backgrounds of cultural and ethnic diversity, these parent groups were extremely responsive to parent educators associated with the centers to provide support for parental self-development and learning.

© Cengage Learning®

It was another 20 years or so before the field of early childhood education expanded again, and with this expansion came renewed interest in efforts to work with parents. Programs for the disadvantaged, including Head Start and other **intervention** programs, appeared in the 1960s and 1970s. Parents were involved in most of these programs (see Figure 4-3). Rodd (1998) refers to the kinds of parent involvement that developed in the intervention programs as taking "a compensatory approach to parental involvement in which **deficit models** of family life were responded to with the provision of interventionist strategies" (Rodd, 1998). Here, the early childhood educators perceived themselves as knowledgeable and parents as lacking the knowledge and skills to create optimal family environments for raising their children. The unfortunate result of working with a deficit model perspective was that the professionals involved did not see the parents as capable of being allies. The professionals were clearly in control—in an uneasy tolerance of the families.

intervention
Process of interfering with particular circumstances so as to change them.

deficit models
Working from the perspective of being inadequate or inferior.

Then in the 1970s and 1980s, changes in the structure of American society brought increasing numbers of women into the out-of-home workforce. With the growing need for child care for families with infants and very young children, attention was again focused on finding ways for parents and teachers to negotiate answers to the questions of how to share children's experiences with parents. There are also questions about how parental interests and needs should be accommodated: How much weight should be given to parental ideas based on their commitment to their own children? How much weight should be given to the judgment of the professional staff based on professional training? Where are the boundaries?

The hesitancy is there, along with confusion about what counts as parent involvement. The early childhood professional stance in the 1970s, according to Rodd, was to improve communication with parents, believing that "parental involvement was a matter of communication and contact" (Rodd, 1998). Then, the philosophy of communication gave way to the philosophy of accountability in the 1980s. Here, parents were perceived as "consumers of a service who possessed rights and responsibilities that early childhood professionals were obliged to meet." Throughout all this, parents were informed or consulted, but there was little partnership or collaboration. Currently, the early childhood education field is in the process of trying to further clarify its professional responsibilities toward families and define appropriate and helpful practices. Rodd suggests that a philosophy of partnership gained momentum in the 1990s as early childhood education professionals recognize that they have "both shared and complementary goals with the parents who are associated with their centers" (see Figure 4-4). There is a recognition that parents and teachers are experts related to children and families, each bringing different types of expertise.

FIGURE 4-4
Caregivers of young children share responsibilities for caregiving tasks with parents.

© Cengage Learning®

empowerment
Enabling; strengthening.

In the partnership approach, cooperative activity is stressed over joint activity, and parents may decide the level of involvement that is compatible with their lives and commitments.

Many factors are driving recommendations for partnerships between families and schools: a concern for parental rights and parental **empowerment** and for program responsiveness to family values and cultural tradition (Powell, 1998); ecological considerations of children and families that see the supportive nature of other systems for the child and family (Bronfenbrenner & Morris, 1998); and imperatives from school systems and government agencies, with a view to supporting the educational process.

Parents were closely involved in the first community public schools established in early America, and then lost that involvement as schools increasingly adopted the factory model of the nineteenth and early twentieth centuries. The National PTA was established in 1897, with a view to advocating for children. The history of real parent involvement in the public schools is actually fairly recent. In 1964, the Secretary of Health, Education, and Welfare supported the concept of parent involvement in a report. In 1968, the Kerner Commission, investigating urban riots, reported that increased community and parental participation in school systems was essential to the successful functioning of inner-city schools. Also in 1968, the U.S. Office of Education program guides suggested that education agencies establish parent advisory councils (PAC) for Title 1 programs. Then, in 1972, the U.S. Office of Education required each Local Education Agency (LEA) to establish district-wide parent advisory councils. In 1986, *Beyond the Bake Sale: An Educator's Guide on Working with Parents* was published—the first official guide for educators. In 1988, the Hawkins-Stafford Amendments provided more specific parent involvement requirements, such as written policies to ensure parent involvement; timely information to parents in a language and form parents can understand; assessing effectiveness of parent involvement and determining what needs to be done to increase parent participation, and holding parent–teacher conferences.

The most recent attempts to involve families in elementary schools and higher have been based on abundant research that continues to link parent involvement with student performance in any number of areas, including test scores, attentiveness, homework completion, reading ability, and other academic achievements (Henderson & Mapp, 2002). Every reform effort, educational interventions list, and much recent governmental legislation have all been focused on family involvement as an important ingredient for success of schools (NCPIE, 2006).

The most recent legislation that links parents with the educational process is the No Child Left Behind Act, signed into law in 2002. This federal legislation and its implications for families and parent involvement will be discussed in more detail later in this chapter.

4-3 Motives and Models for Family Involvement

Just as there is more than one philosophy and model of parent involvement, there is also more than one set of circumstances that motivate the involvement. At least three separate forces have brought home and school together:

■ One motivator for family involvement has been the research on education and child development that underscores the interdependence of parent, child, and schools and other community agencies in providing for optimal development of children. Examples of this include the research on cognitive and social development related to parental interaction and style and involvement with educational systems, especially the intervention programs.

■ A second set of motives is through force of a **mandate**, enunciated by various laws and funding arrangements, that parents play a part in the education of their children. Models of mandated parent involvement include Head Start; Title I and Chapter I funding; the Education for All Handicapped Children Act (PL 94-142) and Amendments (PL 99-451), now reauthorized as the Individuals with Disabilities Act (IDEA: PL 101-576 and 108-446); and NCLB (No Child Left Behind). Other mandates are given by National Association for the Education of Young Children (NAEYC) requirements and the recommendations of other professional organizations.

> **mandate**
> An authoritative order or command; something that must be done.

■ A third influence is community concern and efforts, encouraging parental involvement as a means of improving the schools and strengthening the family, thus eliminating some problems of concern to the community. Examples here include the collaborative approaches to family support and education that have developed nationwide. All these motivations suggest larger issues than the token "bake cookies and go on field trips" approach to working with parents.

Today, many American teachers working with young children do not work in programs that have mandates to include families in a specific way. But the rising numbers of private for-profit child care programs, including child care franchises, family child care homes, and nonprofit child care programs—added to the more traditional nursery school programs—place many early childhood teachers on the front lines of contact between home and school, hopefully establishing a pattern that will continue through the school years. Many other teachers are working in classrooms in school systems or in afterschool child care programs, where legislation and mandates for accreditation and funding ask for partnerships with families. Many teachers are convinced that joining in partnership with families may help them find better ways to create a supportive environment for the developing children in their care (see Figure 4-5).

FIGURE 4-5
It is a community priority to ensure that all young children get a good start to their education.

Therefore, this text will offer a brief overview of the motives behind the various forms of family involvement and point to some of the program patterns and the research done on these.

© Cengage Learning®

4-4 Research on Child Development and Academic Success as Motivation to Include Parents

FIGURE 4-6
Attachment correlates with curiosity, language, confidence, and many other aspects of development.

A lasting result of the intervention programs begun in the 1960s and 1970s is a body of research that describes the effects of various kinds of interaction and environmental influences on development and learning, particularly of young children. Such data impel many educators to press for increased family involvement. Studies suggest that the early years are of utmost importance in setting learning patterns for children and families. More recent brain research emphasizes the crucial importance of the early years in providing stimulation that plays a crucial role in developing the brain after birth. It is almost impossible to overemphasize the importance of parenting in relation to learning language and early literacy and other foundations for later learning.

Attachment—the strong, mutual, parent–child bond that forms during the first two years of life—is correlated with virtually every aspect of development: physical thriving; the exploration, curiosity, and problem solving that are foundations for cognitive skills; the appearance of language and communication skills; emotional security and social comfort; and dispositions of perseverance and self-discipline (see Figure 4-6). But beyond the overall well-being that comes with that warm parental relationship, studies confirm the assumption that specific factors in the parents' (particularly mothers') style have important and lasting impacts on children's learning styles, cognitive growth, and educational achievements. For example, it has been noted that many mothers from lower socioeconomic backgrounds, when working with their young children on a particular task, focus most on getting the job done, with little attention to giving verbal directions, helping develop problem-solving skills, or giving positive feedback. It is not surprising, then, that their young children come to the academic environment less prepared for its learning style and interaction with a middle-class teacher who expects children to be able to follow her verbal directions and solve problems independently.

© Cengage Learning®

BENEFITS OF FAMILY ENGAGEMENT IN EDUCATION (IDENTIFIED BY THE NATIONAL PTA)

- Increased student achievement, regardless of socioeconomic status, racial or ethnic background, or parents' level of education
- Higher grades and test scores, better attendance, and more consistent homework completion
- More positive attitudes and behavior
- Higher graduation rates and more postsecondary education
- Higher expectations by educators for students whose parents are involved
- Student achievement for disadvantaged children whose parents are involved improves and can reach that of children from middle-class families.

■ Children from diverse cultural backgrounds tend to do better when parents and professionals collaborate to bridge the gap between the culture at home and the learning institution.

■ The most accurate predictor of a student's achievement in school is not income or social status, but the extent to which a student's family is able to do the following:

  ● Create a home environment that encourages learning.
  ● Communicate high, yet reasonable, expectations for their children's achievement.
  ● Become involved in their children's education at school and in the community.

From National Standards for Family School Partnerships, *PTA, 2008.*

 ## 4-4a Intervention to Strengthen Parenting Skills

Deficits often have solutions. A long-term study by Hart and Risley (1995) investigated how home experiences influenced children's development. Although all the children in the study started to speak at about the same time, their vocabulary—as measured by the number of different words used—varied significantly. By age three, the children from the professional families had an average vocabulary of 1,100 words; the average vocabulary for children from working-class backgrounds was 750 words; and the vocabulary of children from the welfare backgrounds was just around 500 words. The children heard very different amounts of language. In addition, the study found that the most positive parenting practices included specific ways of talking, including the following:

■ Lots of "just talking" by using a wide vocabulary

■ High rates of verbal approval and few prohibitions

■ High information content in the speech

■ Giving children choices and asking children about things

■ Listening to children and responding to their communication

Positive correlations existed between verbal abilities at age three and later academic success as the children were followed to age nine or 10. Perhaps most striking, the researchers later found that low-income parents who were trained in parenting skills could change their methods of communication, resulting in children's attainments equal to the national average. These researchers concluded that the quality of parenting and communication is the key factor that determines cognitive abilities and accounts for achievement—certainly a finding that should have implications for teachers and families.

HART AND RISLEY'S THREE KEY FINDINGS

1. The variation in children's IQs and language abilities is relative to the amount parents speak to their children.

2. Children's academic successes at ages nine and 10 are attributable to the amount of talk they hear from birth to age three.

3. Parents of advanced children talk significantly more to their children than parents of children who are not as advanced.

Educational intervention programs are deliberately designed to improve children's first learning opportunities by stimulating changes within key elements of their early learning environment, including changes in parental behavior. Those who design programs for young children and families often act on the belief that intervention directed at parents is as necessary as intervention directed at the child. Many programs give parents knowledge about child development, techniques for interacting with their children, advice on health and nutrition, and such self-improvement options as assistance with employment, education, or housing.

Head Start

The Head Start program is the longest lasting of all early intervention programs, having started in the mid-1960s as part of President Johnson's War on Poverty. There have been numerous—and sometimes mixed—reports over the decades (Strauss, 2013). A recent study reports long-term effects, showing four indicators of economic and social success in adulthood: significantly increased possibilities of finishing high school and attending college, elevated earnings, and significantly less likelihood of having been charged or convicted of a crime (Garces, Thomas, & Currie, 2000).

Another recent study, by Ludwig and Phillips (2008), finds strong support for the conclusion that Head Start children typically enter school "ready to learn" and that they can achieve academically at national norms. It goes on to state that their studies refute the long-standing view of a "fadeout" effect of benefits for Head Start children. But perhaps most important, parent involvement emerged as a critical factor in children's retention of IQ gains. The gains also extended to other siblings if the parents were involved. And mothers themselves showed gains in confidence and self-concept, with assumed positive spillover effects for their children. In the recent study, one finding was that many Head Start families steadily declined in their need for public assistance programs, indicating the increased self-sufficiency that results from gains in self-confidence and self-concept. The full impact of a program on children, families, and communities cannot be assessed on the basis of children's scores alone. Likely the most accurate conclusion is that Head Start produces modest benefits including some long-term gains for children, and other benefits for families (Strauss, 2013).

Another measure of national confidence in Head Start and its effects on families was the establishment of Early Head Start in the mid-1990s. Framed as a child development program with comprehensive two-generation services, these programs may begin working with families before a child is born and focus on enhancing children's development and supporting the family as the primary educators of their children during the critical first three years of life. The program is designed to produce outcomes in four domains:

1. Child development, including health, resilience, and social, language, and cognitive development

2. Family development, including parenting and relationships with children, home environment and healthy family functioning, parent involvement, and economic self-sufficiency

3. Staff development, including professional development and relationships with parents

4. Community development, including enhanced child care quality, community collaboration, and the integration of services to support families with young children

An early report of 17 programs participating in the national Early Head Start Research and Evaluation Project (2010) indicates that test scores not only improve over time with this method but also are maintained for several years after the intervention has been discontinued. Effects may be found even in younger children within the family who were directly involved; this shows the impact of new skills learned by the parents. The continuing importance of the Head Start program after more than 45 years is indicated by the efforts to expand the program through congressional funding even in times of government budget cuts.

In Head Start and most other intervention programs, parent participation is now considered a necessary component to effect changes within the family itself and in the surrounding community (see Figure 4-7).

Perry Preschool Project

Other well-known center-based intervention programs include the Perry Preschool Project begun in Ypsilanti, Michigan, in the early 1960s. In addition to disadvantaged preschool children attending high-quality early childhood programs for 2.5 hours, five days a week over a two-year period, teachers visited parents in their homes for 90 minutes every week. The design actually included three different models of preschool programs, including a direct instruction program now called DISTAR; a traditional nursery school program that encouraged children's active involvement in play orga-

FIGURE 4-7
Head Start is an example of an intervention program and also of mandated family involvement.

nized around themes; and an "open-framework" approach, now called the **High/Scope** curriculum. In this rare long-term study, researchers followed 123 children from the preschool program through their fortieth birthdays as of the latest report (Schweinhart et al., 2005). The research initially found that children who had participated in any of the preschool programs showed dramatic gains in intelligence scores over children without preschool experience and that these gains in achievement remained over time at a higher level through their tenth year. Perhaps the most dramatic effect noted in those who had participated in the High/Scope option was the observation that when compared with children from the other programs, participants did very well in a number of measures of social and educational achievement, such as the following:

- Less remedial education

- Twice the rate of high school graduation

- Twice the postsecondary education

- Twice the successful work history

- Fewer arrests

- Fewer teenage pregnancies

- Less welfare dependence or other behaviors that create problems for families and community

- As adults, more likely to be married, own homes, participate in volunteer work in their communities, and hold stable jobs

Carolina Abcedarian Project

The Carolina Abecedarian Project from Chapel Hill, North Carolina, is another intervention program. It began in the 1970s and followed the participants and their families until age 30. The project had a four-way design. At birth, a group of children from poverty-level families was chosen randomly to receive an array of services from birth through age five, including

High/Scope Model
Early childhood curriculum based on principle of children as active learners who plan, carry out, and reflect on learning choices during free choice periods and small group teacher-led experiences to help children focus on key experiences.

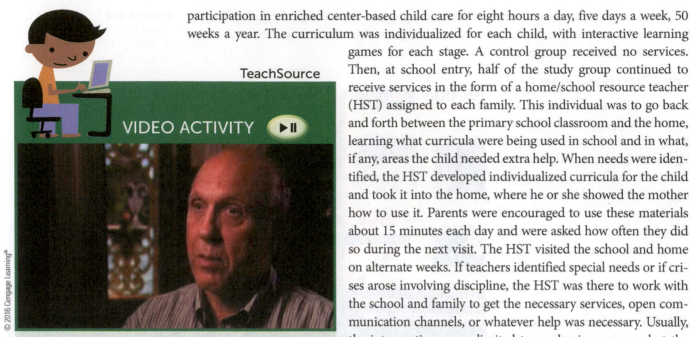

TeachSource

VIDEO ACTIVITY ▶❚❚

After viewing the video *The High/Scope Study: Early Education Does Matter,* consider these questions:

1. How do the life stories of the two men corroborate the long-term findings of the High/Scope study?

2. What are some of the possible reasons for the different outcomes for children?

3. How could this information be used to support early education and family involvement in it?

FIGURE 4-8

As parents get involved in their children's education, children's attitudes and school achievement reflect positive gains.

© 2016 Cengage Learning®

participation in enriched center-based child care for eight hours a day, five days a week, 50 weeks a year. The curriculum was individualized for each child, with interactive learning games for each stage. A control group received no services. Then, at school entry, half of the study group continued to receive services in the form of a home/school resource teacher (HST) assigned to each family. This individual was to go back and forth between the primary school classroom and the home, learning what curricula were being used in school and in what, if any, areas the child needed extra help. When needs were identified, the HST developed individualized curricula for the child and took it into the home, where he or she showed the mother how to use it. Parents were encouraged to use these materials about 15 minutes each day and were asked how often they did so during the next visit. The HST visited the school and home on alternate weeks. If teachers identified special needs or if crises arose involving discipline, the HST was there to work with the school and family to get the necessary services, open communication channels, or whatever help was necessary. Usually, the interventions were limited to academic concerns, but the HST also provided social work services, referring the families to necessary agencies and following through as needed.

Some of the positive benefits noted in the research results of the Abecedarian project (Carolina Abecedarian, 1999; Campbell et al., 2002) include the following:

- Higher IQ detected as early as 18 months of age
- More engagement with persons and objects in the preschool years
- Improved school performance
- Reduced retention in grade
- Fewer risky behaviors at 18 years of age
- More likely to attend a four-year college
- Delayed childbearing
- More likely to have been consistently employed

In the intervention programs, the emphasis for family involvement is on two things:

- Parents as learners, increasing parental knowledge about children and their needs and ways that child development can be nurtured and supported
- Parents as teachers, working with professionals in the classroom and in the home to enhance and extend the professionals' efforts

Some research indicates that the involvement of parents in a program over time is a critical factor in the gains made by children. One reason that the benefits may sustain over time is that family involvement in early childhood education sets the stage for involvement in future school settings. As Bronfenbrenner said:

The family seems to be the most effective and economical system for fostering and sustaining the child's development. Without family involvement, intervention is likely to be unsuccessful, and what few effects are achieved are likely to disappear once the intervention is over (Bronfenbrenner, in Weiss, Caspe, & Lopez, 2006).

Numerous studies also indicate that additional factors related to later school success may be indirectly influenced by parents' involvement in their children's programs. A parental expectation for children's educational attainment and parent participation in school activities has the most consistent influence on children's educational outcomes (Reynolds & Stilafen, 2010). There are documented gains in reading for children whose parents are encouraged to help with reading activities at home (Eldridge, 2001). Children whose parents are involved have more positive attitudes about school, improved attendance, and better homework habits than do children whose parents are less involved (Epstein, 2011; see Figure 4-8). For both preschool and elementary-aged children, family–school involvement is associated with early school success, increased language and literacy skill development, and social competence (Dearing et al. in Amatea, 2013). Parental participation in school activities in grades K–3 is associated with children's educational engagement, high-quality work habits, and task orientation and the long-term benefits of likelihood of completing high school (Caspe, Lopez, & Wolos, 2006/2007). Indeed, literally hundreds of studies suggest the value of involving parents in their children's schools and doing so as early as possible (Henderson & Mapp, 2002; Barnard, 2004; Ho & Willms, 1996). For a full listing of some of this research, see the North Central Regional Laboratory (NCREL) and Harvard Family Research Projects website addresses at the end of this chapter.

The value the home places on school learning is related to differences in academic performance. In fact, it has been found that home attitudes and factors affect the positive outcome of children's schooling twice as much as do socioeconomic factors, and the single most important factor is the self-esteem of the parent.

There are some obvious ways parental self-esteem is enhanced by involvement in their children's programs. The schools seek parents out to include them as an essential part of their children's education. Parents increase their knowledge of the school program and develop familiarity and comfort with the school experience. Improved interaction skills help parents feel more effective with their children and more effective in the parenting role. Parents perceive their own role as important. Experience in leadership skills and decision making, along with fulfilling social interaction with other adults, all add to parents' positive self-image (see Figure 4-9). Head Start evaluations report that mothers who participated claim fewer psychological problems, greater feelings of mastery, and more satisfaction with their present life situations at the end of the program. Surely, spillover effects for children could be anticipated from such positive feelings in parents.

FIGURE 4-9
Experience in decision making may help parents' own self-esteem.

© Cengage Learning®

TeachSource

VIDEO ACTIVITY ▶❙❙

© 2016 Cengage Learning®

After viewing the Video Case *Parental Involvement in School Culture: A Literacy Project*, consider these questions:

1. What benefits from parent involvement does the teacher discuss for the children's curriculum? For the teacher? For the parents?

2. How does the teacher arrange for the involvement?

3. What ideas from the chapter do you find reinforced in this video?

Research that suggests benefits to the development of children and their parents from parental involvement offers powerful motivation to many programs to work toward parent participation. School systems and government agencies believe so strongly in the importance of involving families in their children's education that they develop policies and strategies to facilitate that involvement (Caspe, Lopez, & Wolos, 2006/2007). One important finding is that family involvement is more likely to occur when schools are committed to it.

4-5 Mandated Parent Involvement

When the powers that control funding mandate family involvement as a program requirement, there is no longer any debate about whether to have parent participation. Several legislative efforts have included parent participation as part of the required structure in schools and agencies providing services to children. In addition, recent policies and practice guidelines have proclaimed specific directions for programs to follow in relation to families—sometimes in order to win accreditation or professional status. Several examples of mandated parent involvement will be discussed next.

4-5a Head Start

We have already mentioned Head Start as an example of the research linking family involvement with children's school success. From the beginning, Head Start was required to have "maximum feasible participation" of the families served. Head Start Performance Standards for family support and parent involvement include the following:

- Building relationships with parents as early as possible from enrollment and creating ongoing opportunities for parent involvement throughout the time children are in the program

- Helping families work toward their goals and linking families to or providing necessary services

- Making programs open to parents at any time, involving parents in the development of program curriculum, and providing parents opportunities to volunteer or become staff

- Providing parents with opportunities to enhance their parenting skills

- Helping parents become active partners in accessing health care for their children, making community services more responsive to their family needs, and transitioning their children into school

- Involving parents in program decision making and governance (Head Start Performance Standards, 2010)

Parents are given a concrete means of doing something for their children. The major role of decision maker is emphasized to offer parents opportunities to become competent in running the program. Parents set the standards for the hiring of professional staff—often interviewing and selecting staff. They also participate in decisions on budgetary matters. Parent decisionmakers influence the agency to become sensitive to the culture and needs of the families served.

4-5b Title I

More recent federal initiatives authorize funds as part of Chapter I of Title I (of PL 100-297), reauthorized by the Literacy Involves Families Together (LIFT) Act of 2000 and the No Child Left Behind (NCLB) Act of 2001. Called Even Start, the family-centered education program funds local efforts to improve the educational opportunities for the nation's low-income children and adults by integrating early childhood education and adult education for parents into a unified **family-centered** literacy program. The mandate calls for the following:

- Early childhood education

- Adult basic and secondary education and instruction for English language learners

- Parenting education

- Interactive parent–child literacy activities (see Figure 4-10)

Each program funded by Title I funds must have a plan to involve families. Sample activities and services for families that may be funded by Title I include the following:

- Family literacy activities

- Parent meetings and training activities

- Transportation and child care so parents can come to school activities or volunteer in classrooms

- Parent resource centers

- Materials that parents can use to work with their children at home

An example of the mandated involvement for parents can be seen in a Parent/School Partnership agreement signed by parents whose children were participating in a prekindergarten program funded by Title I resources. In this agreement, parents agree to the following:

1. Make sure my child attends school regularly.

2. Make arrangements for my child before and after school; for example, arrange for an adult to wait with/for my child at the bus stop in the morning and in the afternoon.

3. Keep immunizations/physicals up to date and handle any medical needs that arise.

4. Attend the orientation session for parents.

5. Attend conferences requested by my child's teacher and be available for contact on a regular basis with staff (this may involve home visits, telephone conferences, or school/worksite conferences).

6. Participate in at least four parent/child/staff events during the year.

7. Read with my child and sign the reading log as required.

8. Participate with my child in regular at-home activities designed to promote literacy learning as requested by my child's teacher.

9. Attend a minimum of five hours of family–school partnership workshops offered by the school.

10. Complete and return progress reports so there is open, ongoing communication between the teacher and myself.

Parents are informed that failure to fulfill these requirements may mean their child cannot remain in the program.

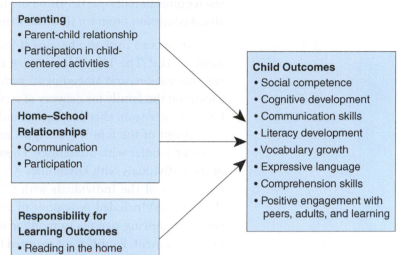

FIGURE 4-10
Processes of Family Involvement and Young Children's Outcomes.

Parenting
- Parent-child relationship
- Participation in child-centered activities

Home–School Relationships
- Communication
- Participation

Responsibility for Learning Outcomes
- Reading in the home
- Parent-child conversations

Child Outcomes
- Social competence
- Cognitive development
- Communication skills
- Literacy development
- Vocabulary growth
- Expressive language
- Comprehension skills
- Positive engagement with peers, adults, and learning

Reprinted with permission from the Harvard Family Research Project at http://www.hfrp.org.

family-centered
Focusing on children and parents as a unit, with the parents becoming active in their children's development—not relating separately to parents and children.

4-5c Education of Children with Disabilities

Parent involvement in plans to provide services for children with special needs was first mandated by PL 94-142, the Education for All Handicapped Children Act of 1975. This law requires parents' participation in planning with professionals to develop an individualized education program (IEP) for their children.

Parents can initiate a hearing if they do not agree with the child's diagnosis, placement, or IEP. The 1986 Education of the Handicapped Act Amendments and all later reauthorizations and amendments added services for infants and toddlers and required a focus on the family for delivery of services. Parents or guardians are included in a multidisciplinary team that develops an individualized family service plan (IFSP), including a statement of the family's strengths and needs in maximizing the development of the infant or toddler with disabilities. These provisions are continued in the reauthorization of the Individuals with Disabilities Act in 1990 and the amendments of 1997. The reauthorization of the Individuals with Disabilities Educational Improvement Act of 2004 (PL 108-446) included provisions to align special education with the NCLB legislation, such as requiring parents to monitor whether the IEP was in line with state standards for achievement. Families are required to be involved with all aspects of planning for the education of their children with special needs. Read more about this in Chapter 14.

4-5d Child Care and Development Block Grants

The Child Care and Development Block Grants, funded by Congress in 1990 and reauthorized and renamed the Child Care and Development Fund (CCDF), is legislation that lays the foundation for a national system of safe and affordable child care. Many provisions of CCDF highlight the importance of parental choice and involvement. The bill preserves the rights of parents in the system by stating that nothing in the bill should be applied to "infringe upon or usurp the moral and legal rights and responsibilities of parents." Parents are given the right to help set child care standards and policies on national, state, and local levels. The legislature sets minimum national standards, including parent involvement, to help parents measure and improve program quality. The bill also funds resource and referral programs to educate parents and the public about child care options and choices, licensing and regulatory requirements, and complaint procedures. These CCDF provisions recognize the importance of including parents in child care systems.

4-5e No Child Left Behind (NCLB) Legislation

The Elementary and Secondary Education Act, commonly known as No Child Left Behind, was signed into law in 2002 (PL 107-10) and has far-reaching effects on educational systems, schools, classrooms, and the children served. Four main goals are behind the law:

- Stronger accountability for results measured by student achievement test scores, with corrective actions to be taken as needed

- More freedom for states and communities to use federal education funds

- Encouraging the use of proven education methods to improve student learning and achievement

- More choices for parents

Teachers should be familiar with all provisions of the law, but we will focus on the choices and opportunities for families mandated by the law. In general, the law mandates that schools give parents the tools they need to support their children's learning, communicate regularly regarding academic progress and available choices for children, provide opportunities for family workshops, and offer parents opportunities to engage in parent leadership activities at school (see Figure 4-11). The intention of the requirements is for parents to play central roles and be actively encouraged to be involved in their children's education.

Parents of children in low-performing schools have new options for making changes for their children. In schools that do not meet state standards for at least two consecutive years, parents may transfer their children to better-performing public schools, including charter schools, within their district, with transportation provided by the district. Students from low-income families that fail to meet state standards for at least three years are eligible to receive supplemental educational services, such as free tutoring, afterschool services, and summer school. Parents can also choose another public school if the school their child attends is unsafe.

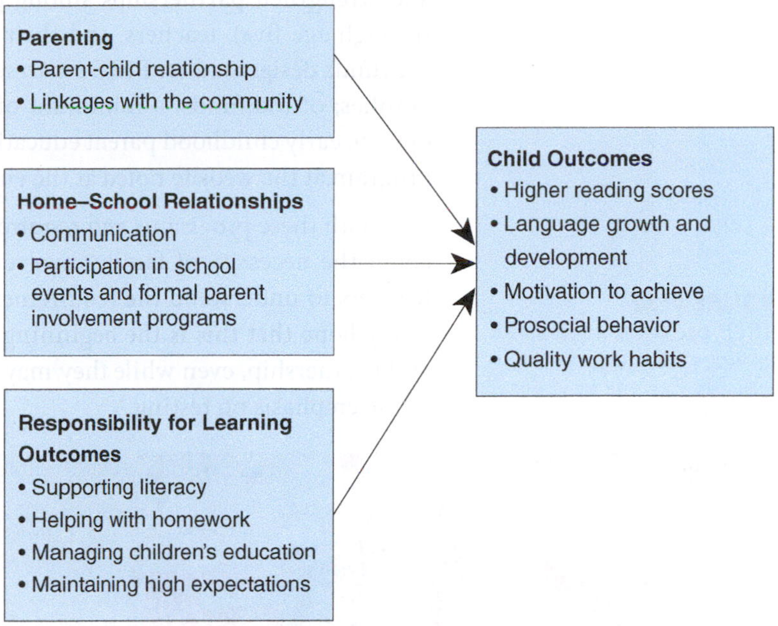

Schools are required to give parents annual report cards that show how well students in each school performed on required standardized tests, broken out by race, gender, disability, and the like so parents can clearly see how well their schools are performing. In addition, parents must be given an annual report about how teacher qualifications at the school meet the law's requirements.

In addition to these family rights, the law makes clear statements about requirements for parent involvement. The requirements include the following:

- A written parent involvement policy that has included parents in creating and evaluating the policy

- Involvement of parents in planning, evaluating, and improving the various programs for parents

- Giving parents understandable descriptions and explanations of the curricula and forms of academic assessments used to measure student progress

- Offering a flexible number of meetings for parents at various times and using funds to provide transportation, child care, and home visits to facilitate parent attendance

- Emphasizing the importance of regular, bi-directional and meaningful communication, including (a minimum of) annual parent–teacher conferences in each elementary school, frequent reports to parents about children's progress, reasonable access to staff, and opportunities to volunteer, participate, and observe in their children's classrooms

- Building the capacity for parent involvement, including providing assistance to understand curriculum content and offer materials and training to help parents work with their children, such as with literacy training and technology

- Educating teachers on how to reach out to, communicate with, and work with parents as equal partners, building ties between parents and the schools

- Training parents to enhance the involvement of other parents

- Sharing responsibilities between home and school for high student achievement

- Coordinating parent involvement activities with Head Start, Reading First, Early Reading First, Parents as Teachers, HIPPY (Home Instruction for Parents of Preschool Youngsters), and public preschools to encourage parents to participate more fully

- Establishing parental information and resource centers

FIGURE 4-11
Processes of Family Involvement and Elementary School Children's Education.

Parenting
- Parent-child relationship
- Linkages with the community

Home–School Relationships
- Communication
- Participation in school events and formal parent involvement programs

Responsibility for Learning Outcomes
- Supporting literacy
- Helping with homework
- Managing children's education
- Maintaining high expectations

Child Outcomes
- Higher reading scores
- Language growth and development
- Motivation to achieve
- Prosocial behavior
- Quality work habits

Reprinted with permission from the Harvard Family Research Project at http://www.hfrp.org.

Parental information and resource centers (PIRC) are to assist parents of children identified for improvement under Title I. These school-based and school-linked centers are designated to help implement effective parental involvement policies, programs, and activities that will improve children's academic success. Another purpose is to develop and strengthen partnerships among parents (including parents of children from birth through age five), teachers, and their children's schools and programs. Fifty percent of the funds designated for PIRC are to serve areas with a high concentration of low-income families; of the funds, a minimum of 30 percent is to be used to establish, expand, or operate early childhood parent education programs. (See the information about the PIRC program at the website noted at the end of this chapter.)

With these provisions and requirements, the act is sending clear messages to schools about the necessity of family involvement programs in all schools. It is important for teachers to understand the requirements of the law and help interpret them to families. Many hope that this is the beginning of a new era of home and school communication and partnership, even while they may have concerns about other aspects of the law, such as the emphasis on testing.

FIGURE 4-12

NCLB provides additional services for students in schools that fail to meet state standards.

Two resources could be particularly useful to teachers trying to help families understand the implications of NCLB for themselves and their children. A fact sheet titled *Choices for Parents* is available to download and print from the Department of Education website; see the references at the end of this chapter. Booklets titled *Models of Meaningful, Productive Parent Engagement* and *Success Stories about Family and Community Involvement* are available from the Learning First Alliance; see information about this website at the end of this chapter (see Figure 4-12).

4-5f Recommendations from Professional Organizations

Beyond these legislative mandates, clear statements issued from several professional organizations point toward inclusion and involvement of parents in schools for young children as a measure of a quality program.

Early Childhood Environment Rating Scale

A tool that is widely used in the United States—and in military child care and other programs around the world—is the Early Childhood Environment Rating Scale, now in a revised edition (Harms, Clifford, & Cryer, 2004). Program administrators, credentialing evaluators, and teachers wanting to identify areas of strength and need for improvement in an early childhood program use the 43 items of the rating scale. One of the items, number 38, is focused on provisions for parents.

The specific indicators identified under this item delineate practices that may be rated from inadequate to excellent. In many states, programs must get at least a good rating to gain a higher standard of licensing or certification. The descriptors that suggest quality are described in Figure 4-13.

FIGURE 4-13

Descriptors that suggest the signs of parent involvement in quality programs.

	Inadequate		Minimal		Good		Excellent	
	1	2	3	4	5	6	7	

PARENTS AND STAFF

38. Provisions for parents

Inadequate	Minimal	Good	Excellent
1.1 No information concerning program given to parents in writing.	**3.1** Parents given administrative information about program in writing (fees, hours of service, health rules for, attendance).	**5.1** Parents urged to observe in child's group prior to enrollment.	**7.1** Parents asked for an evaluation of the program annually (parent questionnaires, group evaluation meetings).
1.2 Parents discouraged from observing or being involved in children's program.	**3.2** Some sharing of child-related information between parents and staff (informal communication; parent conferences only upon request; some parenting materials).	**5.2** Parents made aware of philosophy and approaches practiced (parent handbook, discipline policy, descriptions of activities).	**7.2** Parents referred to other professionals when needed (for special parenting help, for health concerns about child).
	3.3 Some possibilities for parents and family members to be involved in children's program.	**5.3** Much sharing of child-related information between parents and staff (frequent informal communication; periodic conferences for all children; parent meetings, newsletters, parenting information available).	**7.3** Parents involved in decision-making roles in program along with staff (parent representatives on board).
	3.4 Interactions between family members and staff are generally respectful and positive.	**5.4** Variety of alternatives used to encourage family involvement In children's program (bring birthday treat, eat lunch with child, attend family potluck).	

Questions

(1.1, 3.1) Is any written information about the program given to parents? What is included in this information?

(1.2, 3.3, 5.4) Are there any ways that parents can be involved in their child's classroom? Please give some examples.

(3.2, 5.3) Do you and the parents ever share information about the children? How is this done?

(3.4) What is your relationship with the parents usually like?

(5.1) Are parents able to visit the class before their child is enrolled? How is this handled?

(7.1) Do parents take part in evaluating the program? How is this done? About how often?

(7.2) What do you do when parents seem to be having difficulties? Do you refer them to other professionals for help?

(7.3) Do parents take part in making decisions about the program? How is this handled?

NAEYC Accreditation

The NAEYC has developed standards to accredit high-quality programs for young children. The NAEYC governing board approved revised accreditation performance criteria in 2005. Among the program standards, partnerships with families are included as a necessary component. Program Standard 7 says:

> *The program establishes and maintains collaborative relationships with each child's family to foster children's development in all settings. These relationships are sensitive to family composition, language, and culture.*

Rationale

Young children's learning and development are integrally connected to their families. Consequently, to support and promote children's optimal learning and development, programs need to recognize the primacy of children's families; establish relationships with families based on mutual trust and respect; support and involve families in their children's educational growth; and invite families to fully participate in the program. (NAEYC, 2005a)

The specifics drawn from the performance criteria in the section related to families (NAEYC, 2005a, pp. 13–15) can be found on the inside cover of this textbook.

CULTURAL CONSIDERATIONS

Lessons from around the globe

You will have noticed that these discussions have centered on American research, American institutions, and American legislature and requirements. Families who enter American schools and preschools having had experiences in other countries may have encountered similar or very different approaches in working with families. Around the globe, early educators are struggling with how to achieve optimum outcomes with children, including working with families and adapting practices to individual communities. Such studies go beyond the scope of this textbook, but interested students can learn more by studying what is happening around the world, including in the countries from which their immigrant families come. A starting place could be the entire November 2007 and November 2010 issues of *Young Children* [62(6) and 65(6)], in which programs and practices in places as far-flung as Bangladesh, China, South Korea, Estonia, Denmark, El Salvador, and more are discussed.

Read about some of these programs and then reflect on how ideas from other countries can contribute to good practices for children and families with whom you work.

Code of Ethics

The Code of Ethical Conduct and Statement of Commitment, approved by NAEYC's Governing Board in 1989, revised in 2005, and reaffirmed and updated in 2011, includes a section of ethical responsibilities to families, articulating 15 specific principles governing actions and the following nine ideals:

1. To be familiar with the knowledge base related to working effectively with families and to stay informed through continuing education and training

2. To develop relationships of mutual trust and create partnerships with the families served

3. To welcome all family members and encourage them to participate in the program (See Figure 4-14.)

4. To listen to families, acknowledge and build on their strengths and competencies, and learn from families as we support them in their task of nurturing children

5. To respect the dignity and preferences of each family and to make an effort to learn about its structure, culture, language, customs, and beliefs

6. To acknowledge families' child-rearing values and their right to make decisions for their children

7. To share information about children's education and development with families and to help them understand and appreciate the current knowledge base of the early childhood education profession

FIGURE 4-14
One of the ideals of the revised code of ethics is to welcome all family members and encourage them to participate in their children's school.

© Cengage Learning®

8. To help family members enhance their understanding of their children and support the continuing development of their skills as parents

9. To participate in building support networks for families by giving them opportunities to interact with program staff, other families, community resources, and professional services (NAEYC, 2005, 2011)

The 15 principles that are enunciated in this section of the code of ethics are useful in helping teachers determine appropriate professional actions when they face dilemmas in serving families. The principles of the code of ethics related to working with families are accessible online.

OPPORTUNITY FOR SELF-REFLECTION

As you read this chapter, do you find that your own definition of family involvement is expanding? What was your definition until now? What new ideas are you adding to your definition?

4-5g NAEYC Position Statement on Developmentally Appropriate Practice

The revised NAEYC Position Statement on Developmentally Appropriate Practice (Copple & Bredekamp, 2009) makes explicit the professional commitment to:

Appreciating and supporting the close ties between the child and family

Recognizing that children are best understood in the context of family, culture, and society

Respecting the dignity, worth, and uniqueness of each individual (child, family member, and colleague)

These are the statements most directly related to working with families and their cultures, customs, and beliefs. The most recent revision repeats the emphasis on establishing reciprocal relationships with families. The statement maintains:

Practice is not developmentally appropriate if the program limits "parent involvement" to scheduled events (valuable though these may be), or if the program/family relationship has a strong "parent education" orientation. Parents do not feel like partners in the relationship when staff members see themselves as having all the knowledge and insight about children and view parents as lacking such knowledge. Such approaches do not adequately convey the complexity of the partnership between teachers and families that is a fundamental element of good practice. (Copple & Bredekamp, 2009, p. 23)

FIGURE 4-15

Families participate in program decisions about their children's care.

© 2016 Cengage Learning®

Of the five sections in the NAEYC position statement on roles of the teacher, one deals specifically with "establishing reciprocal relationships with families." The guidelines suggest at least the following:

A. In reciprocal relationships between practitioners and families, there is mutual respect, cooperation, shared responsibility, and negotiation of conflicts toward achievement of shared goals.

B. Practitioners work in collaborative partnerships with families, establishing and maintaining regular, frequent, two-way communication with them (with families who do not speak English, teachers should use the language of the home if they are able or try to enlist the help of bilingual volunteers).

C. Family members are welcome in the setting, and there are multiple opportunities for family participation. Families participate in program decisions about their children's care and education (see Figure 4-15).

D. Teachers acknowledge a family's choices and goals for the child and respond with sensitivity and respect to those preferences and concerns but without abdicating the responsibility that early childhood practitioners have to support children's learning and development through developmentally appropriate practices.

E. Teachers and the family share their knowledge of the particular child and understanding of child development and learning as part of day-to-day communication and in planned conferences. Teachers support families in ways that maximally promote family decision-making capabilities and competence.

F. Practitioners involve families as a source of information about the child (before program entry and on an ongoing basis) and engage them in the planning for their child.

G. The program links families with a range of services based on identified resources, priorities, and concerns (Copple & Bredekamp, 2009, p. 23).

NAEYC Standards for Professional Preparation

In 2001, the NAEYC published core standards for initial teacher licensure programs, followed in 2003 by similar core standards for associate degree preparation of teachers. Of the five standards, the second is *Building Family and Community Relationships*. This requires education to enhance experiences so students:

Understand and value children's families and communities.

Support and empower families and communities through respectful, reciprocal relationships.

Involve all families and communities in their children's development and learning (Hyson, 2003, p. 6; see link in references to find complete revised statement).

Specific opportunities to learn these concepts are suggested in the standards, along with ways that students may demonstrate their growth within their college programs.

These standards mean that students enrolled in college early childhood education programs accredited by the NAEYC will be involved in learning about families during their professional preparation.

4-5h National Parent Teacher Association Standards for Parent/Family Involvement

In 2002, the National Parent Teacher Association (PTA) revised the content and title of its family involvement standards. Known as the Family–School Partnership Standards, six standards are seen as essential for any school or program involving parents:

- Welcome all families into the school community.

- Communicate effectively.

- Support student success.

- Speak up for every child.

- Share power.

- Collaborate with the community (PTA, 2008).

It has long been recognized in American society that parents have the primary responsibility for deciding what is in their children's best interest. Public policy now seems concerned with safeguarding family authority in the "education, nurture, and supervision of their children." The increasing official attention to policies involving family matters may lead to more specific mandates regarding family involvement.

4-6 Community Concern for Family Support

The changing demographics of American society that have created changes in the lives of families have focused attention on parents' needs. Families who today may be more isolated, more stressed, and perhaps poorer than ever before need all the help they can get. As communities count the costs of inadequate parenting and family stress in the numbers of teenage pregnancies, school dropout rates, drug addictions and other illnesses, crime rates, and other antisocial disruptions, there is powerful motivation for schools, social agencies, legislatures, businesses, and other concerned community organizations to mobilize and combine efforts for family support. The family is seen as a complex and dynamic system that sits at the hub of and is influenced by other complex systems, such as schools, the workplace, the health system, the human services system, and government at every level. Schools are concerned about the lack of quality preparation for children prior to entering formal education, especially in families not proficient with English, and they recognize that schools and communities cannot do it alone.

Family resource and support programs have appeared all over the country, offering services to parents that may include parenting education, adult education and job training, emotional support, and varieties of child care services. Teachers, psychologists, social workers, other professionals, or other parents run the programs. The difference between the intervention models of the 1960s and 1970s and this more recent family resource movement is that the intervention programs saw the child as the unit for intervention, whereas family resource and support programs see the entire family as the unit for intervention.

The focus is not on intervention as a means of solving a deficit problem but as a developmental service needed by all families, regardless of socioeconomic or cultural background, to support them to optimum functioning, particularly at key points in the family life cycle when stresses, crises, and changes are the norm. The approach is prevention, not treatment. Not all families need exactly the same kinds of support, so family resource and support programs are individualized, flexible, and adaptive. Collaborative efforts between community agencies offering health, welfare, social services, and education meet the family's comprehensive needs.

Strengthening Families is a program started nationally in 2001, and functioning in several thousand early care and education settings, to build research-based protective factors into early childhood systems (Jor'dan et al., 2012). See Figure 4-16 for the basic protective factors defined by the program, and ways that early childhood programs can support these.

FIGURE 4-16
Strengthening Families—Protective Factors.

1. **Parental Resilience: Parents need to be strong and flexible.**

   What it is: Having problem-solving skills; being able to rebound; being flexible; experiencing emotional well-being.

   How early childhood programs build it: Being welcoming and supportive; building relationships with families; meeting one-on-one with families; working with families to develop family goals and identify resources; involving families in decisions about their children and the program.

2. **Social Connections: Parents need friends.**

   What it is: Having a positive peer network, mutual support systems, and community connections.

   How early childhood programs build it: Making space available for families to meet informally; supporting parents in planning events for parents and children; arranging family field trips and family activities outside the center; providing volunteer opportunities; working closely with parent advisory groups.

3. **Knowledge of Parenting and Child Development: Being a great parent is part natural and part learned.**

   What it is: Understanding what children are learning—and what they are capable of learning—at different ages and stages; having appropriate approaches to teaching and guiding children.

   How early childhood programs build it: Making parenting information available in families' home languages; sharing classroom observations with parents; telling parents something positive about what their children did during the day; conducting home visits; offering parenting classes; sending home newsletters; setting up lending libraries for parents; holding parent-teacher conferences.

4. **Concrete Support in Times of Need: We all need help sometimes.**

   What it is: Being able to meet basic needs; having access to program services, informal support, and resources to deal with a crisis.

   How early childhood programs build it: Building relationships with families so they feel comfortable sharing the challenges they face; making space available for staff to meet privately with families; responding to signs of parent and family distress; being connected to and familiar with community services and organizations (e.g., food programs, clothing closets).

5. **Social and Emotional Competence of Children: Parents need to help their children communicate.**

   What it is: Helping children identify and express feelings in positive ways and helping them understand that other people have feelings and needs; teaching ways to resolve conflicts; encouraging friendships.

   How early childhood programs build it: Using social and emotional curricula (e.g., Second Step, Center on the Social and Emotional Foundations for Early Learning (CSEFEL), I Can Problem Solve); offering parenting education opportunities; providing individualized support to parents; helping families understand age-appropriate social and emotional skills and behaviors; encouraging children to express their feelings through words, artwork, and expressive play.

6. **Healthy Parent-Child Relationships: Give your children the love and respect they need.**

   What it is: Bonding with the child; nurturing the child; fostering secure attachment; having a loving, reciprocal parent-child relationship; setting healthy boundaries.

   How early childhood programs build it: Offering parent-child activities and parenting education opportunities.

   Protective factors are adapted, with the authors' permission, from the Center for the Study of Social Policy's second edition of *Strengthening Families—A Guidebook for Early Childhood Programs* (Washington, DC; CCSP, 2008) and from K.G. Wolf's *Living the Protective Factors—How Parents Keep Their Children Safe and Families Strong* (Chicago: Strengthening Families Illinois, Be Strong Families, 2012). The factors are available at www.strengtheningfamilies.org.

4-6a State-Funded Family Support Programs

Examples of state-funded family support initiatives include Minnesota's Early Childhood Family Education program, begun in 1975. Operated by local school districts, this program offers a variety of approaches to enhance the competence of all parents of children birth through kindergarten entrance in nurturing the development of their children: child development classes, home visits, parent discussion groups, developmental preschool activities, newsletters, drop-in centers, toy and book lending, and special services for special populations (such as single parents or Southeast Asian immigrant families). Learn more at the website for Minnesota Early Childhood Family Education.

The Parents as Teachers program in Missouri, also operated through school systems since 1985 and available to all parents, offers information and guidance during the third trimester before birth until the child's third birthday via home visits and individual parent conferences each month, monthly group meetings with other parents, use of a parent resource center at the schools, and periodic screenings for the children. The Parents as Teachers program has been replicated and is now operating within all 50 states. Read more at the website for Parents as Teachers.

Many states have now begun to offer some types of family support services; check what is happening in your own state.

4-6b Individual Community Efforts

Individual cities and communities have also developed various kinds of programs that offer support and education to parents of young children, including efforts to involve families in early childhood programs. Family Focus (one of the nation's first family support programs), in the Chicago area, operates drop-in centers in a cross-section of ethnic and socioeconomic neighborhoods. Parents may choose from various educational and support offerings while other children are cared for in quality preschool and afterschool programs.

AVANCE Family Support and Education Program in San Antonio, Texas, has offered a parent support and education program to predominantly poor Latino families with very young children since 1973. Now also in a number of other cities in Texas, AVANCE tries to create strong families by providing intensive parent education classes that last over a nine-month period as well as offering social support, adult literacy, English language learner classes, basic and higher education, quality early childhood education, personal development, and community empowerment. Read more about AVANCE in Chapter 11.

Other similar programs are springing up in communities all over the country. The Family Resource Coalition of America is a national grassroots organization of over 2,000 community programs that offer information, education, advice, and support to families. The purpose of the coalition is to offer information, models of programs, and funding for communities who want to begin their own family resource and support effort. (For more information, see the Family Resource Coalition of America at the website at the end of this chapter.) A comprehensive listing of family support centers nationally can be found at www.familysupportamerica.org. For sources that describe a number of family resource and support programs in detail, see *America's Family Support Programs* and *Programs to Strengthen Families*.

In addition to offering parents psychological support and knowledge necessary to help them understand their children's development and needs, family resource and support programs have set a model for parents and professionals working together as equals, each respecting, valuing, and supporting the contribution of the other. Such a stance makes a school one of the agencies offering a constellation of services to the family. The school's most important role is to confirm the importance of child development and education and the parent's role in it and not to be a substitute for the family or another source of threat to the unit. The program that shares in child-rearing endeavors with parents may act as a reconstituted form of the extended family, offering parents support and avoiding the isolation of child rearing (see Figure 4-17).

Support for families as extended family just may be the newest role for educational institutions to incorporate. Empowering parents keeps the locus of family power within the family—where it needs to be. As communities focus attention and collaborative efforts to support the family through various programs, the momentum will develop for schools to become increasingly responsive to the needs of families and inclusive of their strengths and resources. As a leader from the excellent schools in Reggio, Emilia says:

> There can be no doubt that the education of a child is of great importance, and this predisposes the parent to being concerned and getting involved. School, which by its very nature is an environment for exchange and involvement, cannot ignore this predisposition. The participation of parents is therefore, by its very nature, one of the fundamental premises of the educational experience, if the school views it as essential and not as an accessory or an option (Spaggiari, 1998, p. 110).

© iStockphoto.com/Kali Nine LLC

FIGURE 4-17
Schools and early childhood programs can function as a new form of extended family.

The traditional method of conveying the image of teacher–parent partnerships was as a triangle with a corner for each of the protagonists: teacher, parent, and child (see Figure 4-18). This design seems inadequate in the sense of a true collaborative partnership, where teachers and families develop reciprocal ties that benefit all, as shown in Figure 4-19. Here, there is no sense of rivalry or separation but rather a united, focused, child-centered effort.

FIGURE 4-19
New model of family engagement.

FIGURE 4-18
Old model of family engagement.

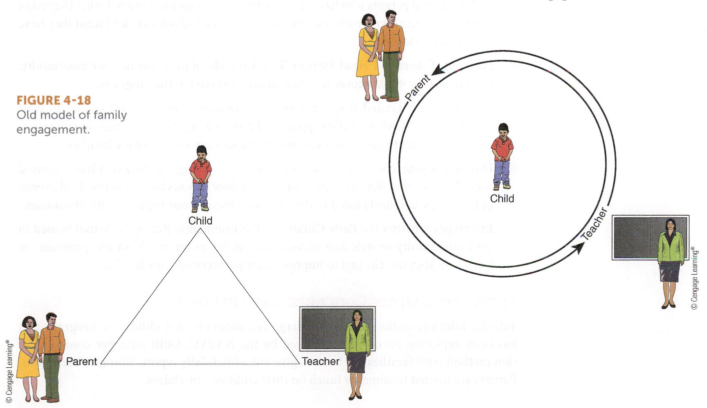

© Cengage Learning®

© Cengage Learning®

SUMMARY

An understanding of family involvement has evolved through various philosophies and historical traditions in preschool and elementary education. Currently, there are three main reasons to consider ways to involve families in their children's care and education:

- Research on family involvement as an optimal factor in child development and learning; family engagement in schools and patterns of communication with their children all correlate with positive results.

- Mandates from government and professional associations, such as recent legislation and accreditation standards.

- Community concern and collaboration for family support programs. The need for strong families has caused communities to create agencies on the state and local level to support parents and their children in many ways.

Student Activities for Further Study

1. Find out if your community has a parent cooperative-style preschool program. If so, visit and discover what aspects parents are involved in.

2. Interview several teachers. Find out the following:
   a. How they define parent or family involvement
   b. What activities and strategies they use to involve families
   c. How much time each week or month they would estimate they spend working with parents
   d. Their opinion of the value of family involvement, considering the time involved

3. Talk to several parents who have children in various schools. Find out what they want in terms of their own involvement with the schools and teachers and what they have actually experienced.

4. Find out if there is a Head Start or Title I preschool program in your community. If there is, visit it to discover how parents are involved in the program.

5. Call your local United Way office or any information and referral service in your community. Ask what family support and resource organizations exist in your community. Contact those agencies to learn what services they offer for families.

6. Discover if your community has any schools for young children that have received accreditation from NAEYC. If so, visit to learn how parents have been involved in each of the program criteria listed in this chapter. Discuss your findings with classmates.

7. Investigate whether the Early Childhood Environmental Rating Scale tool is used in your community or state as a measure for quality programs. Visit any programs to learn how they use the tool to improve their partnership with families.

Apply the Chapter Concepts: Case in Point

Tameka Johnson works in a pre-kindergarten program in a child care program that has been exploring becoming accredited by the NAEYC. Until now, her communication method with families has been to give out a brief daily report, filling in the blanks. Parents are invited to come for lunch on their children's birthdays.

1. According to the accreditation standards discussed in this chapter, what are some additional methods of involving families that she will need to consider?

2. How are these methods also supported by other NAEYC position statements discussed in this chapter, such as the code of ethics and the statement on developmentally appropriate practice?

3. Are these changes mandatory or just what Tameka chooses to use to improve her classroom?

Review Questions

1. Discuss some of the ideas about what constitutes family involvement.

2. List some of the ways parents have been involved historically in schools.

3. Identify three motivations for parent involvement and the underlying ideas.

4. Discuss examples of how research on parenting influences on child development and academic success motivates those trying to involve families.

5. Discuss several examples of mandated family involvement.

6. Describe community motivations and efforts to involve families in their children's education.

Helpful Websites

-   Find information about the No Child Left Behind legislation at the Department of Education's website. Also search there to find *Family Involvement in Children's Education: Successful Local Approaches: An Idea Book* (Funkhouser & Gonzales, 1997). This idea book is offered to stimulate thinking and discussion about how schools can help overcome barriers to family involvement in their children's education—regardless of family circumstances or student performance.

-   Search the website for the National Center for Family and Community Connections with Schools.

-   National Network of Partnership Schools has information on their website for schools and organizations regarding the use of research-based approaches to organize and sustain excellent programs of family and community involvement that will increase student success in school.

-   Search the Head Start Bureau's official website for the report on ongoing research for Head Start: "Building Their Futures: How Early Head Start Programs Are Enhancing the Lives of Infants and Toddlers in Low-Income Families."

-   The Early Childhood Learning and Knowledge Center is a resource with much information about Head Start, including the Program Performance standards.

-   The National PTA's website has information on the national standards for parent–family involvement programs.

-   Search the website of the Family Resource Coalition, the nation's clearinghouse for family support issues.

-   At the website for the National Association for the Education of Young Children, you can find the revised accreditation standards, standards for professional preparation, the code of ethics, and the position statement on developmentally appropriate practice.

CHAPTER 5

Benefits and Barriers in Teacher– Family Partnerships

© Cengage Learning®

Learning Objectives

After reading this chapter, you should be able to:

5-1 List benefits for children when parents and teachers work together constructively.

5-2 List benefits for families when parents and teachers work together constructively.

5-3 List benefits for teachers when parents and teachers work together constructively.

5-4 Discuss various reasons for barriers to relationships.

5-5 Discuss attitudes that may create barriers between parents and teachers.

5-6 Discuss emotional responses of parents and teachers that may cause barriers.

5-7 Discuss external factors in the lives of parents and teachers that may create barriers.

naeyc

Related NAEYC Standards

Accreditation Standards (see inside text back cover for full listing of the Accreditation Standards for exemplary early childhood programs)

1.A.04, 7.A.02, 7.A.03, 7.A.04, 7.A. 05, 7A.06, 7.A.08

Licensure Standards (see inside text front cover for full listing of the Licensure Standards for this chapter)

2b, 2c

The education and care of a group of children are serious responsibilities for any teacher in any school, requiring enormous amounts of time and energy. The prospect of adding to this the role of finding ways to communicate and engage with families may be daunting. Why would any teacher want to add this role? The answer lies in the profound benefits for children, for parents, and for teachers themselves. Everyone in a productive relationship gains and grows. This chapter explores the benefits of establishing a positive working relationship with families and then continues to examine the barriers that are challenges to such partnerships.

Teachers have to see for themselves that the effort of working with families really supports and enhances everything else they do. Whether you have already had experiences in a classroom or are preparing for them, it is vital for you to become convinced that the work in creating and maintaining partnerships with parents will have long-lasting effects and is indeed inseparable from all other teaching roles.

But the complexity of human relationships fosters particular attitudes and behaviors in teachers and parents that may act as obstacles to communicating openly and comfortably and establishing working relationships. These potential barriers must be recognized and understood by teachers who bear the burden for trying to remove as many barriers as possible. As teachers consider the attitudes and emotions that create psychological distance and some of the institutional practices that create physical separateness, they can discover new ways to bridge those gaps.

As the previous chapter pointed out, *family involvement* has a variety of meanings and motivations. Variations in teacher attitudes may help or hinder such endeavors.

Listen to several teachers in various schools and programs; we will see them again throughout the text in various activities with families.

You have already met Jane Briscoe. Jane is 27 years old, single, and has been teaching four-year-olds in a demonstration preschool in a college town since she graduated from the child and family development program at State College five years ago. She describes herself as an extrovert—the oldest of a family of four girls. She believes wholeheartedly in working as a partner with parents. She complains that many of her parents seem too busy to spend much time in the classroom, but she keeps on trying.

Anne Morgan is 35 and a divorced mother of a 10-year-old daughter and an eight-year-old son. She has been working in a pre-K program since her divorce four years ago. Before that, her only teaching experience had been student teaching. Anne is often heard criticizing some of the behaviors of parents at the center, who seem to her to be less than conscientious about their parental duties. She does not encourage or invite parents to be involved in her classroom, although she is always polite when she sees them. When a parent with a problem called her at home in the evening, she complained bitterly to her administrator about the infringement on her private time.

This is John Reynolds's first year of teaching kindergarten. He has had to endure a lot of kidding from friends because they feel it is an unusual career choice for an African American man who played football in college. He is hoping salaries in the field will increase so he can stay in the work that he finds so satisfying. He is deeply involved with the children and is conscientious about observing them and making individual plans to fit in with their developmental needs and interests. However, he feels uncomfortable in his contacts with parents, feeling that they are always watching him. He is unsure how much he should tell them about some of his concerns for the children. One parent asked for a conference next week, and he is afraid this means she wants to criticize. He and his wife expect their first child this year, and he is hoping that may help some of the parents accept him as competent. It is not so much that anyone has openly questioned his competence with the children, but he is sure that is what they think.

Connie Martinez is enjoying teaching in a primary school in a small town, which she chose because of the good master's program at the university nearby. She is working hard to finish her degree at night and says that although she believes in parent involvement, she just does not have any extra time beyond her planning and preparing the curriculum for the children and preparing them for the end-of-grade testing. She has never told anyone, but she thinks too many parents expect that the school and the teachers will "do it all" for their children. She does not believe that taking on the parents' role should be encouraged. Last week, a mother brought in her child, who had just come from the doctor's office, and asked if the teacher could give the first dose of the prescribed eardrops because she had to get right back to work. Connie was annoyed with this example of parents shifting their responsibilities to the teacher. When asked if she believes in parent involvement, she says she is too busy to spend much time with parents.

MiLan Ha came to America as a six-year-old. When she graduated from high school, she was second in her class. After a year of college, she took a job in a preschool and has received some training in workshops. MiLan is a talented artist and encourages creativity with her children. She is a quiet young woman with no close friends on the staff. She lives at home with her parents, an uncle, two nieces, and a younger brother. She dreads the conferences and meetings that are scheduled at her preschool and uses the excuse that her English is not good. In fact, her English is excellent; she is just extremely uncomfortable in social encounters. When parents enter her room, she smiles and quickly turns to the children. The parents feel she is a good teacher but are also uncomfortable with her.

Dorothy Scott has been teaching second grade in a private school for 13 years. She took five years off when her own son was a preschooler. She has quite definite ideas about child rearing and feels most parents do not handle things with their children as well as they should. She believes it is important to hold conferences and meetings to tell parents what they should be doing and does not mind spending extra time to do these things, although she finds it discouraging when parents do not attend or disregard her advice. Some of the parents have asked the director privately if it is necessary for their children to be in Mrs. Scott's room, but unaware of this, she states proudly that she has never had a parent complain.

Jennifer Griffin was hired as an assistant teacher this year after graduating from community college in general studies last spring. She is not sure what she wants to do and felt this would be a job she could do while she was making up her mind. She enjoys the children but finds herself somewhat puzzled by the discipline policies, so she allows the teacher to handle most of the problems that arise or questions from parents. Her major complaint is the few parents who are frequently late in picking up their children. She has told another teacher that she may really blow up at one particular mother the next time it happens.

Jeannie Sweeney runs a family child care center in her home for six toddlers and preschoolers, including her own three-year-old. She started the business seven years ago when her first child was born so she could have some income while still caring for her own children. Her earlier job experience was in retail sales. Although she forms close relationships with most of the parents for whose children she cares, she has had several frustrating experiences lately with one family who have rather different child-rearing values from her own. Despite her request in the parent handbook that children not bring violent toys to school, this child continues to bring action figures that are associated with a television show that Jeannie considers too violent. The parents, when approached, laugh and say Jeannie is taking it too seriously. Jeannie is considering asking them to find other child care because she feels this is undermining her approach to teaching the children.

Eight different teachers have eight different experiences and attitudes that clearly determine the responses and relationships each would offer to parents.

Let us go back and listen to Anne Morgan again. She seems quite definite about her position:

Look, I'm not their parent; I'm their teacher. There's a lot of difference between the two. All I can do is work with the children for the six hours or so they're at the school and in afterschool. After that, they're the parents' responsibility. Goodness knows some of those parents could use some help—some of the things they say and do! I do get annoyed when I work so hard with a child and then see the parent come right in and undo everything I've tried to do. But it's really not my business, I guess. Let them do their job, and I'll do mine.

Anne has apparently decided that there is no purpose in establishing a working partnership between herself and her children's families. Let us examine the areas Anne is overlooking: the benefits to children, parents, and teachers as the adults learn to communicate and collaborate.

5-1 Benefits for Children When Teachers and Parents Work Together

Since children are the focus for both parents and teachers, what do they gain when the adults work in partnership?

5-1a Security in a New Environment

In their early years, children depend on the key adults in their lives to foster first a sense of security and then feelings of self-worth. Parents are, of course, of primary importance here. The attachment in a parent–child relationship forms the basis for a child to trust or not trust the environment.

Most researchers conclude that this parent–child attachment is crucial for the development of a healthy personality. The presence of the mother or another primary caregiver to whom a child is attached serves as a secure base from which to move out and respond to other aspects of the environment. Preferably, when a child moves into the school world, the first important attachment provides a base of security that can be extended to other adults (see Figure 5-1). This task is made easier if the child's familiar, trusted adults are comfortable with the new adults. For example, contrast the effects on these two young children:

FIGURE 5-1
Children can move more easily into new situations from the secure base of those first important attachments with family.

Emma's mother feels nervous around the new teacher. She feels that the teacher is looking critically at some of the things she does, and she does not seem like a friendly person. As a result, she spends little time talking to her, hurrying in and out of the classroom when picking Emma up. She has made some negative comments to Emma's father at home about the classroom situation. Emma's teacher is perturbed by this avoidance behavior and feels annoyed and uncomfortable when Emma's mother darts in and out. Puzzled but aware of the strain between the adults, Emma does not allow herself to relax and feel secure in her new classroom world.

Sandra's parents, on the other hand, looked long and hard before they found a preschool that seemed to match their beliefs about child rearing. They took the time to talk with the teacher at length; they discovered that they shared some leisure interests. The parents and teacher now feel comfortable and trusting as they share conversations daily. Sandra seems to feel that her circle of loved and trusted adults has widened; she moves easily back and forth from home to school.

FIGURE 5-2
Children feel more secure when their parents appear comfortable with their teachers.

A young child's anxiety in a new school experience may be lessened if there is not an abrupt division between home and school. Children thrive when they feel continuity between family and teachers that can be present only when the adults have reached out in an effort to understand and respect each other (see Figure 5-2). (And not incidentally, the child is also offered positive examples of cooperation and social skills in communication.) Just as a teacher's first task in relating to a child is to build a sense of trust and mutual respect, the same task is important in working with families. It is not realistic to expect to like all parents. However, it is essential and possible for teachers to respect all parents for their caring and efforts and their central position in their children's lives. In most cases, parents care deeply about their children. This belief should be the basis for all teacher interaction.

The participation and active involvement of the parent in the school is perceived and appreciated by the child, who can derive from it a sense of security besides seeing it as a model and incentive for his or her own personal growth (Spaggiari, 1998, p. 110).

Many teachers of school-aged children believe that children at later periods of development do not have the same need for their parents in the school setting in order to build their confidence. However, all the research proves over and over again that when families are involved, not only is children's performance enhanced but they also have more positive attitudes about school (Epstein, Coates, Salinas, Sanders, & Simon, 2009).

5-1b Sense of Self-Worth

Children also gain feelings of self-worth if they perceive that their families are valued and respected by others. A child's sense of who he or she is relates closely to the sense of who his or her parents are. If his or her parents receive positive feedback, he or she also feels worthwhile and valued. On the other hand, if a child observes a teacher ignoring his or her parents or treating them with obvious disdain, his or her own self-esteem suffers.

Sandra beams when her teacher comes over to greet her father in the morning and asks how the weekend camping trip went. In her eyes, her teacher and father are friends, and this means her father is somebody special in her teacher's classroom. This makes her feel she has been treated in a special way and is therefore valued.

5-1c Knowledgeable and Consistent Responses

Another benefit for children in a constructive parent–teacher partnership is the increased ability of all adults to guide and nurture a child's development knowledgeably, creating "seamless care" with fewer mistakes and less confusion or tension between home and school (Baker & Manfredi/Petitt, 2004).

Parents and teachers who can comfortably share personal observations, general ideas, and specific reactions expose each other to a wealth of information that may help them provide the most appropriate response for each child. Such an exchange of information surely benefits the child. As families and teachers plan together, they identify and reconcile their understandings of children's needs and their goals for children.

CULTURAL CONSIDERATIONS

Welcoming all families

The presence of families and their welcoming acceptance by a teacher are especially valuable in affirming for children of ethnic and cultural minorities a sense of value for and integration of their own culture in the classroom world (see Figure 5-3). The teacher who makes the effort to learn even a greeting word or two in the language of immigrant families demonstrates such acceptance.

Many teachers still cling to stereotypical expectations that parents from minority or low-income families or families that do not conform to societal norms will not become involved in communication with teachers. However, when they reach out positively and sincerely to all families, they usually discover that their assumptions were wrong: Families want success for their children and will work to support that success. In fact, recent studies indicate that the school success of African American children is directly related to their parents' values and expectations as well as the active participation and emotional availability of their parents (Murphy, 2003). As teachers draw families into the educational process, minority children benefit in self-esteem and academic success. We will talk more in Chapter 13 about classroom practices that convey inclusiveness and welcome to all families.

Reflect on any occasions when you have felt left out. How would these feelings affect minority children and their families?

Last month, Sandra missed her daddy very much when he was out of town visiting his sick mother. At home, she became clingy and demanding of her mother. Miss Briscoe noticed lots of crying at school and easy frustration with everyday tasks. At first, she was puzzled by the sudden change, but when Sandra's mother shared her description of the behavior at home and the temporary change in the family pattern, she was able to help Sandra talk openly about her concern for her daddy. She read a story at group time about a daddy who sometimes had to go away; Sandra took it off the shelf almost daily to read it by herself.

In some cases, teachers and families may work together to provide consistent responses, feeling it may help children's learning if all adults respond to specific behaviors in the same way. For example, when Ricky's response to frustration is to whine, his mother and teacher have agreed they will ignore the whining and redirect his attention to something else. This approach seems to help him decrease the whining.

Many of the gains for children resulting when parents and teachers cooperate, share information, and expand their skills are measurable (see Figure 5-4). Research reveals that children gain in academic skills, positive self-concept, and verbal intelligence when extensive family participation with teachers is required (Weiss, Caspe, & Lopez, 2006).

Children receive three benefits when parents and teachers work together:

1. Increased security in the new school environment
2. Increased feelings of self-worth
3. Increased number of helpful responses and success in appropriate learning experiences

FIGURE 5-3
The welcome and acceptance of his parents are especially valuable for the minority child.

5-2   Benefits for Parents Welcomed into Partnership

What do parents gain from developing a working relationship with their children's teachers?

5-2a   Feelings of Support for Parenting

An immediate benefit is the feeling of support in carrying out the responsibilities of parenthood. As discussed earlier, the changing nature of contemporary life means that many parents are removed from the natural supports of family and roots, traditions, and models when they begin the usually unprepared-for task of parenting. The many questions and uncertainties that occur in everyday activities often make parenting lonely, worrisome, and indeed overwhelming.

Having an adult who cares about their children—to share the good and the not-so-good times of day-to-day life—is extremely helpful in alleviating anxieties of parents of

FIGURE 5-4
When teachers and parents share information, the child benefits.

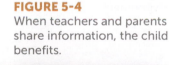

FIGURE 5-5
A parent–teacher relationship can give parents the feeling of being supported in their responsibilities.

© 2016 Cengage Learning®

young children. It has been noted that after mothers have a chance to express their feelings and concerns to others willing to listen with an empathetic ear, they often exhibit more patience with their children, listen more carefully to them, and are more responsive to their needs than before having the opportunity to unburden themselves. A parent–teacher relationship can offer much needed support to parents (see Figure 5-5). In this way, it has been suggested that the child care program and its personnel can function as a new kind of extended family—part of the constellation of community support that each family needs and what Bronfenbrenner has referred to as a **microsystem** in the **ecology** of human development (Bronfenbrenner, 1979).

You will read more about Bronfenbrenner's ideas in Chapter 12. An educator in Reggio Emilia, Italy, where family participation is a hallmark of the excellent programs, expresses it this way: "Families cannot be left to themselves. They need a network of shared responsibility and solidarity that is of benefit and support to them" (Spaggiari, 1998).

microsystem
Small part of a system that forms a unified whole; related to children—bounds of a child's world, such as home, school, Grandma's house, or the like.

ecology
Interaction between the individual and the environment.

 ### 5-2b Knowledge and Skills

In addition, teachers provide a background of information and skill from their expertise and experience in dealing with a variety of children, as well as a model for positive guidance techniques. There is no question that families possess firsthand knowledge about their children, but frequently, the experience of living with them is their only opportunity to learn about child development.

Many parents never have the opportunity to learn relevant developmental information and often misunderstand the nature of developing children. Parents of school-aged children are often at a loss on how best to support their children's academic development. When teachers share their knowledge, they help parents respond more appropriately to their children's developmental needs.

When parents converse with teachers and watch and listen to teachers working with children, they can expand their knowledge and become more effective as parents (see Figure 5-6). They learn informally, comfortably, through the conversation of a relationship. This learning does not threaten parents' self-esteem if the teacher is careful to create a relationship of equals rather than teaching from the lofty pinnacle of old-style professionalism. Parents can learn in an atmosphere of feeling trust and being relaxed.

"You know," says Sandra's mother, "I sure am glad to have you tell me most four-year-olds tend to get a little out of bounds. When she began to spit last month, I was horrified. It's also been helpful to watch you dealing with some of that behavior in the classroom. It would never have occurred to me to be so calm and suggest she go into the bathroom to spit."

 ### 5-2c Enhancing Parental Self-Esteem

It is essential that parental self-esteem develop in a positive way. Parents who believe in themselves are much better at developing and using appropriate parenting skills; parents who feel self-confident are better at providing their children with a secure environment and fostering positive feelings of self in their children. Thus, nurturing parental self-esteem contributes to optimum parental functioning.

Parents who become involved in their children's schooling develop a greater appreciation for their role in their children's learning, enhancing their sense of adequacy and self-worth (Hoover-Dempsey et al., 2005). The most important predictor of children's school success is related to positive parental self-esteem. Studies indicate that there is a definite impact on the development of feelings of competence and self-esteem in parents involved in their children's schools (Epstein, 2011; see Figure 5-7). Empowered parents function at their best.

FIGURE 5-6
Parents learn new skills by watching and listening to teachers communicating with children.

Perhaps one reason for the increase in parental self-esteem is that parents can get specific positive feedback on their functioning as a parent—feedback that is especially meaningful because it comes from an "expert" in child development.

"You know," says Miss Briscoe, "I admire the way you talked with Sandra this morning. You were sensitive to her feelings but also quite definite that you had to go. That approach helped her see where the limit was."

Teachers are powerful people; in many cases, they are the first people outside the family to see children and their parents on an ongoing basis, so their approval is important to parents.

A positive feeling of parental self-esteem is also nurtured when parents feel they are a vital part of their child's school world as well as home world. Teachers who help parents feel included in the education process contribute to parents' feelings of competence and strengthen their social networks. Parents who are included feel able to support their children's learning. This feeling of being necessary and included is helpful for all parents—especially fathers, who often feel cut off by our culture and unimportant to the overall needs of the child.

FIGURE 5-7
Parental self-esteem increases as they are involved in their children's schools.

"You know, Miss Briscoe," Sandra's father said at a recent conference, "I'm very glad you suggested I'd be welcome to come and spend some time any afternoon I can get off work a little early. I really like knowing who the kids are that she talks about at home—just to see what part of her day here is like. It's important to me not to feel as though I have nothing to do with part of her life."

Parents benefit from positive teacher–parent relationships in three ways:

1. Feelings of support in the difficult task of parenting
2. Knowledge and skills gained by parents to help them in child rearing
3. Enhanced parental self-esteem from receiving positive feedback on their parenting actions and feeling they are an important part of their child's life away from home

5-3 Benefits Teachers Receive from Working with Parents

What about teachers, whose efforts to develop a positive working relationship may be the greatest? Are there benefits to justify such efforts? Again, the answer is *yes.*

5-3a Increased Knowledge for Increased Effectiveness

Anyone who has worked in a classroom is aware of the uniqueness of each child's personality and needs. Teachers have learned much that is applicable about the general characteristics of children at particular ages, stages, and grade levels, but to be effective with each child, additional information is needed. Each child comes to the classroom with a history—years of reactions, experiences, and characteristic styles of behaving that are unique. Each family has its own dreams and expectations for its children, its own patterns of behavior and values related to the specific cultural or ethnic ethos from which it comes, and its own structure, relationships, and needs. Teachers need to know all this and learn it early in their associations with children and families. With this specialized knowledge, parents are in a position to assist teachers in working with their children. One way of describing the difference in the kinds of knowledge that parents and teachers have of children is that parents' knowledge is vertical, having developed longitudinally through the child's life; teachers' knowledge is horizontal, encompassing much about a particular age group or grade level. At the point where these two lines intersect, teachers and parents can support each other in a partnership of knowledge (see Figure 5-8). Teachers who build effective communication with families are more likely to meet realistic goals for each child and support each family in reaching their own particular goals.

FIGURE 5-8
Teachers' knowledge is horizontal; parents' is vertical. Where these two points intersect, parents and teachers can strengthen each other's effects.

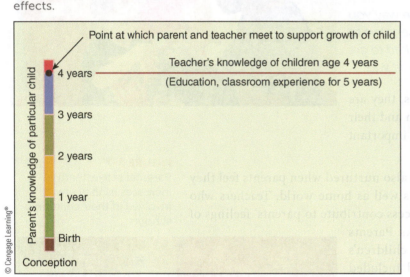

OPPORTUNITY FOR SELF-REFLECTION

If you have spent time in a classroom situation, consider some of the information you would like to have received about children that can come only from their families. Note that here, and comment on how you could obtain this information in your classroom in the future.

At the same conference, Miss Briscoe commented how helpful it has been for her to know, before Sandra's introduction to the classroom, that she was a quiet child who normally took a long time to warm up in a new situation. "Otherwise, I'd have been concerned. But that helped me give her lots of time and support. I was also glad to know she especially liked puzzles—that way, I could plan something special for her during those first days."

In addition, when teachers are open to learning from families, much knowledge about the practical aspects of living with children can be learned. Not only can this help a teacher who has not had the firsthand experience of parenthood but it may also increase the teacher's store of ideas to pass along to other parents.

"You know, I got some really good mealtime tips from one of my parents. Let me share them with you. In fact, the ideas would likely be helpful to everyone—I'll include them in my next newsletter."

5-3b Positive Feedback Increases Confidence

Teachers' self-confidence will grow as positive feedback is received from others regarding their job performance. To have their efforts valued and respected, as demonstrated by parents' positive responses and desire to cooperate, is an important contribution to teachers' sense of professional well-being (see Figure 5-9).

CASTLE SQUARE TEACHERS, WE APPRECIATE YOU!!!

© Cengage Learning®

There is no question that teachers have frustrating and negative experiences as they work with families; there is no such thing as 100 percent success in complex endeavors involving human personalities, needs, and other foibles. But for teachers who honestly and warmly try to reach out to parents, there is enough success for them to realize that their efforts are effective and appreciated. And when frictions arise—as they inevitably will—teachers who have formed relationships with families will be better able to resolve differences.

The reaching out may be difficult, especially for teachers who are not very comfortable in social situations. In fact, one effect of enhanced teacher self-confidence is that personal social skills may develop and expand. Teachers' personal growth is often a byproduct of their experiences with parents that garner positive feedback for them. Involvement with families reduces teachers' feelings of isolation and nonsupport.

Parents involved in schools enhance their views of their children's teachers and schools, often becoming advocates for teachers, urging communities and institutions to establish working policies and personnel conditions that benefit teachers and allow them to do their best for children. Teachers and schools need and deserve the support of families that comes when parents are fully involved.

"For all you do, that's what they pay you? I think that should be brought up with the board."

"Our kids deserve to have better facilities for sports activities. What can I do to help?"

It is evident that the advocacy efforts of teachers to support quality for children's schools and programs can be greatly strengthened when parents recognize the benefits of quality education and join in supporting teachers' efforts.

It is interesting to note that through partnership, teachers and parents may have some of their personal emotional needs satisfied on the subject of competence. Education is a very human partnership. It depends for its strength on how teachers and parents feel about each other and what they do to meet each other's needs.

5-3c Parental Resources for Enriched Learning Experiences

Teachers have only the resources of one person, with individual limitations on time, energy, knowledge, creativity, experiences, and other resources. Families may offer additional resources in all these areas as well as others (see Figure 5-10). Listen again to a view from Reggio Emilia:

"The contribution of ideas, expectations, and abilities offered by families to the schools help the teachers to perceive the link with families as something that enriches rather than interferes.... Even with the best-prepared teachers and in the richest situations, there are areas that can only be realized through sharing and interactive choices"

FIGURE 5-10
More one-to-one attention to children can be available when parents spend time in the classroom.

© Cengage Learning®

(Spaggiari, 1998, p. 111). The learning experiences teachers can offer children in the classroom are multiplied and enhanced by parents who feel invited and included in the educational process. Parents learn a good deal about interacting with their own children and often "teach" very well. Families as a classroom resource will be discussed further in Chapter 10.

Families who are included in the educational process will also continue learning experiences with their children at home, strengthening teachers' efforts. A review of research on the importance of involving parents in the education of their children strongly suggests that the effectiveness of teachers and schools is reinforced and increased by active involvement of children's families (see Chapter 4).

Teachers receive three benefits for working with parents:

1. Increased knowledge, which enables teachers to be more effective with each child

2. Positive feedback, which increases their own feelings of competence in their profession and advocacy of their interests

3. Parental resources to supplement and reinforce their own efforts in providing an enlarged world of learning

The best way for teachers to have an impact, especially a long-lasting one, on the children in their classrooms is to work to strengthen and meet the needs of the whole family. The partnership between teachers and families benefits them both, but most of all, it benefits the children for whom they both care.

Beyond any question, when you work closely with parents you pay a price. You adjust to the other fellow's ideas, sometimes going faster and sometimes going at a slower pace than you desire. But there are rewards in working together that isolation could never bring. Teachers do gain. Parents gain. And children are the real winners. (Hymes, 1975)

5-4 Why Are There Barriers to Teacher–Family Partnerships?

As we have seen, there is potential for families and teachers to offer each other strength, support, and knowledge as they work together for children's benefit. But why does the relationship sometimes never get off the ground? Some of the families and teachers introduced earlier may help demonstrate the reasons.

John Reynolds is quite ready to admit it: He is frankly terrified of the prospect of his contacts with parents in his first year of kindergarten teaching:

> *"Look, I'm just feeling my way with the kids this year. I'm sure those parents are wondering what's going on, and I'm not comfortable with them asking many questions. And I don't even have any kids of my own to draw on that experience. I'm sure they wouldn't even listen to me."*

Connie Martinez shares her negative feelings about the parent involvement philosophy but for different reasons:

> *"Enough time goes into running a good classroom for children without asking teachers to spend even more time on trying to do things for parents. If you ask me, the whole idea is wrong anyway. Parents today are pushing*

their responsibilities off on someone else—always asking the government or somebody to do more for them. How will they learn to do a good job with their own kids that way if we're helping them every step of the way?"

Dorothy Scott shares her pessimism:

> *"I've been working with children for 13 years now, and believe me, the majority of parents just don't seem to care. I've knocked myself out planning meetings to teach them the things they ought to know, and most of them never show up. You tell them what they should do, and they keep on doing things the same old ways. It can be pretty frustrating, let me tell you."*

MiLan Ha will not say much about her feelings:

> *"I really wish I could just work with my children without anyone suggesting I should also be working with the parents. When parents begin to talk to me, I just freeze up and can't think of anything to say. With the children, I'm fine."*

These teachers are expressing strong feelings that will clearly influence any interactions they have with families. But some of the parents have equally potent viewpoints.

> *Sam Leeper says: "That teacher can hardly stand to talk to me. You can see her disapproval written all over her face. I'd like to know who she thinks she is, passing judgment on my partner and me. We're good parents, and we have a strong family."*

> *Jane Weaver is very uncomfortable around the teacher but for different reasons. "She just knows so much. I never went to college, and sometimes, I don't quite understand some of the words she uses when she talks about what she's trying to accomplish with the children. I'm afraid I'd show my ignorance if I said anything. And she's such an expert—she always knows what to do with those children. She makes me feel—dumb."*

> *Mary Howard explains her biggest problem with the teacher: "I feel like a nuisance. I mean, she's always so busy, I hate to bother her to ask her anything. I feel like I'm butting in, and that makes me feel kind of bad. Cynthia's with her all day long, and sometimes, I just feel left out."*

These comments exemplify some of the attitudes that we will explore. Many of these reactions are natural human reactions that constitute a problem only when they are unrecognized barriers between parent and teacher. Simply becoming aware of some of these and why they exist will help.

When considering family–teacher communication, remember that the initiative must come, in most cases, from a teacher. Because this communication takes place in school—a teacher's home territory—it gives the teacher the advantage of his or her own environment, and with this advantage comes the burden of responsibility.

Teachsource

VIDEO ACTIVITY ▶❙❙

© 2016 Cengage Learning®

Watch Bonus Video 1 in the Video Case, *Communicating With Families: Best Practices in an Early Childhood Setting*, where a parent and teacher communicate during morning drop-off time. After watching the video, reflect on these questions:

1. How does the child benefit from this communication?

2. How does the parent benefit from this exchange?

3. How does the teacher benefit from this conversation?

A teacher is responsible for creating an atmosphere open to dialogue. The teacher must recognize not only the experiences and feelings of parents that might stand between them but also analyze personal attitudes and behaviors so no action exacerbates parents' discomfort.

"The teacher–parent relationship is a lot like an arranged marriage. Neither side gets a lot of say in the matter" (Mosle, 2013). In one sense, parents and teachers can be described as natural adversaries—not because of the dynamics of any individual relationship, but because of the nature of the relationship that emerges from the roles defined by the social structure of society. Parents and teachers generally have different perspectives on how to approach and view a child—a difference that evolves from their distinct social and cultural roles. Our culture defines parents as ultimately responsible for their children's well-being. Parents tend to be protective and highly emotionally invested in their children. Their perspective is quite focused on the individual, and they have particular expectations, goals, and intense feelings for their children. Teachers are given the cultural role of rational guide; their perspective can be described as more universal—concerned about children in the context of broad goals of socialization and education (Lawrence-Lightfoot, 2003). A teacher can be affectionate and still able to regard a child with objectivity not possible for a parent—what Katz calls a "detached concern" (Katz, 1995). Katz distinguishes between parenting and teaching in seven dimensions:

- **Role Dimension 1: Scope of Functions**—Parents must play every role related to the care and development of their children—from trips to the dentist and barbershop and making decisions about dance lessons or vacation plans to deciding whether the budget can stretch enough to afford a new pair of shoes. It is their responsibility to make sure that the child is physically healthy, emotionally secure, socially happy, stimulated, responded to cognitively, and reading at grade level—all the while making sure that tomorrow's laundry has been folded! Teachers are concerned about the child's more limited classroom life.

- **Role Dimension 2: Intensity of Affect**—Parents are highly emotional regarding everything that concerns their children—positive and negative. Teachers are only mildly emotional about the same children because they depend less on children in the classroom meeting their emotional needs; children meet many of their parents' psychological needs, so parents tend to be very intense when discussing their children.

- **Role Dimension 3: Attachment**—Parents are deeply involved in the mutual attachment that endures over time and is essential to the child's development. Teachers care sincerely about children, but they do not form deep attachments because they know their relationship is temporary—often lasting a year or less. Parenting is a long-term relationship.

- **Role Dimension 4: Rationality**—Parents are supposed to be quite "crazy" about their children; children thrive when they bask in unconditional love. This may mean that parents cannot move away from their subjective response to matters about their children and become completely objective—the optimal condition for making factual assessments. In contrast, because of their emotional distance, teachers can be deliberate and objective in their analysis of a child's strengths and needs.

- **Role Dimension 5: Spontaneity**—Because of attachment and related emotions, parents often act by emotional reaction in unpremeditated ways. Teachers are more likely to be able to keep cooler heads and can plan and speak with calmer objectivity.

- **Role Dimension 6: Partiality**—Parents are most likely biased on their child's behalf. When teachers complain that some parents seem to believe there is only one child in the classroom, this is a reflection of the parents' **partiality**. However, teachers are expected to show no favoritism toward any particular child.

- **Role Dimension 7: Scope of Responsibility**—Parents are responsible for and responsive to the needs and lives of their individual children. Teachers are responsible for the needs of a whole group of children. Looked at this way, it is not surprising that parents and teachers frequently approach the same issue from different perspectives. Look at the cartoon in Figure 5-11 and appreciate it as you think about Katz's distinctions.

"Did Momma's little angel stretch his potential today?"

© Ingrid Thomas. Used by permission.

Today, more than ever, parents and teachers may experience tension in their relationship because so many very young children are being cared for by other adults, causing an overlap of parents' and teachers' spheres of influence. Much of what caregivers of children in the first three years or so do for them are things also done by parents when they are present; in effect, early childhood caregivers and educators are sharing in parenting. The culture has not yet moved to define clearly the roles within this new context, nor can they *be* easily defined or separated, thus creating an ambiguous situation with unclear boundaries. In addition, many parents feel somewhat conflicted about leaving their young children in the care of "outsiders" for most of the day, which can cloud their communication with caregivers.

partiality
Tendency to favor one person over another.

gatekeeping
Keeping others away from the child—either physically or by subtle interference.

The issue is further complicated by the fact that it is important that young children become attached to adults who care for them during so many of their waking hours in their parents' absence. But attachment is a mutual process. When two or more adults are attached to the same child, they frequently engage in **gatekeeping**—a subtle attempt to undermine the position of the other adult in relation to the loved child.

Gatekeeping is a sign that strong bonds are forming with the child, and although it can be stressful, it is also a good sign (Brazelton & Sparrow, 2002). It is no wonder that the ambiguous roles and responsibilities, complicated by emotional responses of competition, lead to an uncomfortable mistrust of the other that is usually not admitted or discussed and may carry over to relationships with later teachers. An acceptance of the differences and, perhaps, conflicts in the relationship of parents and teachers should not also imply an acceptance of distancing, mistrust, and hostility as inevitable. These responses result from a lack of communication and from mistaking differences for complete alienation.

Although teachers in elementary schools have more clear-cut roles than do teachers working with younger children in child care situations, there has long been a tradition of professional separation and formality when dealing with families.

It is important to remember that when people come together, they do so as individuals whose personalities, past experiences, present needs, and situations all determine their perceptions and reactions. Teachers need to examine sensitively the words and behaviors that pass between themselves and parents; to do so requires self-esteem and a sense of competence, or else teachers will be reluctant to undergo so searching an examination.

This is not to suggest that professional attention and skill can simply remove the difficulties in something as complex as teacher–parent relations or that it would even be desirable to be able to reduce the complexity to following simple formulas. With experience, teachers will come to realize that this complexity adds challenge and richness to the process of professional and personal growth. Loris Malaguzzi, the founder of the early childhood programs in Reggio Emilia (noted for their strong family involvement, among other things) spoke of the value of creative conflict and dissonance:

> Family participation requires many things, but most of all it demands of teachers a multitude of adjustments. Teachers must possess a habit of questioning their certainties, a growth of sensitivity, awareness, and availability, the assuming of a critical style of research and continually updated knowledge of children, an enriched understanding of parental roles, and skills to talk, listen, and learn from parents…. Such relationships are and *should* be complicated. (Malaguzzi, 1998, p. 69)

Many of the barriers to effective parent–teacher relationships can be caused by specific factors, including the following:

turf
Area of familiarity over which one asserts authority.

- The essential differences between teaching and parenting (already discussed) (See Figure 5-12.)
- The question of maneuvering over **turf**
- The issue of trust
- Differences in expertise (adapted from File, 2001)

FIGURE 5-12
There are real distinctions between parenting and teaching.

Distinctions Between Mothering and Teaching in Their Central Tendencies in Seven Dimensions

Role Dimension	Mothering	Teaching
1. scope of functions	diffuse and limitless	specific and limited
2. intensity of affect	high	low
3. attachment	optimum attachment	optimum detachment
4. rationality	optimum irrationality	optimum rationality
5. spontaneity	optimum spontaneity	optimum intentionality
6. partiality	partial	impartial
7. scope of responsibility	individual	whole group

© Cengage Learning®

Some of these barriers may be erected by teacher behaviors and attitudes and others by parents. Other more external barriers may be caused by larger circumstances of the school structure or community. Consider the list of barriers suggested by teachers in Figure 5-13; Figure 5-14 shows barriers that parents have identified. In the following discussion, we will consider in more detail all these obstacles to creating comfortable and effective partnerships. The issue is not to assign blame but rather to find ways of maneuvering around these barriers.

FIGURE 5-13
Teacher identification of circumstances that create barriers.

Why Are Teachers Reluctant to Involve Parents?

- It takes too much time and organization.
- Parents may become too dominant in the classroom.
- Parents may not agree with teachers' methods.
- Teachers feel intimidated by parents' presence.
- Teachers are unsure of parents' expectations.
- Teachers are afraid of parent scrutiny.
- Teachers lack confidence.
- Teachers want to retain their authority, power, and control.
- Parents have unrealistic perceptions of their children.
- Lack of administrative support.
- Lack of communication skills.
- Lack of classroom space.
- Lack of knowledge about how to involve parents.
- Teachers are unwilling to admit they need help.
- Teachers just do not want to deal with parents.

© Cengage Learning®

FIGURE 5-14
Barriers to participation identified by parents.

When asked why they did not participate in their children's school settings, parents identified these barriers:

Not enough time	89%
Feel have nothing to contribute	32%
Do not understand or know how to be involved	32%
Lack of child care	28%
Feel intimidated	25%
Not available during time scheduled	18%
Language and cultural differences	15%
Lack of transportation	11%
Do not feel welcome	9%
Other barriers	21%

© Cengage Learning®

5-5   Attitudes That May Cause Barriers

5-5a   Differences Between Teaching and Parenting

One of the most noticeable differences between teaching and parenting (refer back to the earlier discussion) is that parents' responsibilities are seen as "diffuse and limitless" and teachers' as "specific and limited." This means that parents feel responsibility for everything they do related to their children and the outcomes of the children's behavior or performance. Fairly or unfairly, parents are placed squarely on the hook for these outcomes, even when they occur in the classroom. Thus, parents often feel that they are in the position of having to defend themselves and their parenting actions. Parents generally feel vulnerable.

Being vulnerable makes parents sensitive to implied (or interpreted) criticism. Aware of the cultural myths and facts that place the burden for children's success and positive functioning squarely on parents' shoulders, most parents dread any indication that they are not doing a good job. With many parents uncertain that what they are doing is "right" yet feeling they must prove it is right in order to be accepted as capable parents, defensiveness against any suggestion of need for improvement often results. When teachers speak of a child's imperfections, parents might feel like they are being criticized for those imperfections.

> *Jane Weaver admits: "When I saw the teacher watching me scold Sandra the other day, I felt as nervous as a kid myself. You could tell by the look on her face she didn't like it. Well, I don't care—she doesn't have to live with her, and I do. What does she know about children anyway—she never had any of her own 24 hours a day."*

Regardless of their personal outlook and how they view their own parenting performance, most parents find it difficult to seek outside help, even under serious circumstances. It is incorporated into the self-image of most American parents that they should work things out for themselves as a sign of personal strength, achievement of adult status, and parenting success. Therefore, for many parents, reaching out to share concerns with teachers is contrary to their self-image. For some parents, raising children is a private affair, and many parents feel that they know their children best and do not need teachers meddling in family matters.

Because of their strong attachment, many parents see their children as extensions of themselves; to comment negatively on one is like commenting negatively on the other. Teachers need to remember Katz's observation that it is not possible for parents to deal with information about their children from a rational and objective perspective. Their responses are usually emotional and intense.

> *"It really bothers me when the teacher says Sandra is shy. I've always been pretty quiet myself, and it just hurts to hear her say that."*

When children go to school, parents and children are facing their first big test: "How will he or she—and therefore we—do?" Parents have made a heavy emotional investment in their children and may avoid a teacher as a source of possible hurt and criticism (see Figure 5-15).

Even though teachers do not have the weight of complete responsibility on them, they also can be vulnerable to criticism—or what they interpret as criticism. As John Reynolds expressed it, many teachers would rather avoid parents as a source of possible criticism. This is particularly true of young teachers who fear that their position may not be accepted because of a lack of teaching experience or because they have not experienced parenthood firsthand. Teachers unsure of their own abilities fear any negative feedback that may confirm their inner doubts,

FIGURE 5-15

When children go to school, children and parents are facing their first big test, wondering how the children will do.

dreading parents' discovery of their mistakes or inadequacies. They put invisible "Do Not Enter" signs on their classroom doors to tell parents that their presence and opinions are not welcome.

A consequence of feeling vulnerable is that people become defensive. "Defensiveness is an equal-opportunity pitfall for both professionals and families" (File, 2001, p. 72). When parents become defensive, they can become belligerent and hostile in their attacks on a teacher's skills and knowledge. When teachers feel defensive, they may hide their concerns behind a "professional" mask.

A defensive teacher may depend too heavily on conveying the image of the professional person who knows the answers and is all-important in the task of caring for children. This exaggeration of professional behavior intimidates parents and keeps them at a distance, which may be a teacher's unconscious goal. Such a teacher has a hard time acknowledging the importance of parents' contributions or the right of parents to be involved. When one's sense of being in control is shaky, it is difficult to share power.

> *"After all, I've been trained to do this. I frankly don't see why parents who haven't should be able to plan policies, make suggestions, or interfere with what I do in my classroom."*

Rodd points out that the types of relationships established with families and the level of family involvement appear to be determined by the stage of professional development the teacher has reached.

> At earlier stages of career development and professional maturity, relationships with parents are more likely to be authoritarian and paternalistic, token in nature, and from a deficit perspective—that is, where parents, even those who are considerably older than the staff member, are not thought to possess the knowledge and skills necessary for bringing up their children. (Rodd, 1998)

Exhibiting the aloofness of false professionalism or unwillingness to recognize and respect the parents' significant role masks a teacher's defensive position and uncertainties that the teacher hopes will go unchallenged.

> *Jennifer Griffin says: "I hate having parents watch me—it's worse than the principal coming in. They ask so many questions— it's as if they're just trying to find something I've done wrong."*

When parents perceive a teacher's self-imposed distance of excessive professionalism, they often withdraw behind fear and resentment:

> *"I'd like to ask her some questions, but she never seems to have time. The other day she frowned and suggested I make an appointment to talk with her. Why does she make it such a big deal?"*

It is hard to communicate comfortably across this distinctly cold gap. Parents are reluctant to spend energy in a situation where they feel they are not needed or wanted:

> *"Who's she trying to kid? She really thinks she does a better job with them anyway—why does she even bother to ask parents to come in?"*

5-5b Maneuvering Over Turf

Power is an interesting issue. Individuals can work to exert power *over* others or they can work and communicate in such a way that they *share* power with others. Parents feel they should have power to participate in decisions and practices that involve their children. After all, in their homes and in their child rearing, they have the power and are ultimately the ones with the responsibilities—the ones who have to answer for the final product.

FIGURE 5-16

Teachers have the power in classrooms: What happens when they maneuver with parents over their turf?

But in most schools, teachers work on their own turf: the classrooms where they have the power. Families obviously feel less secure and comfortable in the school setting than in their own familiar home settings. So, the issue becomes whether teachers genuinely want to share the power and find ways to make family members feel a basic sense of equality and mutual contribution (see Figure 5-16).

Teachers who get caught up in this issue of power develop "territoriality"—resentment of having parents invade their turf—and try to draw lines that prevent fearful encounters with parents. Another possible reaction of parents faced with a teacher's excessive professionalism and turf protection is to become aggressive in trying to bridge the gap, further alienating or frightening a teacher by demonstrating "pushy" behaviors:

"There's no way I'm going to let these parents come into my classroom. Mrs. Henderson called the other day and insisted she wanted to come sing some holiday songs with the children. Next, she'll be telling me what to plan. Give them a little power and they'll take over!"

When teachers spend energy on protecting their turf, they may also protect their professional self-esteem by blaming others when they feel their efforts are not producing the desired outcomes:

Dorothy Scott again: "Well, I'm certainly not going to bother planning another open house for people who can't be bothered. Fifteen children in my room, and five parents show up. It's a big waste of my time."

Working with parents is an ongoing process; it takes time and effort to build a relationship—and that relationship is only the beginning. Teachers looking for immediate results from their efforts will be disappointed. If teachers are not prepared to accept the idea that this is an ongoing process and expect immediate evidence of effectiveness, they might be tempted to abandon all attempts rather than leave themselves open to a sense of failure.

As teachers recognize that building relationships is a process that occurs over time and that different parents will respond in different ways—and some not perceptibly at the present moment—they can avoid setting themselves up for a sense of failure.

GETTING RID OF THE MYTHS ABOUT HARD-TO-REACH-PARENTS

These beliefs are central to the cultivation of sustaining partnerships with families:

- All parents have dreams for their children and want the best for them.
- All families have the capacity to support their children's learning.
- Parents and school staff should be equal partners.
- The responsibility for building partnerships between school and home rests primarily with school staff, especially school leaders.
- Professionals must take the first steps.

Ideas from Mapp and Hong, 2010.

5-5c The Issue of Trust

Teachers spend a lot of time discussing the development of trust in the classroom. They are well aware that establishing trust with children is a first step to developing supportive learning relationships. They also recognize that establishing families' trust in their program is critical to families' confidence in the school. But a separate issue is related to teachers' abilities to trust families—to give up the common teacher stance of negative judgments about family capabilities (Adams & Christenson, 2000).

One reason for this is that teachers often find themselves working with families whose experiences and viewpoints may be very different from their own. The majority of teachers are members of the middle class and have experienced little beyond middle-class lifestyles, value systems, and ways of thinking. Teachers encountering parents from a variety of backgrounds, experiences, and viewpoints may fall into the all-too-human tendency to stereotype people, their conditions, and their actions. Discrimination or stereotyping can create major barriers. In addition to overt or covert racism, other types of discrimination are based on differences in sex or sexual orientation, social class, education, marital status, economic status, or language. Even without deep prejudices or bigotry, assumptions made on the basis of stereotypes create barriers that preclude true openness to individuals and their actual personalities, needs, and wishes. It is sometimes easier to criticize and avoid than to try to understand and empathize. Barriers may rise in as many directions as there are classes, cultures, and circumstances. When these barriers exist, they may appear as negative behavior, indifference to the other, or stereotypical assumptions:

> *Connie Martinez talks about some of her families. "Well, of course, the Butlers are college-educated and pretty well off, so I expect them to do a good job with their children. They really don't need much advice from me." (The Butlers are inexperienced and uneducated in child development and guidance, and they are shaken by the breakup of their marriage. They hunger for advice and support.) "Sylvia Ashley's just off welfare, so I don't suppose she'll make the effort to come to a parent conference." (Sylvia Ashley has never missed an opportunity to talk with any teacher who offered it.)*

It is easy for teachers to selectively attend to information that is consistent with their beliefs and self-concepts and to screen out, ignore, or criticize people or beliefs that differ from their own. It is also easy for teachers to become convinced that others should and would do things differently if they only had the same knowledge the teachers have.

Trust includes acceptance of others and putting aside one's own viewpoints as absolutes.

> *Ignoring all the good parenting Sam Leeper and James Parker do, Connie continues to complain: "I really don't see why they let them adopt a child. I certainly wouldn't have if I'd been making the decision. What kind of environment can two gay men offer a child?"*

> *"And speaking of environments, Joshua's father lives with his girlfriend. I've heard Joshua refer to her that way: 'My dad's girlfriend.' Now what does that teach a child?"*

Teachers who disapprove of family lifestyles or approach parents with a patronizing attitude because of cultural differences communicate a feeling of superiority—definitely not helpful in forming relationships as equals. Parents, in turn, may avoid contact with teachers whose manner or appearance, communication style, and expectations are uncomfortably different from their own. In addition, parents from working-class or low-income backgrounds are more likely to view school staff as experts who know what is best for their children's education and do not often assume they have a right or responsibility to intervene in their children's schooling. Such ideas are likely to act as barriers, unless teachers give persistent indications of welcome.

Teachsource

VIDEO ACTIVITY ▶❚❚

Watch Bonus Video 2 in the Video Case, *Communicating With Families: Best Practices in an Early Childhood Setting.* After watching the video, reflect on these questions:

1. What are the potential barriers in this scenario?
2. How is the teacher attempting to remove some of these barriers?

"That teacher, I don't know, she talks too good," explains Mr. Rodriguez.

"You know," says Mary Howard, *"just because I'm black, she talks to me like I live in a ghetto or something."*

Nguyen Van Son is angry. "She's never tried to find out how our children live at home. What we want. I don't want my children losing everything from our culture, and if you ask me, she's ignoring the fact that we have a culture!"

In many schools, invisible (but not imaginary) lines exist based on race and class that prevent effective interaction. Indeed, there may be real differences in backgrounds between teachers and parents. Such distinctions can be less divisive when teachers are careful to behave in ways that diminish the importance of the differences and make an effort to get to know parents as individuals, not as members of a particular ethnic group or social class. Trust works two ways: Parents trust that they and their children will be accepted and treated with respect, and teachers come to trust that parent viewpoints and experiences are valid. Genuine respect results when teachers make the effort to learn more about diversity, as we will further discuss in Chapter 13.

5-5d Differences in Expertise

Very much related to the issue of trust is the topic of expertise. In the early childhood education profession, practitioners are increasingly called on to develop their professional knowledge base. As the profession has developed standards of developmentally appropriate practice, teachers have increasingly become oriented toward a vocabulary and tradition of a common body of expert knowledge. Although this has been a positive step toward increasing professionalism, in some cases, it has also had the effect of distancing teachers from families. Partnerships require teachers to see parents as having expertise about their own children and families. But it is sometimes difficult for teachers to value that expertise because it seems so much less formal than their own professional knowledge. However, family knowledge must be recognized genuinely or the barrier of expert relating to novice will be erected.

5-6 Emotional Responses That May Cause Barriers

The role of expert is one that may interfere with comfortable communication, but teachers and parents also have unique responses and strong reactions to the very role of the other. Parents have their own childhood histories of encounters with teachers and learning experiences. Some of these may be positive, causing the parent to automatically consider a teacher a friend. But for many parents, painful memories of past school experiences cause unconscious responses to a teacher as someone to fear—someone who will disapprove, correct, or "fail" the parent (and child). With such an underlying assumption, messages from a teacher may be interpreted more negatively than the sender intended.

Some parents, particularly in lower socioeconomic families, have had numerous encounters with caseworkers, social workers, and other figures in authority. A parent who has a history of dehumanizing or disillusioning experiences with professional people may already have erected barriers in the form of negative expectations.

On the other hand, teachers need to realize how their unconscious reactions to parents are influenced by their relationships with their own parents. A teacher's experiences that have shaped his or her values about family life may conflict with the reality of parents with whom he or she works. For example, a teacher who feels that mothers really should be at home may not be able to relate sympathetically to a working mother. People alienated by unconscious emotional responses can never really hear or speak to each other clearly.

When teachers dominate as experts, they often create negative emotional responses in parents. One of these is that parents may fear antagonizing teachers by their questions or comments, with the anxiety that a teacher could single out their child for reprisals when they are absent:

> *"I'd like to tell his teacher that I don't like the way she lets the children do such messy art activities, but if she gets mad, she'll just take it out on Ricky when I'm not around. I'd better not."*

A majority of all parents—and even more minority parents—report that they are never sure how well their children will be treated when they leave them in a classroom. With such feelings of uncertainty, it is not surprising that parents fear that speaking out might have a negative effect.

Another emotional response created by the separation between teachers and parents is the fear that teachers will replace parents in their children's affections. Attachment is a mutual process, and the affectionate relationship with their children satisfies many emotional needs of parents. Despite research that shows that additional attachments do not undermine the primary parental relationship (Baker & Manfredi/Petitt, 2004), many parents fear this loss and are inhibited from forming relationships with teachers because of their feelings of jealousy and competition with teachers for their children's regard:

> *"I'll tell you, it makes you wonder. She comes in to give the teacher a good morning hug and not so much as a goodbye kiss for her own mother, who's going to be gone all day. I get pretty sick of hearing Miss Ha this and Miss Ha that at home all weekend, I can tell you."*

There are often ambivalent emotions in such situations: A mother wants her child to be independent and happy away from her, but she resents the perception that a teacher is taking over in the child's regard. Feeling that she is losing her child to other people may threaten the mother's own identity.

Teachers themselves are not immune from competing for children's affections, especially if their own emotional needs are not being met in their lives beyond the classroom. A warm, affectionate bond with each child is important, but when a teacher finds herself thinking that she "can do a much better job with him than his own mother," she has slipped into the dangerous territory of identifying with a child so completely that she sees him only as a child she loves in the classroom, not as a member of the more important world of his family. A teacher who begins to confuse her role with being a "substitute" for parents or a "savior" of children in less-than-perfect situations engenders fear and suspicion. A teacher who needs to feel more important to a child than his or her parents may find it too easy to blame the parents for the child's shortcomings and convey such an attitude in his or her choice of words (see Figure 5-17).

FIGURE 5-17
Teachers must be aware of competing with parents for the child's affection.

"The way you're reacting each time Pete has a temper tantrum is really causing him to have more outbursts."

Teachers need to realize that emotions of jealousy and fear of loss are hidden factors limiting much of what is truly said and heard. If teachers ignore the likely presence of these emotions, they may unwittingly fan such sparks into destructive flames:

"Oh, she was just fine, Mrs. Weaver. She played as happily as can be all day and never asked for you once. You don't need to worry about her missing you."

This may be intended as reassurance, but it will simply confirm the mother's worst fears. Most parents believe that no one else can do the job for their children as well as they can, and teachers who help parents feel they are not being displaced from this important position prevent barriers from being raised between them:

"She went to sleep well at naptime today. That was a good idea you had to bring her blanket from home. I know she misses you especially then, and it helps to have that blanket as a connection for her."

The word *guilt* creeps into many conversations when contemporary parents have a chance to talk freely. The many demands on parents, along with an unrealistic image of perfection and a feeling of not doing what should be done, result in feelings of guilt. This emotion may operate as a hidden barrier; parents feeling inadequate to the task may avoid all possible reminders of this, including the person doing things for their children that parents feel they should be doing—the person who seems so very expert in performance. They may also react unreasonably when receiving unfavorable communication about their children's behavior or abilities. Resentment can creep into the relationship from teacher and parent.

Early childhood teachers have extremely demanding jobs that use enormous amounts of energy, creativity, and emotion for long hours each day. In most cases, preschool teachers are paid much lower salaries and receive fewer benefits than their counterparts in schools for older children. They are accorded less professional status and recognition, even when they have completed the same number of years of training. Although elementary or afterschool teachers may be more highly paid, they too often feel as if their contributions to children's lives go unrecognized by families and the community. Therefore, it is easy for teachers to feel the community in general and parents in particular take advantage of them.

"I don't see why they can't pick their kids up on time—don't they know I have other things to do in my life?"

"Look at her dressed like that. I'll bet she spends more on her clothes in a month than I get paid in six months!"

OPPORTUNITY FOR SELF-REFLECTION

This is a difficult area for teachers to consider, but real honesty can help a teacher identify some of the emotions and attitudes that have been barriers to forming effective partnerships with families. Take some time to think about your own perspectives. Can you identify with some of the issues and emotions that have been discussed so far in this chapter? Write about some of the experiences and examples that come to mind. Continue to think about this subject. Self-awareness will help you move past some of these barriers.

Parents have their own reasons for resenting teachers. It hurts to be removed from their children's lives. The TANF legislation that changed how welfare funds are distributed to lower-income families has meant that many parents have had to leave very young children in the care of others in order to support their families. In classrooms for older children, current testing practices may dictate decisions regarding children's retention or moving to the next grade. These are ways that the political decisions of the country impact families and their relationships with schools. No wonder parents feel resentful in such situations over which they have no control.

When it appears that teachers are making decisions and setting rules that exclude parents from classrooms and communication, parents are left with little recourse but can seethe with resentment toward those teachers. It is also a genuine cause of resentment when parents disagree with some of the decisions made about their children's care and education but feel powerless to influence the teacher or program (Delpit & Kohl, 2006).

Parents and teachers who resent each other will be unable to communicate clearly. Thus, it can be seen that the emotions of guilt, jealousy, and resentment may impede the process of open communication, becoming barriers that keep them from sharing their expertise.

5-6a Personal Factors

Some teachers explain their lack of communication with parents as caused by their own personalities or their discomfort in social situations. These factors require special efforts on the part of teachers, and they should not be accepted as justification for failure to take the initiative in reaching out to parents.

> *MiLan Ha knows that she does not have nearly as much contact with parents as many of the teachers in her center, but she says she cannot help it. She says it should not make a difference because she works so well with the children, but she does wonder what she might do to help the situation.*

Teachers aware of their introverted personalities need to find ways of pushing their own efforts—perhaps setting such specific goals as talking to a certain number of parents each day, or approaching a parent with whom they rarely talk, or saying one sentence beyond "Hello. How are you?" It may help to share feelings of discomfort with coworkers and be encouraged by their support. Some initial success in getting to know a few parents makes subsequent encounters a little easier. Students who have the opportunity to practice communication in classes and field experiences will find that communicating becomes easier with experience.

Teachers need to remind themselves frequently that part of a teacher's responsibility is to work with families as well as children and that parents—because of a lack of familiarity with a school situation—may be far more uncomfortable than the teachers themselves. As the leader in a classroom, teachers are automatically placed in the role of host. Just as a host does not allow guests to flounder, unspoken to and uncomfortable in one's home, a teacher must also take the initiative to converse with parents. It is also important for teachers to keep reminding themselves that personality and social comfort may also affect parent responses.

Too often, teachers interpret quiet parents or those who do not readily engage in conversation as having "attitudes" or thinking themselves too good for communication with the teacher. Personal factors may work from both perspectives. Awareness will help; pushing oneself a bit will help; a little success will help. Personality and social discomfort must not be allowed to interfere with the communication process.

5-7 Barriers Caused by External Factors

As well as internal feelings and experiences, the external circumstances in which teachers and parents find themselves may act as barriers. Recall that teachers' and parents' list of barriers to partnership included several external factors.

5-7a Time

Parents and teachers are undoubtedly under time constraints (see Figure 5-18). If school philosophies and administrative actions do not support working with families, teachers may not receive either the staffing arrangements or the compensatory time that is needed to respond with flexibility to families' lifestyles and working patterns. When staffing arrangements have full-time caregivers of young children arriving after and leaving before parents arrive, part-time floaters may greet parents at pickup or drop-off times, putting a strain on families who need information and the temporary caregivers who do not have it. Parents never have enough time for the demands of their lives, but they will find the time for parent involvement if they feel it is really important.

There are ways to maneuver around time as a barrier (see Chapters 8, 9, and 10 for ideas that do not take large amounts of time) if working together is perceived as important to parents and teachers. In today's world, communication does not always have to be face-to-face. It is more productive to consider time as a real problem and search for creative solutions than to interpret the other's lack of availability as a lack of concern for the child or poor parenting.

5.7b Busyness

Another external factor that may function as a barrier is a teacher's appearance of always being busy. This may result from the realities of caring for the needs of a group of children or from an unconscious desire to keep parents at a distance.

Whatever the reason, the perception that a teacher has too much to do to be bothered by a parent keeps many parents from more than the briefest greeting. If teachers try consciously to dispel this impression of being too busy to talk, there are things that can be done. At the beginning of the day, preparations for classroom activities can be made before the children arrive or by another staff member, leaving a teacher available to talk. Teachers can plan—and have ready for use—activities that children may begin by themselves that require little supervision: puzzles on the table, dried beans and cups to fill in a basin, or several lumps of clay waiting in the art area. Books or writing assignments for older children allow teachers to be free to greet parents. When children begin activities, parents and teachers will be free to talk (see Figure 5-19). A classroom should be arranged so when parents enter, they have easy access to a teacher. Staffing arrangements and physical locations at the end of the day should provide enough teachers to care for children so some are free to talk with parents.

Planning and attention to details convey the message that teachers are there for parents.

5-7c Old Ideas of Parent Involvement

Changes in family structure and living patterns over the past several decades demand changes in the timing, content, and form of family involvement, activities, and expectations. Teachers or schools that continue to offer nothing more than the traditional forms and times for meetings, conferences, and the like—what are called institutionalized rituals, which are so obviously unsupportive of good relationships—fail to recognize the current needs of families.

Examples of institutionalized rituals are parent–teacher conferences scheduled at 10:30 a.m., on the teacher's break, or meetings held every first Tuesday at 6:30 p.m. Administrators and teachers must be aware that their own values and the weight of traditional practices may contribute to any reluctance to change forms of parents' involvement. Schools must examine their practices for evidence of outdated concepts of parent involvement and family needs.

When schools bring families into the planning process, they can articulate the changes that need to be made to accommodate family realities.

FIGURE 5-18
Parents as well as teachers are under time constraints.

© Cengage Learning®

FIGURE 5-19
Writing assignments for older children allow teachers to talk with parents.

5-7d Administrative Policies

Some school and program policies discourage or forbid contact and discussion between parents and staff other than supervisory personnel—perhaps on the grounds that unprofessional contacts may take place (see Figure 5-20). The major difficulties here are that parents are denied the opportunity to build a relationship with a child's primary caregivers and that the designated supervisory personnel are often not available in the early morning or late afternoon when parents need to talk. Such policies effectively deter any meaningful family involvement. In addition, families have likely shared information about their children with the administrator who conducts initial interviews, and this information may not reach the teachers who would benefit from it. If the family establishes a relationship with an administrator only, they may not invest in a relationship with the child's actual caregiver (Baker & Manfredi/Petitt, 2004).

Another administrative policy that undermines formation of teacher–parent relationships is staffing patterns with multiple caregivers or frequent changes in personnel. Although administrators often justify such conditions as necessary for children and staff to learn to be flexible and to meet staffing needs, frequent changes do not facilitate formation of authentic relationships. Administrative staffing policies that provide only a

© 2016 Cengage Learning®

FIGURE 5-20
When administrators have policies that do not support teacher–parent communication, it is difficult for partnerships to develop.

Can you think of an example of an institutionalized ritual that needs to be changed in a school with which you are familiar? Why does it persist? What change can you think of that would remove barriers to family participation?

bare minimum of staff available at arrival and departure times also work against forming effective relationships. Parents quickly recognize that harried teachers are not available for communication. When the administration provides training and practice for teachers to learn how to form relationships with parents, lack of knowledge of how to work with adults is removed as a barrier. When administrative philosophy and policies support family involvement and parents are given clear guidelines for ways they can communicate with staff, parents know what is expected of them and do not retreat because of confusion, anger, or frustration.

All these external factors can be solved with concrete changes in the physical and social environment if they are identified as the cause of some barriers. Indeed, these are the easiest barriers to remove, needing only creative thought and perhaps a little money!

5-7e Personal Problems

From the families' side, the pressure from personal problems can act as a barrier to the parent–teacher relationship. As much as parents care about their children and how they are functioning in the classroom setting, too many concerns about other life matters may require parents' primary attention. Such a parent should neither be condemned for indifference nor ignored because of absence, but instead shown continued support and understanding from a teacher regarding the demands on parents. As teachers take responsibility for linking families with information and appropriate community agencies, problems may be eased.

This barrier for parents can be removed with community support and empowerment of attitudes. Jesse Jackson is credited with saying "Parents must make room in their hearts and then in their house and then in their schedule for their children. No poor parent is too poor to do that, and no middle-class parent is too busy."

In the same way, no teacher who believes in the importance of working as a partner with parents will find the problems so immovable as to abandon all attempts.

It is interesting to realize that teacher attitude about family involvement seems to be a key factor in success. Many teachers tend to blame parents for their low level of involvement, even when other teachers in the same building successfully involve parents in their children's education. It is vital that teachers consider the importance of their own attitudes. The key to removing many of the barriers to parent–teacher relationships is a teacher's mind-set. When teachers believe that there is value in working with families, they will find the time and energy to commit themselves to identifying and dealing with potential barriers. The barriers can be broken by a bit more relaxation, a bit more empathy, and a bit more recognition of the many complex factors that shape life for all of us. As one young teacher once said to an older complaining colleague: "Get over it and get on with it!"

SUMMARY

There are benefits for all—teachers, parents, and children—when parents and teachers work in partnership.

- Benefits for children: increased feelings of security and self-worth and successful learning experiences

- Benefits for parents: feelings of support, helpful knowledge and skills, and enhanced self-esteem

- Benefits for teachers: more information and resources to increase effectiveness with children, as well as increased feelings of competence

Barriers to productive partnerships also are realities that must be recognized.

- Barriers may exist because of:
  - Essential differences between teaching and parenting
  - Questions of maneuvering over turf
  - Issues of trust
  - Differences in expertise

- Attitudes that may create barriers include:
  - Defensiveness
  - Vulnerability to criticism
  - Aloofness and false professionalism
  - Blaming
  - Lack of trust
  - Disapproval of others

- Emotions that may act as barriers include:
  - Fears of others' role, of antagonizing the other
  - Jealousy and fear of loss
  - Guilt
  - Resentment

- External factors that may cause barriers include:
  - Time
  - Busyness
  - Old ideas of parent involvement
  - Administrative policies
  - Personal problems

Student Activities for Further Study

1. Choose one of the teachers described in this chapter. How are you like this teacher? Is there anything you want to change in yourself regarding your attitudes about parent involvement?

2. Talk with a teacher about what he or she feels he or she has gained and learned from establishing working relationships with parents. Compare your findings with the benefits to teachers discussed in the chapter.

3. Do a study of a group of parents in your school. (If you are not currently in a school, use the descriptions of the fictional families in Chapter 2.) Compile a list of potential resources these parents offer the school and your teaching efforts.

4. Examine your own biases. Is there a style or kind of family with which you would be less comfortable working compared to other families? Discuss this idea in small groups.

5. Wherever possible, observe teachers and parents talking together. What nonverbal signs of comfort and discomfort do you see?

Apply the Concepts: Case in Point

Maria Gonzalez is a first-year Head Start teacher. She is enjoying her work but is particularly challenged by one of the families in her classroom. The Martinez family consists of Rosa, a young single mother; Diego, a charming four-year-old who is very shy; and an elderly grandmother who speaks no English.

1. How might Rosa benefit from her daily conversations with Maria?

2. What are some of the things Diego learns as he watches his mother and teacher talk together each day?

3. How might Maria benefit as a teacher by her close communication with this family?

4. Consider any potential barriers that Maria should be aware of and ways these could be overcome.

Review Questions

1. List three benefits for children when parents and teachers work together as partners.

2. List three benefits for parents when parents and teachers work together as partners.

3. List three benefits for teachers when parents and teachers work together as partners.

4. Identify four factors affecting parents and teachers that may act as barriers to the development of effective relationships.

5. Describe four emotional responses that may impair the communication process.

6. List four external factors that may act as barriers.

Helpful Websites

- The National Coalition for Parent Involvement in Education (NCPIE) is a coalition of major education, community, public service, and advocacy organizations working to create meaningful family–school partnerships in every school in America.

- The North Central Regional Educational Laboratory (NCREL) is a nonprofit organization dedicated to helping schools and the students they serve to reach their full potential. This website for parent involvement offers literature reviews and database links.

- The National Education Association (NEA) website has many resources regarding parent–teacher relationships.

Foundations of a Successful Partnership

Learning Objectives

After reading this chapter, you should be able to:

6-1   Identify six attitudes or ideas of teachers that are conducive to forming a partnership with families.

6-2   Discuss concrete actions and environmental factors that are necessary in laying the foundation for a parent–teacher partnership.

6-3   Describe the six types of family involvement identified by Epstein that can be seen in an exemplary family resource center.

naeyc

Related NAEYC Standards

Accreditation Standards (see inside text back cover for full listing of the Accreditation Standards for exemplary early childhood programs):

1.A.03; 7.A.01, 7.A.05, 7.A.06 7.C.01

Licensure Standards (see inside text front cover for full listing of the Licensure Standards for this chapter):

2b, 2c

When administrators and teachers in schools have decided that reaching out to include families is an important part of their mission, they have taken a first step toward creating partnerships. Having made that decision, they can then design the policies and practices to work with families. Every program, responsive to what it knows about its particular population of families, will necessarily create methods of working with families that are unique; thus, many programs may look quite unlike each other in their approaches and still work well in their own situations. Therefore, it would be impractical and not very helpful for this text to set down one specific plan of action for working with families.

However, certain common elements can be found in any program that has some success in reaching families. Some of these include attitudes of the staff involved. Others include the external factors in the school that support teacher efforts. By exploring these common elements, we will be able to determine the essential ingredients of successful partnerships.

In this chapter, we will explore some of the attitudes, behaviors, and other factors that facilitate the formation of a productive partnership between families and teachers. We will also look at an exemplary model for creating partnerships in a center in Fort Myers, Florida.

6-1 Teacher Ideas and Attitudes

Jane Briscoe has become convinced that there are enough good reasons to merit really trying to form partnerships with parents. "Where do I start?" she wonders.

Research regularly points to the critical role of teacher practices and attitudes in encouraging and motivating parents' engagement in the educational process (Downer & Myers, 2010). Because a teacher acts as initiator in forming the partnership, the starting place lies in an examination of some essential teacher ideas and attitudes.

6-1a Concept of Professionalism

Basic to the formation of a parent–teacher partnership is a teacher's concept of **professionalism** and the professional teaching role. One traditional characteristic of professionals is keeping a certain distance between themselves and their clients to allow more objective professional judgments, emotional protection from too many client demands, and enhanced status. But this separateness precludes an uninhibited social exchange between client and professional. With the traditional definition of the professional, teachers see their relationships with families as a one-way process of informing parents and attempting to influence them. In such a relationship, families are passive clients, receiving services, depending on experts' opinion, in need of direction, and quite peripheral to the process of decision making. Such a concept implies that there is a deficit that the professional is trying to rectify—an idea that effectively makes shared understandings and responsibilities impossible. Inherent also in this stance is the idea that authority and power must rest with the professional: power *over* another. A partnership can develop only when teachers create a different mental concept of their role. When early childhood programs value relationship-based care, they understand "professionalism" in a new way, following a model that fosters caring connections between adults (Baker & Manfredi/Petitt, 2004).

professionalism
Display of professional character, spirit, or methods.

Teachers who can accept the partnership concept consider parents to be active members in making and implementing decisions regarding their children and capable of making major contributions. These teachers share responsibility and power, believing that teachers and families have strengths and equivalent, although different, expertise. Such a belief implies reciprocity in a relationship, with parents contributing as well as receiving information and services. Families are viewed not as a problem but as part of a solution to common puzzles; power is shared.

"Partnership models call for a move away from previous conceptualizations that portray people as in need of our expertise and educational efforts" (File, 2001). The belief in partnership is a prerequisite to everything else. It is a challenging idea for teachers to understand that having **expertise** is not necessarily the same thing as providing all the answers and advice to those who do not have the same body of knowledge as the professional. Sometimes, a more appropriate use of teacher expertise involves helping families find their own solutions to the challenges regarding their children. Families have their own knowledge—being the ones who best understand the goals and values they prize for their children, their own traditions, and their community and cultural norms. Teacher skills in identifying and drawing out that parental expertise are part of these new professional skills (see Figure 6-1).

CULTURAL CONSIDERATIONS

Cultural views about partnership

In fact, some cultures—particularly Asian cultures—would find this concept of partnership with a professional to be contrary to their understanding. In those cultures, teachers are so highly revered that parents would stand in awe of their expertise and be reluctant to engage in dialogue or make suggestions. Indeed, some teachers themselves have a cultural understanding of teacher importance that makes partnership difficult.

What are some suggestions for teachers who find themselves facing this dilemma of culturally defined professional separateness?

A partnership can be both exciting and anxiety producing because teachers who function as partners with parents are frequently in a position where so much is untried and without guidelines. But as partners, teachers trust that parents are capable of growth, and in demonstrating this belief, they grow themselves.

6-1b Sense of Self

Teachers who are most able to move into a **collaborative** partnership with families have a strong sense of self. "Developing collaborative relationships is not only a question of implementing some steps toward understanding each other when the potential for

expertise
Special skill or knowledge in a particular field.

collaborative
Working with one another.

misunderstanding arises but also a constant awareness of self and others (Kalyabpour & Harry, 2012, p. 19). Teachers learn to be in touch with and can effectively communicate their feelings. They are aware of their own strengths, weaknesses, concerns, and values; sure of their positions, they are not easily manipulated or threatened nor do they try to manipulate others through fear. Because they respect themselves, they treat others with equal dignity, relate as one individual to another, and avoid stereotyping. They are **authentic** to themselves.

Teachers must consciously clarify their values to understand themselves. When teachers find themselves in professional contexts that are not especially supportive of forming partnerships with families, their personal qualities and ability to reflect may allow them to break through barriers in relationships. As teachers identify their values, they also make opportunities for parents to consider and specify their own values. In a parent–teacher partnership, it is important for both to know themselves and each other and to also know the areas of agreement and disagreement in their value systems. It is not necessary or desirable for teachers and parents to attempt to convince the other of the rightness of their beliefs. What is desirable is for both to feel comfortable expressing their viewpoints.

As teachers believe in themselves and their abilities to create partnerships with families, they demonstrate a perception of **self-efficacy**. Defined as an individual's perception of personal competence, self-efficacy will determine how much time will be spent on an activity, how much time will be spent when obstacles are met, and how resilient the individual will be when faced with adversity (Vartuli, 2005). "High teacher self-efficacy relates significantly to increased levels of family involvement in conferences, volunteering, and home tutoring. Teachers with high self-efficacy are more likely to invite families to become involved in the classroom" (Vartuli, 2005, p. 78).

6-1c Humility

Another attitude of teachers related to the concept of partnership and to the new definition of professionalism is **humility**—the ability to wait, be silent, and listen. Teachers who do not make impossible demands on themselves do not expect to immediately understand each question or to have an instant response.

This is not just a pose of hesitancy but an ability to trust the outcome of the process of communication between individuals that is acquired only when teachers are able to dispense with some professional pretensions and keep truly open minds. This may be called **approachability**; it is demonstrated by behaviors that suggest "We're all in this together—what do you think?" (see Figure 6-2). Teachers with humility are able to step outside standard frames of reference and find creative, novel ways to work with families because they are not limited by believing that only the traditional methods will work. This allows teachers to take a nondefensive "why not" approach to parent requests. In this approach, parent requests are recognized as legitimate ideas to mull over rather than eliciting knee-jerk responses that "we just can't do that" or "our policies state" or even an automatic "yes." Hesitancy and humility result in thoughtful practices and increased trust from families that teachers are professionals who support empowerment and genuine partnership. The attitude of humility also allows teachers to keep on trying when some attempts to work with families have failed.

authentic
Genuine, real.

self-efficacy
Strength of one's belief in one's own ability to complete tasks and reach goals.

humility
Quality of being humble; lowering oneself in relation to others.

approachability
Capable of being approached; accessible.

FIGURE 6-2
The attitude and behaviors of approachability suggest real partnership.

6-1d Compassion

Teachers who can work in a partnership display compassion for themselves and for others. As they attempt to understand parents, they try to realize not just what they are thinking but also what they may be feeling (Figure 6-3). Such sensitivity is a first step toward the development of genuine mutual respect.

The ability to **empathize**—to truly try to understand the perspective and emotional responses of another—is a valuable ability for teachers working with families whose life experiences and motivations are often different from their own. For example, being able to take the perspective of another means recognizing that parents have emotional reasons for refusing to leave promptly after saying goodbye to their child, or getting upset when their children get dirty, or criticizing the school, or any one of many things that irritate teachers who do not attempt to recognize the family's perspective. By its nature, empathy necessitates removing the boundaries that teachers sometimes create around themselves.

There is no question that teachers will encounter families whose socioeconomic backgrounds, life experiences, and cultural values and mores are quite removed from theirs. Differences are guaranteed. So, most teachers must consciously reach out in genuine attempts to understand life from the viewpoint of diverse families—a perspective that they recognize is different from their own. At the same time, teachers must be mindful that *difference* is not synonymous with *deficit*; it is not the goal to encourage each family to adopt the values of the dominant culture. Compassionate understanding means learning about the other in a spirit of openness and acceptance. Chapter 13 will continue this discussion on specifics of teachers working with diversity and how understanding and acceptance help teachers and families.

A useful resource for getting started on raising awareness about differences that could separate teachers and parents is the work of Janet Gonzalez-Mena (2008). She reminds us that when teachers meet someone who obviously does not move in the same cultural framework that they do, they are jarred. An attempt to understand the ideas of parenting inherent in another's culture will lead to a more compassionate approach. As teachers take time to build relationships, to question their own beliefs and biases, to ask more and to assume less, they open the door so families feel comfortable in revealing themselves. Families communicate who they are to help teachers understand the specific knowledge that will best support that family. Understanding the facts of another's experience is still worlds apart from genuinely attempting to understand what experiences mean to them emotionally. Compassionate teachers attend sensitively to the unique reactions of each parent—no matter what the background.

Something should be added to this consideration of teacher compassion. It is often tempting for teachers to become overwhelmed by the complex needs and situations of some families and fall into the "Oh, isn't it awful" syndrome. These teachers can become too emotionally involved to retain helpful perspectives and move into trying to "fix" things for families. Compassion means the ability to understand that families may need the support and understanding of others while they learn to determine their own needs and seek their own solutions.

FIGURE 6-3
When teachers attempt to understand parents' feelings, they are better able to build partnerships.

"Some parents have a hard time letting go."

Used by permission of Keith Larson

empathize
To identify with or experience the feelings of another individual.

6-1e Respect for Others

Teachers who move into partnerships with families express a genuine respect for parents, for their position as the most important people in their children's lives, and for their accomplishments in child rearing. They respect the experiences, knowledge, and expertise that each participant brings to the situation. In so doing, they validate parents and themselves, finding areas of strength rather than of weakness. They also respect the rights of individual parents to define their own needs for the education and care of their children.

They convey this respect by treating families with dignity as individuals, listening to their needs, questions, and requests. It is too easy for teachers to begin to treat parents as "they" or "the parents," and not as individuals. When teachers create a "they," they usually use the annoying behavior of the least agreeable families to complain about with distant condescension. Leaving behind the "they" and coming to know and respect individual parents and families is a helpful stance for teachers striving for partnership. Teachers must try to find ways to meet the individual needs of parents. They may not always agree, but they still can convey the attitude that it is all right to disagree and that they can still work together.

FIGURE 6-4
Respect is shown in taking people seriously.

One teacher describes this attitude as the need to take people seriously:

> Whatever comment or criticism or suggestion a person comes up with, I must assume that it carries that person's individual and cultural perspective and deserves my respect. For example, a parent might say, "If she swears at adults, I want you to smack her face." Then I'd say, "It sounds like you really want her to learn to respect adults. I agree—that's important to me, too. I don't hit children, so maybe we can figure out something we can both agree on." And then we talk. I have to take the lead in finding common ground. (Hoffman, 1997)

The respect becomes mutual as families are encouraged to learn more about the teachers' and school's philosophy (see Figure 6-4).

6-1f Trustworthiness

Teachers consider the concept of being trustworthy for families so parents can build a sense of confidence in the choice they have made for their children's education and in those who are caring for their children. Building trust takes time and effort and is at the heart of comfortable, open communication. It is vital that teachers realize their behaviors can assist in this endeavor or detract from families' ability to trust.

Code of Ethics
Statement adopted by the National Association for the Education of Young Children (NAEYC) in 1989 (revised in 2005, reaffirmed and updated in 2011) to provide guidelines for ethical behavior of professionals.

First, teachers must consider trust building as a two-way street (File, 2001). The section on families in the NAEYC **Code of Ethics** describes the first ideal as "to develop relationships of mutual trust with families we serve." As well as professional commitment to being trustworthy *to* families, there must be a commitment to establish teachers' sense of trust *in* families. This means that teachers must assume that families generally know what is best for their children rather than thinking that if they just knew better—as the professional does—they would do things differently. It means setting aside the typical professional mistrust of families and sometimes also setting aside individual strong ideas. It means finding common ground instead of turning differences into battlegrounds and trusting that parents really care for their children with love that goes beyond professional concern and commitment.

Trustworthiness also implies complete teacher respect of families' rights to maintain their privacy. Often, teachers complain that parents do not tell them what is happening at home, implying that this information is the teacher's right in order to work more effectively with the child in question. In fact, teachers do not need to know all the details of a family's personal life to understand a child; generally, it is sufficient to know that a child is under some unusual stress to respond supportively. It is most likely that families do not share specifics of their personal lives precisely because teachers are not careful to indicate to families their complete respect for parents' rights to control what information they choose to share as well as the confidential way such information would be treated. As teachers gather in the lounge for breaks or in staff meetings for discussion, it is too easy to reveal information casually that ought to be kept purely confidential between teacher and family or even to gossip about assumptions rather than facts. Teachers should realize that they are professionally bound to keep information that families have revealed as completely confidential and then reveal information to others who need to know only after first gaining permission from the family. Except when the situation involves abuse or neglect, families deserve the right to trustworthy privacy.

Again, the code of ethics defines this principle for teachers:

P.2.13 We shall maintain confidentiality and shall respect the family's right to privacy, refraining from disclosure of confidential information and intrusion into family life. However, when we have reason to believe that a child's welfare is at risk, it is permissible to reveal confidential information with agencies, as well as with individuals who have legal responsibility for intervening in the child's interest. (NAEYC, 2011)

When teachers understand this ethical boundary, they carefully convey to families and colleagues their adherence to confidentiality. In addition, teachers should understand that they could be legally liable if evidence of breach of confidentiality were given. When teachers indicate that their relationship is governed by confidence, they often find that parents trust them with information more freely.

Families themselves demonstrate trust when they support decisions made by the schools and respond to overtures and communication from teachers and administrators.

To summarize, teachers trying to move into a partnership with parents must work toward the following ideas and attitudes:

- New image of professional role as partnership
- Strong sense of self
- Humility
- Compassion
- Respect for others
- Trustworthiness

6-2 External Factors for Successful Partnerships

A partnership between home and school has four elements:

- Creating two-way communications
- Enhancing learning at home and at school

- Providing mutual support

- Making joint decisions

All of these can be supported by several other concrete, external factors.

6-2a Administrative Support Systems

FIGURE 6-5
Administrative support helps teachers create partnerships with families.

Support systems are necessary for teachers striving to work with parents. Administrative support and leadership set the tone and atmosphere for involving families in a school. Support for family involvement needs to permeate the school from the top down; without wholehearted administrative belief in the importance of working with families, parents will not understand that their participation is a necessary part of the whole effort. Support may come in the following forms:

- A clearly stated philosophy in a family handbook that values and welcomes the contributions of parents in the educational process

- Training of staff so they will be knowledgeable in techniques of working with adults

- Assistance, motivation, and appreciation of staff efforts

- Providing fair compensatory time and staffing arrangements to support efforts

- Coordinating plans and strategies that emphasize family involvement throughout a school

Such support sanctions and gives power to teachers' efforts (see Figure 6-5).

It is important for administrators to realize that teachers need assistance and support to develop communication skills for working with families. If schools do not provide teachers with strategies and techniques for working with families, the recognition of the importance of home–school partnerships will remain purely rhetorical. Standards for degree programs declare that the skills for building family and community relationships are a required part of a college program of study (Hyson, 2003). Support and education to develop skills are vital components.

It is possible for teachers to create an atmosphere of partnership and involvement on their own, but when the administration of a school supports and recognizes those efforts, they are far more productive. In some instances, the administration actively discourages contact between teachers and families. If teachers choose to remain in such situations, their only recourse may be to work toward convincing the administration of the need to change its stance through (1) the positive experiences and proofs offered by research on the effectiveness of family involvement, as discussed in Chapter 4, (2) using community support and advocacy efforts (such as the NAEYC position statements on family involvement in quality early childhood programs), (3) legislative movements (such as the requirements written into the NCLB legislation for family involvement), and (4) enlisting the efforts of parents to press for their own involvement.

Even with administrative support, working with a cross section of families with individual needs, responses, and demands on teachers' time and energy can be stressful. Teachers can benefit from personal support systems, including colleagues and supervisors, offering the opportunity to recognize and vent feelings of frustration or strain and gain new ideas and perspectives. When teachers are part of working groups that encourage them to try new activities or experiment with new methods for communicating with families, they are more likely to take risks.

6-2b Communication Time

One of the most crucial components in the foundation of a parent–teacher partnership is time for teachers and parents to communicate freely together. Communication time with families may be made available by a flexibility in teachers' time options that fits parents' schedules, such as offering evening conferences, prearranged phone conversations, weekend home visits, and early morning coffee discussions. To have this flexibility, teachers should have their "after-hours" work compensated. When teachers are allowed compensatory time, this is a tangible indication of administrative support for their efforts. Additional staff members or staggered coverage may be required to cover this compensatory time as well as to free teachers to talk with parents at the times communication takes place—when children are dropped off and picked up. Because the frequency of casual communication has a direct bearing on the quality of a teacher–parent relationship, it is worthwhile to set up patterns in staffing arrangements and classroom planning and a variety of opportunities that allow teachers the freedom to talk (see Figure 6-6).

Teachers and schools can become advocates for businesses and employers to allow working parents the time to attend conferences and school functions. In some communities, the Chamber of Commerce has clearly stated that employers should support any efforts of parents to become involved in their children's education. Such a stance helps ease the problem of parent unavailability. Time may be an expensive commodity, but it is worthwhile to the effort of forming parent–teacher partnerships.

6-2c Variety in Family Involvement

Another factor facilitating parent–teacher partnerships is to offer a variety of forms of family involvement and communication. Generally, family involvement increases as communication from the classroom is continual and varied. A school reflects its understanding and responsiveness to the various needs of families by allowing parents to choose when, where, and how to participate. Flexibility in timing increases the variety. You will recall from Chapter 4 that families may be involved in a continuum of methods ranging from low involvement to high involvement. Offering a variety of ways of being involved in a school allows families to participate at a level that meets their current needs. A program ready to meet individual needs, concerns, and interests indicates respect for parents and their value within the program.

TeachSource

VIDEO ACTIVITY

© 2016 Cengage Learning®

After viewing the Video Case *Communicating With Parents: Tips and Strategies for Future Teachers,* consider these questions:

1. How do you see evidence of the administrator's support in this school?
2. What attitudes about family involvement do you perceive in the teachers' comments and actions?
3. What ideas from this chapter do you see reinforced in this video?

FIGURE 6-6
Teachers can find time to talk with parents when staffing patterns provide enough staff to watch children.

© Cengage Learning®

OPPORTUNITY FOR SELF-REFLECTION

If you are working or doing student teaching in a school, consider which of these external factors seem to be present to support the work of teachers with families. Can you also identify external factors that could be improved? What could be a starting step in moving toward improving these?

Someone within each school must take the time to find out what parents need and want as well as what they have to offer and are willing to share (see information about resource files in Chapter 10, and surveys in Chapter 11) and then evaluate the effectiveness of various methods of involvement. Asking parents for their evaluative feedback on particular plans and using suggestion boxes or other formats to encourage parent ideas about the program facets that would be helpful to them persuade parents to see the school as responsive to their needs. Such variety in family involvement opportunities allows parents to accept what is useful and reject what does not match their needs.

As discussed in Chapter 4, Epstein et al. (2009) suggest a framework of six types of involvement for parents, including parenting, communicating, volunteering, supporting learning at home, decision making, and collaborating with the community. Her emphasis is also on considering the challenges to teachers for facilitating each of the kinds of involvement and in redefining the practices available for parents. This is a reminder to provide variety not only in forms of involvement but also in practices responsive to parents' circumstances.

6-2d Information

For a constructive family–teacher partnership, clear understanding and knowledge of what is expected or possible in any school are required. Parents who clearly understand their responsibilities and obligations are more comfortable. Such routine encounters as conferences or home visits will not generate apprehension if parents are familiar with the procedures and their roles in them.

Many schools offer this information to families in the form of a family handbook, which is discussed as a parent receives orientation information and may be referred to later. Administrators and teachers understand that much that is presented orally may later be forgotten, so the reinforcement of written material is essential. A parent handbook should define the general philosophy and services of a program as well as the specific philosophy concerning family involvement, so parents understand the work of a school and how they can be involved. Information is needed regarding a program's policies that concern parents, such as admission requirements, the daily schedule, hours and fees, attendance policies, late pickup policies, health and safety regulations, and children's celebrations. Care must be taken to examine the center's policies to ensure they match the realities of today's families. Many handbooks include general information on the developmental characteristics of children and ways parents can help nurture development and learning.

TeachSource Digital Download

IDEAS FOR TEACHERS:

Parent Handbooks

A handbook may include information about the following:

- Methods used in the classroom and in reporting a child's progress
- Lists of supplies parents may need to obtain
- Ways parents may be (or are obliged to be) involved in a school's activities
- Dates of scheduled meetings
- Names and phone numbers of parent advisory committee members
- Facilities and resources for parents in the school, such as bulletin boards or a parent lounge
- Information about school support and resources for families
- Description of process for parents who wish to raise concerns
- A statement about confidentiality

The handbook needs to be concise, attractive, on a basic reading level, and clearly organized. It requires translation into every language represented by the school's population (see Figure 6-7).

See Figure 6-8 for evidence of parents wanting information, contact, and specifics about how they can help. Figure 6-9 lists the seven elements common in successful family involvement programs.

6-2e Family-Friendly Environments

School staff should take the time to look around the building with the perspective of a rushed parent or a tired grandmother. Does the environment suggest that families are part of the school and should linger for conversation, or does it suggest a coldly efficient institution where families are not meant to stay? The example of the excellent schools and infant-toddler centers in Reggio Emilia in Italy is instructive here. Each school is created with a central piazza, or meeting area, with comfortable seating for adults and interesting things for adults and children to see. With plants, photos, and attractive and intriguing displays of children's work, the environment welcomes families for relaxed greeting and transition times with children and teachers, exchange of information, and mutual enjoyment. When pictures and words are posted about children, their families, and the teachers who work in the school, the implicit message is one of welcome and the importance of all participants. When children's classrooms have areas with couches or stuffed chairs, plants, and soft lighting, tired parents may linger for conversation and opportunities to watch the goings-on.

FIGURE 6-7
Communication with families should recognize the diverse languages of the community.

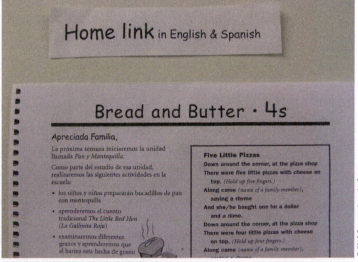

© 2016 Cengage Learning®

FIGURE 6-8
Informal surveys indicate parent needs for specific information.

What Parents Want to Know

Parents Want to Belong

- I want to belong.
- Welcome me to the school; do not shut me out.
- Invite me to school; take the initiative.
- Tell me how I can participate in school activities.
- I would like to be a member of an advisory council or parent involvement committee.

Parents Want Teacher Contact

- I would like my children's teachers to call me.
- Because I work, I need evening teacher conferences.
- Let me know what my children are studying.
- I want to meet the teachers at least once a month.
- Keep communications clear, brief, simple, and not overly technical.
- Contact me about good news, too, not just about problems.

Parents Want Information

- Tell me the philosophy of the school, the channels of authority, and the general goals of each subject studied.
- Tell me the best time to call the teachers, the names of the staff, and their telephone numbers.
- Send me a weekly or monthly newsletter that lists school events, community resources, and enrichment programs.
- I would appreciate parent-education workshops.

Parents Want to Help

- Give me ideas about how to complement what my children are learning in school.
- What are your expectations of my children?
- What can I do to help?

Parents Want Teachers to Love Their Children

- Do something to make my children feel good about themselves.
- Remind yourselves that you are an important influence in children's lives.
- If I complain about something, do not "take it out" on my children.
- Avoid stereotyping children and families.
- Care about my children.

TeachSource Digital Download

FIGURE 6-9
Seven elements common to successful family involvement programs.

Seven Elements Common to Successful Family Involvement Programs

- Written policies and a statement that identifies parent involvement as vital

- Administrative support in the form of funds, space and equipment, time, and personnel

- Training for staff and parents

- Partnership approach—joint planning and goal setting; a sense of ownership

- Two-way communication

- Networking with other programs to share information and resources

- Evaluation of effectiveness of parent involvement efforts

© Cengage Learning®

TeachSource Digital Download

IDEAS FOR TEACHERS:

Creating a Classroom Family Book

Offer parents opportunities to introduce themselves to one another by filling out pages to become part of a classroom family book. With photos, children's drawings, writings, or dictated words, the child's page might include his or her name and birthday and such things as:

- What I look like
- Something I love to do
- How I got my name
- What makes me happy

The family page could include spaces for:

- Who is in our family
- Something special about each person in our family
- Something we like about where we live
- A favorite family dish
- A favorite story we tell in our family

These pages could be added to the classroom family book and kept close to the couch or wherever families relax in the classroom. Such a method includes families from the start, creates a feeling of community, and sends nonverbal positive messages to children and their families of welcome and acceptance of all.

6-2f Communication Skills

Teachers attempting to create constructive partnerships with families need to develop their communication skills. Many teachers are fortunate to have opportunities to speak with parents frequently. However, frequency of communication does not guarantee increased understanding or improved relationships. Clarity may be lacking and

FIGURE 6-10
A teacher's communication style is important in establishing a comfortable relationship.

vocabulary may be different. Unless teachers are aware of different styles and purposes of communication, of how to communicate verbally and nonverbally, to listen and convey attentive caring, and to interpret messages from parents, miscommunication can create real barriers to a partnership (see Figure 6-10).

Some communication styles are almost certain to produce defensiveness: ordering, warning, blaming, advising, extensive questioning, being overly intellectual, and lecturing. Effective teachers learn to avoid these ways of talking. In addition, teachers should practice skills of listening and interpreting and of reading the behaviors in others that indicate how communication is causing them to feel. It is important for teachers to understand that cultural learning extends to daily communication.

Lee Canter, who has developed a program on communication skills for teachers (Techniques for Positive Parent Relationships), suggests that teachers who can communicate their concern for a child will be most effective in eliciting family support (Canter & Canter, 2000). He also suggests that teachers use assertive communication skills that do not apologize for, minimize, or belittle the parent's abilities and concerns.

FIGURE 6-11
Choosing the right words *is* important!

"*Excellent communication skills. Poor choice of words.*"

With experience, teachers will discover that some words convey different meanings to some families, and they will become more precise in their statements and descriptions. Teachers recognizing the social and cultural experiences of their listeners make adaptations accordingly and strive for unambiguous, descriptive words with no emotionally loaded connotations. They avoid professional jargon that may alienate or intimidate—such words as *cognitive, fine motor, and affective*. They paraphrase a parent's statements and their own interpretations—"What I hear you saying is"—to elicit genuine feedback from the parents to verify their understanding. They focus on parents' statements or questions to clarify their primary issues: "I'm confused about …" and "Could you explain that problem again please?" They use verbal reinforcers—"I see," "Yes," "Mmm," or the parent's name—to show they are listening and following what a parent has to say. They practice listening at least 50 percent of the time in discussions or conferences with parents. They realize that open-ended attempts to obtain more information—"Let's talk about that" and "I'm wondering about …"—are more effective than "who," "what," "how," and "when" questions that may feel threatening to the parent. They summarize for parents the ideas discussed (Swick, 2003) (see Figure 6-11).

Teachers need to remember that the verbal message they send accounts for only a small fraction of communication between people. Experts claim that facial expressions have the greatest impact on the receiver (55 percent of the message) and that the impact of voice tone is next (38 percent of the message), leaving only 7 percent delivered by words alone. What's more, in situations in which the sender's facial expression is inconsistent with the words (such as when a teacher says "I'm glad you could come for this conference" but her face shows apprehension or indifference), the facial expression will prevail and determine the impact of the total message (Knapp, Hall, & Horgan, 2013).

OPPORTUNITY FOR SELF-REFLECTION

As you analyze your own communication with others, what areas do you identify that need improvement? Consider the practical strategies you might use to work on your communication.

Eye contact plays an important role in opening or closing channels of communication. Looking at the partner in communication conveys the physical impression of listening, or of seeking feedback, or desire for the other's speech. Looking away may indicate a desire to avoid contact or hide some aspect of inner feelings or an attempt to process difficult ideas. (Although this generalization about eye contact may often be true, keep in mind that cultural factors affect the amount of eye contact offered in communication.) Teachers sensitive to the amount of eye contact offered by parents may be able to perceive when their communication is too painful or too difficult and can alter the message accordingly.

TeachSource

VIDEO ACTIVITY

Watch the Video Case, *Communicating With Families: Best Practices in an Early Childhood Setting.* As you watch the teacher, Mona, interact with the parents, reflect on the following questions:

1. Which of the teacher attitudes discussed in this chapter does Mona illustrate with her comments and philosophy?

2. Which of the teacher strategies for communication mentioned in this chapter does Mona use with her families? How does she avoid the barrier of time?

3. Reflect on the parents' response to Mona's efforts to create partnerships.

Other nonverbal communication for teachers to monitor in themselves and others that may produce effects of distance and discomfort include leaning toward (or away from) the other person; body language that conveys aggressive or closed stances; tone of voice similar to the other person; occasional head-nodding to indicate attention and approval; occasional gestures; smiles; and speech errors or higher speech rates that can indicate anxiety and uncertainty. Even a teacher's style of dress may send a message that could help or hurt the development of rapport.

Such nonverbal cues are sometimes missed if the receiver is inexperienced, temporarily not paying attention, preoccupied with his or her own internal messages, or from another culture where cues may have different meanings. People are likely to base their response to messages on their perception of the source rather than on the message content. Therefore, a prerequisite for effective communication is to relate to one another as individuals and avoid stereotyping. (For further exploration of communication techniques, particularly intercultural communication, the student is encouraged to refer to Ting-Toomey & Chung, 2011, and Martin & Nakayama, 2010.)

As we have seen, family–teacher relationships are complex things, uniting two sets of internal experiences, needs, and responses with two sets of external circumstances. Teachers who expect total success will be disappointed if they measure complete success as full participation by every parent. Parents have unique responses to family involvement opportunities—some families are reached in one way, others in another. And some may be reached at another time—after one teacher's efforts have long seemed to bear no result. So, the measure of success lies not in the numbers responding to any initiative but in the quality of interaction—not in total agreement but in continuing dialogue. Such extended contact allows the growth of comfort and communication as well as the acceptance of ideas. The teacher realizing this is less likely to become frustrated and abandon all attempts (see Figure 6-12).

FIGURE 6-12
Strategies for working effectively with families.

Strategies for Working Effectively with Families

Look for families' strengths and resources.

Identify families' coping strategies.

Build a partnership based on trust.

Listen more and talk less.

Suspend judgment.

Use colleagues and experts as sounding boards.

Build your own support network.

Reflect on your own behavior.

Admit and learn from your mistakes.

Change course when needed.

Write in a journal.

Learn about the family's dynamics.

Think flexibly.

Observe and reflect.

Show positive support for the family.

Interact honestly and authentically.

From Bennett, T. (2007). Mapping Family Resources and Support in Spotlight on Young Children and Families (D. Koralek, Ed.; pp. 20–3). Washington, DC: NAEYC. Reprinted with permission from the National Association for the Education of Young Children.

Consider the following example of a school that uses these principles to form effective partnerships with families.

6-3 Family Resource Center: Fort Myers, Florida

The name clearly states the intent with which this small center on the campus of Florida Gulf Coast University in Fort Myers was created. Planners of this newest member of the state university system in Florida were intentional about providing a resource to serve the campus families—primarily students of the university busy at their studies and work. Of the 40 infants, toddlers, and preschoolers enrolled in the program, approximately 75 percent are from families of university students, another 15 percent are drawn from families of faculty and staff, and the remaining 10 percent come from the community. Five positions are contracted with Head Start—again with priority given to student parents.

The center also serves as a learning and research environment for university students and faculty. Student interns, student assistants, and students volunteering through the service learning program contribute to the family feel by providing low ratios and opportunities for individual interaction. The family atmosphere is enhanced with just three classrooms: one for infants from six weeks through 18 months, where infants each have a primary caregiver; a toddler room for children aged 18 months through three years; and a preschool classroom for three-, four-, and five-year-olds.

The idea of partnership is explicit in the vision statement, adopted by the center staff and families: "… [A] place where a partnership between family and school creates an optimally safe, nurturing, and diverse learning environment, which all children deserve." See Figure 6-13 for the center's mission statement and goals; later in this overview, we will discuss the process of communication of staff and parents that created these documents.

FIGURE 6-13
Mission and goals of the Family Resource Center.

The mission of the Family Resource Center is:

- To promote the social, emotional, moral, cognitive, language, and physical development of each child by
  - Providing support and resources for families.
  - Forming and enhancing nurturing relationships between each child and teacher where each child is cherished for his or her own unique qualities.
  - Creating rich developmentally and culturally appropriate curriculum.
- To build partnerships with families through mutual respect, open communication, and opportunities for active participation.
- To facilitate interactions between and among families.
- To model, convey, and promote high-quality developmentally and culturally appropriate practices in early care and education to families, professionals, and the community at large.
- To create a nurturing and responsive environment that provides resources and supports the personal and professional growth of the Center staff.

© Cengage Learning®

Among the theoretical influences on the director working to implement the philosophy of family involvement in the center is the model of school/family/community partnerships drawn from the work of Joyce Epstein. (See again the discussion of the Epstein model of six types of family involvement in Chapter 4 and in Epstein et al., 2009, in the references.) Although use of the Epstein model has been primarily directed to school settings for older children, it is instructive to realize that the six kinds of involvement are what help make the Family Resource Center an example of productive efforts to create partnerships.

In the Epstein model, the first type of involvement is directed to supporting families with their parenting and child-rearing skills. Reciprocally, this type of involvement also helps schools to understand the unique families they serve.

The center's excellent website offers information to support parent education. There are several articles written by the director and staff, listings of books available for loan in the resource library housed in the multipurpose room, and links to other helpful websites for parents for information and local resources.

An accessible table in the entry area is supplied with magazines about parenting and ideas for family activities. Parents are encouraged to visit in the classrooms at any time, except the quiet time after lunch, and many do because of the proximity of the center to the university classroom buildings. Thus, parents are able to learn new ideas and strategies by observing skilled professionals interacting with their children. Such visits also promote conversations that help professionals learn about each family.

The second type of involvement in the Epstein model is communication. Many opportunities for communication have been created at the center. When parents enter, they must log in on the computer on the front desk before they accompany their children to the classrooms. Often, individual notes and general messages are posted there. Technology enhances communication in other ways. The attractive website includes much information for families, including the *Family Handbook*, with detailed information; the *Policies and Procedures* manual; an online tour; a short video showing the children and staff busy at activities in the center; and other essential information. Parents are given daily sheets detailing the activities of the children's day, and an e-mail copy is sent to parents who might not have access to this firsthand information, such as divorced parents. There are family folders in each classroom for parents to check each day; these contain the daily sheets and any personal communication from the teacher. Parents are also encouraged to leave their instructions and comments for the day in writing for later referral. Pagers are available to families at no charge and must, in fact, be carried by parents of infants so they can be contacted immediately when necessary. Each classroom has a separate telephone number, and parents are encouraged to call when they would like. Parents create and produce the newsletter; currently, faculty and student parents are collaborating on this effort.

Parent–teacher conferences are held twice each year. Teachers keep portfolios of the children's work, discussing them monthly with the children as they consider progress and special memories. These portfolios are shared with families at the conferences. Parents are asked to complete a survey with opportunities to describe things that they most appreciate about the day-to-day care and education their children receive as well as to make recommendations for future practices. Staff discuss these surveys at a retreat as they set goals for the coming year.

And most important, there is a good deal of talk. The friendly, informal atmosphere promotes a sense of community. A faculty father pauses in the university's cafe to share an anecdote from home with the director, and the director responds with her observation of his child from just that morning. Parents are reminded about confidentiality, and there is a sense of respect for all families.

Epstein's third type of family involvement is volunteering. When parents complete the application for the waiting list at the Family Resource Center, they check off this statement: "I understand that parent participation is essential at the Family Resource Center. If my child is enrolled in the center, I will agree to become actively involved in some manner. My participation will be discussed upon my child's enrollment." Parents have choices of action groups that include fund-raising, working on the newsletter or website, designing education and recreation programs, and working on policies and projects.

In addition, the center has a leadership team composed of two parents from each classroom, along with a teacher representative and the director. A representative from the leadership team is selected to represent the group on the board of directors. The leadership team and action groups plan events and projects and work with the director to support the center in various ways.

The volunteer parent participation shows! The outdoor wall of the center that faces the playground is currently adorned with a marvelous painted mural of the environment of Southwest Florida—complete with the kinds of vegetation and animals seen by the children daily. A Head Start parent—and also a talented artist—is creating the mural as part of her volunteer service learning. Parents and grandparents participate regularly in the classroom—often coming to accompany children on walks or join in activities with special visitors, such as the fire department puppet show. When children will be singing at a tree-lighting ceremony, parents meet them on campus to help walk the children there safely. Families contribute many items to the center, including extra clothing, books, and financial gifts to purchase classroom materials. Families share their family traditions and customs in the classroom. As the director describes it: "Every family makes its unique contribution. When nothing is set specifically, their contributions come from the heart."

Epstein describes the fourth type of family involvement as learning at home, where families work with their children on learning activities. Classroom teachers suggest home activities for the Head Start families. As the center compiles volunteer hours, they also tabulate these hours spent in home activities. Last year, the five parents involved in the Head Start contract accrued close to 500 hours spent in activities at home with their children. As families visit the classrooms, they learn strategies and activities they can use at home with their children.

The fifth type of family involvement from Epstein is decision making. As previously mentioned, families are involved in the leadership team, action groups, and board of directors. The mission/vision/goals statement was the product of full collaboration of parents and staff. Look again at the mission statement in Figure 6-13. Notice the wording of the second point under the first bullet. The director tells the story of how staff had worked separately on their mission statement and then met with families to continue to refine the ideas and language. As the group struggled over the word that should follow the phrase "where each child is," one mother suddenly exclaimed, "*Cherished!* It has to be cherished. That so exactly describes what happens between the teachers and children." And *cherished* it was. An important insight from the parent enhanced the overall decision-making process.

Finally, the sixth type of family involvement from the Epstein model is collaboration with the community; in this case, the community involves the university as well as the community. The contract with Head Start has enriched the population of the center, and its services have added opportunities for all the children. The community has been tapped for fund-raising as well as for programs about police and fire safety. Community grants have provided the lending resources and other supports. The center collaborates with the local child care resource and referral agency in family tuition subsidies as well as staff training.

As standards for quality show, it is not possible to provide excellent programs for young children without creating partnerships with their families. Using the Epstein model of the six various types of family involvement, it is clear that one of the reasons the Family Resource Center offers an excellent environment for growing children is the attention to creating partnerships with their families. The vision and clear mission statement of the Family Resource Center guide them to creating the kind of place where families can thrive.

For another description of effective partnerships created in an elementary and middle school, see the description of the Boxberry School and analyze the principles discussed in this chapter that are demonstrated:

THE BOXBERRY SCHOOL AND THE MIDDLE SCHOOL AT BOXBERRY: OXFORD, MAINE

What would schools be like when parents really want to be involved in their children's education? And what would it be like when teachers knew when they were being hired that they would be part of a close community, including families, students, and teachers? The answer to that is found in this small independent school in the foothills of western Maine.

Conceived by a group of parents and grandparents, Boxberry is a state-certified, independent elementary school for boys and girls, with multiaged classes from K–2 and grades 3–5. The school was established to be responsive to individual needs, nurturing the creative spirit of each child, with parents, grandparents, and community members taking the lead in creating the school. The newer middle school was established after a group of parents got together to create an affordable, alternative middle school experience for their children. Both schools develop curriculum based on the Maine Learning Results, integrated around themes (learning expeditions, as they are called in the lower school) that expand in response to the interests and enthusiasm of the students. Learning expeditions may last four to five months with the younger children and perhaps the whole year with older children and are followed by a presentation to families about the work that has been involved during that period.

The current learning expedition of the elementary classrooms at Boxberry is shelter. The direction of this study for one classroom has been yurts, including their origin among the nomadic tribes of Mongolia. They visited a yurt built in the community and worked collaboratively to build mini-scale models in the classroom, geometrically considering how specific shapes make up a shelter or structure. They have also read excerpts from a biography of a yurt builder.

In another classroom, the investigation in the shelter learning expedition began with the study of snake habitats, which then led to an interest in monarch butterflies. On a walk through the woods, they discovered some caterpillars and brought them back to the classroom terrarium. After a student-led investigation of the life cycle of the monarch butterfly, they were able to witness the hatching of two of the butterflies from their chrysalides. Another activity has been to replicate the houses built by the three little pigs and experiment with the wind of a fan to explore stability.

Middle school students last year explored the theme "Where Am I?" and learned a great deal about the geography, geology, history, and concepts about their community. This year, the theme is "food." This kind of challenging interdisciplinary project integrates reading, mathematics, science, social studies, and creative activities and incorporates the Boxberry principle that hands-on learning and field trips foster real-world learning and curiosity. The integrated curriculum is a key feature of the schools.

The other key principle is parent involvement. The curriculum evolves through the close interaction of families with the school. Parents help to brainstorm possible learning directions and resources within the community and accompany the children on the frequent field trips, providing transportation and expertise as appropriate. Parental expertise provides additional curriculum in the school, as parents teach in the areas of art, music, Spanish, health, and literature as well as afterschool activities.

Parental involvement of all kinds, says the Boxberry brochure, is at the core of the program and is a requirement along with tuition. A parent who has been involved in the school since its creation comments: "This is a poor community. For most families, it is hard to think about paying for school beyond the taxes we already pay." The middle school teacher agrees: "If parents are going to pay, at most schools they believe their role has finished when they write the check. That's not the way it is here. This is a parent-run school. If parents are going to send their kids to school here, they have to help run it. This is very different from the public school, where parents, especially middle school parents, are almost forbidden to participate."

Running the school involves decision making. In the middle school, one parent from every family is a member of the board—a system that will likely soon be adopted in the lower school, where the board currently has some elected parents as well as community members. Such participation helps parents develop more awareness of the financial situation of the school. At monthly board meetings, parents decide on school matters and also work on plans for fund-raising—a necessity for keeping tuition affordable. Although some scholarship help is available in the elementary school, middle school families pay the full tuition of $5,500 per year. Because most parents have no expertise in fund-raising, this has been a learning experience. There is a monthly fund-raising event in the community, with a Fall Harvest dinner, a yard sale, a pie sale, Christmas tree sales, and so on. The lower school has an annual "Dozer Days," where construction equipment is available to the community for rides and demonstrations, with paid admission raising most of the funds needed for scholarship assistance.

Parental involvement goes beyond decision making, fund-raising, and curriculum support. The volunteer signup list includes the following:

- Bulletin boards
- Shoveling snow from walks (this is Maine)
- Cleaning the entryway
- Tidying the bookshelves and game area
- Kitchen
- Refrigerator
- Contact with Hannaford's (the local supermarket)
- Contact with Walmart
- Lunch/recess duty
- Bathrooms
- Photocopying
- General maintenance
- Field trip organizer
- Newsletter
- Book orders
- Classroom assistance
- A volunteer coordinator

This list indicates that the Boxberry approach gives parents a down-to-earth way to be a part of their children's school and education.

Parents are in and out of the school on a daily basis. Because transportation is not provided, parents usually accompany their children into the school, pausing to talk with teachers and check their individual mailboxes. Sometimes, they linger to hang out on the playground. Such contact as well as the potluck dinners held every other month, which everyone attends, nurtures social relationships. The middle school teacher says: "We know all the parents so well, we become friends socially. We will be friends after the kids have moved on. This kind of involvement builds community." Community is also built as the older middle school children become Reading Buddies for the younger students. Soon, there will be families that have children in the elementary and middle schools, creating more linkages.

Formal contact with families includes conferences held four times a year in the lower school and three times in the middle school. The conferences include discussion of parents' goals for their children and ideas of what parents would like them to learn more about. Reporting includes written comments rather than grades. Parents and teachers frequently e-mail each other. Teachers in the lower school regularly write up summaries of academic experiences and achievements to provide a springboard for family conversations with children about school and offer suggestions of things to do at home.

The elementary grades offer opportunities for part-time students to participate. Pre-K children—or those not quite developmentally ready—may come on Monday, Wednesday, and Friday mornings. Children who are being homeschooled in the community may come for certain academics and enrichment activities. All this meets the individual needs for particular children and families and the community at large.

To answer the beginning questions about what schools are like when parents want to be truly involved in their children's education and when teachers know they will be working closely with families in a parent-run school, it feels as though there is an undercurrent of connection throughout. The Boxberry School feels like a comfortable home—a community of support for learning. This is quite an accomplishment, springing from the vision of some committed families—the stated philosophy of parent involvement—and offering an example of what exciting learning and strong relationships can offer to children.

From these accounts of two different schools, it is evident that there are multiple methods of working with families. The common thread is the philosophy that families deserve support and respect as they undertake the massive and vital tasks of parenting and that teachers can work most effectively with children when they work closely with families. Each school has worked to find the particular methods that best suit its program and its specific goals, needs, and perception of the needs of the families served. There are some things that work well; in general, methods of working to ensure the fullest communication possible are important. The challenge is always there as teachers and schools continue to reach out to the families they serve.

OPPORTUNITY FOR SELF-REFLECTION

As you think about the schools described in this chapter and others you have encountered, what elements support positive teacher interaction—no matter what the structure, curriculum, or administration of the educational program? In other words, what attitudes and philosophy can you make part of your own practice wherever you teach?

SUMMARY

Specific attitudes are basic to forming a collaborative relationship with families and include:

- New image of professional role as partnership
- Strong sense of self
- Humility

- Compassion
- Respect for others

Concrete steps can be taken and skills can be developed to help lay foundations for parent–teacher partnerships:

- Administrative support to provide collaborative philosophy and tangible assistance with staffing arrangements and time provisions as well as emotional support systems for teachers
- Time created by allowing teachers to interact with parents at crucial points in the workday and compensating them for offering flexible options for parent involvement beyond normal working hours
- A variety of forms of family involvement, allowing parents to select where, when, and how to participate
- Clear explanations of policies, expectations, and openness to welcome families into the educational program
- Family-friendly environments
- Developing and practicing effective communication skills

These components of Epstein's theory can be found in a successful family involvement program:

- Support in parenting
- Communication
- Volunteering
- Learning at home
- Decision making
- Collaboration with the community

Student Activities for Further Study

1. Contact several schools in your community. Ask for copies of handbooks or printed materials for families, and look at the schools' websites. Examine the material to discover any stated or implied philosophies of working (or not working) with families.

2. With your classmates, work on creating a parent handbook that clearly conveys information parents want to know and the attitude of welcoming families into specific participations. (Each student might take on a segment after the necessary information and format have been decided.)

3. With your classmates, generate a list of words, such as those discussed in the chapter on page 160, that might convey different meanings depending on the cultural or environmental experiences of the receiver.

4. Imagine you are a teacher beginning employment at a school. What kinds of guidance, support, and training do you feel you need to become comfortable and capable in areas of working with families? How might you go about getting this assistance? What could you ask for from a supervisor? What questions might you ask a more experienced colleague?

5. When possible, observe a teacher you feel works well with families. What personality characteristics and behaviors do you see? What do you notice regarding the teacher's nonverbal communication?

Apply the Chapter Concepts: Case in Point

Jose Martinez is a second-year first-grade teacher. As he reflected on his experiences in working with families during his first year, he felt dissatisfied. Some parents responded to his overtures to communicate regularly with him via e-mail, and others never responded to any phone call or newsletter that he sent. The number of absences at PTA meetings had puzzled him. Some parents had not even come to the required parent–teacher conference in January. He would like to establish better communication with his families this year and wonders if he will have a better group of parents with whom to work. His colleague— the other first-grade teacher—seemed to have better success than he did.

1. What personal attitudes should Jose consider to create the atmosphere of welcoming communication with families?

2. What questions might he ask the other first-grade teacher to learn how she achieved her greater success in building relationships?

3. What techniques or strategies might help Jose set the tone for forming partnerships?

4. What might Jose discuss with his supervisor in terms of necessary supports for his work with families?

Review Questions

1. Identify three out of six attitudes of teachers conducive to forming a partnership with families.

2. List six external factors important in laying the foundations for partnerships with families.

3. Identify the six Epstein methods of working with families found in exemplary schools.

Helpful Websites

- Visit the site for NAEYC for more on the code of ethics and confidentiality.

- The website for the U.S. Department of Education has much information about involving families in their children's education.

- Check out the websites for the Family Resource Center in Fort Myers, Florida, and for the Boxberry School in Oxford, Maine.

CHAPTER 7

Good Beginnings with Parents and Children

© Cengage Learning®

Learning Objectives

After reading this chapter, you should be able to:

7-1 Identify several steps helpful in establishing a relationship prior to the child's entrance into the classroom as well as benefits and strategies for each step.

7-2 Describe the separation experience for children and parents, and discuss a teacher's role.

Related NAEYC Standards

Accreditation Standards (see inside text back cover for full listing of the Accreditation Standards for exemplary early childhood programs)

1.B.05; 7.A.02, 7.A.06, 7.A.08, 7.A.09, 7.A.10, 7.A.11

Licensure Standards (see inside text front cover for full listing of the Licensure Standards for this chapter)

2b, 2c

Nothing is more exciting or nerve wracking than a child's first day in a new school situation. Children face the challenge of leaving the security of parents and home in order to move into the company of a group of peers, new routines and activities, and a relationship with a new adult. Families experience ambivalence as they mark another milestone of development in their children's lives, insecurities with regard to the decision they have made about the school, and the uncertainties of their own roles as they help their children move into the classroom. Teachers have the excitement of meeting new children and families and the challenge of making sure all the relationships get off on the right foot. With young children, understanding the normal separation process and being able to support parents and children as they undergo the experience is crucial for teachers as they begin to form trust and communication patterns that are the foundation for meaningful relationships. This chapter considers the initial steps to establish a partnership between home and school as well as among parent, teacher, and child. (For the purpose of clarity, in the discussion in this chapter, unless names are used, we will assume the teacher is female and that the parent and child are both male.)

Although separation is not usually a consideration when older children begin new relationships with teachers each year as they move from grade to grade, there are still important considerations for teachers who want to establish comfort and communication with students and families right from the start.

7-1   Establishing Positive Relationships Right from the Start

Some strategies may vary from school to school, but the principles of getting off to a good start are unchanging. Teachers of older children should consider how to use and adapt the ideas in this chapter to achieve good beginnings with children and families. First impressions can have lasting significance. Early attitudes and behavior patterns will determine later limitations on a relationship or what direction it will take. Families and teachers who begin working together with particular expectations and understandings are likely to continue in that mode. Because it is often difficult to change patterns of behavior once they have become habitual, it is important to involve teachers, parents, and children in a program of gradual orientation, information exchange, and increasing familiarity. No matter what children's ages, new school experiences are crucial steps for them. If these steps are facilitated by the adults around them, it is to the children's benefit and therefore indirectly to the benefit of the adults. Between the time when parents first contact a school and the time when their young children finally settle in is an important period for teachers to lay the foundations for successful family involvement. An orientation process has several purposes:

- To make a child's transition to school as easy and pleasant as possible

- To demonstrate to families that they are welcome in the educational program and can learn to feel comfortable there

- To help parents understand the school's goals and practices

- To give teachers a chance to learn from parents about a child and the family situation and to learn their concerns and goals for their children

Whether a child is entering a family child care home, an early childhood or Head Start center, a school that includes children with special needs, an afterschool care program, or a new elementary school classroom, the beginnings are still critical in establishing comfortable communication and patterns of partnership. We will use one of our case study families and teachers to consider some ideas to involve families, as Connie Martinez first meets Sylvia Ashley and Ricky. Although this describes the situation in a child care program for preschoolers, teachers who work with older or younger children will find principles they can *adapt* to their setting. In any situation, time and family circumstances may dictate modification of these ideas, but teachers striving for effective relationships with parents and children will see them as a goal toward which to work.

7-1a Choosing a School

The first contact between families and a school is generally initiated by parents in their search for an appropriate facility for their child's care. (An obvious exception to this is when children are assigned to a particular school in a school district. Here, parents often have no choice in the matter, and it is up to the school and teacher to give families an appropriate welcome and information about the school and plans for the year so parents can be pleased with an assignment in which they had no choice. However, with the NCLB legislation, parents in many more school districts and communities are finding themselves able to make choices.) Usually represented by the director or principal, the school has the dual responsibility of encouraging families to make the most appropriate educational choices for their children and sharing information about the school's philosophies and practices so parents can see if this particular school matches their needs. In initial phone calls, interviews, or tours of the school, the focus should be on the family and what they want for their child. Thus, the initial conversations focus on relationships instead of taking care of business only, and they lay the foundation for ongoing partnerships. Information concerning parental responsibilities and opportunities for participation should also be included at this time.

FIGURE 7-1

The school's obligation is to give families the information they need to make thoughtful decisions about their child's education.

In selecting a school for the early years, parents need to consider more than the usual consumer issues of convenience and cost. If this is their first experience in early childhood education, they may not yet be aware of the variations in educational philosophy, practices, and parental rights and involvement that exist in preschools within any community, as well as the variety of choices that may exist within their school system. Some child advocacy groups and schools offer parents a guide for questions and a checklist for observations to emphasize their key role in making this decision. In many cases, parents feel panicky about finding care for their children in time to begin employment, and they are willing to assume the best, rather than closely examine and evaluate situations. When they are driven by desperation or lack of knowledge or money, many parents are quick to accept the unacceptable. The task of early education programs is to give families the information they need to make thoughtful decisions and encourage them to see their responsibility in making them (see Figure 7-1). Figure 7.2 is a sample checklist for parents that can be adopted for any school.

FIGURE 7-2
Sample Guide for Parents

Sample Guide for Parents

	YES	NO
THE STAFF		
Are staff members friendly and enthusiastic?	_____	_____
Do staff members seem to like and relate well to the children and to each other?	_____	_____
Are staff members required to have special training in child care?	_____	_____
Is there a staff in-service training program and other opportunities for continuous skill development?	_____	_____
Are parent conferences held regularly?	_____	_____
Do staff members welcome questions and inquiry?	_____	_____
THE PROGRAM		
Are teachers required to make daily lesson plans?	_____	_____
Is the daily schedule posted?	_____	_____
Is the program schedule balanced between active and quiet periods?	_____	_____
Are there varieties of materials and equipment ready for use and accessible to children—indoors and out?	_____	_____
Do children have choices about activities?	_____	_____
Do the activities foster the children's physical, social, intellectual,and emotional growth?	_____	_____
Do the children know what to do?	_____	_____
Do the children receive individual attention from the caregivers?	_____	_____
Does the center have a policy on discipline?	_____	_____
Do you agree with it?	_____	_____
Are records kept about children and their development?	_____	_____
Are snacks and meals nutritious and well balanced, with menus posted?	_____	_____
Are the parents linked to the daily life of the program?	_____	_____
THE PHYSICAL SETTING		
Are there comfortable, relaxed areas for resting and naps?	_____	_____
Is the center bright, clean, comfortable?	_____	_____
Are the outdoor and indoor areas safe and free from hazards?	_____	_____
Is there enough space for free, easy movement?	_____	_____
Does the setting allow for group and individual activities?	_____	_____
Does it provide possibilities for privacy?	_____	_____
Is there appropriate, clean equipment for different age groups?	_____	_____

THE PHYSICAL SETTING

Quality care provides:

- A caring, pleasant atmosphere
- Care by an adequate number of well-trained caregivers
- A program that responds to each child as an individual
- Experiences that facilitate exploring, skill development, and learning
- Support for, communication with, and involvement of parents

Consider what is best for your child. If you are not satisfied with the care found, continue your search. You are the parent: The choice is up to you.

Adapted from Child Care Resources, Inc., Charlotte, North Carolina

Programs also have a responsibility to try to understand families' needs and values. The NAEYC has developed five brochures to help parents consider **developmentally appropriate programs**: *A Caring Place for Your Infant* (#548); *A Caring Place for Your Toddler* (#509); *A Good Preschool for Your Child* (#517); *A Good Kindergarten for Your Child* (#524); and *A Good Primary School for Your Child* (#579). Also see the websites listed at the end of this chapter.

> **developmentally appropriate programs** Programs that base their decisions about curriculum, care, routines, and guidance on knowledge about development of individual children and the needs of their families.

In many schools, parents are invited to observe a teacher in action with her present class before deciding whether to enroll their children. Such a practice sends two clear messages to parents: (1) The school respects their judgment and obligation to know exactly what arrangements they are making for their children. (2) The school is proud of what it does and wants parents to see it for themselves. Families are justified in being suspicious of a program where such visiting is not encouraged or allowed.

It is preferable to enroll a child whose parents have carefully considered the issues important to them and their child, matched them with all the available options, and can now choose a particular school on the basis of meeting needs. Too many decisions are based on cost alone. Schools for young children have a responsibility to help families realize the full extent of their decision-making role. Once parents choose a school, their next contact moves beyond the administrator as general spokesperson to meeting the specific teacher(s) with whom their child will begin.

Let us look at the beginning for Sylvia Ashley and Ricky.

In Sylvia Ashley's case, social services had suggested the center for Ricky, and Sylvia went to look it over and talk to the director. As always, she had Ricky with her. "We're delighted that Ricky will be entering our school, Mrs. Ashley. Because he'll be entering our group of three-year-olds, let me take you down to meet Connie Martinez, our lead teacher in that class. Then, you two can find a convenient time to get further acquainted."

7-1b First Encounter—Teachers and Parents

The first conversation between parents and a teacher is best scheduled when parents can come without their child. Parents will be free to talk without concern for their child's response in a new situation, and a teacher can concentrate on helping parents become comfortable without her attention divided between adults and child. This is ideal, of course, and teachers will adapt to realities.

Sylvia had told Connie that she had no one to leave Ricky with, so Connie was not surprised when Ricky walked in with his mother. Connie got two puzzles, a book, crayons, and blank paper and helped him settle in a corner distant enough that he could see his mother but not overhear the conversation. As Connie thought about this later, she realized it was the first time she had ever conducted the first conversation with the child present. It certainly was far from ideal, but she had at least had some time to talk freely with this new mother.

This first meeting has several purposes. One is to permit a parent to share initial information about an entering child. Many schools ask families to fill in a questionnaire about their child's social and educational history. Parents may fill this out at home and bring it to the meeting. In practice, if teachers and parents talk their way through a completed questionnaire, parents often supply additional information in a more easily remembered way. Consider the sample questions for teachers to ask parents, as shown in Figure 7-3.

As parents talk, teachers can gain an impression of the relationship between parent and child, how a child has reacted in other new situations, and how parents feel about enrolling their child in the program. This establishes a precedent of cooperation and of sharing information, with families making important contributions and teachers listening. Teachers can also use this opportunity to acquire family resource information so they

TeachSource Digital Download

FIGURE 7-3
Sample Questionnaire Information on Routines

EATING

- As a rule, is your child's appetite excellent, good, fair, or poor?
- Does your child eat alone or with the family?
- List your child's favorite foods:
- List foods that your child especially dislikes:

SLEEPING

- Approximate time your child goes to bed:
- Approximate time your child wakes in the morning:
- Your child's attitude at bedtime:
- Usual activities before your child goes to bed:

Elimination

At what age was training started for:

- Bowel control _____ Response to training:
- Bladder control _____ Response to training:
- What words does your child use when stating the need for elimination?

Language

- What language do you speak to your child at home?
- Are any other languages spoken at home or in your family?
- How comfortable is your child speaking in new situations?

OTHER INFORMATION

- What do you enjoy most about your child?
- How does your child usually react to new situations?
- What activities does your family enjoy most?
- Has your child been separated from either parent for a long period?
- If so, how did your child react?
- What things repeatedly cause conflict between parents and children in your family?
- Is your child happy playing alone?
- List the ages and genders of your child's most frequent playmates:
- List your child's favorite activities:
- Is there something that your child has just learned that is important to him or her?
- What would you like your child to get out of this year's program?
- Does your child have any medical conditions we should be aware of?
- Is there a favorite friend or relative your child might talk about—real or imaginary?
- What does your child do when upset, and how is he or she best comforted?
- Does your child have fears or worries that we should be aware of?

© Cengage Learning®

FIGURE 7-4
Knowing this child loves play dough helped the teacher get her off to a happy start.

© 2016 Cengage Learning®

can plan for involving families in the classroom. When asking questions, teachers must let parents know how this information will be used and assure parents of the confidentiality of their communication.

Many ideas discussed in this initial conversation may be helpful in increasing a new child's comfort in the first days in school (see Figure 7-4).

"I see here that you mentioned Ricky likes to sleep with a favorite teddy bear. Do you suppose you could bring that along to leave in his cubby for naptime? It might feel good to have something so familiar. Pictures of you and his brother to put in his cubby might help, too."

This first meeting allows parents to ask specific questions about the classroom:

"Yes, there are four other boys who have entered the classroom quite recently, so he won't be the only new one."

"Well, our morning snack is really a hot breakfast, served about 9 each day, so if he doesn't eat much in the early morning at home, he won't have to wait too long."

Parents can help prepare their child for becoming comfortable in the classroom if they have accurate knowledge about what will happen and what to expect.

The first meeting also allows parents and teachers an early chance to get to know each other on a one-to-one basis.

CULTURAL CONSIDERATIONS

Names and titles

Teachers should be aware of cultural differences in the use of names and titles. Some families may be uncomfortable using first names. Some families might want their child to say "teacher" without a name, as an appropriate sign of respect in their culture. By all means, teachers should discuss names and titles with families, and assess their comfort.

"You're going back to school—good for you! That's great. You'll certainly be busy, but I'll bet you'll find it's worth it when it's all over. I'm taking some classes at night, too, so we can complain about it together."

This is a good time to establish clearly what teachers and parents will call each other. If this subject is never discussed forthrightly, there is often awkwardness, with the result that neither calls the other anything.

"Most of the parents call me Connie, although the children call me Miss Martinez. Then, may I also call you Sylvia? Are you comfortable with that? I'm just more comfortable with first names."

During this time, a teacher can inform parents about the rest of the orientation schedule, fix a time for the next visit, and discuss separation patterns that children and parents frequently experience. This establishes the precedent of a teacher casually informing and educating as well as empathizing with parents.

"It's a good idea to get Ricky started a week or so before you have to start your classes. You know, we find a lot of our three-year-olds take a couple of weeks or more to feel comfortable letting Mother leave. Please feel free to stay in the mornings as long as you can, but if he's upset when you leave, don't worry—we'll give him lots of special attention. I know it's hard for mothers, too, but we'll help each other along."

By raising the issue of separation in advance, a teacher gives parents the opportunity to prepare themselves and their children for the transition. Many teachers find it helps to give parents a handout on separation to consider later at home. See Figure 7-5 for a sample handout for parents covering separation.

TeachSource Digital Download

FIGURE 7-5
Handout for Parents on Separation

Handout on Separation

We know that you want to help your child get off to a good start in beginning school. Young children often experience difficulties with separation from their significant adults in new situations. They may cry or cling or behave differently than you are used to. Be assured that this is a typical, normal response and that these behaviors will slowly stop as children (and you) get more comfortable with the new situation. Some things you could do to support your child at this time are:

- Accept and respect your child's temporary unhappiness. Say things such as, "I know you're feeling sad when Dad leaves, but you will have a good time, and soon, you won't be so sad."

- Give yourselves enough time in the morning. Children often get anxious when rushed.

- Have pleasant conversation as you travel about some of the things your child enjoys about preschool.

- Remind your child of the predictability of your pickup arrangements, tying your return with an event, such as after naptime, and then arrive when you have said.

- Establish a pattern of what you will each do when you enter the classroom each day.

- Encourage your child to do as much as he or she can independently during the arrival process—for example, if your child is old enough, walking into the classroom him or herself.

- If you can stay for three or four minutes, help your child find an activity to focus on.

- After you have said you will go, make your goodbye prompt, affectionate, and positive. Do not ever be tempted to sneak away while your child is occupied.

- Have your child's teacher step in to help with goodbyes when you give the sign that you are ready to go.

- Avoid the temptation to pressure your child not to cry or to offer bribes for "good behavior." Learning to cope with sadness is important for your child.

- Let the teacher know if there are particular routines or objects that bring comfort to your child. The teacher will be helped by this knowledge.

- Understand that the process of learning to trust new people naturally takes time. The teacher will be glad to discuss your concerns with you; together, you can make plans to meet your child's needs.

© 2016 Cengage Learning®

FIGURE 7-6
Teachers may hold group orientations for parents.

© 2016 Cengage Learning®

Studies show that parents' verbal explanations are the most important influence in how well children adapt to a new situation.

In situations in which a school starts an entire new class of children at the same time, such as in kindergarten, elementary school, or afterschool child care situations, it works well to have an orientation meeting for all new parents to cover the common information all will need (see Figure 7-6).

A good video for such a group orientation for kindergarten parents is *Kindergarten, Here I Come!* by Educational Productions (2001). This lets a teacher offer information to the entire group and enables parents to meet each other right from the beginning. It can be reassuring to talk to other parents and find they are not alone in their concerns about leaving their children in a new environment. Such an initial meeting allows teachers to get parents of elementary-aged children on their side by talking about plans for the year and how the parents can get involved to support their children's learning. Because this

TeachSource Digital Download

IDEAS FOR TEACHERS:

Beginnings In Elementary Schools

To get off to a good start, elementary teachers can try doing the following:

- Send a personalized postcard or welcome letter to every student.
- Make a phone call to each child.
- Have an open house event for children and families as an orientation to school.
- Plan a welcome parents meeting. Ask each family to complete a questionnaire to help learn about children's interests, hobbies, and strengths.
- Hand out copies of daily schedules, menus, and contact information, providing copies in home languages.
- Call parents after the first day of school to let them know how things began.

meeting will not allow individual conversations about particular children, teachers can have a signup sheet for later telephone calls. While group orientation meetings may give welcoming information and a positive beginning to the relationship, individual meetings between parents and teachers offer opportunities to gain specific information about a child, answer personal questions a parent might not raise in a group, and establish the parent-teacher relationship.

So, this first brief meeting of parents and teacher establishes the patterns of relaxed communication and of mutual informing and asking—all important for the working relationship to grow.

7-1c First Encounter—Teachers and Children

It is best if the first meeting between child and teacher can occur where the child is most comfortable—at home. Whenever a child has to get used to a new concept, such as school and new adults caring for him, he can adjust when fortified by the security of familiar people and surroundings. This first visit, scheduled at a family's convenience, may be brief—15 minutes or so—but the child will have a chance to briefly socialize and observe his parents doing so. One teacher likes to read a children's book to the child and then later have it available when the child visits the classroom as a tangible link to that first visit. Others bring photo albums of the classroom to create interest in coming to play there. Some leave a video for child and family to enjoy after the visit and ask that it be returned to school. Others take pictures of the child and family to place in the child's cubby as a reminder of home and family. Any teacher who has experienced such an initial home visit will remember the comfort this gives children timidly entering a new classroom and recognizing an already familiar face: "You've been to my house." Children's feelings of security are enhanced by seeing that their parents and teachers are forming a relationship (see Figure 7-7).

FIGURE 7-7

When children meet teachers for the first time in their own homes, they are more comfortable.

© Santiago Cornejo/Shutterstock.com

Parents are also reassured by watching a teacher's sensitive approach when children are timid. When teachers speak quietly and get on children's eye level (being sensitive to cultures where eye-to-eye communication is not respectful), parents recognize that their children are being treated as special people. Parents pick up on that caring feeling and are appreciative that someone has taken the time to help their child feel comfortable. Increasing numbers of elementary school teachers are making initial home visits. (Home visits are discussed further in the Appendix.)

The brief visit also offers a teacher a glimpse of the parent–child relationship and a child's home learning environment.

Sylvia had been reluctant to have the teacher make a visit to their apartment, but when Connie explained it might help Ricky feel more comfortable with her (so far, he would not speak to this stranger), she agreed. Connie scheduled the brief visit for late afternoon, after learning Ricky's big brother would be home. And that did help. Terrence talked to the teacher and encouraged Ricky to show her their bedroom. Ricky smiled and waved goodbye when she left.

When home visits are absolutely not possible, a teacher can write a letter to the family and include something special for the child—perhaps her photo. This can be a tangible tie for the child and this new person.

TeachSource

VIDEO ACTIVITY ▶❚❚

© 2016 Cengage Learning®

View the first 2 minutes and 35 seconds of the video clip, *Partnership with Families: Home Visits*. After viewing, reflect on these questions:

1. How do the teacher's comments support the ideas about initial home visits from the chapter?

2. What are the benefits to children of initial home visits, noted by the teacher?

3. Note the emphasis on family along with children in these home visits. Why is this important?

HOME VISITS FOR FIRST ENCOUNTERS

- Are at the invitation and convenience of the family
- Are brief, social events
- Are focused on the child–teacher interaction
- Are used to bring or take materials to create a first home/school link
- Are opportunities to invite parents to talk about their children's strengths and interests
- Are opportunities to begin building comfort and to learn about each other

---

7-1d First Visit to a Classroom

During a home visit, a teacher can arrange a time for a parent and child to visit the classroom. It is best if a child can visit before first coming to the classroom to stay. This visit also will be brief—a chance for a child to see and become interested in a new environment (see Figure 7-8).

Ricky and his mother came to visit in midmorning—two days after the home visit. He said hello to Connie and let her show him around the room. He especially liked the big fire truck. When the other children came in from the playground, he clung to his mother but watched intently. He turned down the invitation to come to the table for juice but joined his mother when she sat near Connie and drank juice. He nodded when Connie told him that next time he could stay longer and play with the fire truck.

TeachSource

VIDEO ACTIVITY ▶️❚❚

© 2016 Cengage Learning®

Watch the video entitled *Creating a Family Friendly Environment: Beginning of the Year Practices.* [http://ceng_ca_post.vpg,com/cen1/cen1_case13_orc1_v1.mov]

After viewing the clip, reflect on these questions:

1. Consider which of the practices discussed in this chapter are illustrated in the video clip.
2. Discuss how the various strategies will help parents, teachers, and children.
3. How do the parents in the video respond to the teacher practices?

FIGURE 7-8
When children have the opportunity to visit the classroom with their parents, they can get comfortable enough to get excited about returning.

It is sometimes overwhelming for a young child to enter a classroom full of other children busy with activities. For this reason, it may be a good idea to schedule this visit when children from the classroom are outside, playing in a gym or another area with another teacher, or at the end of the day when fewer children are present. Then, a child is free to be welcomed by the teacher he has met, shown that he will be a part of this classroom (having a cubby with his name and picture on it is a good idea), and given a chance to investigate the toys and equipment. It may work well to have a visiting child join the group briefly for a snack or cup of juice. He can then enjoy the eating experience and have a chance to see other children without being called on to participate.

Ideally, the parent stays in the classroom during this visit, offering the child a secure base from which to move and sharing pleasure in new discoveries. Parental concerns may be allayed by observing the teacher and child interact and seeing how the classroom functions. This visit gives the parent specifics to discuss at home to continue to prepare the child for this new experience.

Introductory school visits are important. If necessary for the family's schedule, the visit could be at 7 a.m. or at 6 p.m. to allow the parent to stay the entire time. This step is too important to skip. A visit is in the child's best interests and, ultimately, in the family's, even if it is inconvenient.

If an entire class of entering children is new, teachers may schedule brief opportunities for a group of five or six children to come in for "tea parties" and a chance to look around the classroom. Breaking a class down offers teachers a chance to interact with each child while saving teacher time (see Figure 7-9).

(see Figure 7-9)

FIGURE 7-9
It is helpful when the teacher has time to interact with individual children.

7-1e   Child's Entry into a Classroom

The groundwork is laid for a child's entry into a classroom. Teachers and parents need to remind themselves how much there is for a child to become accustomed to in a school experience: the "hows" of interacting with a large group of children; the new rules and practices of a classroom; leaving parents and becoming comfortable with another adult. (Teachers should let parents know that children facing all this may act out afterward in the secure environment of home.)

Because these adjustments can be exhausting for a child, it is helpful if his first days in a classroom are as abbreviated as possible, allowing for the family's schedule. For example, if a child is beginning a full-day child care program, it is helpful if he is picked up at the end of the morning for several days and then slowly extend the schedule to include lunch, nap, and then the afternoon. Even older children entering a new school situation may show signs of exhaustion and stress initially. Children entering a half-day program will benefit from attending for half the morning at first. A school that enters its whole class at one time can shorten the entire schedule for the first week or so, gradually extending from one hour to three hours. The people most inconvenienced during this **easing-in** period are parents, so it is important

easing-in
A schedule of gradually increasing the amount of time a child spends in a classroom so the child does not spend a full period at the beginning.

TeachSource Digital Download

IDEAS FOR TEACHERS:

Helping Children Adjust to a New Classroom

Consider creating a handout to offer to parents who are helping their children adjust to a new classroom. Here is an example:

You're Welcome to Stay Awhile!

As you and your child get used to life in our classroom, feel free to stay if you can. Here are some things you could do:

- Help your child develop a morning routine of putting things in the cubby.
- Find the child's name tag and move it to our "We're Here" board.
- Wash hands in the bathroom.
- Look around at each interest center to notice new materials.
- Go say good morning to our fish Henry.
- Choose a book and read to your child and any other child who wants to join you.
- Say goodbye and leave without lingering when you are ready—teachers will help your child say goodbye.
- Feel free to call or stop back and see us later in the day when you have time.

FIGURE 7-10
There is much to get used to in this new school environment, such as pouring your own milk.

that they understand the rationale for this approach and its benefit for their children in building feelings of comfort and security (see Figure 7-10). Some schools offer a place where parents can have a cup of coffee during these shortened days, waiting and conversing with other parents. Other family members, such as grandparents or older siblings, may be able to assist during the easing-in process if parents' work schedules are inflexible.

Teachers should make every effort to accommodate family needs and pressures by modifying steps and timing and at the same time explaining the importance to the child of the visits and easing-in. Many parents will find the time, even if they did not originally believe they could do so, or find another family member who can help during this period if parents are not free. Nevertheless, some children will be left "ready or not." For children whose parents cannot or will not stay, teachers should do what they can to help trust form. They may send preliminary notes or talk on the telephone. Teachers may suggest that the family bring transitional objects and pictures into the classroom. If teachers believe this process is important, they will convey this impression to families.

After the teacher suggested it, Sylvia had decided to let Ricky stay for two mornings before she left him for the whole day. The first morning, he cried hard as she left; Connie encouraged her to stay a little longer if she wanted, but she just hurried away, feeling a little sick herself. He was very quiet when she went back to get him before lunch, but after his nap, he told her and Terrence a little about playing with the fire engine. The next morning, he cried for about 10 minutes, but as she stood in the hall, she heard him stop. The third day, she and Terrence went together to get him after his nap. Connie said he had had a hard time falling asleep, but she had rubbed his back until he drifted off. Sylvia was starting to think Ricky might be all right.

OPPORTUNITY FOR SELF-REFLECTION

If you have had opportunities to work with families in any capacity, think about your first encounters. What seemed to work well as you got to know each other? What would you do differently next time?

Parents as well as children need special attention during this transition time. A teacher's evident concern and specific comments do much to further a sense of partnership as she takes the time to communicate with families before and after school (see Figure 7-11).

Every day when Sylvia came back to get Ricky, she looked eagerly for the teacher. Connie always tried to leave the children with her assistant briefly and come to tell her what Ricky had played with and how he seemed to feel.

Through the orientation process, no large amount of family time is spent; most of the visits are half an hour or less and can be worked into a parent's employment schedule. For a teacher, this time can be scheduled into a normal teaching day, with coverage from an assistant. The adults need to realize the priority of a child's growing security and try to fit in as many steps as practicable. In addition to a child's security, it is important to set patterns of teachers and parents working together in home/school transitions and discussing a child's needs. As they work together, parents and teachers will get to know each other and start to build trust that will help in the future—a good beginning for all.

FIGURE 7-11
Parents and children need special attention during beginning times.

"You know," says Sylvia, "Ricky is going to get along all right at the school. I really like the teacher; she's helped me a lot to get used to things. I won't have to worry so much."

7-1f Transitions Within Schools

Attention should also be paid to the new relationships and comfort that must be built when children move from one classroom to another within a school. Often, schools offer helpful initial orientations for children and families but neglect to recognize that change within the school should also be approached with sensitivity to the feelings involved in changing relationships. Often, children or adults resist a change, and the resistance comes precisely because time and thought have not gone into a gradual transition. Appropriate transitions may include the following:

- Advance notification to the current primary caregiver at school and family that change is approaching

- A conference between the new primary caregiver and the family

- Current and new caregivers developing a schedule for the transition process, which may take a month or so depending on the child's age and response

- A visit to the child in the current classroom by the new caregiver

- A visit by the child and the current caregiver to the new classroom

- A gradual visitation schedule for the child to participate in the new classroom and then return to the current classroom

- Gradual participation in routines of the new classroom: mealtime, naptime, and the like

- Regular communication (telephone or face-to-face) among the parents and current and new caregivers about the child's response to the transition process

- A written report that details the process and reactions of all involved

- Opportunities for children to maintain contact with beloved caregivers left behind (Baker & Manfredi/Pettit, 2004)

Attention to everyone concerned will allow relationships and communication to flourish.

© Cengage Learning®

7-2 Dealing with Separation Experiences

The emotional responses to a new school experience may be heightened by the **separation anxiety** experienced by most children and parents. The mutual parent–child attachment, developed during the early years of a child's life, means that adult and child feel more secure in each other's presence. A removal from each other's presence causes concern and changes in behavior for both.

separation anxiety
Feelings of sadness and discomfort experienced by children and adults when apart from one another. Separation anxiety is most common in children under four years.

What behaviors are expected of children experiencing separation? Many children up to age three or so will cry and be sad when a parent leaves. Even older children may find the initial leaving difficult. Sometimes, this sadness continues off and on for a good part of the day; some children continue this pattern of crying for weeks or, occasionally, months. A child may come in quietly in the morning and then begin to cry later (see Figure 7-12). Such delayed reactions may occur days or even weeks later. Some children find times like mealtime or naptime particularly hard as they are reminded of home routines. Many children experiencing separation difficulties cling to a teacher and participate little. Separation problems are also demonstrated by an increase in dependence or disruptions and changed behavior patterns at home, such as resisting bedtime, out-of-bounds talk with parents, new and assertive ways of behaving, and "games" that play on parents' guilt. Some children demonstrate regressive behaviors, reverting to thumb-sucking, bed-wetting, or other earlier behaviors. And some children exhibit "very good" behaviors—no signs of upset; just controlled passivity. School-aged children may show their anxiety about a new situation by complaining of symptoms of "school phobia," including stomach upsets and headaches as well as irritability and fatigue at home.

FIGURE 7-12
Children may come in quietly and then begin to cry later in the morning.

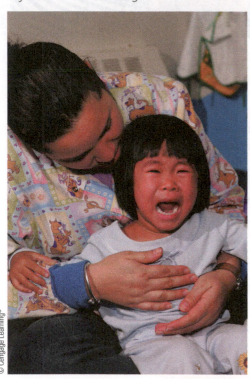

These behaviors are considered usual for a child experiencing separation, and the duration of the behaviors varies with each child. Although they require special considerations, the behaviors are not cause for alarm. Teachers need to be matter of fact in their expectation of these behaviors so they reassure parents of their normalcy and temporary nature. Experiences, circumstances, and temperaments are different for each child. Children who have rarely been left by parents may react quite differently from those who have had lots of babysitters or group encounters. The child who approaches each new situation with zest and enthusiasm may leave parents without a backward glance, whereas the child who is slower to warm up in new situations may appear unhappy for quite some time. Most young children have this period of stressful adaptation to supplemental child care away from their parents. But once they understand that regular separation from parents does not imply their loss, the problematic behaviors subside (Gray, 2004).

OPPORTUNITY FOR SELF-REFLECTION

Consider separation experiences you have had in your life. Recall, if you can, your first beginnings in a school setting or in staying away from home overnight. What feelings can you identify? How did you express these emotions? How did adults around you respond to your feelings? If you are now a parent, recall the first time you left a child in the care of another person. What were some of your concerns? Remembering personal experiences often increases teachers' ability to empathize.

Parents often have a difficult time with separation, too (Merrill, 2010). This is a time of ambivalent feelings: satisfaction that their child is more independent, fear of becoming displaced in their child's affections, and sadness at the changing status in their relationship. Parents may feel concern that their child no longer needs them and jealous of the person he appears to need. They may be concerned about how their child is cared for in their absence and about this change being too disruptive to their child's life and their own, as evidenced by upset behaviors (see Figure 7-13).

FIGURE 7-13
Parents may linger to be sure their child is going to cope in their absence.

© 2016 Cengage Learning®

> *"Look, I thought it was going to work out fine at this center, but now I'm not so sure. Janie screams every morning when I leave and clings to my neck. I can hear those screams all day. I'm afraid of her changing; she's always been such a happy child. And I worry—I wonder whether anybody's looking after her when she's so upset. I miss her, too. But I'd hate to think I was one of those clinging mothers who can't let their kids go."*

A parent may be struggling with more than his own separation feelings. A first-time parent may still be negotiating the developmental task of becoming a new parent—totally responsible for another human being. If he is beginning a working situation, he may be feeling great pressure for his child to adjust to the care situation as quickly as possible. Getting his child adjusted is not an option; it has to work!

A teacher is in an important position to help parent and child deal with separation emotions and behaviors. The aim is for a teacher to remember that she is doing not just what works best but also what best strengthens a child. Teachers' attentions need to be directed to parent and child because the way they treat the child affects the parents, and the way they treat the parents affects the child. Some basic strategies follow.

7-2a Prepare Parents for Separation Behaviors

Prepare parents in advance to accept separation behaviors and emotions as normal. Parents are more open about their concerns if they realize that a teacher is not judging their child or themselves negatively for experiencing separation anxieties.

Information about separation, such as shown in Figure 7-5, should be a component of every orientation packet and interview. Discussing possible behaviors and feelings and helpful strategies ahead of time prepares parents for what may happen and how they can best support their child.

> *"Most children Janie's age have a hard time at first saying goodbye to parents. We expect it. You're the most important person in her life, and it will take a while for her to realize she can be fine when you're gone. In fact, though they don't show it as freely as children, most parents find this a fairly major adjustment, too. I'll be here to help you both however I can. These are concerns we'll talk about each day."*

7-2b Welcome Parents into a Classroom

Help parents feel welcome to stay in a classroom as long as this is helpful to a child. Some teachers have found it helpful to prepare a handout for parents suggesting some things they could do in the classroom during those first few days (as seen in the Ideas for Teachers box). Parents and children may benefit from not having a rushed goodbye in the morning, by slowly helping a child get interested in the classroom activities, and by having a parent

CULTURAL CONSIDERATIONS

Expression of emotion

It is important for teachers to realize that expression of emotion is one behavior that has big cultural connotations. Some children (and their parents) have been taught from birth not to demonstrate or express feelings. Some parents may punish or shame their children for crying or otherwise showing tears or upset. Some parents will also interpret their children's emotional reactions as signs of disobedience to parental wishes. Rather than impose teacher understanding of how best to support separation behaviors, it is important that teachers learn about the cultural expectations held by the children's individual families. This suggests the importance of teachers adopting the posture from the beginning as learners, understanding children's home and community practices. Asking how their child feels when separated from the family may be a good conversation starter to determine parents' responses to emotional issues as well as to learn whether children have even experienced separation. Many children from Hispanic backgrounds will not have experienced separation until beginning school because their care may have been shared among members of the extended family. Emotional responses and separation experiences are hugely determined by culture, and teachers will benefit when they learn this from families.

In his classic book *Beyond Culture* (1981), Edward Hall talked about the world being divided into those cultures that prepare their children to be independent individuals—in effect, cutting the apron strings—and cultures that do not emphasize independence and prepare their children to remain closely tied to the family instead. Teachers need to learn the cultural values that are important to beginning families.

see his child receive a teacher's attention. This approach will help a parent feel a part of his child's school world.

Creating a cozy corner near the entrance—perhaps a loveseat and small table with a few curiosity items, such a music box, a rain stick, minerals with magnifying glasses, or family photograph books—might help give parents and children a few pleasant moments together before departure.

"Janie, maybe you'd like to show your mommy the puzzle you did yesterday."

"We've got some nice, soft play dough on the table over there. Maybe that would be fun to do together for a few minutes."

"Perhaps you'd like to find a book to read together before you say goodbye."

Parents look to teachers for cues about what their role should be in helping their children settle in. As teachers provide directions to families, parents will be able to act confidently with their children. Allowing a child to decide when parents should leave the room— "Shall Mom go now or after our story time?"—may help a child experience self-confidence.

Teachers can help parents and children plan together for the next day's parting and move toward establishing a regular morning routine.

"The two of you might like to decide before you come tomorrow whether she'll give you a hug at the door or after she's put her things in her cubby."

Some classroom teachers help children develop the fun ritual of "pushing" their parents out the door; once again, the children feel a measure of control in the goodbye.

In general, teachers must let parents know they will follow their cues concerning their desire or ability to stay. But an alert teacher picks up on the times a child is ready to move away from his parent who is lingering—perhaps due to his own needs. Here, a teacher can help a parent leave.

"Mrs. Smith, since Janie's starting to play, it might be a good time to tell her goodbye. You and I can watch her from outside if you'd like."

Helping a parent create **parting rituals** may especially help those parents who linger and seem determined not to leave in any clear fashion. As some teachers note, "It's almost as if they can't leave until they have seen the child get upset." This may indeed be so, although likely at an unconscious level. In these cases, teachers should reassure parents of how important they are to their children—help the parent notice the child's delight when the parent returns at day's end. This is a place for empathy—understanding how much these parents may need comforting themselves (see Figure 7-14).

It is important that teachers make decisions regarding the timing of actual separation in such cases, where a child's readiness precedes a parent's. When parents are feeling ambiguous and shaky, they may need or appreciate such help. However, when a parent is unable to respond to such a direct approach, it is probably an indication that the point of personal readiness for separation has not yet arrived, and teacher patience and support are necessary. It is also important for teachers not to become impatient with the process and arbitrarily set their own time limit. "Two weeks is long enough for any child or parent to get used to this!"

Should parents stay away? Some children do not seem to need their parents' presence at times of transition as much as others do, although they are usually quite agreeable to their presence in the room. However, there are also children who get so habituated to a particular pattern, such as parents staying at school, that it becomes even harder for them when their parents finally do leave. Parents of these children might do well to concentrate efforts at home to prepare for the leave-taking. The best policy seems to be one that would allow parents to stay as long as is necessary and helpful to the child. Teachers and parents will need to discuss individual children's characteristic responses to decide on the best plan.

An important concept for teachers and parents to consider is that parents must see their own anxiety as separate from that of their child's; in other words, the reactions of a parent may not be identical to a child's feelings, and it is important not to project those feelings onto a child. It can set up long-lasting problem patterns if a child learns to give a parent a demonstration of his reluctance to be left before a parent feels satisfied that he will be truly missed. A parent may be more able to deal with personal emotions with an awareness of whose problem it is.

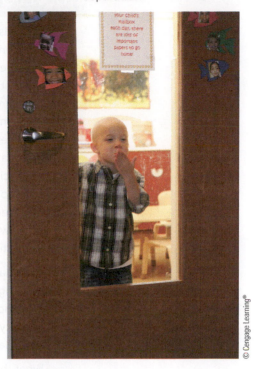

FIGURE 7-14
Creating a parting ritual, such as blowing a kiss at the door, may help ease separation.

© Cengage Learning®

parting rituals
Expected behaviors and activities repeated each day when saying goodbye.

7-2c Develop Children's Trust in Parents

An important step in a child's working through the separation process is to learn to trust that parents will reliably leave and then return. Teachers may need to help parents become aware of behaviors that can foster this sense of certainty.

Although it may be less painful at the time, it is not a good idea for parents to slip away unnoticed while a child is distracted. A child left in this way cannot help but become a little dubious about a parent's trustworthiness. Teachers can help parents realize the

WHAT DOES BRAIN RESEARCH TELL US ABOUT SECURE ATTACHMENT AND BRAIN DEVELOPMENT?

Science tells us that the brain is most plastic for the first two years after birth. During this time, the primary caregiver acts as an "external psychobiological regulator of the experience-dependent growth of the infant's nervous system" (Malekpour, 2007). These early social events are imprinted into the neurobiological structures that are maturing during the brain growth, and thus have long-term effects. Specifically, the early maturing right brain is dominant in the first three years of life. This area of the brain is involved in processing social–emotional information that facilitates attachment functions, as well as regulates affective states, enabling the individual to cope with stress. The maturation of these right-brain capacities is experience dependent, and this experience is embedded in the attachment relationship between the primary caregiver and the infant. Thus, there is a direct link between secure attachment and development of right brain structures with regulatory functions, with resultant adaptive infant mental health, or the opposite, a negative effect on these structures and functions.

The relationship between interpersonal events in early development and a later capacity for change is due to the direct impact of the early social environment on the maturation of the limbic system—the brain areas responsible for the organization of new learning and the capacity to adapt to a rapidly changing environment. Thus, early interpersonal events have long-lasting effects.

What this means is that a responsive, nurturing environment that allows the infant and young child to develop strong attachments to a few caregivers enables the child to build neural connections within the brain that encourage emotional stability—obviously a factor when entering into new situations and relationships.

1. Discuss the relationship between the child's first attachments and later adaptation to new situations, such as entering child care or school.
2. How is attachment theory related to separation experiences?
3. Consider some practical implications of this information for supporting children and parents at the beginning of a new school experience.

need for a definite leave-taking and not allow "sneaking out." Repeated, predictable good-byes strengthen children's beliefs that parents will come back (Balaban, 2006).

"I know it bothers you when she cries as you leave, but it's really better for her in the long run to know she can rely on you to go and come just as you say you will. I'll help her say a quick goodbye to you."

In the same way, parents may not realize the importance of picking up a child at a predictable time. Even a short time elapsing after a parent's expected arrival will seem like a very long time to the child. It is best for parents to equate their return with a scheduled event and absolutely keep to it, especially during this transition time (see Figure 7-15).

"After you eat your snack, I'll be back to get you."

"Remember, Sally, your dad told us this morning that he'd come back to get you after snack. I know you're missing him. Come with us while we have our story, and then we'll be getting ready for snack."

7-2d Discuss the Separation Experience

It is helpful to discuss and validate the emotional responses to separation openly, with empathy. Such an approach frees child and parent to realize that their feelings are recognized and accepted and can continue to be communicated. Keeping "stiff upper lips" is too costly in terms of emotional health.

"I know you're sad when your mom leaves, Janie. It's a little scary, too. But I'll be here to look after you until she gets back, and we can have a good time, too."

"It will take a little while to get used to our classroom, but I'll help you—and so will your new friends."

"Most parents have some pretty mixed feelings about their children starting off in school. It can be kind of sad and scary, I'm sure."

Small touches can demonstrate to parents and children a teacher's empathy: a midmorning phone call to let a parent know that his child who was screaming when he left is now playing happily with play dough; an extra minute to share the day's events fully with a returning parent; talking with a child throughout the day about what he will have to show Daddy when he returns; taking dictation for a note the child would like to write to an absent parent. Yeary (2013) speaks of promoting *mindfulness*—using strategies that keep a child connected to her family throughout the day, so that children understand that loved ones care for her all the time, and even when not present, they are held in their parents' minds. All of these can show children and parents that teachers are there for them and that they can listen, understand, and help.

Teachers who understand separation anxiety and its manifestations will not become irritated or offended by the behaviors of children or parents. They will not take the tears or anxieties personally—as indications that their classrooms are not good places. They will not scold crying children nor ignore the tears and sadness. They will enter empathetically into the child's experience, attempting to feel the fears that they feel. They will understand that time and support will solve most separation problems.

FIGURE 7-15
It is important to a child's sense of security to be picked up on a predictable schedule.

7-2e Special Attention to Parents and Children

Special attention to parents and children is warranted at this time. Teachers may choose special children's books about separation and new experiences to read to children or lend to parents for home use. For ideas, refer to the Books about Starting School and Separation box.

BOOKS ABOUT STARTING SCHOOL AND SEPARATION

Ahlberg, J. & A. *Starting School.*

Albee, S. *I Don't Want to Go to School.*

Amoss, B. *The Very Worst Thing.*

Aseltine, L. *First Grade Can Wait.*

Baker, C. F. *My Mom Travels a Lot.*

Barkan, J. *Anna Marie's Blanket.*

Barkin, C., & James, E. *I'd Rather Stay Home.*

Berenstain, S. & J. *The Berenstain Bears Go Back to School.*

Berger, T. *A Friend Can Help.*

Bizen, B. *First Day in School.*

Blue, R. *I Am Here: Yo Estoy Aqui.*

Boelts, M. *Little Bunny's Preschool Countdown.*

Bram, E. *I Don't Want to Go to School.*

Brand, J., & Gladstone, N. *My Day Care Book.*

Breinburg, P. *Shawn Goes to School.*

Bunnett, R. *Friends at School.*

Burningham, J. *The Blanket.*

Burningham, J. *The Friend.*

Calmenson, S. *Late for School!*

Chalmers, M. *Be Good Harry.*

Civardi, A. *First Experiences: Going to School.*

Cohen, M. *The New Teacher.*

Cohen, M. *See You Tomorrow, Charlie.*

Cohen, M. *Will I Have a Friend?*

Coles, A. *Michael's First Day at School.*

Cooney, N. *The Blanket That Had to Go.*

Corey, D. *You Go Away.*

Crary, E. *Mommy Don't Go.*

DeGroat, D. *Brand-New Pencils, Brand-New Books.*

Delacre, L. *Time for School, Nathan!*

Eastman, P. *Are You My Mother?*

Elliott, D. *Grover Goes to School.*

Harper, J. *A Place Called Kindergarten.*

Harris, R. *Don't Forget to Come Back.*

Henkes, K. *Owen.*

Hill, E. *Spot Goes to School.*

Hines, A. *Don't Worry, I'll Find You.*

Howe, J. *When You Go to Kindergarten.*

Hurwitz, J. *Rip-Roaring Russell.*

Johnson, D. *What Will Mommy Do When I'm at School?*

Kantrowitz, M. *Willy Bear.*

Lionni, L. *Little Blue and Little Yellow.*

London, J. *Froggy Goes to School*

Mannhein, G. *The Two Friends.*

Mayer, M. *Frog, Where Are You?*

Milord, S. *Happy School Year!*

Molnar, D., & Fenton, S. *Who Will Pick Me Up When I Fall?*

Moncure, J. *A New Boy in Kindergarten.*

Oh, J. *Mr. Monkey's Classroom.*

Park, S. *Sumi's First Day of School Ever.*

Penn, A. *The Kissing Hand.*

Rogers, F. *Going to Day Care.*

Rockwell, A. *My Preschool.*

Siegers, L. *Kevin Goes to School.*

Simon, N. *I'm Busy Too.*

Smath, J. *Elephant Goes to School.*

Soderstrom, M. *Maybe Tomorrow I'll Have a Good Time.*

Sperring, M. *Wanda's First Day.*

Stiles, N. *On My Very First School Day I Met …*

Stoeke, J. *The Bus Stop.*

Sturges, P. *I Love School.*

Tompert, A. *Will You Come Back for Me?*

Warren, C. *Fred's First Day.*

Wells, R. *My Kindergarten.*

Wells, R. *Timothy Goes to School.*

Wild, M. *Tom Goes to Kindergarten.*

Wingest, S. *Tucker's Four-Carrot School Day.*

Wolde, B. *Betsy's First Day of Nursery School.*

Yolen, J. *How Do Dinosaurs Go to School?*

For more titles, a good reference to consult in the library is *Books to Help Children Cope With Separation and Loss* by Joanne E. Bernstein (R. R. Bowker Co.).

They may stay close to children, holding their hands at transition times, holding them on their laps when they are sad, and talking with them often (see Figure 7-16). Teachers should talk about what will happen next in the classroom and where parents are now. They may hold monologue-type conversations, not pressuring children to respond. They may write notes from children's dictation to the absent parents; this helps ease the children's feelings and shows that teachers can listen and help. They will encourage children to hold a transitional object from home or parent—holding Mom's scarf is reassurance that she will return. All of these techniques help children learn that teachers are there for them and that sadness is accepted and can be channeled into work and play. They will make opportunities for parents to tape record brief messages to leave in the classroom for children to listen to and encourage parents to bring family photos to school for a special book or to hang in the child's cubby.

© Ingrid Balabanova/Shutterstock.com

FIGURE 7-16
Teachers will stay close to children who are experiencing sadness.

Sometimes teachers are concerned that this special attention to a new child will short-change the other children. It is useful to remember that individualizing responsive care for children means not always giving the same thing to all the children at the same time. The other children likely do not have such acute needs at this time. Furthermore, they are learning valuable lessons about compassion, feelings, and adult trustworthiness. Teachers may call parents during the day with positive information to reassure them: "Jon has a new friend. He's been playing in the block corner with David all morning." They may send pictures by e-mail of the child involved in activity and include a note describing the activity and naming the children playing with their child. Other teachers suggest giving parents a written outline of the day's activities on the first day they leave their children so they can check the schedule and imagine what their children are doing. Gartrell (2000) suggests that all teachers make a telephone call at the end of the first day. Certainly, in elementary or afterschool situations, this could begin the relationships that so often are not established. All these gestures indicate to parents that teachers care enough to make sure they are being included in these first adjustments. Teachers must try to empathize with some of the mixed feelings that parents have when their children begin their first school experiences.

Some teachers find that in order not to foster dependence, some of this special attention and support can be supplied by pairing a new child with a special friend—someone who has already adapted to the classroom and has a personality that would enjoy helping nurture a new child. A new parent can be introduced to a parent who has weathered the stress of separation. But dependence is less of a concern than fostering feelings of comfort and confidence.

All beginnings are important. The long-term effects of establishing parent–teacher relationships with clear patterns of empathetic communication as well as a child's successful adaptation justify taking these careful steps.

SUMMARY

Ideally, good beginnings include the following:

- A meeting with a school's administrator to consider what a parent is looking for in a preschool and how this matches a school's philosophy and practices.

- An introductory conversation between a parent and an individual classroom teacher. Specific information about a child and classroom is exchanged. Further orientation plans are formed.

- A brief home visit so a teacher and child can meet on a child's secure home base.

- A brief visit of parent and child to a classroom—specifically planned for a time when a teacher is free to interact with the child.

- An easing-in schedule so a child can slowly adjust to classroom life on less than a full-time basis.

- Carefully planned transitions when children move to new classrooms within a school or the community.

It is important for teachers to recognize and help with separation issues by doing the following:

- Prepare parents to understand and recognize separation behaviors.

- Welcome parents to stay as long as is helpful for children.

- Help children develop trust in parents and the situation.

- Discuss the feelings of separation.

- Give special attention to both parents and children.

Student Activities for Further Study

1. With your classmates, role-play the following situations, with one of you being a teacher who is trying to get to know, support, and establish a relationship with a parent who is enrolling a child in your center:

   a. The parent says the child has never been left with anyone else in three years.

   b. The parent seems very reluctant to answer any questions about the child.

   c. The parent asks if she can stay until the child stops crying—"It may take a while." The parent seems very tense.

   d. The parent says he really does not have time for the teacher to visit or have an extended conversation with the teacher or allow the child to visit or "ease-in."

   e. The parent seems frightened of the teacher.

2. Role-play the following situations, and have your "audience" discuss a teacher's role in helping parent and child during separation stress:

   a. A teacher with a parent whose child is screaming and clinging to the parent's neck; the parent started a new job two days ago.

   b. A teacher with a parent whose child is screaming and clinging to the parent's neck; the parent starts a new job next week.

   c. A child says goodbye happily; the mother stands at the door looking very sad.

d. Two hours after the parent left, the child begins to cry and says, "I want my daddy."

e. The parent begins to sneak out while the child is distracted with a toy.

3. Ask several parents how they chose their early childhood programs. Did they visit? Were they were looking for any particular features? What convinced them this was the place for their children?

4. Look at the information forms that parents fill in at your school and several others. Do the forms really allow the parents to begin to share their particular knowledge of their children? What additional questions might be helpful?

5. With a partner, plan the beginning activities for orientation of children and their families to a fourth-grade classroom. Write a beginning letter and list any other materials used.

Apply the Chapter Concepts: Case in Point

Isabella Sanchez, age four, is the only child of a single mother, Loretta. They share an apartment with another family that also recently emigrated from the Dominican Republic. Loretta is beginning a training program for data entry, which she hopes will lead to full-time employment. Neither Loretta nor Isabella speaks much English. Loretta has enrolled her daughter in a family child care home in her neighborhood.

Isabella did not speak and she hid her face when her mother went to the home to make the initial arrangements.

1. Put yourself in the position of the child care provider. What are some of the issues to which you need to be sensitive in beginning relationships with Isabella and her mother?

2. What plans would you recommend to help Isabella adjust to your program?

3. How would you get the information about Isabella and her family situation that you would like to have as you begin work with her?

4. Imagine what some of Loretta's concerns are as she begins to leave her daughter at the family child care home. How would you respond to these?

Review Questions

1. Describe an ideal process of orientation to a program for a child and his or her parents.

2. Discuss why each step of the orientation process is beneficial and what strategies a teacher may consider with each step.

3. Identify several behaviors typically associated with separation problems in young children.

4. Discuss several teacher behaviors that help parents and children adjust to separation.

Helpful Websites

- The mission of the Association for Childhood Education International (ACEI) is to promote and support in the global community the optimal education and development of children—from birth through early adolescence—and to influence the professional growth of educators and the efforts of others who are committed to the needs of children in a changing society. Information about good beginnings is available on the Association website.

- National Child Care Information Center. This organization has a helpful website with many resources and links about child care, early education, and families.

- The focus of the National Association for Family Child Care is to provide technical assistance to family child care associations. This site has helpful information about good beginnings.

- The American Academy of Pediatrics is committed to the attainment of optimal physical, mental, and social health and well-being for all infants, children, adolescents, and young adults. Information is available on this site about school beginnings.

- The website for the National Network for Child Care offers information on choosing child care.

CHAPTER 8

Informal Communication with Families

Learning Objectives

After reading this chapter, you should be able to:

8-1 Identify ten communication methods for conveying information, interest, and support to families, and discuss details for implementing each method.

naeyc

Related NAEYC Standards

Accreditation Standards (see inside text back cover for full listing of the Accreditation Standards for exemplary early childhood programs)

1.A.01; 4.E.03, 4.E.06; 7.A.09, 7.B.02, 7.B.05, 7.B.06

Licensure Standards (see inside text front cover for full listing of the Licensure Standards for this chapter)

2b, 2c

Effective relationships are built on trust and open communication. Finding methods to communicate regularly with families is a challenge for teachers who already have many responsibilities within their classrooms. Obviously, face-to-face conversations are most important in communication, and we will explore how to provide opportunities for these. But in addition, other strategies help keep information flowing both ways. In the age of technology and social media, teachers can find many creative methods to enhance contact with families. This chapter examines a variety of methods of informal communication that teachers can use to build relationships with families.

8-1 Ten Communication Methods and How to Implement Them

As teachers begin to work with parents and children, it is important to establish and keep open communication lines. As previously discussed, the initiative for opening a dialogue should come from teachers. By approaching families, teachers demonstrate their willingness to adapt to individual differences in personality, preferences, abilities, and time constraints that may result in different responses to the same method. For example, a busy parent may barely glance at the parents' bulletin board while rushing by but enjoys reading a newsletter at home, whereas a parent who is uncomfortable speaking English may eagerly read everything offered on the bulletin board that has notices in her language as well as English. For this reason, teachers should use as many communication methods as they can. Most are not time-consuming; a few minutes a day may be sufficient to work on ideas for the next newsletter or bulletin board, to update a website or blog, to send several individual notes, or make a few telephone calls. Most teachers probably do not take time to use a multitude of methods, feeling that one or two will get the message out. In actuality, many teachers are surprised when they learn that parents feel uninformed about the daily life of the classroom. A national parental perspectives study conducted by the National Association for the Education of Young Children (NAEYC) found that although most parents are highly satisfied with teachers, they rate parent–teacher communication among the lowest of satisfaction measures and the most common area in which the relationship might be improved (Olson & Hyson, 2005). Parents want regular communication with teachers, do not feel that they always receive it, and wish teachers would reach out more. It is important that teachers recognize this need and use a variety of methods to communicate.

one-way communication
Communication sent from school to inform families without expectation of response.

two-way communication
Communication designed to elicit dialogue between home and school.

Communication strategies can be one-way or two-way. **One-way communication** from a class or school can inform families about events or plans or attempt to educate parents. This is the traditional method that many schools have used to communicate with families. It is important because parents need and want to know what is going on, but a real sense of partnership grows through **two-way communication**, which encourages and facilitates true dialogue, with families actively reacting and responding

Devices can be incorporated into many communication methods that are normally one-way to expand them into two-way communication. In fact, expanding many ideas that have been traditionally used may make them interactive.

With the diversity of languages used in our country, communication can be a challenge but should not be a barrier as teachers learn words in other languages, find interpreters, and utilize local and online translation services for written materials.

Teachers working in school settings have been influenced by traditional methods of communicating with families—those "ritualized and institutionalized" ideas: parent–teacher conferences scheduled for precisely 15 minutes and open house nights, when all parents are invited to the classroom at the same time, leaving no time for individual contact. Especially in school settings where teachers may not have the luxury of daily contact, teachers must work to move beyond these encounters that yield few channels for communication. They must find their own ways of creating communication *between* school and families rather than continuing the tradition of sending messages *from* schools *to* families. The ideas in this chapter may help teachers from child care and preschool settings through elementary school.

FIGURE 8-1
When children are brought to school by bus, teachers have to work hard to maintain regular contact with families.

8-1a Daily Conversations

No matter what other informal strategies teachers use as alternatives for establishing communication with parents, these should not replace personal contact. Nothing is as important as personal, face-to-face conversation for building relationships.

> *Connie Martinez says, "I don't have time for too much else, but I do a lot of talking to parents every day."*

Frequent daily conversations when parents drop off and pick up their children are extremely important in building trust by fostering a sense of familiarity. A study of frequency of communication between parents and caregivers indicated that the highest frequency of communication occurs at the "transition point" when parents leave and pick up their child at a center. There is an obvious problem when children are brought by a carpool or bus; teachers in these situations have to work harder to maintain regular contact by e-mail, telephone calls, or notes (see Figure 8-1).

Important things happen during these brief exchanges. Parents want to know that their child is known and recognized as a person. To see a teacher greet their child personally by name is reassuring. Parents also want to be greeted by name themselves.

> *"Good morning, Pete. You look ready to play today. I've put some of those new little cars that you like in the block corner. How are you this morning, Mrs. Lawrence? Pete's been telling me about his new bedroom—you must be pretty busy at home these days."*

This can be a time for brief but substantive exchanges on child- and family-related issues. Studies indicate that these conversations may be the most frequent form of parent involvement, although the substance of the conversations may not progress beyond social niceties. The topics discussed most frequently are child related, including child–peer relations and child–caregiver relations. However, when communication is frequent, the diversity and number of topics discussed by parents and teachers increase, pointing to the need for frequent conversations to build relationships. With greater frequency, the number of family-related topics discussed increases. More than social conversation is needed; quality care and progress in education demand that home and school coordinate their efforts and exchange information regularly (see Figure 8-2).

FIGURE 8-2
Daily opportunities for conversation help build relationships.

transition times
Times when children and families are arriving at or leaving the school.

But nothing happens if there is no contact. One researcher found that the average length of conversation between caregiver and parents at **transition times** was 12 seconds! Sixty-three percent of all "conversations" were greetings or other small talk with no real exchange of information. In nearly half of the situations observed, the parent and teacher did not even greet each other. Clearly, this is no way to begin or to build a relationship.

The frequency and quality of these daily contacts depend primarily on factors in classroom routine and school policy that can be planned and regulated. In preschool settings, staffing patterns need to provide enough staff available to talk when parents arrive at the beginning and end of the day. Preparing materials before parents arrive or saving cleanup for after parents depart keeps a teacher's attention from being diverted from the door as parents arrive. If teachers provide simple, open-ended materials that children can use with no adult assistance, neither parents nor teachers will have to devote full attention to the demands of children. When both members of a teaching team are in the classroom, making definite assignments for either child care or adult conversations clarifies expected behaviors for teachers and parents. It is a good idea for the teachers in a team to take turns being responsible for conversations with parents, thus allowing parents to develop relationships with both and not feeling they have no one with whom to talk when one teacher is absent. (The obvious exception to this is primary caregiving arrangements for younger children; here, the primary caregiver is the person who communicates regularly with the same families in his group.)

It can present a challenge when only one member of the teaching team—often the assistant—is culturally and linguistically congruent with the family and the lead teacher is not. It helps when the team has formed a trusting relationship with each other and power is truly shared. Then, the dynamic is set for the assistant to use his language expertise and cultural knowledge to help the family communicate with the classroom, and that communication is shared with the partner.

FIGURE 8-3
When teachers create the expectancy for conversation, parents usually respond.

The atmosphere created by teachers and staff can either open or close opportunities for informal chats. The teacher who says "Hello. How are you?" and turns to busy himself elsewhere indicates his unwillingness to prolong the contact. A teacher who asks a broad question or makes a comment that invites response—"Looks like you've had a busy day"—and stands by the parent, obviously ready to continue, creates an expectation of conversation (see Figure 8-3).

Some teachers complain they can never think of anything to say when a parent comes in. These teachers might consider what they most enjoy about a child and share these observations. It is difficult for most parents to resist a conversation that begins by focusing personally on their child. What else can teachers use to initiate conversation? Parents would love to hear about a favorite song, book, or activity; new things their child is interested in; or their child's playmates. Get started—other ideas will come.

Teachers striving for daily contact with all parents are helped to perceive their own patterns by keeping an informal tally (on a file card in a pocket or on a paper taped to the wall) briefly recording who was spoken to, for how long, and the topic of conversation. This often identifies a parent who was slipping in and out unnoticed or with whom the teacher never felt comfortable enough to progress beyond the "How are you?" stage. Once teachers have identified a deficiency, they can work on solving the communication gap.

Some observations indicate that almost 30 percent of child care parents do not enter a school when leaving their children for the day. A clear and firm policy about parents accompanying their children to a classroom is needed, stressing to families the need for safety and a child's emotional security as well as the importance of making daily contact with a teacher (see Figure 8-4). Studies show that as the frequency of communication between parents and teachers rises, communication attitudes become more positive. A policy that facilitates and supports this contact is beneficial.

FIGURE 8-4
A school policy requiring that parents accompany their children to the classroom facilitates daily contact with teachers.

© Cengage Learning®

One center posts a sign-in sheet on the parents' bulletin board just by the door. Rather than signing in just the time of their child's arrival, which most schools do, this sheet provides a space beside each child's name for parents to fill in the phone number at which they can be reached that day.

Sample Sign-In Sheet

Child's name:
Arrival time:
Brought by:
Will be picked up by and time:
Contact phone number:
Today's comments:

Space in the last column allows for parents' regular comments. A device like this makes routine the concept that parents will come in each day. Classrooms that find parents are not coming in may also relocate the sign-in sheet so parents have to come into the classroom.

When teachers regularly communicate with parents whose first language is not English, they may find it useful to add an app to their phones, such as Google Translate, to find the words that will help them communicate clearly.

Teachers may need to help sensitize families to the concept that conversations about children should not take place over children's heads as if they cannot understand the meaning or the fact that they are being discussed. By modeling such respect for children's feelings, teachers help families grow in their understanding of children's needs and emotions. Teachers also demonstrate a professional emphasis on confidentiality of conversations. It is appropriate to direct conversations that turn to specifics involving children or families to another time or place.

"I'd like to talk more about this with you—could we step outside for a minute?"

"This is important information that I'm not comfortable talking about right here—can we find a few minutes this afternoon for a phone conversation?"

Some teachers are afraid that by encouraging parents to talk that they will begin a flow of conversation they will be unable to cut off, and the conversation will interfere with accomplishing certain tasks and operating the classroom smoothly. In most situations, this is not the case; parents' own pressing demands limit their available time. In situations where parents completely accept an invitation to talk and spend long periods in a classroom, teachers should realize these parents are showing a need for companionship and feelings of belonging and try to find ways to meet this need. Teachers may suggest that parents join in an activity or find a way of linking one parent with another.

"I've enjoyed talking with you, but I must get busy mixing the paint now. If you can spend a little more time with us, I know the children in the block corner would enjoy having you play with them."

"Mrs. Rodriguez, let me introduce Mrs. Brown. Your boys have been very busy working together this week. Have you been hearing about the social studies project at home?"

When parents ask teachers for lots of detailed information at a busy dismissal time, teachers may answer briefly and then set up an arrangement to give more information later by note or telephone. If these dismissal requests happen repeatedly, it may help the parent to become aware of classroom needs if teachers have children almost ready to leave when the parents arrive. When teachers realize that daily conversations are valuable, they are more likely to find creative ways of dealing with potential problems like this, rather than cutting off all forms of communication.

Occasionally, teachers can encourage parents to spend a few extra minutes in the classroom with their children by making a cup of coffee or juice available at the beginning or end of the day. No elaborate preparation is necessary to make parents feel welcome. Children can show things to parents or play as parents chat with teachers and other adults. Such an occasion offers a brief chance for everyone to relax together and is supportive for parents and teachers. Chapter 10 will discuss opportunities for family members to become involved with visits and activities in children's classrooms. Every such involvement brings new opportunities for conversations between teachers and parents.

FIGURE 8-5
Electronic communication works well to reach parents busy at work in their offices.

© Cengage Learning®

Teachers who work in elementary schools may discover that a majority of their children arrive by bus or are dropped off in carpool lines. This does not allow daily conversations with families. Rather than assume that communication is impossible, these teachers can find other forms of communication, such as those discussed later in this chapter.

Although daily conversations are probably most important in the context of other plans for family involvement, they should not be seen as an end in themselves; other arrangements are needed to ensure the development of trust and full communication. Nevertheless, beginning steps toward openness are perceived in daily interaction.

8-1b Electronic Communication

Now that most teachers and families have access to computers, tablets, smartphones, and e-mail, electronic communication offers another option for two-way communication. Some teachers send out daily classroom journals to their parent address list so parents can read about events from the leisure of their offices or homes. Others use e-mail to send reminders, an electronic newsletter, or personal notes. With the ease of a reply button, families can quickly respond (see Figure 8-5).

In the era of instant messaging and texting, teachers should nevertheless be aware that professional decorum, including appropriate spelling and grammar, should be maintained—much as if the teacher were sending traditional print matter.

Often teachers have created their own websites and classroom pages. Through attractive links, teachers can post photo stories showing many aspects of the process of classroom life and learning. Daily homework assignments or educational activities can be posted here for parents to check (Huseth, 2001; Bauch, 2000). A family response link can elicit comments, questions, and feedback (Mitchell et al., 2009). For examples of teacher websites, see the end-of-chapter websites that can assist teachers in creating and maintaining their classroom links.

In setting up websites, teachers must be mindful of privacy and protection concerns. Use of photographs and student names must be carefully monitored for permission and discussed with families. Even if photos or video are used only within the classroom and families, parents must give prior permission and be comfortable with the planned use.

Although electronic technology offers additional options for communication with some families, teachers should also be aware of its limitations and be cautious regarding its use. Despite the ease of communication, teachers should be cautious of disrupting parents too frequently while they are working. It is important also to be mindful of misinterpretations that could happen when e-mails are fired off in annoyance. When a subject is delicate, educators would do well to pick up the phone or schedule an in-person meeting (Mosle, 2013).

Some families do not have equipment or technological skills to access information electronically. Therefore, teachers should make sure that information offered electronically is also offered in a variety of other ways. Even some teachers are still intimidated by the world of computer technology. There may also be a sense of removal that could inhibit development of relationships. Nevertheless, for many families today, checking e-mail is so automatic that use of this method could ensure frequent contact (Ray & Shelton, 2004).

One teacher describes her experience in using her digital camera to help the children make slide shows on the computer for families to view during arrival and departure times (Gennarelli, 2004). Another teacher established a lending library of DVDs to help families learn ways to help their children build foundational skills at home (Mass & Cohan, 2007). Another exchanges text messages with an apprehensive mother of an infant to provide frequent reassurance through the day. Still another describes how a virtual pre-K becomes an interactive educational resource in English and Spanish that bridges classroom with hands-on home activities and community experiences (Narvaez, Feldman, & Theriot, 2007). Current technology, such as Skype, social media sites, blogs, and other commonly used resources, allows teachers and families to create innovative ways of communicating.

TeachSource

VIDEO ACTIVITY ▶❙❙

© 2016 Cengage Learning®

Watch the second video, *Teacher Perspectives*, from the *Communicating With Parents Using Technology* series. After viewing the clip, reflect on these questions:

1. How can uses of technology enhance teacher–parent communication?

2. What are some of the benefits of using technology for communication with families?

3. What are potential issues involving the use of technology?

8-1c Telephone Calls

For teachers who cannot be in daily contact with families, the telephone offers an opportunity for personal conversation. For teachers who have not had an opportunity to visit with parents or children before the first day of school, a telephone call may be a friendly overture to introduce the teacher to the family and express pleasure at having their child in the class (Barbour & Barbour, 2004). Sometimes, teachers use phone calls to indicate concern if a child is absent for several days (see Figure 8-6).

FIGURE 8-6
When worried parents can check in by phone, they feel more comfortable.

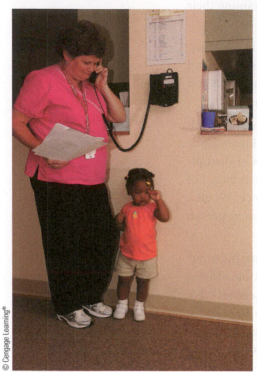

© Cengage Learning®

"Hello, Mrs. Rodriguez. I just wanted to let you know we've missed Tony at school. Has he been sick?"

A most important use of the phone call is to share positive personal observations about a child. Imagine how a child's parents would respond when, tired after a long day at work, they receive a call telling how their child helped a new child in the classroom or said something insightful or funny. Knowing that past experience with schools leads parents to assume that there is a problem when they receive a phone call, teachers let the parent know immediately that everything is fine and that the call is to say hello and tell them something they probably would like to know.

"It's really showing how you have been working with Ryan at home on his math skills. He got a perfect score on our multiplication test today!"

"I know you've been worried about Ricky's appetite, so I wanted to let you know I've noticed him doing much better at lunch lately. Today, he ate two helpings of macaroni and cheese."

Such phone calls take only a few minutes, but they let parents know about a teacher's interest in and knowledge of their child, and they go a long way in establishing positive teacher–parent relations. The telephone facilitates two-way communication. Teachers should be mindful of using good telephone manners, clearly introducing themselves and stating the purpose of the call, asking the parent if this is a good time to talk briefly, and pausing for parents to be able to participate in the conversation.

These are "no problem" telephone calls. They can be very effective with families of children in elementary school. However, it is not a good idea to initiate conversation on the telephone about problems that teachers and parents need to address. Without being able to see parents' facial expressions, it is difficult to gauge their full response. Difficult conversations are best handled face-to-face.

Parents may be comfortable asking questions about progress or behavior they might not otherwise raise. Using the telephone is especially important to connect with parents who are not in frequent contact with the teacher, either because of work schedules or transportation arrangements. Communication opportunities can be further increased by the establishment of a telephone hour when parents can feel comfortable calling a teacher. One teacher chose an evening hour once a week; another chose a naptime hour when other staff were available to supervise her children. When teachers have some control over when telephone calls will occur, they intrude less into their personal life. And when parents know about this regular opportunity, they will usually respect the appointed time.

Many schools around the country are making an innovative use of the telephone to increase interaction and communication between school and home. Each teacher records a one- to three-minute message at the end of the school day, summarizing learning assignments, stating homework assignments, and including suggestions to parents for home learning. (This is useful for parents who do not have Internet connections by which similar announcements can be posted.) Parents can call and hear the message at any time and can also leave a message for the teacher. This "transparent school" concept has been found to substantially increase the number of parent contacts with the school. Students from the "frequent user" homes showed a significant increase in homework completion (Bauch, 2000).

8-1d Personal Notes

A teacher sending a personal note home with a child can also accomplish sharing positive personal observations or anecdotes.

> *"Jonathan told me today that his grandpa is his 'best buddy.' I thought Grandpa might like to know."*

> *"Tina scored the winning basket during our afterschool game with the third-graders. We were all thrilled!"*

Notes tend to be perceived as one-way communication, but a teacher may design them to invite response.

> *"I wanted to let you know I've noticed Ricky is eating more at lunch lately. Have you also noticed an increase at home?"*

OPPORTUNITY FOR SELF-REFLECTION

Consider your typical style of social interaction. Do you let others initiate conversation, or are you more likely to take the first step? Would you call yourself an extrovert or an introvert? Rate your level of comfort in unfamiliar social situations. Now reflect on what these patterns mean related to the professional efforts you will have to make to set the expectation for regular communication with the families you work with. Where will you have to concentrate your efforts?

Parents are always pleased to know that their child has accomplished some new skill and doubly pleased when the teacher takes the time to share the positive event with them. Parents' reinforcing comments to children after reading such notes also help children perceive that parents and teachers are working together. A teacher once reported that her note about a child's accomplishment was sent across the country to Grandma in California for display on the refrigerator. A few words have a lot of power to create positive family relationships.

Some teachers use preprinted "Happy-Grams," filling in the blanks:

> *"_____ has been doing a good job at _____."*

However, this type of note lacks a personal tone. All notes, e-mail messages, and letters should be personalized. Adults should be addressed by name and title or first names if the teacher is on a first-name basis with the family. Teachers should be sure they use the correct names, recognizing the different family structures of individual children. It is also better when teachers refer to children by name rather than "your child." Teachers can end the notes by writing their first and last names or their first name if that is the basis of the relationship (Lee & McDougal, 2000). Personal notes take only one or two minutes to write. If a teacher sends out two or three a day, each child in a classroom might take one home within one or two weeks. E-mail can make the process even quicker.

Sometimes, a note can accompany a sample of the child's work to explain or expand on the idea. For example, for parents who are new at appreciating the stages of art young children move through, it might lead to more productive conversation between parent and child if the teacher makes a comment:

"This is the first time Seth has made a closed scribble with his paintbrush. That shows that his small muscle coordination is really improving. He enjoyed the red paint today, as you can see!"

Notes back and forth may be exchanged in a notebook or file folder kept in each child's cubby or book bag. It is worth the effort to find a translator for a note sent to parents whose home language is not English. Personal notes of appreciation to parents who have shared materials, time, or ideas reinforce a teacher's expression of pleasure.

RIGHT NOW

Pick up a pen and write one or two specific sentences that a parent might enjoy receiving about his or her child. Now look at the clock. Chances are it took you less than two minutes—time well spent!

8-1e Bulletin Boards

Bulletin boards offer another form of reaching out to parents. Often, parents who have a low frequency of communication with teachers use other sources of information, such as bulletin boards.

A bulletin board needs to be clearly visible in an area well traveled by parents—preferably just outside a classroom—so families can make a clear connection between the information offered and the teacher as the source. Placing the board just outside the room also prevents congestion when parents stop to read the material. The board needs to be labeled for "Parents" or "Families" so parents realize this is information meant for them. Eye-catching materials, such as snapshots of children, classroom activities, and samples of work, invite closer attention. Using different colors of paper or fabric as backgrounds is a visual indication to families that there is a change in bulletin board offerings.

The information offered by a bulletin board will be chosen by a teacher as he or she listens to parents' questions and comments or finds areas where they need resources or help (see Figure 8-7). Occasionally, bulletin boards may offer guidelines on choos-

TeachSource Digital Download

IDEAS FOR TEACHERS:

Bulletin Boards

One practical hint is to place several layers of paper on the board when creating the first board for the year; the next background is already in place when the current display is removed. Enlarge articles for the bulletin board when photocopying because larger print is easier to read and is eye catching. Longer articles, recipes, or directions for making things can be offered in a folder of "takeaways." The empty folder offers proof to a teacher that a bulletin board is used. Emphasize new material by a visual change—new pictures or background colors.

ing books or toys; on childhood diseases and immunization needs; nutritious menus appealing to children; suggestions for movies, television, or local events; developmental information or solutions to family problems; or handouts or recent articles that prepare or follow up on a topic under discussion at a parents' meeting. The NAEYC publication *Family-Friendly Communication for Early Childhood Programs* (Diffily & Morrison, 1996) offers brief educational pieces that could be used for bulletin boards or newsletters. Topics include explanations of good early childhood education philosophy, explanations of typical classroom activities, literacy ideas, ideas for learning at home, positive guidance, tips for homework time, and other family/community issues. See Figure 8-8 for sample ideas.

Sometimes, a sequence of bulletin boards can be planned—for example, one on how to choose good books for children, followed by one on library resources for parents and children. A third board on using books to help deal with childhood problems also can be planned.

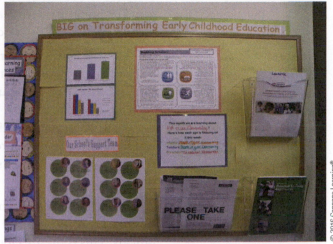

FIGURE 8-7
Bulletin boards are another way of providing information for families.

© 2016 Cengage Learning®

TeachSource Digital Download

FIGURE 8-8
Sample Bulletin Board Ideas

Developmental issues for a particular age in a classroom:

    Toilet learning and separation for under three years old

    Promoting imaginative play for preschoolers

    Television for your school-aged child

    Helping your child cope with bullies

Educational issues:

    School readiness

    Preschool literacy

    How preschoolers learn math

    Value of play

    Whose homework is it?

Parenting issues:

    Discipline

    Healthful snacks

    Bedtime routines

Community issues:

    Family activity schedules at the library, YMCA, or children's museum

    Community resources for family support or health

    Educational opportunities

Adult issues:

    Tax tips for working families

    Support for single parents and families in transition

    Finding time for you and your family

© Cengage Learning®

Bulletin boards can offer support to parents in the form of a wry cartoon or two, reminding parents that a teacher understands the childhood foibles confronting them. A bulletin board or part of one can be provided for parent contributions, such as offers to babysit or exchange outgrown winter coats or requests for carpool drivers. The bulletin board may be used for interactive communication if teachers ask or encourage parents to ask questions that demand others' answers.

Many teachers who are influenced by the documentation that is an integral part of the Reggio Emilia approach now use their bulletin boards for daily communication about the meaningful work that children are involved in. They post pictures, sketches of constructions, recorded conversations, and children's art or writing, along with brief comments, captions, and progress notes. Not only does such documentation enable families to stay abreast of ongoing work, but it also provides opportunities for teachers to engage parents to consider appropriate learning activities and children's development.

If a school has enough room, a separate area for parents close to the main reception area can be provided with comfortable chairs, a coffeepot, and interesting periodicals. This is the area for storing resources available for parents to check out, such as parenting books, children's books and toys, videos the teacher has taken of the class, and so on. (If space is a problem, such materials can be stored in a rolling cabinet

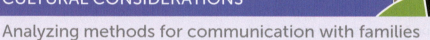

CULTURAL CONSIDERATIONS

Analyzing methods for communication with families

As teachers analyze their methods for communicating with families, they must be mindful of who would be excluded from the methods they choose. Consider these questions: In which families might adult literacy be an issue? Which families might have difficulty reading English? What could be done to enhance any reading experience, such as adding photos? What families would not have access to computer technology? What can be done to provide easy access to information for them? Which parents are not comfortable conversing in English, and what modifications can be made for them? Which cultural backgrounds might mean that fathers (or mothers) do not consider themselves necessary to the school communication process? What family structures or other needs might need to be accommodated by having duplicate sets of information or materials sent to more than one address? Cultural, socioeconomic, and family structure differences such as these should be part of analyzing teacher communication for maximum effectiveness.

A disproportionate number of people with low levels of literacy are members of minority groups or of low socioeconomic status. While typical handouts sent from schools are written at the tenth-grade level, many recipients might be, at best, third- or fourth-grade-level readers (Kalyanpur & Harry, 2012). This clearly has relevance when teachers are working with immigrant families and minorities of low educational level because teachers will have to rely on communication methods other than written.

placed in a central spot during pickup and drop-off times.) Having a space for parents is a concrete reminder that parents are welcome to stop, relax, and enjoy what the school has to offer.

8-1f Daily News Flash

"What about the parents who are in and out quickly?" wonders Dorothy Scott. *"Is there any way to give them classroom updates?"*

There are a number of ways of connecting with parents who are too busy for conversation. A **daily news flash** is one method of letting parents know what is going on and sharing information that teachers want parents to know (see Figure 8-9). In a prominent place outside the classroom door or near the main entrance for parents waiting in the carpool line is a large board—perhaps a chalkboard, a whiteboard, a bulletin board, or a corner of one—that briefly describes one thing children have done or talked about that day.

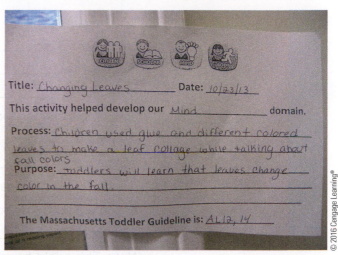

FIGURE 8-9
A daily news flash is a quick report for families on the day's events.

© 2016 Cengage Learning®

"This morning, we blew bubbles outside."

"We learned a new song today about squirrels."

"Tommy's mother had a new baby boy last night, so we talked a lot about babies."

"Today, we talked about Rosa Parks."

"We learned how to do a Google search today—ask your child for a demonstration."

Classroom daily news flashes are not earthshaking, but they offer something tangible from the day that parents can pursue with their children. Most parents are grateful for these bits of news that make them feel a part of the day and help them connect with their children with a specific comment or question rather than the vague "What did you do today?"—likely to be answered unsatisfactorily with "Play" or "Nothing."

Some centers post a board or memo pad for teachers to write personal reports on each child's day. This can be especially useful if there is a change in staff during the day, so families have reports from all staff involved with their children.

Tommy: A busy morning, great block building; very sleepy after naptime

Sarah: Quiet this morning; enjoyed talking with Jamie at lunch

Seth: Sad for a short time after Dad left and then busy with play dough; hard time sleeping at naptime, so rested, then read a book

LaTonya: Loved our new song "Alice the Camel"; discovered broccoli is all right!

Many programs use daily information sheets for individual children and families, with a section on top for parents to fill out at the beginning of the day to update staff about how the child is feeling, and a bottom section to tell families how the child's day went (see Figure 8-10). It is important that there be space and opportunities to offer meaningful and specific information rather than being a perfunctory checklist. Here is a sample:

daily news flash
Brief written news of the day posted for families.

TeachSource Digital Download

FIGURE 8-10
Daily Sheet

Child's name _____ Date _____

Last night's sleep _____ hours

Awakened at _____

Breakfast _____Mood _____

Special information today:

Comments/questions _____

Will be picked up by _____at _____

Meals and snacks today _____

Appetite (circle one) good fair poor usual

Bathroom activity _____

(*Note:* This might be more specific for infants/toddlers or for children in the toilet-learning phase.)

Naptime: Slept from _____until _____

Activities enjoyed today _____

Particular events _____

Comments/questions _____

_____

_____

_____

© Cengage Learning®

All such efforts convince families that teachers are paying some personal attention to their children and that teachers are really trying to keep in touch. Many schools and programs have a message center with a pocket or mail slot for each family to receive daily reports, notes, or other communication.

8-1g Newsletters

Another communication technique involves sending regular newsletters to all families. Newsletters have four main objectives:

1. To keep families informed about classroom activities and plans

2. To give parents insights into the educational purposes underlying classroom activities

3. To enhance children's and parents' abilities to communicate with each other

4. To reinforce and extend learning from school into the home

Parents are often frustrated when attempting to learn directly from their children what has gone on in school, and newsletters can help solve this problem. The newsletter could describe events that have occurred since the last newsletter, upcoming activities and explorations and ways parents can help with them, or practical examples of how parents can reinforce learning at home. Newsletters may be sent by e-mail and hard copy, as well as posted on the bulletin board.

Newsletters need to be fairly short—one printed page is enough—so parents do not set them aside unread, thinking they are too time-consuming. Newsletters sent regularly—

monthly or biweekly—will not get too far behind on current activities. They need to be neat, attractive, and display great care for correct grammar and spelling. Have someone else check your correspondence for errors before distributing it to parents. A professional appearance is necessary when teachers are trying to have parents accept the importance of what they do.

> *We had an exciting snack time last Thursday. The children watched in amazement while the popcorn popped—right out of the popper onto a clean sheet spread on the floor. The children enjoyed their snack of popcorn and milk. We are trying to emphasize healthful snacks. If you would like to join us for snack or have an idea that would be fun and healthful for snack, please share it with us.*
>
> *I know some of you have been frustrated in trying to understand the newest songs your children have been singing this fall. Enclosed are some words so you can sing along. [Words added.]*

> *We have begun working on word problems in math. Please help your child focus on the logic. Your role might be to help him or her draw a picture to illustrate the words, such as "Hannah's apple is bigger than April's but smaller than Daniel's. Who has the biggest apple?"*

> *Dear Parents,*
>
> *You will likely have heard from your children that the end-of-grade tests will be held next week. We are trying to help the children relax about these, so please do your part at home. Don't talk about the tests too much, and reassure your child that all the material on the test is material that will be familiar. Make sure your child goes to bed early the nights before the tests, and see that there is lots of time for breakfast and an early arrival at school.*
>
> *When the test results come back, we will explain them to you in a personal note.*
>
> *Thanks for your support,*
>
> *John Roberts*

TeachSource

VIDEO ACTIVITY ▶❚❚

© 2016 Cengage Learning®

After viewing the video [Bonus video 3 in Teach Source Video Case] *Communicating with Families: Best Practices in an Early Childhood Setting*, reflect on these questions:

1. What kinds of information are included on this bulletin board, and how does this support teacher goals for working with families?

2. What features on the bulletin board attract attention?

3. What features indicate teacher desire to include all families?

Teachers often complain that parents will not read their newsletters or notes anyway, so they question the effort put into preparing the materials. Although that may be true of some parents, the majority of families want to know about things that pertain to their children. Therefore, it is the teachers' responsibility to inform parents and in a way that is easy to read, reliable, and accurate. Letters should be dated and signed so families know with whom to speak if they have questions.

Although there is no substitute for the personal classroom news that each parent wants or the addition of simple explanatory comments for subtle education from a familiar teacher, busy teachers may occasionally find that they want to insert an article produced by another professional.

TeachSource Digital Download

IDEAS FOR TEACHERS:

Newsletter Tips

Make letters visually interesting with:

- Bold headings
- Graphics
- Changed typeface
- Content divided into sections or enclosed in boxes
- Bullets for important points
- Care toward details of spelling and grammar

Capture attention and build a sense of community by:

- Offering a question for families to pose to children to trigger memories of classroom events
- Using dialogue or anecdotes with children's names
- Adding a question for parent response, compiling responses in the next newsletter
- Announcement of family and community events
- Recognizing special parent involvement and contributions
- Encouraging parents to run their own idea corner, edited by a parent
- Providing a regular question-and-answer section, where teachers answer parent questions for everyone

Some of these are available commercially, as in the NAEYC publication *Family-Friendly Communication* mentioned earlier, or in the letters to families included in *The Creative Curriculum for Preschool, 5e* (Heroman, et al., 2010).

Some teachers find that newsletters offer an opportunity for self-evaluation because they answer the questions parents ask concerning what they have been doing and why. Others use a collection of the newsletters for the orientation of new parents because the pages present a summary of classroom activities throughout the year (see Figure 8-11).

8-1h Traveling Backpacks, Libraries, and Circulating Literacy Activities

Teachers can make contact with parents by sending home with a child a "traveling backpack." On a rotating basis, each child has the privilege of overnight or weekend use of several items selected from the classroom. A child may choose a favorite book to have her parent read or a puzzle she has just mastered to show. Depending on a teacher's knowledge of the socioeconomic background of the families involved, one or more of the items might be to keep—a lump of cooked play dough, with a recipe for making more later; construction paper for use at home; or a teacher-made matching game. Some teachers include a class-made book with pictures and names of each child in the class; parents enjoy associating faces with the names they hear from their children and seeing the visual record of classroom daily life. It can extend home/school connections when teachers provide space at the back of the book for families to write a note back to the children (Gennarelli, 2004).

Most children are pleased to be able to show their parents something that has been enjoyed at school, and a child's enthusiasm often guarantees that the materials will be used and discussed. Children who have been taught that the traveling backpack is a special privilege are also usually responsible about the care of these "school things." The bag

FIGURE 8-11
A sample of an attractive
and brief newsletter.

MARCH NEWSLETTER

A TRIP

On Thursday,
February 25,
the class went
for a nice
walk to Dunwood
Clinic. Mrs. Stallings showed us
interesting areas of a doctor's office.

OUTSIDE ACTIVITY

Swimming has been a lot of fun
for the class. It gives everyone
a nice outing even if it has been
cold. Thanks to Mrs. Huntley and
Miss Jones for knowing when it
was too cold to go.

CLASSROOM STUDY

For several weeks we have been studying
community helpers. It is interesting to learn
about firefighters, police, doctors, and others,
and how important they are to us.

COMING SOON

In the following
weeks the circus
will be coming to
town. We will be
working with
different areas of
the circus.
Animals, performers,
and others will be
recognized. This is
always an exciting
time for all.

UPCOMING EVENT

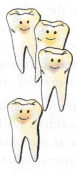

In March Mrs. Houser will come
and talk to the class about good
dental hygiene. We appreciate
her coming in and spending time
with us, especially discussing
this important area of health.

THANK YOU

Thanks to each of you, as parents,
for taking the time to come to
covered dish suppers, spending
time in the classroom, and
many other things that you do.
With your help and support the
year goes a lot smoother.

can also be used to exchange teacher and parent notes. A teacher may suggest "homework assignments" that parent and child can enjoy together: "Help your child find a picture of something big and of something little" or "Help your child count out two crackers to bring—one for him or her and one to share with a friend."

Another teacher may use the backpack to support a family **literacy activity** that is later shared at circle time; one teacher used "Traveling Polly," a stuffed parrot sent home with a notebook for parents to record Polly's adventures when she visited with their children

literacy activity
Activity to promote the
development of oral
communication skills
and an understanding of
print communication.

TeachSource Digital Download

IDEAS FOR TEACHERS:

Traveling Backpack to Promote Literacy

Suggestions:

- A book about a bear, a stuffed bear, and a blank page for child and parent to write their own bear story.
- A book and a blank tape for a parent to use to record a story.
- A tracing of the child's foot that has been cut out of cardboard and a list of things in the house. Parent and child measure and list the things that are longer and those that are shorter than the child's foot.
- A calendar with spaces for parent and child to write in special family dates and hang in the child's room.
- A collection of pads, markers, envelopes, and stickers for child and parent to write mail to send to family members.

at home. Read about a traveling doll named Heidi and some of the stories families wrote about her visits in Spicer (2000). As children dictate their stories to their parents and then hear their teachers read the stories aloud, literacy and family connections are made. Family Involvement storybooks are another way of enhancing home/school relations (Mayer, Ferede, & Hou, 2006). Still another idea is to fill the backpack with books, activities, and suggestions that are related to the theme being explored in the classroom, to extend school learning into the home (Santos, et al., 2012).

FIGURE 8-12

Family literacy is supported when books are sent home in a traveling backpack.

Offering parents the opportunity to borrow materials they can use with their children is further evidence of caring. A stock of paperback children's books—perhaps those no longer used in classrooms or homes—may be borrowed for use at home. Numerous classrooms are using a rotating system to encourage family literacy (Couse, 2003; Hammack et al., 2012). Good children's books can be sent home one at a time in a plastic bag. When the books are returned to school, another book is selected from the collection until all the children in the classroom have read the books and then a new collection is begun. A family journal accompanying the book helps parents and teachers communicate about children's progress and pleasure in reading with families (see Figure 8-12). Parenting books and children's toys can be available for loan to parents and children.

Another idea for circulating materials between home and school is to have classroom videos available for checkout. Teachers record such classroom activities as a cooking activity or story time, special visitors and events, and conversations. Children check out the videos to share at home with their families, with an attached comment sheet on which families can respond. Their comments are then shared with all the children back in the classroom. (The videos may be used in other ways, such as for open houses, for parents who are sitting in the parent lounge, and to play over local access cable stations.)

Another circulating form of communication could be letters sent home by teachers and school-aged children and answering letters from their parents. Teachers add a letter to all children's circulating notebooks each week about classroom learning activities. Then, children add their own drawings and written letters, and parents can respond. Not only does the growing notebook document the varied learning and writing progress during the year, it also gives children meaningful opportunities to develop their own communication skills and draws parents into seeing the real evidence of their children's learning.

All these kinds of materials circulating between home and school promote communication between classroom and family and suggest appropriate and enjoyable learning activities for parents to do with their children, thus involving them fully in the educational process.

8-1i Classroom Displays

Teachers who want to promote communication with families about the learning and development of their children use many opportunities to inform families about daily activities and their purposes. They hope that constant display of children's ideas, questions, and learning will "hook" parents into exploring important topics with their children and their children's teachers. So, they regularly create displays that inform and communicate, such as these examples:

- An area to keep children's three-dimensional work with clay or small construction materials for parent viewing, with brief written explanations of the concepts and skills demonstrated.

- Posting chart paper with individual children's answers to daily questions, written by the teacher or beginning writers. Questions might be "Where is your favorite place?" "What do you want to do when you're older?" and "What's the hardest thing for you to do?" Answers are intriguing to parents and could begin conversations about children's reasoning skills (see Figure 8-13).

FIGURE 8-13

Posting charts of children's words, questions, and experiences keeps families informed and models uses of literacy for children.

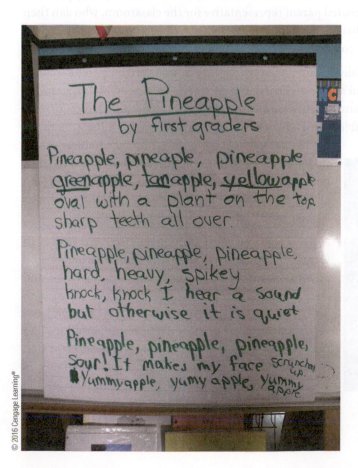

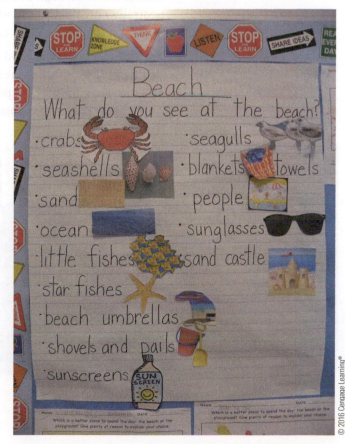

- Pictures of individuals and groups at work, posted with brief explanations or children's words quoted.

- A list of what went on in an area during the week.

  Example: Our math activities this week:

  - *Graphed our favorite crackers at snack time*

  - *Counted to see how many cups we would need for lunch*

  - *Measured feet to see who had the biggest and smallest*

  - *Weighed different kinds of seeds*

  - *Voted to choose our goldfish's name (Sparkles got 11 votes.)*

- Quotes of children's intriguing conversations and questions.

- Displays of children's favorite books, with quotes of children's comments.

- Displays of children's writing and drawing.

 ### 8-1j Suggestion Boxes

It is useful for teachers to devise several methods of obtaining feedback from parents about the classroom, their goals, and the methods of involving them in the program. Various tools can be designed for parent evaluation—from checklists, to fill-in-the-blank forms, to rating scales, for example, "Check which of the following have been useful to you this month: newsletter, bulletin board, daily flash, daily conversations." Parent interests can be surveyed; we will talk more about this in Chapters 10 and 11. A suggestion box should be prominently located and its use encouraged. Some parents are reluctant to raise issues with teachers directly and may be more comfortable with the anonymity of forms or printed material. Other parents, less comfortable with literacy, may prefer to communicate through a designated parent representative for the classroom, who can then neutrally raise the issue. In whatever form, this is a demonstration of openness to parental input that teachers want to encourage (see Figure 8-14).

If teachers list the good ideas contributed by parents in newsletters, parents realize that their ideas have been read and appreciated. Newsletter references to the suggestions also provide a means of explaining when or how the suggestion will be acted on or why some things may not be possible. Remember that what is important in all these methods is the attempt to keep families informed about events that are part of their children's daily lives and to communicate the teacher's willingness to enhance parent–child–teacher relationships.

The ideas discussed in this chapter are not time-consuming, and most do not require a great deal of formal planning. Teachers who use newsletters and bulletin boards often keep a file of ideas, articles, and clippings for future use and save things from year to year. Teachers should realize that these contacts provide vital, ongoing links between families and teacher that are irreplaceable for building knowledge of and comfort with one another and evidence for families that their involvement is welcome.

FIGURE 8-14
Suggestion boxes encourage families to give their input to teachers and schools.

SUMMARY

A parent–teacher partnership is strengthened as teachers utilize the following informal communication methods with parents:

- Daily conversations
- Electronic communication and use of technology
- Telephone calls
- Personal notes
- Bulletin boards
- Daily news flashes
- Newsletters
- Traveling backpacks, libraries, and other circulating materials
- Classroom displays
- Parent suggestion boxes and other evaluation methods

Student Activities for Further Study

1. If you are in a classroom situation, keep a tally of the parents you speak to at drop-off and pickup times each day for a week. (A file card in your pocket can be used conveniently to jot down names.) Are there any families with which you are missing contact? Do you know why? Are there any parents with whom you have little conversation beyond hello and goodbye? Do you know why? What circumstances create difficulties in finding time to talk in this particular classroom situation? Might any alternatives help solve the problem? Then, keep a tally of other methods of communication you have used, such as e-mail, notes, or telephone calls. What does this information suggest to you?

2. Observe the encounters as teachers and parents meet each other at drop-off and pickup times. What nonverbal clues of comfort or discomfort do you note? How do teachers use space to convey messages of welcome or distance? Are names used? What topics are discussed? What are children doing as parents and teachers talk?

3. Write and distribute an e-newsletter for your classroom. (Let families know what has happened recently and why it happened or how the children reacted to it.)

4. Design and create a bulletin board with a theme that you feel would be helpful to a group of parents.

5. Plan a brief, personal note that you could write to each parent, sharing something positive about each child.

6. Talk with an elementary school teacher to learn what methods of communication he or she uses.

7. Write a welcome letter to send to the families of your second-grade class before school opens. Have the letter translated to send it to the ELL parents in the classroom by using an app or website resource for translation.

Apply the Chapter Concepts: Case in Point

Jennifer Marden is beginning a new school year and has set a goal of trying to improve her communication with the families of her kindergarten class. She has realized that nine of the 18 children in her room will ride the bus, so she will rarely see their families. Three of the children will be dropped off by fathers on their way to work, so she will see only one parent out of each of those families—and often very briefly. The remaining six families will have regular contact because they bring their children into the classroom, although she knows that three of these families speak limited English. Last year, Jennifer used a bulletin board as her primary method of communication.

1. Discuss some of the factors Jennifer needs to consider as she selects methods of communication with her kindergarten families.

2. What are the potential problems in limiting herself to the use of the bulletin board for communication this year?

3. Identify some communication methods that might be appropriate in Jennifer's situation.

4. What can Jennifer do to enhance communication with the families who speak little English?

Review Questions

1. Identify 10 techniques teachers may use to convey information, interest, and support to families.

2. For each technique identified, discuss two ways to implement it.

Helpful Websites

- The National Education Association connects school, families, and communities. Check out their website.

- The Colorado Parent Information and Resource Center website includes articles about parent–teacher communication.

- The website for the National Institute on Out-of-School Time has good information about communication.

- SchoolNotes, a part of Education World, has a website that allows teachers to create their own web pages.

- The Scholastic website has many resources for teachers, including information about ways to communicate effectively with families.

- Search for free translation services online, from organizations such as Free Translation.

- My Classroom Connection has a teacher-friendly online website for classrooms; it offers a free trial and a small fee per year.

- Virtual Pre-K is an early childhood resource for educators, child care providers, community members, and families that connects early learning from the classroom to the home and community.

CHAPTER 9

Parent–Teacher Conferences

Learning Objectives

After reading this chapter, you should be able to:

9-1 Identify four reasons for holding regular parent–teacher conferences.

9-2 List four factors that facilitate productive parent–teacher conferences.

9-3 Describe four strategies for a successful parent–teacher conference.

9-4 List six pitfalls to avoid in parent–teacher conferences.

9-5 Discuss strategies for managing difficult conferences.

9-6 Outline a method to evaluate the parent–teacher conference.

naeyc

Related NAEYC Standards

Accreditation Standards (see inside text back cover for full listing of the Accreditation Standards for exemplary early childhood programs)

1.A.01; 4.E.03, 4.E.05; 7.A.01, 7.A.06, 7.A.08, 7.B.01, 7.B.04, 7.C.02, 7.C.04

Licensure Standards (see inside text front cover for full listing of the Licensure Standards for this chapter)

2b, 2c

Besides regular informal contact and conversations, teachers need to provide opportunities for purposeful in-depth conversations with parents in conferences. Such structured meetings let families and teachers learn new information, assess their progress toward mutual and separate goals for children, and continue to develop their relationships. Such benefits do not occur without planning and preparation on the part of teachers and parents. Because these conversations cover a wider range of topics than the briefer daily encounters, teachers need to ready materials, questions, and observations to make good use of the time. Arrangements will also need to be made for parental time and participation. With preparation, practice, and care in communication, parent conferences need not be a matter for apprehension.

In this chapter, we will examine techniques that are part of a teacher's attempt to structure productive situations for the exchange of information, questions, and plans.

9-1   Importance of Regular Conferences

Casual conversations are extremely important, but the more formal arrangement of parent–teacher conferences offers additional opportunities for families and teachers to work as partners. But conferences are often not used by many schools unless there are problems. The reasons for this include both fear and misunderstanding of the purposes of conferences.

Some negative feeling about conferences may come from the fact that an infrequent parent–teacher conference may be virtually the only contact between them. Ideally, a parent–teacher conference offers an opportunity for the free exchange of information, questions, and ideas, which can be accomplished best after a relationship is already established. All the earlier contacts and communications are helpful prerequisites for a successful conference. Teachers should make it a goal to have some type of contact with every family before conference time. In some cases, circumstances may prevent the formation of a prior relationship; however, this is no reason to avoid scheduling a conference to begin the communication process.

Unfortunately, many parents and teachers view conferences as a last step in dealing with negative behavior. If it is assumed that parents and teachers meet only when behavior is a problem, no one can anticipate such a meeting with pleasure. Parents' history of conflict or success in their own early school situations may lay the groundwork for this assumption. Some will recall negative experiences when their own parents were called in for conferences. Most of this reluctance stems from the many years that school systems for elementary-aged children and beyond had infrequent parent–teacher contact, and most conferences happened only when virtual strangers came together rather defensively to clear up some difficulty.

Many school districts are now giving reports on student accomplishment during parent–teacher conferences. But because of the time pressure on teachers who may have to speak with parents of 25 or more students, these conferences often become purely perfunctory, one-way, mostly statistical reports, with little opportunity for real participation and offering of information and insights by parents.

To be productive, it is important that conferences be seen as a routine and necessary component of the ongoing coordination of information and efforts in a teacher-family partnership.

"Oh, sure, I understand how important it is for parents and teachers to talk," says Connie Martinez, *"but I don't really see the need to get so formal as to have a conference. I talk to most of my parents every day. And these are, after all, preschoolers. It's not like we have to talk about reading and math test scores or anything. So, why should I have conferences?"*

"With everything I have to do," moans Frances Blake, a second-grade teacher, *"now they want me to sit down with every child's family? Where will I find the time for that? And half of them won't come anyway."*

It is important to hold regular parent–teacher conferences for several reasons, regardless of a child's age.

9-1a Provide a Developmental Overview of the Whole Child

Conferences provide an opportunity to examine the overall progress of a child in a detailed and organized way. In daily conversations, particular accomplishments or aspects of development may be discussed. This may be a new ability—such as climbing up the slide or learning to write his name—or a different behavior—such as a decrease in appetite at lunchtime or shyness around other children. Particular problems may catch the attention of a teacher or parent—a new tendency to cry when mother leaves or an increase in toileting accidents or temper outbursts; such matters are frequently discussed in daily exchanges. But a complete look at a child's development is not possible in these brief encounters.

In elementary school settings, it is too easy to concentrate solely on children's test results and academic progress, omitting consideration of other important aspects of the students' overall development, such as relationships with peers and physical development. Conferences provide opportunities for parents and teachers to move beyond the daily specifics and limits of the prescribed curriculum to an objective examination of total development.

9-1b Provide Time and Privacy

Conferences provide uninterrupted blocks of time and an atmosphere of privacy—two essentials for facilitating the sharing of information and formulating questions and plans (see Figure 9-1). Regardless of a teacher's commitment to talk with parents, the demands of caring for a group of children may emphatically pull a teacher away from a conversation. And in elementary classrooms, bells control the set schedule.

Parents often postpone talking about their concerns because of their awareness of the demands for a teacher's time:

"I'm concerned about Jason's complaints that the other kids are picking on him, but all the teacher had time to do was tell me his test scores and suggest he spend more time with math homework. The other parents were arriving for their conferences."

Knowing they have time for just talking is important for parents and teachers. Privacy is also needed to facilitate comfort in talking. Teachers who are trying to model sensitivity and respect for children's feelings usually prefer not to discuss them within their hearing or the hearing of other children. Although there are occasions when teachers feel it is appropriate to include an

FIGURE 9-1
Conferences give teachers and parents time to talk away from the demands of the classroom and children.

© 2016 Cengage Learning®

FIGURE 9-2
Some schools hold parent–teacher–child conferences.

older child in a parent–teacher conference and indeed some schools regularly hold parent–child–teacher conferences (see Figure 9-2), every conference should be considered separately, thinking of the individual child and the material for discussion.

Parents are often understandably reluctant to ask for help with parenting issues or to discuss concerns when other adults might interrupt them. In the situation where teachers are seeing parents one after the other in their classrooms, they need to find a way to extend privacy for all. Although teachers attempt to include extended family members and others involved in the child's life in conversations to share and learn information, they do so only with the parents' permission. Laws and professional ethics standards require that teachers always be completely mindful of confidentiality.

9-1c Increase Mutual Knowledge

The unhurried flow of conversation in a conference setting allows an exchange of questions and information that brief contacts at the beginning or end of a classroom day simply cannot.

> *"You know, it wasn't until after we'd gone through the developmental checklist and Mrs. Butler saw how well Sam compares with average four-year-olds that she told me how worried she's always been that he'd be slow. It really helped me understand why she's been asking so many questions about getting early academics started in the classroom and doing so much at home. It was a relief for both of us to be able to talk about how well Sam does and to know what she really wanted to talk about was the best ways to stimulate learning in the preschool years."*

> *"It really helped me to have some time to talk with Hannah's dad. I've been concerned that she had no interest in reading independently because she just daydreams when we have our reading period. He told me that her grandmother has just died and that she always read fairy tales to Hannah. I think now I have a way to reach her."*

Misunderstandings and concerns can surface only in longer conference conversations, with time to reflect on what each participant is saying. Conferences offer opportunities for clarification and deeper explanations of many issues. For teachers, conferences offer opportunities to get additional pieces of the puzzle. They often gain new information and insights from those who know children best and are aided in the endeavor to get to know children deeply.

Teachsource

VIDEO ACTIVITY ▶❚❚

Watch the Bonus Video, *Using a Family Journal to Promote Communication With Parents,* from the Video Case, *Home School Communication: The Parent–Teacher Conference.* After watching the teacher explain why he establishes communication before conference time, reflect on these questions:

1. Why would conferences be difficult if the teacher had not established communication beforehand?

2. How does the family journal help establish comfort before conference time?

3. Can you think of other ways teachers could establish regular communication before conference time?

9-1d Formulate Goals

Conferences can provide an important basis for formulating future goals and working plans (see Figure 9-3).

© 2016 Cengage Learning®

FIGURE 9-3
Conferences help teachers and parents formulate goals for children.

"She decided, during our conversation, that maybe her teaching sessions with Sam at home weren't the best idea. I said that in the classroom, I was trying to provide lots of books about dinosaurs—his current interest—and was trying to be available to read one to him each day. She thought she'd try something like that at home. We decided to get back together in three months and see whether this method was helping him enjoy books more."

"Hannah's dad told me they had bought tickets to the children's theater production of Cinderella. I told him I would be sure to get a copy of the book for her for independent reading."

Conference situations contribute to a sense of mutual knowledge and respect and enhance a parent–teacher partnership to a child's benefit.

FOUR REASONS FOR REGULAR CONFERENCES

- To facilitate a balanced examination of all aspects of development
- To provide uninterrupted time and privacy for conversation
- To facilitate a free-flowing exchange of questions and information and to increase mutual knowledge and respect
- To provide the opportunity to formulate and coordinate goals and plans

---

9-2 Groundwork for a Successful Conference

Such goals are not met without effort. There are important components to successful parent–teacher conferences.

9-2a Explain the Purpose of a Conference

Administrative policies and explanations help clarify the routine nature of parent–teacher conferences and the responsibilities of the participants. In teacher job descriptions and parent handbooks, a statement about the purpose of regular conferences, an indication of when they will occur—such as November and May—and a description of probable content will make this procedure better understood. Offering examples of the topics that will be discussed and questions parents may want to ask helps to dispel any misconceptions about conferences. Parents who are informed during orientation when they enroll their children that conferences are part of a school's regular communication process do not immediately assume there is something wrong when asked to a conference, nor are they afraid to take the initiative when they want a conference.

Parent conferences are a routine part of our school life. A parent conference does not mean that your child is having a problem in the classroom. A parent conference is a time for parents and teachers to exchange thoughts and ideas as well as a progress report from the team of teachers on all aspects of your child's learning and development. The teachers may ask you questions about how your child plays at home, any special friends, and so on. You will be able to ask the teachers about any aspect of his or her learning or development in or out of school and share any information that would help the teachers. Feel free to request a conference any time you would like one. We will schedule conferences in November and May. [Sample from a hypothetical parent handbook.]

9-2b Plan for Uninterrupted Time

Carefully selecting conference times is important: Parents and teachers have needs to be considered and must have a voice in choosing the time.

Teachers should first decide when they are most free to leave a classroom under the care of another teacher or assistant. In preschools, naptime is often convenient. Other possibilities may be early morning, when children filter in slowly at different times, or late afternoon because children's departure times are staggered and there are fewer for whom to care. Some teachers find they are available during outdoor playtime, when other adults can supervise on the playground. In elementary schools, whole days and evenings are sometimes set aside for conference times, enabling teachers to offer parents a range of choices for appointments. Offering a flexible conference schedule allows parents to fit in their work schedules and other family commitments (Seplocha, 2007).

FIGURE 9-4

It is desirable to have both parents in a two-parent family present at a conference.

For families where both parents work, it may be necessary to offer the option of evening or weekend hours. This may sound like a great inconvenience for a teacher, but being flexible enough to meet parents' needs indicates a real commitment to the idea of family involvement. It is desirable to have both parents from a two-parent family present so questions and information are not dealt with secondhand. In too many cases, mothers come to conferences alone (see Figure 9-4).

Specific invitations to fathers and accommodations to their schedules demonstrate that teachers value the participation of fathers and increase the probability that a conference will be fruitful. Any adults who have primary care for a child should be included; this may mean grandparents, stepparents, and other adults in the household.

In team teaching situations, it is rarely possible for both

CULTURAL CONSIDERATIONS

Gender roles defined by culture

Awareness of cultural expectations about male and female roles in children's education is important for teachers. For example, some families from predominantly Muslim Middle Eastern countries would not expect to have the mother play a dominant role in communicating with the teacher or the school, and she would be unlikely to attend a conference. In contrast, many Asian fathers from such countries as Korea, Japan, and India believe that the children's education is the responsibility of the mother and would not be comfortable being asked to the school setting (Bang, 2009). Rather than assume that both parents should automatically come to conferences, or should be involved in conversations, teachers should follow family customs and wishes, while trying to make both parents comfortable. This awareness of cultural customs will also help teachers not to automatically assume that the other parent is not interested.

Consider situations where you know culturally defined gender roles influence communication. Are you comfortable accepting these variations? Assess methods for facilitating maximum communication.

teachers to be free to join in the conference. It is a good idea for teachers to alternate responsibilities for conferences so parents do not come to think of only one teacher as the one with current knowledge of the child. Members of the team should schedule time to discuss information to be shared as well as what is learned during each conference. It is also important that conferences not be scheduled too tightly in rapid sequence. If parents see other parents waiting for their turn, neither they nor the teachers will likely settle into relaxed, productive conversation. In addition, teachers will not have time between meetings to jot down brief notes and reminders.

Having decided on available conference times, teachers may suggest to parents that they find a specific time convenient to their own schedules. These invitations can be made in person or by telephone. Merely posting a sign-up sheet eliminates the personal touch and tends to deemphasize the importance of a conference, as well as missing carpool parents. Personal contact also helps teachers find out if there are scheduling problems. When a sheet is posted, after a spoken invitation, it should make obvious the abundant choices of days and times, allowing for different working schedules, days off, giving employers advance warning for a long lunch hour, and the like. Teachers need to make it clear that they are anxious to be as flexible as possible in accommodating the needs of parents. If teachers are clearly willing to adapt a schedule to parents' needs, they will find responsive parents.

A sign-up sheet might look like the one shown in Figure 9-5a.

Figure 9-5b illustrates a sign-up sheet that is less of an invitation to a parent.

FIGURE 9-5a
A good example of a sign-up sheet for conferences.

Notice

It's time to get together to discuss your child's development. Please sign up for a time convenient to you. If you can't find one here, let's find one together.

    Naptime 12:30–2:30 p.m.

    Arrival time 8:00–9:00 a.m.

    Departure time 3:30–5:00 p.m.

I can also arrange to be available from 6 to 7:30 p.m. on the following days:
M–13, T–14, W–15, Th–16, M–20, T–21, W–22, Th–23.

Tommy

Luz

Seth

Jenny

Isaac

Akwanza

Pete

Ramon

Matthew

Hannah

Emma

© Cengage Learning®

FIGURE 9-5b
A less appropriate example.

Time to Sign Up for Conferences

Any Monday, Wednesday, or Thursday between 4 and 5 p.m.

© Cengage Learning®

Do you see the problems in the second sign-up sheet?

- For parents who cannot be off work between 4 and 5 p.m., it looks as if they have no other possibility, and the teacher does not much care to be either understanding or helpful.

- For busy parents, it looks as if this conference may be scheduled almost any time, so there is no motivation to set an appointment now.

- It is too easy to walk by and leave blank a sheet of paper that does not seem specifically meant for you. It is much harder to ignore the message when your child's name is there with a space beside it.

- Parents who do not come into the school may not know it is conference time.

When frustrated by parents' seeming indifference, teachers might consider these details.

Teachers and parents must remember that young children are sometimes upset by a change in their routine. Especially for very young children, it is useful to schedule conferences for times when children can leave with their parents rather than see the parents leave again without them.

9-2c Plan a Private Location

Planning a quiet, private location is important. In most schools, this may mean coordination among staff members for use of available space—staff room, conference room, empty classroom, or another arrangement. All that is really needed are two or three comfortable, adult-sized chairs, perhaps a table on which to spread papers or coffee cups, and a door that can be closed and posted with a sign—"Conference in Progress. Do Not Disturb." Teachers need to convey that the conversation will be strictly confidential (see Figure 9-6).

The physical environment probably least helpful to the conference goals is a formal office, with the teacher sitting behind a desk; the separation of one participant from the other by a desk conveys avoidance. A desk can act as a barricade between parent and teacher; it implies that the person seated behind it is dominant. These are not the nonverbal messages teachers want to send as they try to establish a partnership with parents. Remember that parents will arrive at the conference feeling nervous and fearful. A relaxed setting can help put them and the teacher at ease (see Figure 9-7).

9-2d Plan Goals to Be Discussed

In preparation for a conference, teachers must set their goals and devise plans for meeting each goal. Because one goal for every conference is undoubtedly to share information for a developmental overview, teachers need to accumulate the resources they will use to guide this discussion. A simple developmental evaluation tool, which evaluates children's accomplishments in several areas, including gross motor, fine motor, language, concepts, self-help skills, emotional development, and social skills, can be used at the preschool level. Elementary teachers may have the outline of a district report card but must ensure that it addresses all areas of development.

The use of a developmental assessment tool in a conference with parents ensures that the conversation covers all domains. The checklist also offers concrete examples of what is usually expected at broad stages of development, thereby educating parents as well as helping them to consider their children's behavior in an objective way (see Figure 9-8).

Other materials may be used to reinforce this developmental information visually and concretely for parents. Samples of art illustrate the refinement of small-muscle skills, new concepts, or new stages in a child's art. Samples of writing or lists of books read may demonstrate emergent literary skills. Examples of daily work collected over time offer parents a perspective on progress. Photos of classroom activities may indicate children's interests or interactions. Aware of

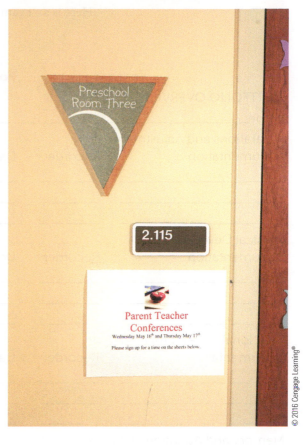

FIGURE 9-6
A sign on the door helps preserve privacy for parent–teacher conferences.

© 2016 Cengage Learning®

FIGURE 9-7
A relaxed atmosphere sitting at a table rather than behind a desk creates an impression of partnership.

© iStockphoto.com/Chris Schmidt

developmentally appropriate practices, many teachers today are maintaining portfolios on children to be able to assess their development and learning broadly, with natural methods, rather than by artificial test situations. A portfolio may include samples of work, anecdotal notes from observations, and checklists of observed skills and development.

Here is an example of the contents in a portfolio (Nilsen, 2013):

Portfolio Checklist

PORTFOLIO OVERVIEW SHEET

Name_____ Birth Date_____

Separations and Adjustment Documentation	Recorder	Date	Self-Care Documentation	Recorder	Date
_____	_____	_____	_____	_____	_____
_____	_____	_____	_____	_____	_____
Physical Development Documentation	Recorder	Date	**Social Development** Documentation	Recorder	Date
_____	_____	_____	_____	_____	_____
_____	_____	_____	_____	_____	_____
Emotional Development Documentation	Recorder	Date	**Speech and Language** Documentation	Recorder	Date
_____	_____	_____	_____	_____	_____
_____	_____	_____	_____	_____	_____
Memory and Attention Span Documentation	Recorder	Date	**Cognitive Development** Documentation	Recorder	Date
_____	_____	_____	_____	_____	_____
_____	_____	_____	_____	_____	_____
Literacy Development Documentation	Recorder	Date	**Creativity—Art and Blocks** Documentation	Recorder	Date
_____	_____	_____	_____	_____	_____
_____	_____	_____	_____	_____	_____
Creative—Dramatic Play Documentation	Recorder	Date	**Self-Identity** Documentation	Recorder	Date
_____	_____	_____	_____	_____	_____
_____	_____	_____	_____	_____	_____
Group Interactions Documentation	Recorder	Date	**Interactions With Adults** Documentation	Recorder	Date
_____	_____	_____	_____	_____	_____
_____	_____	_____	_____	_____	_____

Other Documentation

_____

_____

_____

Four Reasons For Regular Conferences

SUGGESTIONS FOR FURTHER READING

Cesarone, B. (2000). Parent–teacher conferences. *Childhood Education, 76(3)*, 180–5.

Child Care Information Exchange. (1997). Beginnings workshop. *Child Care Information Exchange*, 116. The entire journal deals with conferences, including conferences with parents of infants and school-aged children and cross-cultural conferences.

Croft, C. (2010). Talking to families of infants and toddlers about developmental delays. *Young Children, 65(1)*, 44–6.

Flannery, M. (2004). Turning the tables: In a twist on the traditional parent–teacher conference, teachers are inviting somebody else to run the show—their students. *NEA Today, 23(3)*, 36–42.

Rudney, G. (2005). *Every teacher's guide to working with parents*. Thousand Oaks, CA: Corwin Press.

Seligman, M. (2000). *Conducting effective conferences with parents of children with disabilities: A guide for teachers*. New York: Guilford Press.

Stevens, B., & Tollafield, A. (2003). Classroom practice: Creating comfortable and productive parent/teacher conferences. *Phi Delta Kappan, 84(7)*, 521–31.

Reproduced with permission of author. Nilsen, B. (2010). Week by week: Plans for observing young children *(5th ed.). Florence, KY: South-West College Publications.*

Sharing the portfolio at conference time provides real evidence to parents of the process of learning (Martin, 2009).

Teachers present anecdotal observations in such a way that parents will feel encouraged to comment on or react to them. Parents are not told precisely what an observation might imply about a child, but the data are presented for mutual discussion and consideration.

Anecdotal records are also useful in describing to parents—and not evaluating—aspects of behavior that are of concern. One of the best reasons for using such records in a conference is that they offer tangible evidence of how well teachers have paid attention to a particular child, which is important to every parent.

In addition to planning what to share, teachers should prepare a list of questions to ask so they will be sure to learn from a conference. One teacher's list follows:

Questions to ask:

- *Bedtime routine and time?*
- *Which friends does he or she talk about at home?*
- *What are favorite home activities?*
- *Which parts of the day are discussed at home?*

Making a brief outline of the topics to be discussed is helpful to teachers and parents. A teacher will not forget items of importance as the conversation continues. An initial sharing

FIGURE 9-8
It may be helpful for teachers to use lesson plans and developmental checklists to illustrate information.

© Cengage Learning®

of the list of topics with parents and asking for their additions will indicate to parents that they have more than a passive listening role to play, and may prevent them from beginning too quickly to discuss problems before a balanced overview is achieved. If there are delicate issues to be raised, teachers will want to particularly plan how they will talk about these subjects. A mental rehearsal of the conference plan will help teachers be more confident.

"Let me tell you some of the things I plan to cover today. We'll go through the school's developmental checklist so you can see how Pete's doing in all areas of his development. I also wanted to tell you about some of his favorite classroom activities and friends. There are a couple of areas we're particularly working on—his participation at group time and doing things for himself—so I'll tell you how that's going. Now let me add the questions you've brought in today. This will help us make sure we get it all covered."

Some teachers find it helpful to send home a form to parents to ask for specific things they want to talk about at the upcoming conferences. In this way, the teacher learns of parents' concerns and can plan to discuss those issues and have available related materials. A sample conference letter appears in Figure 9-9.

FIGURE 9-9
Sample conference letter.

Parent–Teacher Conference Letter

Dear Parents,

As the day of our scheduled parent–teacher conference draws near, we need to collect our thoughts about your child so our time can be put to good use. The following questionnaire is designed to assist me in covering all areas of concern to you and to me. Please take a few minutes to complete and return it to me *prior* to our conference. Remember, this is *not* an evaluation; it is a *sharing* of information about a child that we both care about.

Thank you for your cooperation.

1. My child communicates the following to me at home about school:

   a. Relationships with children and adults:

   b. Favorite activities and areas of play:

2. I see my child's areas of strength as:

3. I feel that my child needs to develop skills in:

4. I would like to discuss or have more information on:

5. Have you considered the whole child—social, emotional, physical, and intellectual?

6. What else have you been wondering lately?

Reprinted with permission. Cathy Griffin, Dutch Neck Presbyterian Church, Princeton Junction, New Jersey.

Teachers may also suggest ways families can set goals and prepare for a conference. This may be accomplished in two ways. The first is the letter or handout previously mentioned to stimulate parents' questions. Whatever form this takes, the clear message is that parents can expect to talk about any issue or concern.

The second idea is to suggest that parents spend a brief period observing a classroom before a conference—perhaps joining a group for lunch before a naptime conference or coming into the classroom earlier before a late afternoon appointment. Here again, a simple list with a few questions can guide parents in watching their children, the activities in which they are involved, their interaction with others, a teacher's methods, and so on. Such observation often stimulates immediate responses or questions or it may allow parents to see some of the behaviors that a teacher will later discuss.

A class newsletter before conference time could be devoted to reminding parents of actions they can take to help prepare for conferences. Suggestions might include setting their own goals for a conference, creating their own lists of questions and topics for discussion, setting a time to observe in the classroom, or talking with a school-aged child about their concerns.

The organization of anecdotal records and developmental assessments in preparation for a conference should take a small amount of time because these are materials that should be an ongoing part of a teacher's tools for individualized goal setting and planning in the classroom curriculum and are likely organized on the teacher's computer. A last review and organization of the materials will help teachers see they are prepared; pencils and paper should be added for teachers and parents to use for any notes. Being confident in their preparation leaves teachers free to initiate the social interaction of a conference (see Figure 9-10). Until teachers have prepared for and conducted many conferences, it is probably useful to use a checklist like the one in Figure 9-11 to ensure complete preparation.

FIGURE 9-10
Being prepared for a conference is a basic step toward helpful communication.

TeachSource Digital Download

FIGURE 9-11
Checklist for teachers preparing for parent conference.

Conference Preparation

1. _____ Time scheduled.

2. _____ Coverage in classroom arranged.

3. _____ Staff lounge reserved.

4. _____ Organization of anecdotal records and portfolio.

5. _____ Handout sent for parent preparation.

6. _____ Parent contacted for observation appointment.

7. _____ List of questions prepared.

8. _____ Outline of topics prepared.

9. _____ Plan for opening examples.

10. _____ Environment prepared—snacks, writing materials, privacy sign.

© Cengage Learning®

GROUNDWORK FOR A SUCCESSFUL CONFERENCE

1. Teacher and parent understanding of the purpose and their roles
2. Planning for uninterrupted time, agreeable to teacher and parent
3. A relaxed and private physical environment
4. Planning of goals and organization of materials

9-3 Strategies for a Successful Conference

Preparation for conferences has been discussed at length because setting attitudes and atmosphere conducive to full partner participation is vital. Now let us consider the conference itself.

9-3a Help Parents Feel at Ease

It is a teacher's responsibility to help parents become comfortable and at ease. Teachers are on familiar territory; parents are not. Unless parents are made to feel comfortable, their discomfort may be such a distraction that communication is hindered. A few minutes spent in a pleasant greeting and casual conversation is time well spent. An offer of juice or coffee may be appreciated by a weary parent as well as help create more social ease.

"I appreciate your taking the time to come in today. Pete's been telling me about your camping trip plans. Sounds like you're going to cover a lot of territory!"

Although teachers need to recognize parents' likely fears when entering a conference situation, most teachers also feel some apprehension when approaching conferences. Certainly, advance preparation and thinking through goals, questions, ways to phrase things, and possible conflicts will lessen this, as will experience. Getting to know parents as people will also make conferences less formidable. Awareness and acceptance of inevitable nervousness on the part of teachers and parents will help teachers be sensitive to the emotional atmosphere.

9-3b Begin with a Positive Attitude

As teachers turn the conversation toward the child, they begin with a positive comment about the child. It is important to indicate to parents at the outset that you like and appreciate their child. Parents are more likely to accept later comments—even constructive criticism or concerns—if the conference begins with everyone obviously on the same side and with a teacher's clear indication that she has paid specific attention to a child and knows him well. A positive opening comment also removes any lingering concern a parent may have about the purpose of a conference.

"I'm enjoying having Pete in my classroom. I think one of the things I most enjoy is his enthusiasm about everything! I wish you could have seen him this morning when he was talking about the plans for your trip—eyes sparkling and words just tumbling out!"

OPPORTUNITY FOR SELF-REFLECTION

Think about any experiences you have had with parent–teacher conferences. Perhaps your experiences have been as a parent, as a teacher, or as a child hearing about a conference afterward. Identify some of the emotional responses you had about the conference. How do you think these earlier emotions and experiences affect your present attitude toward holding conferences as a teacher?

9-3c Encourage Parent Participation

Although teachers clearly guide the conversation through the planned topics, they should be continually aware of the principle of partnership and try to draw a parent into participation at all times by frequently asking **open-ended questions**:

> **open-ended questions**
> With no fixed answer; unrestricted.

"So, he's achieved all these self-help skills except for shoe tying, and we're working on that. What kinds of things do you see him doing for himself at home now?"

"What kinds of things have you found that interest him for independent reading?"

The use of questions will help a parent expand on a statement so teacher and parent can get a clearer picture:

"When you say you're having problems with her at mealtime, could you tell me a bit more about some things that have been particularly troublesome at dinner recently?"

"When you say you've been having a hard time interesting her in reading, can you tell me what kinds of things you've tried?"

Teachers who want to help parents assume the role of "expert" on their child use questions to guide parents toward thinking about possible courses of action instead of telling them what to do:

CULTURAL CONSIDERATIONS

Silent parents

Assuming that teachers are using these strategies to involve parents in dialogue about their children, many can be puzzled when parents remain silent. It may be useful to consider some of these culturally driven possibilities:

1. When teachers use first names at the time of introductions, many Asian, Native American, and African American families may expect more formal forms of address at a formal conference.

2. Many Native American and Asian families expect to have authority figures tell them what to do about their children, and they may believe that a proper response is respectful silence.

3. Many parents from Asian and Native American cultural backgrounds may prefer to remain silent rather than discuss what they consider to be family problems.

4. Some people from other cultures may have a lack of trust in what is perceived as an authority figure (Kalyanpur & Harry, 2012).

Before deciding that silence means parents are not interested in working with teachers, it is important for teachers to consider possible cultural messages of silence. How can you clarify the meaning of silence? What nonverbal cues would you look for to evaluate comfort level?

"What are some of the things you've tried when she's begun playing with her food?"

"I wonder if reading could be tied in with some of his other interests?"

They encourage parents to continue talking by **active listening**. This is the technique of giving sensitive attention and picking up a speaker's verbal and nonverbal messages and then reflecting back the total message empathetically for a speaker's verification (see Figure 9-12). Techniques involved in active listening include paraphrasing and reflecting.

Paraphrasing involves restating what another person has said in slightly different words. This is a useful method of checking whether the other's meaning has been understood as well as eliciting more information.

Parent: "We've always believed in eating with the children, but lately, Pete's been giving us such problems that I'm tempted to give up."

Teacher: "Mealtime with Pete has been unpleasant lately. It sounds to me like mealtime has become a time of day you really don't look forward to."

Parent: "Oh, it's been nothing but nagging to get him to eat and fussing about his dawdling. It's awful!"

Reflecting offers feedback on the emotional meaning of a message. It is necessary for teachers to put themselves into the position of the other person, to be able to feel as

active listening
Technique of sensitively picking up on a speaker's verbal and nonverbal messages and reflecting back the total message for the speaker's verification.

paraphrasing
Restating in slightly different words what another has said.

reflecting
Giving back to a speaker words that convey the listener's impression of the speaker's meaning.

FIGURE 9-12
Active listening
involves reflecting and
paraphrasing.

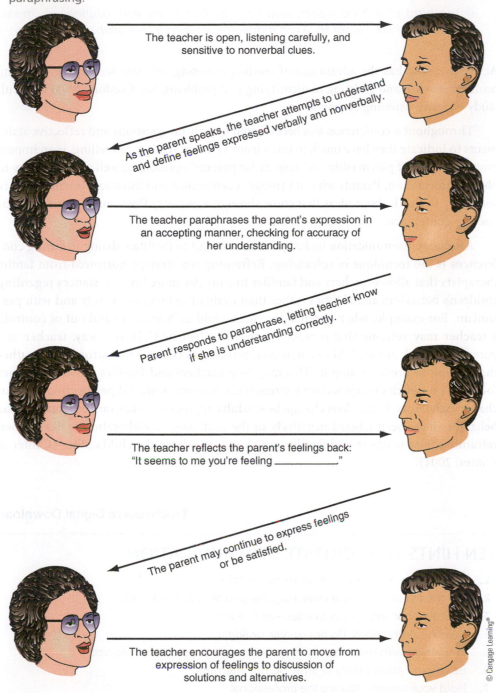

The teacher is open, listening carefully, and sensitive to nonverbal clues.

As the parent speaks, the teacher attempts to understand and define feelings expressed verbally and nonverbally.

The teacher paraphrases the parent's expression in an accepting manner, checking for accuracy of her understanding.

Parent responds to paraphrase, letting teacher know if she is understanding correctly.

The teacher reflects the parent's feelings back: "It seems to me you're feeling _____."

The parent may continue to express feelings or be satisfied.

The teacher encourages the parent to move from expression of feelings to discussion of solutions and alternatives.

© Cengage Learning®

he does, and to see the world as he is now seeing it. This involves accepting the feelings of a parent without judgment and reflecting the feelings back to him in a way that lets him know the teacher understands. When a teacher is not just quietly attentive but also is responsive to the feelings behind the other person's words and body language, active listening encourages fuller communication. As a teacher reflects her understanding of a parent's message, the parent is often stimulated to continue talking about a situation, allowing for a deeper understanding of feelings for teacher and parent.

Teacher: "It really seems to concern you that he's not developing good meal-time habits."

Parent: "Well, you know, it does bother me. I guess because I used to be something of a food fusser, and I remember some very unpleasant meal-times as a child. I want to avoid it developing into a real problem with Pete—if I can."

Active listening has the advantages of sending a message of clear acceptance, defusing hostile behavior, and assisting in identifying real problems. See Gordon (2008) for a full study of active listening concepts.

Throughout a conference, teachers depend heavily on questions and reflective statements to indicate they have much to learn from a parent. Asking, not telling, is an important indication of partnership and respect for parents' opinions as well as a good way to obtain information. Parents who sit through a conference and listen to a teacher talk are less likely to think about ideas that come through a one-way flow—or to come back for another conference.

reframing
Shifting from a negative perspective to a perspective that recognizes strengths by choosing different words and frames of reference.

Another communication technique that is useful to facilitate dialogue during conferences is the technique of **reframing**. Reframing is a strategy borrowed from family therapists that allows teachers and families to consider more hopeful stances regarding children's behaviors and abilities rather than evaluating them negatively and with pessimism. For example, when parents describe a child as "too active and out of control," a teacher may reframe that perspective to being "spirited." In this way, teacher and parents can look at the child in a new way, working to channel that strong spirit rather than trying to break or stop it. This may help teachers and families move away from focusing on deficits to appreciating strengths. Changing a mental perspective may not change behaviors, but it does change how adults approach a situation, especially if the behaviors have been labeled negatively in the past. More collaboration is likely when reframing puts teachers and families on the same side as the child's allies (Canter & Canter, 2001).

TeachSource Digital Download

TEN HINTS TO FACILITATE COMMUNICATION

1. Stop talking. You cannot listen if you are talking.
2. Put the person talking at ease. Help the person feel free to talk.
3. Indicate your willingness to listen—nonverbally.
4. Remove distractions. Do not doodle or fidget.
5. Empathize with the person talking. See the other person's viewpoint.
6. Be patient. Allow plenty of time. Do not interrupt.
7. Hold your temper. You are the professional.
8. Go easy on argument and criticism, which would make the other person clam up.
9. Ask questions. This shows you are listening and helps develop points.
10. Stop talking. This is first and last because everything depends on it.

9-3d Summarize for Parents

There is much to talk about when parents and teachers get together. But teachers must be mindful of the time pressures on busy parents and keep a conference to the scheduled time. If more areas arise that need to be discussed, it is preferable to make a second appointment. Too much information at one time may be burdensome and not fully absorbed.

As a conference ends, it is again a teacher's responsibility to summarize the main points discussed as well as any projected plans. It might be useful to offer a written copy of any assessment tool that the teacher discussed and to offer writing materials for the parent to make final notes. If the teacher also takes notes, this will make it easier to write the conference summary later. It is a good idea for parents and teacher to leave the conference knowing each has a specific action to perform. Parents need to leave a conference feeling their time was well spent; a summary to reinforce the discussion is useful. Once again, it is especially appropriate to be positive about parents' efforts and contributions (see Figure 9-13).

FIGURE 9-13
Offering parents a written summary of any assessment information is helpful.

© Cengage Learning®

"Thank you for coming in today. I've certainly appreciated your sharing so much helpful information about Pete. As you've seen from our assessment, he's doing very well in every area. I'm particularly glad to know of your concern about mealtime so I can support your efforts here. Your plan of trying a time limit sounds good. Do let me know how it goes."

jargon
Vocabulary peculiar to a particular profession or group.

9-4 Pitfalls to Avoid for a Successful Conference

In addition to paying attention to these strategies, teachers need to be aware of and avoid specific pitfalls.

9-4a Avoid Using Technical Terminology

When teachers explain developmental progress to parents, they must be careful not to use educational jargon or technical terms that are not easily understood and can create distance between the adults. Parents are not likely to listen to someone talking over their heads and are understandably reluctant to ask for clarification of terms.

Not: *"He functions well in the Piagetian sensorimotor stage."*

Rather: *"He is a very active explorer. Every time we offer him new material, he examines it very carefully from every angle."*

Not: *"She did fairly well on her Denver."*

Rather: *"We use this set of questions to see how the children are doing at their developmental level, and she did well, as you'll see."*

Not: *"He scored in the 47th percentile."*

Rather: *"He is doing about as well as the average first-grader in reading."*

Teachsource

VIDEO ACTIVITY ▶❙❙

© 2016 Cengage Learning®

Watch the Video Case entitled *Home, School Communication: The Parent–Teacher Conference.* Then respond to the following questions:

1. Which specific benefits of parent conferences discussed in this chapter do you observe in this video clip?

2. How could this conference help the parent? Help the child? Build the parent–teacher partnership?

STRATEGIES FOR A SUCCESSFUL CONFERENCE

Following these general strategies can help teachers achieve a successful conference:

1. Teacher taking initiative in putting parents at ease
2. A positive beginning and ending
3. Give-and-take in conversation, facilitated by a teacher's questions and reflective listening
4. A summarizing of areas discussed and action to be taken

9-4b Avoid the Role of "Expert"

Teachers should be careful not to set themselves up as experts on any child. Such a stance prevents the growth of a working partnership; many parents feel shaky enough in the business of parenting without facing a teacher who seems to "know it all." Rather than peppering their comments with advice that focuses on "shoulds" and "musts," teachers need to avoid such authoritarian dogmatism. The implication that if one disagrees, one is wrong will inhibit discussion.

To avoid the appearance of being a dogmatic expert, teachers need to be cautious about the phrases they use as they share knowledge. Many teachers say "lots of parents find" or "some of my parents have told me;" they find these phrases more easily accepted than "I think," which sounds too dominant. Teachers need to help parents realize that there are few absolutes in child development and guidance; some things work in one situation and others in another.

Certain areas of concern to a parent may be far beyond a teacher's scope of knowledge and competence. It is necessary for teachers to be straightforward in admitting this and to know when to refer a parent to an expert:

> *"I appreciate your concern about Billy's language. Let me give you the number of the people at Speech and Hearing. They can answer your questions far better than I can."*

> *"You know, I'm not quite sure about those admission test score systems. Suppose I check with the school and let you know?"*

If teachers feel another could answer questions better, they may invite the administrator, psychologist, social worker, or co-teacher to join a discussion. Contrary to what some teachers believe, when they confess their limitations, it tends not to demean them but instead earns them respect in parents' eyes for their honesty.

9-4c Avoid Negative Evaluations

Knowing how closely parental self-esteem is tied to others' perceptions of their children, teachers must be sensitive to avoid the appearance of being critical or negative about a child's capabilities. Certain key words trigger defensive feelings in parents, and parents who feel defensive are unable to communicate and cooperate fully. Here are some words to avoid:

- Problem—"I'm having a *problem* with Jimmy."
- Behind—"Jimmy is *behind* in language."
- Immature—"Jimmy is more *immature* than the rest of the class."

- Never; can't—"Jimmy *never* finishes lunch with the others; Jimmy *can't* do most of our puzzles."

- Slow—"Jimmy is *slow* at learning."

- Failing—"Jimmy is *failing* all his spelling tests."

Remember the reframing discussed earlier? This is the place to consider the positive aspects of a situation rather than focusing on negatives or limitations.

Such labels as *hyperactive, learning disability,* and similar terms should also be avoided. Many of these terms have been adopted and overused by the general public. Because teachers do not have clinical training, it is not appropriate for teachers to hypothesize diagnoses.

- Labels—"Sometimes, I wonder if Jimmy isn't *hyperactive.*"

Comments that are objective observations rather than subjective characterizations are more helpful and more easily received:

> **Not:** *"Jimmy doesn't like art." (subjective)*
>
> **Rather:** *"Jimmy usually chooses to play with blocks, building large buildings and adding trucks and people to the scene. I have seen him choose to use art materials twice in the past two months." (objective)*
>
> **Not:** *"Jenny is not a very friendly child." (subjective)*
>
> **Rather:** *"Jenny usually plays by herself at recess. I have seen her turn away if another child approaches." (objective)*

When teachers merely describe specific behaviors, completely adhering to facts and foregoing the temptation to add their own interpretation of factual observations, parents are left to draw their own conclusions. This offers objective information without implying evaluation or criticism. Teachers have a responsibility to help parents think positively about their children, and negative judgments are simply not useful. Any parent would react emotionally to hearing these. Parents need teachers who can offer realistic and constructive, not destructive, comments (see Figure 9-14).

FIGURE 9-14
Teachers need to offer information in an objective way without implying evaluation or criticism.

"One of the things we're working on with Jimmy is...." A comment such as this does not imply negative evaluation, such as being behind or a problem, but states action that can be taken. Because behavior is complex, it would be impossible as well as unproductive to assign reasons or blame for a particular behavior.

This is an example of an unhelpful statement: "Jimmy has been having so many temper tantrums because your husband has been out of town so much lately." The statement is not necessarily true, certainly not helpful, and so personal and pointed it could alienate a parent from a partnership. An observant teacher watches parents' body language to notice if there is an emotional reaction to what she has said. Some body messages to watch for include facial expression, tightening or withdrawal of the body, the degree of relaxation of hands and body posture, and change in position (see Figure 9-15).

9-4d Avoid Unprofessional Conversation

Teachers need to be sure a conversation remains professional, although warm, and centered on the adults' common concerns related to a child. Teachers must never discuss other children and parents in a conference with another parent; to do so would make parents question if their own conversation is confidential.

> **Not:** *"You know, Mrs. Smith has been having an even worse time with Janie—she had a terrible tantrum the other day."*

This might have been intended as a reassurance, but is probably unsettling to the other parent who hears it.

FIGURE 9-15
This cartoon teacher demonstrates the error of an extremely negative focus during the conference.

> **Rather:** *"Many parents find that four-year-olds can get quite out of bounds."*

Teachers should not ask personal questions except when they are absolutely related to a concern being discussed about a child.

> **Not:** *"How do you spend your spare time on the weekends?"*

> **Rather:** *"I've been wondering what time Jimmy goes to bed—he's been very sleepy in the midmorning."*

> **Not:** *"Just how do you and your ex-husband get along?"*

> **Rather:** *"Are there occasions I should know about when Sally will be in contact with her father?"*

When parents turn a conversation to personal matters not directly related to their children, teachers need to make it clear that their only role is to listen supportively if the parent needs to talk—of course ensuring confidentiality—and to refer to more expert community resources if a parent seems interested.

> *"I'm sorry to hear that you and Jimmy's father have been having some difficulties. If it helps you to talk about it, I'll be glad to listen. I can also suggest a couple of agencies that could be really helpful during such a difficult time."*

It is inappropriate to cut this parent off completely; teachers are sometimes so oriented to children's problems that they do not realize that parents have to deal with their own exhausting problems.

Sometimes, especially in a conference with two parents present, teachers can get caught in the middle of a family disagreement:

> *"Mr. Jones, my husband and I just don't agree about disciplining Bobby. He spanks him whenever he misbehaves, but I don't believe in spanking kids. What would you say?"*

There could only be future difficulty in working with this family if the teacher were to take sides. His answer needs to be helpful and neutral:

> *"Discipline is a broad subject, and even many experts don't agree. I think families have to make up their minds and do what's right for them. If it would help, I can tell you some of the things we do in the classroom and why."*

Teachers' awareness of their roles as professionals may help them avoid these pitfalls. Professional ethics also require that teachers not share students' personal family issues with other teachers except when necessary to understand children's behaviors or situations. The information teachers learn about families must be protected within the school and within the community. When teachers see parents away from school in public places, even quiet conversations can threaten confidentiality if others are nearby and could overhear.

"That's the bad news. There isn't any good news."

Courtesy Bob Vojtkol.

OPPORTUNITY FOR SELF-REFLECTION

Imagine that you are a parent in a conference, and the teacher says to you, "Jennifer can't ever stand in line without causing trouble." What might be your response? How could the teacher have changed her language to avoid this response?

Again imagine being a parent, and this is what you hear: "Susan is very selfish. It's obvious she has never been taught to share. I think you should work on this." What is your immediate mental response as a parent? How could this have been presented differently?

9-4e Avoid Giving Advice

It is easy for teachers to make the error of giving unasked-for advice to parents; teachers may see a need and have a fairly good idea what could help. But advice from others is seldom effective; only when parents reach a personal conclusion do they become committed to action. Just because a parent mentions a problem, a teacher should not conclude that the parent is asking for a solution to that problem. A teacher is likely not to know the full complexity of the situation and may give inappropriate suggestions. A teacher does not tell the parent what to do at home—partly because the teacher will not be there to help carry out the action. A survey of parents (Olson & Hyson, 2005) found that parents regard advice giving as intrusive, preferring instead to receive information in a cooperative, respectful manner, within the context of the relationship and based on sharing of information. Giving advice tends to distance a teacher from the parent. Parents might quietly listen to this advice while inwardly fuming:

"Who does he think he is? A lot he knows about it anyway—this is my child, not his."

Giving advice may usurp the parent's right to decide and may also detract from parents' feelings of competence and self-worth. Giving advice may also be dangerous; when the "expert's" suggestions do not work, the expert gets the blame and future mistrust. A more effective teacher role may be to help parents move through several steps in problem solving and discovering options that they may follow.

Teachers should remember that time spent helping parents find their own best solution is time well spent in enhancing parental competence and avoiding disrupting a relationship or partnership. It is easy to fall into the trap of giving advice to parents when they ask for it—probably because it is a good feeling to know you have the answer someone else needs! The best way to avoid such a pitfall is to make several suggestions and turn the thinking process back to the parent:

"Some of the things we've tried in the classroom for that are ..."

"Let me pass along some ideas that have worked for other parents.... Do any of those sound like something that could work for you?"

It is appropriate to help parents understand that in guidance, there is seldom one right answer. Parents should be encouraged to come up with their own plans, which they are more likely to carry out than a plan handed to them. If teachers remember that one of their goals is to enhance not only parenting skills but also parental self-esteem, they will realize how important it is to be speculative in offering suggestions, not dogmatic in giving advice. "If I were you, I'd …" is definitely not the most helpful phrase because it implies such an absolute and sure position.

9-4f   Avoid Rushing into Solutions

Another easy error for either parents or teacher is to feel that all problems must be solved and conclusions reached during a designated conference period. Changing behaviors and understanding is a process that takes time and cannot be artificially rushed to fit into a brief conference. It is better to suggest the need for time:

"All right—both of us will try to watch and see when these outbursts occur. Maybe then we can work out some appropriate response. Let's plan to get back together and talk again next month."

TeachSource Digital Download

PITFALLS TO AVOID FOR SUCCESSFUL CONFERENCES

1. Overly technical terminology or jargon
2. Playing the role of an "expert"
3. Negative or destructive evaluations about a child's capabilities
4. Unprofessional conversation: about others, too personal, or taking sides
5. Giving advice—either solicited or not
6. Trying to solve all problems on the spot or trying to force agreement

---

It is also a mistake to assume that parents and teachers will always be able to agree and work together and that a conference is a failure if the teacher is unable to "convert" a parent to her understanding. Different experiences, personalities, value systems, and needs influence how readily each can agree with the other's viewpoint. Child-rearing values and practices are culturally embedded (Seplocha, 2007). A successful conference is one in which there are opportunities to learn more about diverse cultures and parents' hopes for their children as well as to exchange and accept various insights, including those that conflict.

9-5   Difficult Conferences

Communicating about difficulties stretches teacher abilities and parent emotions. It is vital that teachers do considerable planning—making a series of observations, reviewing notes and documentation, listing strategies and "what-ifs," perhaps even role-playing with a director or coworker to try responses to different parental reactions. It may be useful for teachers to consider the analogy of throwing a ball, which may be accomplished simply without a great deal of thought or planning, as opposed to throwing an egg covered with oil. The ball could be considered the typical, casual communication passing between teacher and parent, and the slippery egg could symbolize the communication about matters that have significant consequences for children and their parents. In throwing a slippery egg, the thrower is much slower to deliver the object; the egg is thrown with much more care, with careful preparation and observation of the catcher's readiness and ability to successfully receive the egg. Planning for delivering difficult information must be done with as much care as for throwing slippery eggs (Leading Edge, 1998). As in all conferences, teachers will start with sharing positive information.

During the conference, teachers need to focus on identifying the concern they share with the parent for the child. It is important that teachers already have laid some groundwork in previous conversations; the concern should not come as a complete surprise to the parent. Teachers should make sure they indicate that they are sharing the concern to support the child's development and to get some ideas on how to best meet children's needs. Teachers must empathize with the emotional responses of a parent hearing difficult news:

"It makes you extremely angry to hear that Bobby may not yet be ready for kindergarten. I imagine there's some disappointment for you, too?"

"I know it can be hard to hear unwelcome news. Is there any way I can help make the disappointment easier for you?"

"I want to help you find the best plan for Bobby. My biggest concern, as I know is yours, is to have a classroom experience next year that will contribute to his growth."

It is vital for teachers to say that they are not being critical but just reporting what they have seen and clearly citing specific classroom incidents and behaviors and what has been tried so far. A nonjudgmental stance is crucial. It is important for teachers to emphasize how what they are seeing is affecting the child. No matter how gentle the teacher is in broaching the matter, anger is a likely response—perhaps masked as hostility or blame. If parents have trouble accepting information, it is not uncommon for them to employ the defense mechanisms of projection—"If only you could teach better, he wouldn't have this problem"—or denial—"Don't you dare tell me my son has a problem." If parents become verbally abusive or irrational in anger, it is impossible to communicate effectively. At that point, a teacher's task is to defuse the anger so communication can begin. To do this, it is crucial that the teacher not become defensive or angry in return. Retaliating verbally, arguing, and retreating from the parents' anger are not helpful responses. A teacher needs to remain calm and speak softly and slowly. Active listening will allow parents to see their own words and feelings from the other's viewpoint. Teachers must demonstrate an acceptance of the parents' right to their opinions (see Figure 9-16).

Marshall Rosenberg has written about a process of nonviolent or compassionate communication that involves four principles: observing what is actually happening in the communication in a particular situation;

TeachSource

VIDEO ACTIVITY ▶‖

Watch the Bonus Video titled *Making a Recommendation for Specialized Testing* found in the Video Case, *Home, School Communication: The Parent–Teacher Conference*. After watching this video, reflect on the following questions:

1. How does the teacher approach the difficult topic to help the parent be receptive to the idea?
2. How does the teacher follow up on the parent's response?
3. What does this make you think about presenting difficult information to parents?

FIGURE 9-16
Effective teachers demonstrate an acceptance of parents' different viewpoints and opinions.

understanding how one feels when observing the action; understanding what needs of the individual are connected to those feelings; and making specific related requests (Rosenberg, 2003). Handling an expression of hostility this way will help a teacher work with a parent on the areas of disagreement instead of losing the issues in personal attacks or emotional responses. (Specific examples of how to work with hostility will be discussed further in Chapter 15.)

Teachers must respect the time it takes parents to process the knowledge and implications of difficult communication about a child. If, in spite of teacher efforts, parents choose to ignore the communication, teachers must realize that is their right. In the future, parents may be able to follow through on recommendations or agree to referral to a specialist.

Sometimes, parents need to hear concerns and recommendations several times before they are able to act on them. Denial for at least a while is a healthy coping strategy, enabling the parent not to become overwhelmed by pain. It is also important that teachers not become overwhelmed by guilt, disappointment, or frustration with parents who do not immediately respond and act on their children's behalf. Teachers must remain available to continue supporting and documenting the concern. Even if parents deny, teachers are not absolved of the responsibility to support and care for the child and family. Teachers also must realize that there will inevitably be unhappy endings.

9-6 Conference Evaluation

Soon after a conference is over, it is a good idea to summarize the information gained and plans made.

> *2/1/14. Conference with Pete's mother. (Stepfather unable to come due to work schedule.) She is concerned about Pete playing with food at meals.*
>
> *Topics discussed: LAP assessment. Preparation for new sibling due 5/2. Pete's readiness for kindergarten. Mother's concern about Pete playing with food at meals.*
>
> *Plan:*
>
> 1. *Share info rmation with co-teacher.*
> 2. *Observe Pete at lunch—move seat near mine.*
> 3. *Talk with mother again in two months.*

Figure 9-17 illustrates an example of a parent conference report form.

It is also useful for a teacher's professional growth to evaluate her own participation in the conference by asking herself such questions as the following:

- How well did I listen?
- How well did I facilitate parents' participation?
- Did I offer enough specifics?
- Was I positive in beginning and ending the conference?
- How comfortable were we in the conversation?

With experience, teachers grow in the process of facilitating an effective conference.

It is appropriate for a preschool teacher to hold conferences to discuss developmental progress and goals at least every six months because change occurs so rapidly at this time. For the needs of particular families and children, conferences may be held more

TeachSource Digital Download

FIGURE 9-17
Parent Conference Report Form.

Parent Conference Report Form

Name of child: _____

Participants in conference: _____ Date:_____

Child's strengths observed in classroom by teacher: _____

_____

_____

Child's needs observed in classroom by teacher: _____

_____

_____

Child's strengths observed at home by parent: _____

_____

_____

Child's needs observed at home by parent: _____

_____

_____

Suggestions for action at school: _____

_____

_____

Suggestions for action at home: _____

_____

_____

Follow-up plan: _____

_____

_____

Other: _____

_____

Teacher's signature_____

Parent's signature_____

© Cengage Learning®

---

frequently at the request of either parent or teacher. In elementary schools, it is also ideal to hold twice-a-year conferences, and in some cases, children may be included in the conference (Young & Behounek, 2006).

Remember that nonattendance at a conference does not necessarily indicate disinterest in the child or the school. Instead, it may reflect different cultural or socioeconomic values, extreme pressures, or the stress of family or work demands. A teacher's response to nonattendance should be to review the possible explanations for nonattendance, see if different scheduling or educational actions will help, persist in invitations and efforts, and understand that other methods of reaching a parent will have to be used in the meantime.

TeachSource Digital Download

IDEAS FOR TEACHERS:

Tips for Successful Conferences

1. Prepare carefully before the conference by considering the individual child's progress and documentation.
2. Ensure privacy.
3. Provide an informal setting.
4. Be mindful of parents' time.
5. Establish rapport.
6. Begin on a positive note.
7. Encourage the parents to talk.
8. Listen attentively.
9. Develop an attitude of mutual cooperation.
10. Delay making suggestions yourself.
11. Encourage suggestions from the parents.
12. Summarize points covered.
13. Make plans together for future actions.
14. End on a note of continuing cooperation.
15. Make notes about the conference after the parents leave.

SUMMARY

- Parent–teacher conferences provide:
  - Time for parents and teachers to talk privately
  - Consideration of all aspects of a child's overall development
  - Opportunities to share information about particular interests, needs, or problems that may concern either parents or teachers
  - Opportunities to formulate goals
- Factors that facilitate communication include:
  - Teacher and parent understanding of the conference's purpose and their roles
  - Planning for uninterrupted time, agreeable to teacher and parent
  - A relaxed and private physical environment
  - Planning of goals and organization of materials
- Strategies for successful conferences include:
  - Teacher taking initiative in putting parents at ease
  - A positive beginning and ending
  - Give-and-take in conversation, facilitated by a teacher's questions and reflective listening
  - Summarizing of areas discussed and action to be taken

- Pitfalls to avoid in conferences include:
    - Overly technical terminology or jargon
    - Playing the role of an "expert"
    - Negative or destructive evaluations about a child's capabilities
    - Unprofessional conversation about others, too personal, or taking sides
    - Giving advice—either solicited or not
    - Trying to solve all problems on the spot or trying to force agreement
- Difficult conferences require:
    - Preplanning and consideration of presentation
    - Sensitivity to parents' responses
    - Active listening
- Careful planning and evaluation of conferences will help teachers grow in the skills necessary for effective parent–teacher conferences.

Student Activities for Further Study

1. With your classmates, set up a role-playing situation in which one of you is a teacher and one is a parent. Remember to concentrate on facilitating a dialogue in the conversation by the teacher's questions and active listening. Your "audience" can help you evaluate and suggest other possibilities. Try these situations and any others you have encountered:

    a. A mother asks how to prepare her three-year-old for a new baby.

    b. A teacher is concerned about a recent increase in a child's aggressive behavior.

    c. A parent is worried about his seven-year-old son giving in to playground bullies.

    d. A teacher wants to find ways to help a first-grade English language learner develop confidence in the classroom.

   For ideas, refer to the Suggestions for Further Reading box. With a partner, brainstorm many possible teacher responses to these comments and questions from parents. Then, decide which is most appropriate and why:

    a. What I want to know is, when are the kids in your classroom going to do some real work, not just this playing?

    b. I don't know if I should tell you this, but my husband has left us, and I don't think he's coming back.

    c. What should I do about my second-grader and his obsession with video games?

    d. I certainly don't want my first-grader held back because of some test score.

2. After reading the following record, develop an outline for sharing this information with parents during a conference:

   Judy is three years and six months old and is much smaller than the other children in her classroom. She speaks indistinctly—often not more than two words at a time. She plays by herself most of the time and in fact seems to shrink back when other children or most adults approach her. She has well-developed fine-motor skills and is extremely creative when she paints.

> *Despite Judy's well-developed fine-motor skills, her self-help skills lag behind, and she often asks for assistance in the bathroom and in simple dressing tasks. She enjoys music and often sits for long periods listening to records with earphones.*

3. Additional ideas for role-playing/brainstorming to practice conference communication skills

   a. A teacher is concerned about coordinating toilet-training efforts

   b. A mother comments that her four-year-old son is being very "bad" lately

   c. A father is concerned about his son; he feels he is not as advanced at four as his older brother was.

   d. A mother asks you what to do about her toddler biting

   e. I honestly don't know how you do it—kids this age drive me crazy.

   f. Do you think my Sarah is slow? She doesn't seem to me to be talking right.

   g. Well, I don't agree with your soft approach. I say, when kids are bad, they should be spanked.

   h. What's the best way to get a child to go to bed?

4. Steps in finding solutions

   a. Identify the problem, including agreeing that there *is* a problem.

   b. Identify options for responding to the situation. Multiple solutions can be generated by the parent and professional brainstorming together, and no one's suggestions are ignored or put down. Teachers must set the stage for openness and encourage parent participation.

   c. Discuss the advantages and disadvantages of each option.

   d. Teachers and parents should choose a solution to try first.

   e. Discuss a plan to help implement the idea.

   f. Agree to meet again to evaluate how the option is working.

Apply the Chapter Concepts: Case in Point

Abigail Jenson is a five-year-old in a kindergarten classroom. Abigail lives with her mother and grandmother and sees her father every other weekend. Now that it is January, her teacher, Lukeisha Richardson, is becoming concerned about Abigail's solitary play behavior and developmental level. Abigail can identify only two colors and the letters that begin her first and last names. Her mother was unavailable during the last conference period, but Lukeisha feels it is time they met to discuss Abigail's development. The teacher has many questions that she would like to ask the mother:

1. What are some of the reasons Abigail's mother may have been unavailable during the last conference period? What could Miss Richardson do to make it more likely that the mother would be able to meet for a conversation?

2. As the teacher prepares for this conference, what are some issues she needs to take into account?

3. Suggest a first sentence or two that might help set a positive tone for the conference.

4. Describe several potential pitfalls that this teacher needs to be careful to avoid.

5. What would you see as a hoped-for result of this conference?

Review Questions

1. Identify three of four reasons for holding regular parent–teacher conferences.

2. List five of eight factors that facilitate productive parent–teacher conferences.

3. Describe four strategies for a successful parent–teacher conference.

4. List four of six pitfalls to avoid in parent–teacher conferences.

5. Discuss several considerations and strategies for difficult conferences.

6. Understand how to evaluate the parent–teacher conference.

Helpful Websites

- All these organizations and their websites offer helpful tips for teachers and parents in conferences.

- The website for the Colorado Parent Information & Resource Center.

- The website of the National Education Association has much information for teachers and parents.

- The website for TeacherVision has several components, including the Family Education Network (FEN).

- The website of Teachers' Network has several articles with tips on parent–teacher conferences.

Families in the Classroom

Learning Objectives

After reading this chapter, you should be able to:

10-1 Discuss several advantages and potential problems of working with parents in a classroom.

10-2 Identify methods of encouraging family involvement in the classroom.

10-3 Discuss methods to facilitate parent observation.

10-4 Describe methods of utilizing families as resources for classrooms.

10-5 Discuss the teacher's role in supporting families in the classroom.

naeyc

Related NAEYC Standards

Accreditation Standards (see inside text back cover for full listing of the Accreditation Standards for exemplary early childhood programs)

1.A.02; 2.A.04, 2.L.03; 3.F.06; 6.A.04; 7.A.02, 7.A.03, 7.A.07

Licensure Standards (see inside text front cover for full listing of the Licensure Standards for this chapter)

2c

One traditional way families have been involved in their children's education has been as volunteers in the classroom. The parent cooperative preschools that began in the first decades of the twentieth century believed that including parents in classrooms educated them and also extended the learning experiences available to their children. Certainly, bringing families into the classroom does this and gives families the opportunity to understand the program through firsthand observation. But in many cases, parent participation in classrooms has deteriorated into assignments of unattractive tasks rather than seen as yet another method of developing communication and working partnerships.

There are many roles parents can play within the preschool and elementary school classroom—from observer to assistant. This chapter examines these roles and considers ways teachers can make parents' participation enjoyable and productive for everyone, including their children. Planning, preparation of all participants, and positive attitudes will help teachers draw families into the educational process of their children.

10-1 Advantages and Potential Problems

There is a lively discussion going on in the teacher's lounge. Jane Briscoe has just announced she has a parent coming in to play the guitar at group time. MiLan Ha says nothing; she's never had a parent in, but Anne Morgan has told Jane she's just asking for trouble.

"It's a disaster when a parent comes in; the whole routine gets turned upside down, and worst of all, I guarantee you the parent's child will act up dreadfully."

Connie Martinez agrees. "One of my parents came in last year and brought a cake and balloons for everybody on her daughter's birthday. When the birthday girl's balloon broke, she burst into tears, and her mother slapped her. I was furious, but what could I do? Now I just ask them to have parties at home."

Jane looks thoughtful and a little worried, too.

There is no question that bringing families into a classroom adds responsibilities for teachers as they cope with various aspects of behavior and reactions of children and visitors. Teachers often object to having parents in the classroom for professional and personal reasons.

Involving parents in a classroom for any reason demands extra time and effort from a teacher because there are plans to make and fit into the routine. The best use of parents' time and skills must be determined, and children and parents must be prepared for their roles in the unusual event.

Jane Briscoe admits it took several conversations with Mr. Butler to learn about his guitar-playing skill and then more to convince him that the children would enjoy having him come and that he would know what to do when he got there! She's also had to reschedule the visit twice to fit around his working schedule and has spent considerable time helping Sam understand his dad will be coming for a visit but that Sam will be staying at school and not leaving when his dad goes back to work.

Teachers often have professional reservations about parents' functioning in a classroom. Teachers may be convinced that parents who do not have a teacher's education will behave inappropriately with children, especially with their own children, and therefore put teachers in the awkward position of observing unsuitable adult actions in their own classrooms. Some teachers still mistakenly believe that they alone should be the resource for learning in the classroom rather than valuing the potential contributions of others—despite all the evidence that children's learning is enhanced by their families' involvement.

Connie Martinez sighs. "I could have predicted that child was going to get over-excited with that whole birthday party hoopla. What I didn't know was that her mother would react so angrily. I was embarrassed not only for that child but also that the other children saw that happen in my classroom."

Teachers may be concerned that parents will behave unprofessionally in other ways, such as discussing children with others outside the classroom or making inappropriate remarks to other children.

Another teacher concern results from their knowledge of young children's reactions when adjusting to changed routines. Some teachers who perceive a child's overexcitement or distress when a parent leaves the classroom after a special event feel the experience is too disruptive to be beneficial.

"Look, it's a nice idea, but in practice, it's too upsetting. Children can't understand why their parents can't stay the whole time, and it undoes a lot of adjustment."

Teachers may also have personal qualms about parents being on hand to observe their actions for an extended period. Whether it is true or not, many teachers feel that they are constantly watched and evaluated when parents are present and therefore feel uncomfortable throughout a visit, feeling the need to perform.

MiLan says, "Frankly, I don't need the additional stress of having a parent watch me through the whole morning."

Considering these objections, are there reasons for including parents in the classroom that outweigh the disadvantages? There certainly are great benefits for parents, children, and teachers.

For parents, spending time in a classroom is the best way to understand what is going on in a school (see Figure 10-1). Parents have often equated school with purely cognitive learning and are sometimes surprised and dismayed to learn that good early childhood classrooms emphasize more than academic learning. Parents of children in elementary school may not realize how much teaching methods and curricula have changed since their own school days. Seeing what is actually happening gives them more respect for the real learning that is taking place.

Mr. Butler, the guitar-playing father, helps explain this. "It was good to see what they do at their group time. Those kids are really learning to listen—to take turns talking and participating. Then, they had their snack. Several children were responsible for getting the tables set, and they did it just right. And they poured their own juice, and not a drop spilled. Then, they all tried these vegetables in a dip; at home, Sam would never have touched the stuff, but there with his friends, he did."

FIGURE 10-1
For parents, spending time in a classroom is the best way to understand what is going on in a program.

FIGURE 10-2
Most parents enjoy getting to know their children's friends.

And Mrs. Murphy says after a visit to her first grader's classroom: "I realized the difference between what writing meant when I was in school and what it means in Kathleen's classroom. We used to spend hours practicing forming letters, one after another, across the page. Kathleen spends time writing in her journal every day. She makes lots of mistakes in spelling, and the letters aren't very neat, but she is learning how to express her ideas. It's amazing."

Such firsthand knowledge provides a ready basis for discussion with teachers and leads to parental support of classroom practices and the teacher.

In a classroom, parents can see how their children are functioning with peers and other adults. They can also observe typical behaviors and skills for a cross section of children the same age, increasing their understanding of typical child development and education. This observation may also enable parents to see firsthand the kinds of problem behaviors that teachers may want to discuss later:

"You know, it's kind of reassuring to find out that most two-year-olds grab things from each other. I'd been thinking mine was particularly aggressive."

"Now I can talk with the teacher about how I should help her with her writing—all that misspelling has been bothering me."

Being in a classroom also gives parents a feeling of satisfaction as they contribute to learning, are welcomed by a teacher, and are recognized as important adults by their child and his or her friends—a real ego boost. Most parents enjoy getting to know their children's friends (see Figure 10-2).

"I'd never play my guitar for a group of adults, but the kids loved it, I must say."

"Every time I come, I really can see how my listening to children read one on one is helping them as well as the teacher."

FIGURE 10-3
Children feel special and important when their parents are in the classroom.

Children also feel special and important when their parents are in a classroom (see Figure 10-3).

"That's my daddy," beams Sam as his dad leads the singing with his guitar.

"My mom helps out in our classroom sometimes," says Kathleen.

Such good feelings probably have a more lasting impact than the transitory distress for a young child caused by a parent saying goodbye twice in one morning. Children's feelings of security increase as they see parents and teachers working together

cooperatively, with each respecting the other's contribution. Children see how important education is to their parents when parents support it with their presence. Children also benefit as parents gain in understanding the process of learning and children's interaction skills.

Teachers as well as children gain through the expanded opportunities for learning that other adults bring into a classroom. Parents' skills, knowledge, interests, and talents add up to lots of possible resources for curriculum learning and more than expanded opportunities. Countless recent studies underline the vital importance of family involvement in children's classrooms at all levels. Around the country, elementary schools are trying their best to bring family and community partners into the classroom for meaningful work: to read to children and be part of other literacy efforts, to tutor children, to work with children on special projects, or just to be a lunch buddy. Everyone, from the principal to the PTA, now recognizes that family involvement—and not just the "room mother" who arranges parties—enhances teachers' instructional efforts.

"I really like to give them as much music as I can, but I don't have a musical bone in my body. There's no substitute for having a real instrument in the classroom. From me, they get a lot of records."

"I really appreciate Mrs. Murphy coming in to have children read to her individually. There's just never enough time in the day for me to get to every child who needs my help."

Having an extra pair of hands in a group of children often allows activities that just are not possible without enough adults (see Figure 10-4). In primary classrooms, parent volunteers provide individual support and instruction.

Classroom visitation by parents gives teachers another chance to see parent–child interaction and parental attitudes:

"It's interesting to me to see Sam and his dad together. Mr. Butler is very comfortable in the nurturing role."

"Kathleen really strives to do her best work when her mother is visiting."

Teachers perceive family involvement in a classroom as evidence of support of their efforts because parents gain empathy toward a teacher and the problems of teaching a group of children. It is professionally and personally rewarding to deepen parent–teacher partnerships through such cooperative efforts:

"I really enjoyed having Mr. Butler with us, and I appreciated his interest in sharing some time with us. You know, he said when he went home, he shook his head and said he didn't see how I do it all day, every day."

"Mrs. Murphy said to me, 'I wish more parents would come to volunteer in the classroom. I don't think we'd hear so many complaints about the teachers and schools.'"

FIGURE 10-4
When parents go along to help, a special trip is possible.

© Cengage Learning®

FIGURE 10-5
In primary classrooms, parent volunteers provide individual support and encouragement in learning new skills.

It is true there are potential problems when parents are involved in a classroom. However, the following advantages make it worth the effort:

■ Parents gain firsthand experience of the school and of their child's reactions in a classroom as well as feelings of satisfaction from making a contribution.

■ Children feel special when their parents are involved, feel secure with the tangible evidence of parents and teachers cooperating, realize the value their parents place on education, and gain directly as parental understanding and skills increase.

■ Teachers gain resources to extend learning opportunities, observe parent–child interaction, and feel supported as parents participate and empathize with them (see Figure 10-5).

OPPORTUNITY FOR SELF-REFLECTION

If you are a parent, have you had experiences visiting your child's classroom in a child care program or school? What insights did this visit give you about your child, the teacher, and the classroom? What circumstances made you feel comfortable or not? Welcome or not? If you are not a parent, ask these questions of a friend or family member who is.

10-2 Encouraging Family Involvement

There are many different ways to involve parents in early childhood classrooms. Nonworking parents can be regular volunteers assisting teachers in **parent cooperative nursery schools**, Head Start programs, or other programs set up to educate parents and children. When parents regularly assume auxiliary teaching roles, it is advisable to prepare them for this experience with a training program. Then, issues of teaching philosophy and goals, children's behavior and learning styles, and appropriate adult guidance and interactive techniques can be explored so parents entering a classroom clearly understand their expected roles. A training program may include classroom visits, workshops, orientation discussions, handbooks, and guided observation.

Many other parents—particularly those who work—may visit a classroom infrequently for planned social events and opportunities to observe or as an extra resource. Teachers can facilitate family involvement in the classroom in a number of ways.

parent cooperative nursery schools
Nursery schools in which parents participate along with paid professionals or are involved in decision making and maintenance of the school.

© 2016 Cengage Learning®

10-2a ◦ Exploring Resources and Needs

Before establishing any plan to bring parents into a classroom, teachers need to gather information about the families to discover which family members can be involved, interests and

FIGURE 10-6
A father's musical instrument may add a resource to the classroom.

experiences that can be shared, and time resources (see Figure 10-6). Some of this information can be gathered informally as teachers learn about families during initial interviews, home visits, and casual conversations with parents and children. Other information may be gathered more formally by the use of questionnaires and application forms to acquire written responses to specific questions.

A brief background questionnaire may ask parents about the following:

1. *The names and ages of other children and family members in the home,* to learn whether grandparents or teenaged siblings are available to come in occasionally (see Figure 10-7) or if young children keep a parent too busy to visit

2. *Occupations,* to learn a little about working hours and days off (to see if there is available time) and jobs that are of interest to children or that offer interesting field trip possibilities, that can provide scrap materials and expertise for classroom use, or that can help other parents

3. *Interests and hobbies, pets, travel, and cultural or religious backgrounds*

A wealth of resources can be obtained by asking these few questions. As teachers accumulate information, it is a good idea to organize it into a **resource file**, with a card or page for each family. This file can be easily updated as new information is accumulated. Tentative plans for using these resources throughout the year can be noted, along with times parents are free to come to school. See Figures 10-8a, b, and c for sample resource cards.

resource file
File of information about each family and ways they can be potential resources for a classroom.

FIGURE 10-7
A grandparent may have time to visit the classroom.

Some teachers invite parents at the beginning of the year to sign up in their areas of interest, making it clear that this is an option to welcome families who are willing and able to visit. "*Inviting* families' involvement in contrast to *expecting* it is a subtle yet important difference" (Souto-Manning, 2010, p. 83). Parents certainly do not need teachers to make them feel guilty if they are unable or choose not to participate. Options might include the following:

- Going along on field trips

- Being a guest reader

- Helping in the classroom with special projects, such as woodworking or cooking

- Working with individual children who might need particular assistance and tutoring

- Coming into the classroom to talk about their work or interests

- Bringing in a pet

- Recording books on tape

- Preparing classroom materials at home, such as cutting out collage pieces or making journals

- Making telephone arrangements for children's visits in the community or to parents' workplace
- Doing online research to assist the teacher with activities and resources

These last contributions do not require classroom visits (adapted from DeSteno, 2000 and Souto-Manning, 2010).

FIGURE 10-8a
Sample Resource Card File

Butler, Bill and Joan (divorced)

Other child: Lisa—4 (in center)

Bill: Salesman, Angel Stone, 8:00–5:00; can be flexible in morning sometimes; usually out of town Wednesday and Thursday

Joan: Secretary, South West Telephone; 8:30–5:00, Monday–Friday; access to old computer sheets, discarded telephones

Interests: Joan—tennis, needlepoint, Chinese cooking; Bill—plays guitar, golf

Possibilities: Bill—play guitar—Chanukah celebration (December; Bill is Jewish); Joan—ask for paper—stir-fry vegetables (spring)

Note: No social for parents on Wednesday or Thursday

© Cengage Learning®

FIGURE 10-8b
Sample Card for Weaver Family

Weaver, Bob and Jane

No other children

Jane: homemaker

Bob: production in furniture factory, 7:30–4:30, Monday–Friday

Other: Grandparents in neighborhood, retired. Grandmother likes to cook.

Interests: Jane—gardening, sewing; Bob—volunteer fireman

Possibilities: Jane—help with planting (spring)—cloth scraps—free most days (field trips); Bob—wood scraps—bring fire truck or uniform, late afternoon

Grandparents—invite grandmother to cook with us

© Cengage Learning®

FIGURE 10-8c
Sample Card for Ashley Family

Ashley, Sylvia.

Terrence—9.

Sylvia: Job training program, 9:00–4:00, for next nine months

Possibilities: Invite for late afternoon time

Come in to read informally with children

Invite Terrence to throw ball with children on playground

© Cengage Learning®

CULTURAL CONSIDERATIONS

Involving all families

With the varied work schedules of family members, it may be impossible to get all family members into the classroom. Teachers should be aware of constraints on family time, such as the needs of younger children or care of older family members, and not interpret a lack of participation as disinterest or indifference. A welcome and invitation should be made to all families, believing that all families can make a contribution and can benefit from classroom visitation.

In the case of immigrant families, or families with limited English, teachers should be sensitive to the fact that families may be working hard to try to figure out the customs of the school or early education program that appear very differently from what they have been accustomed to. They may have the attitude that the professional knows best and not believe they have a role to play. Teachers should take care to explain the routine and practices of the classroom, talking clearly and using plain language. Teachers can act as interpreters of the culture of the school, helping the parents become comfortable in the new environment. Also remember that older children may feel embarrassed by their parents' accents or awkwardness and will be sensitive to indications of the teacher's approval and respect for their parents.

As families become comfortable, they will have much to add in helping all the children in the classroom learn about their unique culture and family life. And, in turn, they will be able to help other families adjust to the culture of the classroom, thus becoming an ally of the teacher in creating a sense of classroom community.

Consider how you might discuss feelings of discomfort with school-aged children before their families visited. Also consider one specific action a teacher could take to help immigrant families feel comfortable during a classroom visit.

10-2b Encourage Informal Visits

How do teachers get parents into a classroom? At first, casual, unstructured visits are often best because parents feel no pressure to perform a role and no demands are placed on their time. If allowed to get comfortable in a classroom, they will enjoy interacting with the children, other parents, and teachers.

Reserve Time

Designating one morning or afternoon every week or so as open for visiting creates a welcoming atmosphere. Parents are encouraged to spend an extra few minutes while dropping off or picking up their children—or more if they can stay—to join in or observe some activities and perhaps have a drink or snack prepared by the children. Parents enjoy coming to a school to briefly participate in their children's work. Such a regular occurrence demystifies for children the idea of having parents in a classroom and allows parents to stay occasionally as their schedules permit. These visitations require little effort on a teacher's part beyond the usual setting up of activity choices that require little supervision or assistance so teachers are free to move about. The casual nature of such visits means that only a few parents at a time are in a classroom, thereby avoiding overcrowding that may be too stimulating for children. There is also less chance of children feeling left out if their own parents are not there because activities go on as usual, and many other parents are also absent. The clear message of just sharing an ordinary day is relaxing as well as reassuring to parents that the classroom is always open for their viewing.

Birthday Celebrations

Most schools for young children have a special way of celebrating children's birthdays. Inviting parents to be present for the celebration can make it even more special. This may mean having the celebration at a time suited to a parent's schedule. Most parents enjoy an event that centers on their child. When classrooms have specific guidelines for celebrations, parents will not be drawn to compete in parties or make decisions deemed unsuitable for the group of children.

Because particular foods may not be acceptable to all families, for religious or health reasons, many programs move the celebration away from a focus on such food as cake or ice cream. For families whose religious beliefs preclude birthday celebrations, many classrooms have moved away from the party idea toward acknowledging the importance of meaningful events in the child's life. For example, one teacher asked parents to help prepare a "growing" display, showing pictures of the child at various ages—perhaps adding toys or clothes that had been used as the child grew. It seems appropriate for a birthday to be a celebration of the child's life, including the people and things that are important. In this spirit, all families could join in a developmentally appropriate celebration.

Personal Invitations

Some teachers include a "Family of the Week" component in their classroom plans. Specific, personal invitations made to an individual family may include siblings and other family members. The child whose family comes is host for the day, getting chairs for parents and siblings, serving them drinks and snacks, showing them around the room, discussing the art and writing on the walls, and so on. Families are asked to share something about their lives with all the children—whether it is talking about jobs or other interests or something that the family enjoys doing together. When each family is invited in turn, most will make a special effort to come as their child is honored. Some schools call these "family days" and ask families to schedule them early in the school year. Not only is this a useful way to draw parents into classroom life, but it is also a concrete model of demonstrating multicultural diversity and the uniqueness of all families.

Lunch Invitations

Families can be invited for lunch in their children's classrooms or cafeterias. Most schools do not require much advance notice to set an extra place for lunch; this offers another chance for a social visit and a special treat for a child (see Figure 10-9). Having Mom, Dad, or Grandpa as just theirs for lunch, away from other siblings, may be fun. Parents get an opportunity to see firsthand how teachers help children develop appropriate table behavior and self-help and conversational skills and encourage tasting a variety of foods. In elementary school, parents enjoy the opportunity to eat along with their children's friends and then may have a few minutes to join in classroom activities.

FIGURE 10-9
Parents may just come for lunch or to enjoy classroom life.

Special Occasions

Whether it's for a family tea party, early morning coffee, or a picnic lunch, most families try to respond to invitations made to a whole group. With various family structures, it can create problems or discomfort when invitations are made to "fathers only" or "mothers only." Parents with particular work schedules may be unable to accept, and children who do not have the specified parent in their lives will feel left out. Even when well-meaning teachers say "That's all right. You can bring Uncle Joe or your grandpa," children still feel that this is only second best if the day is named specifically for fathers.

In planning to include all families with sensitivity to potential barriers that would prevent or limit attendance at particular events, teachers should consider what they know about the children and families in their classrooms (Kieff & Wellhousen, 2000). They should consider the following:

- *Family structures:* Who are the primary caregivers for the children? Teachers should remember to include divorced parents, grandparents, blended families, foster parents, same-sex parents, family members with disabilities, and teenaged parents.

- *Family cultures:* What do they know about the children's family religious backgrounds, holiday celebrations, dietary restrictions, languages spoken, and views on child rearing and education?

- *Family lifestyles:* What do they know about the daily challenges and routines affecting each family, such as employment hours, transportation, caring for elderly or disabled family members, unemployment, income and education level, reading ability, access to telephones and computers, and latchkey child care?

When teachers become sensitive to the reasons many families may not be able to participate easily or comfortably in typical classroom involvement activities, they may change traditional ways of trying to involve families in classrooms. "Doughnuts with Dad" or "Muffins with Mom"—long mainstays of inviting parents into classrooms for snack as well as working on literacy skills for preschool and primary teachers—may need to give way to invitations for Lunch with Special Adults. If teachers use such tools, they are less likely to

TeachSource

VIDEO ACTIVITY ▶❚❚

Watch the video *Parents as Classroom Resources.* [http://ceng_ca_post.vpg.com/cen1/cen1_case12_orc1_v2/mov] After watching the video, reflect on these questions:

1. What ideas from the chapter regarding using parents as classroom resources are illustrated?

2. Consider the different ways parents are used as resources in the classroom and how these ways fit with the different needs of parents.

3. Consider which words of advice from teachers you would like to remember for your own classroom.

TeachSource Digital Download

FIGURE 10-10
Family Involvement
Planning Worksheet.

Family Involvement Planning Worksheet

Name of activity/event: _____
Proposed date and time: _____
Location: _____
Targeted participants: _____
Consider the following descriptors to identify family-related factors that could create barriers and prevent or limit the participation of families. After identifying possible barriers, adapt the activity or event to include all families.

Family Structures
Consider who are the primary caregivers for the children. Consider the presence of younger and older siblings living at home:

❏ Divorced parents ❏ Split families ❏ Same-sex parents
❏ Single parent ❏ Foster parents ❏ Family member with disability
❏ Grandparent(s) ❏ Legal guardian ❏ Teen parents
❏ Blended family ❏ Widowed parent ❏ Other_____
Possible barriers include: _____

Family Lifestyles
Consider the daily challenges or routines affecting the children and each family:

Possible barriers include: _____

Family Cultures
Consider the cultural aspects of each family; avoid stereotypes:
❏ Religious backgrounds ❏ Nonverbal communication styles
❏ Holiday celebrations   Eye contact
❏ Dietary restrictions   Gestures
❏ Views on child rearing   Touching
❏ Languages   Proximity during conversations
     ❏ Other _____
Possible barriers include: _____
How the activity or event can be adapted to include all families represented in the class or school: _____
_____
_____

TeachSource Digital Download

FIGURE 10-11
Common barriers and
possible modifications
checklist.

Common Barriers and Possible Modifications Checklist

Barriers	Modifications
Time	❏ Breakfast meetings
	❏ Weekend events
	❏ One event scheduled over a number of days
	❏ Open invitations
Transportation	❏ School bus or van
	❏ Carpool arranged by teacher or parent volunteer
	❏ Buddy system among families
Child care	❏ School-provided child care
	❏ Child care provided by parent organization
	❏ Buddy system among families
Decorations/celebrations	❏ Artwork created by children in the art center
	❏ Artwork generated during a theme/project study
Curriculum	❏ Opportunities for children to make multiple gifts and cards and to pick their recipients
	❏ Family members share expertise and culture
	❏ Bias-free curriculum
Food	❏ Multiple menus available
	❏ **Buffets**
	❏ Picnics
Printed material	❏ Translate copies
	❏ Make audiotapes
	❏ Make telephone calls
	❏ Use voice mail or e-mail
Special guest	❏ Guest not specified by role
	❏ A pal or friend
	❏ Open invitations to extended family members or a noncustodial parent
Expense	❏ Support provided by community businesses underwriting the event or materials needed
Misunderstanding the role as parent volunteer in the classroom	❏ Volunteer training sessions
	❏ **Specific** routines created
	❏ Recorded or printed instructions
Misunderstanding the parental role in home-extension learning activities	❏ **Specific** routines created for home-extension learning activities
	❏ Parent workshops to explain activities
	❏ Demonstration tapes
	❏ Demonstrations during home visits
Discomfort in school situations	❏ Alternative home visits or neighborhood meetings
	❏ Buddy systems among families
	❏ Small group meetings

offend or create barriers to family involvement in classroom activities. Such tools as those found in Figure 10-10 and Figure 10-11 will help teachers plan family involvement activities.

Walking Report Cards

Walking report cards (Anderson, 2000) provide opportunities for family members to walk with a child through a series of classroom centers and activities. Adults can then observe the child's performance in various activities. Teachers select specific materials and tasks to set out that will highlight children's developing abilities.

Some teachers add the walking report card to portfolio assessments and regular parent–teacher conferences as additional methods of sharing information with families. Teachers say that families enjoy the opportunity to see their children in action. Walking report card visits work well in preschool and elementary school.

Drop In and Read (DIAR), See Our Successes (SOS), and Other Invitations

Many elementary teachers are establishing regular family involvement events to help showcase children's work and accomplishments. For example, DIAR days are when family members are invited to drop in and read with children and have their children read to them. SOS events are to enjoy displays of writing or math or see children's long-term projects. (Any creative teacher can invent an appropriate acronym.) When teachers schedule such events for several days at different times, families are more likely to be able to participate. Sometimes, such an event could be combined with a potluck supper, providing social opportunities as well as meeting teacher goals of informing families. When children are involved in inviting their families, many parents will make an effort to please their children.

Zoo Day

A "zoo" day when families are asked to bring pets provides a good situation for getting parents to share and volunteer their resources (see Figure 10-12).

FIGURE 10-12
A pet from home may be interesting to all children.

Parents often find their own ways of becoming involved in classroom life when allowed to take the initiative. See Figure 10-13 for a list of volunteer opportunities that one school offers to stimulate family thinking about the variety of contributions they can make.

TeachSource Digital Download

FIGURE 10-13
Help parents to see that there are many ways they can be involved.

Volunteer Opportunities

- Answer phones—any help would be appreciated, even a couple of hours a week. This would free the staff to work on lesson plans and so on.

- Rock the babies—it is good for them and you!

- Read stories—the staff would love to have some new faces (and voices) to read to the children. If you are a good storyteller, please come and share your life experiences or childhood remembrances.

- Watch children during naptime (from 1:00 to 3:00 p.m.). Teachers need a break and could use the time to work on lesson plans or future projects.

- Assist with center events—go on field trips, help with staff appreciation week, and so forth. Our field trips are fun! Some of the latest ones have been to Discovery Place, the Nature Museum, the circus, the opera, and the like.

- Give career mini-workshops—come in for an hour and tell the children about your job, show them the tools you use, and so on. The older children are very interested in what grownups do all day!

- Sponsor a field trip to your workplace—this does not have to be difficult. Children can come in the center vans and tour your workplace. This kind of field trip is a real adventure for them.

- Provide some assistance with typing/computer service. The center always has a need for newsletters, meeting notices, and so on.

- Donate toys or clothes—playground toys are especially needed.

- Bring store-bought treats for the children (state regulations do not permit home-baked goodies). Watermelon and ice cream are especially popular with this crowd.

- Help with cutting out materials and/or decorating bulletin boards.

- Repair furniture, equipment, or toys.

- Sew doll clothes or costumes.

© 2016 Cengage Learning®

10-3 Encourage Parent Observations

Parents who are comfortable in a classroom may accept an invitation to spend a short period observing. This is beneficial for all parents—particularly for parents with special concerns about their children or questions about the school—in anticipation of an extended conversation at a later conference.

Observation periods are most productive when parents and children are prepared for their roles. Teachers may explain to children that parents will be coming "so they can see all the fun things and work we do in the classroom." Children can also be told that the visiting adults will probably want to sit at one side and not play or talk for a time. (It is ideal to have an observation booth or window where visitors can observe undetected. But not many schools boast such an opportunity, so parents and children will have to accustom themselves to the others' presence.)

Parents and teachers should be aware that children may act differently in the presence of parents. It is helpful to discuss this openly and to suggest that parents observe on several occasions to accustom their children to the practice. Parents should also feel comfortable leaving if their children are having difficulty with their presence. Teachers can reassure parents that such behavior is normal and that the parents can try coming again at another time.

FIGURE 10-14

It is ideal for a parent to be able to observe in an informal setting, such as the playground.

© Cengage Learning®

Observing outdoor play is a good first step for children and parents (see Figure 10-14). Outdoor play may offer more natural opportunities for children to play freely without feeling they are being watched, and parents may also be more comfortable outdoors. In elementary classrooms, parents can sit apart, watching children and teachers busy with their normal routines and assigned tasks.

Many parents feel uncertain about their role as an observer and may feel more secure when given verbal and written guidelines for helpful classroom behaviors and points for observation. Figure 10-15 is a sample form that may be used.

A parent with particular concerns should be given individual guidelines. Parents who observe on several occasions will appreciate having an observation booklet with specific points on each page.

TeachSource Digital Download

FIGURE 10-15

An observation guide may be helpful for parents.

Welcome to Our Classroom

The children will be delighted to see you and may need a gentle reminder that you've come to see them at work and play. A crowd could make it difficult for you to observe or jot down questions.

1. Observe your child and as many others as you can. This can be a learning experience about

   - Your child and how he or she relates to other children and the learning activities

   - What children the same age as your child are like

   - How the teacher guides each child

2. Observe your child and several others. Notice how they

- Respond to other children
- Use language
- Choose activities, and how long they stay with each activity
- Solve problems and obtain assistance

3. Observe your child's particular interests and interactions.

4. Observe the teacher in a variety of activities. Notice how the teacher

- Relates to each child
- Handles difficult situations
- Prevents problems and guides behavior

5. Write down any impressions, surprises, suggestions, or questions you would like to discuss later.

© 2016 Cengage Learning®

10-4 Parents as Classroom Resources

As teachers get to know the families they work with, they become aware of parents' wealth of experience that can be used to deepen children's understanding of the world around them. Parents should be invited into classroom experiences to involve and include them, not merely to exploit them as an extra pair of hands to complete chores in the classroom. Parents are resources in a variety of ways. Parents' competence, creativity, and knowledge should be respected so they will be involved in tasks that are worth doing and from which they can gain a sense of accomplishment and make real contributions. The learning opportunities when parents work with individuals or small groups are innumerable.

Parents may be invited to find a time convenient for them to visit a classroom and share an experience. When appropriate, children may also be able to visit a parent at work or at home.

10-4a Jobs

Many parents' jobs are interesting to children when demonstrated along with the "tools of the trade." Visitors may be a dental hygienist with a giant set of teeth and toothbrush, a truck driver complete with a truck, a hair stylist, or a carpenter with tools. Even parents who have more ordinary jobs sometimes work in places that make wonderful field trips. A tall glass office building with an exciting elevator ride up to see the view, a company next to a construction site or a shopping mall or neighborhood store may have a cheery parent to greet the children as they explore the different places people work.

Elementary school teachers can incorporate such learning experiences into their plans for social studies units or to extend literacy and math curricula.

10-4b Hobbies

Parents with particular interests and hobbies may offer fascinating substance to a curriculum. A violin player, an avid camper with backpack and pup tent, a gardener, a cook, a dancer, a cyclist, or an artist all have enthusiasm and skills to share with the children. A parent who enjoys using a video camera may record children busy at play—fun for the children to see replayed and interesting for parents to view later at a parent meeting. Most adults, even if initially hesitant, enjoy themselves thoroughly as children respond with zest to the new activities (see Figure 10-16). Such interests expand the curriculum in elementary and preschool classrooms.

FIGURE 10-16
Many parents will enjoy sharing their interests with children.

10-4c Cultural or Religious Traditions

Multicultural experiences are promoted within good early childhood classrooms. Children need to learn respect and value for the unique differences among people. Families may help a teacher offer firsthand experiences for children in exploring customs, foods, or celebrations of a variety of cultural or religious traditions. Activities like the following can be woven into a classroom curriculum to enrich and stimulate learning for children:

- Chanukah songs, games, and foods from a Jewish parent
- A Chinese parent demonstrating the use of a wok and chopsticks
- Spanish children's songs taught by a Mexican parent
- The sharing of some family treasures by a Vietnamese parent
- An African American parent explaining the traditions of Kwanzaa celebrations
- A Native American parent sharing a craft artifact
- Mementos brought back from vacation travel

More important, inviting families to share aspects of their lives and cultures lets teachers demonstrate respect for the diverse family backgrounds in a classroom. Children and their parents receive a self-esteem boost when they share a representation of their own lives. All children benefit as they learn to enjoy and accept the aspects of uniqueness and universality in multicultural experiences. We will talk more about this in Chapter 13.

10-4d Extended Family

Knowing the makeup of each family will help teachers find resources beyond the parents. A retired grandmother who enjoys reading stories to children, a teenaged brother who can help with throwing balls on the playground, a baby who can be brought to visit for a bath or feeding, and other family members can provide additional experiences.

10-4e Field Trips

If parents are coming to help out on field trips, they should be given specific duties. Teachers will give parents a list of the children they are expected to keep track of and should make sure the children wear name tags and know whose parent they are with. All safety rules must be clearly established so parents understand necessary practices, such as car seats, seat belts, and supervision. Parents should understand the goals for the field trip and all guidelines for children's behavior before setting out. Information is the key to parent comfort and helpfulness as well as productive and safe field trips.

Teacher planning of the complete field trip beyond the aspect of parent assistance is beyond the scope of this text. For more on this topic, see Carroll (2007).

10-4f Time

One resource provided by many parents is time. A parent coming into the classroom is helpful when an extra pair of hands is needed. Walks or field trips, classroom parties, or more complicated projects become possible when teachers can count on additional assistance from parents. Many classrooms today are encouraging family presence as an important component of literacy experiences. When parents come into the classroom to read to large or small groups of children, they model the pleasurable and useful aspects of literacy.

Sometimes, parents are more comfortable offering to share time instead of demonstrating a talent. As parents interact with children, they are often drawn into an activity they have done at home—supervising cooking experiences, carving a jack-o'-lantern, or playing a game (see Figure 10-17). It is also important that parents' time not be wasted. Teachers need to have materials ready for their use and be efficient in explaining classroom routines and activities so parents do not feel they are just waiting for something to happen.

Sometimes, parents would rather use at-home time to support classroom activities. Parents can launder and mend dress-up clothes and toys, use personal computers to type newsletters, make phone calls to remind other parents of meetings, or prepare simple classroom games.

10-4g Materials

Families who are unavailable to come into a classroom may still provide resources in the form of materials to be used in classroom activities. Scraps and throwaways from jobs (office materials, Styrofoam packing bits, wood scraps), scraps and discards from home (kitchen utensils, dress-up clothes, magazines, fabric pieces), and recycled or natural materials that can be used for collections to sort or for math materials all make a contribution that allows parents and teachers to feel a sense of cooperation. Some teachers regularly post a list of "Treasures Wanted" via a newsletter or bulletin board, such as the one shown in Figure 10-18.

TeachSource Digital Download

FIGURE 10-18
Parents may feel involved when they contribute materials for classroom use.

Contributions from Home

Throughout the year, we can always use:

- Writing supplies—envelopes, paper, postcards, small notepads, and any sizes of paper, including computer paper
- Appliance boxes and cardboard boxes of all sizes
- Yogurt containers for paint
- Discarded clothing or costumes for dress up
- Small appliances to take apart
- Wood for the workbench
- Fabric, yarn, and large needles for sewing
- Collections of buttons, nuts and bolts, or other small objects
- Ideas for local field trips

Parents outside a classroom will feel involved as they prepare materials for classroom use. Tracing and cutting out pieces for teacher-made games is something a parent can do at home and feel important and valued.

10-4h Special Skills

Families may have skills or knowledge that can be drawn on as resources beyond the classroom to support the school or to offer to other parents. Architects, builders, or landscape designers can contribute to playground design; accountants or businesspeople can help with budgets, insurance, and tax matters; medical personnel can set up first aid kits and procedures; particularly handy parents can repair toys as needed; "bargain hunter" parents can aid the person who purchases for the school, answering such questions as "Where can we get the best deal on sand?" Knowledgeable parents are possible resources for parent meetings or workshops: A high school counselor can lead a discussion of communication techniques; parents who have successfully negotiated divorce and remarriage can share insights on stepparenting; an accountant can discuss tax tips for working parents; a parent with older children can advise on the intricacies of the school system and understanding tests.

10-5 The Teacher's Role in Supporting Families in the Classroom

As teachers invite families to participate in classroom learning activities, they need to concentrate on their skills for working with adults. Teachers need to be able to relax and enjoy the contributions of others to their classrooms without feeling threatened by any attention transferred from themselves to visiting adults.

As specific information is given to parents, they will feel more comfortable knowing what is expected of them. Parents should know what time frame to plan on and that it is acceptable to leave or stay as their schedules allow. It is helpful to confirm all arrangements in writing so parents have a concrete reminder of an event to fit into their schedules:

> *Dear Mr. Butler,*
>
> *We are looking forward to your visit to our classroom next Friday, February 2, at 9:15 a.m. The children will have snack at 9:45, so that will give you about half an hour to sing songs with us. We'll probably have some favorites to request, too! Please feel free to stay and have snack with us if you're able. See you next week.*
>
> *Sincerely,*
>
> *Jane Briscoe*

> *Dear Mrs. Murphy,*
>
> *I appreciate your offer to help in our classroom on Thursdays this semester. The children have individual reading time from 9:00 to 9:30 a.m. This would be the best time for you to be able to read with individuals. I will have a list on my desk each morning of children who would benefit by having you listen to them read.*
>
> *This is such an important support to their learning, and they will enjoy the time alone with you. We look forward to seeing you next Thursday and hope you will feel free to stay as long as you are able to participate in our day.*
>
> *Sincerely,*
>
> *John Roberts*

Teachers should immediately greet parents coming into a classroom and make them feel welcome by introducing them to the children and pointing out an area to sit or begin their preparations. Parents appreciate knowing beforehand exactly what they will be expected to do. Avoid vague suggestions that they "join in." For example, if the parent is helping with a cooking experience, demonstrate how to help prepare children for participation: washing hands, rolling up sleeves, putting on a smock. The teacher might demonstrate how to show children the recipe to follow and how to involve the children in measuring and stirring. After working with one child, the teacher can stand back and let the parent take over, still being available if needed. Even if parents are just coming to share time in the classroom, they will be more comfortable if teachers help them get started.

FIGURE 10-19
This father has been made comfortable to participate with children in the block corner.

"Our children love for someone to read to them. If you just sit in that chair in the book corner, I'm sure you'll have children joining you before long. There are two small chairs there, too, to limit the number of children to two. Usually, they'll move on to something else when they see the chairs are filled. There'll be about half an hour before we clean up for snack."

See the additional specific suggestions for involving parents in and out of the classroom in DiNatale, 2002 and Souto-Manning, 2010 (see Figure 10-19).

When parents come into the classroom frequently, it may be helpful to have specific work cards that indicate which part of the room to be responsible for, suggestions of questions or comments to facilitate learning, cleanup responsibilities, and so on. See Figure 10-20 for sample work cards. Teachers may also hold a volunteer orientation, giving handouts that explain how the classroom or school functions as well as policies and philosophy (Sullivan, 2006).

Teachers should watch parents for signs of discomfort or indications of how much they want teachers to help them out in uncertain situations. When teachers prepare parents for potentially disruptive situations that could occur, especially if their own children are involved, parents are more likely to feel

FIGURE 10-20
Sample work cards.

Block Area

Thanks for helping in the block area today.

—Limit to four children.

—Sit in the small chair.

—Enjoy conversation about the buildings.

—Good questions are open-ended: Tell me about your building.

What do people do in your building?

What is your building called?

—If children argue, ask if they can work the problem out.

—Children are responsible for returning blocks to shelves—encourage effort.

Art Area

Thanks for helping in the art area today.

—Set out four chairs to limit participation.

—All children put on smocks.

—Children use displayed materials freely and independently.

—Children may use any other materials from the art shelf.

—When children ask for assistance, demonstrate and then see if you can encourage them to try again.

—When children ask you to make them something, tell them you would rather watch them make it.

—Sometimes, children busy at work do not have time for conversation.

—Respond as they initiate conversation, and use comments to describe their work, such as "Wow, you glued so many pieces" or "You certainly used a lot of green in your painting."

—Children may continue using materials, making several creations, as long as no one else is waiting for a turn.

—Ask if they would like to write their name on their work or if they would like your help.

—Remind children of where to place work for drying and to wash hands and hang up smocks when finished.

Reading Buddies

Thanks for coming in to be a Reading Buddy today.

—Find the red folder with the names of children scheduled for reading buddies today.

—Find the first child (all children wear name tags).

—Invite the child to come to Quiet Corner to read with you.

—Ask the child whether he or she would like to read to you first or have you read to him or her; let the child choose a book.

—When finished reading, converse about the story.

—Switch roles, with you being the listener this time.

—When children get stuck on a word, supply it for them.

—Move down the list of reading buddies. Enjoy.

comfortable at school. Teachers help children of visiting parents understand that Mom or Dad will be helping all the children and will have special things to do today. This helps to clarify the visiting parent's role for the child. Occasionally, a child of invited parents reacts by showing off or clinging and being possessive of her parent's attention. It is a good idea to warn parents ahead of time that this may happen and that a teacher is prepared for it and will not mind. Parents should also be reassured that a teacher will step in if necessary to remind a child of classroom rules so parents will not feel the full burden of guidance is theirs and perhaps react inappropriately because of embarrassment. In the classroom, teachers should enforce classroom rules. This understanding helps clarify adult responsibilities.

> *"It's so special when parents come in that sometimes we get some unusual behaviors. No problem. If Sam forgets our rules, I'll just remind him."*

The unusual event may cause a young child to get upset when his parent leaves, even though separation is not normally a problem. A teacher needs to comfort him and to reassure the parent that the classroom visit was still a great idea even though there were a few tears at the end. The positive feelings for child and parent far outweigh any brief distress.

Parents like feeling that they are making a valuable contribution to a classroom. Many parents will try to find the time for a visit if they feel truly needed and wanted. A note of appreciation from the teacher and children afterward, pictures of the event displayed on a bulletin board, a mention of the event as a classroom highlight in the next newsletter—all these convey to parents that their time was well spent.

SUMMARY

Parents, children, and teachers all benefit when families are involved in classroom activities.

- Parents gain firsthand experience of the school and of their child's reactions in a classroom as well as feelings of satisfaction from making a contribution.

- Children feel special when their parents are involved, feel secure with the tangible evidence of parents and teachers cooperating, realize the value their parents place on education, and gain directly as parental understanding and skills increase.

- Teachers gain resources to extend learning opportunities, observe parent–child interaction, and feel supported as parents participate and empathize with them.

Advantages likely outweigh disadvantages, which include:

- Disruption of normal routines

- Children's distress or unusual behavior

- Stress of another person in the classroom

Families may be involved as:

- Casual visitors, to participate in classroom activities, meals, or celebrations

- Observers, to extend their knowledge of children's functioning in a classroom

- Resources, to extend and enrich opportunities for the children

Observation may be facilitated by:

- Preparing children and parents for their roles

- Offering an observation guide

Using parents as resources in the classroom will be helped by:

- Exploring resources by learning about families' jobs, time, cultural and religious backgrounds, and interests
- Creating parent resource files with relevant information

Teachers will help parents be effective volunteers by:

- Helping them become comfortable in the classroom
- Being specific about classroom tasks
- Moving in to take charge when needed

Student Activities for Further Study

1. If you are working or interning in a classroom, gather information about parents—family composition, jobs and details of what is involved, hobbies and interests, and religious and ethnic backgrounds. Find out whether families have access to any materials that are useful in your classroom or have particular periods of time free. Organize this information into a resource file. (If you are not presently in a classroom, use the fictional family information described in Chapter 2 to make a sample resource file.)

2. Use your resource file to:

   a. Make a hypothetical plan for how you will use your resource knowledge to invite families into the classroom for particular activities, events, and curriculum topics throughout the year.

   b. Invite three different parents into your classroom if possible.

Remember that it will be your role to prepare parents and children for what to expect; play hostess in making parents feel comfortable in the room, and guide children's behavior. Use this as an opportunity to observe parents and children in the classroom and the effect of the visit on each.

Apply the Chapter Concepts: Case in Point

Read the following letter written to parents and then answer the questions that follow.

Dear Parents:

There will be a special Mothers Luncheon on Wednesday, December 8. It will be held in our kindergarten classroom from 12:30 to 2:00 p.m. The cafeteria will serve barbecued pork at $5.00 a plate. We are asking moms to donate baked items for dessert. The kindergarten class will entertain after lunch, singing Christmas songs from around the world. Please plan to attend.

1. As you put yourself in the place of parents receiving this letter, what is your initial response to this invitation?

2. As a single mother who works a full-time and a part-time job and has trouble making ends meet, what is your response?

3. As the custodial father of a child whose biological mother lives in another state and whose stepmother travels out of town frequently in her work, what is your response?

4. As a Middle Eastern Muslim immigrant family that speaks little English, what is your response to this letter?

5. Considering the barriers you just identified, how might this invitation be changed to be more inclusive?

Review Questions

1. Describe at least one advantage for children, parents, and teachers when teachers work with families in the classroom and any one of three disadvantages.

2. List at least two methods of encouraging parental visits to the classroom.

3. Describe at least one method to facilitate parental observation in a classroom.

4. Discuss at least two ways families can be used as resources in a classroom.

5. Describe aspects of the teacher's role in facilitating parents' classroom contributions.

Helpful Websites

- The Colorado Parent Information and Resource Center (CPIRC) has been created to help families and schools work better together to ensure that children succeed in school.

- The mission of the National Association of Partners in Education is to provide leadership in the formation and growth of effective partnerships that ensure success for all students.

- The National Coalition of Parents in Education is a coalition of major education, community, public service, and advocacy organizations working to create meaningful family–school partnerships in every school in America.

Parent Education

Learning Objectives

After reading this chapter, you should be able to:

11-1   Discuss what is meant by parent education.

11-2   Discuss a rationale for parent education.

11-3   Identify several assumptions and considerations regarding parent education.

11-4   List steps in planning and implementing parent education programs.

11-5   Describe ways parents can function as advisers and decision makers.

naeyc

Related NAEYC Standards

Accreditation Standards (see inside text back cover for full listing of the Accreditation Standards for exemplary early childhood programs)

7.A.09; 7.A.12; 7.A.13; 7.A.14; 7.B.02; 10.A.01; 10.F.04

Licensure Standards (see inside text front cover for full listing of the Licensure Standards for this chapter)

2b; 2c

A traditional way of trying to reach families in school systems has been to hold occasional meetings. Generally, the meetings are designed to give information to large groups of parents. Frequently, parents will attend an initial meeting; however, the aspects of large groups are usually unappealing, so future attendance is less likely. This is unfortunate because it continues the distance between home and school and fails to give parents assistance that may be truly helpful. Until children come with complete instruction booklets or the education system becomes less complex, parents will continue to need information and ideas to support their child rearing and involvement in their children's learning. Many parental needs for support, social contact, and information may be satisfied in parent meetings.

This chapter explores how schools can offer more than that traditional meeting so families may be more likely to participate. In addition, parents should be invited to get involved in the decision-making aspects of a school program. Teachers also will consider the educational facet of working with families.

11-1 Understanding Parent Education

Anne Morgan and Dorothy Scott do a lot of things differently in their classrooms, but they agree on one idea: Neither of them wants to attend the school's parents' meeting next week. Dorothy sounds quite cynical about it: "Look, I've been going to parents' meetings for 13 years, and it's always the same thing. A handful of parents show up—always the same ones—the ones who are already doing a pretty good job and don't need to hear the guest speaker anyway. I'm just getting tired of the whole thing."

Anne is also disappointed with the results of the last meeting she attended. "If there's one thing the parents need to understand, it's the terrible effect of television on their children. So, after they listened to the man we invited to speak on that topic, do you think I noticed any difference in what my children tell me they've watched? It doesn't seem worth the effort."

Even their director seems less than certain of the value of the parents' meetings she continues to arrange. "It does seem there must be something else we could do to attract more families."

Traditionally, *parent education* is defined as "intervention to help parents function more effectively in their parental role" (Auerbach, 1968). Swick expanded this to "any effort to increase the development and learning of parents in carrying out the diverse roles they perform," including the personal dimensions of marital roles and relationships and personal needs as adults (Swick, 1985).

Traditional parent education has consisted of various methods for giving parents information deemed necessary by professionals. The traditional approach stresses information and training that is directly related to parent–child interaction or school success. The model is that of competent professional dispensing facts to a less competent parent. This one-way model implies a passive audience and a need to overcome a deficit in parental knowledge. Such a stance increases parental self-doubt: It is not surprising that parents frequently engage in these educational approaches with minimal enthusiasm or maximal avoidance! Such a parent education program can make parents feel powerless and dependent on the advice of professionals. The system through which they are educated is itself an important part of any parent education program. The usefulness of many informational programs is hindered by procedures that point to the authority of professionals and the incompetence of parents.

In fact, teachers may learn much from families about themselves and their children and their diverse communities. As they present themselves as open to learning, both parties are educated reciprocally.

Although some programs refer to all efforts at parent involvement as **parent education**, the term is usually used to refer to specific attempts to offer knowledge and support to parents in hopes of increasing parenting effectiveness. Parent education has taken many forms, for different purposes, with varying results. Specific programs may be planned for particular groups, such as first-time parents, expectant parents, future parents, teenage parents, single parents, parents of children with special needs, and grandparents (see Figures 11-1a, 11-1b, and 11-1c). This listing of diversity could go on. In considering models that may be most effective, we need to examine attitudes and practices that support and strengthen parents' sense of competence and the reciprocal partnership with teachers.

parent education
Specific attempts to offer knowledge and support to parents in hopes of increasing parenting effectiveness.

(a)

(c)

(b)

FIGURE 11-1
Parent education must meet the needs of various family structures, including single parents, grandparents, and those from diverse cultures.

11-2 A Rationale for Parent Education

Why all this concern about parent education? And just why should schools and teachers be involved?

11-2a Need for Family Support

In the past couple of decades, a major direction for programs for parents has been the development of family support programs (Kagan, 1995). This broad approach to parent education focuses on all of family life and emphasizes developing support systems for families. The changing terminology increasingly used indicates the change in emphasis and structure; besides *parent education*, terms include the following:

- Parent empowerment
- Family education
- Family life education
- Parent support
- Family support (Kagan, 1995)

A goal is to help families prevent problems and optimize their functioning, motivated by the belief that families receiving support are empowered to act on their own behalf. Family support programs include and embrace other principles:

- A recognition of the need to work with the entire family and community
- A commitment to regarding the family as an active participant in planning and implementing educational programs
- An acknowledgment of the importance of nourishing cultural diversity
- A focus on strength-based needs assessment and programming

The Family Resource Coalition promotes family empowerment programs and offers information about local funding methods and organization models. (For more information on the FRC, see Chapter 4.)

11-2b Information and Interaction

Perhaps the main functions of a parent education curriculum are (1) to stimulate parents to examine their relationship with their children more closely and (2) to encourage interaction among parents and between families and school staff. Although the education of parents is primarily for the benefit of the children, the parents' own development can also be enhanced in the process of interacting with other adults (see Figure 11-2).

The term *education* is part of the problem because it connotes the formal study of facts associated with a narrowly cognitive academic world. In reality, the subject of parent–child relations and education is not usually so much concerned with facts and knowledge as it is with concepts, attitudes, and ideas. The content of any educational program may be less important than the methods of bringing families together to widen their horizons, sensitize them to feelings in a parent–child relationship, and to the role of families in supporting their children's education.

A vital realization for teachers is that teachers play critical roles in supporting families to be optimally effective in supporting children's development and learning. Teachers become involved in family education as yet another professional opportunity to help parents develop their skills as children's first teachers and nurturers, with children ultimately benefitting.

A broader consideration of parent education implies a dynamic learning process in which families are active participants, growing out of parents' interests and needs, and in which parents participate as individuals. Research-based information increasingly suggests that the ways parents see their parenting roles and interact with their children directly influence how young children learn to think, talk, solve problems, and feel about themselves and others. Therefore, parent education needs to offer a broad variety of services designed to complement families' responsibilities and knowledge and to increase their understanding of children and their educational needs.

FIGURE 11-2
Parents generally enjoy the opportunity to share their experiences with other parents.

© Jamiehooper/Shutterstock.com

FOCUS OF PARENT EDUCATION

Parent education focuses on the following:

- Educational experiences to give parents new knowledge and understanding
- Support for parenting roles
- Support for marital roles
- Support for self-awareness and personal growth
- Support for adult roles and relationships within the community
- Opportunities to question habitual ways of thinking and acting
- Help to develop new methods (where needed) in relationships with children
- Understanding of family roles and responsibilities toward their children's school success

---

11-2c   Samples of Predesigned Parent Education Programs

Several popular program models have been developed for widespread use and have been used primarily in workshop sessions with parents. These include Parent Effectiveness Training (PET), Systematic Training for Effective Parenting (STEP), Active Parenting, the AVANCE parenting education curriculum, and the curricula from the Center for the Improvement of Child Caring.

Parent Effectiveness Training

Thomas Gordon developed a course and wrote a classic book with this title. The method focuses primarily on helping parents develop communication skills that allow them to act as counselors to children regarding their behavior and feelings and resolve conflicts between parents and children. Parents are taught techniques such as active listening, I-messages (as discussed in Chapter 15), and no-lose methods of conflict resolution. Although the principles of communication are adaptable for use with children of any age, many of the examples used in the curriculum are of communication with elementary-age children. Note also that similar training for teachers is given in Teacher Effectiveness Training. (For more information about Parent Effectiveness Training methods, see Gordon [2008] and the related website listed at the end of this chapter.)

Systematic Training for Effective Parenting (STEP)

This program offers a structured curriculum based on the child management principles of Alfred Adler and Rudolf Dreikurs. Communication methods and such nonpunitive discipline techniques as natural and logical consequences are emphasized, along with skills for developing responsibility, decision making, and family problem solving. Programs for using STEP methods for parents of children younger than six and for parents of teenagers have been developed and are also available in Spanish (Dinkmeyer et al., 2008 and 2007b). (For more information about STEP methods, see Dinkmeyer et al., 2007a, and the related website listed at the end of this chapter.)

Active Parenting Now

Active Parenting Now offers a number of parenting programs in structured sessions with trained leaders. The program claims to "emerge from the concepts of psychologists such as Alfred Adler, Rudolf Dreikurs, and Carl Rogers, and go beyond groundbreaking programs like PET and STEP to make parenting education easier to teach—and more compelling to learn—than ever before" (APN newsletter). Tested techniques such as I-messages, active listening, and natural and logical consequences are emphasized, along with basic understandings of causes of misbehavior, formation of self-esteem, and helpful praise and encouragement in developing responsibility. Curricula include Active Parenting of Teens; Active Teaching; Parents on Board: Building Academic Success Through Parent Involvement; 1, 2, 3, 4 Parents!; Cooperative Parenting and Divorce; and Spanish language versions of the major programs. For more information on Active Parenting Now, contact Active Parenting Publishing at its web address (listed at the end of this chapter).

CULTURAL CONSIDERATIONS

Matching programs to cultural values

Programs that appeal widely to middle-class parents may be quite unappealing for lower-income parents or parents from cultural backgrounds that may not value **democratic models** and open expression of feelings. This is not to suggest that the information and ideas proposed by these predesigned education programs would not benefit all parents. But even the best information may not be helpful if the model conflicts with a family's cultural values and experiences. Rather, teachers and administrators should consider carefully the methods and style of instruction to ensure that parents are learning in styles and circumstances that match their cultural values and experiences and their comfort levels (Fine & Lee, 2000). Examples of such culturally relevant programs follow.

Consider this idea further by asking three different people what style of meeting they prefer, and then reflect on how culture influences their answers.

democratic models
Models in which power is shared.

AVANCE Parenting Education

The AVANCE Parenting Education Curriculum has become a model as one of the first family support and education programs in the United States and one of the first comprehensive, community-based programs to target at-risk and Latino populations. In working with the parents of infants and young children, AVANCE offers parenting education, social support, adult basic and higher education, early childhood education and youth programs, and personal development. The parenting curriculum includes an intensive nine-month set of parenting classes. Topics include an overview of parenting, prenatal care, infant needs, physical, emotional, and social needs of young children, childhood illnesses, nutrition and the young child, children's behavior, cognitive and language development, self-awareness, and goal setting. The curriculum, now available for sale and replication in other communities, suggests that although it was designed for high-risk Hispanic families, it is also effective in African American communities and Native American communities. For more information, see the website for this program listed at the end of this chapter.

Center for the Improvement of Child Caring

This organization is a private nonprofit group that sees its role as being a major organizer of the Effective Parent movement. Two of the programs they have developed are designed specifically for minority parents. Effective Black Parenting is described as a "culturally relevant skill-building program for raising proud and confident African American children." A step-by-step curriculum leads participants through 15 three-hour sessions, teaching parenting skills that respect African American patterns of communication and recognize the roots of the extended black family. African proverbs guide the topics, and role-playing of home situations is used. Los Ninos Bien Educados is a parent education program developed specifically for Spanish-speaking and Latino-origin parents, dealing specifically with traditions and customs in child rearing and with adjustments being made as families acculturate to life in the United States. These programs are available through the Center for the Improvement of Child Caring at its website, which is listed at the end of this chapter.

11-3 Considerations and Assumptions for Planning Education Programs

It is often tempting for teachers to use formats or activities planned by others. Using a ready-made manual or suggestions sometimes seems more efficient and removes the additional responsibilities of planning and preparing activities. A number of resources are available; see Rockwell and Kniekamp (2003) and Kyle, McIntyre, Miller, and Moore (2005) for examples of such resources. However, the great danger is not matching ideas or activities to the particular group of families with whom a teacher or administrator is working at a particular time. Although time-consuming, the only way to plan activities that are truly meaningful is to work with the knowledge of a unique group. Resources may be useful to provide ideas that teachers can adapt rather than simply adopting them.

In planning parent education programs, it is important to consider the intended population, the relationships among the school staff and the participants, and the social context (see Figure 11-3).

11-3a Matching Programs to Parent Characteristics

We have noted that parent education methods often used with groups of middle-class families do not necessarily transfer to low-income parents. For example, group discussion methods may have limited appeal. Planned programs must recognize and respond to the

FIGURE 11-3
Strategies for Parent Education, with Challenges and Suggestions

Strategies for Accessing Community Resources
Parent Resource Lending Library

Advantages	Challenges	Suggestions
■ Contains items that reflect topics of interest to families	■ Finding appropriate space	■ Brainstorm and compile initial resources through team effort and then assign one or more staff members to keep the library updated.
■ Includes national, state, regional, and local resources of interest to all families, not just those who have children with disabilities	■ Keeping the library up to date	■ Ask families what information they are especially interested in.
	■ Setting up and maintaining a checkout system	■ Make a basic list of contents that tells where items can be found in the collection.
■ Offers different kinds of materials: books, booklets, videotapes, audiotapes, and training materials	■ Finding/creating identical resources in Spanish or other home languages	■ Include local resource directories.
		■ Collect pamphlets from agencies and programs in your area.
■ Allows family members to browse at their leisure		■ Look for and collect information from agencies that serve specific ethnic or language communities.
■ Lets families know that you are there to support them as well as their children		■ Collect and organize pamphlets in binders by using pocket inserts or house them in file boxes or drawers.
		■ Post upcoming community events on bulletin boards or send home the information with the children.
		■ Bookmark useful websites at the classroom computer station.
		■ Print information from websites or lists of URLs to add to the library.

The Public Library

Advantages	Challenges	Suggestions
■ May have more resources and more up-to-date items than a center can acquire	■ May not be easily accessible or convenient for some families	■ Work with your local library in setting up a resource section about young children, including children with disabilities.
■ Offers public access to the Internet	■ May not have resources available in other languages	■ Provide families with library hours of operation, resources available, and other information.
■ Has knowledgeable staff to assist family members in finding information		■ Regularly visit the library to see what is new and available.

Parent Meetings

Advantages	Challenges	Suggestions
■ Can invite individuals from multiple agencies to take part in a resource fair ■ Can invite speakers from local resources	■ Not always convenient for parents to attend	■ Publicize meetings well, including issuing personal invitations. ■ Participate in a community resource fair, and advertise it to families. ■ Invite families and staff members from other programs or centers to hear your speaker(s).

From Kaczmarek, L. A. 2007. A Team Approach: Supporting Families of Children with Disabilities in Inclusive Programs. *In D. Koralek (Ed.),* Spotlight on Young Children and Families *(pp. 20–3). Washington, DC: NAEYC. Reprinted with permission from the National Association for the Education of Young Children.*

needs and wishes of the individual participants. This suggests an active role for parents in determining content and method of learning, as well as sensitivity to cultural contexts for child rearing and communication.

11-3b Changing Relationships Between Professionals and Families

There is an increasing trend toward equal relationships between program staff and parent participants. Administrators or teachers do not always play dominant roles or make all decisions. Professionals who work with parents take on a collaborative partnership role rather than a professional-as-expert role. This puts staff into the role of facilitator of goals and activities that are jointly determined by parents and staff. Such an understanding focuses more on adult education within the relationship than purely parent education, assuming that parents and teachers educate each other. Parents build on their strengths as individuals, and professional facilitators are also learners.

11-3c Attention to the Social Context of Parenting

Increasingly, it is recognized that social networks and support are important for parents in their parenting role. Families who receive adequate social support are more capable of carrying out their functions. Traditional parent education programs rely on disseminating information to parents, but the parent support approach assumes that social ties will positively assist parent functioning (see Figure 11-4). Professionals who work with families in groups facilitate the group members' ability to share ideas and experiences and to support one another.

Parent education involves making available to all parents the necessary support and attitudes that do the following:

1. Encourage them to use and depend on what they know.

2. Encourage them to share their experience with other parents.

3. Support what they are doing.

4. Expose them to new ideas they have not considered.

These ideas eliminate the connotation that parent education is associated only with deficit models of parenting and emphasize the need to support and help *all* parents.

FIGURE 11-4

The social ties formed with other parents at parent education programs may be as important as the information.

© Cengage Learning®

11-3d Assumptions Underlying Parent Education

A philosophy of parent education that involves parents actively in a dynamic situation makes these assumptions:

1. Parents can learn. Parenting behaviors are not determined by the unfolding of instinctive reactions but are learned behaviors that can be acquired or improved with effort. The more parents know about child development and the effects of parent–child interaction, the more they examine what they do and why they do it, and the more skillful they become in displaying appropriate behaviors.

2. Parenting is an area in which a knowledge base exists pertaining to effective types of parent behavior. Studies and research have indicated specific parental attitudes and actions that result in specific responses from children. It is important to state here that there is no unanimous agreement about what knowledge should be taught in any parent education program; however, the knowledge base is there for whatever areas need to be addressed.

3. Knowledge alone is not sufficient to develop parenting competence—that is, all major efforts at parenting education deal in some way with emotions and attitudes. Feelings about family and parent–child dynamics run deep. Attitudes about power, authority, reciprocity, and related issues are often more influential than facts. Parent education must provide a vehicle for dealing with facts and feelings.

4. No matter how well educated, well adjusted, or fortunate in their social and economic arrangements, all parents need help with learning how to cope with the parenting role and to support their children's growth and development. This need is intensified by current changes in living styles for some as well as at particular stages of the family's life cycle for all.

5. Parents want to learn. Parents care about their children and will participate when they believe they are helping their children toward future success in school and life, or are doing something that makes them better parents. It follows that if parents do not participate in available education programs, they are not yet convinced of a program's value to their children or to themselves. Also, specific stresses in parents' lives must be alleviated to enable parents to involve themselves in learning and change.

6. Parents learn best when the subject matter is closely related to them and their children. All parents have unique experiences in the relationships and circumstances of their lives and need to make specific applications of new ideas to their situations. This places the basic responsibility for growth and change within each parent because each identifies particular needs and motivations. No person or agency outside the parent can decide what that parent needs.

7. Parents can often learn best from one another. A negative expression of this idea is that parents are adults who resist being told what to do by a stranger—even an expert; parents also frequently resist being told things by experts they do know. Learning from the common experiences of other adults who are perceived as peers can be meaningful because parents remind each other of what they already know and increase their feelings of self-worth as they empathize and understand.

8. Parents learn in their own way. Basic educational principles point out individual differences in pace, style, and patterns of learning. A dynamic program offers flexible approaches that allow parents to proceed as they feel comfortable, to concentrate on what they find significant, and to participate actively to the extent that they are able. Professionals who work in parent education must understand principles of adult learning.

OPPORTUNITY FOR SELF-REFLECTION

As an adult, have you been involved in educational experiences that did not recognize these principles of adult learning? What was your reaction when treated without respect for your own needs or particular interests in learning? How can those experiences help you plan meaningful, respectful parent education?

Some of the more typical problems that parent education programs have to address can be prevented or resolved with more attention to the implications of these assumptions. These problems include the following:

1. Initial recruitment problems or lack of interest. Attention to program content and format, program time, transportation, child care, and other support services can all help here.

2. Conflict in views and values. Collaborative discussion and planning can help turn differences in ideas and attitudes into stimulating situations that can cause parents to examine their own positions more deeply.

3. Group management problems. Administrators and teachers have to learn skills necessary to work with adults. Part of the training should be a change from the professional stance of domination to group process techniques.

11-4 Planning and Implementing Parent Education Programs

Families must be actively involved in planning the educational programs in which they will participate. A collaborative effort in which teachers and parents function as partners in needs assessment differs from the traditional approach of a professional making these decisions alone. There are numerous ways to facilitate this.

11-4a Initial Parent Involvement

Parents may come together for such purely social occasions as potluck suppers, brown bag lunches, or parents' breakfasts. As comfort levels increase and relationships grow, the general discussion among the parents may narrow to particular interests and concerns. Teachers can help parents structure a program that evolves directly from the discovery of common needs and questions. Teachers are then acting not as "experts" but as resources as families define their own needs. It is a natural progression for parents to become involved because they already feel welcomed as a member of the group of parents.

Remembering that family education may be broader than merely focusing on children's issues, programs may bring parents together to learn skills in which they have indicated interest; see some of the choices on the sample interest survey shown in the Ideas for Teachers feature., such as using the Internet or financial planning and investments. As the monthly meetings become popular, interest may cycle back to parenting topics.

FIGURE 11-5
Families must be actively involved in planning the educational programs in which they will participate.

To involve parents directly in planning education efforts, schools may structure a meeting soon after the school year starts specifically to generate and discuss ideas that parents are interested in pursuing. At this initial meeting, parents can take an active role if staff members ask one or two parents to help plan and lead the first discussion (see Figure 11-5).

© Cengage Learning®

Answering an assessment questionnaire or survey is one way of receiving input from parents on their interests and needs for future parent programs.

The disadvantage to using a survey form is that some parents may have difficulty with the reading and writing aspects of it or may not bother to return it. If the survey is also posted on the parent bulletin board and on the school website, parents may respond on their own time. The form lacks the personal involvement of individuals in a discussion, but at least a survey conveys the message that parents' ideas are needed and wanted and can yield a lot of helpful planning information. Parents will pay attention to subsequent announcements of meetings that they have helped to plan (Stephens, 2007).

TeachSource Digital Download

IDEAS FOR TEACHERS:

Create a Survey to Learn Parents' Interests

Parent Education Interest Survey

As we plan our parents' meetings for this year, your ideas are needed. Let us know if you would like to learn more about the following topics.

1. Rate the following topics:

Interest:
———————————
Great Slight None

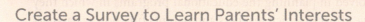

Discipline for self-control
Using the Internet
Sibling rivalry
Nutrition and children
Financial planning and investments
Understanding No Child Left Behind
   Legislation and what it means to you
Getting ready for school
Choosing good books and toys
Sex education
Normal preadolescent development

Preserving family stories

Being an only parent

Television and its effects on children

Language development: What is
    normal and what is not

Cooking quick suppers in a wok

Resources in the community: Where
    to get help for what

When to call the doctor

Avoiding your child's "I need" trap

How to make your child responsible
    for his or her own homework

Please add topics of interest to you: _____

_____

2. Circle the day that fits your schedule: M T W Th F

3. Indicate the time of day that is best:

Lunch hour

Right after work

Evening—7 or 7:30

Thank you for your help. Watch for coming notices.

Teachers are often tempted to plan programs based on what they believe parents need to learn. But unless parents are motivated by a current need to gain particular knowledge or skills, they may reject plans imposed by teachers—no matter how important the ideas are. Parent education programs have a greater likelihood of effecting change if they are sensitive to and design activities around the basic assumptions and beliefs parents hold regarding child rearing and education. Reports of successful parent education efforts point out that in each case, the curriculum is not preset and prescribed but follows the interests and needs identified by families—that is, programs start where the parents presently are, rather than where teachers think parents should be. Only parents can accurately define this starting place by expressing their needs and interests. They can also keep the program responsive to differences of culture and class.

11-4b Selecting the Style of a Meeting

Group size and style of meeting must be considered when providing for parents' comfort and an opportunity to talk with other parents. Studies find that the most important variable in parent attendance and participation in meetings is group size; smaller groups create feelings of closeness, community, and ownership of the endeavor. Other studies indicate that meetings involving families of just one class are preferable to meetings that involve the entire school; bringing together a dozen or so parents with children of similar ages or grade levels facilitates the sharing of experiences and concerns (see Figure 11-6). The advantage to large group meetings is that a timid parent can listen without feeling pressure to participate; the disadvantage is that individual needs are

FIGURE 11-6
Bringing together a small group of parents with children of similar ages or grade levels facilitates the sharing of information and concerns.

© 2016 Cengage Learning®

often not met because not all parents will have the opportunity to ask questions related to their particular situations or gain the satisfaction of sharing with other parents.

Because parents learn from each other as well as from professionals, the style of a meeting should encourage such interaction. Greater changes may occur in parents' behavior and attitudes following discussions within a group of parents than following lectures. This requires a reconceptualization of the roles of administrators, teachers, and parents in parent education, emphasizing the importance of parents speaking to each other and putting professionals in the role of consultants, supporting instead of instructing. When parents identify a need that requires an expert, teachers can help locate and invite suitable resources.

 ### 11-4c   The Teacher's Role in Setting the Style of a Meeting

A teacher's role in a parent discussion group is first to provide a structure that helps establish a warm atmosphere of informality and friendly sharing and then to function as a facilitator of group discussion. Such a leader displays several traits:

- Acceptance, support, and encouragement for all parents in a group to express themselves

- Objectivity, to avoid taking sides in most discussions

- Tact, to protect each parent's right to discuss in a nonthreatening environment

- Alertness to both verbal and nonverbal responses of group members, using that feedback to guide a discussion and maintain group morale

Heavy utilization of media or lecture techniques does not allow parents to participate or teachers to function in a learning role, whereas group discussions or small group work formats do. When fun and interesting activities are paired with the sharing of information, meetings will be more enjoyable (Lashley & Giannoni, 2010). (See Figure 11-7.)

TeachSource Digital Download

FIGURE 11-7

Sample Plan for a Meeting to Satisfy Parents' Needs for Participation and Social Interaction

1. Welcome and introductions—use the round-robin format to talk with at least three people and then introduce the last person with whom you speak.

2. Discuss the purpose of the evening: to answer parents' questions and concerns about the No Child Left Behind Legislation; overview of activities.

3. Break into groups of four to five members, with chart paper and a marker. Appoint one member to record the group's questions, comments, and concerns. Allow 15 minutes for this discussion—more if needed.

4. One member from each group will present the main points of their discussion and post their questions.

5. The facilitator (the director of the parent information and resource center located behind the school) will summarize the questions and lead a discussion that provides relevant information.

6. Leave time for further questions and discussion.

7. Break for refreshments and informal conversation.

8. Tour the parent information and resource center.

Notice how the plan in Figure 11-7 allows informal parental interaction and participation as well as providing information to address parental concerns and letting parents explore the resources that can continue to support them.

Teachers can structure the initial meeting of parents to ease interpersonal communication. Name tags, with reminders to identify parents and connect parents to their children, help parents make initial connections.

Icebreaker games or activities may start a conversation (see Figure 11-8). However, it is important to remember that teachers are dealing with adults, not children, so a teacher must learn techniques that are appropriate for adults. Most adults would feel discomfort at being asked to participate in children's songs until after the group moves to a level of familiarity with each other. More ideas for icebreakers can be found in Ukens (2008) and Bloomfield (2009).

Teachers can demonstrate the philosophy that parents' meetings are another way of working with the whole family by involving children in making refreshments or decorations during a classroom day, by asking children to leave a picture or note for their parent to find, or asking parents to make a picture at the meeting to leave in a child's cubby for the next morning. Children may write letters to entice their parents to come to a meeting.

The prior existence of a social network of friends and relatives correlates with a lower level of attendance at regular group sessions and special events for parents. In other

TeachSource

VIDEO ACTIVITY

© 2016 Cengage Learning®

After viewing the Video *Toddler Tutoring,* consider these questions:

1. Plan a parent meeting that uses this video as a springboard for discussion about appropriate learning for preschoolers. Outline the format for the meeting.

2. Recognizing that parents may have different viewpoints about this topic, how will you ensure a balanced discussion? Plan three open-ended questions to facilitate discussion.

3. What other methods of parent education might be appropriate follow-ups for this meeting?

FIGURE 11-8
Icebreaker Activities.

1. Ask participants to find someone who:
    - Has the same number of children
    - Has the same birthday month
    - Was born in the same hospital
    - Has the same middle name
    - Has the same favorite food
    - Has the same favorite TV show

2. Pair up participants to share the stories of how they were given their names. They can use this information to introduce their partners to the group.

3. Ask participants to find a partner to share their worst memories of school. When the group reconvenes, ask for a few volunteers to tell their partners' stories. When the laughter dies down, names can be shared.

4. Create small groups, and give them chart paper and markers. Ask them to create a group drawing incorporating characteristics of their least favorite teachers. Group members must all contribute ideas to whoever volunteers to draw or represent them.

words, parents without reciprocal ties to other adults are more eager for the support and interaction with adults in parent education settings. This may be especially true for single parents (see Figure 11-9). The opportunities for social interaction and new relationships provide incentives for some parents to become involved in such a parent education group.

FIGURE 11-9
Single parents may be especially eager for interaction with other adults in parent education settings.

11-4d Selecting a Time for a Meeting

Stresses and concerns of daily life may prevent some parents from involving themselves in parent education activities. Teachers need to be conscious of any accommodations they can make to help alleviate some of these problems.

Meetings may be more convenient if parents help select the dates and times. Sometimes, parents' attendance is precluded by child care demands; providing child care may allow a family to attend. This is why many successful parent education efforts of full-day programs occur during the lunch hour or late afternoon while children are still in their classrooms. Transportation difficulties may keep parents from participating; parent committees can set up carpools or arrange meetings in more central locations, or parents may come to school on the bus with their children for a morning meeting. Some programs that are located close to parents' worksites, such as employer-sponsored child care, take the parent education program right into the office building during lunch hour. Such assistance lets parents become involved and is evidence that teachers understand some of their problems.

FIGURE 11-10
A relaxed atmosphere and activities with children before the parents' discussion create enjoyable participation.

Traditionally, parent meetings for elementary schools have been held in the evening. For working parents, evening meetings are often difficult to attend; after a long day at the job and then taking children home to prepare supper and getting through the evening routine, going back to school becomes quite unattractive. Many schools find success in providing an evening meal—a covered-dish supper or a spaghetti dinner—when parents come to pick up their children (see Figure 11-10).

Parents, children, and teachers could relax together after a workday and enjoy a social occasion without parents having to worry about hurrying home with tired, hungry children. The children can play or do homework supervised in another room while parents continue a more serious discussion. Parents and children can still get home early in the evening after a pleasant and productive time for all. (Figure 11-11 has a list of

FIGURE 11-11
Books to Help Teachers and Parents Plan Discussion.

Books about Topics That Teachers and Parents May Enjoy Discussing

Bernstein, J. (2007). *10 Days to a less distracted child: The program that gets your kids to listen, learn, focus and behave.*

Faber, A., & Mazlish, E. (2004). *Siblings without rivalry: How to help your children live together so you can live too.*

Gurian, M., & Sterns, K. (2010). *Boys and girls learn differently: A guide for teachers and parents.*

Hurley, C. (2009). *The six virtues of the educated person: Helping kids to learn, schools to succeed.*

Karres, E., & Looman, D. (2000). *Violence proof your kids now.*

Louv, R. (2008). *Last child in the woods: Saving our children from nature-deficit disorder.*

Maxwell, S. (2008). *The talk: What your kids need to hear from you about sex.*

Phelan, T. (2010). *1-2-3 Magic: Effective discipline for children 2–12.*

Tomeo, T. (2007). *Noise: How our media-saturated culture dominates lives and dismantles families.*

Weissbourd, R. (2010). *The parents we mean to be: How well-intentioned adults undermine children's moral and emotional development.*

Willard, N., & Steiner, K. (2007). *Cyberbullying and cyberthreats: Responding to the challenge of online social aggression, threats, and distress.*

See other ideas about family–teacher book discussions in Dejong & Burton, 2013.

---

books that might provide useful resources for teachers and parents planning discussions of particular topics.)

Schools centrally located to parents' workplaces find that asking parents to "brown bag" it occasionally for a lunch meeting brings parents together while children are busy at school. Such meetings recognize the many demands on parents' nonworking time.

Busy, weary parents are more likely to attend meetings where the time frame, announced in advance, will not be much more than an hour and will begin and end promptly. It is helpful to announce meetings well in advance (a month at minimum), with weekly, then daily, reminders. Coordinating plans and arrangements takes time, so staff should assume parents are not able to come on short notice; at least two reminders are appropriate. Attention to physical comfort, with adult-sized chairs, light food and beverages, and a relaxed, uncrowded atmosphere, creates optimal conditions for concentrating on a discussion.

As parent education discussion groups evolve, the participants will more strictly define their purposes and goals. It is important to the ongoing success of such programs that parents and teachers occasionally evaluate whether activities are meeting the intended goals. Remember that the effectiveness of any parent education program is measured not by how many people come (the "bodies in the building" assessment) but by the effect the program has in changing attitudes and behaviors and increasing parental competence. An evaluation should center on how a program works for those who attend and what additional steps can be taken to include others.

For such teachers as Anne Morgan and Dorothy Scott, who have been part of a traditional "professional giving information" type of parent education program, it may require determined effort to accept the concept of parents choosing, guiding, and actively participating in a discussion. But such forms of education give strength and power to parents as they gain confidence in their own ideas and abilities.

CULTURAL CONSIDERATIONS

Parent education for immigrant and migrant parents

Every community now realizes that the school population includes many children and families who are newcomers to our country, bringing their own culture and language with them. It is estimated that more than 10 percent of schoolchildren are English language learners (ELL)—some areas of the country have even higher percentages. This presents additional considerations for involving their parents in education programs. Migrant parents are often very concerned with survival, working long hours just to support their families. Many immigrants are suspicious—rightly or wrongly—that involvement with schools will bring official scrutiny about their legal status. Many immigrant parents come from cultures that tend to leave school activities and contact to the professionals. Often, migrant parents are not educated or comfortable in a school setting. And still more do not have the language ability to communicate comfortably with teachers and others in education programs.

Schools that have successfully involved parents whose first language is not English have held themselves accountable to meet the multiple educational and other needs of migrant parents. They have reached out to immigrants and their families where they work and gather to let them know what educational resources are available to them. They have recruited bilingual teachers who can gain parents' trust by meeting them at their language level. They have offered or created linkages to programs that can help parents earn a GED or classes for learning English so parents can improve their own work opportunities, better help their children with homework and literacy for school success, and better communicate with teachers and the school system.

Meeting specific parental educational needs for English-learning parents may take precedence over other goals for parent education involvement (Lopez, Scribner, & Mahitivanichcha, 2001).

For some teachers, who have their own ideas about needed parent education, these ideas may be difficult.

Reflect on your own response to the idea of focusing parent education for immigrant parents on immediate survival needs.

11-5 Parents as Decision Makers

Some schools involve parents as advisers and policymakers. Parent membership on parent councils or policy boards brings them into decision-making positions that may affect their children and the communities they represent. The exact roles of decision makers may vary according to the regulations of the school or agency involved (see Figure 11-12).

Federally funded programs, such as Head Start and Title 1, have federal guidelines and local regulations to govern parental roles on advisory councils that have 50 percent parent membership. These roles are active, with the power to decide on budget matters, curriculum, and hiring. Parent cooperative schools generally allow their parent boards to make all policy decisions.

Many school districts have now established parent advisory or decision-making councils for each school site. Variously called Parent Advisory Councils (PACS), Site-Based Councils, School Improvement Councils (SICS), and Local School Councils (LSCS), these bodies usually include parents with teachers and staff to serve on the council.

Other parent councils in some public and private educational settings may function as purely advisory bodies, with decision-making powers vested in professional personnel. A parent advisory council can be a first link to successful communication and collaboration between staff and families. As the staff works with the parents on the parent advisory council, there is less of an impression of "experts" advising or controlling the situation. The difficulty may be that the parents who are invited to participate may not fully represent the diversity of parents in the school or may be volunteers who may feel most comfortable in the school setting. Schools must try to include all voices represented in the school community.

© iStockphoto.com/ Chris Schmidt

FIGURE 11-12
Parents are involved as decision makers in some schools.

Many parents are eager to have a voice in their children's schools. Effectively involving parents in cooperative decision making can benefit everyone. Children benefit as schools shape their offerings to fit community character and need. Parents assuming leadership roles develop skills that benefit themselves and their communities and increase their confidence in their abilities to shape their children's lives. They may also demonstrate more support for a school as they perceive a closer connection between its functioning and their own goals. Parents who feel they have a vehicle to voice their concerns will not withdraw or resort to negative methods of making themselves heard. As parents learn more about how a school functions and why, they learn more about children's needs. Administrators and teachers benefit by the expansion of their viewpoints with the addition of parents' perspectives. They also may find their efforts are strengthened with the addition of parent understanding, advocacy, and support.

In poorly planned parent advisory situations, a variety of problems may surface:

- Conflicts about how to conduct the organizational process
- Power struggles among parents vying for control of a group
- Confusion about the responsibilities of group members
- Disagreements over institutional philosophies and goals

When an organization develops a trusting relationship among its members and helps develop group communication and planning skills, parents participating in the decision-making process develop important relationships between home and school. Specific guidelines for and clear understandings of parent action are most helpful. The real advantages of involving parents as decision makers should encourage professionals to find methods that avoid conflict and misunderstanding.

SUMMARY

Parent education refers to:

- Specific attempts to offer knowledge and support to parents in hopes of increasing parenting effectiveness.
- Parent education has taken many forms, for different purposes, with varying results

Parent education is necessary because:

- Every family needs support.
- Every family needs information and interaction with other families.

Assumptions regarding parent education include:

- Parents can learn.
- A specific body of knowledge exists that can help parents become more effective.
- Knowledge alone is not enough. Attitudes and feelings must be dealt with.
- All parents need education and help.
- Parents want to learn.
- Parents learn best when the subject matter is closely related to their particular circumstances.
- Parents can often learn best from one another.
- Parents will learn at their own paces and in their own ways.

In planning and implementing parent education programs, considerations include:

- Active family involvement in planning
- Surveys of family interest and availability, as well as style of meetings matched to participants
- Concern for family needs for transportation, child care, and socialization

As decision makers, parents may be involved:

- In advisory meetings to support school functioning
- On boards, mandated or otherwise

Student Activities for Further Study

1. Attend a parent meeting at your own or any other school. Notice efforts made to promote social comfort and interaction; physical arrangements and services, such as child care, seating, and refreshments; planned activity, amounts of interaction, and parents' responses to it. Find out how and when the meeting was publicized. Discuss your findings with your classmates.

2. If you are working or interning in a school, devise a survey form to assess parents' interest and needs for making future program plans. After you obtain the responses, analyze the information and then devise several plans that match parents' expressed needs and wants. If you are not currently in a classroom situation, work in pairs to devise a questionnaire and then answer it as each of the hypothetical families in Chapter 2 might. Analyze the information, and devise several education plans that match those needs and wants.

   For the parents' meeting:

   - List the purpose of the meeting.
   - List the instructional strategies you will be using and the materials and equipment you will need.
   - Describe the room arrangement you will use.
   - List the tentative schedule, with approximate times for the events.

- List five questions you would expect parents to discuss about this topic.
- List five questions you might use to stimulate discussion about this topic.

3. Plan a simple icebreaking social activity for the beginning of a meeting. Demonstrate and discuss this with your classmates.

4. Contact several schools in your area, including one that has a Head Start or another federally funded program if one exists in your community. Find out whether parents participate in any advisory capacity.

Apply the Chapter Concepts: Case in Point

The faculty at Jackson Early Childhood Center has always had one required parent meeting each year, held on an evening in January. For the last two years, fewer than one-third of the families were represented in attendance, even though they know it is expected of them. The teachers have been discouraged by this lack of response. One outspoken parent told her teacher recently that she did not plan to attend again because the meeting was a waste of her time.

1. What would be the most helpful response to this parent? The least helpful response?

2. How could this parent's response be useful to the faculty and administrator as they plan this year's parent education meeting?

3. What are some questions the faculty should be asking as they try to change the situation?

4. Brainstorm a list of strategies that might help in the planning process.

Review Questions

1. Discuss what is meant by "parent education."

2. Discuss a rationale for parent education.

3. Identify several assumptions regarding parent education.

4. For each assumption, describe a corresponding implication for planning parent education programs.

5. Describe how parents may act as advisers in a program.

Helpful Websites

- Parent Effectiveness Training's mission is to provide people worldwide with the communication and conflict resolution skills necessary for creating effective and lasting relationships in the workplace, in families, and in schools. Find information about related resources at their website.

- The Center for the Improvement of Child Care (CICC) is a private nonprofit community service, training, and research corporation and a major supporter and participant in a nationwide effective parenting movement to improve the overall quality of child rearing and child caring in the United States.

- Active Parenting's programs provide parents with the skills to help them develop cooperation, responsibility, and self-esteem in their children. Get more information at their website.

- AVANCE provides innovative education and family support services to predominantly Hispanic families in low-income, at-risk communities. Much information is available on the website.

- Systematic Training for Effective Parenting (STEP) has become a source of widely recognized and used parent education materials in North America.

- The mission of the American Academy of Pediatrics is to attain optimal physical, mental, and social health and well-being for all infants, children, adolescents, and young adults. Information on this site could be useful for designing parent meetings on a variety of topics.

- The National Center for Family Literacy helps parents and children achieve their potential together through quality literacy programs. The NCFL works with educators and community builders to meet the educational needs of disadvantaged families.

CHAPTER 12

It Takes a Village: Teachers, Families, and Communities

Learning Objectives

After reading this chapter, you should be able to:

12-1 Discuss the importance of community.

12-2 Discuss corporate involvement in family, education, and child care issues.

12-3 Describe current legislative initiatives that shape policy affecting families, schools, and children.

12-4 Discuss community collaborations that support families and children.

12-5 Identify and discuss advocacy roles for teachers and families.

12-6 List three ways the community can provide resources for teachers and families,

naeyc

Related NAEYC Standards

Accreditation Standards (see inside text back cover for full listing of the Accreditation Standards for exemplary early childhood programs)

2.L.05; 2.L.08; 6.B.02; 7.C.05; 7.C.06; 8.A.02; 8.B.01; 8.C.01; 8.C.03; 8.C.05; 8.C.06

Licensure Standards (see inside text front cover for full listing of the Licensure Standards for this chapter)

2a; 2c; 6e

As communities reel from the impact of troubled families crumbling from change and stress, everyone realizes that healthy families are essential. Furthermore, it is in the best interests of everyone in the community to support families so they are effective in their child-rearing functions. When families—isolated and struggling—are left on their own to do what they can without the support of the larger community, the community bears the brunt of the family's failure. The entire village that it takes to raise a child, about which we have heard so much in recent years, realizes that the vision that supports children, families, and the institutions that serve families is a vision that impacts us all.

In this chapter, we examine the ways the community at large affects schools and the families they serve and the ways that teachers and families may function as advocates for child and family issues within the community. Together, teachers and families have the power to inspire community support that will mutually benefit them, their schools, and the children for whom they care. As children learn to live within their communities, they contribute to the communities that support them and their families.

12-1 The Importance of Community

Children live in many worlds. Home and family, schools, the neighborhood, and the community beyond shape their lives. Just as every family is unique, so, too, is each community.

Children exist in the context of community, depending on a multitude of adults who touch their lives directly through relationships and indirectly through the decisions they make that affect children and families. In the words of former First Lady and Secretary of State, Hilary Rodham Clinton:

> Adults police their streets, monitor the quality of their food, air, and water, produce the programs that appear on their televisions, run the businesses that employ their parents, and write the laws that protect them. Each of us plays a part in every child's life. It takes a village to raise a child.
>
> I chose that old African proverb to title this book because it offers a timeless reminder that children will thrive only if their families thrive and if the whole of society cares enough to provide for them. (Clinton, 1996)

In the best of circumstances, the many worlds of children are complementary and reinforcing, and each world is supported by the other, forming a circle of protection around children. As we have seen in earlier discussions, when teachers and families create real partnerships, their spheres of influence overlap and form a caring community around students. The Harvard Family Research Project refers to the need for *complementary learning* for children to be successful—an array of linked learning supports around them, including families, early childhood programs, schools, out-of-school programs and activities, health and social service agencies, businesses, libraries, museums, and other community resources (Caspe, Lopez, & Wolos, 2006/2007).

However, there has been an erosion of social capital over the past decades—within the family and in the larger community. In the family, social capital refers to the presence and availability of adults and opportunities for a range of parent–child communication about social and personal matters. In the community, social capital includes norms of

social capital
Available resources provided by efforts, knowledge, and relationships of people.

social control, organizations for youth sponsored by adults, and a variety of informal social relations between adults and children that allow adults to support children in ways they might not seek from their parents. Many today believe that the erosion of community is fundamental to contemporary unrest and breakdown. The late Urie Bronfenbrenner considered the development of children in all their contexts: at home and in school, in neighborhoods and communities, and within the larger context of such influences as the health care system, the media, and the economy. He noted the silent crisis of contemporary society, calling the present state of children and families in the United States the greatest domestic problem our nation has faced (see Figure 12-1).

FIGURE 12-1
There are real community concerns about the community investment in protecting American children.

Where America Stands

Among industrialized countries, the United States ranks:

1st in gross domestic product

1st in the number of billionaires

1st in per capita health expenditures

1st in military weapons experts

1st in defense spending

17th in reading scores

22nd in low birth weight rates

23rd in science scores

29th in infant mortality rates

31st in math scores

31st in the gap between rich and poor

Last in relative child poverty

Last in adolescent birth rates

Last in divorce rates

Last in protecting our children against gun violence

Adapted from "The State of America's Children," 2012, Children's Defense Fund, 2012.

As society has increasingly centered on advancing one's individual interests, less attention has been paid to a sense of community responsibility for raising other people's children. Specific government actions during the past two decades have removed visible support from some agencies within the community and left individual families to care for themselves as best they could. Most of this government withdrawal has been done under the stance of noninterference in responsibilities that are stated to belong rightfully to families; in reality, families are often left without necessary community supports and resources. During this same period, the number of children and families living beneath the poverty line has increased dramatically. However, at the same time that the rhetoric of individualism and government removal seems to be withdrawing community attention from the family, other interests within the community bring attention back to the family and its needs.

An examination of society's ills brings renewed awareness of the problems that arise when parenting roles are ineffective and the family unit is weakened. The community is left to face problems:

- High student dropout rates from school, with the results being illiteracy and underprepared workers

- High unemployment rates and increasing numbers of citizens living in poverty

- Increasing numbers of adolescent and unmarried girls becoming mothers

- Violence in families and schools as anger and isolation cause painful eruptions

- Higher crime rates and drug addictions that accompany hopelessness and poverty

- Family breakdowns and stress for adults and children that accompany changed family structures

- Different working patterns of parents that take away already small reserves of family time

Considering how to deal with the primary causes of these problems has focused community attention on examining family situations and needs and formulating policies to support children and families.

12-1a Bronfenbrenner's Ecological Systems Theory

The ideas of Urie Bronfenbrenner's ecological systems theory (1979) portray the child developing within the context of five nested, interrelated systems of relationships that form his or her environment (see Figure 12-2). This is the series of connected and interrelated social systems:

- The **microsystem**, which includes the principal relationships and experiences a child has with immediate surroundings. Structures in the microsystem include family, school or child care program, church, and neighborhood.

- The **mesosystem**, which provides the connections between the structures of the child's microsystem. Examples of this would be the connection between the child's teacher and family or between the child's church and neighborhood.

- The **exosystem**, which describes the larger social system that the child does not experience directly, but the structures in this layer impact the child's development by interacting with some structure within the microsystem. For example, the schedules of the parent's workplace or availability of community-based family resources may have a positive or negative impact on the child.

- The **macrosystem**, which describes the sociocultural context—the surrounding cultural values, customs, and laws that affect the structures within which the family functions. For example, if the belief of the culture is that parents are solely responsible for child rearing, the culture is less likely to provide resources for families.

microsystem
Small part of a system that forms a unified whole; related to children—bounds of a child's world, such as home, school, Grandma's house, or the like.

mesosystem
Those events or situations in which two microsystems come together to have impact on development.

exosystem
Settings or events that influence the child's development even though the child has no direct role in them.

macrosystem
The belief systems, lifestyles and options, and patterns of social interchange of an individual's society and subculture that affect development.

FIGURE 12-2
Bronfenbrenner's
Ecological Systems Theory.

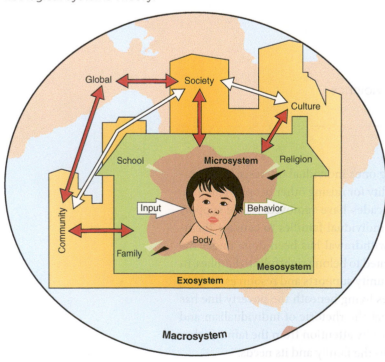

■ A more recent addition is the concept of **chronosystem**, adding the temporal element to these other interactions. This can refer to changes over time in the systems, and the effect of changes in the other systems, such as the timing of a mother returning to work (Downer & Myers, 2010).

These ideas suggest the importance of examining the interconnections among the ideas and structures that surround the child and family. Bronfenbrenner's principles clearly show the connections between values and decisions of the larger community and their effect on children and families, and the importance of the families and schools that exist within larger communities (see Figure 12-3). Research makes it clear that families can only do their job of child rearing when their social and economic needs are met by the surrounding community. Actions taken by communities impinge on the functioning of the family and the school. In turn, actions of families and teachers can influence the community. A vital role for teachers and parents to consider together is their opportunity to be advocates for social practices, legislation, and support for optimal functioning for families and schools. Consider some of the actions being taken within the community that have impacts on families and schools.

> **chronosystem**
> System made up of the environmental events and transitions that occur throughout a child's life, including any sociohistorical events.

FIGURE 12-3
Families exist within larger communities.

© 2016 Cengage Learning®

12-2 Corporate Involvement

The business community has to deal with its employees as family members. Now that about two-thirds of all mothers are in the workforce along with fathers, employers are facing conflicts that arise when their employees are trying to fill the roles of parent and worker at the same time. Concern about child care may interfere with an employee's productivity. Parents may have to be absent from work when child care arrangements fall through, when school is closed, or when a child is sick and cannot go to school. Almost daily, many working parents have events, conferences, or meetings scheduled that mean they must decide whether to be responsible to their employers or their children and the schools. Companies might lose good employees because of the lack of helpful parental leave policies. In fact, research has shown the business world that attention and assistance to parents' child care needs pays off in recruitment, retention, productivity, absenteeism patterns, and morale of employees (Galinsky, Kim, & Bond, 2001).

Studies confirm that family-friendly practices are good for business, making the workforce more committed and engaged and avoiding absenteeism and lack of attention (Connelly, DeGraff, & Willis, 2004). National figures estimate that employers lose $3 billion annually for child care–related absences of parents. Increasingly, employers are coming to understand that they have some responsibility to support the family needs and issues of their workforce and create a corporate culture that allows families to work and care well for their children (see Figure 12-4).

FIGURE 12-4
With corporate support, employees can volunteer time to work in community classrooms.

© 2016 Cengage Learning®

Each year since 1986, *Working Mother* magazine names the 100 Best Companies for Working Mothers. Companies are rated for their flexibility to meet parents' needs, leave time for new parents, child care assistance, elder care assistance, and the number of women occupying top positions in the company. Policies are varied and adapt to parents' needs and may include:

- Backup child care for sick children or during holiday times
- Such flexible work arrangements as compressed work weeks, working from home, job sharing, or reduced hours and gradual return to work after parental leave
- Resource and referral services for child care and other family needs
- Parent education and support programs
- Near-site or on-site child care
- Pretax child care funding arrangements
- Supplements for cost of child care
- Maternal and paternal leaves, with pay

A majority of companies now offer some sort of flexible work arrangements; many also offer maternal/paternal/adoption leave—often with at least some replacement income—and over two-thirds offer some form of child care assistance. Many companies now have policies that allow parents to take personal leave time for participation in their children's schools. Corporate America is rising to the challenge of supporting its workers' families. However, teachers should realize that many employers do nothing at all to support the families of their workers.

An organization that works on issues related to work and family life is the Families and Work Institute. Established as a nonprofit organization in 1989, the institute seeks to address the changing nature of work and family life. As it identifies emerging issues, the organization engages in policy and worksite research and provides data to inform decision making on the changing workforce, changing family, and changing community. Numerous publications are available and more information can be obtained from the Families and Work Institute. See their website listed at the end of this chapter.

The increased awareness of child care, need for educational improvements, and other family needs have brought corporate leaders into discussion and collaboration with other community organizations in efforts to improve services offered to families. Many communities have included corporate leaders in their child advocacy organizations and school systems. With awareness comes policy. Many local chambers of commerce urge local businesses to implement policies that release parents for necessary conferences with their children's schools and for volunteering in the school system. As they become involved in ways to ease the stress of family care for their workers, employers are educating themselves about community, school, and child care needs and becoming collaborators in the private sector.

12-3 Legislative Initiatives

The public sector is also increasingly aware of children's and family issues. After decades of opposing government regulation of child care at any level, Congress finally passed and funded a first-ever comprehensive federal system for supporting child care to address issues of affordability, availability, and quality: the Child Care and Development Block Grants.

Now reauthorized and renamed, the Child Care and Development Fund provides over $4 billion a year in federal funds to states; the states supply additional funds, including some of the funds allotted under TANF. The CCDF provides money to states to do the following:

- Provide child care assistance to low- and moderate-income families, with specifically at least 70 percent for families transitioning off TANF.

- Recruit family child care providers.

- Develop local resource and referral programs to help link families to child care services.

- Train providers.

- Expand the supply of child care.

Unfortunately, because the funds allow for only a small fraction of eligible families to receive child care, much more assistance is needed to meet the needs of low-income families.

Other political initiatives and media campaigns have directed national attention to the needs of working families and the child care community. For the first time, the needs of children have been discussed in weekly newsmagazines and in television specials.

With President Obama having discussed the need for early childhood education in his State of the Union address in 2013 and members of Congress introducing a number of bills to increase federal funds to help families with the cost and quality of child care and to provide incentives for businesses to become involved in child care, hope for additional legislative support is high in the early childhood education community. Teachers and parents can get up-to-date information about current legislative issues from the National Association for the Education of Young Children via *Young Children* or the association's website (listed at the end of this chapter).

12-3a Temporary Assistance for Needy Families

In August 1996, the Personal Opportunity and Work Opportunity Reconciliation Act changed welfare by eliminating the guarantee of cash assistance to needy families with children and by requiring work in exchange for time-limited assistance. Temporary Assistance for Needy Families (TANF) replaced the 60-year-old guarantee of the Aid to Families with Dependent Children (AFDC) program. The TANF legislation was reauthorized in 2006 under the Deficit Reduction Act, with strengthened work requirements (see Figure 12-5).

Although welfare caseloads across the nation have decreased more than 40 percent since TANF was instituted, there is concern that the well-being of children and families is suffering. Most of those losing welfare support are not gaining the remuneration from work that could support a family; former welfare recipients who find jobs typically earn wages below the poverty level (Children's Defense Fund, 2004). More than a third of homeless Americans in urban areas who sought shelter in U.S. cities were families with children (National Coalition for the Homeless, 2006). With more than 20 percent of children in this country living below the poverty level, the TANF legislation may have created additional risks for children and families in the segment of the population that has the least access to good jobs and the support systems that make it possible to work. The political parties have spoken of "cleaning up welfare waste." But along with those possible improvements, they have made enormous changes in the lives of many children and families. With TANF work requirements, many single parent–headed families have very little time to spend with family or for school communication. Teachers will

FIGURE 12-5
TANF has work requirements for parents that increase the need for child care.

© Cengage Learning®

have to monitor the progress and effects on families of this legislation over time; certainly, a major effect already has been to push the need for child care and afterschool care to new limits as more parents move into the workforce.

12-3b Family Medical Leave Act

As we saw in Chapter 3, America lags behind most industrialized nations in parental leave policies for care of children after birth and in their earliest months. Although most European nations offer six to 12 months of paid parental leave with provisions also available for fathers, the United States is the only Western country where an employer does not provide paid leave for mothers and fathers. In 1993, Congress passed the Family Medical Leave Act, which could generate up to 12 weeks of unpaid leave to care for an elderly parent, sick spouse, newborn, or newly adopted child; since then, at least 50 million employees have taken advantage of its provisions. Unfortunately, the bill covers only employers with 50 or more employees, and the economic status of most families creates financial hardship if they go for long periods without salary. Studies show that two-thirds of the employees who needed a family or medical leave but did not take one said they could not afford to take time off without pay. Passage of the Family and Medical Leave Act was a first step in indicating awareness of some community responsibility to support families in times of change. Currently, there is a move to support extension of the act to cover all employers with 25 or more employees; the law does not presently apply to 41 million private employers, or nearly 43 percent of U.S. workers. Some states are funding or exploring methods to make family leave affordable by using unemployment insurance or temporary disability insurance (Hutter, 2000).

12-3c No Child Left Behind Act

The No Child Left Behind Act, signed into law by President George W. Bush in 2002, represented the federal government's most dramatic move to involve itself in education. In an attempt to reform public education, the legislation is stated to be designed to do the following:

- Gain stronger accountability from schools and school systems for educational results.

- Provide more freedom for states and communities.

- Encourage the use of proven educational methods.

- Offer more choices for parents.

The legislation requires standardized tests nearly every year and demands that schools give parents an annual report card that shows how well students in each school performed, with statistics broken out by race, gender, and disability. The law allows parents to choose another public school if their child attends a school that needs improvement or is unsafe. In Chapter 4, we read about this legislation's provisions to involve families in their children's education; this is certainly a positive feature.

The Department of Education publishes results of the tests given to all fourth- and eighth-graders in reading and math in the National Assessment of Educational Progress (NAEP) Long-Term Trends in Academic Progress, or nation's report card. The most recent results indicate only slight progress in reading and math achievement for children of all races and family backgrounds and no narrowing of the gap between white and minority students—one of the stated goals of the NCLB legislation. This kind of data, along with other concerns, earns mixed support and approval for the legislation. Many educators and professional organizations express concern about the narrow focus on test results; they urge a broader approach to considering achievement of children and schools. When the legislation is reauthorized, it is likely that changes will be made. This is a situation that will need careful monitoring by both families and those involved in education as we go forward (see Figure 12-6).

The most recent federal initiative for improving education, the Race to the Top, was funded in 2009. States are awarded funds based on points for satisfying certain educational policies, such as performance-based standards for teachers and principals, complying with Common Core standards, lifting caps on charter schools, turning around the lowest-performing schools, and building data systems. While all of these improvements may benefit the community, few specific initiatives involving families were included in the plan.

In addition to these large federal actions, most states are presently involved in funding some kinds of pre-kindergarten or preschool education and family support services. (See the discussion of some examples in Chapter 4. Be sure to learn what your state is currently doing or considering.)

FIGURE 12-6
The No Child Left Behind legislation requires standardized tests for elementary students to assess school achievement.

© Lisa F. Young/Shutterstock.com

It seems that this is a time of increasing community attention at the legislative level to child care, education, and family issues. At local, state, and national levels, economic and child care policies affect the quality of life and education that parents and teachers can provide for children.

12-4 Collaborations Within the Community

In these times of enormous social problems and limited funding resources, many agencies within the community have found it productive to form linkages to support each other's services. Collaborations come in all shapes and sizes. Public and private funding collaborations and interdisciplinary alliances result from common community concerns. For example, library systems may work with schools and child care centers and health departments that run child health clinics in efforts to get parents involved in literacy for young children. High schools, Planned Parenthood, health departments, and other civic organizations may unite their efforts to combat adolescent pregnancy. Public education, health, and child welfare systems combine efforts to address the needs of poor children and families.

The community-based partnership of the United Way Success By 6® is the nation's largest network of early childhood coalitions and is focused on improving school readiness through community change. With over 350 programs in the United States and Canada, the partnership unites community businesses, governments, service providers, advocates, educators, and families in efforts to ensure that children are born healthy and remain healthy, nurtured, and ready to succeed at school entry by age six. Connections strengthen attempts while preventing wasteful duplication of services. Such linkages also heighten overall community awareness of the problems as citizens and professionals from diverse backgrounds come together to discuss common concerns.

In her important book on efforts to strengthen families and communities, Lisbeth Schorr (2011) describes many individual collaborative programs, noting seven attributes of highly effective programs:

1. Successful programs are comprehensive, flexible, responsive, and persevering.

2. Successful programs see children in the context of their families.

3. Successful programs deal with families as parts of neighborhoods and communities.

4. Successful programs have a long-term, preventive orientation, have a clear mission, and continue to evolve over time.

5. Successful programs are well managed by competent and committed individuals with clearly identifiable skills.

6. Staffs of successful programs are trained and supported to provide high-quality, responsive services.

7. Successful programs operate in settings that encourage practitioners to build strong relationships based on mutual trust and respect (Schorr, 2011).

The forging of coalitions to address specific problems has successfully united those working within government and advocates in the private sector. Marian Wright Edelman of the Children's Defense Fund states the need for this collaboration:

> No single person, institution, or government agency can meet all of our children's and families' needs. But each of us, taking one or more of those needs, can together weave the seamless web of family and community and private sector support children need. We must work together and resist the political either/or-ism and organizational turf-ism that plague so much policy development, advocacy, service, and organizing today. Good parenting and good community, employer, and governmental supports for parents are inextricably intertwined. (Children's Defense Fund, 1998)

FIGURE 12-7
Parents can learn about community resources from teachers.

© Cengage Learning®

Teachers may play an important role in helping link families with community agencies that can provide needed services; teachers work with families to seek help from the community, neither judging nor pitying families that may need resources. Every teacher should know what community resources exist in order to refer families. Often, the local United Way publishes and distributes a directory of all community agencies that provide a variety of services for families. It is also important to use the Internet to access information about national organizations that might be supportive. Frequently, families learn of sources of help only through teachers (see Figure 12-7).

TeachSource Digital Download

IDEAS FOR TEACHERS:

Creating Resource Files

Teachers can collaborate with other staff on compiling a file of pamphlets and referral information for all community resource agencies. The following is a sample of agencies that could be included:

- Hotlines for crisis intervention
- Child care resource and referral agency
- Child abuse prevention agencies and parent support groups

- Educational options within the community
- Head Start
- Afterschool programs—public and private
- Literacy council
- Early intervention services and screening agencies
- Library resources for families, including toy-lending libraries and computers
- Individual and family counseling agencies
- Food banks and other crisis assistance
- Red Cross
- Employment counseling/training
- Women, Infants, and Children (WIC)
- Human services or welfare offices
- Health care services and clinics
- Hospitals
- Mental health/cognitive disability services
- Recreation sources for families
- Planned Parenthood
- Parenting support groups, including for newborns, parents of multiples, adoptive families, children with special needs, and grief support
- Parents Without Partners
- United Way agencies, such as counseling and other services
- Big Brothers/Big Sisters

See Figure 12-8 for a form with the kinds of information that are useful to obtain about community resources.

TeachSource Digital Download

FIGURE 12-8
Use this community resource form to gather needed information for teacher files.

Community Resource Form

Obtain the following information. Where possible, accumulate brochures from the agency.

Name of agency: _____

Address: _____

Telephone: _____

Website: _____

Hours of operation: _____

Name of contact person/supervisor: _____

Services provided: _____

Funding source for agency: _____

Cost of services: _____

Eligibility for services: _____

Method of referral/application: _____

Other information, such as nearby transportation or availability of interpreters: _____

A spirit of volunteerism may spring to life from raised awareness within communities about school and family needs. In some communities, civic organizations and businesses have "adopted" schools, linking volunteers with a specific school or center. Senior citizens find helpful roles as "foster grandparents," giving individual attention to children in early childhood classrooms. "Mentor mothers" pair experienced volunteers with new adolescent mothers. Families and schools alike may reap benefits from such volunteer efforts.

The family resource and support movement discussed in Chapter 4 is a graphic example of the power generated by community agencies forming linkages. Frequently, such programs link to other community services rather than providing the services directly. Such an arrangement is far more cost effective and encourages the optimal use of available resources. A community-established "umbrella" organization can encourage linkages at the administrative level. Networking and providing coordinating mechanisms accomplish this. Thus, conflict and fragmentation in the field are reduced, whereas training, funding streams, regulating mechanisms, and information are coordinated.

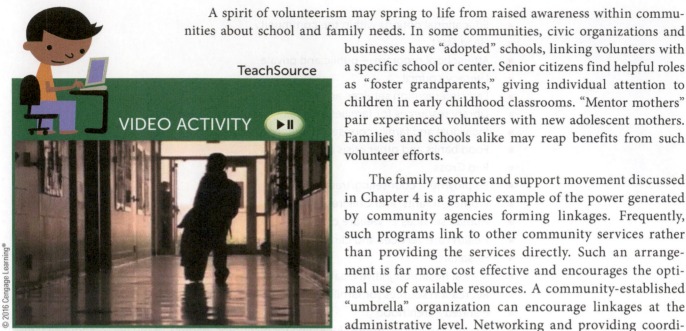

TeachSource

VIDEO ACTIVITY ▶❚❚

Watch *Serving New Immigrant Students and Their Families; the Importance of a School's Community Partners.*

After viewing, reflect on these questions:

1. How are the teachers in the school using community resources to help immigrant families?

2. How does the teacher build a sense of community with immigrant children in the classroom?

3. What additional community resources can you think of that could support immigrant children and their families?

Child care resource and referral agencies across the country offer ways for professionals and families to procure resources and information. They represent avenues for local networking and planning. Most are supported by a combination of funding from city, county, and state budgets, business and United Way contributions, and federal dependent care funds (see Figure 12-9). In large and small ways, decisions made in business, government, and social and medical service agencies affect the quality of life for families and the ways schools can meet family needs. See other information about home–school–community collaborations at the websites of the Comer School Development Program and the Family Involvement Network of Educators described at this chapter's end.

12-5 The Role of Advocate

Because of their positions, teachers and families have the capacity and obligation to influence—by separate and united action—community segments that are making decisions that affect their lives. As those who best know and care about the needs of developing children, parents and teachers are uniquely suited to be **advocates** working to convince the community of what actions must be taken on their behalf.

advocates
Those who defend or espouse a cause.

12-5a Teachers and Parents as Advocates

As people who see firsthand the everyday issues facing children, their families, and the child care and educational community at large, teachers must become advocates within the community. This is a relatively new role for many teachers, who have often concentrated efforts on the direct education and care of children. But it is now obvious that teachers and families must act to protect the interests of children in a climate where laws are enacted in response to loud lobbies from particular interest groups. As those who best understand what is developmentally appropriate and supportive of families' needs and interests, teachers must become articulate proponents of those needs and interests by doing the following:

FIGURE 12-9
Child care resource and referral agencies help link families with quality child care.

- Demonstrate the vital importance of early care and education to the community and articulate a vision of what quality education should include.

- Use influence to persuade local power brokers that early care and education must be near the top of the community's agenda.

- Function as community experts in early care and education to define what needs to be done and influence policymaking on a community-wide basis.

In exactly the same way, teachers in school systems see the impact of family and community conditions and of the emphases in educational institutions on children and healthy development. In the current climate of legislated school reform, teachers have strong opinions about how these situations are affecting excellence in education. To remain silent in the face of clear conflicts with good practice would be to ignore the importance of teachers speaking out as advocates.

Where does a teacher/advocate start?

Become Visible

Perhaps the most important starting place is to realize that our image and definition of an educational professional must change. It is no longer possible for teachers and administrators to concentrate solely on the functioning of single classrooms or schools. Advocates must become involved in the community, caring about and participating in a variety of social and civic concerns rather than simply focusing on their own issues. Educators gain credibility beyond their sphere of influence as they become recognized as positive forces in community action. Teachers can start small, joining local neighborhood or school groups that work to improve the quality of life in the community.

Be Informed

Community issues and policies are developing rapidly and continually. Teachers need to keep informed about problems, issues, and proposals at local levels and beyond and to know how these matters and proposals affect education, child care, and family support.

Teachers can become informed in many ways: newspaper or television reports about legislative and corporate discussion and action; bulletins and statements from professional and advocacy organizations; local hearings; Internet searches and social networking sites; staff meetings; discussions with colleagues; and classes and workshops. The important thing is to demonstrate professional willingness to stay abreast and learn what is going on.

OPPORTUNITY FOR SELF-REFLECTION

What educational issue in your school or community do you feel passionately about? What have you done about it up to this point? Why have you not done more? What else could you do? What supports and information would you need as you become involved in advocating for this issue?

Tell the Story

Many people who are not directly involved with education or young families have no first-hand knowledge of problems and concerns. For example, most citizens probably could not accurately answer questions on why early childhood education programs are important or what types of programs are offered in the community. Even many parents may not understand differences in state licensing requirements, legal adult–child ratios, or staff training requirements. Likewise, many citizens have no current knowledge of how NCLB, the Common Core, and the latest legislation are affecting schools and children. Teachers who have this information can perform an important service in helping others learn the magnitude of the problems and needs. Teachers have the stories to illustrate the information—to give it meaning—and passion in demonstrating the contrasts between what could be and what is. Personal conversations, newsletters, blogs, and letters to the editor are all important in raising community awareness of the issues. It is important for teachers to clarify what their message is, who their audience is, and how they will reach their audience (Jacobson & Simpson, 2007). Making methods obvious and outcomes clear helps the community understand what the vision is, how far from the vision the community is, and the action plan needed to reach the vision. Here, parents can join teachers in their efforts.

The National Association for the Education of Young Children (NAEYC) sponsors the annual Week of the Young Child in communities across the country in April to call attention to the critical significance of the years between birth and age eight. Individual community activities focus on advocacy and information activities. Click on the Week of the Young Child on the NAEYC website for a comprehensive discussion of strategies to enlist community support. The NAEYC has also published an excellent book that discusses specific actions for advocates (Robinson & Stark, 2005) (see Figure 12-10).

Adapt and Replicate

FIGURE 12-10
Teachers and parents can join in Week of the Young Child events.

© Lucy/Shutterstock.com

Every community is unique in its organization, specific population, and problems. But some programs and ideas have worked well in communities around the country. Rather than try to reinvent the wheel, advocates should become familiar with these successful endeavors. The purpose of learning about successful programs is not to simply reproduce them but rather to build on previous experiences, adapt them to the unique community, and improve on the original model. Not every program will work in all contexts and climates of support; it is important to take advantage of the information that already exists about what programs are most effective at various stages of community organization.

As community leaders meet to synthesize their visions and their efforts, agreement about particular directions for a particular community will inform necessary

CULTURAL CONSIDERATIONS

Recognizing the role of advocate

For teachers and parents alike, cultural influences may be a factor in their comfort level in adopting the role of advocate. The expected roles of teachers are dictated by cultural understanding. Likewise, the roles of parents in relation to professionals or others in authority will determine parental willingness to participate in advocacy activities. Expected gender behaviors may also be a factor in whether parents move forward in common efforts. This awareness may help teachers and administrators move with patience when they encounter seeming reluctance from either teachers or parents to engage in advocacy work. As relationships deepen and as understanding of the importance of key issues involving their children develops, parents and teachers may take first small steps that may move them beyond their cultural reluctance.

Can you think of ways that individuals who are overcoming feelings of discomfort with the advocate role could begin small steps toward that role?

adaptations. See the discussion of successful community programs in Clinton (1996), Schorr (2011), Olson (2007), Friedman (2007), and Dickinson, Lothian, and Jonz (2007).

Join Professional Organizations

Teachers become empowered as they unite with others to learn, support one another, define professional goals and standards, and wield political power. Increasingly, the NAEYC is recognized as the professional organization that unites those from various occupations working in the early childhood education field. The professional organization's publication *Young Children*—also available online—is one way for teachers to become informed. The columns "Policy Alert" and "Washington Update" provide current information and calls for professional action.

Recent statements of standards by the organization have helped teachers and administrators define and evaluate appropriate curricula and services within centers. Standards for training and behavior of professionals have been delineated. These actions have helped child caregivers and early childhood teachers to see themselves as part of a profession that is taking steps to prove its value to the community. In fact, the Code of Ethical Conduct adopted by the NAEYC governing board in 1989, revised in 2005, and reaffirmed in 2011 includes a section on specific ideals and principles of teachers' ethical responsibilities to community and society that says, in part:

> Our responsibilities to the community are to provide programs that meet the diverse needs of families, to cooperate with agencies and professions that share responsibility for children, to assist families in gaining access to those agencies and professionals, and to assist in the development of community programs that are needed but not currently available. Because of our specialized expertise in early childhood development and education and because the larger society shares responsibility for the welfare and protection of children, we acknowledge a collective obligation to advocate for the best interests of young children within early childhood programs and in the larger community and to serve as a voice for young children everywhere. (NAEYC, 2011)

The political power of a large professional organization can yield results. In *A Call for Excellence in Early Childhood Education,* adopted in July 2000, the organization made these statements:

- Our nation can and must do better to create opportunities that help all children and families succeed. The time for action is now.

- All communities are accountable for the quality of early childhood programs provided to all children, backed by the local, state, and federal funding needed to deliver quality programs and services.

- Making this vision of excellence a reality will require commitment from and a partnership among federal, state, and local governments, business and labor, private institutions, and the public. As we stand at the beginning of a new millennium, we must join forces to advocate and implement the policies at the appropriate federal, state, and local levels that will lead to excellence in early childhood education programs. (NAEYC, 2000)

For more information about this professional organization and its advocacy role, visit their website, which is listed at the end of this chapter.

There are many other organizations in which membership may be an important part of a teacher's role as advocate. The Children's Defense Fund (CDF) is a private organization supported by foundations, corporate grants, and individual donations to provide a voice for the children of America, educate the nation about children's needs, and encourage prevention of problems. The CDF gathers and disseminates data on key issues affecting children; monitors development and implementation of federal and state policies; provides information, technical assistance, and support to a network of state and local child advocates; pursues an annual legislative agenda in the U.S. Congress; and litigates selected cases of major importance. For more information, see its website listed at the end of this chapter.

WHAT DOES AN ADVOCATE DO?

- Become visible.
- Become informed.
- Tell the story.
- Adapt and replicate.
- Join professional organizations.
- Connect with the community power structure.
- Contact representatives.
- Vote.
- Persist.

The Black Child Development Institute and the Family Resource Coalition, which is referred to in Chapter 4, are other organizations that can help teachers and parents feel united in their community efforts.

Many communities have local advocacy organizations for child and family issues; teachers should find out if their own community has one. There is strength in numbers. Parents can be encouraged to join these and other organizations. A number of websites listed at the end of this chapter have complete listings of organizations for parents. As parents and teachers gain confidence in their ability to speak and influence others, they may find themselves able to link with other community representatives and committees: the local school board, the dropout prevention task force, the council on adolescent pregnancy—whatever opportunities the community offers.

Connect with the Community Power Structure

Before advocates can go into the community looking for support for education and children's issues, they need to identify three things:

1. Who is out there? Identifying the prominent stakeholders in the community who carry clout will help advocates know who can impact policy and programs.

2. Who among them are known personally? In reaching out to community leaders, it makes sense to first advocate with leaders who are already known or acquainted with early childhood issues.

3. Who are the "significant others"? To make a difference in community issues, advocates will have to form relationships with all who are important in the community decisions. Advocates have to identify them, learn their viewpoints, and determine how best to communicate positively with them.

THE NAEYC'S FIVE WAYS TO BECOME A "CHILDREN'S CHAMPION"

1. Speak out on behalf of children.
2. Improve the life of one child beyond your own family.
3. Hold public officials accountable for a national commitment in actions as well as words.
4. Encourage organizations to commit to children and families.
5. Urge others to become children's champions.

From Young Children, 51(5), 56.

FIGURE 12-11
Teachers have to learn who can support advocacy efforts.

Figure 12-11 illustrates this process of identifying the community power structure as a step to connecting with the individuals with whom communication must be opened and collaborative efforts must be joined.

Contact Representatives

As concerned citizens, as professionals employed in specific capacities, and as members of professional organizations, teachers and parents need to contact their legislative representatives and state their positions, along with the specific reasons for their beliefs. Legislators can be influenced as they hear from even small numbers of constituents who speak with passion regarding specific community needs.

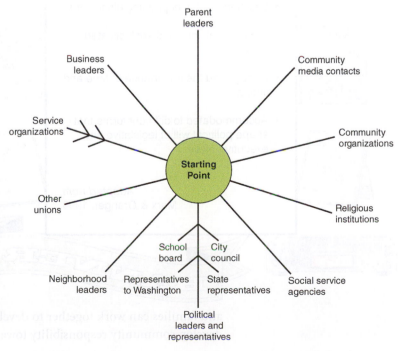

Vote

Advocates must follow up on their interests by learning what responsive actions businesses, government officials, and others who can shape policy have taken. With the power of purchase choices or voting decisions, teachers and parents can express their approval or disapproval of particular actions. As private citizens, families and teachers can support leaders who favor family and education issues (see Figure 12-12).

12-6 Community as an Educational Resource

Schools exist within particular communities, and each community has much to offer as a resource to teachers planning curricula for children in their classrooms. Teachers need to assess what the community can provide. Resources may be categorized as natural resources, people resources, and material resources.

12-6a Natural Resources

Within reach of most schools, teachers may find businesses, shopping areas, transportation systems and depots, construction sites, police and fire stations, parks and recreation areas, churches, zoos, museums, and residential streets. Each one of these offers countless learning experiences. It is a useful exercise for teachers to review the areas within 10 minutes' walking distance of their centers to discover all the places that might be intriguing from a child's viewpoint (see Figure 12-13). For example, there might be an automobile repair business where children could watch cars being elevated and serviced, a bakery with a large oven for many loaves of bread, or a grocery store where children could watch delivery trucks being unloaded before purchasing cooking ingredients to take back to the school. Alert teachers use these natural community resources to design curricula outside and inside the classroom. Elementary teachers will find opportunities for real-life social studies within their communities as children investigate, document, and report on various aspects of community life and work.

In addition to using the natural resources within any community, teachers and parents can take opportunities to help children develop an understanding of community responsibilities as they practice stewardship and protection of the environments and resources around them. Schools and families can work together to develop community action projects that help children develop community responsibility toward others.

FIGURE 12-12
Tips for successful advocacy efforts.

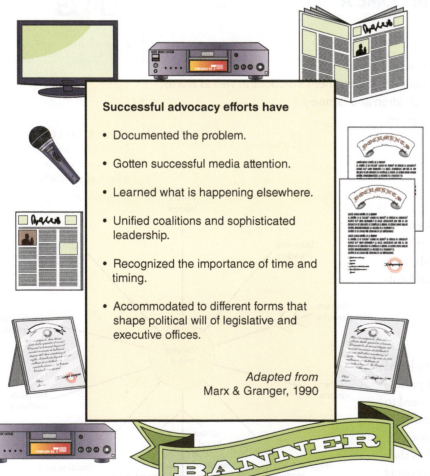

Successful advocacy efforts have

- Documented the problem.

- Gotten successful media attention.

- Learned what is happening elsewhere.

- Unified coalitions and sophisticated leadership.

- Recognized the importance of time and timing.

- Accommodated to different forms that shape political will of legislative and executive offices.

Adapted from
Marx & Granger, 1990

12-6b People Resources

Every neighborhood has its own socioeconomic, racial, and cultural composition. Teachers who familiarize themselves with the customs and lifestyles of the people in the community surrounding their schools may find richness and diversity to share with the children (see Figure 12-14). Parents themselves may be the link to assist teachers in learning the community's people resources as they disclose aspects of their home lives. For example, teachers may find neighbors experienced in ethnic cooking or traditional music who could share their interests with the children. Many community service agencies have representatives prepared to explain the agency to children, such as a firefighter bringing a truck (see Figure 12-15). People resources of all types can enrich a school. (For more about people resources to enhance the curriculum, see Chapter 10.)

Earlier in the text, we discussed the need for adults to mentor and support children in their community schools. Individual attention, coaching, and/or tutoring may help strengthen children's learning experiences in the schools and benefit everyone in the community.

Teachers and parents should also remember that children can learn how they themselves can be resources for their own communities. No child is too young to learn valuable lessons of making contributions to others and feeling responsible as a member of a community.

FIGURE 12-13
Every community has interesting places for children to visit.

© Bikeriderlondon/Shutterstock.com

service learning
The process wherein schools integrate meaningful community service with instruction and reflection to support the learning experience, teach community responsibility, and help develop lifelong community engagement.

Service Learning

Service learning describes the process wherein students learn and develop through active service experiences throughout the community. Schools integrate meaningful community service with instruction and reflection to support the learning experience, teach community responsibility, and help develop lifelong community engagement. Service learning should be part of every classroom curriculum—from preschool throughout a child's schooling. Preschoolers can collect materials for less advantaged families, visit older people in nursing homes, or participate in neighborhood cleanup efforts. School-aged children can learn about issues in their communities and help plan projects to benefit others. See Heiss (2007) and Miller (2010) for ideas. The mutual benefit of people resources in each community should be explored (see Figure 12-16).

12-6c Material Resources

Teachers who make community connections can find their classrooms the recipients of many objects children can use. Fast-food chains may donate cups and napkins and props for dramatic play or school events. Lumber stores may provide scraps for woodworking. Large packing cases from local appliance or furniture stores can be transformed into storage

TeachSource

VIDEO ACTIVITY

© 2016 Cengage Learning®

Watch the learning module video entitled *School Age: Family Interaction, School, and Community.* After viewing the clip, reflect on these questions:

1. How are these community members supporting the school and children's learning?

2. How are the children benefitting from this encounter with older members of their community?

or play spaces. Teachers should make lists of all community businesses and then brainstorm all possible material resources for all the schools in the community. Most businesspeople like to feel they can make a contribution to their neighborhood schools.

Families are often helpful connections in identifying and obtaining material resources. Some communities have established central recycling centers where businesses can donate disposables or other materials that can find many uses in classrooms.

All these community connections can enrich curriculum offerings as well as convey evidence of community interest and support for teachers and families.

The modern world often seems too busy to allow a sense of connectedness. As teachers and families work together as partners, they are in fact forming their own community that can reach out to and support the world around them. As members of the community, teachers and families can do the following:

■ Involve themselves fully within the surrounding community.

■ Work together for improvements in the community that benefit families and schools.

■ Learn about, tell each other about, and use community resources.

■ Understand that the community itself may provide learning resources for schools.

■ Build a sense of community within a school.

FIGURE 12-14
People from the community may enrich classroom activities and offer positive role models.

© 2016 Cengage Learning®

FIGURE 12-15
A firefighter visiting the school is an example of using community resources for curriculum.

© Cengage Learning®

FIGURE 12-16
School-aged children may become involved in cleaning up their community playground.

© Monkey Business Images/Shutterstock.com

SUMMARY

Children exist within the context of communities. Current concerns include:

- Erosion of social capital

- Interactive systems (Bronfenbrenner's theory)

- Problems within the community if families break down

Corporations may become involved with family and education issues:

- Flexible work arrangements and leave policies

- Support for parents volunteering in schools

- On-site or subsidized child care

Legislation supports families and schools:

- TANF

- Family Medical Leave Act

- No Child Left Behind

Collaborations within the community support families:

- Public and private agencies

- Interdisciplinary cooperation

- United Way Success By 6®

Advocacy roles for teachers and parents include:

- Becoming visible and informed

- Telling the story

- Adapting and replicating successful programs

- Joining professional organizations and connecting with the community power structure

- Contacting representatives and voting on particular issues

Communities may provide resources for teachers, children, and families by:

- Families referred by teachers to community agencies

- Children involved in service projects for action within the community

- Teachers using people, natural, and material resources found in the community to extend learning opportunities

Student Activities for Further Study

1. Obtain several copies of *Young Children* from your local college library or online. Examine the table of contents to find articles of interest for teachers of young children. Read the "Washington Update" and Public Policy Report columns. Discuss the current issues with your classmates.

2. Get information from your local or state NAEYC affiliate about program plans for the year and any legislative initiatives in your community that need your support.

3. Discover if your community has a United Way Success By 6® program, a child advocacy group, or other organization to coordinate services for families. Invite a representative to visit your class.

4. Create a community resource file. Obtain current pamphlets and referral information from the community agencies that offer services for families with various needs: economic, social, special medical and educational, recreation, and so on. Your instructor may make assignments for individual class members to report to other students about specific agencies within your community.

Apply the Chapter Concepts: Case in Point

As a teacher of young children, you learn that proposed legislation in your state for a universal pre-kindergarten program is not in the best interest of developmentally appropriate practice in early childhood education programs. The impact of this legislation is a concern to you. As a new advocate, you are unsure how to proceed.

1. How might you get families together to help them understand this issue? Are there others in the community who should be involved in an advocacy effort?

2. What resources might you use to get information and data to support your case?

3. What steps could be taken to lobby for the rights of children and best practice?

4. What could your school do to get support and help?

5. Identify three or four first actions in your campaign.

Review Questions

1. Discuss the importance of community in supporting child development and families.

2. Discuss ways that corporations are becoming involved in family, education, and child care issues.

3. Describe current legislative initiatives that shape policies affecting families, education, and child care.

4. Discuss what happens within community collaborations.

5. Identify and discuss eight advocacy roles for teachers and parents.

6. Identify three ways the community can provide resources for teachers, families, and children.

Helpful Websites

- The Families and Work Institute is a nonprofit center for research that provides data to inform decision making about the changing workforce, changing family, and changing community. The website has information about their publications, including the *National Study of the Changing Work Force* (2008), which is conducted at regular intervals.

- The National Association for Child Advocates (NACA) is a nationwide network of child advocacy organizations working at the increasingly critical level of America's statehouses, county commissions, and city councils. NACA serves as the forum where child advocacy leaders from across the country convene to share ideas, exchange information, and establish links between state and local child advocates and national experts. It also provides a clearinghouse of information about issues affecting children and effective advocacy.

- The Child Welfare League of America is the nation's oldest and largest membership-based child welfare organization and is committed to engaging people everywhere in promoting the well-being of children, youth, and their families and protecting every child from harm.

- The Action Alliance for Children exists to inform, educate, and persuade a statewide constituency of people who work with and on behalf of children by providing the most reliable information about current issues, trends, and public policies that affect children and families. The AAC is a resource for policymakers, children's service providers and advocates, and the media.

- The mission of the Children's Defense Fund is to Leave No Child Behind and to ensure every child a Healthy Start, a Head Start, a Fair Start, a Safe Start, and a Moral Start in life and successful passage to adulthood with the help of caring families and communities. This site has much information about community issues to support family needs.

- The National Campaign for Public School Improvement. Project Appleseed provides parents with the information and resources necessary to become committed to school improvement.

- The National Center for Family and Community Connections with Schools offers research-based information and resources that families and educators can use to effectively connect school, families, and communities to increase student success.

- Family Involvement Network of Educators (FINE), of the Harvard Family Research Project, is a national network committed to promoting strong partnerships between children's educators, their families, and their communities by providing them with research, training tools, and model programs.

- Comer School Development Program, of the Yale Child Study Center, offers many examples of home–school–community partnerships, replicated in more than 650 schools, linking schools with community services.

Working with Families from Diverse Backgrounds

Learning Objectives

After reading this chapter, you should be able to:

13-1 Discuss a rationale for recognizing the importance of culture and working with families from diverse backgrounds, identifying benefits for children, parents, and teachers.

13-2 Describe several specific strategies for teachers welcoming all families.

13-3 Identify methods of resolving cultural conflicts.

13-4 Discuss common cultural and language issues that arise in classrooms and with families of English language learners (ELL).

13-5 Explore specifics of programs for diverse families to identify practices in action.

naeyc

Related NAEYC Standards

Accreditation Standards (see inside text back cover for full listing of the Accreditation Standards for exemplary early childhood programs)

1.A.02; 2.A.08; 2.L.03; 3.F.05; 3.F.06; 4.E.05; 7.A.02; 7.A.04; 7.A.07; 7.A.10; 7.C.02.

Licensure Standards (see inside text front cover for full listing of the Licensure Standards for this chapter)

2a; 2b; 2c

Teachers working in schools today will find that the families with whom they work demonstrate the diversity typical at this time in most parts of the world. Families can come with as many configurations, colors, cultures, and economic class orientations and communicate in as many languages as there are children in a classroom. Many Western nations' cities report that students in the same school may speak close to 60 different languages. A report from the U.S. Census Bureau states that more than one in seven people speak a language other than English at home. "The biggest single child-specific demographic change in the United States over the next 20 years is predicted to be an increase in children whose home language is not English (NAEYC, in Copple & Bredekamp, 2009, p. 2). "By the year 2030, nearly half of all school-aged children will be ELL, the majority of whom will be Latino, with the dominant language of Spanish" (Downer & Myers, 2010, p. 19). Racial/ethnic minorities account for approximately 30 percent of students across the United States (Downer & Myers, 2010). Immigrant populations are rising and comprise one-quarter of all children younger than age six (Souto-Manning, 2013). Approximately 20 percent of children live below the poverty line, and "that percentage increases dramatically for recent immigrant families, families that do not speak English, single-parent families, and those in certain geographical areas of the country" (Espinosa, 2010, p. 10). A recent study by the U.S. Department of Labor projected that by 2050, the U.S. population will include 82 million people who arrived in this country after 1991 or were born of parents who did. This will include two out of every five people in America. Other Western nations experience similar increases in diverse populations. Rather than the "melting pot," a phrase that has been used to describe America, a better metaphor might be a complex tapestry full of variations, colors, and backgrounds.

These statistics make clear what classroom teachers already know: They must be prepared to live in a diverse society, welcoming and working with families from very different backgrounds. Yet 83 percent of the teaching force in America is white, from middle-class backgrounds, and speak only English (Amatea, 2013). In this chapter, we explore how teachers can reach out to families of diverse cultural experiences, respecting their uniqueness, supporting them in partnership, and providing continuity in their children's educational experiences.

13-1 A Rationale for Teacher Attention to Diversity

Consider the children enrolled in Dorothy Scott's classroom this fall. Of the 15, five live with their biological mothers and fathers, although two of these couples are not married. Two live with single, divorced mothers; one lives with his single, divorced father. Two live with one parent and a stepparent; one of these children was born in Asia and adopted by the mother and her first husband. One lives with her grandparents. One lives with a never-married mother and another with two mothers. One moves midweek between the homes and care of his divorced parents. The last child lives with foster parents—the third home he has known in four years. Of these families, nearly all the parents work—many in factory jobs, several in downtown offices, three in professional positions. Parental education levels range from several who have not completed high school to others with college and graduate degrees. One parent receives funds from TANF (Temporary Assistance for Needy Families) and food stamps; two others receive government assistance with medical and child care needs. Eight are children of color, including African American, Hispanic, a family recently arrived from a Caribbean island, and the child adopted from Vietnam. Three of the families do not speak English in their homes. Six of the families own their homes; three others rent a house, five rent apartments, and one lives with other relatives. Two of the children regularly fly long distances to visit grandparents and parents who live apart; six of them ride the bus to the center with their parents, who do not own cars.

Dorothy Scott says that, in her mind, they are all children, and she never notices what color they are, what their families do, or how much money they have. "They're all the same to me. I treat them all alike. Of course, some of these parents do a much better job of raising their children than others, and the ones who need the most help don't do a thing to get it."

What such a statement fails to recognize is that to profess color blindedness and treat all families as if they are the same is unrealistic and disrespectful. It is unrealistic because it does not take into consideration what cultural values and particular experiences mean to people and how profoundly culture influences their approach to life. And it is disrespectful because individuals deserve recognition, support, and acceptance of their unique identities. When teachers do not take the time to learn about the circumstances and experiences that shape each family, they effectively put up barriers to healthy identity formation for children and real partnerships with their parents. They remove themselves from the role of acting as support for families because they do not have the information that would help them understand family needs. Furthermore, they do not follow the guidelines of the NAEYC position statement on developmentally appropriate practice:

> Understanding children's development requires viewing each child within the sociocultural context of that child's family, educational setting, and community, as well as within the broader society. … Here, culture is intended to refer to the customary beliefs and patterns of behavior, both explicit and implicit, that are inculcated by the society in its members. … Every culture structures and interprets children's behavior and development in its own way. Early childhood teachers need to understand the influence of sociocultural contexts and family circumstances on learning. (NAEYC, in Copple & Bredekamp, 2009, p. 13)

Developmentally appropriate practices result from the process of professionals making decisions about the well-being and education of children based on at least three important kinds of information or knowledge:

1. What is known about child development and learning

2. What is known about each child as an individual

3. What is known about the social and cultural contexts in which children live (NAEYC, in Copple & Bredekamp, 2009) (See Figure 13-1.)

NAEYC has also published a position statement called *Responding to Linguistic and Cultural Diversity: Recommendations for Effective Early Childhood Education* (NAEYC, 1996). Here are some of its key imperatives for professionals:

1. Actively involve families in the early learning program.

2. Help all families realize the cognitive advantages of a child knowing more than one language, and provide them with strategies to support, maintain, and preserve home language learning.

3. Convince families that their homes' cultural values and norms are honored.

color blindedness
Professed unawareness of skin color of others.

culture
The various understandings, traditions, and guidance of the groups to which we all belong; the ways of living developed by a social group and transmitted to succeeding generations; the social backgrounds that imbue children with particular forms of knowledge, values, and expectations for behavior.

FIGURE 13-1
Knowing about children's social and cultural contexts ensures that learning experiences are meaningful, relevant, and respectful for children and their families.

© 2016 Cengage Learning®

overt culture
The various beliefs, behaviors, family practices, style of communication, traits, artifacts, and products associated with a particular group of people.

covert culture
Unconscious behavioral or perceptual patterns learned within one's cultural group.

cultural mores
Customs and beliefs associated with a particular culture.

4. Ensure that children remain cognitively, linguistically, and emotionally connected to their home languages and cultures.

5. Encourage home language and literacy development, knowing that this contributes to children's ability to acquire English language proficiency.

6. Help develop essential concepts in the children's first language and within cultural contexts that they understand.

7. Support and preserve home language usage.

8. Develop and provide alternative, creative strategies to promote all children's participation and learning.

9. Give children many ways of showing what they know and can do.

10. Provide professional preparation and development in the areas of culture, language, and diversity.

The revised NAEYC Code of Ethics (NAEYC, 2005a) specifically states in Principle 2.5: "We shall make every effort to communicate effectively with families in a language that they understand. We shall use community resources for translation and interpretation when we do not have sufficient resources in our own program."

Head Start has defined "Multicultural Principles for Head Start Programs." (See Figure 13-2.) These are all strong professional mandates for teachers working with cultural and linguistic diversity to become culturally competent.

At a minimum, culturally competent teachers learn to do the following:

- Acknowledge cultural differences.

- Understand their own culture.

- Engage in self-assessment.

- Acquire cultural knowledge and skills.

- View behavior within a cultural context (Matthews & Jang, 2007). (See Figure 13-3.)

Overt culture refers to the values, beliefs, behaviors, family practices, language and styles of communication, traits, artifacts, and products shared by and associated with a group of people. **Covert culture** refers to unconscious behavioral or perceptual patterns. "Culture provides the blueprint that determines the way we think, feel, and behave in society.… . Culturally determined norms guide our language, behavior, emotions, and thinking in different situations; they are the do's and don'ts of appropriate behavior" (Gollnick & Chinn, 2005). These do's and don'ts are often referred to as **cultural mores**, and individuals are strictly bound by the habits of behavior and belief that their culture has imparted. Culture becomes the lens through which we see and judge the world; it defines what we know, how we behave, and what we believe. Culture is passed on through the first social relationships of the family and through all the additional environmental influences that are channeled through that family's place in the world.

Culture influences specific behaviors and attitudes related to education, such as these:

- The role-modeling of parents as learners themselves

- Educational resources of the home and the uses made of them

FIGURE 13-2
Multicultural Principles for Head Start Programs

1. Every individual is rooted in culture.

2. The cultural groups represented in the communities and families of each Head Start program are the primary sources for culturally relevant programming.

3. Culturally relevant and diverse programming requires learning accurate information about the culture of different groups and discarding stereotypes.

4. Addressing cultural relevance in making curriculum choices is a necessary, developmentally appropriate practice.

5. Every individual has the right to maintain his or her own identity while acquiring the skills required to function in our diverse society.

6. Effective programs for children with limited English-speaking ability require continued development of the primary language while the acquisition of English is facilitated.

7. Culturally relevant programming requires staff who both reflect and are responsive to the community and families served.

8. Multicultural programming for children enables children to develop an awareness of, respect for, and appreciation of individual cultural differences.

9. Culturally relevant and diverse programming examines and challenges institutional and personal biases.

10. Culturally relevant and diverse programming and practices are incorporated in all components and services.

From U.S. Department of Health and Human Services, www.headstartinfo.org.

- The willingness and ability of parents to participate in their children's school experiences

- The nature and extent of parental expectations and demands

- The value placed on educational success and on children's learning efforts

- Attitudes toward the teacher's profession

Culturally determined actions, behaviors, and ways of dealing with people do not have to be thought about; they are automatic. Clearly, teachers must recognize the complexity of cultural influences on the development and learning of the children with whom they work and on the patterns of communication they are striving to develop with families. In addition, they must recognize how their own cultural experiences shape their personal perspective. These concepts encompass yet move far beyond the obvious awareness of racial, ethnic, and linguistic diversity.

FIGURE 13-3
Culturally competent teachers acquire cultural knowledge and skills.

© Zurijeta/Shutterstock.com

In past decades, *culturally different* equated with *culturally deficient*, and many schools attempted to "fix" children according to the standards of the dominant, white, middle-class culture (Souto-Manning, 2013).

Instead, teachers today are urged to consider a strengths-based approach, recognizing that culturally specific values, norms, and knowledge come to the classroom with each child, and there is much to be gained when teachers recognize and learn more about individual family cultural patterns and strengths.

13-1a For Individual Children

"Young children are developing personal and social identities—from both overt and covert messages coming from children's family members, friends, media, and early childhood programs" (Derman-Sparks & Edwards, 2010).

When children and their families are visible in their environments, they are likely to feel they are all right; invisibility brings the opposite conclusion (see Figure 13-4). So, too, does failure to talk about the other differences that children perceive, such as differences in family structure, in socioeconomic status and living conditions, and in culturally driven customary ways of behaving; these may lead to development of pre-prejudice.

FIGURE 13-4
Healthy self-identity results when children of all backgrounds find acceptance in their environment.

© Cengage Learning®

As young children develop a sense of who they are and who their families are in relation to others, they become aware of culture and of the response of others to their cultural beliefs and images. Cultural and racial identity is achieved by age five (Derman-Sparks & Edwards, 2010). Children need to absorb positive attitudes toward that cultural identity from the world around them. These attitudes need to be affirmations of their personal identity—clear messages from the larger society of acceptance and respect for who they are and who their families are. When children find that the images of person and family with whom they identify are either responded to negatively or are oddly missing from the societal images surrounding them, positive self-identity suffers. Teachers and families who are concerned with healthy formation of identity in young children must ensure that children of all backgrounds find evidence of social acceptance of the cultural norms with which they identify. It is important that teachers recognize the value of the individual child's culture and not perceive culturally *different* as culturally *deficient*, feeling they must replace the norms of the family with those with which the teachers are more culturally comfortable. The norms of the family are those with which individual children form their sense of identity and connection.

It is also not healthy for children of the **dominant culture** when recognition of diversity is absent. Children who can find only representations of themselves and their families in the dominant social institutions are at risk of developing a falsely superior identity. This will diminish those whose cultural identity is devalued or omitted by the explicit or implicit policies or structure of the schools.

How can this experience become real to you? Imagine that you are learning to read by using the primer that most adults used in first grade several decades ago. You would be exposed every day to the adventures of a white middle-class family. Father went off to work dressed in a business suit in an appropriate automobile. Mother was also well dressed and was busy caring for her well-maintained home and three blond and blue-eyed children. Dick, Jane, and Sally led the life that privileged children led, with their varieties of toys, pets, and activities. But if your own life experiences suggested different family structures, different places to work and live, and events with people who dressed and looked differently, the implicit message received during that year of daily reading would be that this was desirable—the norm—and that your cultural experience was somehow deficient. Although Dick, Jane, and Sally have fortunately disappeared, there are still too many occasions when children of all backgrounds are not given the clear message that

dominant culture
The culture that is most influential in a society—numerically and by the power of ideas and behaviors.

their unique circumstances are recognized and accepted. One of the easiest ways to do this is to reach out to all families, encourage full participation, and offer a variety of ways to become involved in their children's schools.

Individual children can only be taught and assessed appropriately when their individual cultural context and its impact on their development are appreciated (NAEYC, 2005b). Appropriate assessment requires culturally and linguistically appropriate methods and assessors. If teachers operate under cultural myopia, they may not recognize the culturally different strengths and abilities of an individual child and may, in fact, interpret as problems or delays behaviors that are quite typical within the child's cultural context. Cultural differences can cause teachers to misunderstand children and incorrectly plan their educational experiences.

As families from the cultural minority communicate about their children, they may help teachers understand the children's developmental history and avoid inaccurate assessments or cultural biases in the observers or testing instruments.

CULTURAL CONSIDERATIONS

General characteristics

Teachers must take the time to discover the values of individual families without making assumptions based only on ethnicity. Having said that, it is important to note that teachers can learn general information about Latino, Asian, and African American cultural practices that are relevant to early education (Espinosa, 2010).

Latino families are much more likely to speak their native language at home than are other ethnic groups. Most Hispanic parents report a strong wish for their children to maintain their native language while also learning English. Latino families generally share a set of values that include family-centeredness and family loyalty to the immediate and extended family. Another value is respect, as in politely greeting elders, not challenging elders' viewpoints or entering adult conversations, or interrupting others. Researchers also identify education as a strong value, meaning formal schooling as well as learning the good manners and high morals expected in the family. Latino parents want to be involved in their children's schooling, although language and culturally preferred ways of participating may act as barriers (see Figure 13-5).

Asian American families are a diverse group, with more than 29 distinct subgroups differing in language, religion, and customs (Espinosa, 2010) and with individual diversity related to reasons for migration and hopes and expectations. Most Asian American parents teach their children to value educational achievement, respect authority, feel responsibility for relatives, and show self-control. Self-effacement is traditionally valued in many Asian cultures. Many Asian children are socialized to listen more than speak—and to speak softly. In Asian culture, teachers have higher status than do teachers in America, and Asian children may be confused by informality, expecting considerable structure (see Figure 13-6).

Newly arrived immigrant families—no matter the ethnic origin—have their own sets of challenges. Leaving the old familiar world behind and starting new in a strange culture brings stress, and language difficulties compound that stress. As immigrants make mistakes,

FIGURE 13-5
Many Hispanic parents value their children being respectful and well mannered.

© Cengage Learning®

FIGURE 13-6
Many Asian children are taught to value academic achievement.

© Cengage Learning®

those who consider them ignorant often surround them, and they have lost their familiar support systems. Soon, their children get ahead of the parents in learning the language and figuring out the new ways of living, putting parents in the situation of having traditional roles reversed. Children may be embarrassed by their parents' awkwardness, accents, and difficulties in communication. Immigrant families may be very concerned about identity issues and their children's loss of cultural ties. Teachers may play a very important role in helping parents adjust to the new culture (see Figure 13-7).

The diversity within African American families makes it impossible to generalize about lifestyles, social class structure, or value systems; nevertheless, racial experiences in contemporary America have been a factor in identity formation of African American children. More African American children than non-Hispanic white families live with a single mother and in poverty. African Americans are often raised in extended families that provide many opportunities for social interaction, offering experience with emotional expression and sensitivity to nonverbal communication and facial expression (see Figure 13-8). Many African American families also report the use of corporal punishment when disciplining their children—a "parenting practice often rooted in feelings of love and concern in families who fear for their children's well-being, particularly that of their male children" (Boyd-Franklin, 2006, p. 273).

Knowledge about the cultural background of any group should never lead to stereotyping but instead to sensitive awareness that can help provide more appropriate educational experiences.

Do you understand the difference between stereotypical generalizations about cultural groups and actual information? Getting real information is important for all teachers.

FIGURE 13-7
Immigrant families may be concerned about their children's loss of cultural ties.

FIGURE 13-8
Many social opportunities in an extended family may make African American children sensitive to nonverbal communication.

13-1b For All Children

The statistics presented in the beginning of this chapter make it evident that adults must prepare children to live comfortably in a world filled with diversity. Exposing young children to cultural differences and modeling appreciation and acceptance of diversity enable children to grow up without developing the kind of prejudices and biases that are largely the result of fear and lack of experience. When differences are not acknowledged, talked about, explained, and seen as positive, children sometimes find them frightening and respond to them negatively. Thus, bias has roots in children's early experiences. When adults provide an environment that allows children to explore differences and supports them in discovering similarities as well as respecting differences in others' lives, children are more likely to respond positively to diversity (see Figure 13-9). When the true variety of experiences of the families within classrooms is recognized and voiced, curriculum and learning experiences can become richer. Utilizing the firsthand experiences that families provide allows children to experience variation in culture, not just learn about it passively.

FIGURE 13-9
Children respond positively to diversity in an environment where they can comfortably explore differences and similarities.

When teachers do not incorporate children's cultural experiences into classroom life, all children miss opportunities to promote their social and cognitive growth.

13.1c For Partnerships with Families

Families transmit their culture to their children. Each culture's values and beliefs underlie parenting practices and ways of living and influence children's learning and communication styles.

Cultural attitudes also determine how parents view teachers' roles and their relationship to the teacher. Culture influences some of the factors that can become sources of irritation in teachers. For example, many teachers interpret lack of punctuality as a sign of indifference or hostility; it may also indicate a different orientation toward time in the family's culture. Other cultural orientation regarding gender roles may mean that some parents are uncomfortable with a female teacher or with a teacher's expectation of communicating with mothers in a culture where fathers communicate for the family (see Figure 13-10).

FIGURE 13-10
Teachers and parents who come from different cultural backgrounds may have different expectations about communication in school.

© R. Gino Santa Maria/Shutterstock.com

When teachers and families who do not move in the same cultural framework meet, it is a jarring experience from both perspectives. Janet Gonzalez-Mena, in her important book on multicultural issues in child care, describes what many do when faced with cultural differences:

Because my way seems right, even normal, I tend to judge others based on my own perspective. I may consider them exotic or interesting, or I may consider them weird. But being a polite person who tries to get along with others, I do what I can not to notice. Because my way is normal to me, it seems rude to make an issue of the fact that someone else is not normal. And because I have a whole society behind me giving me the message that "my people" are the standard by which everyone else is judged, I can afford to keep on ignoring what I choose to.

But can I? What does this attitude do to me? It shields me from reality. It gives me a slanted perspective, a narrow view. I miss out on a lot because of my perspective. … What does it do to those who are not "my people" if I continue in this narrow, slanted perspective, ignoring what I consider "not normal"? …

Imagine the harm I can do both to "my people" and those whose differences I ignore when I carry out my job with this biased attitude. … What does it do to people who are different from me to have those differences defined as abnormal? What does it do to people who are different from me to have those differences ignored? (Gonzalez-Mena, 2008)

By ignoring the differences in behavior, communication style, and beliefs created by culture, teachers run the risk of creating real conflicts and barriers to effective partnership with families. The potential barriers to communication arising from culture are real and must be recognized:

- Families may have few basic communication skills in English.

- Families may not be familiar with school systems, including knowing whom to approach about what, or how to arrange appointments.

- Families may have had little experience of being consulted regarding their children's education.

- Families may have become accustomed to superficial conversation—to smiling and passing on—when interpreters are rarely available.

- Families may be anxious regarding approaching figures of authority or disclosing personal information.

- Families may find written communication daunting.

- Families may have expectations of education and ways of supporting children at home that are different from the school's.

- Children from immigrant families may resist their family's involvement, especially older school-aged children who are learning to negotiate the different worlds of home and school and are mindful of the opinions of their peers and concerned lest they appear too different.

CULTURE AND CHILD REARING

Culture Influences:

- Age-related expectations of children
- Concern over children acquiring skills by a particular age
- Sleep patterns and bedtime routines
- Children's roles and responsibilities in the family
- Toilet learning
- Diet and mealtime behavior
- Discipline and guidance
- How parents talk to children and children to parents
- How parents show affection
- Importance of gender identity and traditional sex roles
- Dress and hair care
- Ideas about illness and use of medicine
- Use of supplemental child care
- Acceptance of, meaning of, and response to emotion
- Children's attachment to adults and separation from adults

Adapted from York, 2003.

It is far too easy for teachers who are of one culture to assume that children of another culture are culturally deprived and that their families need to be taught how to better accomplish tasks of parenting. This presents a genuine challenge to teachers to improve their sensitivity to cultural and individual differences and increase communication across cultural divisions. Only in this way can teachers understand that the family's culture is a resource, not a defect. This process is hard work and takes time and effort. Nevertheless, effective schools continue to press for communication across cultural differences to avoid eroding or conflicting with parental responsibility and value systems. True partnerships with families come when teachers genuinely attempt to learn and understand the ideas that are central to each family's experience.

This partnership is essential to children's success within the school. "Researchers have found that the family's involvement in school learning is the most crucial component in Hispanic (and presumably all other) children's school success" (Saracho, 2010, p. 127).

13-1d For Teacher Growth

The past experiences of every teacher are unique, and each teacher is a product of his or her own culture. An essential question for teachers is, "Who am I as a cultural being?" (Souto-Manning, 2013). Working within educational institutions, teachers of whatever culture are generally proponents of the predominant values espoused by the schools—typically the values of the white middle class. These include concepts supporting equality of all; a basic belief in the goodness of humanity; an orientation toward achievement, action, work, and progress; an emphasis on the individual and rights of privacy; an orientation toward direct communication and assertiveness; and an orientation to the future, change, and progress, with an emphasis on efficient use of time (Lynch & Hanson, 2004). Unless they move outside their cultural comfort zone, it is too easy for teachers to feel that ideas and values beyond those of mainstream society are somehow wrong or inferior.

Nevertheless, professional experiences offer individual teachers the opportunity to reach beyond their limited cultural experiences to learn to understand and value diversity. "But I'm not prejudiced!" you may protest. The attitudes that we all learned beginning in childhood deserve honest examination; such examination offers teachers a chance for increased self-awareness and change. And by genuinely trying to explore the ideas, values, and customs that are meaningful to the families with whom they work, teachers are granted real opportunities for personal growth.

Lisa Delpit (2006) has remarked that teachers cannot begin to understand the children in their classrooms unless they can connect with the families and communities from which they come. Part of doing that is to explore personal beliefs about non-white and non-middle-class people. Doing reflective, autobiographical work is an essential part of this exploration, and is essential to teacher growth. See Figure 13-11 for a cultural competence checklist for self-assessment of attitudes and behaviors that are important for culturally competent teachers.

FIGURE 13-11
Cultural Competence Self-Assessment Checklist

Select A, B, or C for each item listed below.

    A = Things I do frequently

    B = Things I do occasionally

    C = Things I do rarely or never

_____ **1.** I display pictures, posters, artwork, or décor that reflect the cultures and ethnic backgrounds of families served by our school.

_____ **2.** I ensure that all printed materials offered to my families reflect the different cultures and languages of families in our school.

_____ **3.** I ensure that printed information disseminated by my school takes into account the average literacy levels of individuals and families in my school.

_____ **4.** When interacting with families who have limited English proficiency, I keep in mind the following:

- Limitations in English proficiency are in no way a reflection of their level of intellectual functioning.

- Their limited ability to speak English has no bearing on their ability to communicate effectively in their language of origin.

- They may neither be literate in their language of origin nor in English.

_____ **5.** I understand that it may be necessary to use alternatives to written communication for some families.

_____ **6.** I avoid imposing values that may conflict or be inconsistent with those of cultures or ethnic groups other than my own.

_____ **7.** I screen books and other media resources for negative cultural, ethnic, or racial stereotypes before using them in my classroom.

_____ **8.** I recognize and accept that individuals from culturally diverse backgrounds may desire varying degrees of acculturation into the dominant culture.

_____ **9.** I understand and accept that family is defined differently by different cultures, and that male and female roles may vary significantly among different cultures.

_____ **10.** Even though my professional or moral viewpoints may differ, I accept families as the ultimate decision makers for supports and services impacting their lives.

Adapted from Promoting Cultural and Linguistic Competency Self-Assessment Checklist for Personnel Providing Primary Health Care Services, by Tawara Goode, National Center for Cultural Competence, June 1989 (Revised 2009). Available at nccc.georgetown.edu.

ethnocentric
Characterized by an attitude that one's own group is superior.

13-2 Strategies for Teachers

To create an atmosphere in classrooms and schools that conveys welcome and acceptance of diversity, teachers and administrators can do many specific things. Some of these are discussed here.

13-2a Examine Personal Attitudes

An important starting point is honest examinations of personal attitudes and assumptions about children and families of diverse configurations and ethnic and class backgrounds. When teachers explore racist and **ethnocentric** stereotypes, they can find ways to change their beliefs about the way families are supposed to look and behave. This can be difficult and painful, but it is a necessary prerequisite for successfully conveying an attitude of acceptance (see Figure 13-12). Often, such explorations include discussing stereotypes, considering where stereotypes come from and what purpose they serve, and identifying ways to talk with others about differences. Only through this process can teachers reach the point of genuine openness to others.

There will be times when teachers experience personal discomfort when facing particular ideas and behaviors of others. It is vital that teachers work with this feeling, identifying what it is that makes them uncomfortable and being clear about their own values and goals that guide them. Accepting others' rights

FIGURE 13-12
Teachers must genuinely examine their attitudes toward others.

© Cengage Learning®

to hold different beliefs does not mean teachers have to let go of their own values. Teachers must accept that there will be different perspectives, and these may be equally valid to the people who hold them.

OPPORTUNITY FOR SELF-REFLECTION

What do you recall of your first experience in perceiving differences among people? Where were you and what were the circumstances? What emotion can you identify as part of that experience? What did you do when you noticed the difference? If you spoke with an adult, do you remember the response? Consider how these events affected your view of diversity.

Many teachers have found it helpful to develop a support group among colleagues who are interested in doing this kind of self-reflective work. Working with trusted peers can encourage a more honest examination and discussion of values, beliefs, and the accompanying inherent biases and prejudices (Derman-Sparks & Edwards, 2010). Support groups can also be valuable to teachers who are seeking ideas on how to reach out to families to become more inclusive of all cultures.

CULTURAL SENSITIVITIES SELF-ANALYSIS

1. Uncover your memories. Remembering allows us to revisit our own experiences and to deal with strategies for transforming our thinking.

   What are some of your first memories about encountering racism?
   Sexism? Classism? Homophobia? Disabilities?
   What was going on?
   How did you feel?
   What sorts of models did you have?

2. Consider your personal journey in coming to understand/accept your own identity.
3. Have you dealt with personal issues and challenges related to your identity?
4. Write down and consider a list of acceptable and unacceptable behaviors for girls and boys and men and women.
5. Consider what you know about your family's cultural background and experiences with discrimination.
6. Consider any time you have experienced cultural shock. What happened? What was your response?
7. Recall the first time you pointed out to an adult that someone in your environment looked different—either from race, gender, age, disability, or another reason. Recall the response of the adult. How did this make you respond to the difference?
8. Consider the following chart that illustrates stages of multicultural growth. Consider your experiences and attitudes, and consider where you are in these stages.

Level of Self Awareness

Stage 1	Stage 2	Stage 3
Only my perspective is right.	My perspective is one of many.	My perspective is changing and being enhanced.

Emotional Responses to Differences

Fear/Rejection/Denial	Interest, Awareness, Appreciation/Openness	Respect/Joy/Enthusiasm/ Active Seeking

Mode of Cultural Interaction

Isolation/Avoidance/ Hostility	Integration/Interaction Acceptance	Transforming/Internalizing Rewarding

Approach to Teaching

Eurocentric/Ethnocetric Curriculum	Learning about other cultures	Learning from other cultures

Evaluate yourself related to risk taking.

Checklist for Sexist Attitudes

1. List the following attributes under the column that you feel each one most accurately describes.

confident	protective	objective	vain	attractive	passive
brave	tough	intelligent	independent	responsible	ambitious
tender	active	forceful	competent	emotional	
strong	timid	considerate	fearful	talkative	
happy	stoic	creative	aggressive	weak	
BOYS	GIRLS				

A Teacher Self-Test for Cultural Sensitivity

1. Am I knowledgeable about and sensitive to my students' cultural backgrounds and traditions?
2. Am I able to respect the children's cultures and backgrounds when they are different from my own?
3. Do I provide a classroom environment that recognizes and respects my |students' culture?
4. Do I find curriculum materials that are culturally appropriate and avoid those that are misleading?
5. Do I let students know when I do not understand something about their culture?
6. Do I encourage students to share their culture with others if they want to?
7. Have I discarded stereotypes so I can support each child's growth as an individual?
8. Do I make every student, family member, and others in the community feel welcome in my classroom?

13-2b Learn about Other Cultures

When dealing with families whose culture is different from their own, teachers must educate themselves about the values, practices, and communication methods that are comfortable for others. How does this education take place? Reading books and articles may help; see the Suggestions for Further Reading box.

SUGGESTIONS FOR FURTHER READING

Bang, Y. (2009). Helping all families participate in school life. *Young Children, 64*(6), 97–9.

Banks, J. (2006). *Cultural diversity and education: Foundations, curriculum, and teaching* (5th ed.). Boston: Allyn & Bacon.

Bradley, J., & Kibera, P. (2006). Closing the gap: Culture and the promotion of inclusion in child care. *Young Children, 61*(1), 34–40.

Burt, T., Gelnaw, A., & Lesser, L. (2010). Do no harm: Creating welcoming and inclusive environments for lesbian, gay, bisexual, and transgender families in early childhood settings. *Young Children, 65*(1), 97–102.

Cho, E., Chen, D., & Sin, S. (2010). Supporting transnational families. *Young Children, 65*(4), 30–7.

Copple, C. (Ed.). (2003). *A world of difference: Readings on teaching young children in a diverse society.* Washington, DC: NAEYC.

Delpit, L. (2006). *Other people's children: Cultural conflict in the classroom* (updated edition). New York: The New Press.

Diamond, K., Okagaki, L., & Kontos, S. (2000). Responding to cultural and linguistic differences in the beliefs and practices of families with young children. *Young Children, 55*(3), 74–80.

Duarte, G., & Rafanello, D. (2001). The migrant child: A special place in the field. *Young Children, 56*(2), 26–33.

Eggers-Pierola, C. (2005). *Connections and commitments: Reflecting Latino values in early childhood programs.* Portsmouth, NH: Heinemann.

Gay, G. (2000). *Culturally responsive teaching: Theory, research, and practice.* New York: Teachers College Press.

Gonzalez-Mena, J. (2010). *50 early childhood strategies for working and communicating with diverse families* (2nd ed.). Boston, MA: Pearson.

Hildebrand, V., Phenice, L., Gray, M., & Hines, R. (2007). *Knowing and serving diverse families* (3rd ed.). Columbus, OH: Prentice Hall.

Huntsinger, C., Huntsinger, P., Ching, W., & Lee, C. (2000). Understanding cultural contexts fosters sensitive caregiving of Chinese American children. *Young Children, 55*(6), 7–15.

Joshi, A. (2005). Understanding Asian Indian families: Facilitating meaningful home-school relations. *Young Children, 60*(3), 75–8.

Kaufman, H. (2001). Skills for working with all families. *Young Children, 56*(4), 81–3.

Klein, M., & Chen, D. (2001). *Working with children from culturally diverse backgrounds.* Clifton Park, NY: Delmar/Thomson Learning.

Lindeman, B. (2002). Speaking their language: Successfully reaching out to immigrant parents. *Instructor,* September, 100–1.

Lundgren, D., & Morrison, J. (2003). Involving Spanish-speaking families in early education programs. *Young Children, 58*(3), 88–95.

Okagaki, L., & Diamond, K. (2000). Research in review. Responding to cultural and linguistic differences in the beliefs and practices of families with young children. *Young Children, 55*(3), 74–80.

Pryor, C. (2001). New immigrants and refugees in American schools: Multiple voices. *Childhood Education, 77*(5), 275–283.

Ramsey, P. (2004). *Teaching and learning in a diverse world: Multicultural education for young children.* New York: Teachers College Press.

Riojas-Cortez, M., Flores, B., & Clark, E. (2003). Los ninos aprenden en casa: Valuing and connecting home cultural knowledge with an early childhood program. *Young Children, 58*(6), 78–83.

Ryan, S., & Grieshaber, S. (2004). It's more than child development: Critical theories, research, and teaching young children. *Young Children, 59*(6), 44–52.

Takanishi, R. (2004). Leveling the playing field: Supporting immigrant children from birth to eight. *The Future of Children, 14*(2), 61–84.

Trumbull, E., Rothstein-Fisch, C., Greenfield, P., & Quiroz, B. (2001). *Bridging cultures between home and school: A guide for teachers.* Florence, KY: Lawrence Erlbaum.

Veselu, C., & Ginsberg, M. (2011). Strategies and practices for working with immigrant families in early education programs. *Young Children, 66*(1), 84–9.

Walker-Dalhouse, D., & Dalhouse, A. D. (2001). Parent–school relations: Communicating more effectively with African American parents. *Young Children, 56*(4), 75–80.

Wardle, F. (2001). Supporting multiracial and multiethnic children and their families. *Young Children, 56*(6), 38–9.

Zepeda, M., Gonzalez-Mena, J., Rothstein-Fisch, C., & Trumbull, Ed. (2006). *Bridging cultures in early care and education: A training module.* Mahwah, NJ: Erlbaum.

FIGURE 13-13
Teachers will learn much about cultural patterns of child rearing through observing parent–child interactions.

Teachers will also realize that cultural heritage is learned and is not innately based on the culture into which an individual is born—that is, individuals of a particular ethnic background whose families have lived for several generations in America may now have a culture that is an adaptation of the earlier culture. Culture is a dynamic system that changes continuously, so written generalities must be viewed as tentative guides at best. Perhaps the best resources for learning are families themselves. Through respectful relationships and careful observation of parent–child interaction and learning how parents care for their children (see Figure 13-13), teachers will learn much about how messages are transmitted verbally and nonverbally and about what is important to the family. Intercultural communication shows real differences in the proximity of people when communicating, in facial expressions and eye contact, and in the desirability of touching another. See Martin and Nakayama (2012), Samovar, Porter, and McDaniel (2009), and Ting-Toomey and Chung (2011) for specifics about

© 2016 Cengage Learning®

intercultural communication and culturally influenced behavior. It is vital for teachers to realize that the general cultural characteristics associated with particular cultural, class, or ethnic backgrounds are meant to be helpful guidelines and are *not* to be interpreted as limited stereotypes. They will recognize that uniqueness and individual patterns are always present. Showing openness and a genuine desire to learn respectfully will help families become comfortable with demonstrating and discussing their family systems and style with the teacher.

13-2c Establish an Environment That Welcomes

When each family first crosses the classroom or school threshold, they should find evidence that their presence is recognized and accepted. Enrollment forms may be a first place to begin to learn about families and to convey the message that diversity in family styles is expected. Rather than having blanks for "mother," "father," and "siblings," schools might change this to "adults in the home" and "children in the home" and "family living out of the child's home," with spaces for families who may wish to add clarifying information. There should be spaces to indicate which language is primary at home as well as other languages used there. Enrollment forms and information booklets should be printed in as many languages as possible; families are often happy to help with translating the information if it has not already been done, and the school's invitation to do so indicates genuine intentions of including all. It is also important to recognize that the limited literacy level in some families may mean that teachers might best attain this information in conversation. Individual teachers may already have visited the family in their home setting and have learned something about the family's neighborhood, work, and living conditions. Often, teachers take a snapshot of the family or ask for a family picture to add to their family picture board—a sure way of including every family.

Teachers use initial visits and survey forms to obtain information that will help the child and family feel comfortable in the new setting and assist the teacher in working more effectively with the child. Learning what language is spoken in the home allows the teacher to obtain the services of an interpreter, to learn a few basic words for the first conversations with child and parent, or to post a welcoming greeting in the family's native language. If the teacher does not know how to add this, parents will often willingly write it if they feel their help would be welcome.

The classroom can appear "culturally safe" to parent and child when materials, pictures, books, and room design reflect family and home experiences. Utensils and clothing in the home living center can reflect the items children might see in use in their own homes; a wok, a garlic braid, or a string of dried chilies for pretend cooking; a pair of work coveralls for dress up; and woven baskets for decor could reflect varied meanings from different homes. Parents can be asked to contribute culturally specific materials, such as empty food containers or hair care products. Dolls that represent the various racial and ethnic traditions of the classroom and community show awareness of differences. Photographs and posters that depict the ethnic heritage, social classes, and family configurations representative of all children in the classroom convey acceptance. Use the checklist in Figure 13-14 for a multicultural classroom that welcomes all.

Displaying books and games that depict particular cultures or represent traditional literature and stories also conveys welcome. All these additions to the environment help children and their parents feel secure and accepted.

Asking families to contribute songs, tapes, and musical instruments representative of their culture's music can help build the diversity of the classroom listening library. Exposing young children to different tonal patterns and rhythms can enhance their musical experiences and build positive acceptance of a wide variety of music forms.

TeachSource Digital Download

FIGURE 13-14
Checklist for a multicultural, antibias classroom.

Consider how your classroom could be improved.

1. Does your classroom have a wide variety of age-appropriate and culturally diverse books and language arts materials?

   _____Yes _____No

   Find examples.

2. Are the cultures in your class and community represented in your books and materials?

   _____Yes _____No

3. Are there books that portray people of diverse cultures in stereotypical or derogatory terms?

   _____Yes _____No

   If yes, which books are they?

   Should they be removed or is there a way to use them with children to broaden their concepts and encourage children to share their experiences?

4. Are the pictures of people on the walls representative of a multicultural community, showing various classes, work patterns, races, and other diversity?

5. Does the curriculum help children increase their understanding and acceptance of attitudes, values, and lifestyles that are unfamiliar to them?

   _____Yes _____No

   If yes, how? If no, what can you do to change it?

6. Are materials and games racially or sex-role stereotypical?

   _____Yes _____No

   If so, how can you change your collection to give strong, positive images?

7. Are the accessories in the block area representative of various cultural groups and family configurations?

   _____Yes _____No

8. Are the people block accessories stereotypical in terms of sex roles?

   _____Yes _____No

9. Are there a wide variety of clothes (everyday clothes, not exotic costumes) of various cultural groups and sex and work roles?

   _____Yes _____No

10. Do the props for dramatic plays represent diverse cultures?

    _____Yes _____No

11. Are the dolls representative of the major racial groups in our country—not just in colors but also in features?

_____Yes _____No

12. Do you use finger plays, games, and songs from various cultural groups?

_____Yes _____No

13. Do cooking experiences encourage children to experiment with foods they are not familiar with?

_____Yes _____No

14. From the following list, check those activities that you do not present to your class:

woodworking _____ active games _____ dance _____

cooking _____

sewing _____ music _____ reading _____

Teachers can plan family get-togethers scheduled for times that are convenient for all parents to attend. A potluck dinner where each family brings a favorite food helps parents meet their children's friends and families and welcomes everyone into the program. Teachers should be aware that recent immigrant families with limited English might be hesitant to attend school activities because of their difficulties in understanding the

TeachSource Digital Download

IDEAS FOR TEACHERS:

Creating Culturally Welcoming Classrooms

- Examine all printed materials to be sure they are inclusive of all family structures.
- Translate all printed materials, notices, and signs into all languages represented in the classroom.
- Provide interpreters.
- Post "welcomes" in languages represented in the program (see Figure 13-15).
- Use family pictures in the environment.
- Display artifacts, pictures, and posters that are familiar to all families.
- Display maps and flags of each family's country of origin (Vesely & Ginsberg, 2011).
- Collect and use music and books from different cultures.
- Allow families ways of sharing their culture in the program.
- Bring families together for comfortable social events.
- Share teachers' and staff's culture.
- Welcome the larger community.
- Participate in collective and meaningful social action.

communication or the educational system. Extra efforts will likely be needed to ensure their comfort and attendance, such as flexibility in scheduling and location and invitations from peers with the same language background.

13-2d Open the Door for Communication about Culture

Teachers will send clear and constant messages that they are interested in learning how a family wants to have their culture represented and supported in the classroom. Remember that we are using the term *culture* here in its broadest sense to indicate the uniqueness of each family in its ideas, attitudes, and values. Some teachers seem to feel that if they are working with a homogeneous collection of white families who have lived in this country for generations, they do not have to concern themselves with culture (Derman-Sparks et al., 2011). But every family is still individual in its beliefs and attitudes, parenting methods, celebrations, and ordinary lifestyle. Teachers can elicit from parents their wishes with regard to their children's care and education, as well as their ideas about how family experiences can enrich the classroom curriculum.

FIGURE 13-15
It is important to establish an environment that welcomes.

How do teachers open the door for such communication? They connect early on and in person. Many teachers interview their parents at the beginning of the school year (Magruder et al., 2013). They ask families about home language practices and their children's talents and interests, as well as their goals for their children and what they want their children to accomplish at school during the year. With young children, they elicit detailed information about family caregiving practices, such as toilet learning, discipline, and so on. They attempt to learn as much as they can about family activities and experiences. They ask families what holidays they celebrate in their homes and how the school can support such celebrations without lessening the families' primary importance. They ask families if they would be willing to share some holiday traditions and practices or other parts of their family life in the classroom. They also ask what holidays the families do not celebrate and in which they would prefer their children not be included. They find out information about places the families have lived and experiences the children have had. And with all this, they let parents know that their primary desire is not to be intrusive but to use this knowledge to preserve and enhance the families' culture and to support parents and their beliefs as the primary influence on the children's lives. They empower families with the knowledge that they can play an active role in helping the school better address the aspects of their cultural heritage that are meaningful to families, rather than smolder resentfully in silence while the institution imposes ideas and activities with which they disagree.

See Figure 13-16 for a survey that teachers can use to learn about family culture.

One important area of sensitivity for teachers is not to make any assumptions about a family's cultural background, priorities, or resources based on limited knowledge. For example, one teacher asked a parent if she would come in to explain Kwanzaa customs to the children, assuming that the family would celebrate that holiday important to many African American families simply because the family was black. Jumping to conclusions that arise from stereotyped assumptions about a family's culture can be avoided when teachers take the time to form relationships that lead to real knowledge of families.

When teachers open dialogue about the issues that are meaningful to families, parents feel freer to ask questions and to talk about conflicts they perceive. As teachers work to see the parents' viewpoint, they model acceptance of differences.

FIGURE 13–16

Getting To Know Your Students

Instructions: Please fill out as much as you can. Do not feel you must answer every question. These questions are meant to make your child's experience in our classroom more enjoyable:

1. Child's name:

2. Father's name:

3. Father's country of origin:

4. Mother's name:

5. Mother's country of origin:

6. What name do you use for your child?

7. How did you decide to give your child this name?

8. Does this name have a particular meaning or translation?

9. Where was your child born?

10. Where else has your child lived and when?

11. How long has your family lived in [name of community]?

12. What language or languages do you use to talk to your child?

    Father:

    Mother:

13. Do you speak any other languages?

    Father:

    Mother:

14. Who else does your child spend time with besides you? (Please include sisters and brothers, aunts and uncles, cousins, grandparents, family friends, and child care providers.)

    Name   Relation to child   Age   Language used with child

15. If English is *not* your home language, please estimate how many English words your child knows. (Circle one.):

    Fewer than 10   0 to 50   50 to 100   More than 100

16. Do you belong to a particular religious group?

17. List the foods that your child likes to eat:

18. List the foods that your child does *not* like to eat:

19. What does your child usually eat with? (Circle one.)

    Fingers   Chopsticks   Fork and spoon

20. How does your child let you know he or she needs to use the toilet?

Please complete the following sentences:

21. When my child is with a group of children, I would expect my child to_____ .

22. When my child needs help from an adult, I would expect my child to_____ .

23. If my child is misbehaving in class, I would expect the teacher to_____ .

24. If my child is unhappy in class, I would expect the teacher to_____ .

25. The most important thing my child can learn in class this year would be_____ .

26. Is there any other information you would like to give us about your family or your child?

Adapted from Tabors, 2008

13-3 Resolving Cultural Conflict

It is inevitable and predictable that when teachers and parents from diverse cultural settings come together, conflict and differences will appear. Culture determines that families and teachers have strong viewpoints about what is good and necessary for children's development. All the most basic acts of daily care and nurturing reflect the cultural values of parents and caregivers, and their expectations are unlikely to match. Although differences are inevitable, it is not inevitable that one cultural view becomes dominant over the other. Gonzalez-Mena (2008) identifies four possible outcomes to cultural conflicts. Three of them involve activity and change to resolve the conflict.

FIGURE 13-17
An example of a cultural conflict could be the caregiver allowing the toddler to feed herself when that was not the desire at home.

13-3a Understanding and Negotiating

The first possibility is that the conflict is resolved through understanding and negotiation, with both sides seeing the other's perspective and finding a compromise. An example here might be the familiar situation where the parent objects to seeing his or her child messy and dirty, and the early educator provides many classroom opportunities for sensory exploration with water, sand, and paint. As the teacher communicates with the parent about why cleanliness is so important to this parent, she learns that this family equates sending children to school clean and well dressed with the parent's respect for education and with the family maintaining decent standards within the community. The teacher is also able to help the parent learn something about good early childhood practice and the importance of sensory experience in early learning. The teacher agrees that he or she will change the child's clothes or cover them well during messy play. The parent agrees to allow the child to do messy play as long as the clothes are protected. Both parties feel they are right (and the other is unnecessarily worried about something that does not seem very important), but they feel that the compromise is satisfactory (see Figure 13-17).

13-3b Learning a New Perspective

The second possibility is that the situation could be resolved when the caregiver learns a new perspective from the parent and subsequently changes his or her actions. The example Gonzalez-Mena offers is of a caregiver who is convinced that the best place for babies to sleep is in a crib in a quiet nap room; this seems to provide optimal rest for most infants. But a baby from a family who is used to sleeping in the midst of an active household is unable to sleep. When the parents express dismay that their child will be isolated and alone in his or her crib, the caregiver discovers their viewpoint and works with the licensing consultant to accommodate parental requests and infant needs. The caregiver changes his or her actions because he or she recognizes and accepts the cultural difference.

13-3c Resolving Through Parent Education

A third possibility is to resolve the situation through parent education. Parents gain knowledge and learn ideas that might be different from their traditional cultural ideas, but they come to see that the new ideas could provide optimal developmental environments for their children. This requires thoughtful, respectful sensitivity on the part of the caregiver—to be very sure that the education relates to ideas that seem essential for children's development, not merely to help the family conform to some arbitrary standard of what is "normal." Gonzalez-Mena's example regards the conflict between parents of infants whose cultural beliefs are that babies should not be left free on the floor to play with toys but instead should be held and involved with human interaction. Rather than stopping floor freedom, the teacher helps the family understand the importance of physical freedom for muscle development and cognitive stimulation. When parents understand this importance, they are more open to learning how they can keep their children safe while they play on the floor. The teacher displays cultural sensitivity to the parents' concerns but finds the developmental issue important enough to pursue.

13-3d Finding No Resolution

The last—and indeed fairly common—possibility in cultural conflicts is that there may be no resolution of the conflict. The worst-case scenario here is for neither family nor teacher to perceive or accept the other's perspective and for both to persist in their

TeachSource Digital Download

IDEAS FOR TEACHERS:

Cultural Dilemmas

When faced with cultural dilemmas, teachers should do the following:

- Analyze the situation. What is the child's experience at home? What is my belief about this? Is the child's welfare at stake?
- Do not blame the child or the family.
- Get information. What does this behavior mean to the parents? What do parents do in this situation and why?
- Realize the child cannot cope with being caught between two cultural expectations.
- Respond to the child and parents as individuals.
- Keep talking and trying to find common ground.

separate beliefs and practices. Children caught in the middle of such separation may be confused and uncomfortable when the practices in the school setting feel very different from what is done at home. The term **culturally assaultive** has been used to refer to such negative experiences because the family's culture is in fact under attack.

A better outcome would be for families and teachers to gain an understanding of the other's ideas, which are treated with respect and sensitivity but without changing the strong beliefs. The achievement is for parent and teacher to learn to cope with the differences, each in a way that is acceptable to the individual. With sensitivity, communication, and working at problem solving, teachers and families may find ways of reconciling cultural differences or at least becoming sensitive to separate perspectives.

13.4 Common Cultural Issues That Arise in Classrooms

Sensitivity to important issues and family concerns helps teachers consider best practices to support culturally and linguistically different families.

13-4a Linguistic Diversity

Communication with families and children is challenged when the primary language of a family is different from the teacher's and that used in the classroom. With the number of immigrant children entering early childhood programs in America today, a vital attitude for teachers is to consider a "nondeficit perspective in relation to linguistic diversity" (Rosegrant, 1992); that is, it is not so much that the child and parent are limited in English but that they are proficient in their primary language while learning a second language. Rather than seeing linguistically different children as less capable, less intelligent, and educationally delayed and their parents as less able to successfully raise their children, teachers must understand that abilities in languages other than English demonstrate competencies that will slowly apply to **English language learners (ELLs)** and also to learning the new cultural and social values associated with the classroom culture. Educators should consider what children could lose in both academic content and social-emotional adjustment if their home language is not supported. It is not a matter of giving up one language and culture in favor of adopting another, but adding other skills and experiences to those that already exist and are important in the lives of children and their families (see Figure 13-18).

culturally assaultive
Behaviors that attack the culture of another by ignoring, failing to accept and respect, demeaning, or attacking the behaviors and beliefs of another.

ELLs English language learners:
Individuals whose first language is not English.

FIGURE 13-18
English language learners need special support as they learn a second language.

© Cengage Learning®

OPPORTUNITY FOR SELF-REFLECTION

Can you recall a situation in which you have been involved in a cultural conflict regarding child rearing—whether in your professional or personal life? What was the conflict? How was it resolved or not resolved? What insights does this give you about culturally determined differences of opinion?

Supporting children's home language while scaffolding their English learning allows children and their families to become bilingual and able to function comfortably in the worlds of home and school. Here are some specific things teachers can do to show respect and to facilitate communication:

TeachSource

VIDEO ACTIVITY ►❚❚

© 2016 Cengage Learning®

Watch the Video Case entitled *English Language Learners: Partnering with Parents to Promote Oral Language and Early Literacy.* After watching this video, reflect on these questions:

1. What suggestions do you see the teacher make about supporting home language use?

2. What concerns and questions do parents of ELL children have, and how does the teacher address them?

3. How does the teacher offer new information and ideas to parents?

- Learn greeting words in the families' native languages. These can also be posted on the wall so other teachers and families in the classroom can use them: "Hello to Eleni and her family is 'Kalimera.' Goodbye is 'Yia sou.'"

- Make a "survival words" chart, getting words with pronunciations from families to place beside photographs of children doing such basic things as eating, sleeping, and using the bathroom. Children will be reassured that they can have basic needs met when the teacher can respond to children's indications (Nemeth, 2009).

- Respect children's names. Children should be addressed correctly to preserve children's sense of self-esteem. Shortening or otherwise changing their names could distort the meaning and deny important cultural heritage (Kirmani, 2007).

- Provide written materials in the families' native languages. Help with translation can often be obtained from others in the community, such as university faculty or students, ESL programs, churches associated with particular cultures, school system personnel, representatives from foreign-owned businesses, international clubs, or bilingual members of the same nationality. Explore your community resources to help find individuals who can help with translating materials or interpreting conversations. There are also many useful websites that offer free translation services from English to a number of languages: Spanish, Italian, French, German, Chinese, Japanese, Russian, Arabic, and many others.

Learn from families what languages are spoken at home and their preferences. A form that elicits such information is seen in Figure 13-16.

- Encourage families to bring family members who can speak English to conferences, meetings, and classroom activities. If there are other parents who also speak the same language, be sure the parents meet. These other parents may be able to support the new families and also act as a bridge for involving them in the school.

- Encourage parents to use their primary languages with their children at home, as they have since birth. Children will quickly pick up the second language in the classroom, and it is vital not to disturb the parent–child relationship and the language in which they are primarily communicating. Teachers acknowledge that there are functions of language beyond exchange of information, such as establishing and maintaining meaningful relationships within their families. A rich home language environment supports important parent–child interactions. Teachers can help parents understand the importance of oral language as a precursor to early literacy development. Encouraging storytelling, rhymes, songs, and folklore enhances children's understanding of components of literacy, such as phonemic awareness, vocabulary development, and comprehension (Isbell, 2002). The language principles learned in one language will help children transfer these to a second language and help them at school. When parents are encouraged to "practice more English at home," the quality of their interaction with their children may be limited. This hurts self-esteem and social competence, and ultimately affects the children's abilities to do well in school. (See Figure 13-19.)

FIGURE 13-19
Teachers encourage parents to continue to use their home language with their children.

© Eprom/Shutterstock.com

- Label objects and pictures in the classroom with all the languages represented in the room. Parents will be happy to supply the words. This will allow the teachers and all the children to enjoy learning new words in each other's languages.

- Make a photograph book or picture sequence that represents the daily life and routines in the classroom. Pictures tell the story when words are not understood. Another strategy is to make a video of the children during the day. Parents can interpret the actions even if they do not understand the language.

- Create many opportunities for two-way communication, particularly with face-to-face contact, such as home visits, conversations at the door, potluck dinners, conferences, and classroom open houses. In this way, the teacher's real attempts to include the families with primary language differences may be seen more clearly, and gestures and body language can help the communication process.

- Make a collection of take-home children's books in the children's primary languages. This will encourage families to reinforce their native languages as well as read to their children. "Parents who cannot read or write fluently in either their primary language or in English still play a critical role in their child's literacy learning" (Ordonez-Jasis & Ortiz, 2006). Teachers can help parents learn how to use wordless books, introducing their children to the functions and pleasures of books.

- Invite family members to teach songs or tell stories in their native languages in the classroom. This will welcome parents' contributions, even if they have limited English proficiency, at the same level as all parents and give a positive message about diversity to all children.

- Read the bilingual book *Tomasito's Mother Comes to School/La Mama de Tomasito Visita la Escuela,* available online at www.hfrp.org. This little book helps communicate to children and parents the expectations for immigrant parents to be involved in the U.S. educational system. Teachers can read and discuss the book in class and send the book home for children to share with their families.

- Be sensitive to not assuming developmental delays or personality difficulties in children when behavior may be limited by the children's language understanding in the classroom as well as by cultural differences. An example is a child who does not make eye contact with a teacher because of cultural teachings about respectful communication. Help children by demonstration, gestures, and support as they become involved in play activities. Also be sensitive to overlooking needs for special attention that can be masked by assuming that the problem is lack of understanding or failure to assess children in ways that consider their cultural background. An example is a hard-of-hearing child who is assumed to be nonresponsive because of the language difference.

WHAT DOES BRAIN RESEARCH TELL US ABOUT DUAL LANGUAGE LEARNERS?

Recent studies indicate that children who grow up in bilingual settings have enhanced activity in prefrontal cortex neural pathways, revealed by MRI. This translates to greater attention focus, distraction resistance, decision making, judgment, and responsiveness to feedback—what are known as the executive functions of the brain. These neural networks of the brain are the latest to mature, with prefrontal cortex maturation occurring long after childhood.

The bilingual brain is highly involved in the cognitive challenge of evaluating between the two competing language systems, with the control and storage networks of both languages being active and available. Thus, the massive activity of evaluating meaning of words, of sentence structure and grammar, and details of pronunciation exercise the executive functions early in deciphering the codes within each language. Just as muscles become stronger with physical workouts, the developing brains of children in bilingual environments seem to build strength, speed, and efficiency in their executive function networks. You can read more about this in Willis, 2012.

1. How does this information support the idea of encouraging parents to speak in their home language with their children?
2. What might be the implications regarding introducing second languages to children from monolingual homes?

- Make the classroom feel safe for children, not allowing any teasing, bullying, or isolation.

- Make families feel welcomed and respected, with abundant information available to them in their home language (Nemeth, 2009).

- Assume that ELL families who do not participate in what teachers perceive to be the "right" ways need more support or teacher effort, rather than that they are indifferent or inattentive to their children's educational needs (Carlson, 2010). Remember that recently immigrated families face many challenges: adapting to a new culture, learning new language, locating suitable housing, getting employment, and adjusting to educational settings and other societal systems (Cho et al., 2010). Teacher support can be very helpful.

13-4b Holidays

Because of religious traditions or cultural backgrounds, many families in schools may celebrate their holidays in their own way, may celebrate holidays that are unfamiliar to mainstream society, or may not wish their children to participate in celebrations that are traditional in many schools. Examples are families that celebrate Buddha's birthday or Chanukah; one that has never heard of Halloween or feels it is contrary to their religious views; one that wants only the religious aspects of Christmas recognized and another who does not want their child to participate in a Christmas pageant; or one that is offended by the teacher's creation of a dragon to celebrate the Chinese New Year as though it were merely a tourist attraction.

Teachers need to be sensitive to the cultural diversity within their classrooms and must think long and hard about building any curriculum around holidays that may not be celebrated or valued by the families in their classroom or holidays that may be difficult for some families, such as Mother's Day and Father's Day. Exploring the issue with families and colleagues can help teachers gain different perspectives and develop new ideas for celebrations.

There is a viewpoint that suggests that early childhood programs may be inappropriate places to celebrate holidays. This approach points out the following:

1. It is extremely difficult to give holidays meaning that is developmentally appropriate for young children because many holidays are based on abstract concepts.

2. Holidays challenge inclusiveness because of decisions about whether to include holidays that represent all the family traditions in a center, what to do if many other traditions are not represented in a center, or what to do when all families do not agree on the celebration or method of celebration of a particular holiday.

3. Many holidays are overdone in any case, with great emphasis on commercialization, leading to uncomfortable situations of competition and pressure on families of limited economic means as well as trivialization of deeper feelings that families may hold.

These are certainly points worth considering (see Figure 13-20).

In *Anti-Bias Education for Young Children and Ourselves* (2010), Derman-Sparks and Edwards encourage schools to develop a holiday policy that spells out the program's objectives and decision-making process in their approach to holidays in the curriculum. They offer guidelines for planning holiday activities:

- Teachers should understand the context of the holiday, including ethnic/cultural/historical origins, what portion of the classroom families celebrate it, and what specifically they want children to learn from the holiday activities.

- Teachers should plan how to equitably respect everyone's traditions rather than treating some holidays as "different" and others as "what everyone does."

- Teachers should invite children to share their own experiences.

- The holidays of every group that is represented in the classroom should be honored, with their agreement and active participation. Participation prevents the holiday celebration from becoming just a "tourist" experience, where the holiday is seen as exotic rather than regular. The participation of all concerned also allows the particular differences in the way individual families within a culture celebrate the same holiday to be respected and demonstrated. When holidays are celebrated without any connection to real people in the children's lives or without anyone in the classroom having ever participated in this holiday before, the danger is that the holiday celebration may deteriorate into a rather trivial and superficial experience that actually works against developing respect for diversity.

- Families whose beliefs do not permit their children to participate in particular holiday celebrations should be included in planning satisfactory alternatives for the children within the classroom. Teachers must guard against feeling sorry that these children are being deprived of some experience that the teacher believes is important. Such an attitude implies that the only desirable cultural beliefs are those tied in with celebration of that holiday—a truly ethnocentric error. By becoming knowledgeable about particular family beliefs and traditions, teachers can help support children in making the explanations to their peers.

FIGURE 13-20
Many families prefer to celebrate their own traditions with their children.

© 2xSamara.com/Shutterstock.com

"Henry's family doesn't celebrate Halloween, so that's why he decided he didn't want to help carve the jack-o'-lantern. He's going to help me wash and bake the pumpkin seeds for our harvest snack. Who would like to help us?"

■ Think and rethink every classroom practice to be sure that everyone's traditions and beliefs are represented throughout the curriculum and activities. Such traditional practices as making Mother's Day cards or Father's Day gifts may be hurtful to some (Campbell, Jamsek, & Jolly, 2007).

There is a thorough discussion of holiday practices in *Celebrate: An Anti-Bias Guide to Enjoying Holidays in Early Childhood Programs* (Bisson, 2002).

13-4c Classroom Curriculum

An obvious way to draw families of diverse backgrounds into their children's early education programs is by inviting them to enrich the classroom curriculum with their ideas and presence. Some parents are reluctant to come into the classroom, fearful that this will identify their child as being "different." Others are unfamiliar with school practices and traditions of involving families. Still others are prevented from participating by time and other circumstances. Teachers need to be able to articulate the benefits for all children and families in becoming comfortable with their differences and similarities. What are some of the ways the cultural diversity of individual families can enrich the classroom? A first essential is obviously for teachers to learn about their children's families through the kinds of methods discussed earlier. Again, when teachers clearly open the door by indicating recognition and appreciation for individual family experiences, parents will likely become comfortable enough to offer ideas of importance to them. Teachers can avoid making assumptions about particular ethnic or religious backgrounds by allowing families to decide which aspects of their family life they will share.

It is vital that teachers include *all* families in enriching the curriculum, not merely the ones who present more obvious cultural differences or those whose first language is English. Parents from sociological groups that have not traditionally been involved in their children's schools or are called only when their children have problems may require particularly persistent invitations. The basic principle that teachers are trying to demonstrate is that all families are unique and special and have their own rich experience to share with others. Teachers can invite parents to do several things to participate:

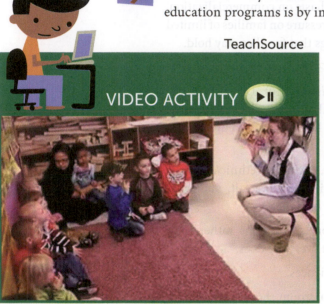

TeachSource

VIDEO ACTIVITY ▶❙❙

Watch the Video Case, *Multicultural Lessons: Embracing Similarities and Differences in Preschool Education,* and read Interview Transcript 1. After viewing the clip and reading the interview, reflect on these questions:

1. What is the approach to holidays suggested by Shelley Outwater? How do her ideas support the aforementioned discussion of holiday practices?

2. Consider several other ideas from her discussion of the values of multiculturalism that you would like to incorporate in your classroom. How do these support the benefits for children and families discussed in this chapter?

© 2016 Cengage Learning®

■ Talk about what makes their family unique—what they enjoy doing together. Children enjoy the storytelling of family members, including grandparents. Stories about individual family experiences help children begin to understand diversity.

■ Bring videos and CDs, photos, art, and artifacts of their home cultures into the classroom to share and discuss. Everybody has something they treasure that has meaning to the family. Even parents who can't come can participate by offering materials.

- Share their experiences with traditional celebrations, literature, dance, and religious ceremonies by activities, discussion, and display. Because these are important to the child and family, other children will gain an appreciation of the depth and breadth of human experience, finding similarities with their own experience as well as appreciating the differences.

- Cook and share recipes with the children (see Figure 13-21). A cookbook of favorite recipes from each family could be compiled. When culturally diverse foods are shared regularly, children may learn new food experiences, see how foods relate across cultures, and feel comfortable sharing their own family traditions with others without fear of stereotyping. Parents can help explain religious or cultural food restrictions that apply to children in the group.

- Share maps, flags, and travel experiences with the children to enliven social studies learning.

FIGURE 13-21
Cooking and sharing food experiences help children see how food connects people across cultures.

- Help identify community resources that may help teachers plan field trips, or invite visitors who can increase multicultural experiences for the classroom. This can be another method of participation for families who cannot visit in person.

- Help teachers evaluate curriculum materials and activities to be sure no stereotypical influences creep in and to make sure all children and families are fairly represented. Conversations about curriculum will help make sure that individual needs are being recognized.

- Help teachers interpret areas of similarity and differences to children.

- Learning about diversity takes thoughtful processing after experiences. As teachers and parents work with children, they can gradually help them sort out the experiences that join us together in humanity. Read more about families in the classroom in Chapter 10.

13-4d What Does Working with Diversity Look Like?

It can be helpful to consider examples of programs that are attempting to work respectfully with culturally and linguistically diverse families. A case example follows.

13.5 Buen Dia Family School

In the heart of San Francisco's Mission District in a narrow townhouse is Buen Dia Family School, offering a full- and part-day developmentally based preschool program for about 40 families with children ages two years, nine months, through six years. Yvonne Gavre, the director who was one of the founders of the program, envisioned a family-like program that could meet the needs she felt children really wanted when they were cared for away from home: a small, "cozy" program where they could be intimately involved with activities that were important to them and where adults could help them feel important.

A visitor immediately feels the home-like atmosphere when entering. There are a couple of large playrooms in front and a large kitchen for eating, working, and displaying in back. The kitchen door opens to the backyard play area, which boasts the rarity of a couple of city trees. A downstairs area is arranged for play and more formal drama presentations (one of the two visiting artists-in-residence is a performance artist, and several parents are involved in theater and film). The director's office upstairs shows evidence of children coming in to play, read, and visit. Because some of the children are present only for morning or afternoon hours, there are never more than 24 children in the school at a time, adding to the home-like atmosphere. Each teacher has his or her own small group of children who come together for snack and small group conversation or activity once in the morning and once in the afternoon.

Another guiding idea was that anyone living in contemporary California should be able to speak Spanish and English, so Buen Dia is a bilingual program, serving a cross section of families with diverse ethnic, cultural, and religious backgrounds. A statement from the parent handbook illustrates the school's emphasis on a multicultural/antibias approach:

We, as teachers, are constantly questioning and revising our own perceptions while developing and implementing an antibias approach in our manner of interacting with children as well as in our basic developmentally based curriculum. We all believe in the value of fairness, self-esteem, and respect for individual differences. A curriculum that emphasizes these is especially critical in a city like San Francisco with its rich ethnic diversity and where 53 percent of families are nontraditional.

Our program integrates not only materials and activities that are sensitive to the uniqueness of each child and family but also includes a conscious way of being, talking, and acting according to the needs of each. We try to make the children feel good and comfortable about themselves, their culture, and their families. ... Throughout the year we celebrate every holiday possible in nonreligious ways and encourage parents to participate in any way they want.

This underlying theme of uniqueness and acceptance of family and individuals is visible everywhere at Buen Dia. Early in the year, the children bring their "Personality Bags," filled with their own special things, to share at group time. A newsletter has explained the concept and purposes of the activity to the parents; one of the purposes is to give the parent and child a time to talk together about "what makes each of them special." Parents sign up on the parent bulletin board for a time and day for their child to share with the group. In the following weeks, children create a "Me Book—Un Libro sobre Mi!" On various pages, children list their school friends, make their fingerprints, and glue a string that is as tall as they are. Each child creates an audiotape of his or her own stories. Some of these can be acted out at group time each day, with the child acting as "director." Staff members have found this activity to be not only a valuable language experience but also a way for children to work on a theme throughout the year in safe surroundings. A book of some favorite stories is published at year-end.

A corner in the front playroom is devoted to pictures of "Our Families—Nuestra Familias." A glance indicates the true diversity of cultural background and family structure. Not only are there single-parent families, but there are also two-parent families with different- and same-gender parents, as well as families where adopted children are of different racial backgrounds than their parents. The director speaks of the school's support of the gay and lesbian families who have been part of the school's population since the beginning:

"We've almost had to throw out all the books that attempt to explain families and babies and come up with our own words. We talk about 'home' daddies and mommies and 'seed' daddies and mommies—when the inevitable discussion arises about 'He doesn't have a daddy' or 'Her mommy looks different from her.'"

A look in the display area tells of parents' involvement in the curriculum. Nahoa's father has just been in to talk about farmworkers and has left behind some pictures labeled

"Farmworkers from a Presentation by Nahoa's Dad, Jesus." Another corner has a section on study of Native Americans, including a clay representation of a Navajo pueblo, a listing of the children who include Native American as part of their heritage, and the story of another father's visit to discuss kachina dolls. Such parent participation is encouraged, not required, but many parents are eager to help extend the children's perceptions and experiences of others. As a result, the children have celebrated Buddha's birthday, Jewish holidays, Dia de Los Muertos, and Kwanzaa. Every year is a bit different depending on the interests and background of parents. The director remarks that they are careful not to assume that parents will necessarily want to celebrate a particular cultural holiday, and they ask each family what they would like to do.

Parents and children visit the center to decide if they wish to be placed on the waiting list; children are admitted with attention to male/female ratio and cultural diversity. At this initial visit, the program's philosophy is explained, and it is suggested to parents that if they are looking for academic emphasis, this is probably not the school for them. Many families have fees subsidized or are assisted by scholarship or alternative payment plans. Parents sign a work incentive agreement, agreeing to work for the center for 25 hours each year in lieu of a fee. Families who do not wish to or are unable to work pay the fee. Possible activities include driving on field trips, participating in monthly cleanup days, buying food, making repairs, writing grant proposals, sewing, organizing the recycling center, working on fund-raisers, and the like. Some parents follow their interests or professions for the volunteer work; a father who is an arborist is involved with sprucing up the playground, and an Academy Award–winning filmmaker mother is making a video about the school.

At the beginning of the school year, there is a big open house, with teachers planning activities for parents to experience what their children do. Throughout the year, there are many small meetings—usually held from 4:30 to 5:30 or 5:00 to 6:00 p.m., with parents choosing the kinds of topics they want to talk about: transitions into school, siblings, and so on. There are three big social events each year. Newsletters are sent out monthly, bringing parents up to date on past and coming events and mentioning specific parent involvement. A newsletter at the beginning of the year introduces the staff of Buen Dia—themselves a diverse lot, with teachers from Colombia, Peru, and France and of various ethnic and language backgrounds and with varied travel and work experiences. Each teacher particularly communicates with the parents of the children in his or her small group daily.

Parents choose this center because of the atmosphere of extended family. Parents and staff talk on weekends, are invited to bar mitzvahs, and stay involved with the school even after their children have moved on to elementary school and beyond. Some middle school "alumni" come in to work in the afternoons. Buen Dia, with its emphasis on the value and uniqueness of individuals and families, creates a supportive atmosphere for its small group of families.

SUMMARY

Because culture has influenced us all in so many ways and without our awareness, working with parents of diverse backgrounds presents major challenges for teachers, as well as benefits:

- For individual children, affirmation of identity, with acceptance and respect for themselves and their families
- For all children, ability to live comfortably with diversity and avoidance of prejudice

- For families, support of their culture and language, and support in understanding how to help their children fit into mainstream culture

- For teachers, personal growth and enhanced ability to partner with diverse families

All families can be welcomed by:

- Teachers becoming aware of their attitudes and learning about other cultures

- Making classrooms culturally safe and familiar

- Opening the door to communication about culture

Cultural conflicts are inevitable, but may be resolved by:

- Understanding and negotiation

- Learning a new perspective

- Parent education

- Finding no resolution, but treating everyone with respect and sensitivity

Families who are English language learners will need:

- Translated materials and/or interpreters

- Encouragement to continue using their home language

- Ways to honor their holiday traditions

Learning about programs that work well with diverse families may be helpful.

Student Activities for Further Study

1. Evaluate the forms and written materials of a school to see how welcoming they appear to be regarding diverse family experiences.

2. Discover the resources available in your community to assist teachers working with parents with primary languages other than English. Investigate churches, university programs, international centers, and so on.

3. Talk with teachers to learn how they make their decisions about holiday celebrations. Consider whether what you learn indicates a real respect for families of diverse backgrounds.

4. Devise a questionnaire that could be used with families to learn more about their ideas about child rearing and home practices. Also consider questions that could help a teacher get insights from families about holidays and celebrations.

Apply the Chapter Concepts: Case in Point

One of the families in Naomi Berg's Head Start classroom this year is an immigrant family from Sudan. She is having a difficult time getting the parents to communicate with her about their child, who is often ill and seems fearful, with eyes always cast down. She brought up this dilemma in her early childhood class at the college one evening and was dismayed when several of her classmates also described families that were creating challenges in their classrooms: a family with two mothers and a child adopted from China, as well as several Latino families who speak little English and seem overprotective of their children.

Their instructor asked them to defer the discussion until next week, and come prepared to identify potential problems and solutions.

1. What might be several causes of tension in working with the families described?

2. What are some of the issues these teachers must consider personally?

3. What are ways that Naomi and her fellow students might suggest to reach out to these families, creating culturally safe environments?

4. Identify two or three starting points for working with each of these families.

Review Questions

1. Discuss a rationale for working with families of diverse backgrounds. What are some of the benefits for individual children? For the group of children? For families? For teachers?

2. What are some specific things teachers can do to ensure that all families feel welcome?

3. Identify and discuss the four possible outcomes in resolving cultural conflicts.

4. Discuss several common cultural issues that arise in classrooms, as well as possible teacher actions.

Helpful Websites

- Teaching Tolerance, Southern Poverty Law Center. This website offers free resources for teachers on developing accepting classrooms.

- Early Childhood Research Institute on Culturally & Linguistically Appropriate Services (CLAS). The CLAS Institute identifies, evaluates, and promotes effective and appropriate early intervention practices and preschool practices that are sensitive and respectful to children and families from culturally and linguistically diverse backgrounds.

- The National Association for Bilingual Education (NABE) is a nonprofit professional organization devoted to representing the interests of language minority students and the bilingual education professionals who serve them.

- NCELA, the National Clearinghouse for English Language Acquisition and Language Instruction Educational Programs (formerly NCBE, the National Clearinghouse for Bilingual Education), is funded by the U.S. Department of Education's Office of English Language Acquisition, Language Enhancement, and Academic Achievement for Limited English Proficient Students to collect, analyze, and disseminate information relating to the effective education of linguistically and culturally diverse learners in the United States.

- The Center for Applied Linguistics (CAL) aims to promote and improve the teaching and learning of languages, identify and solve problems related to language and culture, and serve as a resource for information about language and culture.

- The National Association for Multicultural Education works to foster the understanding of unique cultural and ethnic heritage and promotes the development of culturally responsible and responsive curricula.

- The Center for Law and Social Policy is a nonprofit organization that works to improve the lives of low-income people. Search here for the Breaking Down Barriers study and the study on immigrant families in early education by Matthews and Jang (2007).

CHAPTER 14

Working with Families in Particular Circumstances

Learning Objectives

After reading this chapter, you should be able to:

14-1 Discuss some ways that divorce and remarriage can affect children and families, and discuss ways teachers can be helpful.

14-2 Describe possible emotional responses from parents of children with special needs or disabilities, and discuss ways teachers can work effectively with them.

14-3 Describe typical responses from parents of infants, and discuss ways teachers can work effectively with them.

14-4 Discuss factors that create an abusive situation, indicators that suggest abuse or neglect, and teachers' responsibilities in working with these families.

14-5 Identify ways that classroom teachers can support adoptive families.

naeyc

Related NAEYC Standards

Accreditation Standards (see inside text back cover for full listing of the Accreditation Standards for exemplary early childhood programs)

1.B.12; 3.A.01; 6.A.01; 6.A.03; 7.A.01; 7.A.03; 7.A.10; 7.B.05; 8.A.01; 8.A.03; 8.A.05; 10.D.03

Licensure Standards (see inside text front cover for full listing of the Licensure Standards for this chapter)

2a; 2b; 5b

Every family's situation is unique in its history, emotions, and demands. As such, there is no neat package of services or supports that meets the needs of every family at every time. Teachers find themselves working with families who have specific needs at particular times. The skills discussed throughout this text for working with all families are useful here; in addition, particular attitudes and behaviors will be helpful.

This chapter examines several of these circumstances and discusses helpful teacher responses. One frequent occurrence in contemporary society is the dissolution of existing family structures by divorce. At this critical time, both children and parents need help in making the necessary emotional adjustments. Remarriage and the formation of stepfamilies is another stressful period when sensitive classroom teachers can help. Families who are providing for the special learning needs of children with atypical development or chronic illness face continual stress and emotional adjustment. Families who are adjusting to the demands of an infant and to leaving their little ones in the care of others also have unique needs. Teachers must also be aware of their responsibilities to children and parents when abuse or neglect, substance abuse, or violence is a family pattern. And families created by adoption have their own unique concerns. This list is by no means complete; distinctive issues are seen in families headed by adolescent parents, military families with frequent moves and deployments, and in homeless families—to mention just a few other circumstances in our world today. Teachers are in a position to support them all, through their positive professional relationships.

14-1 Working with Families Undergoing Change Due to Divorce

Dorothy Scott has recently noticed some disturbing behaviors in Sam Butler. He has been quite out of bounds—almost defiantly breaking the group rules and striking out aggressively at other children. She is also bothered by the quiet sadness she sees in him at other times. She knows his parents' divorce is now final and wonders if these behaviors are related and what she might do to help the family during this time of change.

The Butler family is not alone. Currently, nearly one out of two marriages is expected to end in divorce (see Figure 14-1). Two-thirds of divorces involve children; over one million American children experience the divorce of their parents each year. Because about 50 percent of all divorces occur in the first seven years of marriage, the children involved in divorce are often quite young. Five out of six men and three out of four women remarry after divorce—often creating stepfamilies. Half of all children under the age of 13 are currently living with one biological parent and that parent's current partner (Stewart, 2007). Some researchers predict that more children will soon be living in second marriages or in single-parent families than in first marriages.

Such large numbers have led to the societal acceptance of divorce; divorced people are no longer as stigmatized—partly because "no-fault" divorce laws refrain from naming a wrongdoer. Although the societal stigma may be reduced, the pain experienced by children and their parents is not. Perhaps the most positive way to view the divorced family is as a bifocal or binuclear family. In such circumstances, children may have two homes and two major centers of decision making and activity, along with two parents who are no longer living together. An important first step for teachers working with such families is to be informed about the facts concerning divorce and to examine their own attitudes and expectations in order to avoid stereotyping.

FIGURE 14-1
Divorce affects about half of all American families.

There are many myths concerning divorce and its effects, particularly on the children involved. One myth is that children will not be affected by what is, after all, an adult matter. Several researchers have in fact tracked and studied divorced families for long periods after the divorce (Heatherington & Kelly, 2002; Wallerstein & Blakeslee, 1989). At least one study followed the effects on children through 25 years of their lives that followed their parents' divorce (Wallerstein, Lewis, & Blakeslee, 2000). Such research contains many interesting implications for those in positions of support to families experiencing divorce.

Divorce—the second-most stressful experience for families after death—is a critical experience for the entire family, affecting each member differently. To some degree, all family members experience abandonment, trauma, rejection, loss of income, a lower standard of living, and change in many other areas of their lives. However, adults usually also experience relief to be finished with a difficult situation. No children in the study reported they were relieved that their parents were getting divorced—even if the parents were often in violent conflict with each other. Children usually do not consider divorce a relief or a remedy.

Whatever long-term findings show—and they often show contradictory results of divorce—most researchers find evidence that "divorce often leads to a partial or complete collapse in an adult's ability to parent for months and sometimes years after the breakup. Caught up in rebuilding their own lives, mothers and fathers are preoccupied with a thousand and one concerns, which can blind them to the needs of their children" (Wallerstein, 2000). As Heatherington (with Kelly, 2002) puts it, "Divorce destroys the reassuring rhythms and structures of family life, especially those that give a child's life order and predictability." The divorced family is not a version of the two-parent family minus one parent. It is a different kind of family, and the entire family system is strained.

"For adults, divorce brings *a* world to an end; for young children, whose lives are focused in the family, it seems to bring *the* world to an end" (Heatherington & Kelly, 2002). This is a time of bereavement for everyone in a family; the family they knew is gone. One parent usually leaves the home and is less available to a child, and sometimes siblings may also leave. There are no proven guidelines for noncustodial or nonresidential parents. This is an unfamiliar parenting experience for those who move out and see their children on visits.

A mother's working pattern may increase, and a family's living standard is likely to change with increasing economic stress. Although three-quarters of divorcing mothers have child support agreements, only about half receive the full amount ordered; one-quarter receive funds irregularly or less than ordered; and still another quarter receive no support at all. Recent studies have shown that in many states, a woman and her children suffer a drastic drop in income; this drop not only creates a new impoverished class but also may be demoralizing.

Each family member grieves in different ways peculiar to their roles and ages. It is important to be aware of patterns but not to expect all children and parents to react similarly to divorce due to individual personalities, genders, experiences, and outside supports, as well as varying ages and developmental levels in children. See Figure 14-2 to consider all the losses that family members experience.

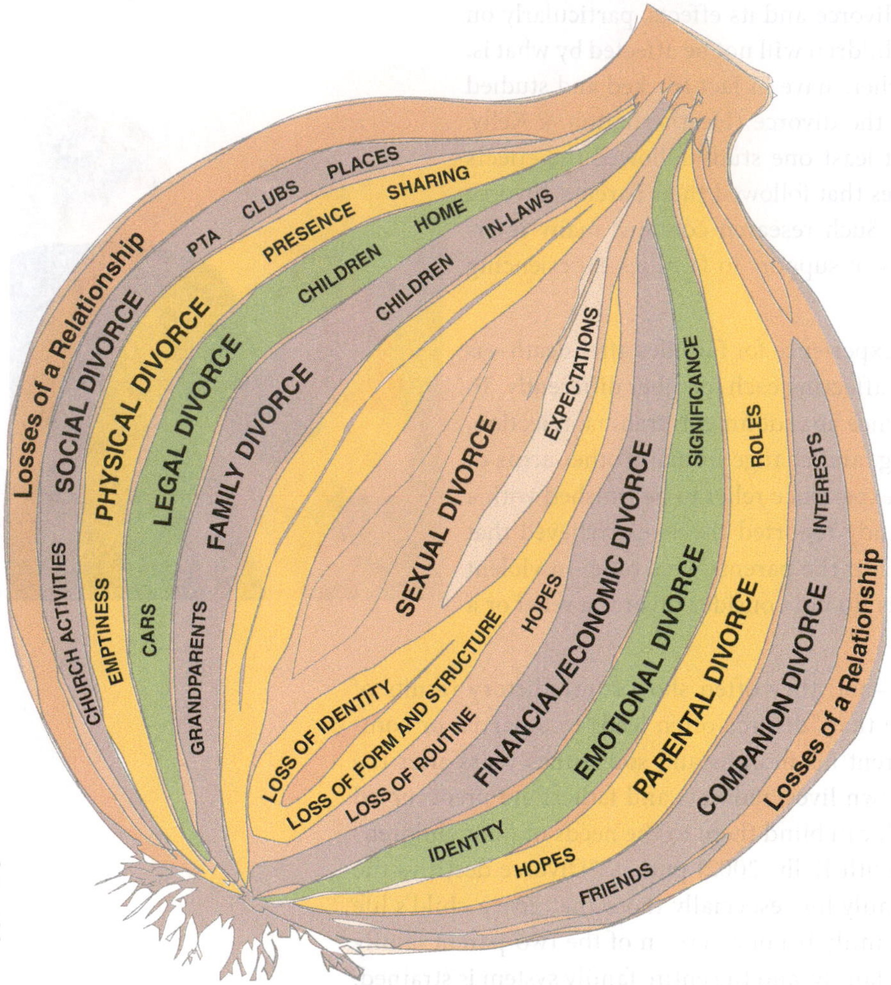

FIGURE 14-2
The "divorce onion": Families undergo many kinds of changes with divorce.

The second myth about divorce explored by Wallerstein (2011) in her 25-year study is that divorce triggers a temporary crisis with the most harmful effects in adjusting to loss at the time of the breakup. Instead, in her studies of adults, she points out that children who grow up in postdivorce families experience not only one loss—that of the intact family—but also a series of losses as people come and go. "Divorce is a life-transforming experience. After divorce, childhood is different. Adolescence is different. Adulthood—with the decision to marry or not, and have children or not—is different." Wallerstein indicates that what may be the solution for the parents' troubles may indeed be the cause of the children's troubles—a disturbing idea for those who would like to advocate for children and safeguard adults' rights to pursue personal happiness.

Although Wallerstein's conclusions have concerned many who work with divorcing families, it is nevertheless important to realize that there may be irreconcilable differences between parents' and children's needs. It is important that the adults who are intimately involved with children realize what a critical point this is for their development. Children are in particularly vulnerable positions at the time of divorce. The mother and father may resolve this life crisis and move on to the next chapter. For children, divorce is not a chapter but a long continuum of life experiences.

Children react with a variety of behaviors—related to their dependent position in a family and age level of intellectual development. In general, preschool children are the most frightened and show the most dramatic symptoms with separation and divorce (see Figure 14-3). Their self-concept seems to be particularly affected, with an increased sense of powerlessness. Their view of predictability, dependability, and order in the world is disrupted. In their anxiety to be sure their needs are met, preschool children may show an increase in dependence, whining, demanding, and disobedient behaviors. In their fear of abandonment, they may have trouble sleeping or being left by adults. Other noted behaviors are regression to immature behavior; separation anxiety and intense attachment to one parent; and guilt, shame, and anxiety about loss of love and safety. Very young children often express the denial stage of grief in rhythmic behavior, such as bouncing, hitting, banging, or kicking; children seem to keep moving so they do not feel the pain. Symptoms of emotional stress may take the form of nightmares, temper tantrums, bedwetting, and unusual fears. In their play, preschool children may be less imaginative, exhibiting less associative and cooperative play and more unoccupied and onlooker play. More aggression is frequently noted. Because of the egocentric nature of their thinking, preschool children often feel responsible for the divorce and behave "better than good," fearing to lose the remaining parent's love through more "bad" behavior. Sometimes, the exact opposite behavior is seen, as a child literally tries to test every limit to see what it takes to lose the other parent. Even infants show such behavioral changes as sleeping and feeding irregularities, clinginess, and lack of trust as they react to tension felt at home. But in the long run, preschoolers may adjust well. They have spent less time in a family riddled with conflict; their experience in the family unit is shorter; and the parents themselves are younger and more able to easily recover.

FIGURE 14-3
Preschool children are generally the most frightened and show the most dramatic symptoms when their parents' marriages break up.

© 2016 Cengage Learning®

Wallerstein (2003) suggests that the most helpful thing for adults to do to help preschoolers is to deal with the child's central fear of being abandoned. They can stress that the child is not losing his or her parents and siblings and that he or she is not at all responsible for the divorce.

School-aged children may show great sadness and despair, fears and phobias, anger, loneliness, shaken identity, and an inability to focus attention on school-related tasks. The growing ability to understand the feelings and perspectives of others allows them to be sympathetic and concerned for their parents. They may feel conflict in their loyalties to each parent. Other behaviors of school-aged children may include nervousness, withdrawal and moodiness, absent-mindedness, poor grades, physical complaints, and acting-out behaviors (see Figure 14-4).

The helpful behaviors that Wallerstein identifies for these youngsters encourage their staying tuned in to life at school. This age can benefit as parents cultivate a sense of a postdivorce family, setting up recreational plans for the child and his or her siblings and friends. By not overreacting to angry outbursts and providing structure, kindness, and rules, teachers can help children get through the divorce experience. Studies show that school-aged children also benefit from school-based discussion groups with a counselor and peers in similar situations.

It is important to keep our perspective about this; Heatherington estimates that 20 to 25 percent of children from divorced families have problems, contrasted with 10 percent of children from nondivorced families who have problems. This is twice the risk, but 75 to 80 percent of children from divorced families do not have problems related to the divorce.

FACTORS THAT CONTRIBUTE TO CHILDREN'S ADJUSTMENT AFTER DIVORCE

- Mental health of parents
- Quality of parent–child relationships
- Degree of open anger versus cooperation between parents
- Age, temperament, and flexibility of child
- Extent to which parents are willing to have the same routines for the child in each home

From Wallerstein, Lewis, & Blakeslee, 2000

Children react best when open conflict between parents is limited and when children can maintain good relationships with each parent individually. The major danger to children is the conflict between parents during and after the divorce. Key factors in children's healthy adjustment are appropriate parenting, including emotional support, monitoring activities, access to the noncustodial parent; disciplining authoritatively; and maintaining

FIGURE 14-4
School-aged children may show loneliness and withdrawal after a divorce.

© Cengage Learning®

age-appropriate expectations. Other factors predictive of positive outcomes include the parents' flexibility and adaptability in redefining roles; availability of social support for family members; and provisions for a secure and predictable environment. The best predictor on children's later well-being is the parents' psychological health and the quality of the parent–child relationship (APA, 2004).

At the same time, parents have their own difficulties. They often feel a double sense of failure for not living up to the American dream of happily ever after and for their unsuccessful efforts to make a marriage work. This may, at least temporarily, decrease their confidence, self-image, and feelings of competence while increasing feelings of anger, guilt, terror, and helplessness. Some of these feelings directly relate to their children as they worry that they have endangered them by their actions. In most cases, there is disorganization of the household; even meeting rudimentary needs seems overwhelming when an exhausted and anxious parent takes on more roles. Parents display a diminished capacity to parent in almost all dimensions, and children feel this most deeply with their heightened state of need. Frequently unavailable to the child, parents at this time exert less consistent and effective discipline, communicate less well, may be less nurturing, and make fewer demands for mature behavior. In the first couple of years after the divorce, children have less regular bedtimes and mealtimes, eat together as a family less, hear fewer bedtime stories, and are more often late for school.

Wallerstein and Blakeslee (2003) point out that parents and children have different tasks to work on during and after a divorce. Adult tasks include ending the marriage, mourning the loss, reclaiming oneself, dealing with strong emotions, venturing forth again, rebuilding, and helping the children. Children's tasks are understanding the divorce, strategic withdrawal, dealing with loss, dealing with anger, working out guilt, accepting permanence, and taking chances on love.

14-1a Working with Children in the Classroom

A family overwhelmed by its own turmoil is greatly helped by the understanding and support of teachers and others outside the family. A teacher can help a child within the classroom and provide information and supportive guidance to parents in a variety of ways.

Maintain a Structured Environment

Children whose lives are in a state of transition are helped by the maintenance of a relatively structured and predictable environment. Some certainty is provided when a child's classroom world is unshaken. Keeping familiar activities and a scheduled routine will lessen some of the negative effects of a stressful home environment. As a child perceives that his or her basic physical and emotional needs are being met, he or she may come to feel personally safe. Part of an environment's stability is demonstrated by consistent expectations. Teachers who firmly and gently maintain limits enhance a child's sense of certainty during this uncertain time:

"I know you're sad today, but we do need to pick up our toys before we can have a snack. Shall I help you, or do you think you can do it by yourself?"

Sometimes, teachers feel so sorry for children and what they are experiencing that they are tempted to be lax on maintaining limits. They may feel that they will help the child by lifting the burden of limits and expectations. Although this is definitely a time for being understanding, it is also a time for gently providing consistent limits.

Encourage Expression of Feelings

Teachers' knowledge of specific areas where these children need attention comes from observing and listening to them in the school setting, rather than making assumptions about problems. Because all children have unique responses to the situation depending on their temperament, support systems, and other factors, it would be unproductive for teachers to assume that all will need the same help or have similar difficulties. A teacher can guide children to work through feelings by opening up an area for discussion and understanding and accepting a child's reactions.

"It can be pretty scary not to have both your daddy and your mommy living in your house together anymore."

"Sometimes, children get pretty mad at their mom and dad when they change a lot of things in their family."

"You're going to your dad's for Thanksgiving? Sometimes, it's hard to do new things, but I'll bet you'll have fun."

Teachers who use active listening skills (discussed in Chapter 9) to listen empathetically can help children release many pent-up feelings (see Figure 14-5). This may be particularly important for school-aged children, who are often reluctant to discuss some of their sadness with either parents or peers. Some elementary schools around the country have had success with establishing support groups for children who are going through divorce to meet and discuss their problems.

© Larisa Lofitskaya/Shutterstock.com

Teachers can also provide classroom activities and materials that offer acceptable opportunities to work through feelings: clay, water and sand play, paint, family figures and props for dramatic play, and books about various family styles may help younger children. Older children may prefer to write in journals or listen to music. Reading books to individuals or small groups of children may help explore the tender topic (Mankiw & Strasser, 2013). Several dozen children's books about divorce have been published; a list of books for preschool children and beginning readers is shown in the accompanying box, Books for Children about Divorce and Stepfamilies.

Privacy and additional opportunities to be alone may help some children, especially school-aged children. Teachers may offer concrete evidence that a child is loved through touch, hugs, and smiles, but they must be careful to discern whether a child might welcome such contact and also take care that a child does not become too dependent on them.

Teachers may discover that some young children need additional help in understanding a family's changed situation; repeated, clear explanations of information supplied by the family may be appropriate. Teachers must remind parents that they need information to be able to help a child, not because they are curious. Parents will be more comfortable sharing information when teachers have previously established a caring relationship.

"Mrs. Butler, I know this is a confusing time for all of you. We find it helps children get used to changes if they get facts they can understand. If you let me know how you've explained the situation to her, I can reinforce it when she brings it up."

BOOKS FOR CHILDREN ABOUT DIVORCE AND STEPFAMILIES

Divorce

Ballard, Robin. *Gracie.*

Baum, Louis. *One More Time.*

Bienenfeld, F. *My Mom and Dad Are Getting a Divorce.*

Brown, Laurene K., & Brown, Marc. *Dinosaurs Divorce.*

Caines, J. *Daddy.*

Carney, K. *Together We'll Get Through This.*

Cofelt, N. *Fred Stays with Me.*

Forrai, M. *A Look at Divorce.*

Gardner, R. *The Boys' and Girls' Book About Divorce.*

Girard, Linda. *At Daddy's on Saturdays.*

Goff, Beth. *Where Is Daddy? The Story of a Divorce.*

Haughton, E. *Rainy Day.*

Hazen, Barbara. *Two Homes to Live In: A Child's-Eye View of Divorce.*

Kimball, G. *How to Survive Your Parents' Divorce: Kids' Advice to Kids.*

Lach, M., Loughridge, S., & Fassler, D. *My Kind of Family: A Book for Kids in Single-Parent Homes.*

Lansky, V. *It's Not Your Fault Koko Bear: A Read-Together Book for Parents and Young Children During Divorce.*

LeShan, E. *What's Going to Happen to Me?*

Lindsay, Jeanne Warren. *Do I Have a Daddy: A Story About a Single-Parent Child.*

MacGregor, C. *The Divorce Helpbook for Kids.*

Masurel, Claire. *Two Homes.*

Mayle, P. *Divorce Can Happen to the Nicest People.*

McCoy, J. *Two Old Potatoes and Me.*

McGinnis, L. *If Daddy Only Knew Me.*

Nahachewsky, T. *What Happened to My Family? A Children's Book About Divorce.*

Nightingale, L. *My Parents Still Love Me Even Though They're Getting a Divorce: An Interactive Tale for Children.*

Prestine, J. S. *Mom and Dad Break Up.*

Rodell, S. *Dear Fred.*

Rogers, F. *Let's Talk About It: Divorce.*

Sanford, D. *Please Come Home: A Child's Book About Divorce.*

Schindel, J. *Dear Daddy.*

Schwab, L. *My Dad Is Getting Married Again.*

Seuling, B. *What Kind of Family Is This? A Book About Stepfamilies.*

Sharmat, M. *Sometimes Mama and Papa Fight.*

Simon, Norma. *I Wish I Had My Father.*

Spellman, C. *Mama and Daddy Bear's Divorce.*

Spellman, C., & Parkinson, K. *When I Feel Good About Myself.*

Stern, Z., & Stern, E. *Divorce Is Not the End of the World: Zoe's and Evan's Coping Guide for Kids.*

Taylor, L. *My Whole Family.*

Venable, L. *The Not So Wicked Stepmother: A Book for Children and Adults.*

Vigna, J. *She's Not My Real Mother.*

Weitzman, E. *Let's Talk About Living in a Blended Family.*

Wilson, J. *The Suitcase Kid.*

Zornes, J. *Patchwork Family.*

Stepfamilies

Ballard, R. *When I Am a Sister.*

Bender, E. *Search for a Fawn.*

Berman, C. *What Am I Doing in a Stepfamily?*

Bowdish, L. *Living with My Stepfather Is Like Living with a Moose.*

Bunting, E. *The Memory String.*

Cook, J. *Room for a Stepdaddy.*

Helmering, D. *I Have Two Families.*

Herman, G. *Just Like Mike.*

Hoffman, M. *Boundless Grace: Sequel to Amazing Grace.*

Holub, J. *Cinderdog and the Wicked Stepcat.*

Jukes, M. *Like Jake and Me.*

Marshall, L. *What Is a Step?*

Monroe, R. *I Have a New Family Now: Understanding Blended Families.*

Park, B. *My Mother Got Married and Other Disasters.*

Parks, C. *The Beautiful Duckling.*

Rogers, F. *Let's Talk About It—Stepfamilies.*

Schwab, L. *My Dad Is Getting Married Again.*

Seuling, B. *What Kind of Family Is This? A Book About Stepfamilies.*

Taylor, L. *My Whole Family.*

Venable, L. *The Not So Wicked Stepmother: A Book for Children and Adults.*

Vigna, J. *She's Not My Real Mother.*

Weitzman, E. *Let's Talk About Living in a Blended Family.*

Wilson, J. *The Suitcase Kid.*

Zornes, J. *Patchwork Family.*

Encourage Acceptance

Teachers can guide children in accepting their changed family structure. In words and actions, teachers demonstrate their respect for each family, stressing how unique each family is. Books or pictures that show only traditional family groupings are not helpful. Teachers want to avoid activities for an entire group that make some children feel uncomfortable, such as making Father's Day cards or gifts. If this is just one of several choices planned for activity time, children can choose whether to participate. As a teacher becomes knowledgeable about family patterns, adjustments will need to be made.

Be Aware of Group Reactions

Teachers may find that other children in a group express or experience anxiety about their own parents divorcing or leaving. It is best to remind children that all families are different; that when grownups have problems, they still love and look after their children; and that they need to tell their parents what they're worried about.

14-1b Working with Parents

As teachers become aware of parents' probable emotional reactions, they will be more able to understand some puzzling behaviors.

> *"Honestly, I don't understand the woman. Every time I ask how Sam has been at home, like if he's having trouble sleeping there, too, she changes the subject. Doesn't she even care that her own son seems upset?"*

Because of their feelings of guilt and isolation, parents may be evasive or hostile when asked innocent questions about a child's daily routine. Often, parents are so preoccupied with their own concerns that they are unavailable to teachers as well as to their children. Teachers must remind themselves frequently that this does not mean they are disinterested.

When teachers are aware of parents' emotional state, they are less likely to become angry at parents' behavior and seeming indifference to their children's problems.

Reassure Parents

FIGURE 14-6
Teachers can reassure parents about the adjustment process.

Teachers who empathize and demonstrate their caring are in a position to encourage parents in helpful actions with their children. Teachers can remind parents that an open and honest discussion of adults' and children's feelings will help, as will clear statements of the facts of divorce and a new living situation. Teachers can reassure parents about the amount of time needed for families to adjust; giving information regarding the grief process and positive outcomes may help alleviate parental guilt (see Figure 14-6).

Teachers can also provide books about divorce for adults, such as those shown in the accompanying box, Suggested Books for Adults about Divorce and Remarriage. Having a lending library of such books readily available in a center is useful.

Keep Requests Light

Teachers must be especially conscious of any requests they make. Asking stressed single parents to "Bring two dozen cookies tomorrow" or "Send a new package of crayons" may be overwhelming in light of the new strains on time and budget.

SUGGESTED BOOKS FOR ADULTS ABOUT DIVORCE AND REMARRIAGE

Ahrons, C. *The Good Divorce: Keeping Your Family Together When Your Marriage Comes Apart.*

Atlas, S. L. *Single Parenting: A Practical Resource Guide.*

BelGeddes, J. *How to Parent Alone—A Guide for Single Parents.*

Benedek, E., & Brown, C. *How to Help Your Child Overcome Your Divorce.*

Berman, C. *Making It as a Stepparent.*

Beyer, R., & Winchester, K. *Speaking of Divorce: How to Talk with Your Kids and Help Them Cope.*

Bienenfeld, F. *Helping Your Child Succeed After Divorce.*

Blau, M. *Ten Keys to Successful Co-Parenting.*

Burns, C. *Stepmotherhood: How to Survive Without Feeling Frustrated, Left Out, or Wicked* (rev. ed.).

Clapp, G. *Divorce and New Beginnings: A Complete Guide to Recovery, Solo Parenting, Co-Parenting and Stepfamilies.*

Coleman, W. *What Children Need to Know When Parents Get Divorced.*

Corcoran, R. *Joint Custody with a Jerk: Raising a Child with an Uncooperative Ex.*

Dodson, F. *How to Single Parent.*

Einstein, E. *The Stepfamily: Living, Loving, Learning.*

Fischer, B. *Rebuilding: When Your Relationship Ends.*

Francke, L. *Growing Up Divorced.*

Galper, M. *Co-Parenting: A Source Book for the Separated or Divorced Family.*

Garrity, C. *Caught in the Middle: Protecting the Children of High-Conflict Divorce.*

Gold, L. *Between Love and Hate: A Guide to Civilized Divorce.*

Gould, D. *The Divorce Decisions Workbook: A Planning and Action Guide.*

Grollman, E. *Talking About Divorce: A Dialogue Between Parent and Child.*

Hart, A. *Helping Children Survive Divorce.*

Hill, G. *Divorced Father: Coping with Problems and Creating Solutions.*

Kennedy, M., & King, J. S. *The Single Parent Family: Living Happily in a Changing World.*

Klein, C. *The Single Parent Experience.*

Krementz, J. *How It Feels When Parents Divorce.*

LeShan, E. *What's Going to Happen to Me?*

Mayer, G. *The Divorced Dad Dilemma.*

Noble, J., & W. *How to Live with Other People's Children.*

Prestine, J. S. *Helping Children Understand Divorce: A Practical Resource Guide for Mom and Dad.*

Salk, L. *What Every Child Would Like Parents to Know About Divorce.*

Schneider, M., et al. *Difficult Questions Kids Ask and Are Too Afraid to Ask About Divorce.*

Sinberg, J. *Divorce Is a Grown-Up Problem: A Book About Divorce for Young Children and Their Parents.*

Teyber, E. *Helping Children Cope with Divorce* (revised and updated).

Visher, E. J. *How to Win as a Stepfamily.*

Wallerstein, J. *What About the Kids? Raising Your Children Before, During, and After Divorce.*

Weyburne, D. *What to Tell Your Kids About Your Divorce.*

Be Aware of Legal Agreements

Teachers should know the legal and informal agreements between parents regarding their children's care. It is important that teachers release children only to people who are authorized to take them. Joint custody is the newest family form, agreed to by parents and courts to soften children's loss. Many states now have an assumption of joint custody.

There are two types of joint custody. The most common form is joint legal custody, in which parents share legal rights to make major decisions for children about education, religious upbringing, medical care, sports participation, and other lifestyle issues. Joint physical custody is becoming more common, in which both parents have substantial and significant time with their children. Sometimes, children divide time between parents' houses by day, week, or month; occasionally, children remain in one place while parents move in and out. Papers regarding the legal agreements, including restraining orders, should be on file in the school office so school personnel know who can pick children up, give permission for medical treatment, and so on.

Although there is still debate about how well such arrangements work for children and families (Wallerstein, Lewis, & Blakeslee, 2000), sharing parenting responsibilities reflects the growing interchangeability of men's and women's roles in the workplace and in family life. Teachers need to be sure they are relating equally to both parents in a joint custody arrangement rather than unconsciously giving more attention or information to one. For example, both parents in a joint custody arrangement may be contacted to arrange for joint or separate parent–teacher conferences.

Both parents should be invited to class parties; it is up to parents to decide if either or both will attend.

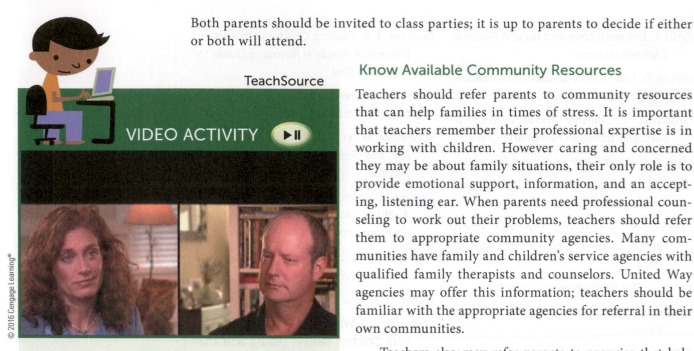

TeachSource

VIDEO ACTIVITY ▶❙❙

After viewing the video clip *Divorce and Children,* consider these questions:

1. How do the children's comments reinforce the textbook discussion of the effects of divorce on children?

2. What are the sources of challenge and stress for children?

3. What are the advantages for the children of the joint custody arrangement? For their parents?

4. How would this understanding help a teacher work effectively with this divorced family?

Know Available Community Resources

Teachers should refer parents to community resources that can help families in times of stress. It is important that teachers remember their professional expertise is in working with children. However caring and concerned they may be about family situations, their only role is to provide emotional support, information, and an accepting, listening ear. When parents need professional counseling to work out their problems, teachers should refer them to appropriate community agencies. Many communities have family and children's service agencies with qualified family therapists and counselors. United Way agencies may offer this information; teachers should be familiar with the appropriate agencies for referral in their own communities.

Teachers also may refer parents to agencies that help families in economic distress—being particularly aware of state and federal resources to suggest. During the divorce and after, family finances may be a severe source of stress.

Another helpful referral is to organizations that provide support and social opportunities for isolated parents and children. One example is Parents Without Partners, an international organization offering single-parent education and support. Many churches offer similar programs. (For more information about Parents Without Partners, see the organization's website.) Parents may also be interested in discovering if their community offers an organization of Big Brothers Big Sisters that provides opportunities for children of single parents to form relationships with interested adults to supplement possible missing relationships in a family. Recent studies show that such mentoring programs may be very helpful for school-aged children.

Teachers should be knowledgeable about the resources of their specific community and have information ready for referral if the opportunity arises. In working with families undergoing divorce, teachers need to be conscious of their own attitudes, values, and

OPPORTUNITY FOR SELF-REFLECTION

Consider any personal experiences you have had regarding divorce and stepfamilies. Identify the emotional responses of the individuals involved and how those emotions affected their behavior. Reflect on experiences you have had working with people experiencing emotional pain. How did you feel as you worked with them? What are you conscious of needing to work on to best support families experiencing divorce or remarriage?

emotional reactions. These personal aspects influence a teacher's ability to function well with parents and children and may cause a teacher to expect more problem behaviors than are really present. Truly helpful teachers do not get caught up in assigning blame or evaluating families negatively. Teachers should remind themselves that everybody is doing the best he or she can. Crisis is difficult, but it presents opportunities for change and growth.

14-1c Working with Stepfamilies

The teacher notices that whenever Pete Lawrence's stepbrothers visit for the weekend, the Monday after is a disaster. Pete is frequently whining and demanding, and his mother always looks frazzled and exhausted. And when Pete was asked to draw his family last week, he drew his mother and sister, then his stepfather, then his "other" father, and then lost interest in the project. She does not know if she should be concerned with this behavior.

About 250,000 families are "recycled" every year—created after the breakup of old families and the remarriage of one or both of the parents; one-third to one-half of these new families have children from either or both of the former marriages. Most of the remarriages occur within two to three years of the end of the first marriage, when children are still coping with the pain and loss of that first family. Such family structures can be complex: The number of possible relationships is multiplied, and the stepfamily is highly influenced by another adult or family, thus having less control over their family life. As one modern writer expressed it, "Today's stepfamily consists of you, me, your kids, my kids, our kids, your ex's, my ex's, even our ex's new mates, and all the kin of these various folks. Stepfamilies give a new meaning to the concept of complex family relationships" (Delia Ephron, in Hildebrand, Phenice, Gray, & Hines, 2007). This complexity is the source of the positive and negative aspects of a "blended" family (see Figure 14-7). The very term *blended* may be part of the problem; it suggests that, as in a melting pot, individual differences will disappear along with the existence of the previous family history—clearly impossible and undesirable. (Blended families are families that have been created by the coming together of previously existing families or parts of them; an example would be a mother and her two children from a previous marriage becoming part of a new family when the mother marries a widowed father who has three children.)

One major difficulty is that parents often feel ambiguity in their roles—unsure of when to step in or to stand back. Here, the only cultural role models offered are distinctly negative—everybody remembers Cinderella's very unattractive stepmother! Being a good stepparent is different from being a good

blended families
A family created by the coming together of previously existing families or parts of them.

FIGURE 14-7
Stepfamilies offer children a complex assortment of relationships.

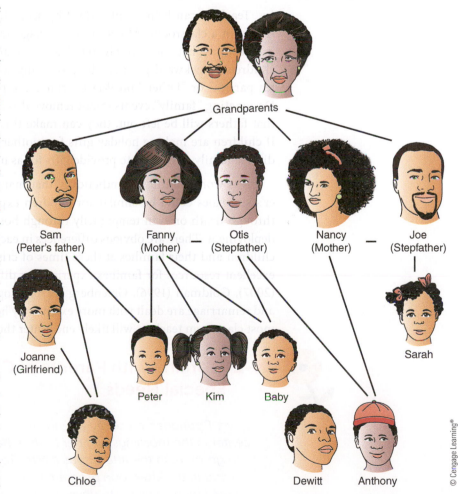

Grandparents

Sam (Peter's father) — Fanny (Mother) — Otis (Stepfather) — Nancy (Mother) — Joe (Stepfather)

Joanne (Girlfriend)

Peter — Kim — Baby

Sarah

Chloe

Dewitt — Anthony

© Cengage Learning®

biological parent, and there really is no model for this. Parents often want to make up for the upset in the original family by instantly creating a close-knit, happy family. The stakes are higher the second time around. For everyone, it becomes more important to succeed.

However, second marriages that include children from a first marriage are more prone to conflict; 60 percent of these end in divorce. Differences in child-rearing beliefs and methods, friction, conflicts with other parents, and children testing the entire situation result in a lot of stress.

Teachers may need to remind stepparents and themselves that there are also positive aspects for the children involved: They have multiple role models and an extended kin network; they may have happy parents, additional siblings, and a higher standard of living; and a new family may offer experience with conflict resolution and flexibility.

In working with stepfamilies, teachers can provide similar kinds of emotional support and information as they offer to adults and children undergoing the transition of divorce. It is helpful to reassure parents that adjustment takes time—usually years—and to provide children with a secure, stable classroom environment.

Many communities may have a local organization of the Stepfamily Association of America to offer information and support to these families. (See the website listed at the end of this chapter.)

Teachers need to be sensitive to family name differences. If John Smith is the stepfather of Billy Jones, he may not appreciate being called "Mr. Jones." Again, teachers need to learn the legalities in each family situation, including who has the right to pick up children or give permission for their care.

Teachers can help a child adjust by accepting the multitude of family styles represented in a classroom. Attention to language and the message it conveys to children is important. What does it imply to talk about "real" parents? Teachers should not put stepchildren in awkward positions by promoting activities that cause confusion. "Mothers' tea parties" or "fathers' breakfasts" can cause problems about who gets the invitation. Designating "family" events might remove this awkwardness. (If teachers are concerned that fathers will be left out, they can make this clear through personal conversations.) If children are making holiday gifts for mothers, encourage stepchildren and others in diverse family structures to provide gifts for as many people as they would like!

It is worth noting parenthetically that many of the children's reactions and teacher's strategies could be similar for children experiencing the stress of loss of a parent through death or even temporarily through hospitalization, imprisonment, or military deployment. There are obvious differences in each situation, but sensitivity to supporting children and their families at these times of crisis is necessary. See the ideas and other excellent resources for families experiencing different kinds of loss in Allen and Staley (2007), Goldman (1996), Greenberg (1996), Hopkins (2002), and Petty (2009). Divorce and remarriage are dealt with more extensively here because of the statistics showing that most classroom teachers will likely encounter those phenomena more frequently.

14-2 Working with Parents of Children with Special Needs

Sylvia Rodriguez presently attends the kindergarten run by the cerebral palsy center in the mornings, but her mother has asked the child care program if she can go there in the afternoons if Mrs. Rodriguez begins to work full time. The teacher in the afternoon program is concerned about this because she has not worked with a child with physical disabilities before.

Working with children with disabilities presents new challenges and opportunities for all, and working with their families raises particular issues. Since 1974, Head Start has been mandated by Congress to have 10 percent of its children be those who have disabilities (Community Services Act, PL 96-644). With the passing of the Education for All Handicapped Children Act of 1975 (PL 94-142), which directed that all children aged three through 18 must be given free and appropriate education in the least restrictive setting, many teachers besides those trained in special education have children with special needs included in their classrooms with typically developing children. The law has been amended and reauthorized several times, with the most recent amendments made in 2004 and the final requirements published in 2006 and 2011.

The same laws directed educators to involve parents in the development and implementation of an **Individualized Educational Plan (IEP)** for their children. Parental involvement was part of the legislated requirements from the first law, although parental roles were initially limited to attending the IEP meeting and consenting to evaluation or placement. However, when the Education for the Handicapped Act amendments of 1986 (PL 99-457) lowered the age for intervention to birth, the law also provided emphatically for significant involvement of and focus on families as essential collaborative members of the intervention team. The Individuals with Disabilities Education Act (IDEA; PL 101-576) reauthorized the Education for All Handicapped Children Act in 1990 and emphasized the concept of the family as expert in creating the **Individualized Family Service Plan (IFSP)**.

The IFSP effectively redefines the service recipient as being the family (rather than the child alone), requires explicit judgments about the family's service needs, and reconstitutes the decision-making team by mandating family representation. The more recent legislation—the amendments of 1997, PL 105-17, and the reauthorization of 2004, PL 108-446—are continuing to strengthen and clarify the intent of involving families fully in the education and decisions regarding their children with disabilities.

A written IFSP addresses not only the needs of the infant but also the strengths and needs of the family related to enhancing the development of their child. Going beyond the IEP model, where goals were often based on professionals' perceptions of the family's needs, the IFSP approach challenges professionals to develop practices that allow families to assess their own needs and encourage collaborative goal setting (see Figure 14-8).

The Individualized Family Service Plan requires the following:

1. A multidisciplinary assessment of the unique strengths and needs of the infant or toddler and identification of the services appropriate to meet such needs

2. A family-directed assessment of the resources, priorities, and concerns of the family and identification of the supports and services necessary to enhance the family's capacity to meet the developmental needs of the infant or toddler

3. A written Individualized Family Service Plan developed by a multidisciplinary team, including the family

In the IDEA amendments, there is discussion of the importance of strengthening the role of parents to ensure that families have meaningful opportunities to participate in the education of their children at school and at home. Parental participation in development of the IEP is also now required.

Individualized Educational Plan (IEP)
A written plan designed to meet the unique educational needs of a child with a disability, as mandated by the Individuals with Disabilities Education Act.

Individualized Family Service Plan (IFSP)
A written plan for providing special intervention services for children under the age of three with disabilities, which includes the family as a primary participant.

FIGURE 14-8
Current legislation includes families in assessing their strengths and needs, and encourages collaborative goal setting for their children.

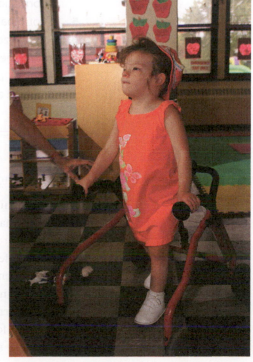

© Cengage Learning®

The reauthorization of the IDEA law from 2004 builds on the educational reforms of the NCLB Act, making public education accessible and excellent for all children with disabilities, including requirements for parental choice and academic results. Other expanded options for parents include the provision that parents, along with the local education agency, may agree to make changes to students' IEPs without having to hold a formal IEP meeting—instead developing a written document for an amendment.

Working with families of children with special needs offers particular challenges to teachers. Because it is now common for children with special needs to be included in most schools and classrooms, all teachers should prepare for working with this special group of families. Teachers and caregivers are important partners with families in the implementation of an IFSP or IEP. It is beyond the scope of this textbook to examine in detail the kinds of exceptionalities—physical, emotional, and cognitive—that teachers might encounter. Rather, that information will be learned in specific courses and reading about children with special needs. Our focus here is on understanding the common emotional responses and challenges that their families face, so teachers realize how best to communicate with and support these families.

The Council for Exceptional Children's *Special Education Professional Ethical Principles and Practice Standards for Special Education Professionals* has a section specifically on "Parents and Families."

Special education professionals:

1. Use culturally appropriate communication with parents and families that is respectful and accurately understood.
2. Actively seek and use the knowledge of parents and individuals with exceptionalities when planning, conducting, and evaluating special education services and empower them as partners in the educational process.
3. Maintain communications among parents and professionals with appropriate respect for privacy, confidentiality, and cultural diversity.
4. Promote opportunities for parent education using accurate, culturally appropriate information and professional methods.
5. Inform parents of relevant educational rights and safeguards.
6. Recognize and practice in ways that demonstrate respect for the cultural diversity within the school and community.
7. Respect professional relationships with students and parents, neither seeking any personal advantage, nor engaging in inappropriate relationships.

Copyright © 2011 by the Council for Exceptional Children.

14-2a Emotional Responses

Parents of children with developmental challenges undergo an adjustment process that is lifelong; many authors liken the complex emotional responses to the process of grieving (see Figure 14-9). The shock of learning that one's child has a disability is frequently followed by feelings of guilt—of somehow being responsible. Many parents experience feelings of denial that may take the form of searching from one professional to another—always looking for a more optimistic opinion or magical solution. Sometimes, denial takes the form of projecting blame onto others or attempting to hide the disability. Anger often follows before acceptance finally takes place. These feelings are often recycled because stages that were previously experienced reappear and influence behavior.

This may happen in response to particular events in the lives of children or their families, such as beginning a new school year or when a sibling is born. This sadness that is part of the life of families of children with special needs has been called *chronic sorrow*. But the recognition of the presence of this grief does not mean the family is maladjusted in some way. Rather, the adjustment experience suggested by Ulrich and Bauer (2003) identifies four levels, as parents become aware of the impact of their child's disability:

FIGURE 14-9
Parents of children with disabilities undergo a lifelong adjustment process.

1. The ostrich phase, which is not denying a disability but not yet fully realizing its impact

2. Special designation, where parents begin to realize their child has special needs and seek help

3. Normalization, where parents try to make the differences between their child and others without disabilities less obvious

4. Self-actualization, where parents view their child as just different while supporting and advocating for their child

Some professionals (Gallagher et al., 2002) caution that we may need to rethink the concept of denial related to families who have learned of their children's disabilities, pointing out that families process information in different ways and at different times. Families may have a range of emotional responses at various times in their lives with their exceptional children.

Although most parents of children with special needs entering school have probably been aware of their child's situation since birth, entering a classroom with children who do not have similar problems may be another reminder that the condition will always exist, necessitating constant adjustment and adaptation. Other emotions frequently experienced by parents of children with developmental challenges are frustration, guilt, ambivalence, powerlessness, and a desire to overprotect.

For many parents, the realization that their child has a disability can be a blow to their sense of self-worth. They are in difficult parenting situations, with many unknowns, and may sometimes feel less than capable. See Figure 14-10 for a mother's words that describe the unknowns as well as the growth experiences of parenting a child with a disability.

Most parents of children with special needs live with increased amounts of stress in their lives, caused by the following:

- The increasing amount of time and energy spent parenting their children—often with no respite

- The economic strain of medical expenses, therapy, and treatment

- The strain of living with complex emotions and shattered dreams

- The isolation that results as families either anticipate or experience social rejection, pity, or ridicule

- The stress of the parent-to-parent relationship—particularly endangered by the amount of time and energy spent on the child with special needs

- Managing the needs and responses of siblings without disabilities

Parents of a child with special needs find themselves trying to maintain the family's integrity as a group with its own developmental tasks while providing for the distinctive needs of their child. There is an enormous impact on family life and future family goals (Smith, Gartin, Murdick, & Hilton, 2006).

FIGURE 14-10
A mother of a child with a disability describes her parenting experience.

Welcome to Holland

I am often asked to describe the experience of raising a child with a disability—to try to help people who have not shared that unique experience to understand it and to imagine how it would feel. It's like this... .

When you're going to have a baby, it's like planning a fabulous vacation trip to Italy. You buy a bunch of guide books and make your wonderful plans. The Coliseum. The Michelangelo *David*. The gondolas in Venice. You may learn some handy phrases in Italian. It's all very exciting.

After months of eager anticipation, the day finally arrives. You pack your bags and off you go. Several hours later, the plane lands. The stewardess comes in and says, "Welcome to Holland."

"Holland?!?" you say. "What do you mean Holland?? I signed up for Italy! I'm supposed to be in Italy. All my life I've dreamed of going to Italy."

But there's been a change in the flight plan. They've landed in Holland, and there you must stay.

The important thing is that they haven't taken you to a horrible, disgusting, filthy place, full of pestilence, famine, and disease. It's just a different place.

So, you must go out and buy new guide books. And you must learn a whole new language. And you will meet a whole new group of people you would never have met. It's just a *different* place. It's slower-paced than Italy—less flashy than Italy. But after you've been there for a while and you catch your breath, you look around ... and you begin to notice that Holland has windmills ... and Holland has tulips. Holland even has Rembrandts. But everyone you know is busy coming and going from Italy ... and they're all bragging about what a wonderful time they had there. And for the rest of your life, you will say "Yes, that's where I was supposed to go. That's what I had planned."

And the pain of that will never, ever, ever go away ... because the loss of that is a very, very significant loss.

But ... if you spend your life mourning the fact that you didn't get to Italy, you may never be free to enjoy the very special, the very lovely things ... about Holland.

No parent is ever prepared for a child with special needs. There are no role models or guidelines to assist parents in modifying their child-rearing practices to match their child's special needs. Parenting is a task that can make people feel shaky under the best of circumstances; parents of children with disabilities often feel insecure in their position.

When teachers increase their awareness of these particular emotional reactions and tasks, insensitive responses can be avoided.

14.2b Parent Relations with Professionals, Teachers, and Others

Many families of children with disabilities already have an established history of relationships with professionals by the time they encounter a classroom teacher. Families of children with special needs learn to allow professionals into their lives to provide the help and knowledge they need. These families also have learned how to enter a professional's world to equip themselves to better help their child.

Some of these earlier experiences with professionals may not have been positive. Parents of children with special needs relate stories of being shuttled from one professional to another, finding a confusing lack of integration between these professional evaluations and services. Sometimes, they feel they have only been partially informed of the findings and prognosis and have not been given complete knowledge of the available resources.

The emphasis on the team approach mandated by PL 108-446 means that parents and various early intervention professionals must now function interdependently and collaboratively. The family is not disabled but has unique capacities for problem solving and coping that need to be recognized. This stance may help parents become less suspicious and hostile when interacting with professionals, including teachers.

A partnership between parents of a child with special needs and a teacher is crucial to the child's optimal functioning. Only when teachers interact with these families do they gain valuable information about the children's developmental, medical, social, and emotional history. In addition, teachers can help families obtain the skills and information necessary for directly working with their children at home. Continuity between home and school is crucial for the optimal development of a child with a disability; efforts to learn and coordinate similar techniques that can be used throughout a child's life are important.

How can a teacher work effectively with these families? Several ideas are important.

Treat Parents as Individuals

Parents of children with special needs want most to be treated as individuals. They want not to be categorized, judged, or pitied, but to be treated with dignity. Teachers who know and respond to parents as individuals show such respect. In fact, parents of children with special needs are more like the parents of typically developing children than they are different—just as children who have a disability are children first, with typical and positive aspects. Families will appreciate being accepted as individuals and as parents and will need teachers' respect for their efforts in helping their children develop to their fullest potential.

CULTURAL CONSIDERATIONS

Cultural interpretation of disability

The culture of an individual family will influence a number of attitudes about any disability, including the meaning of the disability, the family's feelings about professionals and about seeking and receiving assistance, and their attitudes about children, family roles, and interactions (Klein & Chen, 2001). All these culturally determined attitudes influence an individual family's level of acceptance of the disability and their willingness to participate in their child's care plan. As teachers come to know families, they will learn what the disability means in their particular case.

Spend a few moments reflecting on what your culture has taught you about the meaning of disability. How will this influence you in your work with children with disabilities and their families?

FIGURE 14-11
Teachers should help parents focus on the present.

© 2016 Cengage Learning®

Teachers who examine their own attitudes toward children with special needs and their parents will avoid treating them as stereotypes.

Focus on the Present and Future

Teachers must be aware of families' tendencies to project blame and feel guilty for their children's problems. Teachers should avoid discussing the past or the source of a child's disability and focus conversations and plans on the present and future—what actions can best help a child and parent now and in the future (see Figure 14-11). Focusing on the present will help families appreciate children's progress and abilities rather than dwelling on disabilities.

Clarify Information

Teachers may have to reinterpret or reinforce earlier communication from other professionals. Families need information about the disability, services, laws, and policies in order to be able to help their children. Parents who are uncomfortable with medical or educational terminology may ask a teacher to clarify the information. Teachers should remember that their function is to clarify, not comment on, the diagnosis and educational plan.

Teachers working with children included or mainstreamed into their classrooms need to communicate regularly with other members of the professional team who are planning the overall care and methods of treatment. By speaking in plain, everyday language, teachers can help demystify the professional jargon for families. Teachers can also help families as they transition from preschool to kindergarten (Fenlon, 2005). Planning the steps for this transition allows preschool and kindergarten teams to support the family through the transition. Parents of children with disabilities often have questions about how their children's special services will be provided and whether they will have the same kind of support systems they had with the preschool.

Be Hopefully Realistic

Families value teachers' realistic approaches. It is only natural to want to comfort parents with optimism, but raising false expectations is unacceptable. Teachers should offer hope and optimism whenever possible and help parents rejoice in small successes, supporting their hopes and dreams. Specific and frequent reporting to families is helpful here. Teachers should be as positive as possible, striving for realistic optimism. The schools in Reggio Emilia in northern Italy have become famous for their many excellent practices. One is for the positive way they have included children with disabilities in their classrooms. They are called "children with special rights" (Smith, 1998), signifying not a position of helplessness but rather a position deserving extra support. Surely, this is an example of hopeful and realistic viewpoints. As families are hopeful, they can set the bar of accomplishment for their children at challenging levels (Winter, 2006).

TeachSource

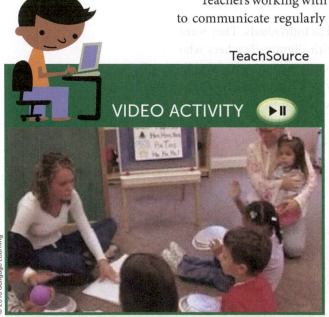

© 2016 Cengage Learning®

VIDEO ACTIVITY ▶❙❙

Watch the video entitled *Preschool: IEP and Transition Planning for a Young Child with Special Needs*. After viewing this video, reflect on these questions:

1. How does this IEP meeting support the family of a child with special needs?

2. How do teachers help the parents learn and feel comfortable about the next steps for their child?

3. What is the atmosphere at this meeting, and how do the teachers create it?

Help Families Let Go

Families must undertake the process of letting go, which is especially difficult when complicated by a desire to overprotect their children—a frequent reaction due to feelings of guilt. Teachers can have an important role in supporting parents as they try to strengthen their children to function independently. Separation and letting go are always hard, but in this case, parents may experience real conflict as they perceive children's dependence.

"I know it must feel almost cruel to have her walk into the classroom on her own—it's such hard work for her. But the light of accomplishment on her face is worth it to see, isn't it? Good for you!"

As teachers help children develop self-help skills in the classroom and encourage children's responsibility in classroom tasks, they support children's feelings of confidence in new abilities, strengthening children's willingness to venture forth on their own. (Incidentally, in classrooms with older children who may feel particular sympathy for the peer with disabilities, teachers must also help others avoid doing too much for the individual who is striving to do for him or herself.)

Increase Family Involvement in the Classroom

Recognizing that parents of children with special needs often feel isolated, teachers should provide opportunities for families to contribute meaningfully in the process of helping their children. Opportunities to observe and participate in a classroom help parents feel included as well as provide firsthand knowledge of their children's functioning and a teacher's methods of working with them (see Figure 14-12). As teachers help families devise and follow through on plans for home training, parents are able to function more effectively with their children.

Teachers must also remember that these parents already have many burdens and expectations placed on them, so it is best to encourage them to become involved in ways that fit into their lives. Teachers should open the door of obvious welcome and let families choose the best ways to respond. In the schools in Reggio Emilia previously mentioned, teachers try to help parents find some projects to help with so they can feel they are contributing to the well-being of their children and the other children.

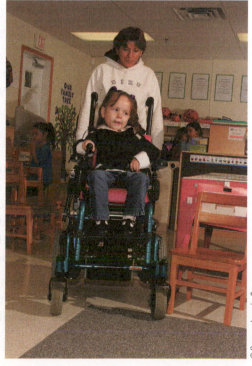

FIGURE 14-12
Opportunities to observe and participate in a classroom help parents feel included.

We want the child with special rights to become part of the classroom routines, and for their parents to see their child in a more positive and capable way and to watch the child participating with others in exciting and interesting projects. Our hope is to avoid negative comparisons and to pay attention to the particular gifts and contributions of each individual. We like the parents of children with special rights to spend time at the center so they can see how their children are making friends; and we also encourage a network among parents of special children. It is good for these parents to find mutual support and to see other viewpoints. (Soncini, in Smith, 1998)

Know Available Community Resources

Teachers must be familiar with all community resources that can be helpful to families of children with special needs. Families who do not know where to turn for assistance will need teachers' knowledge for referrals. Empowering families and supporting them as they develop the skills and knowledge needed to negotiate the system for their children are vital teacher roles. See the websites listed at the end of this chapter for helpful sources of information and support for families and others who care for children with disabilities.

Support Parental Self-Confidence

Recognizing the social and emotional isolation of many families of children with disabilities, teachers should make particular efforts to help them establish social linkages with the outside world. Introducing and involving them in work or discussion projects with other families and arranging for other parents to take the initiative in approaching them are methods for helping these parents reestablish self-confidence in relating to others. See the accompanying box, Books to Offer to Families of Children with Special Needs for suggestions of books that may help these families to realize the common threads of their experiences.

BOOKS TO OFFER TO FAMILIES OF CHILDREN WITH SPECIAL NEEDS

Fawcett, H., & Baskin, A. *More Than a Mom: Living a Balanced Life when Your Child Has Special Needs.*

Gill, B. *Changed by a Child: Companion Notes for Parents of a Child with a Disability.*

Klein, S. *You Will Dream New Dreams: Inspiring Personal Stories by Parents of Children with Disabilities.*

Lavin, J. *Special Kids Need Special Parents: A Resource for Parents of Children with Special Needs.*

Marsh, J., Ed. *From the Heart: On Being the Mother of a Child with Special Needs.*

Meyer, D., Ed. *Uncommon Fathers: Reflections on Raising a Child with Disabilities.*

Miller, N. *Nobody's Perfect: Living and Growing with Children Who Have Special Needs.*

Nasuf, R. *Special Children, Challenged Parents: The Struggles and Rewards of Raising a Child with a Disability (rev. ed.).*

Osborn, S., & Mitchell, J. *A Special Kind of Love: For Those Who Love Children with Special Needs.*

Pover, P., & Dell Orto, A. *The Resilient Family: Living with Your Child's Illness or Disability.*

Sullivan, T. *Special Parent, Special Child: Parents and Children with Disabilities Share Their Trials, Triumphs, and Hard-Won Wisdom.*

York, R. *Touching the Halo: An Emotional and Spiritual Journey of Parenting a Child with Disabilities.*

Many families of children with special needs have found that involving themselves in advocacy efforts on behalf of their own and other children with disabilities is a way of feeling more powerful and able to impact the community and educational systems. Agencies that support children with special needs and their families offer parent support groups to help parents see they are not alone. They also allow them to share and work with others with similar concerns.

Teachers who recognize the emotional reactions and needs of parents of children with special needs are best able to support and strengthen these families' abilities to function optimally for their children.

14-3 Working with Families of Infants

Another group of families with particular needs requiring consideration consists of families of infants.

"Honestly, that Mrs. Henderson! Doesn't she think I know anything at all? You should see the list of instructions she left with the baby this morning—how much to feed, when to feed, what to do if she doesn't finish it all, what it might mean when she cries. I'd be furious if it wasn't so funny."

There are often strained feelings between the caregivers of babies and their parents. The inherent tension that exists between the individualized focus of parents on the well-being of their child and the generalized focus of the program on the well-being of all children is exacerbated by the particular aspects of parental development that are at work in the parents of infants. Teachers who are working with families of infants need to consider the particular emotional responses characteristic of the first stages of parenting. Caregivers also must remind themselves how relatively recent is the phenomenon of many mothers having to leave their babies in someone else's care. In 1950, it was so rare to have mothers of babies working that the Labor Department did not keep statistics on it! Currently, about 35 percent of mothers have returned to work by the time their babies are two months old. More than half are back at work by the infants' first birthdays (Cohany & Sok, 2007). (See Figure 14-13.)

FIGURE 14-13
More than half of all infants have mothers who are back at work before their first birthday, leaving them in the care of others.

© Cengage Learning®

14-3a Reactions of Parents of Infants

The important process of attachment in the first two years of a baby's life is mutual; adults are becoming attached to their babies just as babies are becoming attached to the adults who care for them. Attachment is an enduring process that is cognitive and emotional and is supported by interaction and information involving the senses. When baby and parent are attached, not only do they care for each other deeply, but they also feel more secure and comfortable in each other's presence. This feeling of a special close relationship with the baby is crucial to the beginning parent–child relationship and the optimal development of the baby. But this is also the cause for parents' possessive feelings toward their babies. They do not want to be away from them for too long and are convinced that their babies are not safe with anyone else. For example, this is the reason that mothers leave long, explicit lists of directions that a caregiver may find insulting to his or her intelligence, or demand exactly detailed accounts of every minute of the babies' days away from them. It may help caregivers if they can respect parental anxiety as flowing positively from the attachment process. It is important to realize that parents are always anxious about putting their infants into substitute care. There are usually other emotions involved, too. Most new parents feel guilty or at best ambivalent about leaving their babies for someone else to care for, fearing that the babies might not continue to love them if someone else is caring for them.

WHAT DOES BRAIN RESEARCH TELL US ABOUT ATTACHMENT?

The periods just before birth and just after are crucial periods for brain development. There is an initial overproduction of synapses, the neural connections necessary for brain activity. Synapse creation and elimination are powerfully affected by the infant's experiences. After repeated stimulation, the synapse is strengthened and stabilized. With lack of stimulation, synapses are eliminated. Circuits that process basic information are wired earlier; the development of higher-level capabilities is more difficult if lower-level circuits are not wired properly—hence the importance of the first years in brain development.

Researchers now agree that the infant brain is plastic, designed to be molded by the environment it encounters. Nurturing relationships are central to infant experiences. When the nurturing and responsive relationships of attachment are not provided, elevated levels of stress hormones impair cell growth and interfere with the formation of healthy neural circuits. The early maturing right brain, which is dominant during the first three years of life, is involved in processing social-emotional information, facilitating attachment, and regulating physical and emotional states. "It could be suggested that a responsive nurturing environment that allows the infant and young child to develop strong attachments to a limited number of caregivers enables the child to build neural pathways that encourage emotional stability." In other words, when a baby is held or hugged, brain networks are activated and strengthened; when the baby hears language or lullabies, still other pathways are stimulated. The experiences that lead to attachment also develop the infant brain (Malekpour, 2007). A securely attached infant is able to explore the world to gain still more experiences and stimulation. Thus, it can be seen that attachment and brain development are linked in a circular pattern where each influences the other.

1. Consider how the ideas about infant brain development would specifically influence you in your specific arrangements in an infant program.
2. Describe how the connection between infant brain development and attachment will influence your interaction with families of infants.

Attachment leads adults to engage in what Dr. Berry Brazelton calls "gate keeping"—strategies to keep rival adults distant from the adored infant (Sparrow & Brazelton, 2007). Caregivers and parents all want to do well for the child, but it can end up as a contest of who is best able to nurture or know the child. Jealous competition is not necessary. All the adults are striving for the same end: the child's optimal development. This is a sign that strong bonds are forming with the child; although it can create stress, it is a good sign. This happens within families as well as with outside caregivers.

Within the family, gatekeeping may look like Mom saying to Dad, "Don't lay him down like that. He likes to have his blanket tucked in tightly. Here, I'll do it."

With the caregiver, a gatekeeping mother might say, "Well, she doesn't have any trouble sleeping at home on the weekends when I settle her down."

A gatekeeping caregiver might say, "If you'd just burp her like I do, halfway through her feeding, you'd see that she won't spit up."

Any infant caregiver knows that you do not have to be a parent to become strongly attached to babies, so it is not surprising that tension between parents and teachers in an infant room may be present (see Figure 14-14). What parent and caregiver need to understand is that warm, attentive caregiving is necessary to support the development of attachment, and it is that caregiving that should be the focus, not how much is supplied by whom. Parents and caregivers will be more comfortable with strong child–caregiver attachments if they understand that children can love many people. The child–caregiver relationship will not diminish the connection with parents, which cannot be duplicated in its duration and intensity (Baker & Manfredi/Petitt, 2004). Parents and caregivers who value each other's efforts can move past competition for the sake of the baby.

FIGURE 14-14
When all the adults caring for a baby are strongly attached, tension and rivalry may develop.

Another factor to consider is that new parents are often anxious and tentative as they approach the unfamiliar tasks and decisions of caring for an infant. Very rapidly, they have experienced pregnancy, birth, and parenting, and integrating these experiences is an important developmental task for parents.

Often, they are unsure of how they measure up to the expected standards in their new role. The confident behaviors of a very experienced caregiver may increase the parents' feelings of incompetence by contrast.

developmental task
Appropriate accomplishments at specific stages of development.

Many life adjustments are necessitated by adding a baby to a household:

- New demands on time and money

- Disruptions in the marital relationship and the smooth-running household and careers

- Physical exhaustion from attending to a baby's needs 24 hours a day

- Stress of returning to work outside the home

The parent of an infant is often emotionally and physically stretched with the stress of the new lifestyle and roles.

Brazelton feels that many new parents are in deep emotional trouble due to having to share their babies with others too soon in the development of the parenting relationship. He predicts two possible courses of action for these parents. One is to protect themselves from forming attachments because it will hurt too much to care; the second is to grieve. Grieving, he claims, may be manifested by blaming, anger, guilt, or helplessness, which may lead to the distortions in behavior that infant room staffs see. Child care providers, then, have a special responsibility to help new parents so they will have an opportunity to move into attachment.

> I would press for one more set of stipulations on day care for infants: that the care include nurturing of mothers. Unless a mother is included in the planning for her baby, she will feel shoved out and useless at a time when it is critical that she continue to feel important to him. If she is left out, she is likely to grieve about losing him and may begin to detach at an unconscious level in order to defend herself from her feelings about having to share him. This will make her raw and competitive with his caregivers. (Brazelton, 1992)

14-3b Adolescent Mothers of Infants

The emotional reactions and changes in life roles are different but equally momentous in adolescent mothers. Just imagine the complexity of dealing with the added role of becoming a responsible parent when still reeling with the identity issues of adolescence. The developmental tasks of adolescence and parenthood can easily conflict with each other, meaning that a teenage mother will often compromise one role or fail at both.

CULTURAL CONSIDERATION

When the infant's parents do not speak english

Consider the stress of a parent who speaks a language other than English leaving her infant in a child care center. She knows her baby will be surrounded by unfamiliar sounds and people, and when she returns to pick up the child, her lack of English will make it difficult for her to get information about the baby's day. A child care program can ease this stress for the family in several ways:

- Present a welcoming first impression, using pictures and signs in different languages.
- Learn a few words in the family's language, or send home a list of key words and ask the parents to record them in their home language, such as hello, up, down, change, diaper, clean, juice, bottle, more, hurt, mommy, daddy (Nemeth & Erdosi, 2012).
- Ask parents for familiar objects and music from home for the baby's environment at the center.
- Provide digital pictures of the baby's day.
- Create a message board with key phrases in English and the family's home language, so teachers and parents can point to items for communication.
- Be creative. Find community resources, and online or app resources for translation and communication.
- Welcome volunteers (family members or community helpers) to spend time with the infant.

The usual self-absorption of adolescence means that it may be difficult for these mothers to distinguish the baby's needs from their own. Their expectations of typical child development are often unrealistic, as is their expectation of what the baby can offer them. It is difficult for many adolescent mothers to be patient and nurturing with their children because they need nurturing themselves. Adolescent mothers have to cope with changed relationships with their own parents. Conflict is often increased by their need to rely on their parents for help with the infant's care and for help with their own financial and emotional needs while they need to establish a separate identity as an individual and a parent. There may be strained feelings between the adolescent and her parents related to the early pregnancy. Often, adolescent mothers are emotionally isolated: They are separated from the lives and interests of their peers who are not parents but perhaps still living in the high school world after leaving their infants at the child care center. The majority of adolescent mothers today do not marry the fathers of their infants. Depending on the relationships they have with the fathers of their children, these mothers may also be trying to establish relationships of parenting with other people, who may or may not be willing to accept such responsibility. Assistance is important because teen mothers have multiple risk factors for the future healthy development of their babies, including poverty and lack of education and social supports (White, Graham, & Bradford, 2007).

The sheer number of identity issues precipitated by the arrival of the baby may mean that an adolescent parent is emotionally unavailable to the child care provider, who may be seen as yet another interfering adult. While needing assistance and information to care for the baby, a young mother may resist attempts of caregivers to communicate with her, wanting to prove her independence and entry into the adult role of parent. Some adolescent mothers find it easier to withdraw from their responsibility and are too willing to become dependent on the provider (or their parents), allowing them to take too much responsibility for their infant's care. Either alternative is not likely to be healthy for the formation of an attachment between the adolescent parent and infant, nor for the growth of positive parenting skills. Caregivers who work effectively with adolescent mothers actu-

FIGURE 14-15
Infant caregivers working with adolescent mothers support the dual development of mother and baby.

ally support the dual development of mother and infant and will be challenged to find the right combination of caring relationship and professional support for optimal development of this young family (De Jong, 2003) (see Figure 14-15). It is important to focus on the most positive aspects of the situation, which include the motivation, resilience, and responsiveness of young parents (White et al., 2007).

© 2016 Cengage Learning®

14-3c Teacher Relationships with Families of Infants

Recognizing the emotional responses and needs of new parents, caregivers can do several things to form effective partnerships with these parents. Generally, it is developmentally appropriate to focus on parents and baby as a unit. Helpful infant programs have a **family-centered** approach, recognizing the infant and the family as one unit of care, with the need for child care personnel "to support, respect, encourage, and enhance the strengths and competence of the family" (Sandall, in McMullen & Apple, 2012, p. 44).

Support the Attachment Process

Competition over the children can be transferred into concern for the parents' degree of attachment to their children. Teachers can make sure that infant room practices facilitate the attachment process. The function of good infant child care is to support a family's developmental needs, and attachment is the primary need of infants and parents. Caregivers should be given specialized knowledge about the attachment process and should celebrate the attachment between children and parents (see Bowlby, 1988; Karen, 1994).

Parents should feel welcome to drop in whenever they can (see Figure 14-16). Many parents of infants will come and feed their babies during lunch hours or other free times during a day if they feel welcomed. Mothers who want to nurse or offer a bottle should be provided with comfortable chairs and as much privacy for one-on-one time with their babies as they would like. No matter what a caregiver's personal feelings are about breast-feeding or bottle-feeding, the caregiver's positive attitudes can be very important in supporting a mother's ability to continue to nurse even while her infant is in child care (Perez, 2011). This is not an intrusion into an infant room routine but an important time for parent and baby. The physical environment makes a statement of welcome; creating a parent corner right in the baby room, with soft chairs and an array of helpful books and pamphlets, conveys a warm message that parents are welcome to stay. It is also very important that caregivers and administrators offer clear welcoming messages to fathers in the infant room rather than ignoring them or including them in only a special and artificial role—rather than in the natural role of a parent learning attachment roles and

family-centered
Focusing on children and parents as a unit, with the parents becoming active in their children's development—not relating separately to parents and children.

FIGURE 14-16
Parents should feel welcome to drop in whenever they can.

behaviors. Support both parents in developing rituals that provide meaningful connections between babies and adults (Gillespie & Peterson, 2012).

If parents feel that routines and regulations are not separating them from their babies, they will feel less possessive in their relationships with a caregiver and reassured that their babies' care is satisfactory.

Standardize Informational Procedures

An important responsibility is to enable families to share their information and thus build their feelings of competence in parenting. When parents can share specific knowledge of their infants, they can help create an individualized care plan and be involved in all decisions made about their child. Procedures for passing information back and forth between parent and caregiver must be standardized and clear. Programs keep a written record of such daily occurrences as feedings, naps, diaper changes, activities, and behavior as well as recording developmental progress. They offer parents additional forms and a chance to record information that can help a caregiver, such as the last feeding time, amount of sleep, unusual behavior, or home routine. Keeping this individual form conveniently located—perhaps on top of a baby's cubby—makes its use routine for all adults. When parents are convinced that an infant room staff wants to share with them fully and that the information they offer as parents is important to their baby's day, feelings of anxiety and rivalry often decrease (see Figure 14-17).

TeachSource Digital Download

FIGURE 14-17
Sample information sheet for families to complete.

All about Me

My name is _____.

I like to be called _____.

My birthday is _____.

My parents' names are _____.

In case of emergency, call _____ _____.

I like to sleep on my side, tummy, back. (Circle one.)

I have/don't have a special blanket.

I have/don't have a pacifier.

I like to eat every _____ hours.

I am allergic to _____.

I am afraid of _____.

When I cry, it helps me if you _____ _____.

My favorite thing to do is _____.

I want you to know _____ _____

_____.

Remain Objective

Caregivers of infants need to be conscious of their own feelings toward the infants in their care. This relationship is warm and nurturing on a caregiver's part but brief—probably lasting only through the months of infancy. What these babies most need from a caregiver is support warmly offered to a total family unit as baby and parents work through the process of attachment. The family is at the center of things, with child care being just one satellite of the services the family has chosen to use. There is no place in this relationship for caregivers who disapprove of the decisions parents have made or who think how much better a job they do for a baby than his or her own anxious, inexperienced parents. Parents are the primary people in an infant's life. With connotations of rivalry among adults, a baby will suffer. It is important for caregivers to examine their feelings about authority so they can become sensitive to ways of sharing power without abdicating their role. Loving caregivers realize that the best way they can help infants is to support their parents' growth.

Introduce New Parenting Techniques

Teachers of infants should offer information and ideas to new parents. During their infants' first year, first-time parents are most open to learning basic parenting behaviors that have a lasting effect on themselves and their children. As their relationship develops, teachers should have frequent conversations in which it is appropriate to introduce ideas and answer questions subtly. At the same time, teachers must guard against overt behaviors that suggest parental incompetence contrasted with professional expert knowledge. A teacher in an infant room educates gently—as a friend.

> *"Wow, we should really have a celebration today. When I noticed how hard it was for her to say goodbye to you this morning, I realized this was the first time she's done that. That crying when you leave is a good sign that she loves you very much—that all your hard work these past few months has paid off and that she's become attached to you. This is a very special day."*

Sometimes, the meaningful communication can be done lightly by "talking through the baby."

> *"Tell Mom how you like it when she wraps you up so securely."*

> *"It does make you feel good to see Mommy come back, doesn't it? See how she gets all your best smiles!"*

Pamphlets, books, articles, websites, and parenting magazines should be made available for parents who prefer to get their information through printed matter and the Internet.

　　As an increasing number of infants are cared for by other adults outside their homes, their teachers will have important opportunities to support families and act as resources at this crucial point in their lives. Indeed, by establishing the pattern of sharing care rather than handing a child over to the professionals to be educated, infant caregivers can begin the precedent of reducing the distance and formality often found in school encounters and establishing partnerships.

TeachSource

VIDEO ACTIVITY

© 2016 Cengage Learning®

After watching the video clip *A Parent's Viewpoint: Parent-Teacher Communication,* consider these questions:

1. How does this parent of an infant view her relationship with the teacher?

2. What is the kind of communication that this parent wants with teachers? Why is this so important to her?

3. How would these ideas affect your practice?

Cultural Considerations

Culture influences parenting decisions

As teachers educate, they should also be sensitive to the fact that ideas about parenting are born from cultural contexts, and some practices they would like to introduce may be quite alien or even unacceptable to parents from other cultures (Day & Parlakian, 2004; Im, Parlakian, & Sanchez, 2007). It is important for teachers to hear parents' viewpoints as well as learn their child-rearing philosophies rather than focus solely on information they want to impart. Teachers who are open to communicating with culturally diverse families will come to understand that best practices are not universal but are influenced by the family's cultural beliefs. All of us learn child rearing by watching our own parents and absorbing culturally driven ideas about acceptable behavior for parents in a particular culture. Thus, it is important to avoid thinking that some parenting practices are "right" and others "wrong." Culture teaches us how to parent. For an example of this, see the interesting discussion of differences in beliefs about infant sleep habits in Bhavnagri and Gonzalez-Mena (1997) and the more detailed discussions of ethnopediatrics in Small (2002).

Try writing down three things you believe that parents should do in their care of infants and then compare your list with another person. What does this show you about cultural differences in ideas about child rearing?

14-4 Working with Families When Abuse Occurs

Every time Dorothy Scott reads an article in the paper about child abuse and neglect, she shudders. "What kind of parents could do a thing like that?" she wonders. "Thank goodness we'll never have that problem in our school—not with our kind of parents."

Many teachers believe that in their communities, with their particular populations, they will never have to face this problem. But this is simply not so. Child abuse occurs in every segment of society, among families who look just like everyone else. In fact, it is likely that one in four teachers experienced abuse themselves as children or know someone well who is a survivor of abuse.

Although reporting of cases seems to have improved in recent years due to more public information and awareness, it is still difficult to quote reliable statistics on occurrences of abuse and neglect. The most recent statistics on abuse and neglect indicate a continuing trend to decrease over the past 10 years.

The website of the National Children's Alliance states that reports of abuse or neglect were made on more than three and a half million children nationally in 2011. Experts believe that real figures are probably at least three times greater. Of these cases, about 60 percent of the children are victims of neglect, about 20 percent are victims of physical abuse, 10 percent have suffered sexual abuse, 7 percent emotional abuse—certainly the most difficult to prove—and the remainder a combination. In the case of neglect and physical abuse, nearly 84 percent of the children were abused by their parents, stepparents, or unmarried partners of their parents.

Experts are not yet in agreement whether children who are not abused themselves but are in homes where family violence occurs should be considered maltreated (Edelson,

2001), although many child protection agencies already treat childhood exposure to domestic violence as a form of maltreatment that should be reported, investigated, and result in state intervention. Certainly, in many children, exposure to domestic violence is associated with behavioral, emotional, and cognitive problems that may last at least into young adulthood. Thus, teachers should be aware that many children exposed to domestic violence will themselves need sensitive responsiveness (see Figure 14-18).

It is therefore inevitable that classroom teachers will encounter abuse and neglect and their effects on families. Teachers must understand the dynamics of abusive or violent families and the indicators that suggest a problem may exist, as well as the legal obligations and possibilities for helping a child and her family. Perhaps even more important, teachers must be aware of their own emotional responses to the idea of abuse so they will be able to act in professional and helpful ways with the children and families involved, rather than merely react with personal emotion. Of the reports of suspected abuse and neglect, professionals made nearly three-quarters, with a majority of these reports made by educators and child care personnel. It is vital that educators perceive that they have several roles in relation to child abuse. These roles include a role of primary prevention—as they model positive child guidance and ways to enhance positive self-esteem in children and as they support parents by lending an empathetic ear and providing resources to develop positive parenting skills (Seibel & Gillespie, 2006). Caregivers play a role in secondary prevention when they identify suspected child abuse and report it to the appropriate child protection agency for investigation. They also play a tertiary role in child abuse prevention as they support children and parents when child abuse has been confirmed.

FIGURE 14-18
Schools can raise awareness of the effects on children of domestic violence.

© Kentoh/Shutterstock.com

The Child Abuse Prevention and Treatment Act as amended and reauthorized under the title Keeping Children and Families Safe Act of 2003 (PL 108-36) defines abuse and neglect as "any recent act or failure to act on the part of a parent or caretaker which results in death, any serious physical or emotional harm, sexual abuse or exploitation; or an act or failure to act, which presents an imminent risk of serious harm."

Physical abuse includes the deliberate hurting and inflicting of injuries on children—often becoming more severe over time. Emotional abuse is more difficult to prove, lacking the more obvious evidence of physical injury. Emotional abuse includes all acts of omission or commission that result in an absence of a nurturing environment for a child, resulting in damage to a child's sense of self. It should be obvious that emotional abuse will also accompany any other form of abuse or neglect because the explicit and implicit message is always of the child's lack of worth. Sexual abuse may include any involvement of children in sexual activities for the gratification of the offender, including sexual contact and exploitation of children for pornographic purposes. Neglect occurs when adults do not provide for the physical, emotional, and social needs that are necessary for healthy growth and development (Crosson-Tower, 2009).

NAEYC has issued a position statement on prevention of child abuse in early childhood programs and the responsibilities of early childhood professionals to prevent child abuse (NAEYC, 1997). Adults who are entrusted with the care of children are responsible for their well-being. When this well-being is at risk, the law enables others to intervene on a child's behalf. In this discussion, we focus on the professional's role in working with families to prevent, report, and change patterns of abuse.

What forces cause parents to abuse their children? Many different factors or components in the environment may come together and interact. These include social, educational, cultural, economic, religious, family, and individual circumstances and ideas. Specifically, these factors may include the following:

- The examples of adult control absorbed in their own childhoods
- The cultural messages of the individual community about the responsibilities and styles of "good parents"
- The lack of child development knowledge and skills
- Religious teaching that children are inherently evil and must be broken in spirit
- The isolation of a family that has moved too many times to develop supports

FIGURE 14-19
Parents who were themselves abused can break the cycle of abuse with education and support.

© Denizo71/Shutterstock.com

- A rigid and demanding personality in a parent or a difficult child

Abuse is insidious, continuing in the fabric of families for generations; abused children frequently become abusive adults or the victims of other abusers later in their lives. Abuse is an infection coloring the feelings and attitudes of families, and it destroys normal relationships for the entire family (Barbour, Barbour, & Scully, 2004).

Although it is true that about one-third of children who were abused become abusive parents themselves, it is also true that many children who were abused can, with conscious effort, support, and education, become excellent parents who move beyond abuse and offer positive examples of nonviolent guidance to their own children (see Figure 14-19).

14-4a Precipitating Circumstances

In most cases, the personality potentials for parent and child are present, but a crisis event usually takes place before a parent loses control and abuse occurs.

Often, a family undergoes too much change too fast, with no time to recover before being hit by a new crisis. The crisis may be *economic*—loss of a job, financial problems; it may be *personal*—desertion by a spouse or other marital problems, death of a family member, or other transitional events; it may be the *perception* that a child needs extraordinarily strong discipline; it may be *environmental*—a move, substance abuse, inadequate housing, the washing machine breaking down. Whatever it is, however remote from the child, this event is the last straw, and a parent loses control. Because these circumstances know no socioeconomic or cultural barrier, abusive situations are found in every stratum of society.

14-4b Indicators of Abuse and Neglect

Physical Abuse

There are four general groups of injuries that may result from physical abuse (Crosson-Tower, 2009). These include injuries to the skin and soft undertissues, including bruises, abrasions, bites, and burns; injuries to the skeletal system from direct blows or from shaking or squeezing;

injuries to the head and central nervous system from being shaken or choked; or internal injuries from being punched, kicked, or thrown. Teachers might see such signs as the following:

Physical Indicators of Physical Abuse

- Unexplained bruises or welts, especially in places where a child's physical activity cannot account for them: on the face, throat, upper arms, buttocks, thighs, backs of knees, or lower back
- Bilateral marks or those with unusual patterns that suggest the use of an instrument (belt buckle or electrical cord)
- Unexplained small burns as might be made by match or cigarette, especially on palms, soles of feet, abdomen, or buttocks
- Immersion burns, producing marks like socks or gloves on feet or hands or a doughnut-shaped burn on buttocks
- Rope burns
- Infected burns, indicating a delay in treatment

Behavioral Indicators of Physical Abuse

- Wearing inappropriate clothing to cover physical indicators
- Inappropriate, excessive fear of parent or caretaker
- Unbelievable, inconsistent explanations for injuries
- Unusual shyness and wariness of physical contact
- Extremes of behavior—withdrawal, aggression, regression, depression
- Infants lie unusually still while surveying surroundings

Sexual Abuse

Physical Indicators of Sexual Abuse

- Stained or bloody underwear
- Difficulty sitting or walking
- Frequent unexplained sore throats or yeast or urinary infections
- Somatic complaints, including pain and irritation of genitals
- Sexually transmitted diseases or pregnancy

Behavioral Indicators of Sexual Abuse

- Disclosure
- Regressive behavior, such as thumb sucking, wetting, fear of dark
- Disturbed sleep patterns and recurring nightmares
- Unusual or age-inappropriate interest in sexual matters
- Avoidance of undressing or perhaps wearing extra layers of clothing
- Sudden decrease in school performance or truancy
- Promiscuity or seductive behavior

Emotional Abuse

Physical Indicators of Emotional Abuse

- Eating disorders—obesity or anorexia

- Speech disorders—stuttering or stammering
- Developmental delays in speech or motor skills
- Weight or height substantially below norm
- Nervous disorders—rashes, hives, tics, stomachaches
- Flat or bald spots on head (not necessarily conclusive regarding infants because these often appear in infants placed on backs to sleep)

Behavioral Indicators of Emotional Abuse

- Habit disorders—biting, rocking, head banging
- Cruel behaviors—taking apparent pleasure in hurting animals, children, adults
- Age-inappropriate behaviors—wetting or soiling
- Behavioral extremes—listless/excitable, overly compliant/defiant

Neglect

Physical Indicators of Neglect

- Poor hygiene, including lice, scabies, severe diaper rash, body odor
- Squinting
- Clothing unsuitable for weather or missing key items of clothing
- Untreated injury or illness
- Lack of immunizations
- Height and weight significantly below age norms

Behavioral Indicators of Neglect

- Unusual school attendance and absenteeism
- Chronic hunger, tiredness, lethargy
- Begging for food
- Report of no caretaker at home

Abuse and neglect may include any or all of these indicators and are not limited to these. Remember that in all instances, teachers must be aware of the complete situation and all circumstances, not relying only on appearance of a symptom that may well have a different explanation.

14-4c The Teacher's Role

When a teacher suspects abuse or neglect in a family situation, several courses of action are indicated.

Gather Information

Information gathering and clarifying should occur continually as teachers try to determine if there is cause for concern. Teachers can ask for explanations of injuries or appearances, neutrally inquiring, "What happened to your knee?" or "What did the doctor say about the bruises?" so the child or parent may explain the situation without being put on the defensive. Parental responses may either support teacher suspicions or resolve the question. The administrator should have an opportunity to observe the concerning injury or behavior.

OPPORTUNITY FOR SELF-REFLECTION

Child abuse is an emotionally charged topic. When you hear those words, what is your initial emotional response? What thoughts and images occur to you?

List some words that come to mind when you think of a parent abusing a child; let them flow freely from your mind and pen. Now look at what you have written down; consider how these feelings and attitudes will support or hinder your work with abusive families. What do you need to do to be able to perform at your professional best?

Document Evidence

When teachers become aware of possible abuse and neglect, they must document what they see. Such records indicate patterns for teachers and administrators and may determine their next actions. Documentation is to substantiate any suspicions with recorded evidence and is useful to an investigator. Many schools will have their own forms for such documentation. Otherwise, simple, objective descriptions are all that is required, including the child's full name, the date when the information was recorded, and the date when the observation occurred. Also include the verbatim conversations held with the child or the parent. If concerns are removed after clarification with the family, documentation may be the only step to take at this time.

November 18. Two large bruises, on each upper arm, including distinct finger marks.

December 3. Bright red welts on backs of legs. Child reports father was very angry previous night.

TeachSource Digital Download

IDEAS FOR TEACHERS:

Questions Teachers Can Ask Themselves

- Does the child have a low threshold for frustration, crying over tiny difficulties?
- Does the child's mood shift abruptly without apparent reason?
- Do the parents appear to be hiding something? Do they deny or minimize any observable injuries or give explanations that do not seem plausible?
- Does the child appear withdrawn or depressed or have difficulty making friends?
- Does the child threaten or bully to get his or her way? Is the child timid, passive, or fearful with peers?
- Is the child apprehensive about going home? Does the child express a wish that you were his or her parent?
- Does the child appear sleepy or lethargic at school?
- Does the child frequently have stomachaches or headaches?
- Does the child seem preoccupied or startle easily?

Report to Proper Agencies

Laws in all states and provinces mandate teachers to report cases of suspected abuse and similarly obligate child care workers in most areas. Teachers should check their local regulations for current laws and the appropriate protective agency to which to report. In addition to the mandate of law, the NAEYC Code of Ethical Conduct (2005) clearly states obligations for early childhood professionals. Under the section regarding ethical responsibilities to children, the following principles are directly related:

P-1.5 We shall be familiar with the symptoms of child abuse, including physical, sexual, verbal, and emotional abuse, and neglect. We shall know and follow state laws and community procedures that protect children against abuse and neglect.

P-1.6 When we have reasonable cause to suspect child abuse or neglect, we shall report it to the appropriate community agency and follow up to ensure that appropriate action has been taken. When appropriate, parents or guardians will be informed that the referral has been made.

P-1.7 When another person tells us of a suspicion that a child is being abused or neglected, we shall assist that person in taking appropriate action to protect the child.

P-1.8 When a child protective agency fails to provide adequate protection for abused or neglected children, we acknowledge a collective ethical responsibility to work toward improvement of these services.

In reporting, the burden of proof is not on teachers but on the protective services agency to whom teachers must report; if a report of suspected abuse or neglect is made in good faith (for example, contrasted with the malicious intention of a parent who is trying to discredit another in a custody battle), the reporting adult is protected from liability.

There are instances of teachers and schools who try to ignore the problems they suspect or see in families—perhaps fearing reprisals or parents' anger if they involve themselves in "family matters." Teachers need to accept their responsibility as perhaps the only people who know what is going on with some children and their families and as the only outside advocates a child might have. Teachers need to realize their own legal and moral responsibilities even if they discover their school's policies discourage such active advocacy roles. The Code of Ethics makes it absolutely clear that early childhood professionals have a definite responsibility to act to protect children and that this responsibility takes precedence over other responsibilities to employers or families (P1.1, Code of Ethics):

> Above all, we shall not harm children. We shall not participate in practices that are disrespectful, degrading, dangerous, exploitative, intimidating, psychologically damaging, or physically harmful to children. **This principle has precedence over all others in this Code.**

When reports are made, they should include the child's and parents' full names and addresses; the child's age, sex, and birth date; the name and address of the person making the report; and the name, address, and telephone number of the child care center. Professionals should realize that less attention is usually paid to anonymous reports, according to some overworked caseworkers.

Examine Personal Attitudes

Teachers need to examine their own attitudes to be able to work with these families. Many teachers feel great anger toward parents who hurt their small children or expose them to adult violence. It is important to recognize the existence of this anger and to work especially hard to get to know parents and the circumstances of their parenting in order to develop true empathy for their situations. It is more appropriate for teachers to release some of their negative feelings in conversation with colleagues rather than with parents because parents are themselves in need of nurturing and acceptance, not expressions of anger (see Figure 14-20).

© Cengage Learning®

FIGURE 14-20
It is more appropriate for teachers to release some of their feelings to colleagues than to parents.

However, it is important to remember that confidential material or statements that have not yet been confirmed must be treated with the utmost care and professional responsibility for privacy. A family's reputation could be damaged by thoughtless comments or casual display of papers.

Create an Atmosphere of Trust and Healing

Teachers' concern and caring for children in these troubled families enable them to support children through difficult times. It helps these children to know teachers care for them, are dependable and trustworthy, and are concerned enough to help them and their parents. Such an atmosphere of trust may free children to confide their problems and allow them to feel confident in the ability of other adults to help them and their parents. Children need allies in the classroom who can help them express their anger safely. Play is a vehicle that helps build trust as teachers accept the children's self-expression. These children do not need to hear condemnation of their angry feelings or of their parents, who are the most important people in their lives, no matter how troubled they are at this time.

Teachers can also comfort themselves in the knowledge that they are providing an important model for children, helping them to realize that not all adults are abusive. All this is true whether the children have been abused themselves or have witnessed abuse and violence directed toward someone they love. Children who have been exposed to violence or neglect have experienced a world in which important adults have not guaranteed their safety and well-being. Coming daily to a classroom with different adults who provide a safe and predictable environment can help them experience security. Classroom teachers need to realize the importance of unvarying routines and gentle limits in helping these children make sense of their world and make the classroom an emotionally safe place. Teachers need to be careful to alert these children to any changes in the class schedule and discuss any new or different procedures and prepare them for the presence of new people in the classroom. Teachers should maintain calm and cheerful voices.

Just as young children are particularly vulnerable to the effects of abuse and neglect—even to the alteration of brain development—so, too, are they capable of **resilience** and healing in supportive environments. They need the support and reassurance of caring adults and tools and activities to allow them to transform their memories of fear and helplessness, choosing symbolic ways to control the ways the adults in their memories act and talk. Healing activities may include imaginative play, art and creative activities, or literary experiences. A number of children's books can help children identify with others' pain and give them hope for the future. See the accompanying box, Books to Read with Children about Abuse and Violence in the Family. The adult's role is not to be that of a play or art therapist; the children are themselves capable of processing their own grief, anger, and fears in a supportive environment. (See Figure 14-21.)

resilience
Ability to spring back, adjust, or adapt to stress, misfortune, or change.

FIGURE 14-21

Helpful Behaviors for Teachers Who Become Aware of Abuse

- Remain calm and reassuring.

- Listen without judgment, paying close attention.

- Speak with children privately, positioning yourself at eye level.

- Take the child seriously.

- Allow the child to have feelings.

- Reassure the child that the abuse is not the child's fault.

- Refrain from asking "why" questions.

- Do not condemn the abuser.

- Assure the child that he or she is not alone.

- Tell the truth, and do not make promises you cannot keep.

- Inform the child of the process that must be followed to help keep him or her safe.

- Let the child know you are going to help.

Adapted from Austin, 2000

BOOKS TO READ WITH CHILDREN ABOUT ABUSE AND VIOLENCE IN THE FAMILY

Al-Anon Family Group. *What's Drunk Mama?*

Bass, E., et al. *I Like You to Make Jokes with Me, but I Don't Want You to Touch Me.*

Behm, B. *Tears of Joy.*

Bernstein, S. *A Family That Fights.*

Boyd, C., & Cooper, F. *Daddy, Daddy, Be There.*

Caines, J. *Chilly Stomach.*

Carrick, C. *Banana Beer.*

Cavaciuti, S. *Someone Hurt Me.*

Clifton, L. *One of the Problems of Everett Anderson.*

Davis, D. *Something Is Wrong at My House.*

DiGiovanni, K. *My House Is Different.*

Geisen, C., and Alley, R. *My Body Is Special: A Family Book About Sexual Abuse.*

Girard, L. *My Body Is Private.*

Havelin, K. *Child Abuse: Why Do My Parents Hit Me?*

Hornbum, T. *Hear My Roar: A Story of Family Violence.*

Jessie. Please *Tell! A Child's Story about Sexual Abuse.*

Katz, I., et al. *Sarah.*

Kehoe, P. *Something Happened and I'm Scared to Tell: A Book for Young Victims of Abuse.*

Klassen, H. *I Don't Want to Go to Justin's House Anymore.*

Kleven, S. *The Right Touch: A Read Aloud Story to Help Prevent Child Sexual Abuse.*

McAndrew, L. *Little Flower: A Story for Children.*

Otto, M. *Never, No Matter What.*

Paris, S. *Mommy and Daddy Are Fighting.*

Porett, J. *When I Was Little Like You.*

Sanford, D. *I Know the World's Worst Secret: A Child's Book about Living with an Alcoholic Parent.*

Spelman, C. *Your Body Belongs to You.*

Stanek, M. *Don't Hurt Me, Mama.*

Vigna, J. *I Wish Daddy Didn't Drink So Much.*

Williams, C. *The True Colors of Caitlynne Jackson.*

Winn, C., & Walsh, D. *Clover's Secret.*

Woodson, J. *Our Gracie Aunt.*

Teachers can support children's progress in self-healing activities by posing open-ended questions, such as the following:

- "What happens next?"

- "I wonder what the baby would like to have happen differently?"

- "What makes your dolly happy?"

Healing activities are not used to get information for reports. Rather, they are opportunities for children to process painful memories and experiences in a supportive and caring classroom environment.

Refer Families to Support Groups

Many communities offer agencies and groups to support families under stress. If teachers know about these community resources, they can refer parents on a preventive basis or reassure them after a court's referral. There are agencies that offer support to families in the form of therapy, a 24-hour stress telephone line staffed by trained volunteers, and reparenting education for parents who have abused. One method found to be effective is to give families a "parent aide"—a parent trained in counseling skills who makes home visits and models positive and appropriate ways to interact with children.

In recent years, courts have tended to be less punitive with parents and have concentrated on efforts to help families learn alternative methods of discipline and appropriate expectations. Teachers can wholeheartedly support such efforts. There are benefits for an entire family when families learn new methods of parenting.

Support for these efforts can also come from families who have experienced similar problems. Many communities have a local group of the national Parents Anonymous organization, whose members are formerly abusive parents who meet to encourage each other in their attempts to change their behavior. For more information about this organization, see the website listed at the end of this chapter.

14-4d Working with Substance-Abusing Families and Their Children

Related to the topic of abuse and neglect is the topic of substance abuse in the adults of a family. In fact, an estimated 40 to 80 percent of the families who become cases with child protective services have problems with alcohol or drugs (Child Welfare League of America, 2004). Children in homes where substances are abused are three times as likely to be abused and four times as likely to be neglected as in homes without substance abuse. When parents are addicted to alcohol or other drugs, it means that they are more concerned about obtaining drugs than caring for their children. When parents abuse drugs and alcohol, their children are in an emotionally neglectful environment and are at risk for physical neglect and abuse.

WHAT DOES BRAIN RESEARCH TELL US ABOUT ABUSE AND NEGLECT?

Neurophysiological measurements and brain imaging techniques have shown that considerable changes in brain structure and function are associated with both traumatic abuse and severe neglect. The specific effects of maltreatment depend on factors such as age of the child at the time of abuse or neglect; whether the maltreatment was brief or chronic; the identity of the abuser (i.e., parent or other adult); type and severity of the abuse; and the intervention (Child Welfare Information Gateway, 2009).

Physical abuse can cause direct damage to a baby's or child's developing brain. Malnutrition, both before birth and during the child's first years, can result in stunted brain growth and slower passage of electrical signals in the brain. This is due to the negative effect of malnutrition on the myelination process in the developing brain.

Chronic stimulation of the brain's fear response means that the areas of the brain involved in this response are frequently activated, and other regions, such as those involved in complex thought and abstract reasoning, are less frequently activated. Research on children who suffered early emotional abuse or severe deprivation shows an alteration in the brain's ability to use serotonin, the neurochemical that helps produce feelings of well-being and emotional stability. Global neglect (deprivations in more than one domain, such as language, touch, or interaction with others) leads to significantly smaller brains, due to decreased brain growth, resulting in fewer neuron pathways available for learning. Clearly, decreasing incidents of child abuse and neglect is important for healthy brain development.

1. How would you use this information to inform the community about the connection between brain development and abuse and neglect. What media could you use?
2. Why is understanding brain research a vital part of information to be given to new parents, as well as a preventive factor? Who else besides parents should have this information?

Early childhood professionals can help these families. For parents trying to recover from addiction, it is important that caregivers understand the nature of addiction and the lifetime recovery process. While other professionals will work with the parents on the specifics of their addiction, caregivers can also be involved in a caring, therapeutic type of relationship, nurturing the parent because of concern for the child. When they suspect substance abuse may be a family problem, caregivers must turn to supervisors and other community resources, recognizing the limits of their roles and expertise. Caregivers can learn about referral sources for substance abuse treatment programs in the community and post information about Alcoholics Anonymous and other recovery meeting groups.

With the children of these families, teachers can make a difference in providing an emotionally safe environment that children can learn to trust. They help when they provide daily routines, consistency, and firm boundaries in a world where children can count on little and may have taken on too much responsibility for themselves. Teachers can provide materials and opportunities for therapeutic play, as in art expression and sensitive dramatic play. They can acknowledge children's feelings so children learn to express the emotions they have kept pent up. They may read books about children in families with substance abuse and other sensitive issues—perhaps helping children to tell their own stories to an understanding adult; a list of books appropriate for reading privately with a child affected by abuse or violence is found earlier in this chapter. Above all, teachers must recognize the need to support the whole family during a difficult journey. The reality is that child abuse and neglect, family violence, and substance abuse are problems many teachers will encounter. The best scenario is for teachers to be able to recognize signs of distress and problems, to know their legal and moral obligations and their community resources, and to support families through the agonizing process of evaluation and reconstruction. Building a caring relationship with families is the best gift a teacher can give to an abused child.

14-5 Working with Adoptive Families

As we have discussed throughout this book, every family is unique in its situation, history, and structure. Adoptive families are created by legal agreement, not by biological ties. Parents frequently receive little notice when a child is available for adoption—often after long waiting periods and even longer preceding periods of attempting to conceive a child. Adoptive families are diverse in many ways (Hunt, 2003). Adoptive families are often multiracial, with the rate of transracial adoption doubling in recent years to more than 15 percent. International adoption has seen enormous growth in the same period, with nearly half a million in 2012 (Department of State, 2013) (see Figure 14-22). Single-parent adoption is also on the rise, accounting for about one-third of all adoptions, and many gay and lesbian adoptions are included in that number. Adoptions from foster care have risen—often initiated by black or Latino parents as well as by parents who are not affluent. And stepchild adoptions are common across racial groups and socioeconomic classes. Sometimes, older children who are adopted into families have already experienced such difficulties as death of parents, abuse, neglect, abandonment, or leaving a home or country. Such circumstances create adjustment difficulties for children and their adoptive parents. Although they are a minority of families in a classroom, these families deserve sensitive and supportive responses from classroom teachers.

What are some things that classroom teachers can do?

14-5a Know the Facts

Teachers and administrators need to support parents in the information they have given to their children. "Thinkers and leaders in the field of adoption teach that the more openness and education there is about adoption issues, the better off everyone will be" (Greenberg, 2001). Schools generally need to explain that they are as open with children about adoption as about the myriad other different situations in which children live and may have questions about. Nevertheless, they must be sensitive to information that individual families consider private.

FIGURE 14-22
International adoptions create many new families.

Admission information forms need to have a place to include adoption information about an adopted child or siblings that may be adopted. Teachers must also be sure to find out whether the child knows this, how questions have been answered at home, and whether people in the community are aware of information that the child is not aware of. Greenberg suggests making the comment, "I'd love to hear how you've been telling Annie her adoption story." This is obviously a sensitive area that some parents may be reluctant to answer; teachers must explain to parents their need for information to be sure they are supporting children's comfort and also not lying to children.

© Jaren Jai Wicklund/Shutterstock.com

Most experts believe that adopted children should know they are adopted—given as much of their story as is appropriate for their age and told in a way that is respectful of them, their biological parents, and their adoptive parents. Teachers may have had personal experience with adoption through their own family backgrounds and may need to focus on their own comfort level before helping children explain their circumstances to other children and adults.

14-5b Include Adoption in the Curriculum

When such topics as babies, family trees, types of families, and family resemblance arise in the early childhood classroom, teachers need to include adoption as a concept for children to understand—whether or not there are adopted children in the classroom. The school's task is to normalize children's thinking about the many different kinds of families that exist by promoting discussion and activities that allow children to experience the diversity in family structure and appearance. The accompanying box, Books for Children about Adoption, can help children understand that all children deserve parents who can look after them, and that there can be both joy and pain in adoption. Contemporary books focus on honest, sensitive approaches that look at children's and adults' feelings.

BOOKS FOR CHILDREN ABOUT ADOPTION

Acres, K. *Little Miss Ladybug and Her Magical Red Thread.*

Banish, R., & Jordan-Wong, J. *A Forever Family.*

Bunin, Catherine and Sherry. *Is That Your Sister?*

Burwash, L. *All about Me: Adopted and Special; An Interactive Tool for Parents and Children.*

Carson, N. *My Family Is Forever.*

Cole, J. *How I Was Adopted: Samantha's Story.*

Cosby, E. *A Is for Adopted.*

Curtis, J. L. *Tell Me Again: About the Night I Was Born.*

D'Antonio, N. *Our Baby From China: An Adoption Story.*

Henderson, P. *A Blessing From Above.*

Joose, B. *Nikolai, the Only Bear.*

Kasza, K. *A Mother for Choco.*

Katz, K. *Over the Moon: An Adoption Tale.*

Keller, H. *Horace.*

King, M. *Mutt Dog.*

Koehler, P. *The Day We Met You.*

Kroll, V. *Beginnings: How Families Come to Be.*

Lewis, R. *I Love You Like Crazycakes.*

Lifton, B. *Tell Me a Real Adoption Story.*

Livingston, C. *Why Was I Adopted?*

London, J. *A Koala for Katie: An Adoption Story.*

McCutcheon, J. *Happy Adoption Day.*

Miller, K. *Did My First Mother Love Me?*

Mora, P. *Pablo's Tree.*

Nystrom, C. *Mario's Big Question.*

Patterson, E. *Twice-Upon-a-Time: Born and Adopted.*

Peacock, C. *Mommy Far, Mommy Near: An Adoption Story.*

Rogers, F. *Adoption.*

Rosenberg, L. *We Wanted You.*

Schwartz, P. *Carolyn's Story: A Book About an Adopted Girl.*

Shemin, C. *Families Are Forever*

Sobol, H. *We Don't Look Like Our Mom and Dad.*

Stanley, D. *The Mulberry Bird: An Adoption Story.*

Stinson, K. *Steven's Baseball Mitt: A Book about Being Adopted.*

Turner, A. *Through the Moon and Stars and Night Skies.*

Urbanovic, J. *Duck at the Door*

Wright, Susan. *Real Sisters.*

Zisk, M. *The Best Single Mom in the World: How I Was Adopted.*

See also Miles, Susan G. *Adoption Literature for Children and Young Adults: An Annotated Bibliography.* New York: Greenwood Press, 1991.

Teachers should be aware that some adopted children will not necessarily have photos of themselves as babies and plan accordingly when using family materials in curricula. The once common assignment in elementary schools of creating family trees or interviewing grandparents for information about family heritage can give way to choices for all students, such as Circles of Caring as a more flexible way of tracing family relationships (Hunt, 2003). This activity accommodates variety in all families, not just adoptive families, by putting the child's name in the center of the page rather than the traditional format that assumes one father and one mother in each generation. This allows the tree to connect all the important people to the child, allowing room for diverse family formats, including birth parents (or not).

Some parents whose children are adopted from other countries or cultures may welcome the opportunity to include their children's native cultures in classroom activities. These experiences expand children's thinking about the complex subject of families. Again, teachers should make no assumptions, but explore this topic with each family.

14-5c Talking to Families

Heightening their awareness of parental feelings regarding adoption may help teachers prevent insensitive communication. These parents cannot have their relationship to their children affirmed by appearance: "Your son is certainly the image of his dad." Instead, their relationship must be affirmed in less concrete ways: "The baby really watches you." "Your son really enjoys spending time with you."

Talking about "real" parents is insulting to adoptive families who *are* real parents. Instead, where necessary, teachers can refer to "birth" or "biological" parents and "forever" parents—all of whom are real.

Many adoptive families have limited information about their children's backgrounds or their lives before adoption. Teachers should make it clear that they welcome any information parents can give them but that they are focusing on helping the child and family in the current adjustment. Parents may understandably feel sad or even guilty that there are gaps in their knowledge of the child. In many of the adjustments that occur in families after adoption, parents may feel frightened, worried, angry, and stressed in the new situation. Teachers can help best by providing a supportive listening ear.

As newly adoptive parents are getting to know their children day by day, teachers can assist by sharing objective observations and specific information about what the child is like while under their care. Often, newly adopted children may show great problems with separation. Having already perhaps experienced the loss of significant adults, they may understandably be less than trusting when they see their new adults depart. Families are often very reluctant to cause their children additional pain and will need teacher support through the difficult adjustment process. Help parents understand that their predictable leaving and return will eventually help the children learn to trust again. Parents and children will need particular attention while working on this task.

14-5d Talking with Children

Teachers should be emotionally and cognitively prepared to answer questions from children who have not been adopted as well as from adopted children. Children might have several questions:

- Why do families give up their children?
- Will it happen to me?
- Will it happen again?
- Why do I not look like my parents?
- What was so bad about me that my mother did not want me?
- Why did her real mother not want her?
- Why is his skin a different color than his mom and dad's?

Knowing that questions can create doubt about self and identity for adopted children if not answered helpfully, teachers can be very supportive here, talking acceptingly and matter-of-factly about these issues. Phrases and responses that teachers might use include the following:

- "Being adopted means Lena had another mother before, but her first mommy couldn't take care of her, so Mrs. Peters is Lena's mommy now."
- "Children need to have families who can look after them."
- "Real parents are the ones who feed you and put you to bed and take you places and live with you while you grow up."
- "Grownups sometimes aren't able to take care of their babies, so they make a plan to find a family to love and take care of the baby."

14-5e Offer Resources

Knowledgeable teachers can assist family adjustment by providing books for parents such as those in the accompanying box, Books to Suggest to Families about Adoption, as well as information about support groups and opportunities to meet with mental health professionals experienced with adoption issues. The websites listed at the end of this chapter may provide additional information for teachers and families.

BOOKS TO SUGGEST TO FAMILIES ABOUT ADOPTION

Anderson, R. *Second Choice: Growing Up Adopted.*

Bartholdt, E. *Family Bonds: Adoption and the Politics of Parenting.*

Berg, Barbara. *Nothing to Cry About.*

Brodzinsky, D., Schecter, M., & Henig, R. *Being Adopted: The Lifelong Search for Self.*

Canape, C. Adoption: *Parenthood Without Pregnancy.*

Chase, M. *Waiting for Baby.*

Gilman, L. *The Adoption Resource Book.*

Hormann, E. *After the Adoption.*

Jewett, C. *Adopting the Older Child.*

Keck, G., & Kupecky, R. *Adopting the Hurt Child: Hope for Families with Special Needs.*

Melina, L. *Making Sense of Adoption: A Parent's Guide.*

Melina, L., & Rosia, S. *The Open Adoption Experience.*

Plumez, J. *Successful Adoption.*

Siegel, S. *Parenting Your Adopted Child.*

Tukas, M. *To Love a Child: A Complete Guide to Adoption.*

Watkins, M. *Talking with Young Children About Adoption.*

Wirth, E., & Worden, J. *How to Adopt a Child From Another Country.*

SUMMARY

Teachers often work with families whose circumstances require new sensitivities in understanding the dynamics and emotional responses of parents and children in each situation in order to provide understanding and support.

These include:

- Families going through divorce or remarriage, where children and parents may need opportunities to express emotion and other helpful teacher responses.

- Families raising children with special needs, who may have particular stresses and lifelong emotional adjustments.

- Families of infants, including adolescent mothers, who are learning new roles and adjusting to sharing the care of their infants.

- Families where abuse and neglect are issues. Here, teachers must know indicators and the laws, and respond professionally.

- Families created by adoption, each of whom has individual needs, depending on circumstances and ages of children.

Teachers must also incorporate classroom behaviors that can help children, as well as skills and knowledge to support parents. With sensitive and professional responses, teachers will be able to help the families who need them most.

Student Activities for Further Study

1. Investigate and gather referral information and brochures on any agencies that exist in your community to:

- Assist or support parents and children undergoing separation and divorce, such as counseling services, Parents Without Partners, Big Brothers and Big Sisters, and the like.

- Assist parents and their children with special needs or help in the identification and early intervention process.

- Offer support to new parents.

- Assist, treat, and support families in abusive or violent situations.

- Support adoptive families.

If there are many such agencies, it is useful for each class member to visit one to gather information and report back to the class.

2. Find the state law that defines the legal responsibilities for professionals and para-professionals in schools and child care programs in your state regarding reporting abuse and neglect. Learn about your local reporting agency. It is helpful to invite a representative of that agency to visit your class.

3. Investigate your library resources for parents and children with special needs. Compile a list of these to have available for parents.

4. If children with special needs are included in classrooms in your community, plan a visit to these classrooms or to any specialized schools. Learn what their parent involvement policies and practices are.

5. Role-play and discuss the following situations:

    a. You are concerned by a six-year-old's aggression and regression in your classroom. The father moved out of the home two months ago. You want to discuss the child's behavior with his mother.

    b. A mother wants to tell you all about how terribly she and the children were treated by her ex-husband.

    c. A child in a recent divorce situation seems totally withdrawn and sad. What is your conversation with the child?

    d. A child tells you, "He's not my real daddy. He just married my mother. I hate him." What is your response?

    e. A child tells you, "My dad hit my mom hard. He scares me when he's so mean to us." What is your response?

    f. A child has been observed in explicit sexual activity (not exploration). You want to discuss this with the parent.

    g. A mother of a child with cerebral palsy says, "The doctors say she'll never walk or talk right, but she seems so much better in your class. What do you think?" What is your response?

    h. A mother of an infant says, "My mother visited this weekend and says for me not to pick the baby up so much—just to let him cry—so you shouldn't, either." What is your response?

    i. A mother of a seven-year-old who was adopted as an infant requests that you not mention the adoption to other children and parents in the classroom. What is your response?

Apply the Chapter Concepts: Case in Point

In question 5 under Student Activities for Further Study, you will find nine scenarios based on our cross section of families and others who are experiencing the situations discussed in this chapter. Choose several, and for each, consider the following questions:

1. What are the primary emotions that seem to be at work in the individuals described in the scenario?

2. What are several helpful teacher responses in this scenario? Also, consider any that would be less helpful, and identify why that is the case.

3. Identify classroom activities and materials that teachers should consider providing for children from these families.

Review Questions

1. List several behaviors in children and parents associated with the stress of divorce or remarriage and discuss ways teachers can help children and parents experiencing divorce or remarriage.

2. Identify three possible emotional responses of parents of children with special needs, and describe four ways teachers can work effectively with parents of children with special needs.

3. Discuss typical responses of families of infants, and identify three helpful behaviors for infant caregivers.

4. List two factors that can create abusive situations—any six indicators of abuse and neglect—and identify three responsibilities of teachers in situations involving abuse and neglect.

5. Describe ways teachers can support adoptive families.

Helpful Websites

Divorce and Remarriage

- Kidsturn is a nonprofit organization to help kids and parents through divorce. Their website offers information about workshops and other resources for families.

- Parent Education and Custody Effectiveness (P.E.A.C.E.) is sponsored by the American Bar Association, Family Law Section. The P.E.A.C.E. program is an educational program designed to provide information to parents about the divorce and separation process, hoping this will result in improved parent–child relationships after divorce and a reduction in the number of contested custody, visitation, and support disputes that now face our courts.

- The National Family Resiliency Center (formerly Children of Separation and Divorce Center) (NFRC) is committed to helping children and adults preserve a sense of family, foster healthy relationships, and constructively adjust to change, especially during times of separation, divorce, and other family transitions.

- Parents Without Partners has a website that explains the resources offered by the international organization that focuses on single parents and their children.

Stepfamilies

- The Stepfamily Foundation's mission is to assist in making the family as it is now work.

- The Stepfamily Association of America is a national nonprofit membership organization dedicated to successful stepfamily living. This website provides educational information and resources for anyone interested in stepfamilies and their issues.

- Stepfamily Information. This nonprofit, research-based educational site exists to help co-parents (bioparents and stepparents) build high-nurturance relationships and families with a free online self-improvement course.

Families of Children with Special Needs

- Support for Families of Children with Disabilities has a website that organizes a variety of Internet resources for families of children with disabilities: 1. Getting started; 2. The laws; 3. Parent sites; 4. Specific disabilities; 5. Education; 6. Health; 7. Mental health; 8. Transition to adulthood; and 9. Espanol.

- The worldwide mission of the Council for Exceptional Children (CEC) is to improve educational outcomes for individuals with exceptionalities.

- Family Voices. This website is for parents and caregivers of children with special needs.

- Federation for Children with Special Needs (FCSN) is a center for parents and parent organizations to work together on behalf of children with special needs and their families. FCSN is a coalition of parent groups representing children with a variety of disabilities, offering a variety of services to parents, parent groups, and others who are concerned with children with special needs.

- The mission of the Parent Advocacy Coalition for Education Rights (PACER) Center is to expand opportunities and enhance the quality of life of children and young adults with disabilities and their families based on the concept of parents helping parents.

Families with Infants

- Resources for Infant Educators (RIE), Magda Gerber's organization, is a nonprofit group that has developed and is teaching a unique philosophy and methodology in working with infants. Get information at their website.

- Dr. Berry Brazelton's organization, Touchpoints Center (BTC), offers training at the Child Development Unit, Children's Hospital, Boston. BTC training, based on the work of Dr. T. Berry Brazelton, combines relationship building and child development into a framework that professionals can use to enhance their work with families.

- The website for Zero to Three has much information for parents and professionals on the first three years of life.

Abuse and Neglect

- Prevent Child Abuse America (PCA) advocates for the existence of a national policy framework and strategy for children and families while promoting evidence-based practices that prevent abuse and neglect from ever occurring.

- Healthy Families America (HFA), a national program of Prevent Child Abuse America, has three goals: to promote positive parenting; to encourage child health and development; and to prevent child abuse and neglect.

- The National Council on Child Abuse and Family Violence provides information for public awareness and education.

- The mission of the International Society for Prevention of Child Abuse and Neglect is to support individuals and organizations working to protect children from abuse and neglect worldwide.

- The mission of the Family Violence Prevention Fund is to prevent violence against women and children within the home and community and to help those whose lives have been touched by violence.

- The mission of Parents Anonymous is to seek to prevent child abuse by offering programs where parents and children learn new behaviors and create positive changes in their lives.

Adoptive Families

- The Evan B. Donaldson Adoption Institute is a national organization devoted to improving adoption policy and practice and providing resources for educators.

- The website has information about the National Adoption Information Clearinghouse, from Children's Bureau, Administration on Children, Youth, and Families, contains information to connect professionals and concerned citizens with research and statistics to create permanent families.

- The mission of the Adoption Institute is to enhance the understanding of adoption by educating the public, including educators, about adoption.

CHAPTER 15

Working to Resolve Challenging Attitudes and Behaviors

© Cengage Learning®

Learning Objectives

After reading this chapter, you should be able to:

15-1 Discuss reasons for hostile reactions and considerations in dealing with them.

15-2 Discuss reasons for apparent indifference and considerations in overcoming it.

15-3 Discuss overly involved parents and ways of handling them.

15-4 Discuss several frequent causes of parent–teacher tension and ways of dealing with them.

Related NAEYC Standards

Accreditation Standards (see inside text back cover for full listing of the Accreditation Standards for exemplary early childhood programs)

7.A.01; 7.C.04; 3.F.03

Licensure Standards (see inside text front cover for full listing of the Licensure Standards for this chapter)

2b

Human nature being what it is, teachers occasionally find themselves working with families whose attitudes and behaviors are difficult to deal with, no matter how positive the teacher's attempts have been. Obviously, it is easier to work with some families, particularly those whose values and life experiences are similar to the teacher's. Stress or personality may cause some parents to display responses that range from belligerence to indifference, and either extreme is quite daunting to work with. In addition, any classroom teacher can tell you that particular situations with parents arise regularly enough to become sources of chronic irritation. Such encounters may be so discouraging or threatening that teachers retreat from future efforts to work with families. But when this happens, children's well-being will suffer, so it is important that teachers develop skills and strategies to help counter the negatives.

Contemporary teachers comment that many of today's parents are particularly challenging, exhibiting the following characteristics:

- Less respectful of authority (as are their children)

- More educated and consumer oriented

- Often cynical and distrustful

- Under more stress and feeling guilty about their parenting roles

- Worried that schools will fail to help their children achieve in today's competitive society (Waterman, 2006)

In this chapter, we will consider reasons for parents' challenging behaviors and strategies for handling them. This does not suggest that there are magical solutions to these difficulties. Rather, there are teacher and school responses that may get the teacher through the immediate encounter and policies or procedures that may prevent recurrences. Perhaps most important is the teacher's belief that a partnership with families is important enough to keep on trying.

pedagogical issues
Issues related to teaching.

As professionals, teachers have the responsibility to keep working toward effective relationships with parents, even under difficult conditions. Perhaps the most difficult circumstances arise when teachers and families view a situation quite differently. These differences may center on **pedagogical issues**.

Examples of pedagogical issues might be the following:

- Families who refuse to let their children be tested, despite evidence to warrant it, or who refuse special educational services

- Families who want to push academic work before a teacher believes the children are ready

- Families who do not follow through with their children's homework or projects

- Families who disagree about methods used to discipline their children

- Families who insist that teachers prohibit their sons from playing dress up

Parent–teacher differences may also center on parent behaviors that conflict with teachers' responsibilities for the whole group. These might include the following:

- Families who urge their children to "fight back," knowing it is against school rules

- Families who gossip or make unfavorable comments about other children in the group

Other predicaments for teachers sometimes arise from parent behaviors perceived to put children at risk. Examples of this might be the following:

- A child using foul language that has evidently been heard at home

- An immature child for whom a teacher has concerns about parental "smother love" and overprotection

- A perfectionist parent who makes a child do and redo homework until the child is in tears

- A parent who has failed to show up for several appointments with a teacher to discuss a child's inattention and declining achievement in school

Yet another predicament that often faces teachers is the need to communicate negative information to a parent about a child's behavior, development, or progress at school. This might be the following:

- A child is not ready for the next grade, and retention is recommended.

- A child is extremely aggressive toward other children.

 Add to any of these circumstances the factor of diverse cultural interpretations of a situation, or language limitations that prevent real communication, and we can appreciate the complexity for any teacher.

These situations and causes of strained communication may sound familiar to most teachers. Teachers and families feel extremely uncomfortable coming together to discuss issues such as these. But all of them demand getting past the feelings of discomfort so real communication and problem solving can take place. Too often, teachers facing these situations tend to avoid communication until the problems have escalated to a crisis stage.

CULTURAL CONSIDERATIONS

Problem or cultural context?

Teachers need to open their minds to the idea that what they see as harmful may not be when considered in the context of the culture of the family. Examples of this might include early toilet training or putting infants to sleep on their stomachs, despite the professional's concern about SIDS. In such situations, the key for caregivers is not to jump to immediate judgment but to seek to understand more about the reasoning behind the practice and the total picture. If professionals move to the place where they accept that their ideas are not the only right ones, they can understand a situation in context and learn whether practices are truly harmful. For example, a professional who learns from the family that the stomach-sleeping infant never sleeps alone learns that in that cultural context, SIDS may be less of a risk. In addition, teachers can articulate the information and reasons behind the alternate practices of the school, and from such dialogue, a compromise may develop.

Can you think of a similar situation where families and professionals might have different culturally driven interpretations of appropriate child-rearing practices? Is there a way that both viewpoints could be reconciled?

How does a teacher proceed? A helpful stance is to ask questions, to wonder together with families (Whiteman, 2013). This approach honors parents' knowledge of their children, and puts the teacher and parents on an equal footing. In general, as a teacher contemplates potentially difficult situations, it is important to do certain things:

- Analyze a situation critically from teachers' and parents' viewpoints.

- Change from arguing and persuading to having a dialogue (Gonzalez-Mena, 2010).

- Define the issue clearly, focusing on mutual interests.

- Break a problem into its component parts to see how each person perceives a situation.

- Attempt to find mutually acceptable solutions, based on objective criteria (Fisher et al., 2011).

In some cases, there may be no solution to the vast differences in perspective or emotional response of teacher and parent, and it is left only to agree that there is disagreement, and respect the differences. In other instances, a careful analysis of the dynamics and facts of a situation may help the parties find common ground on which to work together—a win-win solution. Teachers must realize that dealing with attitudes and values is a long, slow process. There are no instant solutions or successes. An understanding of human growth and development, not just child development, is necessary for a teacher working with a variety of adults at different stages of their unique lives. It is too easy for teachers to force parents into a lose-lose situation where any outcome is a loss because the teacher or school has all the power. If parents become defensive and feel that teachers are criticizing them, teachers and parents will suffer from the breakdown in communication. If families feel they are being forced into compliance and acceptance of the teacher's viewpoint, they may become silenced, and teachers will lose the valuable perspective of the parents' knowledge, creating a lose-lose situation. Careful analysis of the conflict from the perspectives of all participants may help teachers move toward professional actions and mutually acceptable solutions—more of a win-win situation.

See the Critical Analysis form in Figure 15-1 for a tool that teachers could use to consider predicaments in teacher–parent relationships.

15-1 Hostility

In a recent conference, Ted Sawyer angrily burst out at the teacher. "My son has never had this problem before with his other teacher. If you ask me, there's something wrong with a teacher who can't get a child to obey her. Don't tell me he needs limits! I think your principal should watch you more carefully!"

As a teacher responds to this attack, it is important to consider several points.

15-1a Hostility as a Mask

Teachers need to realize that not everything that seems like hostility is really so. Sometimes, parents are motivated by genuine concern for their children, and questioning the practices or evaluation of another is a form of healthy self-assertion. The intensity of concern may be expressed in voices that sound angry. Individuals who are not used to being assertive may go too far and appear aggressive instead. Sometimes, parents who feel powerless attempt to grab power inappropriately.

Another emotion that may be masked by hostility is the grief parents feel when realizing that their child has a developmental problem or disability (see Chapter 14). When teachers realize that parents may be overwhelmed and extremely upset by teachers'

FIGURE 15-1
The Critical Analysis Form is useful when reflecting on teacher–parent conflicts.

Critical Analysis Form for Predicaments in Teacher–Parent Relationships

Parent's Perspective

How does the parent describe the problem?

How does the parent seem to feel about the problem?

What do you think the parent expects the teacher to do about the problem?

If the teacher did this, what might be the result?

Teacher's Perspective

How does the teacher describe the problem?

How does the teacher feel about the problem?

What does the teacher expect the parent to do about the problem?

If the parent did this, what might be the result?

Child's Perspective

How might the child see the problem?

How does the child feel about the problem?

If the problem is not resolved, how might this affect the child?

If the problem is resolved, how would that affect the child?

Overall Perspective

What is known about the problem?

What knowledge is applicable?

What principles of ethical behavior are involved?

What are possible solutions?

reports or interpretations, they will realize that parents' defensive reactions are more a method of coping with anxiety and less an attempt to stop the process of getting help for their children.

When teachers directly or indirectly assign blame for a problem, parents may understandably react in hostile ways. Blame ought not to be the focus of any conversation; finding solutions depends on a stance of we versus the problem. Also, parents who feel inadequate or guilty about their effectiveness as parents may strongly resist teachers' comments. It is essential that a teacher think about a parent's emotional position before automatically labeling a response as hostile.

True hostility appears as an individual reacts with anger when dealing with a person seen to be in authority. A hostile person is defensive and suspicious, assumes that others have unfriendly intentions, and therefore feels impelled to strike the first blow. Such hostile reactions often indicate a carryover of childhood attitudes or earlier experiences with authority.

15-1b Hostility Inhibits Communication

When parents are verbally abusive or irrationally angry, it is impossible to communicate effectively. It is a teacher's task to defuse the anger so communication can begin (Jaksec, 2004).

Remain Calm

To be able to work through the parent's anger, it is vital that a teacher remain calm in every way, separating the professional's feelings from those of the parent. Teachers need to avoid being caught up in parents' strong emotions while making an effort to understand what is behind the feelings. Being attacked by an angry parent triggers emotional responses in teachers, including feelings of frustration, fear, helplessness, and anger. Although actual physical danger from angry parents is rare, the verbal abuse is itself unsettling for a teacher to receive. Nevertheless, the teacher's response is critical. It is important that the teacher remain as outwardly calm and unemotional as possible, even though internally emotions may be churning.

Emotional behavior may be escalated if teachers do not attempt to control their own outward responses. The louder and more vehement a parent's voice, the more softly and slowly a teacher should speak, being careful that his or her body language remains open and positive—for example, avoiding the crossed arms or lack of eye contact that suggests being closed to the parent's position. It helps teachers remain calm when they do not interpret the parents' approach as a personal attack, and in fact separate the person from the problem. Instead, the parents' behavior should be seen as a code for expressing emotions that spring from the parenting role. It is very important that teachers not become defensive or argumentative and not retaliate verbally, as in the following negative example:

FIGURE 15-2
If teachers remain calm in the face of parents' strong emotions, they may prevent the hostility from escalating.

"Look, don't you talk to me about my teaching. If you were doing a halfway decent job with parenting, I wouldn't be having these problems in my classroom."

Defensive behavior suggests that the attacker is right and tends to escalate the tension. Responding to a parent's emotion with a teacher's emotion can only lead to an explosive situation (see Figure 15-2). Nevertheless, a teacher must continue to maintain composure by trying to perceive a situation from a parent's perspective and identify with the emotional responses of a parent. It is also important to consider that there are cultural differences in messages and communication styles.

Learning to support parents nonjudgmentally, without losing emotional control, is crucial. Professionals do not have the right to lose control with parents. By taking on the role of teacher, they commit themselves to working constructively with those who need assistance.

Staying calm will help parents see that the teacher is confident that he or she can deal effectively with the issues.

Remaining calm is not an easy task. Teachers are just ordinary human beings, with limits to remaining calm in the face of persistent inappropriate behavior, no matter how hard they try to understand or tolerate it. Nevertheless, if they lose control and treat parents with disrespect, they cannot expect that parents will be respectful of them or that anything constructive will be accomplished.

Acknowledge and Accept the Anger

The first step in working with an angry reaction is to accept it. An expressed feeling is real, no matter how distorted the perception of facts that caused the feeling. Accepting others and their feelings does not mean giving up one's own perspective; it simply means being more sensitive to that of the other (see Figure 15-3). By taking a parent's perspective, a teacher is able to show genuine concern and is more likely to respond appropriately. As a teacher reflects an understanding of a parent's viewpoint, a parent realizes that his or her feelings are recognized:

> *"You're really very upset by my comments about Jacob's behavior, aren't you?"*

The teacher has listened carefully to the concern and listened between the lines, asking "What

FIGURE 15-3
Accepting the parent's feelings does not mean giving up the teacher's own perspective but rather being sensitive to the parent.

is he or she feeling?" Then, the teacher tries to define the emotion being expressed and reflects that understanding back to the parent to see if this is correct. Such feedback acknowledges the parent's anger and may eliminate a parent's need to show more anger because the teacher has clearly picked up on the message. The teacher's reflective comment may elicit a response from the parent that can clarify a concern in terms of specific details:

> *"You bet I'm upset, and I'll tell you, I don't think it's fair to be talking about making him keep rules after all that kid has had on him. With his mom being away with work so much, he's had to deal with a lot."*

When active listening does not evoke an opportunity to hear the reasons behind the anger, a teacher should continue to reflect back an **empathic** perception of a parent's response:

> Parent: *"Of course I'm upset. Anybody would be—to hear a teacher say such things about their child."*
>
> Teacher: *"It really troubles you to hear the kind of comments I made."*
>
> Parent: *"It certainly does. It's just not fair—what do you know about it anyway?"*
>
> Teacher: *"I know there's a lot about Jacob I don't know, and I'm counting on you to help me understand. What can you tell me that would help me?" and so on.*

empathic
Identifying with feelings of another.

Asking meaningful questions can steer the conversation more toward problem solving and less into emotional confrontation.

It is necessary for a teacher to analyze personal emotional responses, determining whether this has become a power struggle and why the issue elicits such strong feelings. Are facts involved or only emotional responses? Making decisions by any of the three Ps—politics, pressure, and power—is a mistake (Waterman, 2006).

Teachers, being human, sometimes overlook details or simply make mistakes in dealing with certain situations. This may become a source of hostility or anger in parents. Teachers need to be prepared to admit the mistake or responsibility openly and honestly to parents, empathize with their frustration and anger, and then share a plan to ensure this will not occur again. Such honesty can mitigate the hostility:

> *"I don't blame you for feeling so upset with me. This was my mistake, and I'm sorry for it. I'd feel angry, too, if it had happened to my child. Here's what I plan to do so this doesn't happen again."*

When teachers are sure they have not made a mistake, they can say "I'm sorry this happened," keeping an open mind about the parent's constructive criticism.

Adhere to Facts

As a conversation proceeds, teachers must be careful that any disagreeing statements concern facts and issues, not personalities. In discussing different viewpoints, participants

TeachSource Digital Download

IDEAS FOR TEACHERS:

Some Don'ts for Dealing with Adversarial Parents

1. Don't interrupt or try to change the subject.
2. Don't take parents' comments personally.
3. Don't focus on things that can't be changed.
4. Don't start thinking of your answer before you have actually heard and understood the concern.
5. Don't try to persuade parents that you are right and they are wrong.
6. Don't come across as a know-it-all professional.
7. Don't overexplain.
8. Don't be so intent on smoothing over a conflict that you achieve only a superficial resolution.
9. Don't be defensive.
10. Don't use blame, control, and power over parents.

should use descriptive statements, not evaluative ones. It is easier to deal with descriptions rather than labels. By being objective and factual in the statements made to families and by having written observations that support the statements, teachers will sound less judgmental or accusing:

> *Not: "Jacob is a very undisciplined, out-of-bounds child."*
>
> *Rather: "I'm noticing that it's hard for Jacob to follow the rule about hitting others. This week, when he was angry with Eddie on three different occasions, he hit him. Do you notice hitting at home?"*
>
> *Not: "Jennifer is very careless in her work."*
>
> *Rather: "If you look at these assignments Jennifer handed in last week, you will see the errors I circled. I have seen her do this work correctly on other occasions. What have you noticed about her making errors?"*

Parents would be more likely to respond to each of the second statements with information and suggestions, whereas the first statements would likely produce defensive, angry reactions. When teachers take care to use words that describe behaviors without adding their own interpretation, they are more likely to engage the parents in dialogue that moves toward problem solving rather than alienating the listener.

Express Concerns Constructively

sandwiching
Presenting an issue of concern with positive statements preceding and following the concern.

Teachers need to remember that angry outbursts may be triggered if they approach parents with problems so directly that the parents' only recourse is to attack back in order to protect themselves. It is effective to use more palatable methods, such as **sandwiching** the meat of a problem between two slices of positive, supportive statements regarding a parent's interest and concern:

> *"I appreciate how deeply concerned you are for Jacob. There's no more important thing for a child than to know his parents care. I'm concerned about his ability to develop some self-control, and I feel sure this is an area that we can work on to come up with some things that might help him."*

Validating parents and their feelings and opinions is a productive way for teachers to align themselves with families, instead of lining up against them.

Using the communication technique of **I-messages** to express concerns allows teachers to express their feelings constructively and so indirectly encourage parents to do so too. An I-message has three basic parts:

1. "When …"—a statement of the behavior that troubles a teacher

2. "I feel …"—a statement of the feeling about the behavior or its consequences

3. "Because …"—a statement of the reason for the concern (Gordon, 2000)

Thus, an I-message sounds something like these examples:

> *"When Jacob hits other children, I feel frustrated because I'm not able to help him understand our rule about everybody being safe here."*

> *"When Jacob forgets our rules, I feel very concerned about his level of self-control."*

> *"When you refuse to discuss these problems, I get upset because the problems seem urgent to me."*

Some of the potential explosiveness is removed when feelings are expressed in I-messages rather than "you-judgments" that focus blame squarely on the other:

> *"You're just not helping this situation."*

> *"You're refusing to admit there's a problem."*

> *"You always take Jacob's side and refuse to listen to what's really happening."*

Respect Families' Concerns

It is important that angry parents know their concerns are taken seriously. These problems are important to a parent and must not be minimized by a teacher. Teachers should nod and say "Hmmm" and give other signs of acknowledging the speaker. Another way to indicate respect for parents' problems is to write down every complaint, allowing them to truly vent their feelings (see Figure 15-4).

When parents slow down, teachers can ask if anything else is bothering them, so their list of complaints can be exhausted. Teachers should wait until the speaker is completely finished before speaking and then read back the list by using the parents' own words; it suggests that the teachers truly value the concerns. Teachers can next ask for any suggestions that parents have for solutions to the problems and write these down, too. This conveys valuing the parents' input, although the teacher is not necessarily committing to follow these suggestions. These actions say that the concerns are important and the parents are being listened to. It is also valuable to state that educators don't have all the answers and need all the help they can get.

I-messages
Verbal expression of an individual's emotional response to a specific situation.

FIGURE 15-4
One way to indicate respect for parents' concerns is for teachers to write down every complaint.

© 2016 Cengage Learning®

Express Teacher Emotions Constructively

If these earlier steps are not successful in stemming the flow of the parent's anger, it is appropriate for teachers to express their own emotional responses to the verbal attacks. It is entirely appropriate for teachers to state something like this:

"I'm feeling disturbed by the tone of voice you're using as we speak."

"I'm bothered that you're not giving me a chance to explain my perspective."

The example of a teacher discussing his or her emotions calmly may help parents calm down.

It is also important that a teacher not retreat from the anger by suggesting "You'd better talk to the director" or "I won't talk to you unless you stop shouting at me." The potential for communication and learning more about a problem is available here and now. As teachers help parents express feelings and perceptions, they both have an opportunity to see the issues from a different perspective.

Reschedule the Meeting

FIGURE 15-5
It may be useful to invite a colleague or supervisor to sit in on another meeting to help facilitate the discussion.

On those occasions when all attempts to reduce the amount of anger and facilitate communication fail, it may be wise to schedule another meeting. No one benefits from an extended angry outburst: not the teacher, not the child, not even the parent. To accept abuse will not remedy the situation, and it is emotionally draining on the teacher to be bullied.

"I don't think we can accomplish anything more today. Could we meet again next Wednesday at this time? Maybe some new ideas will occur to us in the meantime."

It can be useful to invite a colleague or supervisor to sit in on the next conference because some participant at every conference needs to be free of emotional responses and have skills to help the other participants deal with their emotions quickly and fully (see **Figure 15-5**). Checking out a situation with a colleague may also help a teacher see it from a different perspective. If the teacher and parent can come up with a plan for responding to their mutual problem, it is important to schedule another meeting promptly to attempt to follow up on the original conversation as an indication of the teacher's sincere desire to work with the parent. Teachers do well to keep supervisors informed about what has gone on between the parents and themselves.

Anger is a powerful emotion—destructive if allowed to rage unleashed but potentially a strong motivation to examine a situation and work together for understanding and change (see **Figure 15-6**).

OPPORTUNITY FOR SELF-REFLECTION

What experiences have you already had in dealing with people who became angry and aggressive with you? How did you handle it? How did you feel after the encounter? What does this suggest you will have to consider when put in a professional position of dealing with a hostile parent?

TeachSource Digital Download

FIGURE 15-6
Five steps for working through conflicts.

| Analyze | Imagine a walk in their shoes | Confer with a colleague | Meet | Brainstorm solutions |

In a Conflict with a Parent?

Five Steps to Take:

Analyze

1. Analyze your own feelings. Why do you feel so strongly about this issue? Are you emotionally involved? Has this become a power struggle? Are factors other than the child's best interests entering into your thinking about the conflict? If so, what are they?

Imagine a walk in their shoes

2. Put yourself in the parents' shoes. What are they thinking, and why might they look at the situation the way they do? Assuming that they have their child's best interests in mind, why are they behaving as they are?

Confer with a colleague

3. Check out your perceptions. Find a friend or colleague whom you respect but who often sees things differently from you. Describe the situation as objectively as you can. Can your colleague give you any insight into why you and the parent are at odds?

Meet

4. Arrange to meet with the parent. Make all preconference communications as friendly and unthreatening as possible. Do not get drawn into playing out the dispute before you meet. If you are very angry, have someone else look at your notes before you send them or role-play with a colleague what you will say.

Brainstorm solutions

5. Avoid coming to the conference with a prearranged solution. Learn more about the parents' viewpoint. Try to be nonjudgmental. Negotiate. Try to come up with a solution that meets the child's needs. Try to agree at least on the next step.

NEXT STEPS ...

Congratulate yourself if it went well and you learned something new about the child or the family.

If it did not go well, ask to meet with a third party or supervisor.

Stay cool, try to remain objective, and do not take it personally. Keep the child's best interesst as the primary focus for decisions.

15-2 Indifference

Connie Martinez is concerned about a different kind of behavior. There are a couple of parents of children in her classroom that she simply can't reach. They seem apathetic—uncaring about their children's needs or the teacher's attempts to involve them in any way.

"Hard-to-reach" families include those whose physical, social, or psychological distance from the school places extra barriers in the school's or family's path and make communication and interaction even more difficult than usual. "Hard-to-reach" ought not to be a judgment. "In some ways, some of the time, every family is hard to reach" (Epstein, 2011, p. 270). These families may include single parents; less educated parents; very young or very old parents; language minority parents; parents with low incomes; the homeless; families new to the community; immigrant families; parents with such personal problems as alcoholism, drug abuse, or mental illness; parents overwhelmed with family needs; parents working hard just to make ends meet; and parents preoccupied with demanding careers.

There are several possible reasons behind apparent indifference. One may be that the overwhelming pressure in families' lives prevents them from focusing much attention on their child, as much as they care for him or her. Too many concerns about basic physical needs may crowd in. A parent who worries that her resources will not stretch to cover food for the rest of the month and the electric bill has little emotional energy left to care about higher academic or social needs.

Pressure in families' lives can come from the opposite end of the socioeconomic spectrum—from having two sets of career demands and the problems of meshing two schedules, relocating households when told to, and continuing to push up the ladder of success. Sometimes, there is little time or energy left for personal relationships or development. Such parents are often more than willing to entrust child care and education to the professionals and to withdraw to more obviously gainful career pursuits.

Parents who feel particularly uncomfortable due to differences in social class or cultural backgrounds may withdraw from a situation and appear indifferent. Noninvolvement or indifference may indicate an attempt to disguise illiteracy or other problems. English language learners may not be comfortable in situations where their language ability is limited. Some families, including families of some cultural minorities, may have a high regard for teachers and education but feel that education is a one-way street and they have nothing to offer. Some parents in child care programs may see teachers simply as employees in a low-status occupation and feel there is no need for their involvement in a "babysitting" arrangement.

Still other families who seem indifferent may be adults who missed childhood—who are themselves products of abnormal parenting. Such parents spend their grownup years attempting to have their own lost needs met by their children and by doing so raise children whose own needs are never met.

Whatever the reason for families' lack of interest or involvement, most teachers dislike not being able to reach them. As is human nature, teachers who feel unsuccessful in reaching particular parents often withdraw from them, thereby increasing the distance between them. It is common for teachers to shift the blame from themselves to parents:

"Well, I'm sure I don't know what's the matter with them—goodness knows I've tried."

"What kind of parents are they anyway—not even caring about their own child enough to come in for a conference."

These responses do not improve a situation. It is important for teachers to hold the belief that most parents want their children to succeed and do well. It is helpful to adopt an attitude that parents are reachable but that teachers have not yet found ways to reach them. Teachers must not interpret inaccessibility personally. Rejection is something teachers must learn to manage. A positive way to look at rejection is that it is an opportunity to reconsider methods or redirect energies. The key is not to give up but to consider other ways of getting through, reminding oneself of specifics about this particular family's circumstances.

Teachers must assess the reasons for families' unavailability and consider various ideas to overcome it. It is vital that teachers not fall into the trap of making stereotypical judgments about the involvement or abilities of families, particularly those who are disadvantaged socioeconomically. Such stereotypes would prevent teachers from truly reaching out to involve all families.

15-2a Personal and Economic Pressures

For families overwhelmed by economic and personal pressures, there is little probability of their becoming involved or less "indifferent" to their children's needs as long as these external pressures exist. The most positive action for a teacher is to be an advocate for these families, referring them to appropriate community agencies for assistance. Such concern and help will lay the basis for trust in a relationship that may develop as these parents' other concerns are lessened.

15-2b Career Interests

For parents busy with their own career interests, teachers may emphasize particular techniques to reach them—newsletters or e-mail that can be read at their convenience or perhaps occasional bag lunches, with their children issuing the invitation and planned with plenty of advance notice. Opportunities to talk with other upwardly mobile families may be appreciated as a source of support.

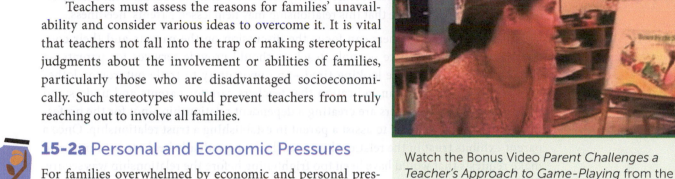

TeachSource

VIDEO ACTIVITY

© 2016 Cengage Learning®

Watch the Bonus Video *Parent Challenges a Teacher's Approach to Game-Playing* from the Video Case entitled *Home-School Communication: The Parent-Teacher Conference.* After watching the video, reflect on these questions:

1. There appears to be a real difference of opinion between the teacher and the parent. Should there be a win/lose about this situation? Why or why not?

2. Is this a demonstration of hostility or just different approaches to the issue? What is the teacher's response? Would you have done anything differently? Describe alternate actions and the rationale for them.

15-2c Cultural Differences

With families who may remain distant because of discomfort with social or cultural differences, teachers must be warm, friendly, and casual in their contacts. It may be important to consciously simplify speech styles and vocabulary.

Other families from similar cultural and language backgrounds who are more comfortable in a school setting can be helpful in making contact with these parents and personally inviting and accompanying them to informal events. Casual social activities or hands-on workshops (making toys for their children or materials for the classroom) provide less threatening experiences and give a sense of being important in their child's education.

Through genuine indications that a teacher needs and values family participation, parents who feel they have nothing to offer may see that education is not as formidable or as unimportant as they had believed. Persistence can pay off here.

15-2d Emotional Pressures

Perhaps the greatest challenge to teachers comes in attempting to reach parents who are less sensitive to their child's and a teacher's needs because of their own overwhelming emotional needs. This can be any parent at any particular time of his or her life. Teachers must realize that their expectations for these families to understand and be involved are often unrealistic. Parents need to grow themselves before they can understand the need for their involvement or what their child needs in parenting.

What they need is nurturing. These parents need to be accepted for who they are, encouraged for whatever they have done, reinforced for any strength and efforts, and helped to feel understood. As teachers slowly establish a climate of trust with these parents, they should recognize that this relationship may help lessen parents' neediness.

In conversation, teachers can focus the discussion on the parents and their concerns and interests. Where possible, teachers should provide services for parents—a cup of coffee when they're looking tired—an opportunity to trade outgrown clothes with another family—as an indication that teachers care for parents and understand their needs. In fact, teachers are creating a dependent relationship—not for the professional's needs but as a way to assist a parent in establishing a trust relationship. Once a parent exhibits trust in the relationship, a teacher can gradually begin to set limits and make requests that would have been too frightening before the relationship was secure. It may be a long and trying struggle, but by responding to parents' needs, teachers may be able to reach parents who are "unreachable" in ways teachers had first expected to involve them.

There is an important consideration for teachers about parental underinvolvement. Some have expressed a current concern that families want teachers and schools to just fix all students' needs and problems, leaving it all to them and not giving their own support and efforts in collaboration. This is a line that teachers and schools must draw, realizing what their roles are and making it clear that they will not go it alone. Collaboration is a key to their children's success. Parents have equal responsibilities with teachers, and effective partnership schools make this message explicit.

15-3 Overly Involved Parents

To teachers struggling to get families involved in the school or even indicate an interest in their children's welfare, the predicament of overinvolvement might seem a lesser problem. But parents who are too involved in a school situation may hinder their children's move toward independence or do the wrong thing at the wrong time, disrupting their children and the class. A phenomenon that many teachers note today is the many parents who are totally involved in their children's lives—often called "helicopter parents," hovering over their children—anxious to see that they achieve and develop as quickly as possible and ready to tackle any obstacle they perceive on their children's behalf. They often refuse to believe their children are not the brightest and best, and insist on overprotecting or demanding special privileges for them (see Figure 15-7). They may be so overinvolved that they are hindering their children's learning, as they work all night on projects for them or virtually do their homework. They are sometimes the parents who "know it all" and are full of recommendations or criticisms. Certainly, they do not want to hear a teacher's realistic observations of their children. Sometimes, these parents just get in the way of orderly classroom procedures as they linger to talk indefinitely despite a teacher's need to care for the children or set up activities. How does a teacher respond to these behaviors?

Understanding a parent's behavior is a first step to tolerating or dealing with it. A teacher must get to know a particular parent to assess the individual situation and motivation.

15-3a Reluctance to Separate

Many parents are overwhelmed because of their own reluctance to separate from their children. Being uncomfortable with separation is a natural experience in the developmental stages of parenthood, but a positive resolution of the conflicting feelings is important for child and parent.

These parents may need particular reassurance that their child is being well cared for. Regular and specific reporting of information helps, as will personal notes and phone calls to share anecdotes about the child. This communication reassures parents that individual attention is paid to their child and also that they are not losing contact with their school life.

FIGURE 15-7
Many parents today are overly involved in their children's school lives.

Empathizing frankly with a parent's feelings can bring separation into the open:

"I know there must be a lot of mixed feelings about seeing her grow up— rejoicing at all the new things and sadness at the idea of the little one left behind. It must seem to you sometimes like you're not as close as you once were. But it's just different, isn't it? Believe me, you're still the most important person in her world. Why, just the other day...."

Teachers should encourage parents to share their feelings and thoughts. Such communication allows teachers to reassure and subtly remind parents of a growing child's needs:

"Hard as it is for you, the most loving thing a parent can do is to allow the child some room to move on, feeling stronger about being able to function without you. She needs to know you have enough confidence in her that she can be all right, for a while, without your presence."

When presented with the idea that it is for their child's welfare, many parents try harder to let go.

15-3b Unmet Personal Needs

Parents who are overinvolved because of unmet personal, social, or emotional needs benefit when a teacher responds with genuine appreciation and praise for their efforts. It is counterproductive to try to stop this involvement because it is so important for a parent's emotional health, as well as potentially helpful to a school.

When a parent's overinvolvement in a classroom becomes a problem to a child and teacher, his or her efforts can be redirected to other areas that are less disruptive—another classroom, working to involve other parents, or preparing materials. The particular strengths of families should be identified and utilized fully—always with sincere appreciation for the value of their contribution. Positive ways to contribute may be found—an extra pair of hands at lunchtime in the infant room, a cozy lap for an upset toddler, gathering the dress-up clothes that need mending, reading with a child who needs extra help (see Figure 15-8), or calling other families to remind them about an upcoming meeting. Such efforts are not disruptive to a child's independent functioning and allow a parent to feel important to a school.

FIGURE 15-8
Helping children who need extra support may be one way for overly involved parents to contribute.

15-3c Insecurities

For parents who "know it all" and want to share that knowledge, a teacher may need to indicate frequently that he or she considers parents to be the real experts on their particular children. Sometimes, a parent acts this way out of insecurities caused by real or imagined perceptions of a teacher's competence and dominance in a situation. When a teacher emphasizes partnership and defers to parental knowledge of their children, parental feelings of unimportance may diminish:

"You know, parents really know their own children best. I need to know all I can about Johnny, and I appreciate your sharing your knowledge. What can you tell me about his projects at home?"

Sometimes, a parent's information can be acknowledged and shared with others:

"That's a good tip about those children's books. Could you write that down so I can add it to next month's newsletter? I think a lot of parents would like to know."

Teachers have to realize and acknowledge that in many cases, parents really are more knowledgeable than they are. As parents' knowledge and contributions can be directed in positive channels, their urge to criticize and complain may diminish.

When the "know-it-all" parent is unable to hear a teacher's points, a teacher must exercise skills of assertiveness and state his or her position clearly, without belittling a parent's ideas or antagonizing and hurting. Teachers who recognize the complexity of human behavior know that a situation may be perceived in a variety of ways, and it is healthful to air all perspectives. This realization often prevents becoming too aggressive in presenting one's views. Assertiveness in a discussion may be helpful; aggressiveness will likely be destructive.

If reluctant to accept the validity of another's viewpoint for information, a parent may be more susceptible to information conveyed by less personal means. Making pertinent articles available to parents allows them to absorb the ideas and make them their own; an exposure to new ideas is accomplished without the resistance that can be inherent in personal discussions.

15-3d Lingering to Talk

For a parent who lingers indefinitely to talk, a teacher should draw clear limits while still making the parent feel welcome. After a few minutes of talk, when other responsibilities press, the teacher can say, "I enjoy talking with you, but right now, I need to get over to those children at the water table. We'd love to have you stay if you have a few extra minutes. Perhaps you'd like to sit near the book corner—there's always someone looking for a story to be read." This reassures parents that their presence is welcomed and provides a chance for them to be useful in classroom life. If they are uneasy about leaving their children, it allows them to observe a teacher and see how busy he or she really is. If such patterns continue, a teacher may need to say frankly:

"I really want to talk with you, Mr. Parker. It's important to me to hear from you. But arrival time is so busy that I'm not able to give you my full attention. Let's see if we can find some time to talk that's less hectic for me. I can be free at my break this afternoon at 3:30."

Specific guidelines help a parent realize the many facets of a teacher's responsibility.

15.4 Frequent Causes of Tension Between Parents and Teachers

In addition to troubling attitudes and behaviors, several situations frequently arise in schools, causing irritation for the staff involved. Let us consider some ways schools can deal with these situations.

15.4a Late Parents

Among recurrent problems that annoy teachers in child care and afterschool programs is the frequent late arrival of parents picking up their children. At the end of a long and tiring day, this becomes a final insult for hardworking teachers and is a cause of resentment and relationship breakdowns. If teachers confront parents at the time of lateness, there is potential for explosive responses on both sides.

This is one situation that is probably best handled by administrators rather than by teachers themselves (see Figure 15-9). It is important to stress timely pickups in the family handbook and in orientation information. Some programs ask parents to sign a contract agreeing that because staying with children after school closing times is a personal service to the family, late fees will be paid directly to the teachers who use personal time to stay and care for children. Other programs find that a late fee must be more than modest because some parents find it worthwhile to pay a small fee and have extra time. A substantial fee, such as $5 for every five minutes, often eliminates the problem. With parents who are habitually late, some administrators find it necessary to ask parents to make contingency plans or provide lists of people who can be called to pick up children when parents are late. Termination warnings and follow-through may be a final step. It is important for late policies to be strict, clearly communicated, and consistently administered by those in charge, leaving teachers and children free of the emotional issue.

FIGURE 15-9

It is usually best to let administrators handle the issue with late parents.

© 2016 Cengage Learning®

15-4b Releasing Children to Adults Who Are "Under the Influence" or Noncustodial Parents

A very uncomfortable and potentially dangerous situation arises when teachers are asked to release children under their care to adults they suspect to be impaired by drugs or alcohol or to an adult who does not have legal custody of the child.

The best protection against such occurrences is to have written policies that are discussed at the time of enrollment. Complete information about people permitted to pick up children should be on file with a verifying signature, and parents should understand that any changes must be made in writing, with a signature that can be compared. Identities should be confirmed with picture identification. Teachers should not hesitate to delay the departure to confirm the legitimacy of any person's claim. Certified copies of court orders regarding custody should be made available for the school's files; verbal requests of one parent to prohibit access of another parent are not valid without a court document. Teachers should not be put in a position of having the responsibility to decide which parent has legal custody without such a document. If asked to release children to noncustodial parents, teachers should try to reach the custodial parent and law enforcement if necessary to protect all the children in the teacher's care as well as him or herself.

If a teacher feels that the adult picking up a child is not in a condition to be driving, he or she can call other authorized adults, call law enforcement officials, or pay for a cab (a requirement for reimbursement can be part of a parent contract). In either case, the concern is to protect children under teacher care.

15-4c Lack of Respect

Many teachers complain that parents fail to treat them with respect. Especially in the child care environment, some parents seem to feel that teachers are merely employed lackeys and deserve no particular esteem at best—or at worst, downright contemptuous rudeness. Rather than the former belief that teachers were doing important and worthwhile work, when parents more often valued their efforts and opinions, many parents today seem to display lack of courtesy to teachers. Unfortunately, their children often echo this attitude. Such a lack of civility colors all communication between home and school. What can teachers do about this problem? (NEA, 1999).

It is important that teachers themselves realize the significance of the work they do with children and families. Their demeanor and attitudes best convey to others how deserving of respect they are. Succumbing to others' disrespectful behaviors would be an unfortunate loss for society and education. Demonstration of administrative support and valuing of teachers may be an important message for the community.

It is vital that teachers continue to treat others with respect—no matter how rude or demanding they are. This example may go a long way toward helping parents and children see more appropriate models of interaction (see Figure 15-10).

15-4d Sick Children

Another frequent cause of home–school friction is parents' disregard for policies that exclude sick children. It is, of course, understandable that families are sometimes overwhelmed by the difficulty of finding substitute care for sick children when parents feel that they must be at work themselves. Nevertheless, teachers cannot be expected to allow sick children into their classrooms, knowing the danger of the spread of infections and the special needs of children who do not feel well enough to participate in the usual routine. Clearly stated policies may help with this problem. Family handbooks and orientation information should state specific conditions that demand exclusion from the classroom as well as expected parent responses when they are called to pick up sick children. It is probably useful to require parents to file plans and names of providers for sick child care during the application process. Many parents would not consider this eventuality until a time of crisis unless directed to do so at the outset.

Teachers can and should empathize with parents who are torn between their child's and employer's needs while gently focusing on the sick child's needs and holding firm to policies:

FIGURE 15-10
It is vital for teachers to treat parents with respect—no matter how rude or demanding they are.

© Cengage Learning®

"I know how hard it is to have to be at work when you wish you could be home looking after Sandra. I also know how difficult it is to find someone who will agree to look after a sick child. I wish we could help you, but our policy on her staying home for at least 24 hours after a fever is there to protect Sandra—she just won't feel up to being here, and her health is extra vulnerable, too."

It is important not to interpret parents' actions in bringing sick children to the center or reluctance to leave work to come and get a sick child as poor parenting or a sign of indifference. It is more likely desperation at the role conflicts of parent and worker. As staff discover community resources that can assist parents needing care for sick children, administrators can post the information and notify parents.

Care of sick children of working parents has become a community issue. Some companies and communities have created linkages between medical facilities and personnel and the child care community to ease the problem. This is surely an advocacy issue that teachers and parents can work on together.

15-4e End-of-Day Problems

When parents, children, and teachers come together at the end of the day, problems can be created by the transition and magnified by fatigue. Children sometimes test and evade parents, almost as if challenging them to take charge again. Parents sometimes demand information and answers from teachers, again appearing to challenge how the day has actually gone. From their side, teachers may have reports of negative behavior they feel are necessary to make. Fragile relationships can be stretched at this time.

What can teachers do to make the end of the day less stressful for everyone? Part of the solution may lie in preparation for the transition. Quiet activities such as reading books or working puzzles should fill the last period of the day. This way, teachers and children can have a calm period at the end of the day. While children are quietly occupied, teachers can be free to do some of the closing chores so they are not feeling rushed in hectic cleanup when parents arrive. Teachers can post summaries of the classroom or each child's day so parents can get some answers to their questions by reading the notice board or individual daily sheets when they enter. If teachers help children gather their belongings or get partly dressed for departure, this helps parents and children move toward going home.

The end of the day is probably not the best time to discuss behavior problems. Parents who are continually given negative reports about their children at pickup time are not being helped to feel positively about either their children or the teachers. Teachers need to avoid the temptation to give daily reports of negative behaviors when everyone is tired and least likely to be receptive to sensitive discussion. A better strategy is to arrange a later sit-down discussion:

> *"Mrs. Rodriguez, I think it would be useful for you and me to have a chance to talk away from the classroom. I know you've had questions about Maria, and there are some things I'd like to share, too. Can we find a time this week? Perhaps if you'd come in 20 minutes or so before your usual time, I could arrange for Miss Phillips to be in the classroom."*

Such a conversation is likely to be more productive than an at-the-door confrontation between harried parents and teachers.

15-4f Parents Who Ask for Special Treatment

Teachers are frequently annoyed by parents' requests for services or attention for their children that go beyond typical classroom practices.

> *"Jane's father asked if we can let her stay in today when the other children go out to the playground because she's just getting over her cold."*

> *"Jeremy's grandmother wants him not to take a nap today because they want him to sleep in the car when they leave for their trip. Now how am I supposed to do that—he'll bother everybody else."*

> *"Another toy from home—her mom says she just wanted to let her bring it, even though she knows it's against our rules."*

Rather than simply being irritated and refusing the requests arbitrarily, teachers may need to remember that early childhood programs are there to provide support services for families, and families have a right to define some of the individual services they need. Teachers should consider how a requested service might be provided rather than immediately refusing. Could Jane stay in with another class? Could Jeremy spend some time with books in the director's office? A cooperative stance may find a solution satisfactory for everyone.

Requests that have no solution need to be explained to families so they understand the problems their requests make for the center. When policies have been clearly communicated in family handbooks before the request, teachers can refer to the policy as they state the decision rather than making it a personal teacher decision. Existing policies mean that parents and children come to understand that teachers' treatment is evenhanded and not open to favoritism, yet applied with sensitivity to individuals.

> *"We'll keep her toy in her cubby so it will be safe. She can show it to her friends at group time and then we'll put it back. I know you'd both be sad if it got lost or broken. Remember our policy about toys from home."*

It also is important to remember that families do have individual, unique needs, and arbitrary refusal of all special requests does not recognize this.

15-4g Disagreement Over Readiness

A current issue that is emotionally charged for the parents and teachers involved is the issue of **readiness** for children moving on—usually into elementary school situations.

> *"I can't believe it. We've been planning all along for Lisa to start kindergarten this fall—her birthday is in August, well before the cutoff date. And at last I was planning to go back to my job full time—my boss and I have been counting on it. Then, the teacher calls me in for a conference and tells me she's not 'ready'—all because they gave her some test and she couldn't tell the difference between uppercase and lowercase letters. Letters, for Pete's sake. She's as smart as can be, and she gets along just fine with other kids. I can't believe they can do this to us."*

readiness
Characteristics, skills, and dispositions that make a successful student; particularly used when talking about moving into kindergarten.

More and more families are getting the kind of news that Lisa's mother received. As school programs need to demonstrate improved quality and accountability, there is a growing tendency to use standardized test results to dictate placement decisions. The requirements of NCLB legislation mean that schools are often looking ahead to future end-of-grade tests and therefore demanding certain knowledge before children enter school. School systems nationwide are using various tests to assess children prior to or after the kindergarten year. Unfortunately, this often leads to practices that are inappropriate when considering the age and developmental level of the children involved (Graue, 2001). Testing narrows the curriculum as teachers try to prepare children to succeed on tests. Many important early childhood skills are not easily measured by standardized tests, so social, emotional, and physical development and learning are not given equal importance in decisions about readiness. Standardized group and individual testing is inappropriate for young children, who often do not have good test-taking skills, such as sitting still, being quiet, and following a series of directions—often to write or make particular marks. Young children are growing and learning so rapidly that there is great potential for obtaining inaccurate test results and thus mislabeling children. Children who are English language learners are especially at risk for misassessment with testing in the early years.

The best information about readiness comes from systematic observations by trained teachers, along with information from parents, who know their children better than anyone else and should be active participants in the assessment process (Caspe, et al., 2013; Elicker & McMullen, 2013). What this means is that teachers as well as parents should work against practices that exclude children's own parents from providing meaningful input into decisions that affect families and the educational future and self-esteem of children. Together, they can become advocates of developmentally appropriate practices that are not potentially harmful for young children.

FIGURE 15-11
Parents are often in disagreement with the school's interpretation of readiness.

If teachers find themselves working in situations that use arbitrary test results to decide readiness, they must realize that parents will find the decisions painful and disruptive to the family's plans and image of the child. Discussions of the findings must be careful and specific so parents carry away no misunderstandings about future prognoses for learning.

Teachers can give families specific information and guidelines about what is developmentally appropriate and what is not—perhaps helping them become advocates working for change in community school practices. Teachers can convey support for the parents' perceptions of their child—always indicating that parents are the real experts on their children. If this sounds as if the recommendation is that the teacher should sympathize with the parent who is left out of the decision-making process and forced to accept the school's view of readiness, that is correct. Teachers should not lend support to practices that are developmentally inappropriate for children and families.

On the other hand, many of today's parents are too focused on their children's academic achievements—often demanding excessively early instruction or methods. This situation demands continual parent education on how children best learn and appropriate experiences. Workshops, discussions, speakers, and offering reading materials may help. When teachers find themselves in disagreement with parents' perceptions of children's abilities and developmental levels, it will be wise to bring in a third party to observe the child and join the conversation. Another perspective may help parent and teacher approach the situation from a fresh viewpoint.

FIGURE 15-12
Many teachers find it useful to spend some time reflecting and writing about difficult experiences.

Finally, teachers who make genuine efforts to understand and solve problems but still find situations that seem to have no solution should remember that they are not alone. Any teacher has had similar experiences that sometimes linger in memory long after forgetting more positive experiences. It is important to learn as much as possible from these negative experiences and to keep on trying!

Many teachers find that recording their feelings, perceptions, and experiences in working with parents is a valuable tool for their own growth (see Figure 15-12). Informal notes or journal entries document concerns, needs, and progress and pinpoint areas that need attention. Such personal notes, meant purely for a teacher's use, provide an emotional release and evidence that his or her efforts are effective.

© 2016 Cengage Learning®

SUMMARY

Teachers may encounter troublesome behaviors and attitudes that are personally annoying and professionally discouraging. In each case, a teacher's first step should be to attempt to identify the feelings or circumstances that might be the cause. A stance that is directed toward solutions rather than accusations is important. Some of these behaviors include:

- Hostility, which may mask other emotions, and requires calm responses
- Apparent indifference, which may come from parent's socioeconomic or work conditions, and is best responded to by assessing reasons for unavailability and finding other methods for communicating
- Overinvolvement, which probably comes from parents' own needs and definition of the parenting role, and requires responses that acknowledge parent needs and protect children's independence
- Specific frequent causes of tension, such as sick children, parent lateness, and requests for special treatment, require thoughtful individual responses

Student Activities for Further Study

1. Role-play and then discuss with your classmates the following situations where teachers are faced with hostile reactions:

   a. "I refuse to talk to you anymore. You're just plain wrong about Sarah—she's a very bright child."

   b. "How dare you ask me so many questions about my child? It's none of your business."

   c. "I want to talk to your principal. If you were doing your job properly, there would not be a problem with Melvin. She should know how incompetent you are."

   d. "If you ask me, you want me to do your job for you. You can't handle him in the classroom, so you want me to get tough with him at home."

   e. "As long as I'm the one paying the bill for child care, I want things done as I ask. I insist that you get busy and teach Barbara to read this year before she goes to kindergarten. Are you saying I don't know what's best for my own child?"

   f. "What is this stuff about readiness? I know my own child. I say she's ready for kindergarten, and I don't care what your test results say."

Apply the Chapter Concepts: Case in Point

Roberta Wolf, a single mother of two children who are kindergarten and second-grade students in your afterschool program, has been late twice this week already. You also know that she was late earlier this month and has not paid those late fees. Just now, you received a call that she was delayed leaving her office and will not likely arrive until 6:30 p.m. Your center closes at 6, and you have a social engagement some distance away at 7 p.m.

1. Use the Critical Analysis Form from Figure 15-1 to consider your responses and possible solutions to this chronic problem.

2. Consider the issue from the parent's viewpoint. What might be some of her emotional responses and behaviors?

3. Consider the issue from the children's viewpoint. How might they react emotionally?

4. From the teacher's viewpoint, what are your feelings and concerns?

5. Identify some possible solutions to this predicament.

Review Questions

1. Discuss possible reasons for apparently hostile responses and considerations for teachers dealing with hostile reactions.

2. Discuss three possible reasons for apparent indifference; for each, identify a consideration for teachers' overcoming indifference.

3. Discuss three possible reasons for overinvolvement; for each, identify ways of working with these parents.

4. Describe considerations for dealing with several causes of parent–teacher tension.

Helpful Websites

- The National Coalition for Parent Involvement in Education is a nonprofit organization that assists and encourages parental involvement in education wherever that education takes place: in public school, in private school, or at home.

- The Association for Conflict Resolution is a professional organization dedicated to enhancing the practice and public understanding of conflict resolution.

- The website for the Center for Nonviolent Communication has information and articles about Marshall Rosenberg's process of nonviolent communication.

- The Conflict Resolution Network is to promote the theory and practice of conflict resolution. The website has information about conflict resolution skills and attitudes.

Appendix

Home Visits to Families and Children

Many students who read this text may never be involved in home visits. Indeed, the only early childhood organizations where home visits are a routine part of the teacher–family partnership are Head Start and Early Head Start. Some Title 1 pre-kindergarten programs also incorporate home visits. But increasing numbers of school districts have established home visiting programs; therefore, many elementary teachers may be involved in doing home visits. This information is provided to those who want to explore home visits further as a part of their family involvement plans.

Home visits may be done to first meet children and families before school entry, at the place where both child and family are most comfortable (Bradley & Schalk, 2013). They may be done as part of planned school efforts to present a focus on partnership in education, or they may be a part of ongoing communication and education plans. An article on the National Education Association website said that most teachers and parents who have been involved in home visiting programs report their home visits have a lasting effect on the child, the parent, and parent–teacher communication. Despite their usefulness, home visits are often a cause for concern for teachers and parents.

A home visit takes teachers out of the familiar classroom world for which they are trained and directly into the diverse worlds in which the children live. Some teacher concerns may include the following:

- A lack of confidence in communicating with parents in their own homes

- Concern about cultural and language differences

- Concern about perceived conflicts in family values

- Child-rearing practices they may encounter

- Worry over personal safety

    Parents also might have concerns:

- Worry about how to behave, with a professional in their home

- Concern about whether the home and family "measure up" to a teacher's standards of environment or parenting skills. "What if my child acts up?" is a common concern.

- Concern about whether the home visit will become intrusive, with the teacher telling them what to do in their own homes and taking too much of their scarce time

    Benefits of home visits generally outweigh such concerns. Benefits include the following:

- Families receive evidence of the teachers' interest and caring for their children and an opportunity to play a more comfortable and dominant role in the home setting. Families also feel more involved in the educational process. In addition, home visits help parents build a sense of comfort with the teacher and the school.

- Teachers have another chance to reach out to families and an opportunity to experience the children's home environments and relationships firsthand, thus gaining information that will be useful in planning for the child's education.

- Children get a chance to build a deeper personal relationship with the teacher in a comfortable home setting. Their learning is increased when teachers are able to frame experiences building on what is familiar, as well as support parents in understanding how to assist their children's learning

There is no question that there are some disadvantages to home visits. These include the additional time involved for both teacher and family because finding available time to meet may be challenging with normal family life and teacher demands. Concerns about safety in some homes and neighborhoods may make teachers uncomfortable. This problem may be alleviated by having teachers visit with a partner.

Successful home visiting programs report that it is essential that visits be voluntary for both parents and teachers, that home visits not be associated with problems or disciplinary action, and that teachers be compensated for their time. Read more about these aspects on the website of the Parent Teacher Home Visit Project.

Essentials for Teachers Making Home Visits

1. Make the purpose clear in explanations to families. Clear explanations may help allay some parental concerns and help the teacher focus on accomplishing the purpose of the visit.

2. Arrange a time convenient for the family. Home visits are usually possible after family work hours or on weekends.

3. Behave as a guest, accepting the family's hospitality. Teachers should indicate no signs of surprise or disdain for the family's living conditions or lifestyle. Teachers are visiting to indicate support, not to evaluate. Dress simply and professionally.

4. Be on time. Plan driving arrangements carefully to avoid being late. Visits may last from half an hour to an hour or so, following the family's lead.

5. Expect distractions. Home life will continue as usual, with phones ringing, demands of children, and household routines. Flexible teachers will relax and help others relax.

6. Use social skills of tact, sensitivity, and interest to help themselves and family participants feel at ease with each another and accomplish the overall goal of enhancing the parent–teacher–child relationship.

7. Follow up with plans from information learned during the home visit. Use information to plan curriculum and family involvement, and to enhance future communication.

8. Send a thank-you note to the family to indicate teacher appreciation for the family's time and willingness to support their child.

9. Complete documentation of the visit. Summarize the visit and record the information that will be useful in future assessment and planning for the child and in formulating family involvement plans.

TeachSource

VIDEO ACTIVITY

© 2016 Cengage Learning®

View the video clip, *Partnership with Families: Home Visits.* After viewing, reflect on these questions:

1. How do the teacher's comments support the ideas about initial home visits from the chapter?

2. What are the benefits to children of initial home visits, noted by the teacher?

3. Note the emphasis on family along with children in these home visits. Why is this important?

Home-Based Educational and Support Programs

In addition to home visits to establish relationships and communication, home visitation programs developed over the past several decades focus specifically on teachers educating and supporting parents and children in the home. The goal of most **home-based programs** has been to help families become better teachers of their children and improve the quality of life for individual families. Typically, home-based programs serve families who are isolated physically or culturally or who would have problems attending a center. Frequently, at-risk families are involved in home-based programs; Head Start began its Home Start Component in 1972, and the well-known intervention programs of the 1960s and 1970s noted in Chapter 4 often included home visits—primarily to families considered at risk because of socioeconomic conditions. Currently, about 5 percent of Head Start programs offer home-based services that include weekly home visits and group socialization programs.

home-based programs
Programs in which a family's home is the primary location for delivery of services to the child and/or the parents

Early Head Start programs, funded in 1995 to serve low-income families of infants and toddlers, have home-based and center-based programs as well as a combination of the two. Programs serving children with disabilities also use home visits frequently; recent attention has focused on visits to families of infants and toddlers with special needs. Some recently established family support and resource programs offer home visits as one of the available options for parent education and support. The primary goals of most home visiting programs are largely preventive: to prevent preterm or low birth-weight infants, to promote healthy child development and school readiness, and to prevent child abuse. The programs all send individuals into the homes of young children, seeking to improve the lives of young children by encouraging changes in attitudes, knowledge, and behavior of parents. In addition, they offer social support, practical assistance, and some education. Programs differ in specific goals, level of services, staffing, and the population served. Some begin during pregnancy; others start later. Programs may work with families as long as two to five years and may schedule weekly or monthly visits.

Some of the most significant models of home visiting in recent family support efforts include Parents as Teachers, the Home Instruction Program for Preschool Youngsters (HIPPY), Healthy Start (Hawaii), Healthy Steps for Young Children, Healthy Families America, Partners for a Healthy Baby, and the Comprehensive Child Development Program.

Various policy and program design decisions determine the content of the home visit. Some programs focus primarily on the child, whereas others include attention to parent and family functioning. If the home visitors concentrate their efforts on working with parents rather than children, they often teach parents how to use everyday caregiving or household situations as opportunities to stimulate learning. When a teacher works with a child, it is a way to model appropriate teaching behavior to parents who are present and involved. All home-based programs assume that parents are the most important teachers of their children during the early years, and the skills they are taught have a long-term impact on all children in a family. In multiple-focus programs, attention is paid to family and parents' needs as well as children's development.

The home visits in these programs require different skills and techniques in addition to those necessary for working with children. In these programs, home visitors are parent educators. The importance of a strong interpersonal tie between parent and home visitor is emphasized in most programs.

For Further Information

For more information about teacher home visits or home-based education programs, the following resources may be helpful:

Print Resources

Bouhebent, E. A. (2008). "Providing the best for families: Developmentally appropriate home visitation services." *Young Children, 63*(2), 82–7.

Bradley, J., & Schalk, D. (2013). "Greater than great!" A teacher's home visit changes a young child's life *Young Children, 68*(3): 70–75.

Gomby, D. (2003). *Building school readiness through home visitation.* Sunnyvale, CA: First 5 California Children and Families Commission.

Klass, C. (2003). *The home visitor's guidebook: Promoting optimal parent and child development* (2nd ed.). Baltimore, MD: Paul H. Brookes.

Smalley, A., & Kush, R. (2003). *Young families at home: A home visitor's guide to young families.* St. Louis, MO: MELD (Parents as Teachers).

U.S. Dept. of Health, Education, and Welfare (Office of Child Development). (2004). *Home visitor's handbook for the Head Start home-based program option.* Washington, DC: Head Start Bureau.

Wasik, B., & Bryant, D. (2002). *Home visiting: Procedures for helping families* (2nd ed.). Mountain View, CA: Sage Publications.

Website Resources

This website for the Center for Home Visiting promotes interdisciplinary research and efforts to support home visiting programs.

This website for the Parent/Teacher Home Visit Project has information about a model for home visits that is inexpensive and easily replicated.

This website for Home Instruction Program for Preschool Youngsters (HIPPY) describes the parent-involvement, school readiness program that helps parents prepare their preschool children for success in school, with services for families delivered by home visits.

This website for Healthy Steps for Young Children, a national initiative that focuses on the importance of the first three years of life, emphasizes close relationships between health care professionals and parents in addressing the physical, emotional, and intellectual growth of children. The programs include home visits.

Glossary

A

active listening—Technique of sensitively picking up on a speaker's verbal and nonverbal messages and reflecting back the total message for the speaker's verification.

advocate—One who defends or espouses a cause.

androgynous—Having the characteristics of both sexes.

approachability—Capable of being approached; accessible.

assertive/democratic—With the weight of predictable authority. See also *authoritative*.

attachment—The strong, affectionate, mutual tie formed in the first two years following birth and enduring over time.

authentic—Genuine, real.

authoritarian—Requiring complete obedience to authority.

authoritative—Showing confident power and the right to command. See also *assertive/democratic*.

B

blended family—A family created by the coming together of previously existing families or parts of them.

C

chronosystem—System made up of the environmental events and transitions that occur throughout a child's life, including any sociohistorical events.

Code of Ethics—Statement adopted by the National Association for the Education of Young Children (NAEYC) in 1989 (revised in 2005, reaffirmed and updated in 2011) to provide guidelines for ethical behavior of professionals.

collaborative—Working with one another.

color blindness—Professed unawareness of skin color of others.

covert culture—Unconscious behavioral or perceptual patterns learned within one's cultural group.

cultural mores—Customs and beliefs associated with a particular culture.

culturally assaultive—Behaviors that attack the culture of another by ignoring, failing to accept and respect, demeaning, or attacking the behaviors and beliefs of another.

culture—The various understandings, traditions, and guidance of the groups to which we all belong; the ways of living developed by a social group and transmitted to succeeding generations; the social backgrounds that imbue children with particular forms of knowledge, values, and expectations for behavior.

D

daily news flash—Brief written news of the day posted for families.

deficit model—Working from the perspective of being inadequate or inferior.

democratic models—Models in which power is shared.

demographics—The statistical data of a human population.

developmental tasks—Appropriate accomplishments at specific stages of development.

developmentally appropriate programs—Programs that base their decisions about curriculum, care, routines, and guidance on knowledge about development of individual children and the needs of their families.

diversity—State of being varied, as by family structure, race, religion, socioeconomic class, primary language, ethnic background, and so on.

dominant culture—The culture that is most influential in a society—numerically and by the power of ideas and behaviors.

dysfunctional—Impaired in function.

E

easing-in—A schedule of gradually increasing the amount of time a child spends in a classroom so the child does not spend a full period at the beginning.

ecology—Interaction between the individual and the environment.

ELL (English language learners)—Individuals whose first language is not English.

empathic—Identifying with feelings of another.

empathize—To identify with or experience the feelings of another individual.

empowerment—Enabling; strengthening.

ethnocentric—Characterized by an attitude that one's own group is superior.

exosystem—Settings or events that influence the child's development even though the child has no direct role in them.

expertise—Special skill or knowledge in a particular field.

extended family—Kinship group consisting of parents, their children, and close relatives.

F

family-centered—Focusing on children and parents as a unit, with the parents becoming active in their children's development—not relating separately to parents and children.

G

gatekeeping—Keeping others away from the child—either physically or by subtle interference.

generativity—A concern for establishing and guiding the next generation.

H

High/Scope Model—Early childhood curriculum based on principle of children as active learners who plan, carry out, and reflect on learning choices during free choice periods and small group teacher-led experiences to help children focus on key experiences.

home-based programs—Programs in which a family's home is the primary location for delivery of services to the child and/or the parents.

humility—Quality of being humble; lowering oneself in relation to others.

I

I-message—Verbal expression of an individual's emotional response to a specific situation.

Individualized Education Plan (IEP)—A written plan designed to meet the unique educational needs of a child with a disability, as mandated by the Individuals with Disabilities Education Act.

Individualized Family Service Plan (IFSP)—A written plan for providing special intervention services for children under the age of three with disabilities, which includes the family as a primary participant.

intervention—Process of interfering with particular circumstances so as to change them.

J

jargon—Vocabulary peculiar to a particular profession or group.

L

latchkey child care—Children caring for themselves at home after school.

literacy activities—Activities that promote the development of oral communication skills and an understanding of print communication.

M

macrosystem—The belief systems, lifestyles and options, and patterns of social interchange of an individual's society and subculture that affect development.

mandate—An authoritative order or command; something that must be done.

mesosystem—Those events or situations in which two microsystems come together to have impact on development.

microsystem—Small part of a system that forms a unified whole; related to children—bounds of a child's world, such as home, school, Grandma's house, or the like.

N

nuclear family—A social unit composed of parents and children.

nurturing—Encouraging, supporting, caring, nourishing.

O

one-way communication—Communication sent from school to inform families without expectation of response.

open-ended questions—With no fixed answer; unrestricted.

overt culture—The various beliefs, behaviors, family practices, style of communication, traits, artifacts and products associated with a particular group of people.

P

paraphrasing—Restating in slightly different words what another has said.

parent cooperative nursery schools—Nursery schools in which parents participate along with paid professionals or are involved in decision making and maintenance of the school.

parent education—Specific attempts to offer knowledge and support to parents in hopes of increasing parenting effectiveness.

partiality—Tendency to favor one person over another.

parting ritual—Expected behaviors and activities repeated each day when saying goodbye.

pedagogical issues—Issues related to teaching.

permissive—Having a low level of demands or expectations for children's behavior; tolerating behavior outside of bounds; a hands-off style of interaction.

professionalism—Display of professional character, spirit, or methods.

R

readiness—Characteristics, skills, and dispositions that make a successful student; particularly used when talking about moving into kindergarten.

reflecting—Giving back to a speaker words that convey the listener's impression of the speaker's meaning.

reframing—Shifting from a negative perspective to a perspective that recognizes strengths by choosing different words and frames of reference.

resilience—Ability to spring back, adjust, or adapt to stress, misfortune, or change.

resource file—File of information about each family and ways they can be potential resources for a classroom.

S

sandwiching—Presenting an issue of concern with positive statements preceding and following the concern.

self-efficacy—Strength of one's belief in one's own ability to complete tasks and reach goals.

separation anxiety—Feelings of sadness and discomfort experienced by children and adults when apart from one another. Separation anxiety is most common in children under four years.

service learning—The process wherein schools integrate meaningful community service with instruction and reflection to support the learning experience, teach community responsibility, and help develop lifelong community engagement.

social capital—Available resources provided by efforts, knowledge, and relationships of people.

spontaneity—Acting from natural impulses.

T

TANF—Temporary Aid to Needy Families—the welfare reform legislation passed in 1996.

Touchpoints model—Model developed by T. Berry Brazelton to support families at key points of disruption during their children's development.

transition times—Times when children and families are arriving at or leaving the school.

trilemma—A dilemma that affects three parties, as in the parent, the child, and the school.

turf—Area of familiarity over which one asserts authority.

two-way communication—Communication designed to elicit dialogue between home and school.

References

Adams, K., & Christenson, S. (2000). Trust and the family-school relationship. *Journal of School Psychology, 38*, 477–497.

Addy, S., Engelhardt, W., & Skinner, C. (2013). *Basic facts about low-income children*. National Center for Children in Poverty. Retrieved on January 16, 2013, from www.nccp.org

Allen, M., & Staley, L. (2007). Helping children cope when a loved one is on military deployment. *Young Children, 62*(1), 82–87.

Amatea, E. (2012). *Building Culturally Responsive Family-School Relations*. Upper Saddle River, NJ: Pearson.

Anderson, G. (2000). A "walking" report card in preschool. *Focus on Pre-K and K, 13*(2), 1–3.

APA. (2004). An overview of the psychology literature on the effects of divorce on children. Retrieved on January 28, 2014, from www.apa.org

Auerbach, A. B. (1968). *Parents learn through discussion: Principles and practices of parent group education*. New York: John Wiley and Sons.

Austin, J. S. (2000). When a child discloses sexual abuse: Immediate and appropriate teacher responses. *Childhood Education, 77*(1), 1–5.

Author. (2010) *Early Head Start Research and Evaluation Project. 1996–2010*. Available online at www. acf.hhs.gov, and search for report by name.

Author. (2010) *Revisiting and Updating the Multicultural Principles for Headstart Programs Serving Children Birth through Age 5*. Early Headstart National Resource Center. (From U.S. Department of Health and Human Services, www.headstartinfo.org.)

Baker, A., & Manfredi/Petitt, L. (2004). *Relationships, the heart of quality care: Creating community among adults in early care settings*. Washington, DC: NAEYC.

Balaban, N. (2006). *Everyday goodbyes: Starting school and early care/A guide to the separation process*. New York: Teachers College Press.

Bang, Y. (2009). Helping all families participate in school life. *Young Children, 64*(6), 97–99.

Barbour, C., Barbour, N., & Scully, P. (2010). *Families, schools, and communities: Building partnerships for educating children* (5th ed., Chapter 9). Upper Saddle River, NJ: Prentice Hall.

Barnard, W. (2004). Parent involvement in elementary school and educational attainment. *Children and Youth Services Review, 26*(1), 39–62.

Bauch, J. (2000). *Parent involvement partnerships with technology*. Nashville, TN: Transparent School Model.

Beadle, A. (2012). *How the zero weeks of paid maternity leave in the U.S. compare globally*. Retrieved on December 23, 2013, from www.thinkprogress.org/health/2012/05/24

Belsky, J. (1986). Infant day care: A cause for concern? *Zero to Three: Bulletin of the National Center for Clinical Infant Programs, 7*(1), 1–7.

Belsky, J., Vandell, D., Burchinal, M., Clarke-Stewart, A., McCartney, K., Owen, M., & the NICHD Early Child Care Research Network. (2007). Are there long-term effects of early child care? *Child Development, 78*(2), 681–701.

Bennett, T. (2007). Mapping family resources and support. In D. Koralek (Ed.), *Spotlight on Young Children and Families* (pp. 20–3). Washington, DC: NAEYC.

Bernard, T. (2013). Standing up for the rights of new fathers. *New York Times*, November 9, 2013: pp. B1, B7.

Bhavnagri, N., & Gonzales-Mena, J. (1997). The cultural context of infant caregiving. *Childhood Education, 74*(1), 2–8.

Bigner, J. J. (2009). *Parent–child relations: An introduction to parenting* (8th ed.). New York: Prentice Hall.

Bisson, J. (2002). *Celebrate: An anti-bias guide to enjoying holidays in early childhood programs*. St. Paul, MN: Redleaf Press.

Bloomfield, S. (2009). *100+ Games, Quizzes, and Icebreakers*. Toronto: Monarch Books.

Boushey, H. (2011). The role of the government in work-family conflict. *Journal of Work and Family*, Vol. 21, 2, Fall 2011. Available online at www.futureofchildren.org/publications

Bowlby, J. (1988). *A secure base: Parent–child attachment and healthy human development*. New York: Basic Books.

Boyd-Franklin, N. (2006). *Black families in therapy: Understanding the African American experience* (2nd ed.). New York: Guilford Press.

Bradley, J., & Schalk, D., (2013). A teacher's home visit changes a young child's life. *Young Children, 68*(3): 70–75.

Brazelton, T. (1992). *On becoming a family: The growth of attachment before and after birth*. New York: Delacorte.

Brazelton, T. B. (2001). The irreducible needs of children: An interview with T. Berry Brazelton, MD, and Stanley I. Greenspan, MD. *Young Children, 56*(2), 6–14.

Brazelton, T. B., & Greenspan, S. (2001). *The irreducible needs of children: What every child must have to grow, learn, and flourish*. Cambridge, MA: Da Capo.

———. (2002). *Touchpoints 3 to 6: Your child's emotional and behavioral development*. Cambridge, MA: Perseus.

Bronfenbrenner, U. (1979a). *The ecology of human development: Experiments by nature and design*. Cambridge, MA: Harvard University Press.

———.(1979b). *Two worlds of childhood: US and USSR*. New York: Pocket Books.

Bronfenbrenner, U., & Morris, P. (1998). The ecology of developmental processes. In R. Lerner (Ed.), *Handbook of child psychology. Vol. 1. Theoretical models of human development*. New York: Wiley.

Brooks, J. (2009). *The process of parenting* (8th ed.). New York: McGraw-Hill.

Brotherson, S., & White, J., Eds. (2006). *Why fathers count: The importance of fathers and their involvement with children*. Harriman, TN: Men's Studies Press.

Brownfield, E. (2001). *The time crunch*. New York: Families and Work Institute.

Bureau of Labor Statistics (BLS). (2013). *American time use survey—2012 results*. Retrieved on January 17, 2014, from www.bls.gov

Caldwell, B. (2001). Déjà vu all over again: A researcher explains the NICHD study. *Young Children, 56*(4), 58–59.

Campbell, F., Ramey, C., Pungello, E., Sparling, J., and Miller-Johnson, S. (2000). Early childhood education: Young adult outcomes from the Abecedarian Project. *Applied Developmental Science, 6*(1), 42–57.

Campbell, K., Jamsek, M., & Jolly, P. (2007). Planning holiday celebrations: An ethical approach to developing policy and practices. In K. Paciorek, K. (Ed.), *Annual editions: Early childhood education 06/07.* Dubuque, IA: McGraw-Hill.

Canter, L., & Canter, M. (2001). *Parents on your side.* Santa Monica, CA: National Education Services.

Carlson, C. (2010). Future directions in family-school partnerships. In Christenson, S., & Reschy, A. (Eds.) *Handbook of school-family partnerships.* New York: Routledge.

The Carolina Abecedarian Project. (1999). *Early learning, later success: The Abcedarian study.* Retrieved on January 24, 2014, from www.fpg.unc.edu/~abc

Carroll, K. (2007). *A guide to great field trips.* Chicago, IL: Zephyr Press.

Caspe, M., Lopez, M., & Wolos, C. (2006/2007). *Family involvement in elementary school children's education.* 2. Retrieved on January 28, 2014, from www.hfrp.org/publications-resources?topic=6

Caspe, M., Seltzer, A., Kennedy, J., Cappio, M., & DeLorenzo, C. Engaging families in the child assessment process. *Young Children, 68*(3): 8–14.

Cherlin, A., & Krishnamurthy, P. (2004, May 9). What works for Mom? *The New York Times,* sec. 4, p. 13.

Child Welfare Information Gateway. (2009). *Understanding the effects of maltreatment on brain development.* Retrieved on August 26, 2013, from www.childwelfare.gov/pubs/issue_briefs/braindevelopment/effects.cfm

Child Welfare League of America. (2004). *Parental substance abuse: A major factor in child abuse and neglect.* New York: Child Welfare League of America.

The children of the Cost, Quality, and Outcomes Study go to school: Executive summary. (1999). Chapel Hill, NC: University of North Carolina.

Children's Defense Fund (1998). *The state of America's children: Yearbook 1998.* Washington, DC: Author.

———. (2004). *The state of America's children: Yearbook 2004.* Washington, DC: Author.

———. (2012). *The state of America's children. Yearbook 2012.* Washington, DC: Author.

———. (2013) *Child poverty in America: 2012 National analysis.* Retrieved on January 16, 2014 from www.childrensdefense.org

Childstats. (2013). *America's children: Key national indicators of well-being, 2013.* Retrieved on January 15, 2014, from www.childstats.gov

Cho, E., Chen, D., & Shin, S. (2010). Supporting transnational families. *Young Children, 65*(4), 30–37.

Chocolate, D. (1995). *On the day I was born.* New York: Scholastic Press.

Clarke-Stewart, A. (1989). Infant day care: Maligned or malignant? *American Psychologist, 44,* 268–269.

Clinton, H. (1996). *It takes a village and other lessons children teach us.* New York: Simon & Schuster.

Cohany, S., & Sok, E. (2007). Trends in labor force participation of married mothers of infants. *Monthly Labor Review, Feb.,* 9–16.

Cohn, D., Passel, J., Wang, W., & Livingston, G. (2011). Barely half of U.S. adults are married. Pew Research and Social Demographic Trends. Available at www.pewsocialrends.org. Retrieved January 17, 2014.

Connelly, R., DeGraff, D., & Willis, R. (2004). *Kids at work: The value of employer-sponsored on-site child care*. Kalamazoo, MI: W. E. Upjohn Institute.

Coontz, S. (2013). The triumph of the working mother. *New York Times*, June 2, 2013: p. SR11.

———. (2011). What is the "Traditional" American Family? Nov. 22, 2011. Retrieved on January 15, 2014, from www.motherco.com

———. (2000). The way we never were: *American families and the nostalgia trap*. New York: Basic Books.

Copple, C., & Bredekamp, S., Eds. (2009). *Developmentally appropriate practice in early childhood programs serving children from birth through age 8* (3rd ed.). Washington, DC: NAEYC.

The cost, quality, and child outcome study: A critique. Final report. (2000). Westport, CT: ABT.

Cost, Quality, and Outcomes Study Team. (1995). Cost, quality, and child outcomes in child care centers: Key findings and recommendations. *Young Children, 50*(4), 40–50.

Couse, L. (2003). "MY book!" Building literacy into family involvement. *Young Children, 58*(3), 103.

Crosson-Tower, C. (2009). *Understanding child abuse and neglect* (8th ed.). Upper Saddle River, NJ: Prentice Hall.

Day, M., & Parlakian, R. (2004). *How culture shapes social–emotional development: Implications for practice in infant-family programs*. Washington, DC: Zero to Three.

De Jong, L. (2003). Using Erikson to work more effectively with teenage parents. *Young Children, 58*(2), 87–95.

DeJong, L., & Burton, M. (2013). Book clubs strengthen family-teacher partnerships and build community. *Young Children, 68*(5): 62–67.

Delpit, L., & Kohl, H. (2006). *Other people's children: Cultural conflict in the classroom* (updated ed.). New York: The New Press.

Derman-Sparks, L., & Edwards, J. (2010). *Anti-bias education for young children and ourselves*. Washington, DC: NAEYC.

Derman-Sparks, L., Ramsey, P., & Edwards, J. (2011). *What if all the kids are white* (2nd ed.) New York: Teachers College Press.

DeSteno, N. (2000). Parent involvement in the classroom: The fine line. *Young Children, 55*(3), 13–17.

Dickinson, P., Lothian, S., & Jonz, M. (2007). Sharing responsibility for our children. *Young Children, 62*(2), 49–55.

Diffily, D., & Morrison, K. (Eds.). (1996). *Family-friendly communication for early childhood programs*. Washington, DC: NAEYC.

DiNatale, L. (2002). Developing high-quality family involvement programs in early childhood settings. *Young Children, 57*(5), 90–5.

Dinkmeyer, D., Sr., McKay, G., & Dinkmeyer, D., Jr. (2007a). *The parents' handbook: Systematic training for effective parenting*. Fredericksburg, VA: STEP Publishers.

Dinkmeyer, D. Sr., McKay, G., Dinkmeyer, J., & Dinkmeyer, D. Jr. (2008). *Parenting young children: Systematic training for effective parenting (STEP) of children under 6*. Fredericksburg, VA: STEP Publishers.

Dinkmeyer, D. Sr., & McKay, G. (2007b). *Parenting teenagers: Systematic training for effective parenting of teenagers*. Fredericksburg, VA: STEP Publishers.

Downer, J. & Myers, S. (2010). Application of a developmental/ecological model to family-school partnerships. In S. Christenson & A. Reschy (Eds.), *Handbook of school-family partnerships*. NY: Routledge.

Duvall, E., & Hill, K. (1948). *When you marry*. New York: Association Press.

Edelson, J. (2001). *Should childhood exposure to adult domestic violence be defined as child maltreatment under the law?* St. Paul, MN: University of Minnesota School of Social Work.

Educational Productions. (2001). *Kindergarten, here I come!* [video]. Find at www.kindergartenhereIcome.com

Eldridge, D. (2001). Parent involvement: It's worth the effort. *Young Children, 56*(4), 65–9.

Elicker, J. & McMullen, M. (2013). Appropriate and meaningful assessment in family-centered programs. *Young Children, 68*(3): 22–27.

Elkind, D. (1987). *Miseducation: Preschoolers at risk*. New York: Knopf.

Ephron, N. (2013) *Heartburn* in *The most of Nora Ephron*. New York: A. Knopf.

Epstein, J. (2011). *School and family partnerships: Preparing educators and improving schools* (2nd ed.). Boulder, CO: Westview.

Epstein, J., Coates, L., Salinas, K., Sanders, M., & Simon, B. (2009). *School, family, and community partnerships: Your handbook for action* (3rd ed.). Thousand Oaks, CA: Corwin.

Epstein, J., Sanders, M., Simon, B., Salinas, K., Jansorn, N., & Van Voorhis, F. (2002). *School, family, and community partnerships*. Thousand Oaks, CA: Corwin Press.

Espinosa, L. (2010). *Getting it right for young children from diverse backgrounds: Applying research to improve practice*. Washington, DC: NAEYC.

Fenlon, A. (2005). Collaborative steps: Paving the way to kindergarten for young children with disabilities. *Young Children, 60*(2), 32–37.

File, N. (2001). Family-professional partnerships: Practice that matches philosophy. *Young Children, 56*(4), 70–74.

Fine, M., & Lee, S. (2000). *Handbook of diversity in parent education: The changing faces of parenting and parent education*. New York: Academic Press.

Fisher, R., Ury, W., & Patton, B. (2011). *Getting to yes: Negotiating agreement without giving in* (3rd ed.). NY: Penguin.

Friedan, B. (1963). *The feminine mystique*. New York: Norton.

Friedman, S. (2007). Coming together for children: Six community partnerships make a big difference. *Young Children, 62*(2), 34–41.

Galinsky, E. (1987). *The six stages of parenthood*. Reading, MA: Addison-Wesley.

———. (1999). *Ask the children: What America's children really think about working parents*. New York: Morrow.

———. (2000). Findings from *Ask the Children* with implications for early childhood professionals. *Young Children, 55*(3), 64–68.

———. (2002). *Navigating work* and *family: Hands-on advice for working parents*. New York: Families and Work Institute.

Galinsky, E., Kim, S., & Bond, J. (2001). *Feeling overworked: When work becomes too much*. New York: Families and Work Institute.

Gallagher, P., Fialka, J., Rhodes, C., & Arceneaux, C. (2002). Rethinking denial. *Young Exceptional Children, 5*(2): 11–17.

Garces, E., Thomas, D., & Currie, J. (2000). *Longer-term effects of Head Start*. NBER Working Paper 8054. Retrieved on January 29, 2014, from www.princeton.edu/jcurrie/publications

Garcia, E., & McLaughlin, B. (1995). Meeting the challenge of linguistic and cultural diversity in early childhood education. In B. Spodek & O. Saracho (Eds.), *Yearbook in early childhood education* (Vol. 6). New York: Teachers College Press.

Gartrell, D. (2000). *What the kids said today: Using classroom conversations to become a better teacher.* St. Paul, MN: Redleaf Press.

Gennarelli, C. (2004). Communicating with families: Children lead the way. *Young Children, 59*(1), 98–9.

Gillespie, L., & Petersen, L. (2012). Rituals and routines: Supporting infants and toddlers and their families. *Young Children, 67*(4), 76–77.

Goetz, K. (Ed.). (1992). *Programs to strengthen families: A resource guide* (3rd ed.). Chicago: Family Resource Coalition.

Goldman, L. (1996). We can help children grieve: A child-oriented model for memorializing. *Young Children, 51*(6), 69–73.

Gollnick, D., & Chinn, P. (2012). *Multicultural education in a pluralistic society* (9th ed.). Upper Saddle River, NJ: Prentice Hall.

Gonzalez-Mena, J. (2008a). Child, family, and community: Family-centered early care and education (5th ed.). Upper Saddle River, NJ: Prentice Hall.

———. (2008b). *Diversity in early care and education programs: Honoring differences* (5th ed.). New York: McGraw-Hill.

———. (2010). *50 strategies for communicating and working with diverse families* (2nd ed.). Upper Saddle River, NJ: Pearson.

Gordon, T. (2008). *Parent effectiveness training: The proven program for raising responsible children.* 30th anniversary edition. New York: Random House.

Graue, E. (2001). Research in review: What's going on in the children's garden? Kindergarten today. *Young Children, 56*(3), 67–73.

Gray, H. (2004). You go away and you come back. *Young Children, 59*(5): 100–7.

Greenberg, J. (1996). Seeing children through tragedy: My mother died today—When is she coming back? *Young Children, 51*(6), 76–7.

———. (2001). She is so my real mom! Helping children understand adoption as one form of family diversity. *Young Children, 56*(2), 90–1.

Halle, T. (2012). *Charting parenthood: A statistical portrait of mothers and fathers in America.* Childtrends. Available at www.fatherhood.hhs.gov. Retrieved January 17, 2014.

Hammack, B., Foote, M., Garretson, S., & Thompson, J. (2012), Family literacy packs: Engaging teachers, families, and young children in quality activities to promote partnerships for learning. *Young Children, 67*(3): 104–110.

Han, W. J., & Waldfogel, J. (2003). Parental leave: The impact of recent legislation on parents' leave taking. *Demography, 40*(1), 191–200.

Harms, T., Clifford. R., & Cryer, D. (2004). *Early childhood environment rating scale* (rev. ed.). New York: Teachers College Press.

Hart, B., & Risley, T. (2003) *Meaningful differences in everyday parenting and intellectual development in young American children* (2nd ed.). Baltimore: Paul H. Brookes.

Hattery, A. (2000). *Women, work, and family: Balancing and weaving.* Thousand Oaks, CA: Sage Publications.

Head Start Program Performance Standards and Other Regulations. Retrieved on January 29, 2014, from eclkc.ohs.acf.hhs.gov/hslc/standards/Head%20Start%20Requirements

Heatherington, M., & Kelly, J. (2002). *For better or worse: Divorce reconsidered.* New York: W. W. Norton.

Heiss, R. (2007). *Helping kids help: Organizing successful charitable projects.* Chicago IL: Zephyr Press.

Helms, A. D. (2000, Feb. 1). Why can't we see Dad as the go-to guy? *Charlotte Observer,* p. D-1.

Henderson, A., & Mapp, K. (2002). *A new wave of evidence: The impact of school, family and community connections on student achievement.* Austin, TX: Southwest Education Development Laboratory.

Heroman, C., Dodge, D., Berke, K., & Bickart, T. (2002). *The creative curriculum for preschool* (5th ed.). Washington, DC: Teaching Strategies, Inc.

Hildebrand, V., Phenice, L., Gray, M., Hines, R., Bubolz, M., & Sontag, M. (2007). *Knowing and serving diverse families* (3rd ed.). Englewood Cliffs, NJ: Merrill.

Ho, E., & Willms, J. (1996). Effects of parental involvement on eighth-grade achievement. *Sociology of Education, 69*(2), 126–41.

Hochschild, A., & Machung, A. (2003). *The second shift: Working parents and the revolution at home.* New York: Penguin.

Hoffman, E. (1997). *Starting small: Teaching tolerance in preschool and the early grades.* Montgomery, AL: Southern Poverty Law Center.

Hoover-Dempsey, K., Walker, J., Sandler, H., Whetsel, D., Green, C., Wilkins, A., & Classen, K. (2005). Why do parents become involved? Research findings and implications. *Elementary School Journal, 106,* 105–130.

Hopkins, A. (2002). Children and grief: The role of the early childhood educator. *Young Children, 57*(1), 40–47.

Howe, N., Strauss, W., & Matson, R. (2000). *Millennials rising: The next great generation.* New York: Vintage.

Hubert, C. (2009, March 10). Number of homeless children on the rise. *Sacramento Bee,* p. 1.

Hull, A. (2003). *Raising America: Experts, parents, and a century of advice.* New York: Knopf.

Hunt, E. (2003). Out of the shadows. *Teaching Tolerance, 24,* 38–43.

Huseth, M. (2001). The school/home connection: Website and e-mail improve teacher/parent communication. *Learning and Leading With Technology, 29*(6), 6–15.

Hutter, S. (2000). Precious time. *Working Mother, 55*(2), 46–48, 108.

Hymes, J. L. (1975). *Effective home school relations* (rev. ed.). Carmel, CA: Hacienda Press.

Hyson, M, Ed. (2003). *Preparing early childhood professionals: NAEYC's standards for programs.* Washington, DC: NAEYC. Complete position statement at www.naeyc.org/positionstatements

Im, J., Parlakian, R., & Sanchez, S. (2007). Understanding the influence of culture on caregiving practices—From the inside out. *Young Children, 62*(5), 65–66.

Isbell, R. (2002). Telling and retelling stories: Learning language and literacy. *Young Children, 57*(2), 27–30.

Jacobson, L., & Simpson, A. (2007). Communicating about early childhood education. *Young Children, 62*(3), 89–93.

Jaksec, C. (2004). *The difficult parent: An educator's guide to handling aggressive behavior.* Thousand Oaks, CA: Corwin Press.

Jamieson, S., & Wallace, L. (2010). *Family strengths.* Retrieved on January 29, 2014, from www.extension. missouri.edu/bsf/strengths/index.htm

Jor'dan, J., Wolf, K., & Douglass, A. (2012). Strengthening families in Illinois: Increasing family engagement in early childhood programs. *Young Children, 67*(5): 18–23.

Kagan, S. (1995, May). The changing face of parent education. *ERIC Digest.* ERIC document 382406. Retrieved on January 29, 2014, from www.eric.ed.gov

Kagan, S., Pwell, D., Weissbourd, B., & Zigler, E., Eds. (1987) *America's family support programs.* New Haven, CT: Yale University Press.

Kalyanpur, M., & Harry, B. (2012). *Cultural reciprocity in special education: Building family-professional relationships.* Baltimore: Paul H. Brookes Publishing Co.

Karen, R. (1994). *Becoming attached: Unfolding the mystery of the infant–mother bond and its impact on later life.* New York: Warner Books.

Katz, L. (1995). Mothering and teaching—Some significant distinctions. In L. Katz (Ed.), *Talks with teachers of young children: A collection.* Norwood, NJ: Ablex Publishing.

Kieff, J., & Wellhousen, K. (2000). Planning family involvement in early childhood programs. *Young Children, 55*(3), 18–25.

Kirmani, M. (2007). Empowering culturally and linguistically diverse children and families. *Young Children, 62*(6), 94–98.

Klein, M. D., & Chen, D. (2001). *Working with children from culturally diverse backgrounds.* Albany, NY: Delmar.

Knapp, M., Hall, J. & Horgan, T. (2013). *Nonverbal communication in human interaction* (8th ed.). New York: Wadsworth Publishing.

Kyle, D., McIntyre, E., Miller, K., & Moore, G. (2002). *Reaching out: A K–8 resource for connecting families and schools.* Thousand Oaks, CA: Corwin Press.

———. (2005). *Bridging school and home through family nights: Ready-to-use plans for grades K–8.* Thousand Oaks, CA: Corwin Press.

Lashley, C., & Giannoni, L. (2010). Optimizing mothers' social networks: Information-sharing strategies. *Young Children, 65*(4): 38–44.

Lawrence-Lightfoot, S. (2003). *The essential conversation: What parents and teachers can learn from each other.* New York: Random House.

Leading Edge. (1998). Washington, DC: NAEYC.

Lee, J., & McDougal, O. (2000, Winter). Guidelines for writing notes to families of young children. *Focus on Pre-K and K, 13*(2), 4–6.

Lino, M. (2013). *Expenditures on children by families, 2012.* U.S. Department of Agriculture, Center for Nutrition Policy and Promotion, Miscellaneous Publication 1528–2012. Retrieved on December 24, 2013, from www.cnpp.usda.gov

Lopez, G., Scribner, J., & Mahitivanichcha, K. (2001). Redefining parental involvement: Lessons from high-performing migrant-impacted schools. *American Education Research Journal, 38*(2), 253–288.

Lucas-Thompson, R., Goldberg, W., & Prouse, J. (2010). Maternal work early in the lives of children and its distal associates with achievement and behavior problems. *Psychological Bulletin, 136*(6), 915–942.

Ludwig, J., & Phillips, D. (2005). *Accreditation criteria and procedures of the National Association for the Education of Young Children.* Washington, DC: Author. Retrieved on January 29, 2014, from www.naeyc.org/academy

———. (2011). *Code of ethical conduct and statement of commitment* (updated an reaffirmed.). Retrieved on January 29, 2014 from www.naeyc.org/positionstatements

———. (2008). *Long-term effects of Head Start on low-income children.* Retrieved on January 29, 2014, from home.uchicago.edu/~ludwigj/papers/NYAS-LudwigPhillips-HeadStart-2008.pdf

Lynch, E., & Hanson, M. (2011). *Developing cross-cultural competence: A guide for working with young children and their families* (4th ed.). Baltimore, MD: Paul H. Brookes.

MacKenzie, B. (2011). Caring for Rosie the Riveter's children. *Young Children, 66*(6): 68–70.

Magruder, E., Hayslip,W., Espinosa, L., & Matera, C. (2013). Many languages, one teacher: Supporting language and literacy development for preschool dual language learners. *Young Children, 68*(1): 8–15.

Malaguzzi, L. (1998). History, ideas, and basic-philosophy interview with Lella Gandini. In C. Edwards, L. Gandini, and G. Forman (Eds.), *The hundred languages of children: The Reggio Emilia approach to early childhood education.* Norwood, NJ: Ablex Publishing.

Malekpour, M. (2007). Effects of attachment on early and later development. *The British Journal of Developmental Disabilities. 53*(2), No. 105: 81–95. Retrieved on January 29, 1014, from www.bjdd.org

Mankiw, S., & Strasser, J. (2013). Tender topics: Exploring sensitive issues with PreK through first grade children through read-alouds. *Young Children, 68*(1): 84–89.

Mapp, K., & Hong, S. (2010). Debunking the myth of the hard-to-reach parent. pp. 345–361. In S. Christenson & A. Reschy (Eds), *Handbook of school-family partnerships (pp. 345–361).* New York: Routledge,

Martin, J., & Nakayama, T. (2012). *Intercultural communication in contexts* (6th ed.). NY: McGraw-Hill.

Martin, S. (2009). *Take a look: Observation and portfolio assessment* (5th ed.). Indianapolis, IN: Addison-Wesley.

———. (2010). *Experiencing intercultural communication: An introduction.* New York: McGraw-Hill.

Mass, Y., & Cohan, A. Home connections to learning: Supporting parents as teachers. In D. Koralek (Ed.), *Spotlight on Young Children and Families.* Washington, DC: NAEYC.

Matthews, H., & Jang, D. (2007). The challenges of change: Learning from the child care and early education experiences of immigrant families. Retrieved on January 29, 2014, from www.clasp.org/admin/site/publications/files/0356.pdf

Mayer, E., Ferede, M., & Hou, E. (2006). The Family Involvement Storybook: A new way to build connections with families. *Young Children, 61*(6), 94–97.

McMullen, M., & Apple, P. (2012). Babies (and their Families) on Board! *Young Children, 67*(4), 42–48.

Merrill, S. (2010). Starting child care: It's a transition for parents too! *Young Children, 65*(5), 60–1.

Miller, S. (2010). Head, hands, heart, and hope: Helping to end global poverty. *Young Children, 65*(4): 64–69.

Mitchell, S., Foulger, T., & Wetzel, K. (2009). Ten tips for involving families through Internet-based communication. *Young Children, 64*(5), 46–49.

Mooney, C. (2009). *Theories of attachment: An introduction to Bowlby, Ainsworth, Gerber, Brazelton, Kennell, & Klaus.* St. Paul, MN: Redleaf Press.

Mosle, S., (2013). The parent-teacher trap. *New York Times*, January 13, 2013: p. SR7.

Murphy, J. (2003). Case studies in African American school success and parenting behaviors. *Young Children, 58*(6), 85–89.

NAEYC. (1996). Position statement: Responding to linguistic and cultural diversity. *Young Children, 52*(2), 4–12.

———. (1997). NAEYC position statement on the prevention of child abuse in early childhood programs and the responsibilities of early childhood professionals to prevent child abuse. *Young Children, 52*(3), 42–46.

———. (2000). *A call for excellence in early childhood education.* Washington, DC: NAEYC. Retrieved on January 29, 2014, from www.naeyc.org/policy/excellence

———. (2005a, 2011). Code of ethics (reaffirmed and updated). Retrieved on December, 17, 2013, from www.naeyc.org/about/positionstatements/ethical_conduct

———. (2005b). Screening and assessment of young English language learners. 2005 Supplement to 2003 joint position statement by NAEYC and NAECS/SDE. *Early Childhood Curriculum, Assessment, and Program Evaluation.* Retrieved on May 12, 2014, from www.naeyc.org/positionstatements

Narvaez, A., Feldman, J., & Theriot, C. (2007). Virtual Pre-K: Connecting home, school, and community. In D. Koralek (Ed.), *Spotlight on young children and families* (pp. 52–53). Washington, DC: NAEYC.

National Center for Education Statistics. (2001). *Measuring father involvement in young children's lives.* Washington, DC: Department of Education.

National Center for Health Statistics. (2013). *Faststats: Unmarried childbearing.* Retrieved on January 16, 2014, from www.cdc.gov/nchs/faststats/unmarry.htm

NCPIE (National Coalition for Parent Involvement in Education.) (2006). *What's happening: A new wave of evidence: The impact of school, family, and community connections on student achievement.* Retrieved on January 29, 2014, from www.ncpie.org/WhatsHappening/researchJanuary2006.cfm

NEA. (1999). What do you do when parents show no respect for school employees? Tips for teachers. *NEA Today, 18*(3), 29–30.

Nemeth, K. (2009). Meeting the home language mandate: Practical strategies for all classrooms. *Young Children, 64*(2), 36–42.

Nemeth, K., & Erdosi, Vi. (2012). Enhancing practice with infants and toddlers from diverse language and cultural backgrounds. *Young Children, 67*(4): 49–57.

News-Press. (2005, March 20). American family like ships passing in dark.

NIHCD Early Child Care Research Network. (1997). The effects of infant child care on infant–mother attachment security: Results of the NIHCD study of early child care. *Child Development, 68*(5), 860–879.

Nilsen, B. (2013). *Week by week: Plans for observing and recording young children* (6th ed.). Florence, KY: South-Western College Publications.

Olson, M. (2007). Strengthening families: Community strategies that work. *Young Children, 62*(2), 26–31.

Olson, M., & Hyson, M. (2005). NAEYC explores parental perspectives on early childhood education. *Young Children, 60*(3), 66–68.

Ordonez-Jasis, R., & Ortiz, R. (2006). Reading their worlds: Working with diverse families to enhance children's early literacy development. *Young Children, 61*(1), 42–47.

Parents and the high cost of child care: 2013 Update. Retrieved on January 23, 2014, from www.naccrra org

Perez, A. (2011). Supporting breastfeeding in your program. *Young Children, 66*(1): 60–61.

Petty, K. (2009). *Deployment: Strategies for working with kids in military families.* St. Paul, MN: Redleaf Press.

Pipher, M. (1996). *The shelter of each other: Rebuilding our families.* New York: G. P. Putnam's Sons.

Powell, D. (1998). Reweaving parents into the fabric of early childhood programs. *Young Children, 53*(5), 60–67.

PTA. (2008). *National standards for family-school partnerships*. Retrieved on January 29, 2014, from www.pta.org/programs/content.cfm?ItemNumber=3126

Rampell, C. (2013). U.S. Women on the rise as breadwinner. *New York Times*. May 29, 2013. Retrieved on January 17, 2014, from www.nytimes.com

Rapoport, R., Bailyn, L., Fletcher, J., & Pruitt, B. (2001). *Beyond work—Family*. San Francisco: Jossey-Bass.

Ray, J., & Shelton, D. (2004). E-pals: Connecting with families through technology. *Young Children, 59*(3), 30–2.

Reynolds, A., & Stilafen, R. (2010). Parent involvement in early education. In S. Christenson & A Reschy (Eds.), *Handbook of school-family partnerships (pp. 158–174)*. New York: Routledge.

Robinson, A., & Stark, D. (2005). *Advocates in action: Making a difference for young children* (rev. ed.). Washington, DC: NAEYC.

Rockwell, B., & Kniepkamp, J. (2003). *Partnering with parents: Easy programs to involve parents in the early learning process*. Beltsville, MD: Gryphon House Press.

Rodd, J. (1998). *Leadership in early childhood: The pathway to professionalism* (2nd ed.). New York: Teachers College Press.

Rosegrant, T. (1992). Reaching potentials in a multilingual classroom: Opportunities and challenges. In S. Bredekamp & T. Rosegrant (Eds.), *Reaching Potentials: Appropriate Curriculum and Assessment for Young Children* (pp. 145–7). Washington, DC: NAEYC.

Rosenberg, M. (2003). *Nonviolent communication: A language of life*. Encinitas, CA: Puddledancer Press.

——— . (2004). *We can work it out: Resolving conflicts peacefully and powerfully*. Encinitas, CA: Puddledancer Press.

Samovar, L. A., Porter, R. E., & McDaniel, E. (2009). *Communication between cultures* (7th ed.). Belmont, CA: Wadsworth.

Santos, R., Fettig, A., & Shaffer, L. (2012). Helping families connect early literacy with social-emotional development. *Young Children, 67*(2): 88–93.

Saracho, O. (2010). The interface of the American family and culture. In O. Saracho & B. Spodek (Eds). *Contemporary perspectives on language and cultural diversity in early childhood education*. Charlotte, NC: Information Age Publishing,

Sauve, R. (2004). *Profiling Canada's families III*. Ottawa, Ontario: Vanier Institute of the Family.

Schorr, L. (2011). *Common purpose: Strengthening families and neighborhoods to rebuild America*. New York: Anchor.

Schweinhart, L., et al. (2005). *Lifetime effects: The High/Scope Perry preschool study through age 40*. Ypsilanti, MI: HighScope Press.

Seibel, N., & Gillespie, L. (2006). Child care as a setting for helping to prevent child abuse and neglect. *Exchange, 169*, 16–20.

Seplocha, H. (2007). Partnerships for learning: Conferencing with families. *Spotlight on young children and families*. Washington, DC: NAEYC.

Shellenbarger, S. (2005, February 18). Both sides in "Mommy War" search for peace. *Wall Street Journal*, D1.

Small, M. (2002). *Kids: How bio and culture shape the way we raise young children*. New York: Anchor Books.

Smith, C. (1998). Children with "special rights" in the preprimary schools and infant–toddler centers of Reggio Emilia. In C. Edwards, L. Gandini, & G. Forman (Eds.) *The hundred languages of children: The Reggio Emilia approach—Advanced reflections* (2nd ed.). Greenwich, CT: Ablex Publishing Corp.

Smith, R., Gartin, B., Murdick, N., & Hilton, A. (2006). *Families and children with special needs: Professional and family partnerships.* Upper Saddle River, NJ: Prentice-Hall.

Souto-Manning, M. (2010). Family involvement: Challenges to consider, strengths to build on. *Young Children, 65*(2): 82–88.

——. (2013). Teaching young children from immigrant and diverse families. *Young Children, 68*(4): 72–80.

Spaggiari, S. (1998). The community-teacher partnership in the governance of the schools. An interview with Lella Gandini. In C. Edwards, L. Gandini, and G. Forman (Eds.), *The hundred languages of children: The Reggio Emilia approach—Advanced reflections* (2nd ed.). Greenwich, CT: Ablex Publishing.

Sparrow, J., & Brazelton, T. B. (2007, September 9). Parent–teacher teamwork benefits kids. *Portland Press-Herald,* G2.

Spicer, T. (2000). Linking home and school—Meet a doll named Heidi. *Young Children, 55*(5), 86–7.

Stephens, K. (2007). Parent meetings: Creative ways to make them meaningful. *Exchange, 175,* 85–8.

Stewart, S. (2007). *Brave new stepfamilies.* Thousand Oaks, CA: Sage.

Strauss, V. (2013, March 5) Does Head Start work for kids? The bottom line. *The Washington Post.* Available online by searching for the title at www.washingtonpost.com

Sullivan, B. (2006). Welcoming volunteers into your classroom. *Exchange, 169,* 53–57.

Swick, K. (1985). Critical issues in parent education. *Dimensions, 14*(1), 4–7.

——. (2003). Communication concepts for strengthening family-school-community partnerships. *Early Childhood Education Journal, 30*(4), 275–80.

Tabors, P. (2008). *One child, two languages: A guide for preschool educators of children learning English as a second language* (2nd ed.). Baltimore, MD: Paul H. Brookes.

Ting-Toomey, S., & Chung, L. (2011). *Understanding intercultural communication.* (2nd ed.). New York: Oxford University Press.

Ukens, L. (2008). *Getting together: Icebreakers and group energizers.* San Francisco, CA: Pfeiffer.

Ulrich, M., & Bauer, A. (2003). Levels of awareness: A closer look at communication between parents and professionals. *Teaching Exceptional Children, 35*(6), 20–4.

U.S. Department of Education. (2004). *A call to commitment: Fathers' involvement in children's learning.* Retrieved on January 23, 2014, from www2.ed.gov/pubs/parents/calltocommit/index.html

U.S. Department of State. (2013). *FY 2012 Annual report on intercountry adoption.* Retrieved on August 27, 2013, from www.adoption.state.gov/content/pdf/2012fy

Vartuli, S. (2005). Beliefs: The heart of teaching. *Young Children, 60*(5), 76–85.

Vesely, C., & Ginsberg, M. (2011). Strategies and practices for working with immigrant families in early education programs. *Young Children, 66*(1): 84–89.

Wallerstein, J. S., & Blakeslee, S. (1989). *Second chances: Men, women, and children: A decade after divorce.* New York: Ticknor and Fields.

Wallerstein, J., Lewis, J., & Blakeslee, S. (2000). *The unexpected legacy of divorce: A twenty-five year landmark study.* New York: Hyperion Press.

——. (2003). *What about the kids? Raising your children before, during, and after divorce.* New York: Hyperion Press.

Warner, J. (2005, February 14). I love them, I love him not. *New York Times*, p. A23.

——. (2006, November 10). The family-friendly Congress. *New York Times*, p. A-25.

Waterman, S. (2006). *The four most baffling challenges for teachers and how to solve them*. Larchmont NY: Eye on Education.

Weiss, H., Caspe, M., & Lopez, M. E. (2006). *Family involvement in early childhood education*. 1, Spring. Available from the Harvard Family Research Project. Retrieved on January 25, 2014, from www.hfrp.org/publications-resources/browse-our-publications/family-involvement-in-early-childhood-education

White, B., Graham, M., & Bradford, S. (2007). Children of teen parents: Challenges and hope. In K. Paciorek (Ed.), *Annual editions: Early childhood education, 2006/2007*. Dubuque, IA: McGraw-Hill.

Whiteman, J. (2013). Connecting with families: Tips for those difficult conversations. *Young Children*, 68(1): 94–95.

Willis, J. Bilingual brains: Smarter and faster. *Psychology Today*, November 22, 2012. Available at www.psychologytoday.com

Winter, J. (2006). *Breakthrough parenting for children with special needs: Raising the bar of expectations*. San Francisco: Jossey-Bass.

Wood, S., & Kendall, R. (2013). *Parents and the high cost of child care, 2013 Report*. Published by www.usa.childcareaware.org

Yeary, J. (2013). Promoting mindfulness: Helping young children cope with separation. *Young Children*. 68(5): 110–11.

York, S. (2003). *Roots and wings: Affirming culture in early childhood programs* (rev. ed.). St. Paul, MN: Redleaf Press.

Young, D., & Behounek, L. (2006). Kindergartners use PowerPoint to lead their own parent–teacher conferences. *Young Children, 61*(2), 24–6.

Index

NAEYC Early Childhood Program Standards and Accreditation Criteria

The 10 program standards define what NAEYC believes every early childhood education program should be, based on research and professional experience. NAEYC uses the standards and criteria to not only define elements of program quality but to also recognize programs that demonstrate the capacity to sustain quality over time. Of the 10 standards, five focus on children, and the other five consider teaching staff, partnerships, and administration. Here, you will find the complete consideration of the standard dealing with families as well as standards in other program components related to working with families and the community.

In the text, you will find these standards referred to as AS (Accreditation Standards).

Standard 7: FAMILIES

Program Standard: The program establishes and maintains collaborative relationships with each child's family to foster children's development in all settings. These relationships are sensitive to family composition, language, and culture.

NAEYC Accreditation Criteria for Families Standard	Text Chapter
7.A Knowing and Understanding the Program's Families	
7.A.01 As a part of orientation and ongoing staff development, new and existing program staff develop skills and knowledge to work effectively with diverse families.	Chapters 1, 2, 3, 5, 6, 7, 9, 14, and 15
7.A.02 Program staff use a variety of formal and informal strategies to become acquainted with and learn from families about their family structure; their preferred child-rearing practices; and information families wish to share about their socioeconomic, linguistic, racial, religious, and cultural backgrounds.	Chapters 1, 5, 7, 8, 10, and 13
7.A.03 Program staff actively use information about families to adapt the program environment, curriculum, and teaching methods to the families they serve.	Chapters 5, 10, and 14
7.A.04 To better understand the cultural backgrounds of children, families, and the community, program staff participate in community cultural events, concerts, storytelling activities, or other events and performances designed for children and their families.	Chapters 1 and 13
7.A.05 Program Staff provide support and information to family members legally responsible for the care and well-being of a child.	Chapters 5, 6, and 11
7.A.06 Program staff establish intentional practices designed to foster strong reciprocal relationships with families from the first contact and maintain them over time.	Chapters 5, 6, 7, and 9
7.A.07 Program staff ensure that all families, regardless of family structure; socioeconomic, racial, religious, and cultural backgrounds; gender; abilities; or preferred language are included in all aspects of the program, including volunteer opportunities. These opportunities consider each family's interests and skills and the needs of program staff.	Chapters 5, 10, and 13
7.A.08 Program staff engage with families to learn from their knowledge of their child's interests, approaches to learning, and the child's developmental needs, and to learn about their concerns and goals for their children. This information is incorporated into ongoing classroom planning.	Chapters 5, 7, and 9
7.A.09 Program staff use a variety of formal and informal methods to communicate with families about the program philosophy and curriculum objectives, including educational goals and effective strategies that can be used by families to promote their children's learning. Staff use a variety of methods such as new family orientations, small group meetings, individual conversations, and written questionnaires, which help staff get input from families about curriculum activities throughout the year.	Chapters 7, 8, 9, and 11

(continued)

NAEYC Accreditation Criteria for Families Standard	Text Chapter
7.A Knowing and Understanding the Program's Families (*continued*)	
7.A.11 Families may visit any area of the facility at any time during the program's regular hours of operation as specified by the procedures of the facility.	Chapter 7
7.A.12 The program facilitates opportunities for families to meet with one another on a formal and informal basis, work together on projects to support the program, and learn from and provide support for each other.	Chapter 11
7.A.13 The program's governing or advisory groups include families as members and active participants. Staff or other families in the program encourage and support family members in taking on leadership roles.	Chapter 11
7.A.14 Program staff and families work together to plan events. Families' schedules and availability are considered as part of this planning.	Chapter 11
7.B Sharing Information Between Staff and Families	
7.B.01 Program staff use a variety of mechanisms such as family conferences or home visits to promote dialogue with families. The program staff asks adults to translate or interpret communication as needed.	Chapter 9, Appendix
7.B.02 The program compiles and provides program information to families in a language the family can understand. This information includes program policies and operating procedures.	Chapters 8 and 11
7.B.03 Program staff inform families about the program's systems for formally and informally assessing children's progress. This information includes the purposes of the assessment, the procedures used for assessment, procedures for gathering family input and information, the timing of assessments, the way assessment results or information will be shared with families, and ways the program will use this information.	Chapter 9
7.B.04 When program staff suspect that a child has a developmental delay or other special need, this possibility is communicated to families in a sensitive, supportive, and confidential manner and is provided with documentation and explanation for the concern, suggested next steps, and information about resources for assessment.	Chapter 9
7.B.05 Program staff communicate with families on a **daily basis** regarding infants' and toddlers'/ twos' activities and developmental milestones, shared caregiving issues, and other information that affects the well-being and development of their children. Where in-person communication is not possible, program staff communicate through established alternative means.	Chapters 8 and 14
7.B.06 Program staff communicate with families on at least a **weekly basis** regarding children's activities and developmental milestones, shared caregiving issues, and other information that affects the well-being and development of their children. Where in-person communication is not possible, program staff communicate through established alternative means.	Chapter 8
7.C Nurturing Families as Advocates for Their Children	
7.C.01 Program staff encourage families to regularly contribute to decisions about their child's goals and plans for activities and services.	Chapter 6
7.C.02 Program staff encourage families to raise concerns and work collaboratively with them to find mutually satisfying solutions that staff then incorporate into classroom practice.	Chapters 9, 13, and 15
7.C.03 Program staff encourage and support families to make the primary decisions about services that their children need, and they encourage families to advocate to obtain needed services.	Chapter 12
7.C.04 Program staff use a variety of techniques to negotiate difficulties that arise in their interactions with family members. Program staff make arrangements to use these techniques in a language the family can understand.	Chapters 5, 9, 13, and 15

(continued)

NAEYC Accreditation Criteria for Families Standard	Text Chapter
7.C Nurturing Families as Advocates for Their Children (*continued*)	
7.C.06 Program staff use established linkages with other early education programs and local elementary schools to help families prepare for and manage their children's transitions between programs, including special education programs. Staff provide information to families that can assist them in communicating with other programs.	Chapter 12
7.C.08 To help families with their transitions to other programs or schools, staff provide basic general information on enrollment procedures and practices, visiting opportunities, and program options.	Chapter 7, 12
7.C.08 Before sharing information about a child with other relevant providers, agencies, or other programs, staff obtain written consent from the family.	Chapter 12
Other Related Standards	
1.A Building Positive Relationships among Teachers and Families	
1.A.01 Teachers work in partnership with families, establishing and maintaining regular, ongoing, two-way communication.	Chapters 1, 8, and 9
1.A.02 Teachers gain information about the ways families define their own race, religion, home language, culture, and family structure.	Chapters 11 and 13
1.A.03 Teachers communicate with family members on an ongoing basis to learn about children's individual needs and ensure a smooth transition between home and program.	Chapters 1, 6, and 7
1.A.04 Teachers are sensitive to family concerns and reassure family members who are concerned about leaving children in non-family care.	Chapters 1, 5, and 7
1.B.12 Teaching staff give one-to-one attention to infants when engaging in caregiving routines.	Chapter 14
2.A Curriculum: Essential Characteristics	
2.A.03 The curriculum can be implemented in a manner that reflects responsiveness to family home values, beliefs, experiences, and language.	Chapters 1 and 10
2.A.08 Materials and equipment used to implement the curriculum reflect the lives of the children and families . . .	Chapter 13
2.L.03 Children are provided varied opportunities and materials to build their understanding of diversity in culture, family structure, ability, language, age, and gender in non-stereotypical ways.	Chapters 10 and 13
2.L.05 Children are provided opportunities and materials to learn about the community in which they live.	Chapter 12
2.L.08 Children are provided varied opportunities and materials to learn how people affect their environments in positive . . . ways.	Chapter 12
3.A.01 Teaching staff work as a team to implement daily teaching and learning activities, including IFSPs IEPs, and other individual plans as needed.	Chapter 14
3.F Making Learning Meaningful for All Children	
3.F.03 Teachers and families work together to help children participate successfully in the early childhood setting when professional values and practices differ from family values and practices.	Chapters 13 and 15
3.F.05 Teaching staff support the development and maintenance of children's home language whenever possible.	Chapter 13
3.F.06 Teachers offer children opportunities to engage in classroom experiences with members of their families.	Chapter 10

(continued)